MARIA
WOODWORTH-ETTER

COLLECTED WORKS

MARIA WOODWORTH-ETTER

COLLECTED WORKS

WHITAKER
HOUSE

MARIA WOODWORTH-ETTER COLLECTED WORKS

Titles included in this anthology:

Signs and Wonders
ISBN: 978-0-88368-299-9 © 1997 by Whitaker House
The Holy Spirit: Experiencing the Power of the Spirit in Signs, Wonders, and Miracles
ISBN: 978-0-88368-548-8 © 1998 by Whitaker House

ISBN: 978-1-60374-834-6
Printed in the United States of America
© 2013 by Author or Ministry or WH

Whitaker House
1030 Hunt Valley Circle
New Kensington, PA 15068
www.whitakerhouse.com

Library of Congress Cataloging-in-Publication Data (Pending)

1 2 3 4 5 6 7 8 9 10 11   20 19 18 17 16 15 14 13

CONTENTS

SIGNS AND WONDERS

CONTENTS

1

EARLY LIFE

I was born in New Lisbon, Columbiana County, Ohio, July 22, 1844, and was the fourth daughter of Samuel and Matilda Underwood. My parents were not Christians; therefore I was left without the religious teachings and influence with which so many homes are blessed. My father and mother joined the Disciple Church one year before my father's death, which occurred in July, 1855. The death of my father was the first great sorrow of my life. He had gone away to harvest in usual health, and I will never forget the night he was brought home, cold in death. Some neighbor children and I were out watching a terrible storm raging, when we saw two strangers approaching the house. They came to bring the sad intelligence of what had happened, and as we looked out we saw the conveyance approaching, bringing the remains of our dear father. It was a terrible blow to our young hearts to see our father carried into the house cold and stiff in death, and my mother fainting as fast as they could bring her to. We children were screaming and the storm was raging in all its fury. Father died of sunstroke; he was only sick a few hours and died praying for his family.

My father was a fine looking man, very intelligent, and full of energy, but addicted to the accursed cup. He could control his appetite very well until he went to a town or city; then when his friends would persuade him to take a drink, he was largehearted and easily persuaded; when he took one drink, he was like a crazy man for more, and thought he was rich, and would give his last penny away. Then when he had no money to buy drink with, he would pawn his clothes and come home to his large family and brokenhearted wife without a penny to buy food, and all in rags. And we little children would run and hide. Our young lives were full of terror and hardships. This is the reason we were left in poverty, with a sickly, brokenhearted mother and eight helpless children; not one in the wide world to come to our rescue.

Yes, I am a *drunkard's* daughter, with all the other dark trials to go through. I have never given this to the public before, but feel led of God to let the world know how the Lord has called and lifted me out of the depths, that He might be all and in all, to prove that no flesh shall glory in His Presence. The Lord must be doing the work, and it is not by human wisdom, but by the Spirit of the Living God.

My mother was left with eight children to provide for and almost destitute. Then began the battle of life with us all. My mother was obliged to seek work in various ways. My oldest sisters and myself had to leave home and work by the week. We had not only ourselves to provide for, but also our brothers and sisters at home. It was very hard for my sensitive nature to go among strangers. I was discontented and homesick. I wanted to go to school where I could learn, for I longed for an education, and I often cried myself to sleep over this matter. I would have my books in the kitchen, where I could read a verse and commit it to memory; then read another, and so on, thus improving every opportunity while at my work. I had no opportunity of going to church from my earliest recollection. My heart went out in strong desires to know of God, when eight years old. Two of my sisters were converted in a Methodist meeting. I went once or twice. My heart was melted with the Savior's love, but they seemed to think children had no need of salvation, and I was kept back.

At the age of thirteen I attended a meeting of the Disciples Church. My family were all Disciples at this time. When I heard the story of the cross, my heart was filled with the love of Jesus. My eyes seemed to be fountains of tears.

I was seated in the back of a large audience, and was the first to make the start to seek the Lord. It seemed so far to the front seat, that it looked like I could never make it, but I said,

> I can but perish if I go.
> I am resolved to try,

> For if I stay away I know
> I shall forever die.

The minister took great interest in me and said many good things to encourage me and prayed that my life might be a shining light. If he could have looked forward and could have seen my life's work for the Master, he surely would have rejoiced to know how kindly he had talked to the poor little orphan girl.

But I did not get converted then. They did not believe in a change of heart and nature; but praise the Lord, He did not leave me in the dark. The next day, as they took me down to the creek to baptize me, there was a great crowd around. I heard someone say, "Maybe she will be drowned." It scared me a little. I thought, "Maybe I might," but I said, "Lord, I will go through if I do": so I asked the Lord to save me fully, trusting myself in His hands; and while going into the water, a light came over me, and I was converted. The people saw the change and said I had fainted.

Then began my new life of peace and joy in a Savior's love. Then I was contented and happy, singing and praising God all the day long. I never went to any place of amusement. I attended four meetings on Sunday and three or four during the week. I did not stay away from meeting once a year unless I was sick. I was more anxious now than ever for an education, for I wanted to work for Jesus and be useful in the vineyard of Christ. Soon after I was converted, I heard the voice of Jesus calling me to go out in the highways and hedges and gather in the lost sheep. Like Mary, I pondered these things in my heart, for I had no one to hold counsel with. The Disciples did not believe that women had any right to work for Jesus. Had I told them my impression, they would have made sport of me. I had never heard of women working in public except as missionaries, so I could see no opening—except, as I thought, if I ever married, my choice would be an earnest Christian, and then we would enter upon the mission work. A few years after this I married Mr. Woodworth.

We settled in the country and thought by industry and honest toil to gain a little of this world's goods to sustain these physical bodies, but my health failed, and everything we undertook seemed to be a failure. I was away from all Christian influence and could not often attend the house of God. Often when hearing the church bells ringing, which had been the signal for me to repair to the house of worship, and knowing that I could not go, I would cry myself to sleep. I had one trial after another, and temptations and discouragements beset me on every side. The angel of death came to our home, and after hovering around for a few days, he bore away our only little boy, a bright, blue-eyed darling. As he was passing away, he looked up and smiled. He looked like an angel and seemed to say: "Mamma, do not weep for me; I am going to a better world." It almost broke my heart to lay him away in the cold grave; but I could see the loving hand of God and hear Him calling me to build up higher, to set my affections on heavenly things and not on the things of the earth.

One year had hardly passed by when the angel of death came again to our home and took away our baby Freddy, and at the same time I lay for weeks between life and death. In all this I could see the hand of the loving Father calling me to leave all and follow Him. About this time our little daughter Georgie was converted. She was about seven years old. She was a great comfort to me. She loved to talk of the goodness of God and our Redeemer. Many happy times we enjoyed talking together of the beautiful home over the river, where her brothers had gone. I did not think she would leave me so soon to join their ranks and raise her voice with theirs in singing salvation to our God, who sits upon the throne, and to the Lamb forever. She was taken sick with that dreadful disease, scrofula, and lingered about eight months. Her sufferings were great, yet she never murmured or complained, but only said it was for her good. She loved to read about Jesus and the beautiful mansions He was preparing, and about the robe and crown that were waiting for her. She would talk to all who came to see her of Jesus and His love, and tell them to meet her in heaven.

She sent messages to her Sunday school teacher and scholars and to her friends far and near to meet her in heaven. For weeks before she died her face was all lit up with the glory of God. The angels seemed to be hovering about her bed. She could hear them singing. Her body was with us, but her spirit seemed to be above the earth communing with God. She was willing to go and be with Jesus, but it seemed hard for her to leave me. She would say, "O Mamma, if you could go with me I would be so happy. I hate to leave you; but oh, say, you will meet me in heaven." I said, "Georgie, I will try." But that would not do. She said, "O mamma, say you will: I cannot die unless you promise to meet me in heaven." I said, "Georgie, by the grace of God, I will meet you in heaven." She said, "Now I am ready; I know you will come, Mamma; I shall always be looking for you, and when you die I am coming for you."

The Sunday before she died she called me to her bedside and said, "Mamma, I am going to leave you this week," and she began to set her house in order. She talked of dying as we would talk of going to visit a dear friend. She gave away all of her earthly possessions. To me she gave her testament; she said would like to see all her friends once more. She selected her burial robe and place to be buried, and requested us to leave room for me to buried by her side. She stayed with us until the last of the week and was frequently heard to say:

> I am coming, Lord
> Coming now to thee;
> Wash me, cleanse me in that blood
> Which flowed on Calvary.

She kept inviting everyone to come to Jesus and be saved. Her sufferings were intense toward the last. When she could not speak, and we would ask her if she was happy and if Jesus was with her, she would smile and nod her head. She thought she was going. She put up her mouth to kiss each one and gasped good-bye between her struggles, saying, "Meet me in heaven;" but she rallied and lived two hours. In this way she talked on until the last, and her face shone with the glory of heaven. Looking up she said, "O Mamma, I see Jesus and the angels; I see my little brothers; they have come for me." And they bore her away in triumph to the heavenly land. It seemed to me that I could see them as they went sweeping through the gates into the New Jerusalem.

It was like death to part with my darling, but Jesus was very precious to my soul. Heaven was nearer, Christ was dearer, than ever before. I had one more treasure in glory.

My health had been very poor all through her sickness. Three weeks before her death, little Gertie was born. She was the picture of Georgie and seemed to have her sweet disposition, and I thought as she grew older she would take her place; but the precious bud was not permitted to bloom in this world of sin. At the age of four months, the angels bore her away where the flowers never fade nor die, there to join her sister and brothers, who were waiting to welcome her at the golden gates. I could say with David that they cannot come back to me, but I will go to them. (See 2 Samuel 12:23.) Praise the Lord for the Christian's hope.

Look to the Lamb of God

If you from sin are longing to be free,
    Look to the Lamb of God
He, to redeem you, died on Calvary,
    Look to the Lamb of God.

CHORUS

    Look to the Lamb of God,
    Look to the Lamb of God;
    For He alone is able to save you,
    Look to the Lamb of God.

When Satan tempts, and doubts and fears assail,
    Look to the Lamb of God;
You in His strength shall over all prevail,
    Look to the Lamb of God.

Are you a-weary, does the way seem long?
    Look to the Lamb of God;
His love will cheer and fill your heart with song,
    Look to the Lamb of God.

Fear not when shadows on your pathway fall.
    Look to the Lamb of God;
In joy or sorrow Christ is all in all,—
    Look to the Lamb of God.

2

PREPARATION FOR SERVICE

From the time of the sad occurrences which have just been narrated in the previous chapter, my health was very poor, and many times I was brought near the brink of the grave. Everyone who saw me thought I would die. But the work the Lord was calling me to do came up before me so plainly that I thought He would raise me up and open the way; and at these times, when I seemed to be hovering between life and death, I would have such glorious visions.

At one time I was praying for the salvation of sinners, and the Savior appeared on the cross by me and talked with me; I laid my hand on His mangled body and looked up in His smiling face. Another time I was meditating upon the love of God in giving His only Son to die for sinners and of the beautiful home He was preparing for those who love Him, when I seemed to float away and was set down in the Beautiful City. Oh, the glorious sight that met my view can never be expressed by mortal tongue! Heaven is located. It is a real city. Its inhabitants are real and not imaginary. If mothers could see their children as I saw them, in all their shining glory, they would never weep for them, but would leave all and follow Jesus. They would let nothing keep them from meeting their children in heaven, where they are shining in dazzling beauty around God's throne and are watching to give welcome to the Beautiful City. I never think of my children as being in the grave. Oh, no. The loved form that we laid away in the cold grave is nothing but the casket that contained the jewel which is now shining in the Savior's crown.

Often now when I am pleading with sinners to come to Jesus and telling them of the love of God, the beautiful home in heaven, of the mansions bright, and of the robe and crown, and of the great multitude who have been washed in the blood of the Lamb, the veil seems to be taken away, and I feel lost in the love and glory of Christ. I feel as though the congregation was left behind, and I was floating upward in a cloud of glory. Oh, the wonderful love of God! The half has never been told. It never can be told. It will take all eternity to tell of the redeeming love in the wonderful plan of redemption to a dying world. Dear readers, will you not give up all and follow Jesus, and meet me in that beautiful land where sorrow will never come?

I do praise God for His loving-kindness to me in always raising up the best of Christian friends in my behalf. In all my sickness and trouble, the ministers and people came from the different churches in the town and had prayer meeting in my room. They prayed in the churches for my recovery. I was willing to die and leave my little girl and boy, feeling that God would care for them, but the work God was calling me to do loomed up before me. All these years God had been preparing me—for I was not willing. I felt like a worm in His sight. It seemed impossible for me to undertake the work for the salvation of souls; but the time had come to promise or die. I promised God that if He would restore my health, and prepare me and show me the work, I would try to do it; I began to get better immediately.

We then moved to a Friends settlement, and they came and took me to church. They had glorious meetings. God seemed to say to me, "I brought you here; go to work." Now the struggle commenced. I was very timid and bound as with chains in a man-fearing spirit. When I arose to testify, I trembled like a leaf and began to make excuses: "O God, send someone else!" Then the Lord in a vision caused me to see the bottomless pit open in all its horror and woe. There was weeping and wailing and gnashing of teeth. It was surrounded by a great multitude of people who seemed unconscious of their danger, and without a moment's warning they would tumble into this awful place. I was above the people on a narrow plank-walk, which wound up toward heaven; and I was exhorting and pleading with the people to come upon the plank and escape that awful place. Several started. There was a beautiful bright light above me, and I was encouraging them to follow that light, and they would go straight to heaven.

This vision left quite an impression on my mind. When the Spirit of God was striving with me to talk or pray in meeting, I would resist as long as I could. Then this awful vision would rise before me, and I would see souls sinking into eternal woe. The voice of Jesus would whisper, "I am with you; be not afraid." Then I would be on my feet or knees in a moment. I would forget everything but the love of God and dying souls. God seemed to speak through me to the people. But I had so much opposition to contend with. My people were opposed; my husband and daughter fought against it; and my whole nature shrunk from going to stand as a laughingstock for the people. But the Lord was showing in many ways that I must go and perform the work He had for me to do.

Several ministers whom I had never seen before told me, at different times, that God was calling me to the ministry, and that I would have to go. I said, "If I were a man I would love to work for Jesus." They told me I had a work to do which no man could do; the Lord was calling me to the West to labor for lost souls. I said, "O Lord! I cannot take Willie with me, nor can I leave him behind." Then the Lord saw fit to take him out of the way; so He laid His hand on my darling little boy and in a few days took him home to heaven. He was the joy of my life. He was nearly seven years old. He was very bright for one of his age—in fact, far beyond his years. He was the pet of the whole neighborhood. He seemed to know when taken sick that he would not get well. He talked of dying and going to see Georgie, who had been dead three years that month. He said that he would have to die sometime and that he would rather go now if we could go with him, that he would never be sick any more or have to take any more medicine. He bid us all good-bye and said he was going to be with Jesus. He died very happy. He had talked and fretted much about his little sister and said he could not live without her. By faith I could see her meeting him at the beautiful gates and welcoming him into the golden city of God. This sad bereavement nearly took my life. The dear Savior was never so near and real to me before. He was by my side and seemed to bear me up in His loving arms. I could say, "*The Lord gave and the Lord hath taken away; blessed be the name of the Lord*" (Job 1:21).

When alone I missed my darling so much that I wept as though my heart would break. Then I would always pray; and as I prayed I would forget everything earthly and soar away by faith to the Golden City, and there see my darlings all together shining in glory and looking at me and saying, "Mamma, do not weep for us, but come this way." I would always end in praising and giving glory to God for taking them to such a happy place. Lizzie, our oldest child, aged sixteen, was all we had left of six sweet children.

In all these trials God was preparing me and opening the way for the great battle against the enemy of souls; and now the great desire of my heart was to work for Jesus. I longed to win a star for the Savior's crown. But when I thought of my weakness, I shrank from the work. Sometimes when the Spirit of God was striving and calling so plainly, I would yield and say, "Yes, Lord; I will go." The glory of God came upon me like a cloud, and I seemed to be carried away hundreds of miles and set down in a field of wheat, where the sheaves were falling all around me. I was filled with zeal and power and felt as if I could stand before the whole world and plead with dying sinners. It seemed to me that I must leave all and go at once. Then Satan would come in like a flood and say, "You would look nice preaching, being a laughingstock for the people to make sport of. You know you could not do it." Then I would think of my weakness and say, "No, of course I cannot do it." Then I would be in darkness and despair. I wanted to run away from God, or I wished I could die; but when I began to look at the matter in this way, that God knew all about me and was able and willing to qualify me for the work, I asked Him to qualify me.

I want the reader to understand that at this time I had a good experience, a pure heart, was full of the love of God, but was not qualified for God's work. I knew that I was but a worm. God would have to take a worm to thresh a mountain. Then I asked God to give me the power He gave the Galilean fishermen—to anoint me for service. I came like a child asking for bread. I looked for it. God did not disappoint me. The power of the Holy Spirit came down as a cloud. It was brighter than the sun. I was covered and wrapped up in it. My body was light as the air. It seemed that heaven came down. I was baptized with the Holy Spirit and fire and power which has never left me. Oh, praise the Lord! There was liquid fire, and the angels were all around in the fire and glory. It is through the Lord Jesus Christ, and by this power, that I have stood before hundreds of thousands of men and women, proclaiming the unsearchable riches of Christ.

The Friends wanted me to travel a year with a minister and his wife and work in revivals, and they would pay all expenses. But my husband was not willing for me to go or to engage in the work any place.

3

PROGRESS IN PREPARATION

I thought I would go through a course of study and prepare for the work, thinking the Lord would make my husband and people willing in some way to let me go out and work. But I could not get my mind fixed on my study. Everything seemed empty and vacant, and I was restless and uneasy.

The dear Savior stood by me one night in a vision and talked face-to-face with me and asked what I was doing on earth. I felt condemned and said, "Lord, I am going to work in Your vineyard." The Lord said, "When?" and I answered, "When I get prepared for the work." Then the Lord said to me, "Don't you know that while you are getting ready, souls are perishing? Go now, and I will be with you." I told Him that I could not talk to the people; I did not know what to say, and they would not listen to me. Jesus said, "You can tell the people what the Lord has done for your soul; tell of the glory of God and the love of Jesus; tell sinners to repent and prepare for death and the judgment, and I will be with you." Still I made one excuse after another, and Jesus would answer, "Go, and I will be with you."

I told Him I wanted to study the Bible; that I did not understand it well enough. Then there appeared upon the wall a large open Bible, and the verses stood out in raised letters. The glory of God shone around and upon the book. I looked, and I could understand it all.

Then Jesus said again, "Go, and I will be with you." I cried, "Lord, I will go. Where shall I go?" And Jesus said, "Go here, go there, wherever souls are perishing." Praise the Lord for His wonderful goodness in revealing His Word and will in such a wonderful way, to such a poor weak worm of the dust. I saw more in that vision than I could have learned in years of hard study. Praise His Holy name. I saw that I must not depend on anything that I could do, but to look to Him for strength and wisdom. "*Not by might, nor by power, but by my spirit, saith the* LORD" (Zech. 4:6). I was to be the vessel of clay God was going to use to His own glory. I was to be God's mouthpiece. I must trust God to speak through me to the people the words of eternal life.

There was all this time a secret monitor within telling me that I should be calling sinners to repentance. I could not get clear of that reflection by day or by night. Walking or dreaming, I seemed to have a large congregation before me, all in tears, as I told them the story of the cross. Thus for months and years did I debate; and yet did I falter and hesitate, and, like Jonah, trim my sail for Tarshish. I thought if I were a man it would be a pleasure for me; but for me, a woman, to preach, if I could, would subject me to ridicule and contempt among my friends and kindred and bring reproach upon His glorious cause.

Always when I had trouble, I would flee to the stronghold of faith and grace and prayer. But when I went in secret to pray, the words seemed to come to me, "You deny me before men, and I will deny you before My Father and the holy angels." Then I would go to my Bible and search for teachings and examples. Who made sport of Miriam when the poet said the following?

> An elder sister led the band,
>   With sounding timbrels in her hand,
> And virgins moved in order grand,
>   And after her they shouting danced.

Again, the Lord put His erring people in remembrance of His great blessing to Israel when He said, "Did I not send thee Moses and Aaron *and Miriam* to be your leaders?" And again the prophets were ordained of God. And when there was trouble on hand, Barak dare not meet the enemy unless Deborah led the van. And the noble woman, always ready to work for God and His cause, said, "I will surely go. God's people must not be a prey to the enemy." "Oh, no; call out the men of Israel; Sisera's mighty hosts are gathering."

As I continued to read my Bible, I saw that in all ages of the world the Lord raised up of his own choosing, men, women, and children—Miriam, Deborah, Hannah, Hulda, Anna, Phoebe, Narcissus, Tryphena, Persis, Julia, and the Marys, and the sisters who were coworkers with Paul in the Gospel, whose names were in the Book of Life, and many other women whose labors are mentioned with praise. Even the children were made the instruments of His praise and glory. (See 1 Samuel 3:4; Jeremiah 1:6; Numbers 22:28.)

The more I investigated, the more I found to condemn me. There was the Master giving one, two, and five talents, and the moral obligation of each person receiving them and their several rewards. I had one talent, which was hidden away.

By the prophet Joel we learn that one special feature of the gospel dispensation shall be, "*Your sons **and daughters** shall prophesy, your old men shall dream dreams, your young men shall see visions; and also upon the servants and handmaids in those days will I pour out my spirit*" (Joel 2:28–29, emphasis added). It seems by the prophet Joel, that the last days were to be particularly conspicuous for this kind of prophesying. We cannot reserve God's decree, for He said: "*Heaven and earth shall pass away, but…the word of the Lord endureth for ever*" (Matt. 24:35; 1 Pet. 1:25). (See chapter 34 on women's ministry.)

Now, to those who are sensitive upon this point, I propose the inquiry: First, Is there not as much to sustain the position that women are called to preach as there is that men are called? If you admit that there is such a call to the ministry, then whence the authority for making the work exclusively for the male sex? What would have been the work of those women who labored with Paul? (Paul's letter to the church at Philippi, 4:3). Second, How could they obey God and not prophesy? (Acts 2:18). Philip had four daughters who did prophesy (Acts 21:9). Was that by divine authority, about thirty-five years after the setting up of the gospel kingdom dispensation? And is it less becoming for women to labor in Christ's kingdom or vineyard now than it was then?

If you determine that there is no acceptable preaching except through a called ministry, who will arrogate to himself the power to determine the calling, seeing that none are invested with miraculous power? But should you deny that there is any divine authority by which the Word is preached, why not offer the most encouragement to those who may labor most successfully? There will be a time when all good workers will meet a just recompense, for it is said: "*Every valley shall be exalted, and every mountain and hill shall be made low; and the crooked shall be made straight, and the rough places plain; and the glory of the LORD shall be revealed, and all flesh shall see it together; for the mouth of the LORD hath spoken it"* (Isa. 40:4–5).

The first meeting that I undertook to hold was in a little town where we had lived some years before, right among my husband's people. It was a cross for me to talk to those people; but I said, in the name of God, and by His sustaining grace, I will try and leave the result with him. As I rose to speak, this text came to mind: *"Set thine house in order; for thou shalt die, and not live"* (Isa. 38:1).

When I began to talk upon the subject, the man-fearing spirit left me, and the words came to me faster than I could give them utterance. My sister-in-law broke down and left the house. We continued the meeting a few days, and twenty claimed to be converted. People were converted all through the neighborhood. One who came to this meeting afterward became my son-in-law.

I continued to keep house and spent as much time in holding meetings as I could, to give my husband a chance to attend his work. I was anxious to raise money for us to go West. I would ride seven miles and hold meeting on Saturday evening and three meetings on Sunday—sometimes in different churches—and then ride home over a hilly and rough road. By this time I would be nearly exhausted and hardly able to walk around to do my work. But the last of the week I would go again; and often through the week I held meetings in the towns around where I was born and raised, where we had lived since we were married.

It was a cross for me to speak before my own folks and the people whom I had always known. But God wonderfully blessed my labors in every place. Wherever I went, the house was crowded. I did not write my sermons or have sketches of sermons. I would take a text and trust God to lead me in His own way. I was holding meeting for a few days where I was raised, and the house was crowded every night. One night I could not get a text. The people came pouring in until the house was packed. I began to get frightened. A brother said to me, "The Disciples are turning out tonight." There I was, with several hundred people before me and no text—nothing to talk about. Everything was empty. I began to plead with Jesus. I told Him He had called me to preach; that here was this starving multitude and I had no bread to give them. To verify His promise and to glorify Himself in manifesting His power to this people, the words came to me, "What are you going to do with Jesus, who is called the Christ?" and also the place to find the text. (See Matthew 27:22.) Jesus seemed to whisper in my ear, "I am with you; be not afraid." I opened the meeting and repeated the text. As I did so the power came and it seemed that all I had to do was to open my mouth. The people all through the house began to weep. I talked one hour and a quarter. The power came as it did when I received the baptism of the Holy Spirit. It seemed as if the house was full of the glory of God. I felt as if I was drawn up over the people. Glory to God for helping a worm of the dust.

For the glory of God and the encouragement of those who are engaged in working for lost souls, to prove that no place is too hard for God, if we only trust Him, I will tell you the victory God gave me at a place called "The Devil's Den." It was distinguished for infidelity and skepticism. There was an old free church in which no one was ever known to be converted. Some of our best ministers had tried to hold meetings here but had gone away in disgust. This place was six miles from home. I had several times refused to go to this place, but at last concluded to go, believing God would shake the foundation of infidelity and that there would be a shaking among the dry bones. A large crowd met me. They had come through mere curiosity, expecting to see me back out. I had to do all the talking, all the praying, and all the singing. But God was there in mighty power. Some of those infidels turned pale and trembled in their seats. For a few days I could hardly find a place to stay. I appointed day meetings; but they said, "Oh, you cannot have meetings in daytime; no one will come." I told them if no one else came, I would go and pray for God to pour out His power upon the people. About the fourth day some were brightly converted. They went to work.

The news spread like fire, and the Christians and singers and ministers came from miles around. There were hundreds who could not get into the house. The doors and windows were open, and the order was so good that I think nearly all the people outside could hear. I held the meeting two weeks, and seventy-five came out on the Lord's side. One old man and his wife, about seventy-five years old, and nine of their children were converted. Nearly all who came out were over twenty years old. Some of the hardest sinners in the whole country were converted. They had to confess that God was there in wonderful power. I organized a Sunday school of one hundred and fifty scholars and put in a man for superintendent who had been a noted drunkard, appointed two prayer meetings for each week, and established meetings every Sunday. Different ministers promised to furnish them with preaching. The people said it was a glorious work, but that it could not last; that when I left it would go down. Bless God. I have heard of only one who went back to the world!

It is now twelve years since that meeting; the Lord has poured out the Holy Spirit as He promised He would in the last days with "signs and wonders" following. He said He would give the latter rains of the Spirit before the notable Day of the Lord came. This was to be given to gather in the last harvest of souls before Jesus comes in the clouds. Many times I have stood before congregations of thousands, preaching or singing, when the Holy Spirit fell upon them and swept over, wave after wave, until the multitudes would sway back and forth like the trees in a forest or grain in a storm. Many of the tall oaks would be laid prostrate over the house or campground; and, like the revival at Cornelius's, many were converted while standing or sitting in their seats.

Many shouted, others wept with a loud voice. Other times the power would sweep over the house in melting power. In a few minutes nearly everyone in the congregation would be weeping, saints and sinners. The solemnity of death would rest upon the people; you could not hear a sound nor see a move; the people were held by the power of God. These outpourings of the Holy Spirit were always followed by hundreds coming to Christ. The Lord has backed up His Word, as I preached it on the apostolic line, with "signs and wonders" and demonstrations of the Spirit.

He has shown me we are in the last days. He has poured out His Spirit in all my meetings. Praise God, no difference how the Holy Spirit came, I knew the Lord was leading. How I realized this: "Not by might, nor by power, but by my spirit, saith the LORD" (Zech. 4:6). Oh, how precious these words of our loving Father: "Open thy mouth wide, and I will fill it" (Ps. 81:10); "Be not afraid of their faces, for I am with thee to deliver thee" (Jer. 1:8); "Thou, therefore, gird up thy loins, and arise, and speak unto them all that I command thee: be not dismayed at their faces, lest I confound thee before them" (Jer. 1:17); "Surely I will be with thee" (Judg. 6:16); and "Be strong and courageous" (2 Chron. 32:7). When I would feel my responsible position and look over the crowded house, I, like Peter, would begin to sink and cry: "Lord, help; Lord, use the clay to Your glory, and give me a message for this dying people."

Some of those promises would come rolling in, accompanied with the Holy Spirit, until I would feel lost in Christ and see nothing but the multitude of dying people rushing on to judgment.

Oh, praise the Lord for His tender care over us and for His wonderful salvation that fills our souls with glory; that takes away the fear of persecution, the fear of man, and the fear of devils; and makes us rejoice in the midst of trials, remembering that *"all things work together for good to them that love God"* (Rom. 8:28), etc.; that takes away the fear of death, and as we look at the grave we hear a shout from Calvary, saying, *"I am the resurrection and the life"* (John 11:25). Death is the gate to glory.

My next work was at Bethel Chapel, St. Mary's Circuit, where I held a revival meeting, which lasted eleven days. The class was in bad condition. There had been trouble in the church for nine years. Sixteen members or more had left the church, but harmony and love were restored to the class, and nearly all who had left came back. Father D., who had been standing out of the church all his life, came out and joined the church, and eleven of his family followed. One brother consecrated himself to the ministry and is now preaching the glorious Gospel. An infidel became convicted and converted and is now in the ministry. One hundred and thirty-five came to the altar; thirty-nine united with the class; Christian workers and ministers came in from all around; and we had a glorious time. The house was filled to overflowing; half the people could not get in. The seekers were trampled upon. We could not get room for the mourners. The altar and the side seats were full, and the night I closed the meeting, there were thirty-two at the altar. It seemed that all who came fell under conviction.

Two young men attended the meeting all through and were deeply convicted. I labored with them day and night. I felt impressed that that was their last chance, and if they did not come to Jesus then, their doom would be sealed. I told them that I believed death was on their track. They turned pale but did not yield. A short time after the meeting closed, they both took sick about the same time, and both were unconscious to the last, going into eternity without a ray of hope. People remembered how I had labored with them, and they thought it was a warning from God for others to flee to a Savior's arms and escape the vengeance of a just God. Oh, it is a fearful thing to die without Christ, to take a leap in the dark and go down into the dark waters of Jordan without Christ to lighten it with His glory.

Sweet Salvation

We went to Pleasant Mills, Indiana, to hold a series of meetings, and there found the class nearly broken up. I could only find six who had any experience; they were discouraged. Even the minister had no hope of it being built up again.

The Baptists were strong there, and there was contention between the churches. A good many of the brothers advised me not to go; but I thought as it was such a hard place, work was needed there worse than anywhere else. I claimed victory before the walls fell. The night I commenced, there were only two members present, though the house was crowded. I spoke from the text, "*I am doing a great work, so that I cannot come down*" (Neh. 6:3). I talked principally to the church. I told them that we were brothers and sisters in Christ, and all were engaged in putting up a building for the Lord, and that each one had a part in the building.

I invited them to come out and help; that it was not only their privilege, but God commanded them to come up to the help of the Lord against the mighty; for we had a great battle to fight and needed every soldier. God has said, "Cursed are those who come not up to the help of the Lord against the mighty" (Judg. 5:23). The churches all came out, and we could not tell a Baptist from a Brethren. Brother B., the Baptist minister, came out and offered to do all he could. Many of them came out in a good experience. Two came to the altar and were converted, and we were all bound together in bonds of love, which I hope will last through eternity. No one seemed to think the church could be built up. They would say, "If any good is done here, it is more than I expect." They had no faith; I could not depend upon them at all.

The third day two old men, about sixty years old, came to the altar for the first time in their lives and were converted; and one young man came out; and they went right to work. Seeing is believing. This fired up the members, and we had a glorious time. The house was filled to overflowing every night. The meeting lasted sixteen days. Fifty-five came to the altar, and I think nearly all were brightly converted.

On Sunday morning I could not find a message. When I got to the church the house was full, and still I had no text. As I stepped to the porch a brother asked me if I would preach a funeral sermon at the hour of preaching, and if so, the procession would be there in a little while. I studied a moment. I thought it was all of the Lord, and I said I would. But I had never preached a funeral sermon. Oh, how I looked to God to guide me to His glory. I knew if God did not speak through me I would be confounded. This text came to my mind: "*I shall go to him, but he shall not return to me*" (2 Sam. 12:23). I turned to the passage in the Bible, and the light of God seemed to shine on the text. It was a child that was dead, and its parents were not saved. They were both convicted and promised me not to stop until they found the Pearl of Great Price. As I stood up and read the text, its meaning unfolded, and the Spirit of God came down in great power. The people were weeping all over the house. Oh, praise the Lord for His ever present help when we trust Him.

While holding the meeting, I visited a man who was sick and unsaved. I talked and prayed with him, and he was sweetly saved. I left him rejoicing in a Savior's love. He was taken into the church but died in a few weeks. He was very happy and resigned. I went to bid him good-bye. He said he was going soon, but would meet us in the Beautiful City above. During his last hours, his friends and neighbors gathered in, and he talked and exhorted them to seek Christ and meet him in heaven. He said the angels and his little child, who had passed over, were in the room. He shouted and praised God until the last breath was gone. His triumphant death convinced some of the hardest sinners of the reality of religion. "Oh, let me die the death of the righteous, that my last end be like his." Our loving Father is calling His children home one by one. Some of us have more loved ones over on the Golden Shore than we have here. They are watching and waiting for us. Shall they watch in vain?

5

SURPRISES

While at Lima, Ohio, I attended a surprise party on Father P., it being his eighty-third birthday. About one hundred and sixty took dinner in a beautiful grove near the house. Several of the oldest settlers in the county were present. After the old gentleman had been loaded with presents, I opened the meeting with singing. Father R., the first settler in Van Wert county, led in prayer. I preached from the text, "We are pilgrims and strangers," after which we had a praise meeting. Nine rose for the prayers of God's people. We closed by singing, "Oh, Think of the Home Over There," and shaking hands. We felt that we would never meet again in that glorious gathering; but if faithful we will all meet on the Golden Shore, where we never more shall say good-bye.

At Brother B.'s request we went to Zion, Olive Branch Circuit, in May and commenced a meeting which continued two weeks. I found a few names on the class book, but they were scattered. Only two or three faithful ones could be found. They, with their pastor, were discouraged. They had so much opposition to contend with that they thought Zion would never rise and shine. But I held on by faith, and the walls began to go up. Although it was in corn planting time, I had meeting day and night. The meetings were well attended. On Sunday the house was full, and in the evening they could not all get into the house. God's people were very much revived, and backsliders were reclaimed, and many came out in the true light.

A few days after the meeting closed, a man was thrown from his horse near the church and killed. I believe it was a warning from God to those who were fighting conviction. He was out of Christ, and no doubt took a leap in the dark. Dear reader, how is it with you? If the pale messenger of death should come for you today, would you take a leap into eternity, and hear the Judge say: *"Depart from me, ye cursed, into everlasting fire...*[where] *there shall be weeping and gnashing of teeth"* (Matt. 25:41, 51) or would you go shouting home to glory? God help you to make heaven your home.

After our visit to those places, I held meeting a few days in a schoolhouse, and fifteen arose for prayers. Six of one family came out upon the Lord's side. A young man, with whom I had labored hard and tried to induce to come to Christ, died very suddenly. He died without leaving any evidence of being saved. His death cast a gloom over the whole neighborhood. His father and the whole family, except his mother, were unsaved. I was particularly interested in this family, but they never came to meeting.

Some of the brothers said I could get the schoolhouse near where they lived. We held one meeting, and they attended. We had services once a week for a month. The mother came out in a very bright experience, and the father and five of the children were happily converted, except one son. He said he was not satisfied yet. They all united with the class at Fairview and are very earnest workers. I think they will be a great help to the church. Brother C. preached at Fairview and opened the doors of the church. Ten were taken in—this family among the number. We then went to the river, where twenty were baptized. I never saw a more beautiful sight. The Holy Spirit came down in great power, and nearly everyone came out of the water shouting and praising the Lord. A very large crowd witnessed the scene, and all seemed to feel the power of God. We then went to the schoolhouse and had preaching in the evening.

I had been holding a few meetings at Bethel and, on coming home, was surprised to see buggies and wagons and people approaching the house from all directions. The dear brothers and sisters and friends were gathering on that day to celebrate my thirty-ninth anniversary. They all brought their well-filled baskets, and the table was burdened with good things. After we had all done justice to the good things with which the table was so bountifully spread, I received quite a number of presents. We then collected in the grove near by, where we spent the rest of the day in religious services. The exercises were opened by the Reverend T., and prayer was offered by Brother W. Brother H. made some appropriate remarks, and excellent addresses were delivered by other brothers, after which remarks were made by some of the sisters. The power of God was wonderfully manifested. I then thanked the people for their kindness, and talked of the Glorious Reunion awaiting us by and by over the river. We then rose and sang, "Oh, Think of a Home Over There." I said we would shake hands while singing, and all think of our home and loved ones over there. The whole congregation wept, and we all felt that if we never met on earth again, we would meet in heaven, where there is no parting and no sorrow.

I held a basket meeting, commencing July 28, 1883, and continuing three days, in the beautiful grove by the side of the river. There was a large attendance and the best of order prevailed. On Sunday about two thousand people assembled in the grove. We had a praise meeting in the morning. It was a glorious sight to see the children of God from all denominations and hear them raise their voices telling their hope of heaven. At the close of this heavenly feast, I preached from the text, "Behold, the Lion of the tribe of Juda, the Root of David, hath prevailed to open the book, and to loose the seven seals thereof" (Rev. 5:5). The power of God was wonderfully present. A deathlike stillness rested over the people, and many of the saints and sinners wept. In the afternoon Brother M. preached on "The Early Dawn of the Church; its Moonlight and Sunlight of Today." At the close we went to the river nearby, and a number were baptized by Brother M. As I looked over the multitude crowding the river bank, my mind went back to the scene at Jordan. In the evening I preached from the text, "Behold, the bridegroom cometh; go ye out to meet him" (Matt. 25:6).

6

DEEP CONVICTION

The Macedonian call from Wood's Chapel, across the Indiana line, being very urgent, I felt the Lord calling. I commenced the meeting under very discouraging surroundings. The house was new. The class had been organized principally of unconverted members. About nine years previous, there had been strife in the church, and the members became scattered.

The class leader, a man tottering upon the verge of the grave, bless God, was reclaimed. His wife and nearly all his family were also brought into the fold. Another brother, who had been a great help to the cause but had lost his power and experience, said he would never again take an interest in religion. The first night the house was crowded, and if ever I needed the prayers of the people, it was then. I was so weak I could hardly get up in the stand. I called on this man to pray. He commenced: "Lord, You have sent her here. If she preaches to the Day of Judgment, no one will be saved," and so forth. I raised my head to see who he was. I said, "My good man, you will change your mind before many days; if you cannot pray for me, I can pray for myself." And I believe it gave me strength and power.

The next night I called on him again, and the people were rejoiced to hear him change his prayer. I received twelve into the church. He was among the first to give me his hand, and he was one of my best friends. Praise God! Those who

worse" (2 Tim. 3:13); "*There* [shall] *come a falling away*" (2 Thess. 2:3); "*Traitors* [will arise] *having the form of godliness, but denying the power thereof: from such turn away.*" (2 Tim. 3:4–5).

As I plead with sinners, how my heart goes out to them in love and pity, knowing that the same message will seal the destiny of some for eternal life and some for eternal damnation. It is a terrible thing to procrastinate until the Spirit leaves us to our doom, until we become past feeling, given over to hardness of heart. "*As I live, saith the Lord* GOD, *I have no pleasure in the death of the wicked; but that the wicked turn from his way and live: turn ye, turn ye from your evil ways; for why will ye die?*" (Ezek. 33:11). Life is set before you without money and without price, but it will avail you nothing unless you accept Him as your personal Savior. The devils believe and tremble on account of the punishment that awaits them.

The Last Lovely Morning

The last lovely morning,
    All blooming and fair,
Is fast onward fleeting
    And soon will appear.

CHORUS

While the mighty, mighty, mighty trump
    Sounds, come, come away:—
Oh! let us be ready to hail the glad day.

And when that bright morning
    In splendor shall dawn,
Our tears shall cease flowing,
    Our sorrows be gone.

The Bridegroom from glory
    To earth shall descend;
Ten thousand bright angels
    Around him attend.

The graves will be opened.
　The dead shall rise,
And with the Redeemer,
　Mount up to the skies.

The saints then immortal
　In glory shall reign—
The bride with the Bridegroom
　Forever remain.

8

GOD'S POWER

I held meeting in the Baptist Church of Hoagland, which continued five days and was attended with wonderful displays of God's power. The other denominations were all prejudiced against this church, for some cause or other unknown to me; and they did not feel like working and sat back. The Baptists were very weak and not in working order. Some of the converts from other places came and went to work with wonderful power.

I never saw such manifestations of the power of God before or since. The house was full of the glory of God. It was like a mist. People fell down in their seats all over the house, overpowered with the glory of God. Sinners came out crying for mercy.

A Universalist, an infidel, and a Catholic, each seventy years of age, were converted. Two of these came out the last night.

The altar was crowded night after night.

There were about fifty converted, and many reclaimed. The work has been going on gloriously. My prayer for the dear people of Hoagland is that they may be kept in peace and love, until God shall say, "come up higher," where we shall meet again.

On Friday evening I held meeting in the Lutheran Church. Several ministers were present from the different places where I had held meetings the year before. They all gave good reports of the success of the meetings I had held on their charges and of the change in the neighborhood. We had indeed a time of rejoicing.

Fourteen ministers were present during this meeting.

In the evening the people came by hundreds. It is said that there were about two thousand on the ground; and although the lights were very poor, the best of order prevailed.

There were two or three hundred persons present who had been converted in my meetings in the past winter. It made my heart leap for joy when I saw their happy faces and heard them speak of their enjoyments in the service of the Lord. Some were aged ones who had been as brands taken from the eternal burning.

The hour for preaching had come. It was a trying moment for me. For we all had such a time of rejoicing, the devil was in the camps. As in ancient times when the sons of men came to worship, Satan came also, as he did in the Garden of Eden, only in a different form, but with the same motive and jealousy. The devil was always jealous of God and His work. In the beginning he rebelled in heaven and tried to take the throne, but God cast him out, "and he fell like lightning." Then when God made Adam and Eve in his own image, Satan came around with his flattering speeches and lying tongue, and by pretending to do a better work tried to destroy what God had done. He has been working on the same line ever since. There never was a glorious work done for God but that the devil came around in person or in the form of a Judas and tried to overthrow it. So, in this case, everything was done to confuse me in order that I would make a failure. My head was aching so that I could hardly see. I had not a moment to prepare or collect my thoughts, and I had never stood before such a multitude.

I felt that I must talk on the deepest subject in the Bible, "The Unpardonable Sin and the Office of the Holy Spirit." I cried, "Lord, help me, and glorify Thyself." The words came: *"And he said unto me, Son of man, stand upon thy feet, and I will speak unto thee....Be not afraid of their faces: for I am with thee to deliver thee"* (Ezek. 2:1; Jer. 1:8). Bless God, I had not spoken five minutes until I had forgotten the roaring in my head and my enemies, who perhaps were praying for my failure.

I forgot everything but the multitude before me rushing on to Judgment. I never had more power and liberty. The subject was revealed to me as clear as day.

The words came faster than I could speak. Glory to God for His loving-kindness and present help in every time of need!

There was an aged minister present who came to me and said surely God was speaking through the clay; he had never heard the subject made so plain in all the points; that people had received light, and that eternity alone would tell the result of that meeting.

I held a series of meetings at Sheldon, Allen County, Indiana, in 1884 in the Methodist Episcopal Church. I found the membership very weak, a good deal of contention among them, and very few in working order. Sheldon was said to be the hardest town in the state. But God can work and give victory if we only exercise present living faith, no matter how wicked and forsaken a place may be.

I went to work, trusting in God and shouting victory. Sinners began to flock to Christ, the church came out for a better experience, and troubles were settled. Some of the brothers from other churches came in and helped with the work. Many who had been in the church for years found that they were only dry bones and came begging for mercy. They afterwards confessed to the church that they had been in the dark, had been trusting in works without an experiential knowledge, and that they were not accepted of God.

A lady who had been in the Disciples church for fifty-one years was converted at home during the meeting. As she shouted all over the house, she praised God and said that this was the kind of religion she wanted.

Mr. B., a popular and talented moral man, came out in a bright experience. The churches had been trying for years to lead him into the lifeboat. He attended the meeting. When I saw him, I felt that he must be saved in that meeting. I worked in different ways, praying day and night for him, and was confident that he would soon be a child of God. One night I felt that the time had come. The house was crowded, and the aisles were full of benches. I climbed over several and made my way to him and asked him if he was not ready to come to Jesus. He began to weep and went with me to the altar. Many shouted for joy. No one could doubt his conversion, for they could see the change in his countenance.

Father S. had not been to meeting for twenty years. He was opposed to all churches and tried to keep his wife and children from coming to the meeting. He was eighty-three years old. His wife was very anxious for his soul's salvation. She showed him my picture and tried to get his curiosity aroused. Finally he came to a day meeting. When I gave the invitation for seekers, he started for the door.

I met him; and when I saw how aged and feeble he was and thought of his lost condition, my heart was melted in pity for him. I felt that God had sent him there to be saved and that it must be now or never. I talked with him until he yielded and went to the altar. In a few minutes he was brightly converted. Soon after he was immersed and united with the Church of God. When he went forward in the ordinance of foot washing, a little boy, who had been converted when he was, washed his feet, and then he washed the boy's feet. It was an affecting sight. Surely he came in at the eleventh hour. He said he was just waiting for the Master to call him home. In the latter part of June he was taken sick and suffered very much. He only lingered a few days. He was patient, kind, and happy, and awaiting for the Savior to call him to his eternal home.

The Midnight Cry

Hark! the cry comes ringing high;
Now the Bridegroom cometh nigh.
Have your lamps all trimmed and bright,
Hearts made holy in His sight.
Joyful raise your minds above,
Fixed upon the Lord of love.
Hark! the warning soundeth high,
Listen to "the midnight cry!"
   (In singing, repeat last two lines.)

Raise the shout of victory,
Glory to the coming King:
Joy to all the saints He brings,
Join the songs which angels sing:
Shout aloud the Victor's praise;
We shall see Him face-to-face,
Hark! the warning soundeth high,
Listen to "the midnight cry."
   (In singing, repeat last two lines.)

Hail Him, then, the pierced Lamb,
Sacred wounds in side and palm;
Worship Him, with holy joy,
Praise Him without sin's alloy.
Saints that sleep, soon He will bring,
Heaven's anthem they shall sing;
Glory to the Lord on high;
Soon we'll meet Him in the sky.
Hark! the warning soundeth high
Listen to "the midnight cry."

9

"BY MY SPIRIT, SAITH THE LORD"

On the evening of the twenty-fourth of August, 1884, we found ourselves in Maples. As we stepped off the train, we were welcomed by several of the dear friends. I had three meetings a day, which were attended with interest, and I felt that God was with us continually. All who came with the right spirit were made to rejoice.

There were fourteen ministers present.

The object of this meeting was to have a reunion, bringing the brothers and those who were converted in the meetings of the year previous together. In this respect we had several hundred converts come together, and all came up to the front and showed what God had done for them.

We had several police on the grounds, and they were not needed, as the best of order prevailed. There was said to be from one to eight thousand on the grounds every night.

On Sunday it was wonderful how the Lord sustained me and gave me courage and strength to conduct all the meetings. I had never addressed such a multitude before. I had a bad cold all the time, but God gave me a voice so clear and strong that I could be heard distinctly all over the grove. Many aged people said they never saw such order and interest at a camp meeting. There was solemnity resting over the people. They always seemed sorry to see the meeting close.

There were many converted. One was an old lady seventy-seven years old, who belonged to the Dunkard Church. Her son and his wife were converted in the winter and are great workers in the vineyard of the Lord. One old man, leaning on his staff, whose locks were white with the frosts of many winters, was converted. I felt he was a brand plucked from the burning. Another brother, sixty years old, who had been trusting to morality all his life, had his eyes opened to see the need of eternal life. The Word says: *"Ye must be born again"* (John 3:7); *"The gift of God is eternal life"* (Rom. 6:23); "[It is] *not by works, lest any man should boast."* (Eph. 2:9).

The last Sunday day, the day I closed, we administered the Lord's Supper in the grove. It was a solemn time. There were the converts with white locks frosted with the snows of many winters, trembling on their staves. There were the lambs of the fold, with their faces shining with the love of God. There were the young men and ladies, just starting in life. There were the middle-aged fathers and mothers, with the great responsibilities of life resting on them, all sitting around the table of the Lord, some for the first time and others for the last.

Called on to Preach

By the earnest request of Brother S., the pastor, I commenced a series of meetings at New Haven, Allen County, Indiana, in the Methodist Church. I realized that I was set down in a valley of dry bones. I found very few Christians; only two or three that could take hold of the work. We held on to God, by faith and prayer, expecting to see the walls fall. They at once began to come to the altar, and came by scores. As many as forty and sixty came at once. We had cast the gospel net and taken in so many fish that we could not get them to shore.

I prayed: "Oh, God, send us help." In answer to prayer, Brother S., the singing evangelist, and others came.

The churches united in the work. We held the meeting part of the time in the Methodist Church, which continued for two weeks, and resulted in hundreds of conversions, most of whom were taken into the churches. A Catholic was converted in this meeting. One dear sister in her seventieth year, and another fifty, who had been church members for years, said they had been deceived, and had been spiritually blind. Now they rejoiced in the God of their salvation.

I never saw so many young men come out in one meeting. Two of them have since been licensed in the Methodist Church.

A little girl, eight or nine years old, came to the altar. I asked her several questions. She said she wanted to be Jesus' little lamb, and very soon her little face was lighted up with the love of God. I asked her if her parents were Christians. She said her mamma was in heaven, but her papa was wicked, that he drank. I told her to talk and pray with him and tell him if he did not come to Jesus he would be lost.

A few evenings after she made her way through the crowded house to the pulpit, I saw the little mite; she was waiting for me to speak to her. I took her in my arms and asked her if she still loved Jesus. She said: "Yes, but papa is sick. I talked and prayed with him, but could not get him to meeting." The trouble was, he was sin-sick. God had sent conviction to his heart. He saw he was a sinner and on his way to hell. I told her to tell him to come to meeting tomorrow; that he might not get well.

He came with her, and I took him by the hand and asked him if his little girl had talked and prayed with him about his soul. He said she had, and began to tremble and weep. I told him he was standing in the way of his child; that he did not want his child to say in the Great Judgment Day, "I never heard my father pray." He went with me to the altar. An old man, who was converted a few days before, prayed with him, and it was not long until he was blessed. They clasped each other around the neck, their white locks like cotton, both weeping for joy. It was an affecting scene. Truly, *"a little child shall lead them"* (Isa. 11:6).

I went from there to Maples and was kindly welcomed in the little chapel by the brothers and sisters. I found a full house and the little band of faithful workers; and they did a great work in the meeting. About fifty of the converts came from New Haven and went to work. As they came up the aisle, their bright and happy faces shining with the love of God, I commenced to sing, "Reinforcements now appearing, victory is nigh."

The people at Maples were acquainted with most of these persons, and they were surprised to see the great change in them, as one after another got up and testified of salvation and the love of Jesus in their hearts, and exhorted sinners to flee from the wrath to come. Two of these were little boys. They had walked from New Haven, five miles, to be at this meeting. They talked like little preachers. We had a glorious time.

The revival commenced at once. We continued the meeting ten days. The power of God was wonderfully manifested.

After Little River, we went to Massillon on Saturday and had three meetings in the church, and the house was crowded. Massillon church has indeed become "*a city...set on a hill*" (Matt. 5:14). Of the hundred that had been converted in the past winter, they told me they were all standing firm. Bless the Lord! They were nearly all there to speak for themselves. Six or seven would rise to their feet at once to speak of the love of Christ.

Oh, how I praised God when I saw the happy faces of the dear brothers and sisters, fathers and mothers, and the young people, who were almost like my own children, so strong and steadfast and determined, by the grace of God, to go on until they got into the beautiful city of God.

While holding meeting at Wood's Chapel, I went with several brothers and sisters to visit an old man who was not able to go to church. He had been seeking the Lord for some time, but was not satisfied. He sent for me. He could hardly wait until I got there. He met me at the door. He was very feeble. The house was full, and we had a very solemn time. The old man was saved; he exhorted and praised God. Two other men were converted, and we were all made to rejoice and praise the Lord. There were shouts in heaven as the angels took the news back that the prodigal was coming home.

One night, at the close of the meeting, a messenger came, saying he was dead and requested me to come and preach his funeral. It rained all night; and when I started, it was still raining. I had to ride eight miles; I was hardly able to sit up. I knew the house would be crowded, and so I found it. I felt very weak, but I trusted in God and looked to Him to give me strength and voice. The words came to me: "*And desire shall fail: because man goeth to his long home, and the mourners go about the streets*" (Eccl. 12:5).

I attended the eldership of the Church of God, which convened at Columbia City, Indiana, in September, 1884, where we met many of the brothers from the different places where we had held meetings. One of the converts was licensed to preach, and two were preaching who had been elected elders in the church.

I was ordained an elder with the authority to administer the ordinances and to solemnize matrimony. My earnest prayer is that I may live low at the Master's feet, as clay in the Potter's hands, fit for the Master's use.

I was called on to preach. It was quite a cross. I had preached in the presence of as many or more ministers, but I was much exhausted from constant labor. I spoke from the text: *"Here am I; send me"* (Isa. 6:8). God gave me liberty, power, and voice. Oh, praise the Lord for His goodness and help in every time of trouble. How wonderfully He has verified His promise: *"Lo, I am with you alway, even unto the end"* (Matt. 28:20).

10

WONDERFUL
DISPLAYS OF POWER

We next went to Little River, Union Chapel, and held meeting from Friday until Sunday evening. The house was crowded, and hundreds could not get in. Many of the converts came from Trinity, Markle, Zanesville, and Zion. They brought the holy fire with them, and sinners were made to tremble and cry, "What shall I do to be saved?" Among those that came to the altar was a Disciple lady, seventy-four years old. She praised God and rejoiced in her salvation. Another dear old sister, sixty-six years old, received a great blessing and went on her way rejoicing.

Sunday morning we had a glorious praise meeting. Over two hundred witnessed for Jesus. After preaching, we went to the river, where forty of the converts were baptized. It was a grand sight. About one thousand witnessed this solemn scene.

From Churubusco we went to Sheldon, Indiana, to visit our only daughter and her family, who had moved from Ohio one year before. We found them well; they rejoiced to see us once more.

I visited the dear people at Trinity and found them all still climbing Jacob's ladder.

I went to Garrison's schoolhouse to hold a revival meeting. It was the week of the election, and everyone was excited. The weather was bad; it was raining; but I went on with the meeting for two weeks.

Fifty came out bright and firm for God. Among these was Brother M., one of the brightest, talented men in the country. He had been a member of Congress.

A Universalist was the brightest conversion we had. Everyone thought he was lost. Nothing ever made an impression on him. I felt that if he was not across the dead line there was hope of him. He was so near there was no time to lose. I worked with him every night. We could not have day meetings. I prayed for him in public. His wife came out bright. I called on him to speak. He said he was glad she came out, as he wanted her to bring the children up for heaven, but to let him alone, as there was no hope for him.

He promised me he would go home and pray. He said he had never tried to pray in his life, but he would try. He kept his word. He began to pray, and God helped him. God turned the light in, and he saw what a sinner he was. He prayed all the next day in the cornfield. That night I went to him and took his hand. He could not speak. He broke down and wept. I told him to come to the altar. He started, but would have fallen if someone had not caught him. He was soon converted and got up and told his experience. He said he had not wept since he was a boy, and he was now forty years old. He had stood by his mother's grave and the graves of his children and never shed a tear. He said it was his last chance. He would have been forever lost if he had refused.

Next I went to Buzzard's schoolhouse, near Huntington, Indiana, to hold a revival meeting. I had heard of this place as being very hard and almost forsaken of God. A number of ministers had labored hard in trying to build up a church but had failed. I felt a desire to go, for I believed many souls would be saved.

Seekers continued to come to the altar by scores, until about one hundred and forty were converted and were very bright, going right to work. Several Dunkards came out, and several church members were converted. Among the converts we counted thirty who were from the ages of fifty to seventy.

I organized a Church of God, and from the results of this meeting the Methodists put up two church houses. There were forty-nine baptized in the river by immersion. They looked like angels and, with many others, came out shouting. This scene was witnessed by hundreds of people on the banks of the river. They seemed to feel that God was there.

On Sunday morning at nine o'clock, the people were coming from all directions to the meeting and assembling in the leafy temple to be present at the closing service of this most wonderful revival.

We spent some time in singing, after which we had a glorious praise meeting. Over one hundred of those who had been converted arose, one after another, telling of Jesus' power on earth to forgive sins and to give them the witness of the Spirit.

Many were received into the church, and we raised several hundred dollars toward building a church. I gave a farewell exhortation to them and closed by shaking hands with them all. It was a hard trial for me; they seemed like my own children. Brothers and sisters, fathers and mothers—we were all weeping together, and many tears were shed. But we looked forward to that great gathering in the mansions fair.

My next meeting was in the country a few miles from Columbia City. The Lord did a great work in that neighborhood. Nearly every house became a house of prayer. Praise God who gives us the victory in every place, over all opposition and persecutions. He convinces the people that He has called and sent me to preach the Gospel with power sent down from heaven, and that He is with me to take care of me and deliver me from the enemies of the Lord and His work.

We next went to Syracuse, Indiana, and held services in a large Union Church. We had a hard battle, but God gave us the victory. The spirit of conviction fell upon the town and surrounding country. Sinners fell as dead men. Others cried for mercy. One night the power of God fell so that the solemnity of the judgment seemed to rest upon the people. The Lord showed me there were some there who would never have another call of mercy. I rose with tears running down my face and told the congregation that death was very near to some of them; that the pale horse was so near them they could almost hear the clatter of his hoofs; and if they left the house that night without making their peace with God, they would be lost forever.

In less than one hour after the meeting, a young man and lady were lying in the bottom of the lake a few yards from the church. They were skating, and the ice broke. They were trying to drive off conviction. I talked to them many times about accepting Christ. I urged them that night to give their hearts to the Lord, to not wait any longer. Many of their friends tried to bring them to Christ that night, but they would not yield. The lady said there was going to be a dance in a few days, and she would wait until after that. They lost their souls and their right to eternal life by turning Christ away and looking forward to a few hours' sinful pleasure. But they were not permitted to attend the dance. In such an hour as they thought not, death came. They fell into the hands of the living God, went into eternity and the judgment to take up the awful wailing: "The harvest is past, the summer is ended, and I am not saved." They were both buried in one grave. The fear of God fell upon the whole community, for many said that I prayed to God to kill them, and that the warning I gave them was from God. Eternity alone will tell how many were brought to Christ in this meeting.

The Great Judgment Morning

(The following is a dream a Salvation Army Captain had.)

I dreamed that the Great Judgment morning
    Had dawned, and the trumpet had blown;
I dreamed that the nations had gathered
    To judgment before the White Throne.
From the Throne came a bright-shining angel
    And stood on the land and the sea,
And swore with his hand raised to heaven,
    That time was no longer to be.
And, oh, what a weeping and wailing
    When the lost ones were told of their fate;
They cried for the rocks and the mountains,
    They prayed but their prayers were too late.

The rich man was there, but his money
    Had melted and vanished away;
A pauper he stood in the judgment,
    His debts were too heavy to pay.
The great man was there, but his greatness
    When death came was left far behind,
The angel that opened the records
    Not a trace of his greatness could find.

The widow was there and the orphans,
  God heard and remembered their cries;
No sorrow in heaven forever,
  God wiped all the tears from their eyes.
The gambler was there and the drunkard,
  And the man who had sold them the drink,
With the people who gave him the license—
  Together in hell they did sink.

The moral man came to the judgment,
  But his self-righteous rags would not do;
The men who had crucified Jesus
  Had passed off as moral men, too.
The soul that had put off salvation—
  "NOT TONIGHT; I'LL GET SAVED BY AND BY;
No time now to think of religion!"
  At last they had found time to die.

11

MANY CONVERSIONS
AND TRANCES

After many invitations from Hartford City, and believing that the Spirit of God was leading that way, I consented to go, and I went believing God would do a great work. I commenced meeting there about the first of January, 1885, in the Methodist Church. The first night it was not known we would be there to commence that evening. They rang the bell, and the people came from every direction and filled the church to overflowing.

The church was cold and formal, and many of the best citizens had drifted into skepticism. I knew that it would take a wonderful display of God's power to convince the people, so I prayed for God to display His power, that the sinner might know that God still lives, and that there is a reality in religion, and this might convict him of a terrible judgment. Five of the leading members of the church said they would unite with me in prayer for the Lord to pour out the power from on high, until the city would be shaken, and the country for miles around. We prayed that Christians and sinners might fall as dead men, that the slain of the Lord might be many. The Lord answered our prayers in a remarkable manner.

The class leader's little boy fell under the power of God first. He rose up, stepped on the pulpit, and began to talk with the wisdom and power of God.

His father began to shout and praise the Lord. As the little fellow exhorted and asked the people to come to Christ, they began to weep all over the house. Some shouted; others fell prostrated. Diverse operations of the Spirit were seen. The displays of the power of God continued to increase until we closed the meetings, which lasted about five weeks. The power of the Lord, like the wind, swept all over the city, up one street and down another, sweeping through the places of business, the workshops, saloons, and dives, arresting sinners of all classes. The Scriptures were fulfilled: *"The wicked flee when no man pursueth"* (Prov. 28:1). Men, women, and children were struck down in their homes, in their places of business, on the highways, and lay as dead. They had wonderful visions and rose converted, giving glory to God. When they told what they had seen their faces shone like angels'. The fear of God fell upon the city. The police said they never saw such a change, that they had nothing to do. They said they made no arrests and that the power of God seemed to preserve the city. A spirit of love rested all over the city. There was no fighting, no swearing on the streets; the people moved softly, and there seemed to be a spirit of love and kindness among all classes, as if they felt they were in the presence of God.

A merchant fell in a trance in his home and lay several hours. Hundreds went in to look at him. He had a vision and a message for the church. The Lord showed him the condition of many of the members. He told part of his vision but refused to deliver the message to the church. He was struck dumb. He could not speak a word because he refused to tell what the Lord wanted him to. The Lord showed him he would never speak until he delivered the message. He rose to his feet, weeping, to tell the vision. God loosed his tongue. Those present knew he had been dumb; and when he began to talk and tell his experience, it had a wonderful effect on the church and sinners.

One night there was a party seventeen miles from the city. Some of the young ladies thought they would have some fun; they began to mimic and act out the trance. The Lord struck some of them down. They lay there as if they had been shot. Their fun-making was soon turned to a prayer meeting, and cries of mercy were heard. The people came to the meetings in sleigh loads many miles. One night while a sleigh load of men and women were going to the meeting, they were jesting about the trances. They made the remark to each other that they were going in a trance that night. Before the meeting closed, all who had been making fun were struck down by the power of God and lay like dead people and had to be taken home in the sled in that condition. Those who came with them were very much frightened when they saw them lying there, and they told how they had been making fun of the power of God on the way to the meeting. Scoffers and mockers were stricken down in all parts of the house.

One man was mocking a woman of whose body God had taken control. She was preaching with gestures. When in that mocking attitude, God struck him dumb. He became rigid and remained with his hands up, and his mouth drawn in that mocking way for five hours, a laughingstock for all in the house. The fear of God fell on all. They saw it was a fearful thing to mock God or make fun of His work. Surely, the Lord worked in a wonderful way in this meeting. The postmaster was converted. All classes from the roughs and toughs to the tallest cedars and brightest talents of the city were brought into the fold of Christ. We took the meeting to the opera house, and it would not hold the crowds, so great was the awakening among the people. Traveling salesmen arranged to return to the city each night. The *Cincinnati Enquirer* sent a reporter to write up the meetings and report daily. Every day the newsboys could be heard crying out, "All about the Woodworth revival." Reporters came from many states and large cities to write up the meetings.

Lawyer C., one of the leading lawyers of the city, was convinced of the reality of the religion of Jesus by seeing me under the control of the Holy Spirit power while in a trance. Sometimes standing with my face and hands raised to heaven, my face shining with the brightness of heaven; other times the tears streaming down my face with mute preaching, pleading with sinners to come to Christ; other times lying for hours, sometimes as one dead, and diverse operations of the Spirit, conscious all the time, but entirely controlled by the power of the Holy Spirit. Always while in these conditions in this meeting, and all others, the fear of God would fall upon the people. Sinners would be stricken down over the house. Many would be saved: they would rush to the altar crying for mercy. Sometimes scores would be converted while God would use me in this way. Mr. C. was the leading lawyer of the state. He was a skeptic and had no use for churches. The ministers had given up all hopes of him ever being saved. When he came and invited us to his house to make our home with them while in the city, people were astonished. He asked me if I would tell him my experience while in a trance. He said he did not ask this to satisfy curiosity, but for light. He said he had confidence in me and would believe what I told him. I knew the Lord was leading in this. I told him more of my experience than I had ever told anyone. While talking, the power of God fell upon us all. I was almost blind with the glory of God.

My hands looked transparent. He broke down and began to weep. We all got on our knees. This was the first time this strong man, this tall cedar, had ever bowed before the living God. In a little while the news had spread all over the city. But that night when he came boldly into the crowded opera house and bowed at the altar, and in a moment another leading lawyer of the city bowed at his side, the excitement and surprise of the people had no bounds. I praise God for victory at this place through our Lord Jesus Christ.

While at Hartford City, calls came from churches in Cincinnati, Fort Wayne, Union City, and many other large cities. They sent one dispatch after another, urging me to come. But God's ways are not our ways; He does not see as man sees. God looks in the heart; man judges from outward appearances. The Lord showed me I must go to a little town fifteen miles away called New Corner. I rode in a sleigh. When I got there, I was so hoarse I could only speak in a whisper and so tired I could not walk without assistance. It was time for meeting. The house and yard were crowded. I could hardly get through to the pulpit. I commenced singing, trusting God to take away the hoarseness and give me voice. In five minutes my voice was strong and clear. I sang in the strength and power of God. I sang two or three hymns. The power of God fell upon me and remained all the week I was there. It could be seen and heard and felt by all who came to the meetings. I preached that night the only sermon while there. After that night I would be interrupted by sinners falling in the congregation. Then there would be a rush to the altar and shouts by the friends of those who were stricken down. In a few minutes the house would be turned into a mourners' bench.

The first night of the meeting, while we were singing, I reached over to shake hands with a man who was standing in the aisle. I asked him to come to Christ. He began to tremble and fell backward. I thought I would not talk to anyone else for fear the people would attribute the power to me instead of God. As I stepped back one of the ministers on the pulpit, the pastor of the church, threw up his hands and fell. The fear of God fell upon the sinners. They thought if the ministers had to go down, there was no chance for them to escape. They tried to get out of the church, but they could not; the house was so packed there was no room to move. Sixty sinners who were near the altar came to the altar; others had to stay back because of want of room. When the minister came out of the trance, he told of the wonderful vision he had, of the horrors of hell and the beauty of heaven. He said heaven was a real city. He saw many of his friends there and talked with them. He saw the hosts of angels. He saw people in hell that he knew on earth.

God showed him some that would go there if they did not repent and be saved in this meeting. This vision stirred the churches and ministers. The ministers came to the altar for a baptism of power. Nearly all their members followed. The second morning they took all the seats out of the church to make all the room they could for the people to stand. They took two rows of seats and made a double altar from the pulpit to the door. They made one on the right and one on the left of the pulpit. These were crowded most all the time, day and night.

Sometimes they were four double. Scores were saved who did not come to the altar. One night there were one hundred and fifteen converted. Nearly all who were saved during this revival, when the Spirit of God came in their hearts, fell under the power or sprang to their feet, shouting the praises of God. Those who fell would lay, some fifteen minutes, some half an hour, some one or two hours, some a day and night, and others longer. They would all come out praising God. I commenced the meetings at nine o'clock in the morning and continued until twelve at night. We could not close, there were so many outside; when one went out, one came in. Sinners were struck down at their homes and along the highways. They were saved for miles around.

Convinced of God's Power

One day fifteen doctors came from different cities to investigate the power and trances. When they came, I was lying under the power of the Holy Spirit. I remained several hours. God used me and others that were in a trance at the same time in a way that convinced them that it was the power of God. One of the doctors was a class leader. He did not want to admit the power was of God. He would have been glad if they could prove it was something else. He came to investigate the trances, but he was called to another part of the house; he went, expecting to find something new. To his surprise he found his son at the altar, who wanted his father to pray for him. He could not pray. God showed him what he was and what he was doing. He began to pray for himself. While praying, he fell in a trance and saw all the horrors of hell. He was falling in. After a terrible struggle, God saved him. He went to work to win souls for Christ. I have heard him tell his awful experience to thousands. Not less than five hundred were saved in one week, and hundreds after the meeting closed, as the result. Men and women were converted miles from the church. Many were struck down and lay like dead men on their way home and miles away from the meeting. Would to God the people could see that it is the mighty moving power of God we need to save the people, as on the Day of Pentecost, when three thousand souls were saved.

The closing scenes of this meeting were very affecting, and the meeting was one of unusual interest, being the last of the series. Many bright testimonies were given by those who were converted.

"No pen, save that of the recording angel, could describe the scenes enacted here tonight. Almost the whole house was transformed into an altar, and cries of mercy from many scores were mingled with shouts of victory. No one can prophesy where this work will end. Many superstitious persons stay away for fear of Mrs. W.'s power to overcome them. Others refuse to shake her hand.

"She came to us, as she does to all her appointments, with the earnest and hearty recommendations of her former neighbors and friends. Letters are now in our midst, and can be seen at any time, from prominent citizens, which sustain her as an energetic, whole-souled Christian lady. Whatever may be said of the trances, there is no denying the fact that her meetings are productive of great good, and that when the sheaves are finally bound for eternity, many will bless the name of the evangelist."

—*Indianapolis Journal*

12

"I WILL WORK AND WHO SHALL HINDER?"

I next went to Summitville, Indiana, and commenced meeting on Wednesday evening, February 25, 1885. The house was crowded the first night. The crowd was made up of infidels, skeptics and scoffers. Many of these scoffers were church members. A few of God's children stood by me praying for victory. Most everyone said, "She will make a failure here," and were hoping it would be a failure. I went in the strength of God, knowing that He that was for me was more than those who were against me. I arose and told them that God was coming in power, that many of them would be at the altar that night, crying for mercy. I saw some laughing, as if to say, you do not know us. I began singing, "Let Me in the Lifeboat." The Holy Spirit fell upon me. God made them be able see the lifeboat on the ocean of eternity, and them drifting away into darkness and despair, down to an awful hell. I led in prayer. When I arose, the silence of death reigned over the house. They were trembling under conviction. While I was preaching, God sent every word like arrows, dipped in the blood of Jesus, to their hearts.

After preaching, I called for sinners to come forward. There was a rush for the altar. It was soon crowded. Those who had opposed me most were the first to come. Some who would not yield were stricken down as dead in different parts of the house. There were many bright conversions the first night. The work went on increasing in interest for one week. About five hundred were saved in the church. The seats were taken out to make standing room. The whole house was a mourners' bench. Many of the worst men in the town and country were saved, and lived earnest Christian lives. Many were saved at home, all around the country, in nearly every house. Some died praising God. Several went out preaching the Gospel. Hundreds have been brought to Christ by their labors.

I commenced meeting at nine o'clock in the morning and closed at twelve at night. Some men arranged to come and break up the meeting. I did not know them nor what they were doing. They came and crowded in at the door. God pointed the leader out to me. With a loud voice I called to him to come to Christ. The fear of God fell upon him. He turned pale as death and started for the altar. When he got halfway, he fell under the power of God. He lay about sixteen hours. The way he talked, and his gestures while lying there, brought the fear of God on all who saw him.

Those who came in with him saw it was a fearful thing to fight against God. They were soon on their knees crying for mercy. When he came out, he had a wonderful experience to tell, which God used to bring many to Christ. He went to work to bring souls to Christ and soon began to preach. Many ministers came and received the anointing power from on high. The power of the Holy Spirit fell upon me the first meeting and remained while I was there. It could be seen, heard, and felt by all who came. Many times the power would take control of me when singing, praying, and preaching. I would be held standing, a spectacle for men and angels. Sometimes I would lay for hours at a time. The holy fire went into all the churches and spread for miles. Hundreds of lost souls were brought to Christ after I had gone to other fields.

From Fairmount we went to Columbia City, Indiana, and commenced meeting in the Universalist Church Thursday evening, March 12, 1885, which lasted about four weeks. Sinners came to the altar the first night. Many made a start for heaven. The interest was so great we engaged the large skating rink, which was crowded. The interest continued until the last. Many who had been saved in my meetings a year previous, and some of the ministers and Christians who assisted me in those different places, came up to the help of the Lord against the mighty.

Called to Preach Divine Healing

The Lord showed me while here that I had the gift of healing and of laying on of hands for the recovery of the sick. I had been working day and night for many months and had no strength only as God gave me each meeting. It would be two o'clock often before I would get to sleep. When God began to show me I must preach divine healing, I could not understand that it was the Spirit of God leading me. For three nights when I was almost dead for rest, I lay awake. God was teaching me a lesson I could not, or would not, learn. I said: "Lord, you know I started out to win souls for heaven, and I have been busy all the time. I have tried to be faithful in every-thing You have given me to do. I am so exhausted with constant labor that I have to be helped many times to rise from my bed."

I thought if I would preach divine healing, they would bring all the cripples in the country, and I would neglect the salvation of souls. The Lord showed me He would take care of the work. I told the Lord if He wanted me to pray for the sick, to send them to the meetings and show me He wanted me to pray for them, and I would. When I made this promise, I had perfect rest of mind and soul. From this time God began to lead me to teach divine healing and prayer for the sick. It is now nine years since, and God has healed thousands of all manner of diseases. Thousands have been brought to Christ by seeing the people healed. The devil tried to make me think there would not be nearly so many saved.

On Friday, April 10, 1885, we left Columbia City for Hartford City, Indiana. At Fort Wayne we were met by Lawyer C., of Hartford City, who escorted us to his house. In the evening we met the Daniel's Band at their nicely fitted-up room and found them all on fire for God, which cheered our hearts. The Daniel's Band arranged to have meetings in the opera house, as I was going to stay over Sunday. At five o'clock Saturday evening, they began to fill the house; and by the time the meeting commenced, the house was full to overflowing, and God greatly blessed the people, and several souls were saved. On Sunday the house was full all day. But Sunday evening was the grandest and most glorious sight I ever witnessed; fully two thousand people were crowded into the hall, and fifteen or more were entranced during the evening, and God was present in mighty power. On Monday we went to New Corner, and in the evening met the Daniel's Band of that place. The house was literally packed, and there were not enough sinners in the house to fill the altar, almost everyone being on the Lord's side.

By very urgent request I next went to Tipton, Indiana. I commenced meeting on Sunday morning, April 26, 1885, at the Methodist Church, and for two weeks we held up the cross of Christ to a dying world, amidst all opposition from professing Christians and the outside world. All hell seemed arrayed against us, but I trusted in the Lord Jehovah to give us the victory. And many hundreds praise God for the meeting at Tipton.

On the second Sunday evening, amidst the most intense excitement, when the altar was filled with seeking penitents, a Mrs. Y. went into a trance, and while in that condition, Dr. P. went to the front part of the house to see the trance for himself. She soon commenced to motion for him to get down on his knees. He fell as one dead. He yielded to the Lord; as he afterwards said, he believed it was then or never. God blessed and saved him.

I never saw such demonstrations of the Spirit and power as at this meeting. Many of the leading church members were struck down or stood held, not able to move, under the power of God, their faces shining with the glory of God. The presence of God was so felt that the fear of the Lord fell upon all the people.

In the two weeks I was there, over five hundred came out on the Lord's side. May they ever be kept faithful to the end of life.

News of the wonderful work of God was spreading all over the country. The interest was so great I could not get any time to rest, day or night. Committees were sent from all parts for me to go and hold meetings in different churches. I was so exhausted from constant work I could hardly sit up. We slipped off to Indianapolis and took boarding in a private house, hoping to rest a few days without anyone knowing where we were; but we had not been there half a day, until several ministers from the city churches came to see me and tried to persuade me to hold meetings in their churches. I told them it was impossible at that time. They then urged me to preach on Sunday, but I had to refuse.

Some came from Pendleton, Indiana, who traced us to our boardinghouse and begged very hard for me to come there, if only for a week. I had only one week before my next appointment. I saw I could not rest there, so I told them I would go. The news of my coming got there a few hours before I did. The preacher's family, and nearly every other, were cleaning house and making garden. Things could not have been more discouraging. I was so weak I had to go to bed until meeting time and then be helped to church. I stayed eight days. The result of this wonderful meeting was that several hundred souls had their names written in the Lamb's Book of

Life, including many leading citizens of the town and county—doctors, lawyers, and merchants. Dr. T., a noted infidel, was converted and healed of diabetes. He is now a member of the legislature of Indiana. The oldest sinners and the hardest were saved.

We prayed for the Lord to convict them on the trains and make them get off, and come and be saved. One afternoon I fell under the power of God and had a vision, and lay until the house was crowded. At night five doctors examined me, and they said I was in a normal condition, and that my pulse and heartbeat were natural, but that it was keeping time with the music. I showed them by signs that they would all be converted and showed them their calling, and they were all made to praise God.

While in that condition I saw three men come in from the train. They were all traveling men.

The people thought that I would not be able to preach, but I arose and stood before a packed congregation. The power of the Holy Spirit was like a cloud on the people. I saw the three men that I had seen in my vision come from the train. They were not sitting together. I went to each one and told them that the Lord had brought them there, and that they would all be converted that night. They were angry at first and said they were going to another city, but something got hold of them, and they had to get off the train. They saw the crowd going to the church, so they came, too. Praise the Lord, they were all saved that night. One told me that he was going right back home—twelve hundred miles—to tell his mother the good news.

After a week or two these men came to another place, where we were holding meeting, and told of the wonderful way they were brought to Christ.

From that meeting the revival swept over that country, and thousands were rejoicing in a Savior's love. The richest men and women were brought to Christ, and they built a nice new church.

For twenty miles around, men and women were struck down in their homes, in business places, and on the roads and streets. Some lay for hours and had wonderful visions. Many went into the ministry or became evangelists.

The Spirit's Power

After long solicitation, which had been kept up constantly for over four months, I next went to Kokomo, Indiana, and for three weeks God wonderfully blessed me and the people of that city.

My first meeting was held in the Friends' Church, which was very large. It would not hold the people. The next day we went to the courthouse. While there, Barnum's show came to the city. The papers said there would be a race between the Woodworth meeting and the show to see who would get the biggest crowd. Hundreds came to the city to go to the show, but when they heard of the wonderful meeting in the courthouse they came there. Once, while the great show was passing, I was preaching and held the crowd. The next time they passed, there were several hundred on their knees in prayer. Not one went to the window. Praise God for such victory through the power of the Holy Spirit. We went from the courthouse to the skating rink, the largest building in the city. About one hundred were baptized. It was said about twenty thousand witnessed this solemn and wonderful scene. The first one baptized was a Methodist minister. About twenty church members who had not thought of being baptized were so impressed they stepped out with their best clothes on and were baptized. The crowds were so large I had to appoint three meetings that night. One was held in the courthouse yard and one on the street. Some ministers took charge of these meetings, and I held services in the rink. The power of God was felt for fifty miles round. Thousands of souls were brought into the light of God. The Sunday we closed, God gave us a Pentecost. The Holy Spirit fell on the multitude that had crowded in the rink and around the door. The power of God had been poured out in all the meetings, and "signs and wonders" followed and rested upon the people. The Holy Spirit sat upon the blood-washed sons and daughters of the Lord Almighty.

In two hours five hundred converts had testified that they knew they were saved by the power of God and happy on their way to heaven. Many fell under the power of the Holy Spirit while speaking. Many fell in all parts of the house. Old men and women wept aloud. Others shouted, and sinners cried for mercy. All classes were stricken down in the meetings, many church members and ministers of different denominations, not only in the meetings, but in the city and miles away. They had wonderful visions of hell and heaven and many of the deep things of God. As they stood and told these visions, the fear of God fell upon the people, and hundreds were convicted and brought to Christ.

One minister on his way home stopped ten miles away with some friends who had been to the meeting; while there, he fell in a trance. The news soon spread. The neighbors gathered in. One left his plow and went in. He had been fighting off conviction. As he looked at his minister lying like one dead, the Spirit of God showed him if he was not converted before he come out of the trance, he would be lost forever. He fell on his knees and called upon God to save him. Others followed. The house became a mourners' bench. Soon their mourning was turned to shouts of praise. Before the minister came back from his visit to heaven, the news had been shouted around the throne: "Sinners are coming home to God." This is only one instance out of hundreds where God has started a revival far away from the meetings, by striking someone down in a trance. The great revival at Cornelius' house was all brought about by two trances—one a sinner, the other a saint—though they were many miles apart at the time. God used three visions to bring about the conversion of Saul. If I would write all the mighty works of God, I would have to write a book for each meeting.

13

THOUSANDS ATTEND CAMP MEETINGS

After closing the meeting at Kokomo, I went to Elwood to visit the dear young converts there and encourage them on their Christian journey. I had a blessed time indeed and found them all standing faithful and working earnestly for the salvation of those around them.

I held a camp meeting at Greentown, Xenia, Willow Branch, ten miles from Willow Branch, Millenor's Corner, and Greenfield, Indiana.

All these meetings were attended by thousands daily, and thousands were converted. A number of church houses were built by different denominations, and a number of churches organized as the result of these meetings.

After closing the meeting in the schoolhouse near Millenor's Corner, we held a camp meeting five miles from Alexandria, Indiana. We were there over two Sundays. This was the most wonderful meeting I had ever held. The congregation was estimated at twenty-five thousand. In the morning before the preaching, there were hundreds of ringing testimonies of present salvation. I then preached about the Holy Spirit power. Before I got through, the power of God fell on the multitude and took control of about five hundred. Many fell to the ground. Others stood with their faces and hands raised to heaven. The Holy Spirit sat upon them. Others shouted, some talked, others wept aloud. Sinners were converted and began to testify and praise God. I was overpowered and carried to my tent. In the afternoon they made a high platform in the grove, so that I could be seen and heard by the multitude. In the strength of God, I arose and stood before the largest congregation I had ever stood before. God gave me a deep subject. I talked nearly two hours. The people all stood. The solemnity of death rested upon the multitude. Some had their bodies healed, and thousands were brought to Christ.

Dr. T. was afflicted with a disease called diabetes. He felt there was no hope for him. The best physicians had given him up, and he was liable to drop any time. He had lost twenty-four pounds in two weeks before his conversion. He came twice to the meeting at Pendleton. He was a noted infidel and horse jockey, and would not allow a Bible in his house. I prayed for God to heal him, soul and body, and it was done, and he went home praising God, feeling he was every whit whole.

He had a large practice, but he found a great deal of time to work for God. He has been a firebrand for God since his conversion, yea, hundreds have been brought to Christ through his labors. He lived many years, and every year on the anniversary of his conversion, he had a meeting in his house, at which there were many conversions. He had great success, became a statesman, and was a power for God. Glory to God for His wonderful works.

Just a word or two from the lips of the father of Sister D., of the vicinity of Alexandria, who, by faith, had been raised almost from the dead:

"For years, with a combination of diseases, my daughter was suffering. Five doctors had given her up to die. For about six months she lay in bed, most of the time not being able to sit up without being propped up with pillows. It was decided by her physicians that there was no use in giving her any more medicine.

"When seemingly the last moments had come, when she could not raise her head, and had to be helped like a child, and was so light her husband could take her on his hands as he would a child, when fully given up to die, and when perfectly submissive to God's will, she raised herself up in bed and was standing on the floor before she knew what she was doing, and then began to walk around the room, a living skeleton. Her husband was very much alarmed, thinking death had struck her, and was looking for her to fall.

"Sister Woodworth was sent for to come and pray for her recovery, but she couldn't come, but while in a buggy, prayed fervently for her recovery. At the same hour Mrs. D. went into a trance, in which she saw Christ surrounded by a bright light and a crowd of sinners to the left. She felt herself raised up, arose from bed, walked out, and ate a hearty supper. 'The prayer of those who abide in God availeth much.'"

This sister went into the field as an evangelist to work for the salvation of souls. We learn that she has had glorious success.

At the close of the meeting near Alexandria, we started on our trip South, stopping for a few days at the beautiful city of Louisville, Kentucky. We journeyed on southward, reaching Memphis, Tennessee, after several days of wearisome travel.

Revival Fire Spreads

We remained in Memphis about one month, holding meetings in several of the large churches. I started four revivals and also worked some with the colored people of that city. On our arrival at Indianapolis, Indiana, I found a letter awaiting, calling me immediately to New York City. We went and for the first time saw the wonderful city—the metropolis of America.

We visited Central Park and many other beautiful places of interest during our stay. We also attended Moody's meetings and assisted in the work.

As I stood on a street of the busy city and looked at the wonderful works of men, I saw the last prophecies fulfilled before my eyes. Chariots rushing over the tops of the high buildings, the cars flying through the air, and stations all around the city built in the air. Looking down from these stations, you see the streetcars jostling one against the other. Every place you look, you can hear the voice of God speaking in tones of thunder: "Prepare for judgment; the angel will soon stand with one foot on the land, the other on the sea, and swear that delay shall be no longer."

Leaving New York, we returned by way of Philadelphia and Harrisburg, Pennsylvania. After leaving these places, we went to Shippensburg and attended the eldership of the Church of God. On Sunday they all insisted that I should preach. It was quite a cross, as my work had been in revivals, and I was very tired after my long journey. They being all strangers to me, I knew it was more needful that God should be with me. The house was filled to the galleries, and the churchyard was filled. There were many ministers present. I talked for one hour from the following words, found in 1 Corinthians 16:22: "*If any man love not the Lord Jesus Christ, let him be Anathema Maranatha.*"

From there we went home with Elder M. to Chambersburg, Pennsylvania, and commenced meetings at that place, with a few hours' notice. I stayed three weeks at this place and had a glorious meeting. Many aged ones were converted, one eighty-two years old, and also many of the best citizens. And the whole church choir was brought into the fold. When I came away, I left five revivals in the city, all having glorious success. Three weeks before, I went to this city a stranger. I had never been in the place before nor held a meeting in the state. The first the people knew of my coming was the ringing of the church bell. The Church of God where I held the revival was in a very bad condition. They had had everything to discourage the few that were left.

One woman was saved at the washtub. She shouted all over the house. A Catholic was struck down in a machine shop where several hundred men were at work. They thought he was dead, or dying. They did everything they could to bring him to, but all their efforts failed. He lay several hours, then sprang to his feet shouting the praise of God. The fear of God fell upon the men who saw him. They had to acknowledge that it was the power of God.

From Chambersburg we went to Huntington, Indiana, stopped at New Bethel, and held a few meetings in Trinity Chapel.

From there we went to Columbia City, Indiana, where I organized a Church of God eight months previous when I was there. I found the church on fire for God. They have since put up a fine church edifice.

From Columbia City we went to Butler, Indiana, where I had a hard battle to fight for my Master, but glorious victory crowned my labors. I organized a Church of God of one hundred members. Nine years have passed since, and the fire is still burning that spread in all directions at that time when hundreds were brought to Christ.

At the close of this meeting, we started to visit my old home in Ohio, after an absence of three years. It was a great pleasure to meet all the loved ones again, especially my aged mother, and hear her say, as I kissed her at parting: "I will meet you in heaven." My prayers have been answered; my mother was converted. At the age of seventy she found her Savior.

On our way, returning from my home in Ohio, we stopped at Cleveland, Ohio. Some of the brothers heard I was in the city and made an announcement for me for one meeting in the Mission Church of that city. I went, and the interest was so great that I continued for some time. Moody was in the city; people had been looking for him for over two months. Everyone was prepared to go. We had large crowds. The interest increased. The power of the Lord was never so manifested in the city before. One businessman was stricken down at his home. He sent to our meeting for some of the workers to come and pray for him. He seemed like a dying man, but he soon came out shouting and went to his place of business. At our next meeting he said he had gone away from our meeting, calling me everything but a lady, and told how God had stricken him down and showed him the pit of hell, and what an awful thing it was to fight against the power and work of God.

A student from one of the Cleveland colleges spoke lightly of the power of God at one of our meetings, and as he was going out of the door, he was stricken down and had to be carried to his home. One of the wealthiest ladies of the city fell in a trance in the back part of the church. Every eye was on her. When she came to, she was converted. She got up and walked through the aisle and told what God had done; then she got down and went to work with the seekers.

A Minister Stricken

One of the city ministers spoke lightly of the power in one of our meetings; that night he went to his church to preach, but God had shut his mouth. He could not preach. He shut the Bible. His mouth was closed. He came back to our meeting the next day to make confession. He said God had brought him down through a wonderful experience, and he wanted to warn the people not to fight the power of God in those meetings. He said he believed God would smite them down and spoke of the time when Saul's daughter made sport of David for shouting and dancing before the Ark of God. God smote her with barrenness.

14

THE HARVEST IS GREAT

After being at Troutman, Pennsylvania, and Harmony, Pennsylvania, we started for Lawrence, Kansas. The Lord wonderfully blessed my labor there. The fire of the Lord began to break out in all directions, and it was hard to resist the earnest pleadings of brothers and sisters to remain and reap the harvest ready to be gathered. The calls kept coming from Indiana, "Come back; your work is not done." The Lord seemed to be calling me day and night to go back.

We went. My first meeting was at Kokomo, Indiana, the seat of war. We pitched our tents and sounded the battle cry, calling for soldiers. They began to come in from the East and West, North and South. We had a grand reunion; several hundred converts of the meeting of one year before were there; also many others, with their bright testimonies that God had kept them through all the persecutions; many had been healed of all manner of diseases. Many of them had gone into the field as evangelists and many as ministers. On one day there were present twenty young ministers, who had been licensed by the different churches, all converts of my first meeting at Kokomo. I could now see why the Lord had brought me back: to encourage and establish these dear workers. Hundreds of souls have been brought to Christ through their meetings.

A preacher came to this meeting, who was dying with consumption, and was healed in the presence of thousands, while we were praying for him. He went out to preach the Gospel.

They have built a fine church edifice at Kokomo and have the most powerful church in the city; also the largest congregations.

Over all opposition and the roaring of the devil and his children, the Lord led us on to glorious victory.

Ministers came from other places, and the young soldiers rallied to the front. The first night while I was leading in prayer, the power swept over the multitude in waves.

Brother D., sixty years old, who had been lame for twelve years, had to walk with a cane or crutch. He could not remain in one place but a short time. Several of us knelt and prayed with him, laying our hands on him. The Holy Spirit fell on him, and the pain left him, the swelling went down, and the callous parts disappeared; he leaped to his feet, shouting, "Glory to God, I am healed." *"The lame man shall leap as an hart"* (Isa. 35:6). He threw his crutch away. It is now about nine years since he was healed; he has testified before thousands; many have visited him; others have written him. He is well now. *"These signs shall follow them that believe"* (Mark 16:17).

Dr. Daggett was the first we ever laid hands on for healing.

In our meeting last August, 1915, in Topeka, Kansas, I was led of the Spirit to tell of this first healing. After I was through, a man came forward and said he was Dr. Daggett's son, and that thirty years ago, he was converted by reading one of my books, a few months before his father was so wonderfully healed, but had never seen me until the meeting in which his father was healed, after suffering from lameness, for many years. His father had a new lease of life and lived many years after.

Surely "God moves in mysterious ways, His wonders to perform." And He is always ready to smile on our work in Jesus' name and to confirm His Word.

On Sunday morning we commenced praise service at nine o'clock, with a large crowd which continued to increase until the grove was a moving mass of living souls. The songs of praise, shouts of joy, and the ringing testimonies came from the old and young, from the white-haired fathers and mothers down to the little boys. When I asked for all those who had been blessed and knew they were saved to raise their hands, not less than five hundred hands were raised, and all shouted, "Praise the Lord." The power came like a cyclone. The multitude swayed to and fro. Sinners were converted on their feet. God's servants were so filled with the glory of God, they could not administer, as the priests of old. Some of their faces shone like Stephen's when he was brought before false witnesses.

My next meeting was at Summitville, Indiana. We pitched our tents and commenced battle. The enemy thought he had this place, and indeed it had that appearance; but the soldiers of the Lord came in companies from all points. Many ministers and converts by the score, who had been converted at my meetings two years previous, came.

15

AN EARTHQUAKE
AT ANDERSON

The sinners and Christian people of Anderson, Indiana, had been making an effort for two years to get me to go to their city and hold a meeting. I had a strong desire to do so, but was unable to go until July, when I commenced a camp meeting at the fairgrounds.

The first night the tent did not hold the people. Nearly all were non-professors, or dead professors, which is worse. I had very little help. Many citizens who had been professed unbelievers made their way through the crowd and stood by us. They encouraged the meeting enough to make the church members blush and bow their heads in the dust. We had hardly strength to stand or voice to speak, but we commenced the battle in the strength of Elijah's God, shouting victory!

I did not ask sinners to come, but insisted on professors coming to the front, but the sinners made a rush and came crowding to the front from different parts of the tent.

Before the meeting closed, nearly the whole city became interested and wanted to do something. Ladies from all the different churches called and invited me to their homes. Every inducement was offered to get me to remain longer, but I had promised to go to Farmland, Indiana, and must keep my appointment. I should have been at Farmland the Sunday previous. I was publicly announced for that time. I sent several other good workers at that time to carry on the work until I could go. On the first Saturday night when I was expected at Farmland, there were two thousand people at the depot to meet me, and they were much disappointed because I sent others instead of going myself. While sitting in the station at Anderson, waiting for the train to take me to Farmland, I was surprised to see one of the evangelists sitting there that I had sent to Farmland. She said she was discouraged and could not do anything there; the people were so hard and spiritually dead. She said she had a vision and saw them all in their coffins and believed they were so dead they would never be raised spiritually. As soon as I got there, one of the other evangelists I had sent there slipped off without telling me she was going.

I had no thought of running. In the strength of God I arose and was helped to the pulpit. I stood trembling, and began to sing. The power came upon me. I prayed and preached, and then called sinners to the altar. To the surprise of all, many came. Soon the shouts of newborn sons and daughters of the Lord were heard over the camp. The altar was crowded, day and night, for ten days with seekers. It seemed almost impossible to close with such an interest, but I had promised to go back to Anderson in ten days. The whole community was stirred, and hundreds were under deep conviction, but I had to close.

In ten days I went back to Anderson and commenced a meeting in a beautiful grove the brothers had secured.

There were twenty-eight conversions the first night of my return. I continued this meeting for three weeks, holding three services each day; sometimes one service would continue on into the next. There were from twenty to fifty conversions each day. Men and women were converted at this meeting from nearly every state in the Union, and went to their homes to carry the tidings of a Savior's love.

There were thousands on the campground every day. The power of the Holy Spirit came as a cyclone, and many times the multitude were swayed as the growing grain in the wind storm. There would be shouts going up all over the congregation. Men and women would be stricken down in every direction and carried to the large platform; it would not hold the slain of the Lord. The scene was beyond description; more than two thirds of the large congregation stood through the entire service; many of them old fathers and mothers, whose locks were whitening for the grave. Many of this class were brightly converted.

Lawyers, doctors, and infidels were brought to Christ, from the "tallest cedars" (see Isaiah 37:24) down to the weakest. Many poor drunkards were lifted up by this meeting, who today are bright citizens. Oh, praise the Lord for the wonderful work done at Anderson. There were thousands of conversions.

Two very old ladies were brought to the meetings who were too feeble to get out of their buggy; and at their request the horse was taken from the buggy, and they were left sitting in it. The buggy was drawn up near the stand, and both old ladies were converted during the meeting. An old gentleman living in the southern suburbs of the city attended one of the meetings and purchased a song book, and after he got home, sat down and read it; while reading, he was converted and broke forth in song and praise, which drew the neighbors to his house. These joined in and were also converted. The singing and shouting of these converts were heard throughout the neighborhood.

These meetings were participated in by as many good men and women as there were in that county, or as can be found in any county.

While hundreds were stepping into the lifeboat and starting for glory, many bright men and women were almost persuaded, yet they would not surrender. I was very much concerned about them. I felt it was now or never with them. The Lord impressed me to say it was the last call and to ask all who believed in prayer to fall on their knees and raise faces and hands to God, and to ask Him to shake the earth, to send an earthquake, if necessary. The people, five hundred or more, knelt in prayer with their hands raised to heaven, and what a wonderful sight it was! All expected the Lord to come near in some wonderful way. The power of God fell in the congregation, and all at once the earth began to shake. There was an earthquake, and it was felt all over the city. It was the time that Charleston, South Carolina, was destroyed, and it reached to Anderson, Indiana. The prayer of faith will be answered, if the Lord has to bring heaven down.

The earth has been shaken at many places so that the multitude swayed and fell.

A lawyer got up one day in the meeting and said he must say a word about the good work that eternity alone would reveal. He held in his hand a letter he had received from his brother, who had been a noted infidel, saying he had never seen me nor attended any of my meetings, but by what he had seen and heard of them from a distance and by reading my book, he was converted and was going into the ministry. He said he had several hundred dollars worth of infidel books, and he had made a fire and burned them. The lawyer who told this about his brother said he was an infidel when I came to the city, but his infidelity was all swept away.

I organized a church in the grove. Two hundred and ninety-five names were enrolled. Hundreds came and took them by the hand in Christian fellowship. It was a sight perhaps no one on the campground had ever witnessed before.

By an earnest request from a number of businessmen of the city, we held the closing meeting on the courthouse steps. As we looked down over the courthouse yard and street, we could see a crowded mass of upturned faces, and from all the stores and windows, all were eager to see and hear. I praise God for standing by me in that trying hour. It took grace and courage for me to stand on those high steps. There were ministers, lawyers, doctors, and reporters all around me. After so many months of constant labor, I was very weak and nervous, but God gave me voice clear and strong. I could be heard blocks away.

While holding meeting at Anderson, the ministers of the different churches at Farmland formed a committee and came to Anderson to try to persuade me to go back. They said they had all seen the good results of the ten days' meeting I had held there, that there was a great change in the community for good, and the churches were wonderfully revived and strengthened, and those who stood back before were now ready to come to the front and do all they could to help me. I felt it was the Lord's will for me to go. When I closed the meeting at Anderson, I went and commenced a camp meeting in a better grove than the one we held the first meeting in, the good results of which eternity alone can tell. Nearly all the ministers of the village came to the front and fought the battle side by side with me.

Hundreds were converted, many aged ones. I don't think there were a dozen converted that were not over eighteen years of age. I think half of all that were saved were forty years of age.

Signs and wonders truly followed. (See Mark 16:17–20.) The Holy Spirit came in slaying, melting, anointing, and healing power.

Praise the Lord for His wonderful works and the great harvest of souls gathered at Farmland.

The ministers and old people said there never had been such a revival in that part of the country, that there had never been such an outpouring of the Holy Spirit, never such signs and wonders followed, never such an ingathering of souls.

16

VICTORY IN A HARD PLACE

After many solicitations by the Christian people of Muncie, Indiana, to come to their city and hold a camp meeting, I decided to do so and went there from Farmland and commenced a meeting on the fairgrounds. It was under very discouraging circumstances that I started the meeting at that place. The weather was cold and dismal, and the hearts of the people colder still; but I commenced, knowing that God would bring wonderful victory. I was nearly worn out with the hard battle at Farmland, and as I had very little help, it looked dreary, but I had faith in God, and He brought me through, *more than* [a] *conqueror*" (Rom. 8:37). The skies brightened, and with the bright skies came the people until the large tent was overflowing. At some services many were unable to get within earshot of my voice.

God was present in mighty power, and hundreds were brought to the Savior's loving arms. Many aged ones were brought to Christ, and scores were healed of various diseases.

Muncie was noted for infidelity and scoffers of religion. They had made their boast many times, saying that I would never come to Muncie, that I was afraid of them. After hearing so much loud talk, I determined to go and let them know what God could do. Many of these infidels and scoffers were the first to fall under the slaying power of God. Others trembled so they could not stand, fell on their faces, and cried to God for mercy. The meeting continued four weeks. The oldest people said there had never been such an awakening; they had never seen such multitudes assembled for the purpose of worshipping the living God. Many converts from our meetings in Hartford City, New Corner, and all through Indiana, and from other states, came to help fight the battle.

Scores of ministers came with their workers. On Sundays the crowds were so great we could not hold the meetings in the tent. They made a high platform on the top of the hill in the grove. When it was understood that the services would be conducted in the open air, such a stampede had never been witnessed by anyone present. Everyone tried to get where they could see and hear. There were no seats, young and old had to stand, but they seemed glad to get a place to stand. Scores of these were very old; they wept and shouted and praised God that they were permitted to live to see a real Pentecost revival. Day after day the power of the Lord swept over the congregation until many times they were shaken like grain in a storm. These meetings, as in all other places, looked like a battlefield; the slain of the Lord could be seen lying all around, and sinners weeping their way to Calvary, amid the shouts of victory and the howling and growling of the enemy that was driven from the field.

Having long felt impressed that it was my duty to commence a work for the Master at the capital of Indiana, we went from Muncie to that city and inaugurated what proved to be the hardest contested battle I ever fought for King Jesus.

God Brings the Victory

On a cold December night, we threw our banner to the breeze in the Meridian Rink, at Indianapolis. I think I am safe in saying no one ever commenced a revival meeting in that place with as little sympathy and as much opposition as we did. The powers of darkness were all in battle array against us, but in the midst of all the trying circumstances and fiery darts thrust at us on all sides by the enemy, we continually looked to Jesus, and, though the battle was long and hard, we had a grand victory.

It was just two weeks before Christmas, and the churches were all having one social after another, preparing to have a big time for the holidays; and most of them were thinking of everything else but a revival of Holy Spirit religion. Nearly all the people had their minds on Christmas, and their time was taken up in some way. I could see multitudes of souls all around, rushing down to an awful hell; I could see the funeral passing every day, many of them taking a leap in the dark. Instead of looking at the dark side of all these things and getting discouraged, I felt my responsibility that much heavier, and said, in the strength of our God, we will go forward. About three days before we went to the city, the United Brethren church house burned down. The minister and his members came up to the help of the Lord against the mighty. The salt of the city, as they heard of the battle, came. Many ministers stood by and worked nobly in the battle. They were never absent if they could get there. We had three services a day. Souls were saved in every meeting. We remained in the rink four weeks; then we went to the Masonic hall.

The house was filled day and night. Hundreds came from the country and other cities. Hundreds of old people were saved, from forty to seventy-five years of age. Some were eighty-five. One old lady was brought twenty-five miles. She was one hundred and three years old. She had fallen and had been badly injured. Her sufferings were so great she could be heard screaming day and night. When she heard of the people being healed, she told her son if he would bring her to the meeting, God would relieve her suffering and heal her. It was a big undertaking in her condition, but he was very proud of his aged mother and anxious to do anything to relieve her. She was carried in. We prayed for her, and she was healed and filled with the power of God. She shouted over the house and praised God and magnified His name in a wonderful manner. When her son rose and told the people his mother was one hundred and three years old, they said, "We have seen strange things today." She was the oldest person I had ever met. A minister who stood very high in the Methodist Church and who had helped us in the meeting, said he had been laboring for lost souls for forty years, had been in many wonderful revivals, but had never seen so many aged men and women at the altar, never saw so many gray heads bowed in sorrow, weeping their way to Calvary.

The closing day (Sunday) of our meeting at Indianapolis was without a parallel as a day of rejoicing among those children of God. The house was crowded all day with those who had been saved during the meetings, and many were unable to gain admittance. A general praise meeting commenced in the morning and continued nearly all day.

At night the building was filled to overflowing at an early hour. Hundreds were unable to gain admittance. I spoke for over an hour on the subject, "The General Resurrection." At the close of the service, we stood for nearly an hour saying farewell and shaking the hands of those we had learned to love during our stay in Indianapolis.

We next went to Greensburg, Indiana, where previous arrangements had been made for us. We started our meeting on the following Saturday night at the opera house. Here, as at other places, we found true Christianity at a discount, and, dear reader, do not be surprised when I tell you that on the first night when I asked those who were on the Lord's side to stand up, no one in the large crowd acknowledged that he belonged to Jesus. This was the start at Greensburg, but before long, scores were on their feet at once, only too glad of an opportunity to tell that they were on the Lord's side.

We continued our meetings for four weeks and had a grand victory for our Master. Several hundred were brightly converted. Many were entranced at the different services, some of them seeing wonderful visions. A merchant's wife who was converted was entranced at one of the services while sitting in a chair. While in that condition, she was the very picture of loveliness. The scene was awe-inspiring and caused the most stouthearted to weep. She came out shouting, having, as she said, seen her daughter in heaven.

Judge W. came to the meeting from Anderson. He told the congregation he felt it a duty he owed to God and the people to come there and tell what the Lord had done for him a hundred miles away in answer to our prayer. He said he was very low with consumption; had given up all hope of getting well; expected to die soon; and that I had appointed a time for prayer and told him to go to the Lord at that time and expect God to heal and baptize him with the Holy Spirit, and we would pray for him at the same time, and it would be done. He said while all alone with God at the time appointed, he was healed. The people saw he was well and strong. He stayed several days at the meeting.

Brother H., a Methodist minister of Indianapolis, was very sick and was instantly healed while we prayed for him. He came to Greensburg and told what Jesus had done for him. While he was talking, the power of God fell upon him. He began to shout, "Hallelujah!" The words rolled out with such power and sweetness that they seemed to come from behind the throne.

At the close of the meeting at Decatur, we packed our tents for the season and returned to Indiana and held a few days' meeting. While there, we met many of those who had been healed of bodily diseases at the meetings a year previous, and in every instance they were strong and well, just as we expected, for God's work is not like man's. It is thorough and lasting.

As we look back over the years of labor for the Master, we remember the many hard battles fought amidst trying scenes and difficulties. Through it all, we have ever kept our eyes on Jesus and been led by His loving hand. No matter how hard the battle, nor how strong the hosts arrayed against us, God has brought us through more than conqueror. All glory to His name.

He Is Coming Soon

How sweet are the tidings that greet the pilgrim's ear.
  As he wanders in exile from home;
Soon will the Savior in glory appear,
  And soon will the kingdom come.

CHORUS

He's coming, coming soon, I know,
  Coming back to this earth again,
And the weary pilgrim will to glory go,
  When the Savior comes to reign.

The mossy old graves where the pilgrims sleep,
  Shall be opened as wide as before,
And the millions that sleep in the mighty deep
  Shall live on this earth once more.

There we'll meet all our loved ones in our Eden homes;
  Sweet songs of redemption we'll sing;
From the North, from the South, all the ransomed shall come,
  And worship our heavenly King.

Hallelujah, amen, Hallelujah, again,
  In a little while we shall be there,
Oh! be faithful, be hopeful, be joyful till then,
  And a crown of bright glory we'll wear.

17

AN AFFIRMING VISION

After attending the eldership at Indianapolis, we went to Anderson, Indiana, to attend the dedication of the new church, which was built by the church I organized there one year before. It is a large, comfortable house. From Anderson we went to Urbana, Illinois, to visit the Daniel's Band. The Band met in Busly's hall, which was crowded, all the standing room being taken, and hundreds were turned away. There was a number of ministers present who took part and spoke of the great work that had been done while we were there before, and was still being done by the Band. Many testified that they had been healed four months and were still well. Some had better health than ever before. Three had been healed of cancer. We saw that the converts were strong men and women in the Lord.

We next went to Hannibal, Missouri, and stopped at the Park Hotel. We rented the rink, paying the rent ourselves. We had one of the hardest battles we ever fought. There was a band of false professors there. No one had confidence in them or their religion. They rushed into our meeting and tried to run away with it. We knew nothing about them, but I saw it was counterfeit. The people of the city saw them taking such an active part and supposed we were just like them. This had the effect of keeping people away. I bore with them as long as I could, hoping that they would see that they were wrong and would walk in the light. But none are so blind as those who will not see. I told them they must fall into line with us or fall out. They would not do either, but did everything that could be done to break up the meeting.

When the people saw that we did not approve of such work, the interest increased until the largest building in the city was crowded and hundreds were turned away. The first convert was an old man, a saloonkeeper seventy years old. Many people followed, among whom were many of the best citizens. The long altar was filled day and night. Sometimes the altar was cleared in a few minutes— all converted or healed—and filled the second time and sometimes the third. They were not only stricken down as dead in the meeting, but many miles away. One man was struck down in a trance at his home and lay in that condition for three days. Several doctors went to see him, but could not tell what was the matter with him. He came out praising God and came to the meeting to tell his experience.

A woman asked the Lord to show her if we were teaching the doctrine of Christ. The Lord showed her in a vision. The platform we used for a pulpit and the altar or mourners' bench, which reached nearly across the rink, were pure white. She saw me and those who were with me clothed in pure white. On the platform she saw some earthen vessels, white as snow, and over all these was a soft cloud of glory, whiter than the driven snow. Over all the vessels she saw in shining letters: "These are my chosen vessels bearing the pure Gospel of Christ in power." Everything you see is pure white, the symbol of purity. She told the vision to the congregation.

Crowning of the Saints

The heavens shall glow with splendor,
    But brighter far than they
The saints shall shine in glory,
    As Christ shall them array;
That beauty of the Savior
Shall dazzle every eye
In the crowning day that's coming by and by.

Our pain shall then be over,
    We'll sin and sigh no more,

Behind us all of sorrow,
  And naught but joy before;
A joy in our Redeemer
As we to Him are nigh,
For the crowning day that's coming by and by.

Let all that look for, hasten
  That coming, joyful day,
By earnest consecration
  To walk the narrow way;
By gathering in the lost ones
For whom our Lord did die,
In the crowning day that's coming by and by.

18

HEALINGS ABOUND

After several other missions, we went to Springfield, Illinois, pitched our tents in Oak Ridge Park, and commenced a union meeting to build up the temple of our God. We made the call for all ministers and Christian workers to come up to the help of the Lord. Not one of the city preachers responded to the call except the Lutherans, several of whom came to the front. We were not acquainted with one person in the city. The voice of God said: "Go, and I will be with you." We lived in our tents, hired a cook, paid all expenses, trusting God to provide all needful help. The first few days the weather was very wet, and everything was against us. Although there were but eighteen persons present the first night, we shouted victory and told them that God was going to shake the city. The interest increased until there were thousands present. The altar was crowded day and night. They came from different states and all parts of the country to be healed of all manner of diseases. They were brought on beds, in chairs, on crutches, in railroad cars, and in cabs, hundreds being healed and converted. There were three that we know of who were brightly converted and died before the meeting closed—a young lady and an old man nearly eighty years of age; another, an old man, saved at his home on his deathbed. Others were converted at their homes, and some in the woods.

A little girl was carried into the meetings in her mother's arms. She was as helpless as a babe two days old. She had spinal meningitis, was paralyzed all over; her brain was impaired; her head dropped on her breast; and she had no use of her back and limbs. She had been sick for six months. For four months she had eaten nothing but a little milk. I laid hands on her and commanded the unclean spirits to come out of her. In five minutes she could sit up straight and raise her arms above her head. In five minutes more she could talk and rose upon her feet, stepped up on the high altar, walked with her mother to the streetcars, went home, and could eat anything she wanted. The next morning she was the first one up, running from house to house telling what God had done for her. It shook the whole neighborhood. This child could not exercise faith and did not seem to know what we were doing. Several children were wonderfully healed and also several infants. One little boy was healed of dropsy, stomach and bowel trouble. His clothes could not be buttoned because he was so badly swollen. The swelling went down at once; his mother fastened every button on his vest and clothes and stood him on the platform where everyone could see what God had done. The little fellow said in a clear, ringing voice that God had made him well.

I must say here, wherever we go God raises up many men and women who make no profession of religion to stand by us. They say if the Bible is true, we are God's children, and they will stand by us for the good we are doing the people in this life as well as the world to come. Praise God, many of these noble men and women are converted in our meetings. They are made to see that God is living and His Word is true. They yield to Him and receive the gift of God— eternal life.

In every meeting God is raising up and sending out many workers with different gifts.

The last two or three days of the meeting, there were twenty or more ministers present from other places. They all came to the front and took part in the battle. Brother S., a Methodist minister, while working at the altar fell in a trance. He lay several hours and was carried away as dead. The night we closed, he told his wonderful vision in a clear ringing voice that could be heard by the multitude. He described the wonderful City of Gold, with its glorious inhabitants. He saw many that he had known on earth; he described the awful gulf of hell and the condition of those who are there; saw the million going there. No one who heard him talk could doubt that he had seen all that he had told them. Many were struck down in different parts of the congregation and at their homes.

An Aged Infidel Saved

Brother W., an infidel, eighty-two years old, was converted and healed of rheumatism. He had been crippled for fifteen years. He arose from his knees, shook hands with those around him, and praised God for saving him at the eleventh hour. He stepped upon the altar and told the people that he had been an infidel nearly all his life. He said that he was one of Robert Ingersoll's first teachers in infidelity; that they had studied and taught infidelity for twenty years. They had made God out a liar; Jesus an impostor; the Holy Spirit a myth; the Bible a fable. He tried to believe man died like the ox and had no soul. He said that he lay in a trance three different times—struck down by the power of God. He did not know then what it was and would not be convinced, but now he knew it was the power of God. He met Ingersoll in 1850. In 1857, he had the first trance. He lay fourteen hours, and it seemed to him that he had died and was buried. He knew when his spirit had left the body for the grave. He saw his friends weeping over the grave, heard them preach his funeral, saw them place the coffin in the grave, fill up the grave, and return to their homes. God did this to show him that he had a spirit that would never die or lose its identity, but he would not believe. Years after he fell in another trance that lasted twenty-two hours. His spirit left the body, was carried away to heaven, and he saw millions and millions of human beings, all clothed in pure white. He heard the sweetest music, saw the most beautiful flowers, and the city with its beauty and grandeur. He could not describe it all. This time he had his identity. His spirit had perfect freedom and liberty. Still he drove off conviction and continued to contend with the Almighty. God came to him again in a vision, showed him the condition of the saints of God in eternity, after this world and everything in it has passed away. He saw the new earth—everything was new and beautiful—adapted to the use and enjoyment of the ransomed army of the Lord.

The first heaven, the real city of God that He has prepared for His redeemed children, will come down and be set in the new earth—something like Washington City is to the United States. God's children will not be confined to the Beautiful City. The whole new earth will be our inheritance. Our bodies will be light, our capacities so great, that there will be no limit to our knowledge. We will be continually exploring new beauties and treasures in the wonderful works of our Father.

And you who call yourselves unbelievers or infidels, trying to make yourselves believe a lie, God have mercy on your souls and help you to see your danger before He permits you to believe a lie and be forever damned.

At the close of the last meeting, it was requested that we stand on the altar and give the congregation a chance to shake hands and bid us good-bye. It was very affecting; nearly everyone, Christians and sinners, came and took us by the hand and said, "God bless you." Many strong men who were sinners broke down weeping and said for us to pray for them.

One old man who had scoffed in the meetings came to the tent and confessed, weeping, saying that he believed it was the work of God.

Another man stood there weeping and said he had stayed away from work to be saved that morning. I believe that he, with others, would have been saved there if I had had time to pray with them. They, with many others, said that they would not stop until they knew that they were saved.

An infidel doctor called that morning. He brought my book and picture and said that he was convinced of the wonderful work and would write to me when he was saved.

A Catholic lady gave me a beautiful basket filled with lovely flowers, nicely arranged, she said, as a token of her love for me and respect of the noble work that we had done in the city. I cannot tell how I appreciated the token of love. She was a lovely looking lady, and as I kissed her, my heart was strangely drawn to her. I felt that I would meet her in heaven where the flowers bloom forever.

My coworkers sang the chorus, "God be with you till we meet again," and they all joined in the singing. All who were standing about the station took off their hats. The singers broke down crying, one after another, until nearly everyone in the station was weeping. Strong men wept aloud, and the power came upon us. I came near being overpowered.

The number of conversions was in the thousands, and we formed a union band of the converts and Christian workers. They met several times a week for the salvation of sinners. The first night they met, there were six in trances and several converted. God was with them in wonderful power. God keep them as shining light is my prayer.

19

A GREAT FIGHT

The next battle fought for King Jesus was in Louisville, Kentucky, August, 1888. Among the many from other states and cities who attended our meeting at Springfield, Illinois, were a number of prominent citizens from St. Louis, Missouri. Among these were Mr. R., a merchant of the famous boot and shoe store, and his mother. They insisted on us visiting St. Louis and stopping with them. We did so and remained there several days. The people were very anxious for us to hold meetings in one of the parks. A number of the businessmen made quite an effort to have us stay, but we felt the Lord was calling us to Louisville. It was quite a cross to leave such a good opening and bear the expenses of the long journey. Not knowing a person in the city, no one to open the way, to board us or help us, bearing all expenses ourselves, which were very heavy, we spent nearly every cent we had, which was about four hundred dollars, before we received a penny. This was walking by faith.

There we were among strangers in one of the wickedest cities in the world. We never thought of being discouraged, but kept shouting "Victory!" knowing that Jesus was leading every step.

When we came to the city, we were very tired after so much hard labor and the long journey, and went seven miles from the city and camped out on the bank of the Ohio River in a small grove to rest. While there we realized that we were soldiers indeed, and, as Paul wrote to Timothy, each of us was called to *"endure hardness, as a good soldier of Jesus Christ"* (2 Tim. 2:3). We did all our cooking on a stove with one small hole. It stood outside the tent. We used a box for a table, benches for chairs, grass for a carpet, and made our beds on the soft side of the floor. We were far from the city and had no way to go back and forth, as the cars did not run that way, so that we were deprived of many comforts. We had money, and we could have put up at a good hotel; but instead we saved it to start the meeting and spent several hundreds of dollars before we received any money. We did this in many places.

I find that the earnest followers of Christ have very little rest here. Like our Master, we must be about our Father's business. We could not get a grove in the city in which to hold religious meetings, though we could have gotten one for most any other purpose. We succeeded in getting the Commons. We pitched our tent in the hot sun. It was the first of August, and we knew that it would be all we could stand to hold a meeting in a tent day and night. But we knew God had called us there and He would take care of us. We moved and pitched our small tents on the Commons to get ready for the battle. Our large tent and most everything we needed for comfort was delayed for over a week, but we did not want to use the Lord's money to board at a hotel. It began to rain the day we camped and continued almost incessantly for a week. The water was over us, under us, and around us. It came up even with the floor. We were a sight for curiosity seekers, some saying we were Gypsies, but there were no children or horses around. Some said we were fortune-tellers, and others that we were artists. But we were none of these, but a band of Pilgrims living in tents like our fathers, and seeking a city out of sight.

Finally a reporter came and interviewed me and gave us a good advertisement in a daily paper. Then the citizens began to call on us. It was not long before they knew who we were and what we were doing. When the large tent and all the small ones had been pitched, they said it looked like a village. It was during the presidential election, and the citizens were having a street fair or a business parade which lasted several weeks. There was a sham battle fought on the Ohio River by moonlight. Thousands came daily from other states and cities. While all these things were against us still it brought many from other states to our meeting. A number were being convicted and saved, who otherwise never would have been.

Amidst all this excitement we never missed a meeting, but held them day and night. The night they had the wonderful fireworks they were only a short distance back of us. The noise was terrible and the devil tried his best to drive us from the field. All classes were there and while all the artillery of hell was turned on us, by the help of God we fought with the fire, sword, and shell from heaven, and won the victory. The two armies had come together. God's soldiers came up in line. I told them to take their eyes off these surroundings and turn a deaf ear to the noise; to lift their hearts to God in silent prayer and I would preach.

God came in wonderful power while we were singing and praying. Many going to the fireworks were so astonished to see such a crowd and such a meeting they were held as under a spell. The tent was crowded. All standing room was taken up inside and hundreds were standing outside. I preached an hour or more. The congregation was so attentive I do not believe they missed a word. Oh, I praised God for victory! Amidst all the noise of the different kinds of fireworks I was not bothered in the least. God gave me voice and power to hold the people as still as if death was in our midst. Glory to God! The devil is mighty, but God is Almighty. Let no one who reads this ever get discouraged in doing the work of the Lord. There never was a meeting held under more discouraging circumstances. Everything was against us; nothing for us but God. He was more than all that was against us.

The colored people were the greatest drawback. The Southern people are so prejudiced against them that they will not permit them to worship with the white people. We gave the invitation for all classes and conditions to come to the meeting. The invitation was accepted by the rich and poor, the white and the colored, church members and all kinds of sinners. The white people said that if the colored were permitted to come, they would stay at home. Then we gave the colored people one corner of the tent and had them sit by themselves. This did not suit the people. Some of the wealthy citizens said that they liked the meetings, would help support them, but they would not do anything if we let the Negroes come. Ministers and professing Christians said the same. They said all evangelists that had been in the city could do no good until they drove the Negroes away. I told them God made the whole human family of one blood. Christ had died for all. Christ said, "Go preach my Gospel to all nations, to every creature." Can we obey God and drive the hungry souls away?

When Jesus sent me out to stand *"between the dead and the living"* (Num. 16:47), He said, "Go where God sends you without respect to persons or places." I told those people who came to persuade me not to let the colored people attend, that I knew if we let them come with the feeling that existed, we would have a terrible battle, but we did not dare drive them away; if we did, the Holy Spirit would leave, and God would hide His face from the work, and it would be a failure. Thank God, amidst all this trouble we shouted victory, knowing that God would overrule all for His glory and do the greatest work ever done in the state of Kentucky. I thank God we had no desire to drive them away but felt glad to have the privilege of leading them to Christ.

God came in such wonderful power it was not long until they seemed to forget about skin color. The altar was filled with seekers, white people on one side and colored on the other.

Sister F., a colored evangelist, whom I had heard of before I started out in the work of the Lord, was present. She was highly esteemed by the people of the East. She had labored with the white people. For years I had desired to meet her. One night I saw her in the meeting, did not know who she was, but called on her to lead in prayer. Such a prayer! She reached the throne, took hold of God in such a way as to shake every member of the congregation, and came near raising them all on their feet. God bless her. She is a firebrand for God. Hundreds of colored people were saved in these meetings, and many bodies were healed. Some had wonderful visions.

We stayed in the city over three months, the interest increasing all the time; when the weather got too cold for our tents, we rented a large hall. Hundreds of souls were converted, and hundreds of bodies healed of various diseases. Persons came on crutches and went away without them. The blind went away seeing; the sick were brought on beds, healed, and picked up their beds and walked off with them.

Trusting in God

We arrived at Springfield, Illinois, at 11:00 p.m. A band of converts met us at the train and took us to a house all furnished for our use. We found a nice supper ready for us. It was like a mother coming home to her children. They had spared no pains to make us feel at home, and as I looked at their happy faces, shining with the Savior's love, I thought of the marriage supper of the Lord, when I shall sit down with the dear children God has given me, who shall come from the East, West, North, and South. Oh, what a meeting that will be!

With such a band of earnest workers to help us fight for God, you may know we had a wonderful meeting. Sinners came flocking to Christ the first night, and the interest continued to increase until the last moment of our stay in the city. Hundreds of souls were saved, and many remarkable cases of the worst diseases and infirmities were healed by laying on of hands and prayer. All classes had been reached—infidels, skeptics, gamblers, harlots, drunkards, dead church members, and moral men. Two members of the legislature bowed at the altar, were converted, and addressed the crowded house, telling what God had done for them and was doing for others. When we left, many said that the work would go down in six weeks—they would all backslide. That is what they say every place we go. But when they saw that the converts were standing firm and had saved more souls the five months we were gone than all others had in the past year, they had to confess that God was with them and doing a mighty work.

Brother W., the noted infidel, and one of Robert Ingersoll's first teachers in infidelity, was converted in Springfield, Illinois. In writing of our first experience there, we gave you his wonderful experience. He attended our meeting in Louisville, Kentucky, and gave his time and strength in winning souls to Jesus. Like Paul, he was telling of his wonderful conversion. He went back to Springfield and had a stroke of paralysis. His prayer was that he might live until we got back. God answered his prayer, and we went to see him. He was very low; taking my hand, he began to weep and praise God. He was perfectly satisfied with his experience. Jesus was all in all to him. He knew that his building of clay was crumbling, but that *"to be absent from the body [was] to be present with the Lord"* (2 Cor. 5:8). He had a mansion in heaven, *"an house not made with hands, eternal in the heavens"* (2 Cor. 5:1). He felt that he was truly a brand plucked from the burning. "God has been so merciful in saving such a sinner at the eleventh hour," he said. When he could not speak, his friends thought him unconscious. Jesus was so precious and was with him all the time. I did not see him pass away, but he sent me his dying message: "Oh, sinners, hear the dying testimony of the converted infidel. Tell Sister Woodworth she was the instrument in God's hands of saving my soul. I have never had a doubt of my experience with God since my conversion. All is well. I thank God that the light of heaven ever shone in my soul." The remains were taken to the hall where we were holding the meetings. I preached the funeral sermon from Ecclesiastes 12:3: *"In the day when the keeper of the house shall tremble, and the strong men shall bow themselves."*

The Odd Fellows buried him, many of whom had known him for years, while he was teaching infidelity. When they heard of his triumphant death, they wept. Many were convicted of their sins and convinced of the reality of religion. Nearly all of the congregation marched out to the cemetery where I made a few remarks at the grave. Strong men were weeping; the power of God fell on all.

We organized a Church of God, appointed two elders and two deacons, and arranged for a new building in which to worship. We closed our meeting of seven weeks in February, 1889. The church continued to hold meetings in the hall where we held our meeting. The Lord gave them many souls. They had a large Sunday school.

Several went out as preachers and evangelists and met with good success.

The ministers of the city met and tried to crush me and the work. They brought history, doctor books, and the devil's works to prove that the power of God had been taken from the church. When they got their ammunition ready, they chose Doctor B. of the Christian church, the great theologian and champion debater, to fire off the cannon. He announced that he was going to prove me a fraud and drive me out of the city on the strength of it. He drew a large crowd and took up a special collection. Many of the citizens took notes and brought them to me. They said it was the thinnest thing they ever heard, and were disgusted. The night I was attacked, our hall was packed, the people thinking that I would denounce him. After the congregation had gathered, God gave me a text, which I had never used before: "*Come and hear, all ye that fear God, and I will declare what he hath done for my soul*" (Ps. 66:16).

I gave a sketch of my experience from my birth to that time. People were weeping in all parts of the house. I do not think there was one there who did not believe God had called me to the work, and that He was with me in mighty power working wonderfully in the midst of the people. I did not intend to reply to Doctor B.'s arguments. I had said that I would meet anyone on the Bible. He had gone outside of it for nearly all his proof. The citizens were very anxious for me to reply. Finally I announced that I would meet him on Sunday night. The hall was crowded, and they said hundreds were turned away.

Dear reader, it was an undertaking to meet this giant. He boasted of his college course, of his education, of his wisdom, of his popularity, and made it appear that I was a poor, ignorant, blinded crank. I am a crank for Christ, and the devil cannot turn me. My trust was in God. I set my face like flint, for God was with me, knowing that no weapon raised against me should prosper, and every tongue raised to condemn me I should confound. When I arose to talk, the congregation was as still as death. I held the paper in my hand that contained Doctor B.'s arguments, referred to one after another, and proved them to be false. He said that I had failed in every scriptural test and that I was a fraud. I said the best proof of our being called of God to preach was the fact that souls were saved. I asked all who had been converted in these meetings to stand up, and over two hundred arose.

I asked all who had their bodies healed by the power of God to stand up, and about fifty stood up. The people said that before I had taken the Bible in my hand, I had cut his head off with his own sword. I met all his arguments on the Bible and did not go outside of it. I proved him to be wrong on every point. Glory to God for victory! With all his boasted wisdom, God chose a weak woman to confound and condemn, and show to the world that it was useless to fight against God or the power of the Holy Spirit. Not one minister stood by me, but all united in opposing and trying to crush me. Notwithstanding all this power of darkness that was arrayed against me, the interest increased daily. Requests came from all the best citizens and from all over the city to stay, saying I had gained such a victory over Doctor B. and all the opposers of the true doctrine of Christ.

Many of the brightest talent in the city were inquiring the way of salvation, but God was calling us back to Louisville, Kentucky. We closed our meeting with many sad hearts and much weeping. We left the next morning at nine o'clock. When we got to the depot, we found a large crowd there to see us off.

Old gray-headed fathers thanked us, with tears streaming down their cheeks, for leading their children to Christ; wives, that their husbands were saved; and drunkards, that they had been saved from a drunkard's grave.

20

"MY COUNSEL SHALL STAND"

We arrived at Louisville, Kentucky in January, 1889, after an absence of about two mouths. We commenced meeting in Bolle's Hall where the converts of the previous year were holding meetings and had been ever since we left the city. We found them at their post. I never saw a braver or more powerful band of workers for Christ, or any more successful in winning souls and building up Christ's kingdom than these Holy Spirit soldiers in the wicked city of Louisville.

I did not leave a pastor or minister who had had years of practice to take charge of these young lambs and carry the work on, but put in charge one that had been converted in the meetings.

We stayed two weeks and I organized a church. It was hard to leave them, but I felt God had prepared them to carry on their own work.

From Louisville, Kentucky, I was led by the Spirit to go to the little town of Shawnee, Ohio, in a valley of dry bones, *"and lo, they were very dry"* (Ezek. 37:2).

This was a mining country, and there were rolling mills, furnaces, and new railroads being built. Nearly all nations under heaven were represented in our meeting. Sometimes eight or ten different languages were at the altar, all praying at once to the one God of heaven who is no respecter of persons or conditions.

God bless the hard-laboring classes who are so often despised by those who call themselves Christians. Jesus said the common people heard Him gladly, and it was so here. But others sat in the seat of the scornful and stood in the way of sinners, and criticized and mocked the plain Gospel of Christ, and denied the power of the Holy Spirit.

One saloonkeeper, who had been in the business nearly all his life, was lifted from the gutter and stood up before the people and praised God for saving a poor wretched sinner like himself.

Many old men and women were plucked as brands from the burning. Some had not been to church for twenty-five years.

One night, eight old, white-haired men were converted side by side at the altar. Skeptics and infidels are saved in all our meetings.

One of the brightest, talented men in Shawnee—an infidel— was led to the altar by a little girl eight years old. He was brightly converted the next day, went into a trance, and had a vision of hell. He saw the awful condition of the people. He had a great influence over the people there and did all he could to lead them to Christ.

The minister and his members stood nobly by us all through the battle. In doing so, his church was wonderfully built up, and he won the respect and love of the sinners. God poured out his richest blessing upon him; he won stars that shine in his crown, while those who mocked and criticized will, unless they give their hearts to God, be lifting up their eyes in hell.

People wonder at me traveling from one place to another, suffering all kinds of hardships, deprived of many comforts of life, exposed to wet and cold, heat and storms. I make this sacrifice for the Lord. Christ is all in all to me. This world is not my home. It has no attraction for me. I am laying up treasures in heaven. I have a mansion there that is built of pure gold, and it can never be destroyed or taken from me. Praise God for the privilege of leaving all to follow Jesus.

Ever since I started in the work, God has been raising up men and women by hundreds who have gone out as ministers and evangelists. The young workers have led many into the fold, who today are happy on the road to heaven. I receive letters from them telling of their trials and triumphs, for they look to me as a mother for advice. I heard from a brother recently who came out in the first meeting I ever held. He went to preaching right away and has been in charge of several churches since. Today he stands as one of the highest in the church.

While holding our meetings in Louisville, Kentucky, my sister, Mrs. S., of Columbus, Ohio, visited us. This was the first time she had ever attended one of my meetings. She had been a church member for years, a teacher in the Sunday school, was trying to do all she could, but was not saved herself. She was enduring religion. When she went to the meeting, God showed her herself as He saw her in the light of eternity. She was nothing but a dry bone in His sight. She never had the love of God in her heart. She was converted and went home happy, rejoicing because her name was written in heaven. She erected a family altar and could pray with her unconverted husband.

After resting, we continued by holding a camp meeting at Shawnee, Ohio. The Lord was present in power to save souls and heal bodies. I organized a Church of God with a large membership.

None had ever seen a woman baptize by immersion. I was the first woman on record, or ever known, to bury the candidates in a watery grave by immersion. Glory to God, He gives strength and power and grace!

Several thousand people stood on the banks witnessing the solemn scene. The meetings were conducted day and night. People climbed in the trees trying to see. The Holy Spirit fell like a cyclone; men and women were tossed as in a windstorm. They fell inside and outside the house. The police standing outside were frightened until they were pale. They said they saw the house shaken, as if in a storm, by the power of God. Hundreds were saved. People were convicted for miles around.

We went back in three months and held meetings in a large tent. Thousands came to the revival, which began at once. Like Pentecost they saw, felt, and heard the mighty power of God. Many gifts and signs of the Holy Spirit were seen everywhere.

A woman fell, struck down, and lay until evening. They took her home, and she lay until the next Sunday, eight days in all; then she came out shouting and preaching; and without taking any nourishment, she came straight to meeting, preached, and told the wonderful experience that she had had.

The fear of God came on the company, and for miles around they said, "We have never seen it in this fashion." They saw strange things, for God visited His people there. It is *"not by might, nor by power, but by my spirit, saith the Lord"* (Zech. 4:6).

It was three months previous to this time that we held the first meeting at Shawnee. God blessed the work. They have three organized churches, one in Shawnee and two within a few miles of there.

21

"MULTITUDES, MULTITUDES IN THE VALLEY OF DECISION"

In the fall of 1889 we felt that the Lord was calling us to California. We obeyed the voice, got ready, and started at once, not knowing one person in that part of the country. I will give a condensed description of our journey to California and of the country. As we traveled along, the cars rolling through one state after another, we noticed the difference in the climate. Some states were given wholly to vegetation, everything green and beautiful; some were mining districts, with vast wealth in minerals of different kinds; many had quarries of beautiful stone, which many of the finest mansions of New York and Chicago are built of. We went rolling on down through the deep canyons and the beautiful valleys. On either side were the high mountains reaching, as it seemed, almost to the clouds. In a little while, we found ourselves passing along over the tops of these mountains. Again we found ourselves sweeping over the plains and deserts. Sometimes for hundreds of miles there was not a shrub or tree to be seen; nothing but yellow sand at times was visible; then again nothing but black sand for miles and miles. As far as the eye could see, the ground was as level as a floor—no vegetation on it. As we came on further into California we saw a great change. The plains were cultivated, covered with grass, trees, shrubs, and vegetation of all kinds. As we looked upon all these grand and wonderful works of creation, our hearts were filled with love and tenderness, and we could look up and say: "My Father, the God of heaven, has made all these."

At last we arrived safely in the great city of San Francisco and stopped at a hotel for a few days. Being very tired from our long journey and summer's work, we felt we must seek a quiet place to rest both mind and body, so we took a journey of sixty miles to Pascadero, a small town in the valley surrounded by mountains.

We commenced meeting in Oakland, California, October 28, 1889. The wet weather had set in. We pitched our tents during a rain, such as was never known in Oakland before. People looked on in wonder and amazement. From a human standpoint, everything looked dark and discouraging. Surely God's ways are not our ways. It takes a great deal of confidence, faith, and courage in God to move forward at His command not knowing one step of the way. Here we were in a strange land, with our money about gone and no means to go back East. We confessed we were pilgrims in a strange country but knew we were seeking a city out of sight. We had no thought of going back until a great work had been done for the Master. We had no fear of suffering for lack of means; we knew our God would supply all our needs (Rom. 8:28).

The meeting was not advertised. The people did not know what was going to be done there. The first night twenty-three came. They felt that God was there. I told them that God had sent us there and a great work would be done there—that hundreds would be saved and in a few days the tent would not hold the crowds that would come to hear the Gospel. Some laughed, as if to say, "I would rather see the crowds in this wet tent than to hear of them coming." All who were there came the next night and brought others with them. Some of God's children heard of us and came to see. They saw and felt that God was there in power and that a great work would be done. One of them went and ordered stoves and had them put in the tent at once. They got lumber and put a nice floor in the tent. Oh, how we praised God for His tender care over us! We could hardly stand the cold and dampness, but now things looked bright and comfortable. The dear Christians seemed to anticipate our wants. It was very cold in our dwelling tents; we had not yet got a stove.

At the close of the meeting one night, as we started from the large tent to our dwelling tents, I said, "I wish we had a warm stove in our tent." As we opened the tent door, to our surprise we found some kind hands had been there and set up a stove and had it red-hot. We were made to give glory to God and say the Lord will provide. We never knew who put it there. In a few days one brother sent in seven dollars' worth of groceries. One gave twenty dollars, another fifty dollars. In this way the dear Lord continued to provide and care for us.

The Christians came from all the churches to the help of the Lord against the mighty, with their prayers and with their means. They advertised the meeting largely in different ways. The interest increased every service. In about a week the tent was crowded.

The first converts were five old persons from sixty-five to seventy-five years of age. The people kept coming to the altar to be saved and healed of all their diseases, old and young, until several thousand were happy in Jesus, and many could testify that Jesus had saved their souls and healed their bodies.

It was a wonderful sight to see hundreds and sometimes thousands crowding around the tent, many times standing in the rain, trying to get near enough to hear the preached word. The Christians said we must have a larger tent to hold the multitudes. They ordered one at once, costing $1,325, with a capacity of holding eight thousand. In a short time it was made and on the grounds, ready for the dedicatory service. The dedicatory sermon was preached by the pastor of the M. E. Church of San Francisco. Prayer was offered by the pastor of the M. E. Church of Oakland. A number of other ministers were present. The congregation was pleased with the services and also the tent.

People came to the meetings from nearly all parts of the world. God drew by His Spirit many of His children from the eastern, western, northern, and southern states. They were baptized with power from on high. They testified that they had never received such blessings and power and light before. They entered the work of God with more faith and courage, never expecting to stop the work until Jesus came for them in the clouds, or by death.

Many sailors came from all parts of the world, together with the captains of the vessels. Thank God, some of the captains and their wives were saved, and many of the sailors and officers.

One captain and his wife and twelve of their crew were saved before they sailed. The captain and wife said they would have services every afternoon on the vessel. They were sailing for the West Indies. They claimed every soul on board for God. They said they expected everyone to be saved before they landed in port.

Many took my books and literature with them. The workers bought hundreds of my books and sermons and scattered them in the ships and sailing vessels. Many were baptized with the Holy Spirit and held meetings on the ships on their journeys over the seas; so the wonderful Gospel and the mighty works of Jesus, through the Holy Spirit, went out and were scattered in many parts of the world.

I never saw so many nations represented in one meeting, nor so many of them brought to Christ. They were saved and filled with the Holy Spirit. Many of these felt God was calling them to their own nation to work for the salvation of souls. Many were called to evangelistic work and were baptized with the Holy Spirit and power. They started back to other nations to preach the glorious news of a Savior's love and of the soon coming of the Lord.

The power of the Lord followed the preaching with signs and wonders. The slain of the Lord were many. Many sinners of all classes were stricken down in their sins. Some lay for hours. Some had visions; they came out brightly converted. Among them was an old man, sixty-three years of age. He gave a short experience one night of his life and wonderful conversion. He had traveled in all parts of the world wherever white man had trod and had visited the Holy Land three times. He had stood in all the sacred spots connected with our Savior's life. He and a party of friends were visiting Oakland at the time of our meeting. They heard of the meeting and came out of curiosity. As he looked over the congregation, he made some light remark to his friends about the display of the power of God and started boldly up toward the pulpit to investigate; but before he reached the pulpit, he was struck to the floor by the power of God and lay there over two hours. While in this condition, God gave him a vision of hell and heaven and told him to make his choice of the two places. He called upon the Lord to save him and said he would choose Christ and heaven. He came to, praising God and realizing he was saved and filled with the Holy Spirit. He had lived over sixty long years in sin and had never made a profession of faith.

This brother came to our meeting at Portland, Oregon, three years after his conversion, and told his experience. He said he had been kept by the power of God, saved and happy and working for the Master in every way he could.

The power of God was over all the congregation and around in the city of Oakland. The Holy Spirit would fall on the people while we were preaching. The multitude would be held still, as though death was in their midst. Many of the most intelligent and best dressed men would fall back in their seats with their hands held up to God, being held under the mighty power of God. Men and women fell all over the tent like trees in a storm; some would have visions of God. Most all of them came out shouting the praises of God.

The tent held eight thousand. It was claimed to be the largest gospel tent in America. It was crowded every night. The day we closed, the police, fearing there might be trouble on account of the crowd, were there in force and said that ten thousand were unable to get into the tent. After the close of the meeting, they said that they had the best of order. Many ministers were present at both the day and night meetings, and they asked all that had been blessed or healed to stand up. Several thousand arose in both services. They all stood and sang praises to God for the great work the Lord had done.

Some of the worst men and boys—those that had given us the most trouble—would not leave until the police had brought them up to say good-bye. With tears running from their eyes, they begged us to forgive them for what they had done and asked us to pray that they might be saved.

22

A MIGHTY WORK

The Lord was calling us to St. Louis, Missouri, in April, 1890, but we wanted to stay in California through the summer, and we had quite a struggle to know what to do. We placed our goods on the cars and were going to Los Angeles, California. That night I received a letter calling me to St. Louis. We sold our household goods and started next morning for St. Louis. No person knew we were coming until our meeting was announced. Surely God leads me in a mysterious way. I cannot have any choice or say I will go here or there, but I must know the voice of God, and where He leads I will follow. Two years prior to this time, the way had been opened in St. Louis. Many of the best citizens invited us to go and hold meetings. They would have taken much of the burden off us, but our dear Lord does not permit us to lean on or trust to the arm of flesh, for the battle is not ours, but the Lord's. (See 2 Chronicles 32:7–8.)

We held meetings in a hall for two months. The first night there were eighteen present. God was there in power. Two were converted. The crowds grew larger every day, and souls were converted at every meeting. A number of remarkable cases of divine healing were wrought by the Lord. We felt we could not afford to board, that we must save our money to pay the expenses of the meeting. We rented rooms in the third story of a private house and did our own cooking. This was very hard on us, but it was the best we could do.

We were invited one Sunday afternoon to hold a meeting in the Union Market. We felt the Lord was leading in this and accepted the invitation. We had a large, attentive congregation. The streetcars were passing by, loaded with people to see the new bridge that had just been built across the Mississippi River.

One old man, a Catholic, heard me preaching. He got off the cars, came to the meeting, and listened attentively; at the close of the service, he was saved. He said he wanted the kind of religion we had. He had a hard battle to fight with his family, who were all Catholics, but he stood firm and said he was determined to make heaven his home. God set His seal on this meeting. Many were convicted. God knows how many carried the good seed away in their hearts, which will grow into eternal life.

It was now the first of June, and we were ready to put up our large tent, which we brought from California. The only place we could get room enough was "Kerry Patch," a place noted for the hoodlum element, where they gathered from all parts of the city. People have been shot down or robbed or stoned here, any hour of the day. There were two large Catholic churches, one on each side of the tent. One was about a block away, the other about two blocks. For five months we lived in our small tents without a shade tree.

The Christians tried to persuade us not to pitch our tents in "Kerry Patch," and after we had them up, they tried to have us move away from that wicked and rough element, but we felt God had led us there. We rented the ground for three months, having paid seventy-five dollars for it. The Christians said there had been several show tents put up where ours stood, and the rough element cut the ropes and tore their tents down. They said if they would cut the ropes of a show tent, surely a gospel tent would have no chance at all. We said God has placed us here and by His grace we will stay. Many of our best friends were afraid to let their wives and daughters come and felt they were running a great risk in coming themselves, as the congregation was stoned coming and going. Sometimes the stones went flying through the tent. They did not know what a camp meeting was, but thought it was some kind of a show. Most of these people had never been to a church. The first night the tent was crowded. Men stood on the seats with hats on, cigars and pipes in their mouths, coats off, and sleeves rolled up. Women had old dirty aprons and dresses on, bareheaded and bare-armed. They would shoot off firecrackers, and when we sang, they sang louder; when we prayed, they clapped their hands and cheered us. They had pistols and clubs and were ready to kill us and tear down the tent. It looked like we would all be killed. Several ministers tried to talk, but they were stoned down or their voices drowned out. It looked like surrender or death.

It was an awful sight to see a little band of Christians, sitting nearly frozen to their seats with fear, surrounded by a mob of wild fierce men and women, many of them half drunk, their eyes and faces red and inflamed. Every effort failed and we could do nothing with them. I said to my coworkers, "We will never give up, and if they take us out of the tent before we are ready to go, they will take us out dead." I told them to lead in prayer one after the other, and the God of Elijah would answer.

A sister knelt on the pulpit pale as death, her hands and face raised to heaven, and in a clear ringing voice asked God to save and bless the judgment-bound multitude. A feeling of the awful presence of God began to fall on the people. Another sister followed in prayer; then I arose and stood before them. I raised my hand in the name of the Lord and commanded them to listen. I said the Lord had sent me there to do them good and that I would not leave until the Lord told me to, when our work was done. I told them the Lord would strike dead the first one that tried to harm us or to strike us with a dagger. If any tried to kill us, the Lord would strike them dead. The power of God fell, and the fear of God came upon all the multitude. The sweat came on their faces, and they stood like as though in a trance; the men began to take their pipes out of their mouths and their hats off. The women began to cover up their bare necks and arms with their aprons. They felt as if they stood naked and guilty before God. They began to get off the seats and try to sit down, but some fell and lay like dead. Others stood with their mouths open. One Catholic said that I struck him down and showed him hell. Tears ran down many faces through the dirt, leaving streaks. They stood like they were afraid to move, and they all passed out quietly. After that the hoodlum element always respected me. Many would take off their hats when they passed me; but they stoned the people coming and going to the meetings and threw stones through and over the tent for some time, until we got them conquered in the name of the Lord and the help of the police.

The citizens took it in hand and went after the police for not doing their duty, for they were afraid of the mob element. The chief of the police came and told me I would be protected if he had to send out the whole police force. The soldiers at Jefferson Barracks said we were doing a great work, and if the police would not protect me, they would.

The ground near our tent had always been used by the hoodlum element from all parts of the city. They would come together on Sunday and bring kegs of beer. Several companies of baseball players were included in these Sunday gatherings. On the first Sunday that we held a meeting, when we began to sing, nearly a thousand of these rough-and-toughs came rushing into the tent with their bats and balls. There were old men, middle-aged men, young men, and children. Some were dressed in baseball uniforms, some in rags, some were drunk, some with pipes in their mouths, and some with cigars. They stoned the tent and stoned the people coming and going to the meeting.

The next Sunday they came as usual, but the chief of police with several police came and drove them away. Oh, praise God for such victory! The neighbors had been tormented nearly to death. These roughs of the city were there every day and especially on Sunday. They said if the meetings did not do any other good, it had relieved them of an awful nuisance. With the kindness of the police and the power of God, those who came to the meeting and would not be tamed were driven away, the rest quieted down; then the civilized people came, many who had been afraid to come before. We do not blame them for being afraid. It was only by the grace of God we stood through the showers of stones. Some of the worst characters on earth came to the meeting. If God had not protected us we would not have left that campground alive. Glory to God, He never leaves His children.

The women and children began to wear cleaner clothes, came with their bonnets on, and left their dirty aprons at home. The men shaved and combed their hair and came with their families. They said the meeting was doing good and that their wives and children were getting more tidy and keeping their homes cleaner. I told those who opposed the meeting that if it did no good except to clean up some of their citizens and better their moral condition, I thought it a good work, and they ought to give us a helping hand. Many of the best citizens came to the meetings and were astonished at the great victory we had gained over the rough element and the good order maintained.

The tent held eight thousand. There were meetings every day and night for five months. There were thousands outside the tent, but they could see and hear. We had six small tents, besides the large one, and it looked like a little town. I slept, and so did my helpers, like babes in our tents. Oh, praise the Lord for His care and protection!

Many were carried in and got up and walked out. The blind shouted for joy; the lame threw away their crutches, leaped and rejoiced, and said, "Oh, I am healed!" The deaf and dumb clapped their hands, while tears of joy ran down their faces. Children who had never walked ran about praising the Lord. Some—both young and old people—who were perfectly helpless, received a shock from heaven's battery that sent life through their limbs; they clapped their hands and jumped and cried for joy.

A Great Battle Fought for the Lord

Many were baptized with the Holy Spirit and received many gifts; all the gifts were manifested by the Holy Spirit. Many received the gifts of healing; the casting out of devils; some of miracles; of visions; of the gift of the Holy Spirit by the laying on of hands; some received the gift of new tongues and spoke very intelligently in other languages, *"as the Spirit gave them utterance"* (Acts 2:4). He gave them to know what they were speaking.

The Lord called one man by name and told him he must go to many nations to give them the light and to speak to them in their own languages, and gave him the gift of writing the interpretation. He also saw many visions. The Lord revealed the deep things to him. Since then he has preached to many strange people of all nations. They would weep and cry out and say, "We will serve the Man who died for us."

A little girl was brought to me one day; she was altogether helpless, could not talk or walk and had no use of herself. I prayed for her. The crowd was great as there were hundreds trying to step into the pool, so we told them to take her out a little and let her try to walk, for she might walk at once, or they might have to teach her, like any other child learning to walk. After a while, they came back with her. She was walking and talking, but they could not understand a word she said! Praise the Lord, she had the use of her whole body; she was walking and talking in a strange language or tongue. She was filled with the Spirit and as bold as a lion in the power of the Holy Spirit.

I stood her on the platform, and she began to walk about and preach. With hands uplifted, pointing to heaven, and stamping her foot, she preached to the astonished multitude, showing what great things the Lord had done for her, for she spoke some words in English.

They said it was the greatest battle ever fought in the Mississippi Valley of religion against science, the works of man, and the powers of darkness. The whole city was shaken. Missions started in many places. The different churches began to have street meetings and to visit the prisons and hospitals as they had never done before.

The people told us we would never stay the three months, that we would lose that money; but, praise God, we stayed the three months and then engaged the ground for two more months.

The man who owned the ground was a Catholic. He was so pleased with the change in the neighborhood for good he said he would let us have the ground free of charge. The interest of this five months' camp meeting in "Kerry Patch" was widespread. It reached from the Atlantic to the Pacific and across the ocean. I received letters from a minister in Scotland whom I had never met, inquiring about the wonderful work of God he had heard about. He sent a letter for publication in favor of the meeting. I received letters from prominent ministers in Canada; from Pittsburgh, Pennsylvania; from Indiana; and all parts of the country, inquiring about the great work God was doing in St. Louis. People came two thousand miles to be saved or to have their bodies healed. Some of the physicians said they knew there had been six hundred persons healed. They said many of these had been given up by the best physicians of St. Louis. It was true that thousands were saved and hundreds healed instantly and saved at the same time.

While holding this meeting, a boy was brought to us, who had been caught and thrown into a dog wagon by the dogcatchers, and frightened nearly to death. He went mad and would have awful mad spells, or fits, every night or day; sometimes more often, for a period of two years past. All that medical skill could do had been done but to no avail. It was a peculiar case; the mother told me that doctors from Germany had tried to cure him but had all failed, and that all hopes of ever doing so were given up. At times he was all right. He heard about the meetings and begged his mother to take him.

She brought him one Sunday. She had him in the great crowd near the outer edge of the camp when he took one of his mad spells, and he was snapping and biting at everyone. The people were panic stricken, so they gathered him up as quickly as possible and took him to my small tent. There he caught hold of the heavy canvas with his teeth and bit and chewed a hole in it, several inches each way. Hundreds saw all this.

I told her never to bring him back, for we would all be arrested; but he was better after that and begged his mother so hard that one night, as I was working at the long altar, preaching to hundreds, there she stood by my side with her boy. I was so scared, but I saw how much faith she had in me. The boy looked so pitiful that the Lord gave me faith to pray for him, and he was completely healed.

Nearly the whole city knew about the condition of the boy, and when they heard that he was healed and his mind perfectly restored, they all wanted to see him. I would ask him to come up on the big platform, and he would step out so manly and tell that the Lord had saved and healed him, and had filled him with His Spirit.

Years after, when I went to the city over Sunday, he would come walking down the aisle to the pulpit with a lovely bouquet of flowers.

The mouths of the gainsayers, scoffers, and liars were stopped. Thousands of souls were saved. Several police, many Catholics, many Germans, and people of other nations were represented at the altar, weeping their way to Calvary, and soon joined in the song with the blood-washed company.

The weather became too cold for our tents. We rented a church building down in the best part of the city. We started a mission of over four hundred members. The interest in the meetings had continued to increase all summer, and when we went into the church, God was there in mighty power, with signs and wonders following. Sinners could hardly keep still until the invitation was given for them to come to the altar. They came by scores, among whom were some of the worst drunkards. A number of Catholics, and indeed, all classes, were brought to Christ.

23

PERMANENT RESULTS

After revisiting two or three towns, our next meeting was held in Anderson, Indiana, in January, 1891. We found the Church of God we organized over four years before still alive for God. We had very large crowds; many were unable to get in. The dear Lord wonderfully poured out His Spirit in saving and healing power.

A sister had met with an accident over five years before in which her hip had been injured. It had withered away until she had not been able to be out of bed for three years. For a while she had gone about some on crutches. She had other diseases. Some of her friends took her to the altar. When I saw her, she was lying there prostrate. I saw she was in a terrible condition, but I knew there was nothing too hard for the Lord. I told her to put her trust in God. I prayed for her, and she arose perfectly healed of all her diseases and went shouting around the house. She left her crutches in the church and walked home.

Another sister was healed of a terrible cancer on one side of her face, head, and eye. She was healed instantly. All signs of the cancer soon disappeared.

We gave glory and praise to God for His glorious presence in the meeting. I felt very much rejoiced and encouraged by meeting so many who were saved five and six years before in this state, who were not only happy themselves, but were working in so many different ways to bring others to Christ.

At Muncie and Anderson, I met twenty-one licensed ministers who were converted or anointed in our meetings for the work. Some are ministers in the Church of God, some in the M. E., U. B., Friends, Baptists, and Newlights.

From Anderson we went to Pendleton, Indiana, to hold meetings in the United Brethren Church for three days. A number were converted and several healed of bodily ailments.

A farmer living near Pendleton was healed in our meeting six years before. He had been in the asylum three or four years. He would get a little better for a few days, then be worse than ever. His friends brought him to the meeting. He was converted and healed instantly. He went home and took charge of his farm. He has been a businessman and a Christian since then. Eternity alone will tell the results of the one week's meeting at Pendleton nine years ago and this three days' meeting.

From Pendleton we went to Indianapolis, to visit the Church of God, which we organized nearly five years before. When we arrived at the church, we found the large building crowded. The church was all in harmony and on fire for God. We continued the meeting for five days, had two meetings a day during the week and three on Sunday. The house was crowded day and night, and many were turned away. The interest was so great we had to request the young people to stay away and give room for the older. The altar was crowded day and night with seekers—some for salvation of the soul, some for the healing of the body, and some for the anointing of the Holy Spirit. The power of the Lord was present to heal both soul and body. A number of God's children received the baptism for service. They obeyed the command of Jesus: *"Tarry ye in the city of Jerusalem, until ye be endued with power from on high"* (Luke 24:49).

Among those converted were two men eighty years old. One had been afflicted most all his life. He was healed and converted at the same time. There never was a brighter prospect for a revival in any place than at Indianapolis. But we were compelled to leave, as our appointments were already made in advance.

We went from Indianapolis to Springfield, Illinois, to hold a two weeks' meeting for the Church of God. We found the church all in harmony and love, ready for the meeting. Many souls were saved and bodies healed of diseases of many years' standing. Notwithstanding that the houses were packed to almost suffocation, the best of order prevailed.

From Springfield, Illinois, we went back to St. Louis, Missouri, in February, 1891, and found our friends waiting for us with our rooms warmed and dinner ready. We commenced meetings the same night with a crowded house. All the members of the mission, with many friends, were present to welcome us back to their city. I organized the mission into a Church of God, with a membership of over two hundred. All classes thought the work would prosper better as a church than a mission. Many of those fellowshipped were among the best citizens. The revival is being kept up the year around, with meetings every night.

From St. Louis we went to Canton, Ohio. The children of God had been calling us for two years to come and help them. We held meetings in the tabernacle one month. We found some brave soldiers of the cross who were willing to make any sacrifice to see sinners brought to Christ. The last place where I kept house was at Canton. It was there I gave up all for Christ and started out in His vineyard. It required a great deal of grace and courage to hold meetings among my own relatives, the most of whom had never heard me preach. But God gave me grace and courage to boldly declare the unsearchable riches of Christ. Many of my old acquaintances were brought out into the light.

From Canton we went to St. Louis and spent one night with the Church of God. The house was filled with Christians and friends to welcome us again.

From St. Louis we went to Topeka, Kansas, and pitched our tabernacle in the City Park. The first month we were interrupted many times by the rain and storms, and hence could not hold meetings more than half the time. The rains were very heavy. There were from two to three thousand people present one night, and the next night we could have no meeting because of the rain.

One night, just as the congregation was gathering for service, a heavy storm came up and the rain fell as if being poured out of buckets. The thunder rolled as I had not heard it for years. The vivid lightning, flash upon flash, illumined the sky like a large blaze of fire. The storm came so suddenly that it was impossible to lower our tent, which it struck and tore one end almost into ribbons. We were left with a poor shelter in time of storm. We put it up again the best we could, and when the wind did not blow too strong, we had services in it. One side of it was a protection from the sun, but when the wind blew too strong, we held services in the open air. We went there among strangers at our own expense. It cost us about three hundred dollars to go and get the meeting started. It was a great trial and test of faith to stand and see our tent destroyed, but God's grace was sufficient. In the middle of this we never became the least discouraged or fainthearted, but praised God in the midst of the tempest. We could say, "*The* LORD *gave, and the* LORD [has permitted to be] *taken away*" (Job 1:21). We are only the Lord's stewards. The tent was His, the work was His, and we are His. "*All things work together for good to them that love God, to them who are the called according to his purpose*" (Rom. 8:28).

The next day (Sunday) great crowds came out to the meeting, and seeing the destruction of the tent, the sympathy was aroused of both saint and sinner. Many of the best citizens came to the front and began to raise money for a new tent. They soon purchased a tent. We dedicated it to the Lord. Notwithstanding these difficulties and many others that were in the way of the meeting, God was with us in power from the beginning, and the spirit of conviction rested upon every congregation.

Word of God Honored

The people were hungry for the Word of God. They sat during the sermon, which was an hour or more, and paid the best of attention. The city was wonderfully stirred. Many got out their Bibles, which no doubt had been laid away for years untouched, and searched to see if these things were true. All classes of sinners came home to God. A number of bodies were healed of different diseases, and a number laid as dead under the power of God. Men and women looked on in wonder, turned pale, and said, "We never saw it happen like this." It was noticed here, as every place we labor, that more than half who are saved are past middle age and many are aged.

A number of drunkards were saved—some of the worst characters in the city. One man when drunk was the terror of the city. Now all these are earnest workers for the Lord—a joy to their families and those around them. The Lord not only saved the outbroken sinner, but also those who were living moral lives.

Many members of different churches were made to see that they had only a profession. Now they know they are born of God, His Spirit bearing witness that they "*are the children of God, and if children, then heirs; heirs of God, and joint-heirs with Christ*" (Rom. 8:16–17).

One sister had belonged to church from childhood. She was considered one of the best workers. When she came to meeting, she found she had never had a change of heart. She came to the altar like any other sinner and cried to God for mercy, and, bless His dear name, He did not disappoint her. Salvation came streaming down in her soul. In giving her experience, she said she thought all these years she was, like Job, perfect; but now she knew if she had died, she would have been lost forever.

Another sister was converted, and after she arose from the altar, she said she had been a church member for eleven years. During these years she thought she was a Christian. She came to the meeting and was so deeply convicted that she prayed all night.

Many others of the same experience were brought to the Lord. This is evidence that what we are teaching everywhere we go is true; there are thousands in the churches today who think they are all right, think they have eternal life, but are in a lost condition. May God have mercy on blind leaders and false teachers, and send something to arouse them before they and their followers go down to hell together. There are thousands of ministers today who *"have healed the hurt of the daughter of my people* [only] *slightly, saying, Peace, peace; when there is no peace"* (Jer. 8:11). They are promising the people liberty when they themselves are servants of corruption. They have left Christ, the fountain of living waters, and have hewn out cisterns, broken cisterns, that will not hold water. They are teaching the people the form, but denying the power. The Lord says, *"Ye scornful men that rule this people...ye have made a covenant with death, and with hell are* [you in] *agreement....Your covenant with death shall be disannulled, and your agreement with hell shall not stand"* (Isa. 28:14, 15, 18).

The people are dead in trespasses and sins, and these false teachers are making them believe they can go to heaven without being made alive to God by His Spirit. They are making them believe there is no hell, doing away with future punishment. The Lord says they are teaching the people to hide behind a refuge of lies, but in the storm of God's wrath these refuges shall be swept away, and they, with their followers, will have no hiding place. May the Spirit of God come upon every reader and cause you to search your heart in the light of God and eternity to see if you are hiding behind these refuges of lies. If so, you are on quicksand; unless you come to Christ and receive life, there is a fearful doom awaiting you.

The meeting continued to grow in interest until the close. God gave us such wonderful victory over all opposing elements that most of the prejudice gave way, and the masses said, "This is the work of God." Christians came from all the churches and praised God for the great work He did. Hundreds begged us to remain longer. We organized a Church of God with over two hundred members.

The last day of the meeting will ever be remembered by many. The tent was full. Several hundred testified to the power of God to save the soul, and many to the healing of the body. Jesus said, *"Ye are my witnesses"* (Isa. 43:10, 12). It made our hearts rejoice to hear so many ringing testimonies.

At the closing service I preached from these words: *"Little children, it is the last time"* (1 John 2:18). The congregation seemed to realize that we were parting to meet again at the Judgment. Sadness rested upon the multitude as I exhorted the Christians to stand firm and hold out to the end, pleaded with the sinner to come to Christ before it was too late, and thanked the different classes for every act of kindness shown to us while we were engaged in the great battle against the powers of darkness.

Christians and ministers from different churches thanked God we ever came to their city and through us God had done such a wonderful work.

We felt the Lord was calling us to work in the state of Florida. We shipped our goods from Topeka, Kansas, to Jacksonville, Florida. We went by the way of St. Louis and stopped and held meetings for the Church of God for five days. It was then one year and six months since I preached the first sermon in St. Louis, and the meetings had been going on every night since. It was nine months since I organized the church. We found nearly all the converts faithful and the church prospering spiritually and financially.

I wept for joy as I listened to the wonderful testimonies, how God had saved and kept them all these months. Many of them had been drunkards as low down as they could be. You could see no trace of a dissipated life. Many who had been hopeless invalids for years, those who had been lame and deaf and blind, afflicted with all manner of diseases, praised God for making them every whit whole and keeping them well.

Many Healed

We visited Florida, New York City, Ohio, Illinois, Oregon, Kansas, and then we commenced meeting in St. Louis, April 6, 1893, in the Church of God Bethel. We found a large crowd present to welcome us back, and amid the tears and shouts of joy, we felt we were at home. We were made to rejoice to find the church in a good spiritual condition, also for the beautiful house of worship that was dedicated while we were at Salem, Oregon, this being the first time we were permitted to meet in it. As we looked at the beautiful building and saw this was the result of the battles we commenced in Kerry Patch amid the howling mob and showers of stones, we realized it is not by might nor by power, but it is by the Spirit of God. Hear Him say: *"I am the Lord, the God of all flesh: is there anything too hard for me?"* (Jer. 32:27). For three years Elder S. has had charge of the church and has had meetings every night. After handshaking was over, we then had an altar service. A number came and bowed, seeking Christ in the forgiveness of their sins; others for the healing of the body. The power of the Lord, thank God, was present to save the soul and heal the body. Some shouted aloud and gave glory to God; some wept for joy and fell prostrate under the power of the Lord. We could say, like Peter on the Day of Pentecost: *"Having received of the Father the promise of the Holy Ghost, he hath shed forth this, which ye now see and hear"* (Acts 2:33). The interest increased daily. Six persons came over three hundred miles to attend the meeting; they remained three or four days. All received a blessing from on high; some had their bodies healed. One was healed of catarrh of the stomach of five years' standing. He was healed instantly. They said, "We never saw it in this fashion," and went home to tell what great things the Lord had done for them.

One sister came to the meeting with a blood tumor she had had for over a year. The physicians said she could not be cured. I laid hands on her and prayed for her; she was healed in a moment. *"The prayer of faith shall save the sick, and the Lord shall raise them up"* (James 5:15), says God's Word. A girl fourteen years of age was healed of spinal disease she had suffered with for two years. She was in the hospital for treatment, and the physicians said she could not get well. She came to the meeting all strapped up in braces, and she was saved and healed instantly. Her mother took off the braces and carried them home. The child came back to the meeting in the evening perfectly well and praised God for saving and healing her. The saints shouted victory, and God shook the city with a cyclone of His power, so that multitudes were moved by the presence of God.

We received many letters from people in different states who, by hearing of the wonderful work God had done, were brought under conviction for the salvation of soul or healing of their bodies, begging us to pray for them that they might be saved or healed in their homes. Many came hundreds of miles to attend the meeting.

In every meeting the power of the Lord was present to heal soul and body. He backs up His Word where He says, *"And these signs shall follow them that believe"* (Mark 16:17). The priests and scribes said of Peter and John, *"that indeed a notable miracle hath been done by them is manifest to all them that dwell in Jerusalem, and we cannot deny it"* (Acts 4:16). Many in the city of St. Louis, after watching the work for the past four years, like the priests and scribes, have confessed that many miracles have been done.

We were pleased to find a brother and sister engaged in a meeting in evangelistic work in that city who were converted and healed in our meeting in Oakland, California. Time and space will not permit me to tell of the many wonderful works the Lord did in the Church of God in Bethel during this meeting. We remained in the church until the first of June and then erected our tent in the southern part of St. Louis. From the first the meeting was attended by from one to three thousand. Many came from other states to enjoy the meetings and to eat at our Father's table, which was so bountifully spread under the tent. Some were saved; others were healed in body and went home rejoicing. An evangelist who had been afflicted with rheumatism for over thirty years came nearly one hundred miles and was healed instantly, which caused him to leap and shout. The next day he walked several miles over the city.

A man who had met with an accident in a shop three years before had suffered great agony. Twenty-two physicians had treated him but could do nothing for him except to relieve the pain a few moments at a time. His friends brought him to the meeting one afternoon. The pain and swelling left his body. He gave God the glory. His wife was saved, and his little boy was healed of neuralgia of the heart. They now say, *"As for me and my house, we will serve the LORD"* (Josh. 24:15).

A Bohemian lady, eighty-two years old, had been crippled all through her body with rheumatism for many years and had to wear bandages on her limbs; she was saved and healed. The pain and swelling left her body at once; the power of God took possession of her body, her youth was renewed, and she shouted and praised God. While we did not understand her language, many were made to weep to hear her shout and to see the tears of gladness running down her dear old face. She went to work to bring her family to Christ. The next day she brought two of them to the altar, and they were saved and healed. One was healed of St. Vitus's dance, the other of consumption. Next she brought her daughter, fifty-nine years old, and two sons followed. Several others of the family accepted Christ. Although she accepted Christ at the eleventh hour, she has won a number of stars for her crown.

We have told only a few of the wonderful cases of divine healing that God wrought in the tent meeting.

The healing power was not confined to the tent alone, but many people in the city, and in other states, were healed instantly while we were engaged in prayer for them in the tent. Many drunkards were saved, and the appetite taken away. Many were saved who had been church members for years.

Thousands Saved

Space forbids writing of missions at Ohio, Indiana, California, etc., and I give a summary of first fourteen years' work.

It is over fourteen years since I started out to stand between the living and the dead, to point sinners to the Lamb of God that takes away the sins of the world. I have been going from one battlefield to another almost day and night. During this time I have traveled about thirty-five thousand three hundred and twenty-two miles, held meetings in thirteen states, and have stood before hundreds of thousands. The power of the Holy Spirit has gone out from these meetings all over the United States and been felt in many places across the mighty deep in awakening power. God alone knows how many thousands of souls have been born into the kingdom of our Lord Jesus Christ and how many bodies have been healed by the power of the Lord. Thousands from the age of fifty to eight-five have been saved; some were past ninety. More than two thirds who have been converted were past middle age.

Hundreds have gone out as ministers and evangelists in America and to nearly all nations, to the West Indies and Africa. Hundreds of those who have been blessed in the meetings have died in the triumph of living faith. Many of these were very aged, plucked as brands from the eternal burning. Many said with their last breath they would be waiting and watching for us at the beautiful gates.

I can say with Joshua, in all the promises the Lord has made, He has never failed in one, but has been with me in every trial and given grace and mercy. He has conquered all my enemies and glorified His name again and again. What He has done in the past He will do in the future. I will trust Him and go forward until He calls me from labor to reward. If we, as ministers and churches and individuals, have passed through many trials and persecutions and have borne them patiently for Christ's sake, we will in no wise lose our reward. Jesus said, "*Rejoice and be exceeding glad; for great is your reward in heaven*" (Matt. 5:12). We ought to thank God we are counted worthy to suffer for Him. "*If we suffer* [for Him], *we shall also reign with Him*" (2 Tim. 2:12) in glory. We know we belong to the company who are going up through great trials and tribulations, having our robes washed in the blood of the Lamb.

When the herald shall shout, "*Behold, the bridegroom cometh; go ye out to meet him*" (Matt. 25:6), what a sight will burst on our raptured vision, as we see the King of Heaven coming! Jesus came to save us from the curse of sin, to restore all that was lost by the Fall. Jesus died in the prime of life, in the strength and vigor of manhood. We shall be like Him; these humble bodies shall be changed and made like unto the glorious Son of God, not to be unclothed, but clothed with immortality. (See 2 Corinthians 5:1–4.) Oh, what a happy meeting that will be! Whole families and friends will rise up from the old churchyards and clasp each other in a long embrace, which will last forever; parents and children shall meet, husbands and wives, brothers and sisters, friends and neighbors, pastors and flocks. Those who are alive will be changed in a moment, set free from the effects of sin, and be clothed with the glory of heaven.

24

THE GOSPEL,
THE POWER OF GOD

After various journeys in several states, the account of which space forbids, we went to North Liberty, Iowa, to hold a meeting for the Church of God. We had a large crowd the first night, which continued to increase every service until the close. Thousands came daily, and souls were saved, and diseases healed from the first.

Many came forty to seventy miles over land in buggies and wagons, from the other meetings we had held. They told how the Lord had saved their souls, and many of them had also been healed by the power of God and made every whit whole. They had been given up by the best physicians to die. Their ringing testimonies convinced the people that God was with us in mighty power. They saw these people were saved soul and body and filled with the Holy Spirit. Nearly all the ministers of the Church of God were at the meeting and many from other churches, viz., M. E., U. B., Congregational, Christian, and others. Many of them bowed at the altar to be anointed with power from on high. Several were healed of different infirmities. The people came from every direction; forty-five, seventy, and a hundred miles through dust and heat.

Praise the Lord, He led many in visions to these meetings in as strange a manner as He led Cornelius and Paul, and as when He saw the man of Macedonia, with his hands raised, crying, "*Come over...and help us*" (Acts 16:9). He saw at once the Lord was calling.

Hundreds came to the altar crying, "*What must I do to be saved?*" (Acts 16:30). Forty at once. Sometimes the shouts of scores of the newborn babes rang out, which made the heavens ring. People from thirty-five to seventy-five came to Christ by scores, but some of the brothers began to get discouraged about the young men and women not coming. There were so many in that community, and the worst of them were very wild; they had tried hard to save them but could not. They wanted this meeting more for their sake. I told them to have faith in God; there would be a breakthrough among them. Thank God there was. The worst came first, and then others followed until there were scarcely any left.

Sinners were struck down and came out praising the Lord, and as their companions looked at them lying as if they were dead, it put the fear of God on them. Some had visions of hell and the Judgment, others of the broad road of destruction; others of the ladder reaching to heaven, whiter than snow, and the white-robed saints going up with the angels all around them. Christian men, women, and children fell and lay for hours. Some lay all night. Some were struck down in their homes, and many were healed. The holy fire spread all over the surrounding country and went in all churches.

I must again omit several accounts. From St. Louis, Missouri, I went to Lisbon, Salem, and Canton, Ohio. I held meetings in the tabernacle six years before in Canton. This time I held services in the Church of God. Most of the church had been converted when we were there before. The minister who had charge of the church was called to the ministry and anointed for the work at our meeting held in the tabernacle.

The Established Work of the Lord

From Canton we went back to St. Louis and stayed a short time with the Church of God. I felt the care and responsibility of the church was too much for me with the work I am called to do as an evangelist, so I gave the church with five hundred members—which I had cared for for five years—to the care of the southern Indiana eldership of the Church of God, which they gladly received. I am no longer responsible for the prosperity of the church. The church and the work we have done in the hands of the Lord is more established and appreciated by the people of St. Louis than ever before.

Eternal Good

During our meeting at this place, the editors of the different papers stood by the work and gave grand reports of the wonderful works the Lord was doing in the city. God bless them, they will never know the good they did until eternity, when the books are opened and all will be rewarded for the good they have done. The interest continued to increase until the close. The night we closed, the house was packed to the outside door at six o'clock, and many were turned away. The altar was filled with seekers to the last.

25

MANY MADE
SPIRITUALLY ALIVE

From Mount Pleasant we went to Carroll, Iowa—two hundred and fifty miles northwest—to hold a meeting for the Church of God. We were kindly received by the pastor and his wife and also the church. As we entered the church the first night, we found a large congregation awaiting our coming. When we walked up the aisle, they were so rejoiced to see the Lord had answered their prayers in sending us to them that they sang, "Praise God from Whom All Blessings Flow." Souls were converted the first night, and every day and night for five weeks, the shouts went up to heaven from those who had been born into the kingdom of our Lord and Savior, Jesus Christ, and from those who had been made whole in body of all their diseases. People came from all parts of the country and were saved. Several came seven hundred miles and were saved and healed.

There were many ministers present at this meeting, and they did what they could to push the car of salvation on. The day we closed, the people took a vote to have us come in the summer with our tent. The vote was unanimous. One of the elders of the church said God gave him a vision of the work at Carroll some years before. He saw the multitudes on the brink of ruin and that they must be gathered to Christ soon. The Lord showed him he would be used of the Lord to bring the meetings about, that they would bring the multitude to Christ. He fell under the power of God one night in our meeting and saw a cloud of glory resting over the pulpit. God showed him this was the meeting and work he had seen in the vision. I think he said he had the vision three years before. He told the people not to doubt that the work was of God. Oh, praise the Lord for the wonderful victory He gave us at this place!

Youth Renewed

The next place at which we held a meeting was at Dedham, thirteen miles from Carroll. We held the meeting in the Methodist Episcopal Church. The town was well named, for the people—at least most of them—were dead spiritually. Almost all the help we had was from those who had attended our revival at Carroll. The converts and other Christians from Carroll came thirty and forty at one time and marched to the front like brave soldiers.

One day kneeling side-by-side at the altar, there were one woman sixty years of age, one seventy-five, and an old man seventy-three; they were all saved about the same time and arose praising God for saving them at the eleventh hour. They shouted and leaped around like as though they were sixteen years of age. Their youth was renewed.

Many of the leading businessmen of the town and surrounding country and many of the best farmers were brought to Christ. People came to this meeting from the surrounding country on the cars and in buggies.

A lady came almost two hundred and fifty miles from Mount Pleasant, Iowa. She had been healed at our meeting at Columbus Junction about eight months before of cancer of the stomach. Seventeen doctors had given her up to die. Since her healing, she had gained fifty pounds and is now well and living in the state of Iowa. Her testimony cannot be doubted; God carried conviction to the people's hearts as she stood up and declared what the Lord had done for her and how wonderfully she was healed.

26

TRUE LIBERTY

After missions at Arthur, Iowa, and North Liberty, we went to Muscatine, Iowa, about fifty miles from Iowa City. We pitched our tent in Park Place on the same spot where we held a three weeks' meeting one year before. The crowds were large and the interest good from the first. When the battle cry was sounded, "To arms, to arms," companies of blood-washed soldiers, who had been redeemed from the hands of the enemy in the different fields where we had fought the battles of the Lord the year before, came up to the help of the Lord against the mighty. Some of these brave soldiers came one hundred miles. Many came over land fifty and sixty miles.

On the Fourth of July, the second day of the meeting, we had a grand reunion. Scores of young men and women drove through the dust and heat from North Liberty, Iowa; they gladly turned away from all the Fourth of July celebrations and came to be witnesses for Jesus. When the multitudes saw the self-denial of these converts, young and middle-aged and aged up to eighty, and heard them tell how God had saved and kept them by His power, they had to confess the Lord was with them. Some had been saved from the drunkards' gutter, from the gambling dens, from infidelity, and many from a dead "profession of faith" and brought into the real light and spirit of the Lord Jesus Christ. The city of Muscatine was stirred, and the country for miles around. They said, "The Lord is in our midst in great power." The man who was taken to our meeting at Iowa City on his deathbed and so wonderfully healed came to this meeting and told the people he had been well and working hard every day since he was healed. Several came with him. One man who came with him was healed of diabetes and stomach trouble; he was a great sufferer.

The woman who was healed of cancer of the stomach at Columbus Junction, over a year ago, and who had been given up to die by seventeen doctors, attended this meeting and testified before thousands that she was still well. The lady has been out working for Jesus ever since she was healed. She has conducted a number of tent meetings, and the Lord has been with her and blessed her labor.

A lady who had been healed of a tumor in one of our meetings the summer before was at this meeting and told how she had been healed, and had been perfectly well ever since.

Conviction fell on the people, the fear of God made them tremble. The children of the Lord said, "We had a Pentecost." Praise the Lord! As Brother Talmage said, "We ought not to be looking at a dead Pentecost of the past, but we ought to have thousands of Pentecosts all along the way." One day a woman was brought to the meeting on two crutches. She had not walked a step without them for eleven months, and for four months was confined to bed. Her sufferings were so great, she could scarcely endure them. The doctors gave her no hope. As I laid hands on her and prayed, the power of God came upon her. Saved and healed, she sprang to her feet, walked back and forth through the tent, clapping her hands and praising the Lord. She left her crutches in the tent and walked away. She attended the meeting until the close and was always ready and happy to testify how Jesus had healed her. Her minister and many members of the church of which she was a member went to her house and came away and reported that she was well.

One of the leading members testified in the tent that he heard of her walking without her crutches; he did not believe it and said he would go and see, and if she was not, he would denounce divine healing. To his surprise, when he went to her home, he found her doing her own work, perfectly well and free from pain. She had no use for her crutches. He left the house praising God instead of denouncing divine healing. He praised God that he was convinced that He was just the same today as in the days of the apostles. Several women were healed of decay of the ovaries, a disease nothing can reach or cure but the surgical knife, and then they nearly all die in or from the operation.

One of the women who was healed of this disease refused to come to the altar to be saved when asked, but the Lord struck her down in the congregation. She lay like she was dead. At the same time, her husband was at the altar seeking Christ. In about an hour, she leaped to her feet shouting. She said she was saved and healed. The doctors had all given her up. They said the only thing that might possibly save her life would be an operation, and then she had but little hope. They told her she was in danger of dying any day of hemorrhages. They said it was not possible for her to live longer without the operation. The day she was saved she had been to see the doctor about putting the operation off until the weather got cooler, but he urged her to have it done at once. She asked him if she would live through it; he told her he did not know, she would have to risk it. She came to the meeting in a very sad state of mind. She knew she was not ready to die, but when the Lord struck her down, she yielded herself soul and body to Him, and she was saved and healed. She rose to her feet perfectly well and happy. The Great Physician cured her without the knife.

She came to the meeting through rain as well as sunshine and did all her own work. Her face shone with the glory of God as she told how Jesus healed and saved her.

A lady came over one hundred miles, greatly afflicted with a tumor in her throat and one under her arm. She had had no use of her arm for eight years; it was always cold and looked like the hand of a corpse. As I prayed and told her in the name of Jesus Christ of Nazareth to stretch forth her hand, she did so, and it was made whole like the other. She clapped her hands above her head, giving glory to God. She told the people her hand had been asleep for eight years, but was made whole. She testified often and told she was well, that she could feed herself and comb her hair, and that she had been baptized with the Holy Spirit. A lady in Muscatine, who had a withered hand for fifteen years, was healed. The bone of her wrist was raised, and the fingers were drawn crooked. The hand had been cold and helpless all these years. I took hold of her hand and prayed, and in a moment it was whole as the other. The woman was healed in the presence of several thousand men, women, and children, who wept and shouted for joy at this manifestation of God's power, just as they did when Jesus was on earth.

One day a lady came to the meeting suffering greatly from a fractured arm and shoulder, and her wrist had been broken and her fingers crushed, for she had fallen down a long flight of steps with all her weight on her arm and hand. She was very heavy, and she met with this accident eight months before. The arm and hand were very much swollen and inflamed. The doctors gave her no hopes of ever being able to use the arm or hand. Before she came to the altar, she rose and told the congregation her condition with tears in her eyes and said she believed the Lord would heal her. When we prayed for her, the people crowded around the altar to see what would happen; when they saw her begin to move her fingers and hand and saw the swelling going down and saw her raise that arm and stretch it forth, then clap her hands together shouting, "I am healed," they could scarcely believe their eyes. Big, strong men who were sinners wept and said, "Surely God is here." The saints shouted, and the fear of the Lord came upon all who saw her. She stayed at the meeting several days and testified of what Jesus had done for her.

One Sunday while waiting for the streetcar to take us to the park for the afternoon meeting, we saw the black clouds gathering; there was a great storm coming. The tent was two miles from the city, and there was no shelter any place around. I felt anxious to be at the tent with the rest. I began to pray for the Lord to protect them, to be around them like a wall of fire, and protect them from harm. While praying, the words of Paul came to me that he spoke while on the sinking vessel. You remember he said that the vessel would be wrecked but no lives would be lost. I did not understand it, but as we got off the cars, we saw the storm just ready to burst in all its fury. The tent was crowded, they had neglected to put down the side walls, and it was too late now to put them down. They were having testimony. The interest was so great that they did not know the storm was upon them. I stepped upon the pulpit and told them the storm was upon us and not to try to get away, but just sit still and put all their trust in God and He would save us. Just as I said this, the storm struck the tent, and the ropes broke close around the pulpit where I was standing. The side poles were flying and cracking. I fell and lay upon the pulpit; all the other ministers and sinners were knocked off; the congregation saw all this; they saw the tent with the two large center poles falling. They saw the tent would soon cover them. Many thought I was killed; when I saw the tent going down, then I knew what the Scripture meant that the Lord gave me in answer to my prayers, that the tent would be wrecked or go down, but no lives would be lost. No one was struck with the poles, and no one was hurt.

The storm continued. It seemed we would be carried over the treetops; for nearly an hour it looked like the rain would come in torrents, but there was only a little shower. Everyone felt the Lord had wonderfully protected us. A man was lying in front of the pulpit under the power of God when the storm came up; the pulpit fell over him, also a pitcher of water and a lot of flowers fell upon him, but he lay through it all praising God!

The Sunday before we closed there, there were nine thousand people on the ground, and the Sunday we closed there were ten thousand. In the morning meeting, there were one hundred and thirty testimonies of the healing of the body and hundreds of the salvation of the soul.

The Triumph of a Living Faith

On the first day of January, 1902, I married Mr. S. P. Etter of Hot Springs, Arkansas. Then we went back to Iowa, where I had labored several years before. We held meetings for seven weeks in Muscatine in the fairgrounds. This was the third camp meeting held by us in that city. The meeting was very deep spiritually from the first. The Lord put His seal on it with great signs and wonders, saving souls and healing bodies. Many who had been brought out in a deep experience some eight years before had died in the triumphs of a living faith; so the Lord's work is established around this part of Iowa, and many are living today that the best medical skill failed to cure. Their lives were spared to their loved ones, and parents spared to care for their children.

Many are preaching the Gospel and scattering the fragments over the land, giving the Bread of Life to starving souls.

27

MIDWEST HEALINGS AND SALVATIONS

In 1903 I held meetings in the beautiful Prospect Park for three weeks and had good success. Many were born into the kingdom of our Lord and Savior, Jesus Christ, and many were healed of all their diseases. The interest was great when we closed, but we had to do so because the weather got so cold and wet. I baptized in the beautiful lake; a large crowd witnessed the sublime scene. As one after another came up from the watery grave and the power of the Lord was manifested, we all were made to rejoice in the presence of the Lord. Several came from Muscatine and Andalusia and were baptized, and they felt that they were well paid for the sacrifice they had made in coming so far. We went from there back to Andalusia, where we held the last meeting in the large tent. The Lord had been there in great power; the surrounding country was stirred; many were saved and God backed His Word with signs and wonders; many were healed, and many fell prostrated under the power of God and received wonderful blessings.

We went back the second time at their urgent call so that the work might be more firmly established. While we were away, the people of Moline went on with the work, and the interest was so good that they opened the way for us to come back. I felt sure the Lord was calling.

We commenced our work in Warr Hall. The first four weeks there were thirteen hundred bowed at the altar; I prayed for each with laying on of hands, and nearly all were converted or reclaimed; and nearly all were healed of from one to a dozen diseases. The power was present just as it was in the days of Christ and the apostles—we do not read of any place where the work was greater—sixty at the altar for healing, all at once in the afternoon meeting. Nearly everyone got up rejoicing, showing by their testimonies that they were perfectly well. Many people in the gallery shouted or waved their hands; sometimes nearly the whole house was weeping at the wonderful miracles that were done before them all.

The scenes were wonderful. Every meeting they could hardly wait until I gave them the opportunity to come to the altar; then there would be a rush. They brought them in chairs, on cots, and on pillows; the blind, lame, deaf, dumb, and the paralytic; those dying with consumption, tumors, cancer, blood poisoning, catarrh of the stomach and lungs, or all through the blood; broken bones and everything else—all chronic diseases that could not be cured by any earthly power—they laid them at the feet of Jesus. As at Peter's great revival, they tried to get near enough for his shadow to fall on them, so it was here—everyone tried to get nearest to me, like those at the pool of Bethesda, to get into the water first. One after another they were healed; sometimes in an hour everyone would be up rejoicing. The people looking on saw large tumors and goiters go and cancers disappear; children got up and walked who never had walked before. They saw the deaf hear, the dumb speak, those that had never heard or spoken before. They wondered and were amazed, and they gave glory to God for His great power and love for suffering humanity.

Police Help

The police force took quite an interest in bringing the afflicted in ambulances and carrying them in on stretchers. One man was perfectly helpless with inflammatory rheumatism. He could not move his fingers and was in great pain with fever. He was saved and healed and walked upon the platform, then walked out and down to the police station. When the officers came for him, he was gone. They laughed and took the cot and went out. Infidels and all kinds of sinners who had never before believed in God were convinced of the reality of the religion of Jesus and were converted.

A doctor, one of the finest men in the city, when he saw so many of his patients healed, was converted and became an earnest worker.

Men and women of all kinds, both businessmen and others, came for healing and received the double cure. The superintendent of the Business Colleges of the Tri-Cities brought his father from a distance, who had to use an ear trumpet. He went away with his son with his hearing restored. Scores of Catholics were converted and healed. One nun who had been lame and afflicted with heart disease for fifteen years, but could get no help anywhere, was saved and perfectly cured. She came back and gave glory to God.

Some Jews, one the wife of a rabbi, came for healing. When she first came, she asked if she could be healed without any mention of Jesus. I told her no, she could not. She said she did not want anything to do with Jesus. She was badly afflicted and had suffered much for many years. I talked some to her, and then she went away; but she came back in a few days, was saved and healed, and confessed Christ in public, praising Him for His wonderful works.

Many Swedish and German people and other nationalities came. We could not understand each other, but they were healed and converted.

Two boys were brought from the deaf and dumb school. The deaf and dumb spirits were cast out, and they both talked and heard perfectly. Three mutes came—two men and one woman. All received their hearing and speech. The woman was healed of other diseases, two of which were heart trouble and a tumor. When her husband saw she was healed and that the tumor was gone, he cried and praised the Lord.

A woman in Moline came with a cancer; she had been given up to die by all the physicians. Her mother died with cancer. Her clothes just hung on her—she could not bear anything to touch her because the least pressure would make her vomit. When I saw the condition she was in, so emaciated and deformed, I threw back her wrap and told the people to look at her, she was dying with a cancerous tumor, but the Lord was going to heal her and take it all away right then. She could not kneel down, so I told her to sit on the altar and that God was going to heal her now. I laid my hands upon her and in the name of Jesus of Nazareth, I commanded the unclean spirits to go out of her. All the pain and misery, the cancer and the tumor, all passed away. She arose before all who had been watching from the gallery down, praising the Lord, and saying she was perfectly healed. She came back and testified to being made whole and well.

Shouts arose from the gallery and all over the hall. Strong men wept, and men and women came and knelt at the altar saying, "I believe there is a God; I want to be a Christian."

A lady came from Iowa, almost dead with a tumor; the specialists of Chicago and St. Louis had given up on her. The pain was so great that she could not be still one minute. When she came to the meeting and to the altar, we laid on hands and in the name of Jesus of Nazareth commanded the tumorous spirit with all its works and pain to come out of her. She was made whole and arose shouting and praising God, who had so wonderfully healed her. She stayed several days without a sign of the tumor, gave many ringing testimonies, and started home to tell what great things the Lord had done for her. The audience looked on in wonder and amazement at the mighty miracles God was performing at our hands.

A woman brought her boy, six years old, full of tumors all over his body—the most awful sight you ever saw, so deformed. They were in his throat and in his windpipe; he had a bad cough with it, nearly choking him to death; he had been treated by twenty doctors and had three operations performed. He could not rest for a minute, night or day. From the first time we prayed for him, he never suffered any more, and he slept like a baby! He was quiet day and night. The people could see how fast the tumors were disappearing. It was a great mountain, but in the name of Jesus it was removed and cast into the sea.

Scores of deaf people of all ages were healed—those born deaf, from babies to forty or fifty years of age. Others whose eardrums had been destroyed in different ways had them restored and were made to hear. A lady from South Dakota had been deaf in one ear for forty years, and her arm had been paralyzed for nineteen years; she could not raise it to her head, but she was instantly healed.

Over two thousand came or were brought to the altar. We prayed for them, and most all were converted or reclaimed. Nearly all were healed of from one to a dozen chronic diseases. Hundreds were converted and healed at the same time, receiving the double cure, salvation for soul and body, like the paralytic son to whom Christ said: "Son, your sins are forgiven: arise, take up your bed and walk." Which is easier to say, "Your sins are forgiven," or, to say, "Arise and walk"? (See Mark 2:9–11.) You see, one was as easy for the Lord to do as the other, and He did both at once, for He *"Himself took our infirmities, and bare our sicknesses"* (Matt. 8:17).

The Lord intended the healing of soul and body to go together, in order that the world might believe He is the same now as He was then (Heb. 13:8), and so they might know that the Lord loves us as He loves His Son.

Remarkable Healing, a Great Miracle

There was a boy seven years old, who had never walked; he was born insane, blind, deaf, and dumb; he was always pounding his head and beating himself like the maniac among the tombs. They tried everything, including the best medical help, but the doctors could not locate the cause, and they said he would never have any sense; but praise the Lord, He says, *"Behold, I am the Lord, the God of all flesh: is there any thing too hard for me?"* (Jer. 32:27).

Praise His holy name, *"All things are possible to him that believeth"* (Mark 9:23). We told the parents if they would give themselves and the child into the hands of the Lord, I had faith that the Lord would heal him. They were Catholics. The Lord has performed the greatest miracle ever known; for me, there is no case of healing in the Bible record as wonderful as this boy.

The man born blind was considered a great wonder; then the man at the Beautiful Gate, who was healed of weak ankles and who was born lame, was considered a great miracle; but this child was born blind, deaf, and dumb, and had no mind; now he can hear and see perfectly. God has given him a bright, intelligent mind; he laughs and plays and walks around in front of the pulpit every day in view of all the congregation; before he was healed, he had spasms, as many as twenty a day, but now he is well and happy. In healing this child, God has put His seal on this work and proven to the world that I am called and sent of God, that the Lord is using me in a wonderful way to do His will in these last days.

The power of Elijah is working among the people with mighty miracles, signs, and wonders, showing that the coming of the Lord is near at hand, even at the door. (See Malachi 4:5–6.) He is preparing the bride, mounting her on the white horse of power, ready to meet the Bridegroom.

28

WORLD'S FAIR TIME

We received pressing calls to come to St. Louis to hold meetings during the World's Fair. We felt the calls were from God to go where all the nations of the earth were represented and gathered together. It was a good time to gather the children of the Lord together in one place. Here we might receive the Pentecostal power, the anointing, the early and later rain in the same month, as the Lord promised to give those who asked in these last days. Thus, the called and chosen, with the power of the Holy Spirit, would scatter out from here to all parts of the world, spreading the true doctrines of our Savior, Jesus Christ, giving the last call, blowing the gospel trumpet, and giving the last warning that the Great Day of the Lord is near.

We remained in the city over six months, holding two meetings a day. The Lord was with us in power from the first meeting. Many hundreds were brought out in a higher experience and were made to rejoice in the saving and healing power of God.

All kinds of diseases were driven out of the bodies of men, women, and children, proving that Jesus is just *"the same...today"* (Heb. 13:8), the Great Physician to heal both soul and body, to give the double cure—saving power for the soul and healing power for the body—and that *"these signs shall follow them that believe;*

in my name shall they cast out devils…They shall lay hands on the sick, and they shall recover" (Mark 16:17–18). The Lord Jesus purchased these blessings on the cross and left them in His will for all who will meet His conditions. *"Himself took our infirmities, and bare our sicknesses"* (Matt. 8:17), and *"By his stripes ye were healed"* (1 Pet. 2:24).

A woman who was born blind received her sight. Her eyes were red and swollen, and she suffered great pain.

Children were healed that were sick from birth; some of them crippled or lame from birth.

Several men and women who were deaf all their lives received their hearing. Many lame and crippled with paralysis or rheumatism and spinal troubles, others with infirm spirits, were made to praise God. Many were struck down by the power of God and had visions.

The people continued from day to day to look on in wonder and say, "We have seen strange things today." Many would weep, others turn pale, when they saw the power of the Lord was present to save and to heal.

Many came from hospitals, given up by the best doctors in the city as incurable. They were saved and healed. Some of them soon went to hard labor, proving what great things the Lord had done for them.

Wonders Worked

(Reprinted from the *Apostolic Light*, of Salem, Oregon)

St. Louis, Missouri—Rejoice with us in the goodness of our God and Savior, for He has been very gracious to us. During the last two months, at Sister Woodworth-Etter's meetings alone, hundreds have been saved, and a greater number healed. Most of the latter were chronic cases; many only came after the doctors had pronounced them incurable. One woman had spent $500 on her child for healing. Several hundred have had hearing restored; some had been paralyzed, others had tumors, consumption, and withered limbs, and were healed.

Yesterday during the afternoon meeting, the Lord Jesus bowed the heavens and came down. Many were under the power. Two women and a girl were struck down unconscious and lay on the floor. The girl came to after an hour and said she was saved and had the witness of the Spirit. The second woman lay unconscious for about two and one-half hours, with both arms raised to heaven. When she was recovering, she sang praises unto God in the Spirit and warned sinners to repent. The third woman lay unconscious until the evening meeting, about four hours, and said she had a message for us from the Lord, the substance of which I wrote in stenography, so you have it direct from the throne of God. She said:

"I was carried away and was with Jesus in heaven. I saw my parents there, and my children who had gone before me, and others I knew. *Some are dead that I did not see;* they were cast into the outer darkness. A man who had been put to death by cruel men, and whom I had been burdened about for months, I saw; he had been executed by men and was in heaven. Some I had never thought to meet in heaven, I saw. Others who were thought to have died innocent, I did not see.

"The Lord said to me, 'Go back and warn the people of My coming soon. If they spit in your face, say Amen; and I will be with you. Wonderful things will be done in the meetings at St. Louis. There will be a hard battle, but hold up My power; and sinners, make your peace with Me before it is too late.'"

Visions of the Coming Lord

We rejoice daily at the marvelous manifestations of the presence of God in our midst. I never saw such wonderful works as those God has wrought in Sister Woodworth-Etter's meetings during the last two weeks. God the Father is glorifying Jesus Christ, in healing all manner of diseases, in saving souls, in giving peace and love and joy to repentant sinners. *"Ye are also helping together by prayer for us, that for the gift bestowed upon us by the means of many persons thanks may be given by many on our behalf"* (2 Cor. 1:11).

The Lord Jesus is pouring out His spirit on these meetings. He showed it to one sister in a vision, and we at the meetings see it. About a dozen have fallen as dead, lain for hours on the floor, and had visions and revelations. Sometimes the Spirit will take possession of a man just after he has finished singing, with hymn book in hand and hand upraised, and hold him as a statute for fifteen or twenty minutes; others standing up or kneeling have been held in this way. Yesterday two women were converted sitting in their seats and got the witness of the Spirit and knew they were born from above. Sister Etter herself went under the power at the afternoon meeting, on March 24, and had to be laid on the platform for over an hour. She had a vision, and the Lord showed her many things, especially with regard to the immediate future of the work in St. Louis.

All those who have had visions and revelations bring back the message to warn the people that Jesus is coming soon, that sinners make their peace with Him, and that those who are saved need to get established and anointed with power and sealed with the knowledge that He is coming soon. May they may be found faithful and true at His appearing.

All who have had revelations while under the power bring back the message that our Lord comes very soon. Praise His name. What a glorious time that will be for His saints.

We made a visit to St. Louis. The Lord was there in great power; there were wondrous miracles of healing, and the Holy Spirit power was manifested in many signs and wonders, in speaking in other tongues with the interpretation, and with heavenly songs.

One sister was almost carried by the power of God from the platform into the congregation. She stood there and had a wonderful vision and spoke in many different languages.

A young boy was struck dumb and deaf and blind. After three days his sight returned while they were praying for him, but his hearing and speech did not return until a month after. While he was deaf and dumb, the Lord wonderfully used him and gave him many visions and revelations. He prophesied of earthquakes, of fire, and of floods, and they have come to pass.

A Swedish sister was entirely under the power of God and spoke in many different languages and gave the interpretation. She gave many prophesies that will reach right on until the Lord comes. Many of them have come to pass.

Another sister was wonderfully baptized and sang an anthem in Greek and one in Latin. She sang a heavenly song that could be heard far away. It sounded like as though it came from heaven. She spoke in several different languages and stood up and preached while tears streamed down her face.

Another young lady received her baptism and spoke in eight different languages. She spoke many times afterwards when the power took possession of her, and everyone knew it was the power of God.

Speaking in Tongues

While preaching and explaining Pentecost—how they too spoke in other tongues—the power of God took possession of me, and I began to speak as the Spirit gave utterance in other tongues. I spoke in three different languages, preaching the wonderful works of Pentecost in other languages. I sang several songs in the Spirit and laughed in a manner resembling the laughter of several other nations.

All who received the baptism with speaking in other tongues received great power.

A young girl came to the meeting and made fun of the workers, but the Lord saved her and showed her the darkness of Roman Catholicism, and she gave a wonderful testimony of how the Lord had delivered her.

The Lord appeared to her in a vision and told her to go to the suburb where she had previously lived on the next day, and He would give her many souls. He showed her in a vision those He would save.

She obeyed and went the next day and called on one of her old friends. They expressed surprise at seeing her look so happy, for before her conversion she hardly ever smiled and was dissatisfied and unhappy and used such rough language. They said, "What has happened to you? You look so happy. We want that kind of religion too." She told them how to get it, and they went to praying. God sent His power, and pretty soon they all fell over and lay for fifteen or twenty minutes. A little girl, about nine years old, ran about the house shouting and saying, "Mama, I see Jesus; I see Jesus." They all came out brightly converted and shouting, ten in all, including the hired girl.

Then she went to another house, and they said the same thing; they saw such a great change in her and asked her what she had done, and she told them she was converted. The power of God came on her while she was speaking, and she began to preach to them while under the power of God. When she came to, she found they were all overpowered; they lay for a while and came out shouting the praises of God, nineteen of them in all, as neighbors had been called in.

After this, as she was walking down the street, she met a girl friend, who was going to a dance hall to attend a committee meeting to arrange for a picnic next day. She was invited to go along; at first she refused, but the Lord showed her to go.

When she got there, she found it was one of the places she had seen in her vision. When she began to speak, the power of the Holy Spirit came on her, and she preached to them, and when she had finished, they were all twenty of them lying round on the floor like a battlefield. She prayed for them, and they all came out brightly converted.

Forty-nine were saved that day, of whom forty-eight were Roman Catholics and one a backslidden Methodist.

Another time she was impressed to write to Mrs. V., who had a daughter who was born deaf and dumb, and who seventeen months ago was run into by a streetcar, the result of which was she was paralyzed from the hips down, and the doctors put her in plaster of Paris cast.

Mrs. V. brought her daughter to St. Louis and called and asked the sister to come and pray for her. She went and, as she was praying, fell under the power of the Holy Spirit and talked with the daughter, using the deaf and dumb language—although she did not, and does not, know a single letter of it—telling her how to give herself to the Lord. Then when the sick deaf-mute prayed, she also fell under the power of the Holy Spirit and *spoke*, saying, "I see Jesus; He said, 'You can walk,' and reached out His hand." She took the tips of His fingers and rose right up out of bed, the cast breaking, and walked across to her father. As she reached out and touched him on the forehead, he too fell under the power of God and was saved, as well as seven others.

The next day she went home and spoke over the telephone to a friend who had been crippled, using crutches for sixteen years. She would not believe that a girl born deaf and dumb could hear and talk, but she said, "It is Agnes," the name of another friend of hers.

She replied, "Come over and see." When the cripple entered on her crutches, and saw Verne healed, she cried, "If you can walk, I can too," and threw away her crutches and walked.

A sister was suffering from appendicitis, gallstones, and another disease. One day she became unconscious and remained so until nine o'clock P.M. The people she lived with had her removed to the city hospital. When she came to, she found herself in bed there, and they told her she would have to be operated on.

An operation was performed, and twenty-five stitches were taken. She got so bad after it that she could not see nor speak, and they put a death screen round her, as is customary when a patient is about to die. A doctor and a nurse were watching for her to die.

A sister from the mission came to visit her and said, when leaving, "We will pray for you to be healed at nine o'clock," and two nurses standing by heard it.

During the day she got worse, her limbs turning black up to the elbows and knees, and her fingers stiff; she also had hemorrhages, the blood coming out of her mouth, nose, and ears, so that her clothing was saturated with blood. Shortly before nine o'clock, all her limbs stretched out, as when a person dies, and the nurse, believing her dead, went and told the doctor, "She is gone." He came to see and found her sitting up; he was astonished and told her she must lie down. She said, "I am healed;" he told her she was out of her head, but she insisted God had healed her, and at last he saw that it was so.

The next day twenty-nine doctors came to see her and said, "It was the most wonderful case we have ever known. She is perfectly healed." They had not known of anyone else to recover from that operation.

In such cases the stitches are never taken out before fifteen days, but in her case, since she was healed, they were taken out the fourth day.

When visiting day came, since she had no visitors, the medical superintendent of the hospital said he and his wife would be pleased to visit her. They came, and as they sat by her bed, she told the story of her conversion, and there were tears in his wife's eyes.

29

MANIFESTATIONS OF THE SPIRIT

After fifteen years I went back to Indianapolis, my husband, Mr. Etter, accompanying me. There he stood bravely with me in the hottest battle, and since the day we were married, he has never shrunk back. He is foremost when the battle is hottest; he will defend the Word and all the gifts and operations of the Holy Spirit, but he does not want any fanaticism or foolishness. He takes the best care of me, in and out of the meetings. It makes no difference what I call on him to do. He will pray and preach and sing and is very good around the altar. He does about all of my writing, and he also helps in getting out my books and looks after the meetings, in and outside. The Lord knew what I needed, and it was all brought about by the Lord, through His love and care for me and the work.

We pitched a large tent in the southern part of the city, and the news soon spread of our being in the city. Our old friends and children in Jesus began to come to our help. The meetings were good from the first. Sinners began to flock to Christ, and shouts of victory began to ascend to the Great White Throne, "The lost is found, the dead alive." (See Luke 15:24, 32.)

Many fell under the power of God and had wonderful visions. There were great signs and wonders and demonstrations, including speaking in unknown tongues. Sinners were struck down like dead men and women. The Lord wonderfully used little children to bring sinners to Christ. While the Holy Spirit had full control, He, the Holy Spirit, would lead them out through the congregation and reach for this man or that woman; they would give them their hand and go straight to the altar with them, with their eyes closed all the time. All knew that they were led by the Lord; some were converted before they got to the altar—some prophesied things that have since taken place.

The weather began to get quite cool, so we went down into the city to Peniel Hall, on 11th and Senate, and all followed. The Holy Spirit was present in great power, with gifts, signs, and visions, following the laying on of hands. There were visible signs of light and glory on the pulpit and through the congregation, seen by the natural eye by some. Saints said they had never been in such a meeting or felt such power of God or of the Holy Spirit.

Converted and Healed

The next year we went back to Indianapolis and pitched the tent on the same ground; and it was about the same time of the year. The revival spirit from the last year was still with them, so the work commenced at once with crowds and interests. The work was much greater than the last year. They were ready to come up and help against the enemy. The crowds were greater, and the interests deeper. Many were waiting to be healed or saved. There were new soldiers coming into the ranks every day and greater miracles of healing.

One woman was brought one hundred miles in a rolling chair. She had been confined to her bed for over seventeen years and had had twenty-five doctors. They did not know her case, nor could they do anything for her from the first, but could only quiet her a little. Sometimes she could not stand on her feet or turn over in bed. A man from her town had been in our meeting in St. Louis and was healed there. He went home and went to see her and told her. She knew him as a bad rheumatic. He went in without any crutches or help, a happy, converted man. He took one of my books with him and gave it to her to read. After seeing him and reading the book, she was converted. She saw that she had never been converted before, though she had been a church member about all her life.

She had been anxious for her husband to get converted. When she saw her condition, she said, "Lord, must I go to Indianapolis to be converted and healed?"

"Yes," she said, "I must be taken." It was taking her life in her hands to run the risk of the journey, but her husband brought her to the meeting, and she was converted and healed; and her husband was also converted. He went to her shouting, and she commenced shouting, and she sprang out of her wheelchair, a healed woman. Then there was shouting all over the tent. When he took her arm and walked up to the platform and stood before the great audience, it was the first time that they had stood together for over seventeen years. They were both tall and stately looking, and he was prouder of her than when they stood as bride and groom. Everyone in and around the tent was glad. There were many tears of joy from hard faces. We sang, "Let the Hallelujahs Roll," and had a wave offering of praise, using handkerchiefs and hats. It looked as if every hand was raised with shouts of praise.

The people at her home thought they would bring her back in a box, dead; but when they heard she was coming home well, nearly the whole town was at the river wharf to welcome her home. She went there to the church in that town for the first time in over seventeen years, and she stood up and preached and told what great things the Lord had done. Her husband's brother had been preaching for many years, and this brother joined him in the ministry. Since then he and his wife have gone out together to hold meetings.

A man had a vision of this tent and the work twenty years ago, and of riding in electric cars to and from the tent. He described the meeting, and he had seen me. The Lord used him in many ways to bring sinners to Christ. He promised the Lord he would do anything He asked. One night he was going home, and it was very dark. He went into an alley to pray, as the Lord led him to do so, and as he knelt down and prayed for lost men, there were two men secreted in a shed close by. The Lord led him to pray for wicked men and women. While doing so, he heard a noise inside the shed, and the men came up behind him from where they were. They threw their arms around him and confessed they were waiting to rob, and if they were caught, murder. They had poison and intended to die rather than to be taken. Right then and there, they were converted and started for their homes, happy men.

This meeting was a greater success than the one a year before. Many ministers that we knew, who had started out as ministers and evangelists from my meetings ten and fifteen years before, came from all parts to see me and be in the meetings. Among them were many converts and workers, in all ways, in the Master's vineyard. Oh! We had such love and fellowship! The power and presence of the Lord was manifested in gifts, demonstrations, operations, and callings, with mighty works of the Holy Spirit.

One sister spoke in unknown tongues all night. This was before the Holy Spirit fell at Los Angeles, California. A minister came to see me. He said he had been converted through a minister who was converted through me. He had heard so much about me that he had come fifty miles to see his grandmother.

Last summer, eight years after, we came back and held a tent meeting for several months; and several hundred were saved and healed of almost every disease. Cancers, tumors, blindness, and deafness; cripples were brought in or came in on crutches; some were in a dying condition; all received the divine touch and were healed by His power; they walked, shouted, and praised God. Many were baptized with the Holy Spirit.

A woman was brought from Cincinnati, dying from cancer. The doctors sent her home to die. She was in such an putrid condition that the odor made people sick. It was in June and very warm, and the flies were thick over her dress. She was a Christian and was ready to die, but the Lord said she should *"not die, but live, and declare the works of the LORD"* (Ps. 118:17). In less than ten minutes after I began to pray, she was completely healed; she jumped and shouted; the odor stopped with the discharge, at once. She remained a week and went to work.

We closed the meeting and went to Maxwell, a little town twenty-three miles east of Indianapolis. The Lord drew the people from all parts; though it was a little town, there were two thousand souls at a time there on Sundays and more on the last Sunday.

Next we went to Ohio, then came back to Indianapolis, commenced meeting in the Christian Church, and remained about eight months. People were saved and healed from the first. They came from Chicago and other cities, and from all around for several hundred miles, and were saved, healed, and baptized with the Holy Spirit. We witnessed many miracles of healing as remarkable as those wrought in the days of the early church. We will give one testimony. It is now about four months since this brother was healed, and he has not had a pain since, nor sickness, no inconvenience whatever. He is a well man, who was made so at once by the power of God. He had piles for thirty years, had them cut and burnt off four times; then cancer commenced. He got so bad that he had to sit on an inflated ring and had to have his wife flush his bowels twice a day, to use a long syringe and tube and two quarts of water at each time. Then he would bleed, and it was so offensive she could hardly do it. The bowel was all gone on the left side for ten inches up; the backbone was bare, having no flesh on it on the inside; he had rheumatism also and was a sinner. God converted and healed him all at once, in less than fifteen minutes. He was sixty-four years old. He was baptized with the Holy Spirit and is now one of God's little ones. *"There is nothing too hard for* [our God]" (Jer. 32:17).

(Reprinted from *The Latter Rain Evangel* of Chicago, from an article by Elder F. F. Bosworth, of Dallas, Texas)

On my return home from the Stone Church Convention, I spent three days with Mr. and Mrs. Etter in their home and attended the services. At the close of the first service seven were prayed with for healing and all seemed healed in a few minutes. One sister (an elderly lady who had broken her hip two years before), suffering great pain and unable to step on her right limb, was brought to the meeting. Her daughter and I helped her into the meeting. When hands were laid on her in prayer, she was instantly healed and walked perfectly, and continued to walk to the services during my stay in the city.

Mrs. Johnson, living on East Jefferson Street in Indianapolis, was born deaf and dumb and is now nearly fifty-two years old. She had never heard a sound nor spoken a word. When Sister Etter, in the name of Jesus, rebuked the deaf-and-dumb spirit and commanded it to go out, the woman was completely delivered. She can now hear perfectly and is learning to talk for the first time.

Clyde Gray, a barber in Indianapolis, was stone deaf. When Sister Etter commanded him to hear in Jesus' name, his ears were opened so perfectly that he had to hold his hands over them at first when the choir sang. Pauline Winters, an eight-year-old child, born blind, was instantly healed in these meetings. Five volumes have been written of Mrs. Etter's work as an evangelist, and it is doubtful if there is any record written since the Acts of the Apostles that is so wonderful.

Raised from the Dead

1104 Broadway, Indianapolis

About five weeks ago, one Sunday night, I was attending the meetings, and was sitting listening to Sister Etter preaching when I turned real sick, and a voice said to me, "Come with me." I went outside the church, a sister accompanying me, and the same voice said again, "This is death, come now, go with me."

That was the last I remembered on earth, only I thought of my son in the army and that no one would know where to send to notify him of my death.

Presently, it seemed to me I was in heaven, in a place where there was such light and rest and joy. I heard singing and all kinds of different instruments.

I saw my earthly father and children, and talked with the Lord, and then a voice said, "You can go back for a while," and then I heard Sister Etter's voice calling on me in the name of the Lord.

—*Mrs. Sarah Nelson*

Sister Woodworth-Etter says, on that occasion, there was a commotion, people going out to help and some coming back. She asked, "What is the matter?" As they did not wish to harm the audience, they said, "She has fainted." Sister Etter said, "She is all right; and even if the Lord should take her, she is ready. I wish the rest of you were as well prepared."

After quite a while, they carried her body in and said, "She is dead!" "The pulse has ceased to beat." There was no motion of the heart, the body was cold and limp, and the face that of a corpse. Sister Etter gathered the others around her, and spoke of Jesus being the Resurrection and the Life, and prayed and called on her in the name of the Lord, and she opened her eyes.

When she opened her eyes they were yellow, and she did not seem to know anything at first; but sat in a big arm chair looking like a corpse. Later on in the meeting she expressed a desire to testify, which she did. She has been attending meeting ever since and working daily.

Indianapolis, January 6, 1915

I can testify that the Lord can heal.

I was healed of cancer of the rectum. Two doctors of this city pronounced it a hopeless case. Not even a hospital case—my age and the advancement of the disease—said I would get no benefit from an operation. My age then was sixty-five years.

The left side of the rectum was eaten away. I was a total wreck physically. Didn't know what a night's sleep was, no appetite, my whole nervous system was completely broken down. On the ninth day of January, 1912, I went to where Sister Etter was holding meetings, at 17th Street and Martindale Avenue, this city. I was a total stranger—did not know a person in the house except my good wife who had gone with me—as I was unable to go out alone.

When Sister Etter gave the altar call, I went to the altar, knelt down, and the brothers and sisters laid on hands and prayed for me and rebuked the diseases in Jesus' name. When they laid their hands on my back, I shuddered, for I was so sore and tender I could not even bear my back bathed. I just had to take a sponge and squeeze the water out gently on my back, as the cancer had almost eaten through. But praise God, He took all soreness away. Something just seemed to drop on the sore spot; it seemed like four or five layers of plasters. It was so real in my mind that I put my hand to my back to see how thick they were. I was not at the altar more than fifteen minutes until all pain and soreness was all gone; that awful burning sensation left and to this day has never returned—about thirty-one months, almost three years since I was healed—not a trace of the diseases left. I have been free from aches and pains; have never had a day of sickness since the day God so wonderfully healed me. On the same day I was also healed of rheumatism in my right arm and shoulder. My arm was drawn to my side; I could not dress myself. The Lord straightened my arm out, and it is still straight. Praise the Lord forever. Oh, glory to Jesus, He can save, and He has power to heal, and He does heal. Oh, I can never tell how happy I was when Jesus touched my body and healed me. I jumped up over the altar, took off my coat, and put it on again— something I had not been able to do for weeks. I said if the Lord could stop pains and aches in a moment, He was the one for me to look to.

I had an inflated rubber ring I had to take with me, for I could not sit down on the softest feather pillow, as the rectum was so sore and tender.

I let the air out of the ring; boxed it up; hung up the syringe. I was using three quarts of warm water night and morning in the bowels; three pills each evening and other medicine every two hours. I had nearly two weeks treatment in the house—I threw it all out—haven't taken a dose of any kind of medicine since the day I was healed, nor would I take a dose for the whole world. The Lord has proved to me beyond a doubt that I don't need any more; He has shown to me that He has power over man, over sickness; just trust and obey Him. My bowels never moved for five weeks, but I kept on eating just the same; never had a better appetite or felt better in my life. Praise His name forever. I am twenty pounds heavier today than I ever weighed before. The Lord cured me of the drink and tobacco habit, also saved me at the same time. Oh, glory to Jesus forever.

—*John N. Armstrong*
953 Dorman Street
Indianapolis, Indiana

Indianapolis, January 6, 1915

To Whom It May Concern:

I, the undersigned, can testify that each and every word of the above statement of Mr. Armstrong's is true to the letter. I am his wife, also am a nurse. I took care of him when he was suffering and being eaten up with that awful cancer.

There was a large hole eaten out in his hip and the bowel discharge would drop into that hole, and I would be compelled to use my own hands to lift out the discharge, and the cancer smelled so bad that many times I would get deathly sick and several times came near fainting while working with him, but praise God, He healed my husband; healed him to stay healed. The flesh is all filled in now where the hole was eaten in his hip. He is in perfect health; works twelve hours a day, six days a week.

—*Mrs. John N. Armstrong*
953 Dorman Street
Indianapolis, Indiana

30

SIGNS AND WONDERS IN DALLAS, TEXAS

(Reprinted from *"Word and Witness,"* from a report of
Elder F. F. Bosworth, Dallas, Texas, August 11, 1912)

It has been about two weeks since our dear Sister Etter joined us in the meeting, and we give glory to God for the way He has used her every night in preaching and demonstrating the wonderful Gospel of the Son of God.

The interest and power increases every night. Last night there were thousands of people in and around the tent. Sinners look on and weep, as they see the sick and afflicted healed by the power of God every night. Among those healed last night, before the great audience, was a mute, thirty-six years old, born deaf and dumb. He came from Oklahoma and was instantly healed in the first meeting he attended last night. Sinners wept when they saw he could hear and shout praises to God.

Yesterday morning a wonderful miracle was wrought on a fifteen-year-old orphan boy, Emmett Martin. His right arm was paralyzed when he was one year old so that he has never been able to raise that arm above his head or to open and shut his hand. His other arm was in splints and in a sling, badly injured by falling off the streetcar a week ago. The bandages and splints were removed and the arm instantly and perfectly healed; and then when Sister Etter in the name of Jesus commanded him to stretch forth the paralyzed arm, it was also instantly healed! He raised both hands above his head and clapped them together and shouted praises to God. He was gloriously saved at the same time and was in the meeting again last night and testified before the great audience.

An invalid lady from Mesquite, Texas, was carried into the tent the other night. Having been an invalid four years with rheumatism all over her body, she could not comb her own hair or raise her arms.

The lame, the blind, the deaf and dumb, the palsied, the paralytic, cancers, those suffering from operations, and others dying with incurable diseases have been wonderfully converted and healed by the power of God. Sinners are converted and flock to Jesus for salvation; and Christians are baptized with the Holy Spirit.

I wish all the saints in the Pentecostal movement had a copy of Sister Etter's book. It is such a help to faith! There has been no such record written since the Acts of the Apostles recording such continuous victories by the Lord in our day over sin and sickness, as this book.

—*F. F. Bosworth*

The Acts of the Holy Spirit

(Reprinted from the *Daily Times Herald*)

At the apostolic meeting, hundreds of people are being healed—acres of people are at the tent every night. We don't have to believe what the papers have said about Mrs. Etter in California, Iowa, or Indiana; but go to the tent, see with your own eyes, and hear with your own ears the mighty works of God. People are coming from Oklahoma, Arkansas, and Georgia to be healed.

Elmer Hooper, thirty-six years old, from McAlester, Oklahoma, born deaf and dumb, healed instantly.

Mrs. Chelve Mallock, 3112 Boulevard Street, Dallas, Texas, last stage of consumption, perfectly healed.

Come on, "Bud," don't stand back on your old graveyard "theology" and miss the blessing. God is in Dallas working miracles. Everybody is coming, everybody praising God. Methodist, Baptist, Presbyterian, Campbellites, and Catholics. If you stand off one hundred yards in the edge of the crowd, you might suppose that John the Baptist had been resurrected or John Bunyan or John Knox or John Calvin or John Wesley, and the crowd had old time religion.

Perfect Healing

(Extracts reprinted from *The Bridegroom's Messenger*, Vol. 5, No. 120)

God is still wonderfully displaying His power in Dallas, Texas, bearing witness to the preaching of the Gospel *"both with signs and wonders, and with divers miracles, and gifts of the Holy Ghost"* (Heb. 2:4). Throngs pack the large tent at every service, many of them coming from other states. Already great numbers of people have come from one hundred to two thousand miles, bringing their sick and afflicted. Letters are pouring in from all parts of the United States and Canada, as many as forty in a single day, inquiring about the meeting and requesting prayer for healing.

A man came several hundred miles, suffering with three broken ribs caused by a fall. As impossible as it may seem, when hands were laid upon him and the prayer of faith was offered, immediately the soreness left, and the broken ribs, the ends of which had turned inward, came into place and knitted together spontaneously; and although a few minutes before he flinched from pain when Sister Etter laid her hands upon his side, after healing he could pound upon these ribs with his hands—the healing was perfect. He was also a backslider and was wonderfully reclaimed.

A full-blooded Choctaw Indian woman came from Oklahoma, a great sufferer for thirty-eight years with a running sore on her foot, caused by a cow stepping on it when she was sixteen years of age. It was a mass of proud flesh, and the odor was almost unbearable. She was kept awake at nights and could not bear the weight of the covers on this foot. By the laying on of hands, God instantly took away all pain, and the foot in now healing up.

Last Sunday, Brother Bosworth baptized thirty-nine more in water and the power of God was present in a mighty way. A great crowd witnessed the scene.

More than one hundred and twenty-five have received the baptism in the Holy Spirit during the past two months, eight received the baptism on last Saturday night, twelve one Sunday. There have been as many as fifty baptized in the Holy

Spirit in one week, many receiving it in their homes. For two months the mighty power and presence of God has been present in these services in a marvelous way.

Increasing Wonders of God

The meetings are increasing in interest and power, and the people are coming from many states. A man got here yesterday morning, coming from Indianapolis, Indiana, on purpose to attend this meeting. Another from the Pacific coast, some from Illinois, Michigan, and other states. Many drive forty and fifty miles, and they were here yesterday from Galveston, Houston, and many other towns in Texas.

On August 12, three men brought a man, dying with consumption and fistula, two hundred miles in a baggage car on a cot. He came from Mercury, Texas, and looked like a dead man when they carried him into the tent on the cot. He was in the very last stages of tuberculosis, and nothing much but bones. When prayed for, the power came, and he jumped from the cot and ran up and down before the people, praising God. He returned home sitting up like other passengers, and he is gaining four pounds a week, and the fistula was healed over the next morning and never had to be dressed again. The county was stirred, and about twenty-five more have come from that vicinity. Night before last a delegation from that county came with two deaf and dumb mutes. One was thirty-four years old and the other a beautiful looking young lady of seventeen years. God opened the ears of both. The young lady was saved and healed at the same time, and she is very happy. They were both at our home this morning, and I played on the organ for them. Many others have been healed of deafness.

Yesterday was the most wonderful day I ever saw in this work. God came with the melting and slaying power. Twenty-one were struck down like Paul by the power of God and lay from one to ten hours. They had wonderful visions of heaven and of Jesus and all came out with shining faces and filled with the love of God. Twelve of these received the Holy Spirit and spoke in tongues for the first time. I never saw such power displayed. It looked like a battlefield to see them fall and lie as dead. God said, "The slain of the Lord shall be many." Sinners look on and weep as they see the wonderful works of God.

A woman seventy-five years old, suffering with rheumatism twenty years, was brought two hundred miles and was healed in the first service. She came through the healing of the consumptive referred to above.

A boy, who had been totally deaf from birth, was brought by his father from Martinsburg, Texas. God healed him perfectly, and his parents have written back to us that his hearing is perfect, and he is learning to talk.

A woman from Palmer, Texas, was healed of pellegra and filled with the Spirit at the same time. She was given up by the physicians. She is still here in the meeting and is well. A man from Blue-ridge, Texas, sixty miles from Dallas, had suffered ten years with cancer all over one side of his face and neck. He suffered so he had to be taken from the meeting. He could not talk on account of the awful suffering from moving his jaw. When Sister Etter prayed for him, the power came, and he was healed. The pain and all the burning and stiffness left instantly, and he could turn his head in any direction without pain. He got up on the altar and preached to the people. His friends told me yesterday that the cancer was healing up, and he is getting well.

The night before last a Catholic lady came into the meeting for the first time. She was deaf in both ears and could not hear a sound as the choir sang. She was instantly healed and could hear an ordinary conversation. Saturday night a lady was brought from Beaumont, Texas, dying with tumor. The doctors said she would not live forty-eight hours. She was instantly saved, healed, and baptized in the Spirit, and leaped and praised God before the people. Sinners look on and weep, and then make their way to the altar.

I said that Sunday was the most wonderful day I had ever seen. Last night was still more wonderful. No tongue or pen could describe that meeting. Three deaf and dumb mutes—fifty-four, thirty-four, and seventeen years old, and all strangers to each other—hugged, kissed, wept, and shouted for about a half hour because God had opened all their ears, gave them their voices, and saved them all. The great audience looked on and wept, and as many as could crowd into the vacant space at the front of the platform sought God for salvation, healing, and the baptism. Many were struck down by the power of God and had wonderful visions of Jesus, and many received the baptism in the Holy Spirit as at Pentecost. Some are stricken down in their homes. I wish you could see how these deaf and dumb mutes looked at the choir, making signs to each other that they enjoyed the singing and the instruments. The delegation that came with the deaf and dumb mutes returned with them this morning, saying that they were going to bring another mute, and perhaps some other afflicted ones. A preacher last night who came with them got up and told how he had known the deaf and dumb young lady from birth and loved her as his own daughter.

Miracles of Healing

(Reprinted from *The Latter Rain Evangel* of Chicago, U.S.A., October, 1912)

God is truly working in a wonderful way in Dallas, Texas, in the meetings conducted by Mrs. Woodworth-Etter and the pastor. During the first week in September about fifty were baptized in the Holy Spirit, besides many bright conversions and miraculous healings.

We quote the following from a private letter received from an eyewitness under date of August 22:

"There are about five thousand people in attendance every night and on Sunday nights many more. The sick and afflicted are coming from all parts of Texas, and some have come from Oklahoma, Alabama, Georgia, and Louisiana. They are coming on trains, covered wagons, and every way they can. Oh, the pitiful sights! How they make my heart ache! Sometimes it is more than I can bear when I see as many as four or five in one service nearly eaten up with cancer or consumption and given up by all earthly aid, and as a last resort they come to the Lord.

"The first night I was here, there were four brought in on cots in a dying condition, several in roller chairs and many afflicted who were able to walk. I saw two on cots get up and walk when prayed with. Some who were thought to be dying have jumped right over the end of their cots, leaping and walking and shouting all over the tent after the prayer of faith was offered. I will mention one or two remarkable cases:

"A woman here in Dallas, dying from a double affliction of cancer of the stomach and tuberculosis of the lungs, a living skeleton, given up by all the best physicians of this city, was brought to the meeting on a cot and thought she would die before Sister Etter could get around to her. When prayed with, she was healed instantly of both afflictions, arose from the cot, and shouted and praised the Lord. She is coming to the meeting every night and testifying. She is still very thin, but the disease is killed, and she is gaining weight every day.

"A boy, brought from Beaumont, Texas, several hundred miles away, suffering from epileptic insanity, was healed instantly, and a few days afterwards a businessman from that city, coming to the meetings in Dallas, testified that the boy was sound and well.

"A little waif, a newsboy on the streets of Dallas, strolled into the meeting with one arm paralyzed and the other broken from jumping off a streetcar a few days previous. Oh, how deserted and pitiful and dirty and forlorn he looked! It says in the Word when our father and mother forsake us, then the Lord will take us up (Ps. 27:10), and He truly did that little fellow. Sister Etter laid her hands upon him and prayed, and he was instantly healed. With the arm that had been paralyzed, he began to tear off the splints and bandages from the broken arm without anyone telling him. He threw both hands towards heaven, raised them high, and shouted and praised God, and I have seen him in the services nearly every night since. He testifies before that large multitude and has two perfectly well arms to show what the mighty power of God can do."

We also give the following clipping from the *Dallas Daily Times-Herald* of September 7, 1912:

"Hundreds in Dallas and all over Texas and many other states have already been healed in this meeting of all manner of diseases and afflictions by the power of God, in answer to *'the prayer of faith'* (James 5:15). Many have been brought over one thousand miles and have been wonderfully saved and healed. The lame, the blind, many deaf and dumb, the palsied, the paralytic, consumptives, those suffering with cancers, tumors, fistulas, pellagra, operations, many with epilepsy, and invalids for years are praising God for healing for soul and body.

"Perhaps never before was there such a scene as that witnessed by the great audience Monday night, when three deaf and dumb mutes, fifty-four, thirty-four and seventeen years old, all strangers to each other, hugged, kissed, wept, shouted, and praised God for perhaps twenty minutes, because He had opened all their ears, gave them their voices, and saved their souls. Sinners look on and weep and make their way to the altar. Sunday, God came in slaying power and twenty-one, like Saul, were struck down by the power of God and lay from one to eleven hours. They had wonderful visions of heaven and of Jesus and all got up with shining faces, filled with the love of God. The tent looked like a battlefield for *'the slain of the Lord* [were] *many'* (Isa. 66:16). This power has continued all the week, and sinners have been struck down in their homes several miles from the tent. Hundreds in Dallas have been filled with the Holy Spirit as at Pentecost. Perhaps in no other place in the world is God so wonderfully displaying His power at the present time."

Mrs. Clay E. Martin, one of the deaf mutes who was healed, gives a written testimony as follows:

"I am now fifty-four years old. My father and mother were first cousins.... Myself and two sisters were born totally deaf and dumb. I was born at Jonesville, Lee County, Virginia, educated at Staunton, Virginia, under Prof. J. J. Covell. I was a teacher in Prof. Van Nostrand's deaf and dumb school at Austin, Texas, at the time my uncle Ben D. Martin was state senator under Governor Coke. On Wednesday, July 31, 1912, I went to the wonderful meeting in the large tent at the corner of Parry and Fletcher streets. When Sister Etter put her finger in my mouth at the root of my tongue and then in my ears, commanding the 'deaf and dumb spirit' to come out, God instantly opened my ears and gave me my voice.... Oh, it seems so wonderful to hear everything."

The Prayer of Faith

Wonders of God

During this revival hundreds have been saved and healed. The blind have seen, the deaf have heard, the dumb have spoken, broken limbs have been restored, incurable diseases like cancer, consumption, and pellagra have been healed. The Word of God has gone forth in power, and the Lord has confirmed it with "signs following."

About twelve hundred have received the baptism of the Holy Spirit as on the Day of Pentecost, each one speaking in other tongues as the Spirit gave them utterance. During our month's stay here we have seen the dear Lord mightily manifest His healing power at different times. A brother came down from Missouri, very far gone with consumption. He had taken to his bed because he was so weak, but the Lord told him to come to Dallas and He would heal him. As Sister Etter laid hands on him, rebuking the disease in the name of Jesus, it went at once, and the brother was able to give an overflowing testimony the next day.

A sister came down from St. Paul who had been an invalid for two years, ever since the birth of her baby. She had all kinds of internal trouble, but the prayer of faith by Sister Etter put everything right, and the Lord raised her up from the couch on which she lay. She ran up and down the tabernacle praising the Lord. In her testimony she said that previously she had been so ill that it was only with difficulty she could move from her bed to a chair in her room. She stayed a little while longer in Dallas, during which she became strengthened in spirit, soul, and body, and the Lord baptized her with the Holy Spirit. She writes from St. Paul telling how well she is.

Another sister came down with the worst case of goiter we have ever seen. She had been under many physicians and a specialist, and her case was pronounced incurable. When her mother decided to bring her to Dallas, the doctor said the train journey would probably kill her. On the first night she came, Sister Etter called on the name of Jesus, and the disease was cured. (We notice that in almost every case Sister Etter dealt with the disease as if she was dealing with the devil himself.) At once the sister was delivered, the pain left, and she was able to exercise her swollen neck. It seemed as though the swelling subsided considerably at once, although the swelling had not all gone before she left Dallas. She is able to give a very blessed testimony. For the first time in a long time she was able to sleep peacefully, she was able to walk thirty-two blocks to and from the meetings every day, whereas before she came she could not walk more than two blocks, and that with difficulty.

At another time a man who looked as though he was dying, suffering internally with appendicitis, came into the meeting, the Lord not only healed his body, but also saved his soul. Salvation means the double cure—it really means *wholeness*—and you cannot limit it to the part of the entire being, as we have often done in past times.

Sister Etter has gone to San Antonio, starting meetings there the first of January. We hear the Lord is blessedly confirming His Word with signs following. Her farewell service took place on the last Sunday of the old year and was one of the most blessed services we have ever attended. Many times while giving her message, she was so overcome with emotion she had to stop. Especially pathetic was her farewell to Brothers Bosworth and Birdsall, "these two dear boys," as this mother in Israel called them. She appealed to all to stand by them. The power of God seemed especially on this dear sister that night, and as she laid hands on sick ones and seekers, they one and all seemed to come mightily under the power of God, becoming prostrated before the Lord.

Yours in the boundless love of Jesus,

—*Stanley H. Frodsham*

Note: Brother Frodsham was an editor from Bournemouth, England, visiting the meeting in Dallas.

The Authority of God's Word

His Mighty Power

(By Carrie Judd Montgomery, Editor, *Triumphs of Faith*, Oakland, California)

My husband and myself are just leaving Dallas, Texas, after a most interesting time at the meetings that are being held here in this city at the large tabernacle (recently built to take the place of the tent). Mrs. Etter has been there five months holding meetings and will remain until the first of the year, when she goes to San Antonio, Texas, for a series of meetings.

Mrs. Etter is an old-time friend of ours. When we first knew her, she was in the midst of a very remarkable revival work on the Pacific coast, where many thousands were saved and many were healed. We were delighted to meet each other again after the lapse of many years. She extended to us a most loving welcome and gave us seats on the platform by her side.

We have already published reports of these Dallas meetings, which we knew were reliable, but it has been a joy to attend them for ourselves and to witness the mighty power of God convicting and converting sinners, healing sick bodies, and baptizing saints with the Holy Spirit. We could only make it possible to remain for a few days, but in that length of time we saw much that we shall never forget. As we entered the tabernacle on Saturday evening, we saw a crowd of rejoicing people at the front. We learned later that a deaf and dumb man, about sixty years of age, had just been instantly healed and saved by the power of God through Mrs. Etter's command of faith, as she bade the deaf and dumb demons to depart in Jesus' name. Another man who had been healed of deafness was pointed out to us; as he was singing a hymn in unison with the others with eyes closed, it was evident how well he could hear. We saw one lady who had been stone-deaf, but after prayer was offered for her, the ears that had seemed dead began to have life in them, and she could hear loud sounds near her. Some people are healed at once and others gradually, but Mrs. Etter feels that if they have been receptive as she has prayed *"the prayer of faith"* (James 5:15) for them, that they have only to hold on in faith and continue to praise God on the authority of His Word, and the symptoms will surely pass away. There really are so many healings day by day that only the more remarkable ones attract attention.

Mrs. Etter's greatest concern is to have people "get right with God" in their souls, and then she tells them they will be healed. When they come to her with more desire for physical healing than for the spiritual healing, she refuses to pray for the healing of their bodies until their souls come into right relationship with God. This undoubtedly is one great reason of her success. Another reason is that she believes in working for the unifying of all the members of the body of Christ, and therefore she does not preach mere theories but holds up a living Christ, receiving all who are honest in their hearts and purposes towards Him, even if they do not yet see the truth just as she teaches it. She also avoids laying stress upon certain words or expressions, with which the enemy is trying to cause divisions in the body of Christ. Therefore there is no contention or strife in these meetings, but love and unity.

It is interesting to note that Mrs. Etter teaches healing in the Atonement (in the same way that we were taught by the Holy Spirit Himself many years ago). She also encourages all the saints to press on for more power from God to do the miraculous works that Jesus said believers should do in His name.

Mrs. Etter is one who speaks with no uncertain sound, and we have never seen anyone else rebuke disease and demons with such heaven-sent authority and power. It brought a new wave of spiritual joy to our hearts to hear the way in which these cruel demons were ordered to depart. Perhaps it is needless to say here that when people get their eyes on the instrument that God uses, instead of upon Himself, they do not receive healing. On the other hand, those whose gaze of faith is upon the Savior alone often receive healing through the application in faith of the anointed handkerchiefs or tracts sent out from these meetings. Some periodicals have ridiculed this means of reaching the sick, but God is wonderfully using them just the same; and as He wrought special miracles by the hands of Paul (see Acts 19:11–12), He is doing the same now for those who trust Him. So many of God's children are sick everywhere that the need is most urgent, and the unbelief is so great that often in isolated places those suffering saints cannot get one near at hand to offer *"the prayer of faith"* (James 5:15) for them.

Mrs. Etter preaches the Gospel in great simplicity and power, backing up all her remarks by quotations from the Word of God. The altar services are very remarkable, as saints and sinners gather around in deep earnestness, seeking God for their individual needs. The power of God falls upon them, and it is wonderful to note the changes that come over the faces of the seeking ones, as the light dawns upon their souls. The power of God often prostrates them, and even little children are seen "under the power," apparently unconscious to all but God and with their little faces shining like angels'.

There were people present from many different states in the Union.

The night we left there were three remarkable cases of healing: one of goiter, one of cancer, and one of deafness. The lady with goiter was suffering very much with the choking or suffocating sensation occasioned by it. Mrs. Etter commanded the enemy to depart, in Jesus' name, and soon we saw her turning her head freely from side to side, while the swelling seemed mostly, if not entirely, gone. The pain and swelling of the man's cancer was also taken away in a few minutes.

It is stated that about three hundred and fifty have received the Pentecostal baptism, with the sign of speaking with new tongues.

There is usually a great solemnity in the meetings, and the faces of the people are very earnest. With the exception of the altar service, where many are often praising or praying at once, the meetings are conducted very quietly. All tendency to wildfire or fanaticism is entirely discountenanced.

Perhaps the explanation for the solemnity of these meetings is that there is continual teaching about the soon coming of the Lord for His bride, and exhortations to get ready. One dear brother, Reverend H. C. Mears, who has preached the Gospel for over forty years, came to fight the work, but became convinced that it was of God; he received the baptism of the Holy Spirit with the sign of tongues, and afterwards God gave him the most wonderful visions of heaven and of what the Lord is preparing for His people, and also visions of the coming of the Lord. It is most inspiring to listen to the revelations of the coming of the Lord which have been vouchsafed to this dear brother. His spirit is so loving and gentle, he reminds us of what the Lord Jesus said about Nathaniel, "Behold an Israelite indeed, in whom there is no guile."

Claiming the Promise

"Behold, I give unto you power to tread on serpents and scorpions, and over all the power of the enemy: and nothing shall by any means hurt you" (Luke 10:19).

At a recent meeting at the time just after the call for all needing prayer to come to the altar had been made, Sister Etter had been praying for many round the altar, and God wonderfully healed them all; and as she was praying for a lady, there was a scorpion lying two inches away from her hand.

She saw it and went to knock it off, and it stung her. The pain seemed to run all through her and go to her heart. The finger got red, and the Lord showed her it was a fatal and poisonous sting, and nothing but the Lord could help her. A brother killed it, and several of the saints saw it and went right to praying. She claimed the promise that we should have power over serpents, and all fear left her.

The people were waiting for her to heal them. She hung on to the Lord and His promises, and the pain began to stop, and she went right on praying for the sick, and nothing was left but the mark of the sting. The hurt was perfectly healed.

Brother S. B. Finley says: "While attending these meetings I have a number of times seen the most beautiful flashes of light, like lightning, with some of the most brilliant colors, including most beautiful purple. There were great waves of light resting over different ones in the meeting.

One night there appeared a light like a white star and a two-edged sword going out from Sister Woodworth-Etter's mouth, while she was preaching and there were like flames of fire in rainbow colors around her, at the same time.

Another night there appeared a very large white cross. It stood before me in the skies as I was about to go to church, with many white roads leading up to it.

The prophet Joel (chapter 2, verse 28) speaks of these signs following God's people. (Also see Acts 2:4–5.)

A brother came to these meetings who had been a holiness preacher for eight years past; he had been fighting this work for about three years; finally the Lord showed him he had to make a final decision, and he decided to walk in the light. He, his wife, four sons, and a daughter, and her husband, all received the baptism of the Holy Spirit, since they attended these meetings. The power of God often comes on two of the sons, and while prostrated under that power, they have glorious visions of the eternal world. One son was healed of a swelling in the head. After he was prayed for, it ran off and away and has not hurt him any more. The power of God comes upon them also in their own home; the Spirit of God speaks through them in other tongues, and they have visions.

One woman had a tumor in her face and jaw for many years; she was in an awful state and could hardly take any nourishment. She came back and testified that it had all disappeared and the side of her face was straight like the other.

A man brought his wife on the way home to die, given up by all the doctors. She had cancer of the mouth, and she was saved and healed. At once the swelling all went down, and the soreness went, and she had the perfect use of her mouth. She came back the next day to testify that she was healed.

Continuous Revival

Great Numbers Following

Having, during the past five years, read and re-read volumes 1 and 4 of "The Life, Work, and Experience of Mrs. M. B. Woodworth-Etter," which record the wonderful acts of the Holy Spirit in her evangelistic meetings during the past thirty-five years, we became very anxious for her to come and help us in the work at Dallas, Texas. For many months we had been conducting Pentecostal meetings every night there, during which time there had been a continual revival, many being saved, healed, and baptized in the Holy Spirit according to Acts 2:4.

Feeling that it was God's plan for her to come, we wrote her concerning it, and in April 1912, I visited her meeting, then being conducted in Indianapolis, Indiana. During the three days' visit, I witnessed some wonderful healing by the power of God and met personally many who were wonderfully healed by the laying on of hands. Brother and Sister Etter also felt that God was leading to Dallas, so they came and began labor with us on July 25, 1912.

Throngs packed the large tent from the first, two or three thousand often standing around the tent. Great numbers of the sick and afflicted came and were brought on cots and in different ways, reminding us of the scenes described in the Gospels when our Lord was upon earth.

Night after night, as soon as the invitation was given, all the available space around the fifty-foot altar would be filled with so many who were suffering with diseases and afflictions and others who were seeking salvation and the baptism in the Holy Spirit, that it was difficult to get in and out among them. For several weeks there have been too many seeking healing to be prayed for, and some each night have had to go away disappointed and come again.

There were so many sick that there was always a rush for the altar as soon as the invitation was given. Many have been wonderfully healed before the service began, and sometimes there has been no preaching—nothing but the altar service.

A hundred seekers often come to the altar at one time. Many have been saved and healed at the same time and have got up shouting and clapping their hands. Many who were not saved came to be healed. After listening to the Gospel, they have realized that their souls were in a worse condition than their bodies and have dropped the matter of being healed until they made their peace with God.

The news of victory went out, and hundreds have already come from all over the United States, many bringing their sick hundreds of miles, some on cots in the baggage cars. Twenty states have been represented in a single service, coming on purpose to attend the meetings. Many ministers have come and gone and have received greater faith and power for the service of God. Many members of churches have come for healing, and God has shown them that they had never been born of the Spirit.

In almost every service for nearly three months, the slaying power so common in the day of Finney, Jonathan Edwards, and others, has been manifested, often "the slain of the Lord" covering nearly all the altar space in the front of the tent. Many most wonderful visions and revelations, often throwing light on the coming of the Lord, have been given to those thus slain by the power of God. Many have seen balls of fire and lights in and around the tent (Acts 2:3 and 26:13). Some of these have been sinners. Jesus has appeared to many in the meetings, and many have at different times seen a great host of angels just above the audience.

In one service, several at the same time saw and heard the awful explosion of the mine near Constantinople and screamed out at the same time; so this and a number of awful battles in Turkey and other calamities have been seen and told in the meeting before they appeared in the daily papers.

We praise God for bearing witness to the Gospel, not only with signs and wonders and diverse miracles, but also with gifts of the Holy Spirit.

In accordance with Acts 19:12, handkerchiefs have been anointed and sent to the sick in all parts of the United States and Canada, and many have been wonderfully healed at the time the handkerchief was applied to their body. Others have been saved and healed while reading the reports of the meeting in the religious papers.

Besides great numbers being wonderfully saved and healed, about three hundred more have received the baptism in the Holy Spirit during the last three months, speaking in other tongues as the Spirit gives utterance. Over one hundred of this number were from other states and towns. A number of these were ministers. We have just lately moved into our new, large, frame tabernacle, seating one thousand people, and Sunday hundreds were turned away, unable to get into the building. During the past few days, people have come from the Atlantic to the Pacific to attend the meetings. We see no reason why still greater victories should not be given during the months to come. There has been a continuous revival here ever since February 2, 1911.

I have heard many preachers who could very eloquently point out what Christianity should be and the wonderful possibilities of faith, but I know of none who, during the whole period of their ministry, have had the faith to as wonderfully demonstrate the truth of Christ's declaration that *"He that believeth on me, the works that I do shall he do also"* (John 14:12), thus, *"By manifestation of the truth commending* [herself] *to every man's conscience in the sight of God"* (2 Cor. 4:2).

Although the revival here has continued every night for many months, the interest and power continues. Last night, hundreds were turned away, unable to get into the new tabernacle, which seats a thousand people.

Sister Etter is always seeking and is continually urging the saints to seek more of God. Concerning the doctrine that she preaches, nothing needs to be said, for, as it was in the first century, God Himself bears witness, *"both with signs and wonders and divers miracles and gifts of the Holy Ghost"* (Heb. 2:4).

Joyfully expecting to meet the readers of this book in the clouds, when mortality shall put on immortality, and we shall be changed in the twinkling of an eye, and in our glorified bodies shall be forever with the Lord and with the redeemed, I am,

Your brother in Christ,
—*F. F. Bosworth*

Greatly Beloved

A minister of the Gospel, who has been in the Lord's work for eleven years past, writes:

We have met with most of the leaders of the Apostolic Faith Movement, but never before met with anyone so deep in wisdom and in the knowledge of the things of God as Mrs. Woodworth-Etter.

Never have we seen the power of God manifested to such an extent as in these meetings. Her preaching is always in the demonstration of the Spirit and in power.

One can sit and feast on the strong meat of the kingdom, which she, a servant of Jesus, is giving to the household of faith here.

At one meeting at the time of the altar call, she laid hands on and prayed for God to baptize some seekers with the Holy Spirit, and three in succession so prayed for fell and lay prostrate under the outpouring of the Holy Spirit and received the baptism. It is noticed that after she has prayed for certain ones and laid hands on them, the power of the Holy Spirit comes upon them, and they speak in other tongues as the Spirit of God gives them utterance.

She has a quick and accurate perception of the needs of the seekers, and can help and lead them into the kingdom in a few minutes, where it would take most other workers hours, and then probably without attaining the same results.

We have met with numbers of people from various cities who have been saved and healed in her meetings, and also independent, unbiased witnesses who confirm our conclusion, that she knows God and the workings of His Spirit better than anyone that we have ever met.

As to her capability and qualification to take charge and lead a meeting: after her thirty-five years of active evangelical work under the direct instruction, supervision, and guidance of God Himself, she stands unequaled in that respect as far as the writer and his colleagues have been able to ascertain.

We have excellent grounds for believing that, like Daniel, she is *"greatly beloved"* (Dan. 10:19) of our heavenly Father and that, like John the Beloved, she constantly leans on Jesus' bosom.

At times while the meeting is going on, the Spirit of God will come down in an exceptional manner and envelop her like a cloud. She at such times is transformed in appearance, and the fashion of her countenance changes. Standing motionless for several minutes with the light of heaven streaming radiant in her face, she sees the unseen and invisible Lord, as well as the angelic hosts and other spiritual things within the veil, which are hidden to others. As when the high priest entered into the Holy of Holies, she leaves the congregation, waiting until she returns in spirit, and ministers once more to them.

At such times the fear of God and strong conviction falls noticeably on the whole congregation, for they cannot but understand the manifestation of the Spirit, and they act more reverently even than at other times, because of the more vivid realization that God is present in their midst, when seeing the visible operation of His Spirit in this way.

The Deep Things of God

In January, 1904, I heard that Mrs. M. B. Woodworth-Etter and her husband were going to hold divine healing meetings in St. Louis, and I went to their first meeting with a friend. The mode of conducting the meeting and some of the doctrines taught were entirely new to me, but I knew at first sight that it was all of God and that they were servants of God.

I helped in the meetings, two meetings each day, for more than six months. I saw miracles of healing and many prostrated under the mighty outpourings of God's Spirit from heaven; I saw them lying with the light of heaven on their faces, happier and more divine looking than anyone that I had ever seen. I saw them rise up after awhile with their faces shining, full of praises to God, and heard them tell of the glories of the eternal world that they had just seen. I saw the visible manifestation of God's presence in many supernatural ways constantly.

The first time that I ever heard the Spirit speak in other tongues was in a meeting she was holding in Moline. A sister who had been used of God to do important evangelistic work said, referring to the tongues, she would believe after she had heard. Sister Etter told her she would be speaking in other tongues that very day, and in the afternoon the Holy Spirit came on her in the meeting, and she commenced to sing in other tongues with a very powerful voice. The singing was solemn, sad, and impressive. I never heard anything more so; it reminded me of the lamentation of the women at the cross of Jesus and of Jesus weeping over Jerusalem. We afterwards learned that an earthquake was taking place at that very time at Kingston, Jamaica, which the Lord showed to another sister in the meeting.

From Moline I went to Muscatine; I found there an assembly that had been meeting ever since Sister Etter had held her last meetings in that city. Brothers and sisters were there who had been healed at that time, and they had been well ever since; and there were others who had, through her teaching, been firmly established in the deep things of God. I told them of how God was pouring out His Spirit elsewhere and speaking through some in other tongues and exhorted and taught them.

A short time after, the Spirit came on an aged brother, and he began to speak in other tongues. This made the others hungry, and most of them commenced to seek for the same manifestation, and all received after various intervals, except one or two.

The Spirit did not speak through me until October 1908, when He spoke for about an hour and a half and sang two songs through me. All glory and praise to God forever.

The Lord always backs up her preaching with the visible signs of His presence, which shows that Jesus is working with her, confirming the preaching with the signs accompanying and following.

She has the "power" of the Holy Spirit, or the gift of the Holy Spirit by the laying of hands and prayer; so often I have seen it, especially at St. Louis, Indianapolis, and Dallas. Just lately out of ten whom she prayed for in succession, the Spirit came on them in such power that they all fell prostrate and lay around the altar.

Of Brother Etter, I have seldom met a brother so entirely free from insincerity at all times. He speaks the truth in his heart, without guile or hypocrisy, and is ever ready to ratify and endorse his wife's preaching; he is equipped in every way for the work that God has called him to. (See Acts 13:2.)

I know of no one God has so highly honored. I look to see her occupy a high position in the kingdom of our Lord in heaven, and I have lived in their home for months at a time.

While I was in the work in England, I got so hungry to be in their meetings again, that having received an invitation from them to come and again help in the meetings, I came clear across the Atlantic Ocean direct to their meetings and have been working with them since.

Yours, trusting alone in the atoning blood and merits of Jesus.
—W. J. Mortlock, Evangelist
England

"In Dangers Oft"

Beloved, think it not strange concerning the fiery trial which is to try you, as though some strange thing happened unto you: but rejoice, inasmuch as ye are partakers of Christ's sufferings; that when his glory shall be revealed, ye may be glad also with exceeding joy.   (1 Pet. 4:12–13)

Jesus said they hated Him without a cause. The real children of God are clothed with light and power, with the Holy Spirit from heaven, sent from the eternal throne of God. The world does not know us, because it did not know Him, so the devil brings all his forces into the battle against Jesus and His saints. But He that is in us is greater than all that are against us, and the Lord will fight our battles, if He has to bring down all the armies of heaven.

When the prophet Elisha was surrounded by the enemies of the Lord, his servant was frightened because he was sure his master would be killed. The prophet of God, however, was calm; he looked up to God and said, "Open the young man's eyes." His eyes were opened, he looked around, and saw the armies of the Lord with horses and chariots of fire: all the artillery of heaven surrounding and protecting one little prophet of God. (See 2 Kings 6:17.)

They said to Paul, "*This sect…every where it is spoken against*" (Acts 28:22). The Gospel preached by the Holy Spirit, with signs, stirs the devil and his hosts in these last days. They lay pits and traps to catch us as they did to our Savior, at the time when they were going to throw Him over the hill to destroy Him, but He slipped away. The devil hates me with perfect hatred and has tried many times, and in many ways, to kill and destroy me. I only escaped by the ever present, watchful, loving care of my Lord. He said, "*Fear not: for I am with thee*" (Isa. 43:5). It means everything to know that God is with us.

I have been in many places where my life was not worth a straw, but I always stood firm. I have been in the greatest dangers, but bless and praise His holy name, He always came, with the hosts of heaven, and in such a way that the fear of God fell on them, whether it was one or a howling mob. Sometimes they could not move; sometimes they fell like drunken men; others ran, and they were glad to escape with their lives and liberty. In all these trials God got the victory, for all knew that the Lord was with me, and with us, and fighting His own battles.

Help in Times of Trouble

California is a great place for wickedness and for men and women to hide from the law. In the great crowds that attended our meetings, they told me there were murderers there and all kinds of other outlaws. They mixed through the crowds with concealed weapons, ready to kill or fight at the least thing that did not suit them. The brothers built a high board fence around the back of the pulpit where I stood; they did not tell me why, but they were afraid I would be shot while preaching.

Some were saved and baptized with the Holy Spirit, and some of their friends, objecting to this, let the devil take charge of them. They sent a letter with a sketch of a skull and crossbones, and also one of a heart with a dagger stuck through it and the blood dripping down. The writers just gave me just so long a time to take my crowd and to get out, or they would tear down our tents and kill us all.

For a while I trembled and did not know what to do. We had been having three meetings a day for many weeks, and I was prostrated with the steady work, the responsibility of the meetings, and worry, never knowing when a mob would come and rush in on us or if some coward would slip in on us at night, for we all slept in our little tents. We had six small tents, not affording much protection.

I called a few of the brothers who had power and influence and showed them the letters. They gave the matter into the hands of the police, and the police watched for them. About two o'clock A.M., a wild mob slipped up, and they were surrounding our tents, ready to kill us all and destroy the tents. They thought they had it all their way, but before they knew anything more, the police had them surrounded.

I did not know what plans had been laid, but felt so sure the Lord would protect us that the helpers and I went to our tents, went to bed, and were asleep when the mob came. Oh, we can be calm and praise the Lord amidst the tempest!

At another time for some reason, some of the drunken police got mad at some of the workers, and they hated us all. It was dark and rainy, and they gathered up a mob and were going to tear down the tent and mob us all. They left part of their number outside some distance from the tent; the rest came in and were to give the sign for those outside to rush in on the tent.

I did not know what plans had been laid, but felt secure. The brothers kept their plans from me; they were prepared to protect me and to die if necessary.

A lot of big, burly police came running in with their raincoats on and their billy clubs hidden under their coats. Some sat down where they entered, some scattered, others stood. I was frightened, for I knew and felt we were in danger; they looked so mad and mean as if they would tear us in pieces.

The Spirit of the Lord came on me. I stepped up on the altar and stood looking at them, then began talking as the Spirit gave utterance. I began to walk slowly down the long altar that led down among them, talking as the Spirit gave utterance with power. The Holy Spirit had control of my whole body—arms, hands, and feet. They could see and feel the awful presence of God in their midst. They knew that I, of myself, would not dare to defy or stand before them or talk to them in such a way. The fear of God fell on them; they were afraid of me. I felt like as though I had turned to be a giant and believed that if they had moved towards us, that God would have smitten them dead. They stood as if they were paralyzed and did not give the signal to those that were outside, but went out solemnly. Oh, praise the Lord for victory through Jesus, our Lord and Savior! We never had any more trouble. There is none like our God to deliver. "*Touch not mine anointed, and do my prophets no harm*" (Ps. 105:15).

Opposers

Awful judgments have fallen upon those who laid hands upon the ark. Under the Law it was instant death to those who touched the ark or laid their hands on it. When anyone willfully lays his hands on the Holy Spirit work of God today, it is spiritual death to that man or woman. Take Michal (David's wife) as a warning. She was smitten with barrenness to the day of her death. David was dancing in the Spirit before the ark, and she despised him for so doing. Sometimes it is instant death. Many places where we have held meetings, it has come to be a common saying, "Just watch that man, and see what will happen to him." Sometimes in a few days, or often in a year or two, they will write, telling me of some awful judgments that have befallen those who sinned in this manner. Many times it put the fear of God on those who knew and noticed these things.

Many editors and preachers who failed to take warning of God's dealings with Uzzah and Michal have gone down in disgrace. Many who had large congregations and large salaries have had to leave in disgrace on account of some sin, or because the congregation broke up and his people left him. Many editors have gone to ruin, have got into trouble, have gone to drinking, become insane, or committed suicide. *"Offenses will come: but woe unto him, through whom they come!"* (Luke 17:1).

During one of the meetings, a man had a crowd around him and was making sport of the works of God and saying awful things about me and the power. All at once he fell to the ground, a helpless man, stricken with paralysis; his face was drawn, his tongue out, his eyes rolling, and he was in that condition until he died, which he did in a short time.

The fear of God was on all that saw him, knowing that it was the swift judgment of God.

When thou passest through the waters, I will be with thee; and through the rivers, they shall not overflow thee: when thou walkest through the fire, thou shalt not be burned; neither shall the flame kindle upon thee. (Isa. 43:2)

Strong in the Lord

We held several meetings in Kansas, near the Oklahoma line, out on the prairies at a place some distance from a small town. The power of the Lord came down like a cyclone. Men and women fell in their homes and in other places in and around the meeting. Many of the rich and of the best people, including the farmers around, were converted. There was a church college in the town, and some of the members got condemned and angry.

A lady who had been at the meeting went to the Methodist Church on a Sunday and fell prostrate under the power of the Holy Spirit. They tried to bring her out from under that power. They poured cold water on her and did everything they could to bring her out. When she would come out a little, they would persecute her for going to our meeting, and she would go back under the power; she continued that way all day and night. They got so convicted and enraged they could have killed me. They called the authorities together to see if I had broken the law in any way so that they could find a flaw to catch me, and then they sent the sheriff and others to where I was boarding to arrest me. But I told them that according to law they could not and that, in the name of the Lord, I would not go and they could not take me. They went away cursing and said they would get me yet. They also said that I must go with them to the girl's house and bring her out of the spell that I had put her in. They said she was crazy and that her father would kill me.

I told them if they would let her alone, she would soon come out, that I had no power to hurt her or to take her out from under that power. They were also working among the cowboys, getting them enraged, telling them I was driving people crazy. We heard their threats and knew they were gathering a mob, and we had no place to go. I told them to stand with me in the name of the Lord. I said that our God would fight our battles. We would trust Him to reach out His hand in some way and put the fear of God upon them. Those attending the meeting said they would die if necessary, but they would never run or surrender. We knew our only hope was in God. Those who had made themselves my enemies expected to kill or take me a prisoner. The brothers knew that I was the one they were after, and they counseled together and decided they would protect me if they had to fight with chairs or anything they could get.

They came as we expected and were told that we were all nervous and trembling. We heard the shouts as they were coming down the roads on horseback, firing pistols as they came. They had on rough clothes and big hats. I said, "Be brave." We commenced singing, and they came and surrounded the tent. Then they would get together in bunches and would act wild, as if they were going to rush in on us. We sang and prayed, and the dear ones tried to keep me in the middle of them and hide and protect me as much as they could. I commenced talking, and they saw the power of the Lord was on me in a wonderful manner. I was in the Spirit, and all fear was gone. I talked to them like to little children, and they began to settle down, and a calm was coming over them.

They had us surrounded so that we could not get away or get out. To my left I saw the man that came that day to arrest me, with a couple of others. The Lord led me out on the platform, right out to those men. I reached out my hand to them and smiled. The leader said, "We saw you today." I said, "Yes, I think you did; I am glad to see you here," and I was, for all fear was gone, and I saw that I had won the victory. I continued, "I hope you will like the meeting so well that you will come again." They could have pierced me through with a knife or have dragged me off, except the hand of God was on them. They could not move. I shook hands with some more of the others, then went back to the pulpit and talked and cried.

I saw there was a group led by the father of the girl. Their great hats were pulled over their faces, waiting for the crowd to leave. They said, "You must go with us and take the girl out of that spell." I looked to Jesus a moment before answering them. I felt the power of God on me, and I marched out right up to the father, reached out my hand, and spoke so kindly that he was surprised. He stood still and looked at me, and the rest were looking on at us. He began to tremble, the power of God fell on them, and the lion was tamed. I asked him if he had been cross to her and abused her for coming to the meeting and for being under the power; he said that he had. "Didn't she talk to you and want you to be a better man?" He said, "Yes, she did." "Then you abused her and she went under the power of God again?" Every time he said, "Yes." I said, "Don't you know it is your fault that she stays that way? Don't you think that if you will go home and listen to what she tells you, that she will soon be all right?" He broke down and said, "I know she is right; I ought to listen to her; she is all right, and so are you." "Then you go right home and tell her she can serve the Lord."

They all shook hands, and I showed the congregation that we could all breathe easier and that henceforth we would all be stronger in the Lord. He surely fought our battle. We had no more trouble, and the meeting continued with great success. Praise God for His wonderful presence and power in every time of need.

In other places I have been in great dangers, many times not knowing when I would be shot down, either in the pulpit, or going to and from the meetings. Many times I have been followed and eavesdropped on. Often bands of wicked men came in to kill or to tear up the meetings. Their looks and very appearance are sufficient to terrify, but I said I would never run nor compromise. The Lord would always put His mighty power on me, so that He took all fear away and made me like a giant. He always stood by me in every way. If in any way they had tried to shoot or kill me, He would have struck them dead, and I sometimes told them so.

The power of the Lord was on me, something like it was on Jesus, when He drove out the mighty men, the moneychangers in the temple, with a little cord whip or rope. There was nothing to make them afraid but the awful presence of God. The fear of God always made them leave, and the same is true today; sometimes they fall like dead men. The Lord always pointed these people out to me when they were in the crowd and showed me our danger.

Dear reader, we are now in the dark days. Many who read these lines will have to go through great danger and persecutions, also hard trials; but be true to God, stand for His Word and honor, and glorify His name. He will protect and deliver.

We can have the faith that we will live until Jesus comes. Claim the promise that He will shield us from all dangers, from all the arrows of the enemy, and from the pestilence: *"There shall no evil befall thee, neither shall any plague come nigh thy dwelling"* (Ps. 91:10). The promises contained in the ninety-first Psalm are for all of God's true children in these last days. Oh, glory to His name who lives forever and ever, who is able to deliver His children *"out of all their troubles"* (Ps. 34:16)! Then why should we fear when storms arise and trouble comes? (See Matthew 8:23–27.) We must have trials to perfect us for our future home.

Prophecies Made and Fulfilled

While holding meetings in California, the Lord showed me that great destruction and an earthquake were coming.

Soon after, the papers were ablaze with the pictures of the awful earthquake and holocaust in San Francisco and the surrounding country. I had told them God always sends mercy before judgment. I told them that they rejected mercy and that they would be visited next with destruction and judgment. The earthquake soon followed, and the fear of God came on those that remembered the prophecy. Both prophecies were fulfilled in a week, and I lived to walk over the ruins.

A woman who had been baptized with the Holy Spirit and healed of a broken leg saw and told the people about the awful storm that was coming. Her prophecy was fulfilled just two weeks from the day she said it would come.

While holding meetings in Louisville, Kentucky, the Lord was visiting the city in great mercy and power, but so many rejected the Spirit and went over to hardness of heart. The Lord showed a sister there of the storm that was coming and that shortly afterwards struck the city and did much damage to property, and in which many lives were lost.

This same sister saw the destruction of the Titanic. She saw the vessel go down ten or more days before it sank, with its hundreds of souls on board. She saw it sink out of sight. She saw them first lower the lifeboats and saw them helping the passengers down into the boats, saw the men drag a man who had hidden in a lifeboat out and kill him and throw him into the sea. She was very excited at seeing the awful disaster, and her husband was frightened by her cries, so vividly did she see the disaster.

Walking in the Light

In David's town, God bless you,
Behold an infant cried;
It was the world's Redeemer,
Salvation drawing nigh.

CHORUS

In the light! In the light!
We are walking in the light of the Lord.

King Jesus came from heaven,
Lost sinners to redeem,
The Spirit is my witness;
I've plunged the healing stream.

He baptized me with power,
And with the Holy Spirit:
Like He did His apostles
On the Day of Pentecost.

My soul is filled with glory,
"Good Lord" I'm bound to shout,
The cleansing blood of Jesus
Has ruled the devil out.

Sinner your soul is darkness,
Your heart is black with sin,
While Jesus' hands are bleeding,
He knocks, oh, let Him in.

The moment you accept Him
Your darkness will be light:
He'll tune your heart for singing
To walk within the light.

31

A VISION OF THE COMING OF THE LORD

O n March 24, 1904, when I fell under the operation of the power of God, while praying for the healing of the last one at the altar, I saw the Savior on the cross and sinners coming to Him. I saw steps leading across to the pearly gates of heaven. All those who plunged into the fountain were at once placed on the steps. Each one carried a light, which grew brighter as they went higher. There was not a spot of defilement on their robes. I was made to understand that they were the light of the world, that their lamps were lighted in heaven. They had Christ in their souls. Each one had a bodyguard of angels of God escorting them on the upward journey. At the top of the steps were the pearly gates, where the heavenly hosts waited to welcome the pilgrims of earth.

I also saw that the world is in great darkness and that saints are very few. *"Many are called but few chosen"* (Matt. 22:14) or will accept. Many were under conviction but trusted to water baptism, to confirmation, or to church membership; but unless they are carrying the light from God, they are worse than an open sinner.

The whole world lies in great darkness, except just a few. I saw the preparation in heaven and earth for the soon coming of Christ. Heaven seemed to be in a commotion. The Lord was marshaling His hosts, getting the horses and chariots ready. The armies of heaven were moving, and the gates were open. An angel came out of the gates blowing a great trumpet; the Savior was taking the lead with all the glory of heaven, shouting to the saints in a loud voice that awakened the dead.

The Lord showed me He was judging His saints, separating the wheat from the tares, that the household of faith was getting their portion of meat in this time, God's due season. The angel was sealing the last ones of the members of the bride with the seal of the living God. They were a little flock, and the last one would soon be sealed, then the Lord would come in a cloud of glory to take His bride to the marriage feast, or supper.

May God help all who read this vision to take warning and repent, for the Judgment of God is at hand.

A Vision of the Hand of God

While holding a revival in Fostina, Ohio, in March 1894, I had a vision of God while I was in my bed. I thought I was in a day meeting, and was standing by the pulpit. Some man in the congregation spoke in a loud voice, saying, "Sister Woodworth, look at the hand above the door." I looked in that direction, and right above the door, coming from the vestibule, I saw a large hand, wrist, and part of the arm. The wrist was bare for several inches. There was a soft, flowing sleeve that hung down about eight inches. It was white and very soft looking. The fingers were all bent a little, except the little and index fingers. They pointed out each way. The hand and arm were lovely. The sleeves and all were white and shining. The hand and arm moved about and pointed all over the congregation again and again, then pointed the index finger to me and waved the hand and fingers as if beckoning me or calling me to come. The hand continued to move over the people and then pointed. Every eye saw the wonderful hand sight. I cried out in a loud voice, "Oh, that is the hand of God!"

There was a very large window on the same side of the house. The transom was open, and a hand just like the other came through the transom and did just like the other, both warning and pointing the people to me. Both lovely hands pointed over the house and then to me. I cried out again and again, "Oh, that is the hand of God!" They both went away at once.

It seemed the congregation could not move. Then I said, "Oh, I believe it is the hand of God, and it means something wonderful to the people and especially to me." Just then I saw through the transom of the same window and clear up to heaven, a path twenty feet or more wide. It reached from heaven down and was full of stars and light. As I looked, I saw one of the hands and nearly all of the arm with the flowing, soft sleeve come out of heaven and come down the shining path. Then without stopping it came across to the window, through the transom, and over the congregation, with the index finger and arm pointing to me. The finger touched me on the forehead. The little finger or thumb, or both, touched my face. The hand and arm waved over me. I felt the everlasting arms and the soft sleeves around me. Everyone saw it then. It went straight across the congregation and out of the window and up to heaven without stopping. I cried out with a loud voice, "It is the hand of God. It was the everlasting arms." I said, "God is going to reveal Himself to me in a wondrous way, writing His laws on my mind with the finger of God. Perhaps He is soon going to take me home." The devil had also come to make me believe I was going to die, but I said, "No."

The Lord showed me the vision is concerning the soon coming of Christ. The warning, the hands pointing over the people, then pointing them to me and to heaven, was God drawing the people to me to get light on the speedy coming of our Lord and to get ready to meet Him; that it would be only a few years; that I would pass through several changes in my life and work; that would be for my good and the glory of God. This vision was not of Christ, but of God who inhabits eternity; the Father of our Lord and Savior, Jesus Christ. The great fatherhood and love of God was revealed to me as never before, as a personal God. God is as much a person as Jesus Christ. Jesus said, "I am the express image of my Father's person." God is a spirit form. He alone had immortality, but through Christ's obedience unto death on the cross, He brought life and immortality to light.

It was the arm of God and the finger of God that touched my forehead. He showed me He would seal me with—and reveal unto me—the wisdom of God and the knowledge of His glorious plan of the ages: the winding up of this harvest; of the calling and preparation of the bride; of the soon coming of Christ, the Bridegroom; that the Gentile door will soon be closed; and of the great time of trouble that will follow the Rapture or ascension of the bride.

All who are left will go down in or through this great day or time of trouble that the angel Gabriel told Daniel of—such as never was or ever shall be again. The whole world will be taken in a snare at the winding up of that awful time with the great battle of God Almighty with the armies of the earth, when He comes back with His saints to set up the glorious millennial kingdom, which will last one thousand years, when Christ and His bride shall judge the nations.

In that vision the Lord gave me a special call for this work: to give the household of faith their meat in due season; to give the last call to the Gentile sinners, the last call to the marriage supper of the Lamb, for His wife is about ready to enter into the marriage relation, and the door will be closed never to be opened again; and to get those who have been called to be established, to be faithful and true, that they may be anointed with the Holy Spirit and with power, and sealed with the proper knowledge of His coming and of their great work during the millennial reign of one thousand years, when the saints shall judge the world and angels, when all the families of the earth shall be blessed.

The Lord showed me He would enlighten and reveal these things to me by His Word; through the Spirit He would write them on my forehead, or in mind and heart. He touched my mouth with His thumb and finger, showing me He would put words in my mouth and give me wisdom to explain these things as fast as He gave them to me; that this was, and is, His due time when we must know these things. He put His loving arms around me, showing His loving care and protection, that He gave me a new lease of life for this work, which was to be devoted to this preparation work of warning the people and getting the bride ready.

I have been very near death several times, but the memory of the wonderful vision has inspired me to new life. I have been wonderfully enlightened during all these years. I understand all these things better every day, as God is leading me to separate the wheat from the tares with His Word and by His Spirit. Christ, the Great Reaper in white, clothed in power, is with me in this great harvest work. He gives me the light every day. The time is very short! The Lord is showing me many things along this line. I never loved the blessed loving Father so much as now. I never had an idea that His plans were so great and glorious. Oh, praise His name forever!

The Lord revealed to me in this vision many vicissitudes and changes that I would pass through in the following four years of my life. These revelations have and are being fulfilled.

God Never Changes

It has been fifteen years since the Lord gave me this vision. Read it carefully, and see if you do not see the hand of God and know that God gave the vision. See how the Lord gave me courage to prophesy how He was going to use me to write another book and send it out quickly. In four months' time we had out ten thousand of the sixth volume of a new book called *Acts of the Holy Spirit*.

This book has gone over almost the entire world, and different parts of it have been translated into several languages. The Lord has blessed the book far beyond all expectations, in enlightening and convicting and stirring up people of all classes to seek more of God. We get letters from all parts of the world asking for help for both soul and body. We get thousands of handkerchiefs asking us to pray over them, just as "*God wrought special miracles by the hands of Paul: so that from his body were brought unto the sick handkerchiefs or aprons, and the diseases departed from them, and the evil spirits went out of them*" (Acts 19:11–12). God is working today the same way, and we receive letters from across the seas and also from the Atlantic to the Pacific shouting, "Glory to God! I am healed and filled with God!"

Many times they are healed while we are praying for them; and many times while they are reading the letter, the power of God falls on them and they apply the handkerchief. They are healed immediately, and very often they are converted, and some have received the baptism of the Holy Spirit, and at the same time many of the worst diseases and the worst cripples are made to leap and praise God for perfect healing.

In the last two and a half years, I have traveled over twenty-two thousand miles. This is the month of May, and I have received calls from twenty-seven states and one from Washington, D.C., and two calls from Canada, to hold conventions or camp meetings for one month or more, and many from small places in these states.

Please read carefully the different accounts of the meetings and see the wonderful work God has wrought, and you will have to confess that God gave the vision and that the vision and the prophecy have come true. Then be very careful how you receive these great and marvelous works of God, for He has taken one of the weakest of all to confound the mighty so that no flesh shall glory. (See 1 Corinthians 1:27–29.) God is continually revealing to His children the mysteries of the kingdom, which are hidden from the "*wise and prudent*" (Matt. 11:25).

God's children have supernatural revelations and see visions: otherwise the Bible could not be the Word of God, for it is the result and record of visions.

Someone said that they thought that those who said they had had a vision just imagined it. If that is so, after the Crucifixion, Mary did not see Christ, but only imagined it; and when she saw the two angels, she just imagined that also; and when Jesus appeared to her, why, she just imagined that. If that is so, the apostles who testified that they saw Him only imagined they saw Him; and after that, when Jesus was seen by the five hundred brothers, seen by all of them at the same time, why, those five hundred men just imagined it, imagined all together, at precisely the same time. (See 1 Corinthians 15:6.) And everyone that saw Jesus after His resurrection from the dead just imagined it. On what grounds then do you believe that Jesus rose from the dead if you reject supernatural testimony? Spiritual things *are spiritually discerned* (1 Cor. 2:14).

After receiving the new birth into the spiritual kingdom, God's children know those things that are mysteries, and forever secret and hidden from the eyes of the simply natural, unregenerate men, however wise, learned, and intelligent they may be, and to whatever high degree of acumen and understanding they may have attained.

When Elisha's servant at Dothan saw that the city was encompassed by a host of horses and chariots, he came to his master and said, *"Alas, my master, how shall we do?"* Elisha prayed, *"Open his eyes, that he may see."* And behold the mountain was full of horses and chariots of fire about Elisha (2 Kings 6:15–17). If Elisha's servant could see, why shouldn't we?

Paul had a vision in the temple; Peter had a vision on the housetop; John the Revelator and numerous others had visions.

One of the elementary and fundamental doctrines of the Christian religion is "The Immutability of the Omnipotent God," or, in ordinary parlance, it is the fixed belief that God has not changed, and will not change, in His dealings with mankind as long as this dispensation lasts; that He is all powerful, and that He has not lost any of His power during the centuries that have elapsed since the days of the early church; that He is still faithful and true to fulfill all that He has promised to do, on the conditions specified in His Word; that He has not lost any of the love that He once had for mankind; and that under the same circumstances and conditions will do as much for us as He ever did for anyone else.

We repeat that the doctrine and belief in "The Immutability of the Omnipotent God" is one of the fundamental doctrines of the Christian religion, which has been adhered to all down the ages, by the Christian church of all denominations; and that no one can deny that God reveals Himself in visions to His servants and remain an orthodox Christian.

Visions of Elder H. C. Mears of Things to Come

I saw the awful destruction of the world. It was thundering and lightning. It was raining and hailing. The water was all gushing in all directions. There were crowds of people, but it seemed as though there was not a saint on the earth. It was dark physically and spiritually. There were great armies of people and multitudes of soldiers dressed in uniforms. There were also people running and rushing in the streets in every direction.

I also saw bolts of lightning falling from heaven that struck the houses, which flew to pieces in every direction.

At another time there were a great many of us here all worshipping God. We were all in white, but some seemed whiter than others. Those who were white were translated and went up, and the others who were not white enough looked and longed to go up, but were not white enough to be caught away from the Great Tribulation to meet the Lord in the air. I recognized a few of them.

There are some of you not white enough before God, while you are claiming to be His followers. I learned from this that some of you professing Christians would be left behind.

One night I saw the Beast mentioned in the thirteenth chapter of Revelation. At another time I saw Enoch and Elijah, the two witnesses. Their names were written on them. Oh, the power that they had! We were lifted up above the world. There were fires of judgment flashing all over the world. Oh, the groaning and wailing that there was at that time!

A wonderful power raised up at last, and those prophets seemed to be killed. They dropped and lay, and then a cry was made. Later I saw them get up.

Another time I saw an angel as he passed along, sealing the servants of God. He said, "Hurt not the earth, neither the sea, nor the trees, until we have sealed the servants of our God in their foreheads."

Another time I was away from here in the Spirit and was in the city of Jerusalem. I have seen pictures of that place, and I was there. There I saw the Savior dying on the cross, amidst a great crowd. Oh, the pain that was on His face! I shed tears looking at Him.

Again, I saw my Savior, sitting upon a dazzling throne; and saw the blazing, sparkling crown upon the head of Him who bled and died for me.

Many of the saints in the Dallas meeting had visions of Christ as a glorious King, coming in His royal majesty with all the hosts of heaven for His bride, and of the changing and Rapture of the redeemed of the Lord. They saw them rise with shouts of gladness, mingled with the music of heaven. And some had glorious visions of the marriage supper and saw the table with the feast spread and the brightness of the saints as they gathered around.

Jesus was seen coming on a white horse with the banner, *"King of Kings and Lord of Lords"* (Rev. 19:16), with all His saints riding on white horses, with the armies of heaven coming back to earth again to the great battle of Armageddon, where the Antichrist and his army will be destroyed, and Christ will set up His everlasting kingdom, and the saints will reign as kings and priests for a thousand years.

The Lord is revealing things to come both on earth and in heaven. In all our meetings, the fire of God is seen on heads as *"cloven tongues"* (Acts 2:3), and lights are seen over and around the platform by many, both saints and sinners. Jesus has been seen walking and standing in the midst.

All these terrible wars that have shaken the whole world in the last two years and almost covered the lovely lands of Europe with blood and the slain were prophesied in the Dallas meeting, less than a year beforehand, and many other things that have come to pass.

The Lord greatly used Brother Mears. He had visions of many large meetings that I would hold soon in this country from the Atlantic to the Pacific, in the large cities, on the mountains, and in the valleys, in the largest buildings, and also in large tents. He saw the crowds standing around and perceived them coming to Christ by hundreds, and saw the slain of the Lord as if on a battlefield. He also saw the sick were being healed by scores and hundreds.

Oh, I thought that could not be possible! Surely I could never travel and endure so much hardness and responsibility, but it has all been fulfilled. I have traveled over twenty-two thousand miles since I was in Dallas. He also prophesied about the book called *Acts of the Holy Spirit*. He said God would greatly bless it and that it would be sent quickly to all parts of the world. Ten thousand copies have been scattered over land and sea, and now, at the call of the people and the leading of the Lord, I am sending out a new book, which is the seventh volume, entitled, *Signs and Wonders That God Hath Wrought*.

Sustaining Power

It could be truly said, as Peter said on the Day of Pentecost, this that you see and hear and feel is the promise of the Father, the wonder-working Holy Spirit (Acts 2:33).

With great *"signs and wonders"* (Acts 5:12) the Lord has stretched forth His hand in working mighty miracles, healing all manner of diseases, casting out demons, laying the people out as dead. Many of the meetings look like a battlefield: sinners struck down in their sins, and saints lying as dead, like John (Rev. 1:17). The saints have been given great visions and revelations and prophecies from heaven.

The Holy Spirit has been seen as cloven tongues, as rays of light, and as a great cloud of glory over the pulpit and the altar, and the Lord has been seen by many walking through the tent and about the altar.

Thousands of people are stirred and are writing to us for help, both spiritual and physical. The Macedonian cry is, "Come, come and help us, or send help."

God has called the saints, the brothers in the ministry, and the evangelists and workers from all parts. They have all fallen in line and rejoiced in the unity and love and power of God in our midst, and went away feeling convinced of the need of more power of the living God in us and through us and in our midst.

At the end of five months as we are about to close our work here, the interest, which has been increasing from the first, is now deeper and the presence of God is more manifest than ever.

As we are expecting to leave soon, the people are improving the opportunity and rushing here from all parts.

Twelve just arrived from Canada, one from England, and others are on their way.

The Lord showed a brother in a vision that the bands of angels who sang at the birth of Jesus were singing through the saints.

The Lord is manifesting His presence more and more to His children and encouraging us in every way that we may be ready and be weaned away from the world and be ready for His soon coming.

I have every reason to praise the Lord that He has wonderfully sustained me during these five months; I have been laboring, very hard, not only in the meetings, but also outside of meetings.

I would say to the reader that the contents of my books are as a drop in the ocean compared to the many meetings and wonderful things that have never been mentioned and no account given of them.

I am sending books forth in the name of the Lord. The Lord showed me that I must make haste and get the books out, for He is going to send them all over the world. They will not only be used to help to gather the saints together and prepare for the marriage and the great work of the future, but it will be a great help to those who are left to go through the Tribulation.

I ask the prayers of all the saints who will read these lines that I may be kept continually in His will and covered with His mighty love and power; that God through me can finish the work that He has called me to do that He may have all the glory.

—*Mrs. Woodworth-Etter*
December 12, 1912

32

QUESTIONS AND ANSWERS ON DIVINE HEALING

Q. What is divine healing?

A. Divine healing is the act of God's grace, by the direct power of the Holy Spirit, by which the physical body is delivered from sickness and disease and restored to soundness and health.

Q. Have we any promise in the Bible that divine healing was ever intended to be an attainable blessing to the people of God?

A. Yes. There are many such promises. We find it given to the people of Israel in a special covenant promise. *"If thou wilt diligently hearken to the voice of the Lord thy God, and wilt do that which is right in His sight, and wilt give ear to His commandments, and keep all His statutes, I will put none of these diseases upon thee, which I have brought upon the Egyptians; for I am the Lord that healeth thee"* (Exod. 15:26). *"And ye shall serve the Lord your God, and He shall bless thy bread and thy water; and I will take sickness away from the midst of thee"* (Exod. 23:25).

Q. Does the Bible prove that any of the people of God ever enjoyed this blessing?

A. Yes. We read that even before this covenant blessing was promised, the physical condition of the people was perfect, which indicates plainly that God had a special interest in their health. There were at least two and one-half million people in the Exodus from Egypt, *"and there was not one feeble person among their tribes"* (Ps. 105:37). Moses enjoyed this blessing in a special manner (Deut. 34:7). So also did Caleb in an unusual experience of preservation and health to an old age (Josh. 14:10–11). David personally knew of the benefits and blessings of healing (Ps. 6:2; 30:2; 103:1–4). Whenever Israel lived up to the covenant conditions, they all had the benefits of healing and health (Ps. 107:20; 2 Chron. 30:20). Hezekiah had a personal experience of the same (2 Kings 20:1–5).

Q. Was this blessing ever promised to anyone else than the Jews?

A. Yes. It is given in prophecy as a redemption blessing, which, together with all other gospel blessings through Christ, is offered to both Jew and Gentile (Gal. 3:27–29).

Q. What does prophecy say about divine healing?

A. There is more said about it in prophecy than we have time at present to read, but I will just quote a few verses, and the rest can be read at your leisure. *"Then the eyes of the blind shall be opened, and the ears of the deaf shall be unstopped. Then shall the lame man leap as an hart, and the tongue of the dumb sing"* (Isa. 35:5–6). This very prophecy is referred to by Jesus Himself in Matthew 11:5–6, where it was daily being fulfilled, *"The blind receive their sight, and the lame walk, the lepers are cleansed, and the deaf hear, the dead are raised up, and the poor have the Gospel preached to them."* Another very plain prophecy is found in Isaiah 53:4: *"Surely he hath borne our griefs, and carried our sorrows."* The fulfillment of this wonderful voice of inspiration is found in Matthew 8:17: *"Himself took our infirmities, and bare our sicknesses."* It is admitted by all reliable translators and the most eminent Hebrew scholars, such as Barnes, Magee, Young, and Leeser, that Isaiah 53:4 in its literal rendering corresponds exactly with Matthew 8:17. We see, therefore, that the latter is a direct reference to the former. Then the beautiful prophecy of salvation and healing is found in the following verse, Isaiah 53:5: *"But he was wounded for our transgressions, he was bruised for our iniquities: the chastisement of our peace was upon him; and with his stripes we are healed."* These prophecies all point to the redemption work of Jesus, which finds its center in the cross. The apostle Peter refers to this verse just quoted in the following language: *"Who his own self bare our sins in his own body on the tree, that we, being dead to*

sins, should live unto righteousness: by whose stripes ye were healed" (1 Pet. 2.24).
The following references will enable you to see that more is said in prophecy
about healing: Isaiah 42:7; Isaiah 61:1, fulfilled in Luke 4:18–21; prophecy in
Malachi 4:2, fulfilled in Matthew 4:16; Luke 1:78–79. These are all fulfilled
in redemption.

Q. Do you believe that the Bible teaches divine healing as a redemption blessing?

A. Yes. Do you not see how plain this is made in the prophecies just quoted
and in their fulfillment? Jesus worked in every respect, in His life, ministry,
death, and resurrection, just according to the redemption plan. His words
and deeds are the divine expression of this redemption plan, and we can
clearly see that healing for the body is placed upon an equality with healing
for the soul. Both are obtained upon the same grounds, obedience and faith.

Q. Can a person possess salvation without healing?

A. Yes, he may. While both are obtained by faith, yet they may not both be
obtained by the same act of faith. Jesus will be to us just what our faith takes
Him for.

Q. Did Jesus heal everybody?

A. Yes, all who came to Him in faith. Read Matthew 4:23–24 and Matthew
12–15.

Q. But they did not seem to have faith, did they?

A. Yes. If you read the references just mentioned, you will notice the people
came to Him for healing and followed Him. At Nazareth, His own town,
where He had been brought up, He could do no great work among them,
"because of their unbelief" (Matt. 13:58). At Capernaum, where some of the
most remarkable healings were wrought, the people were a believing people.
Out of nineteen of the most prominent individual cases of healing in the
ministry of Christ and the apostles, there are twelve of these where their faith
is spoken of. The rest are mentioned sufficiently plain to show that faith brought the
healing in every case.

Q. Did not Jesus heal arbitrarily, for the sole purpose of establishing His
divinity?

A. No. He healed according to the law of redemption and because of His great
compassion for suffering humanity (Matt. 14:14).

Q. Didn't divine healing cease when Jesus finished His earthly ministry?

A. No. It was more wonderfully manifested in the ministry of the apostles after the Day of Pentecost. See Acts 5:12–16; 3:1–16; 14:8–10; 9:17–18; 8:6–8; 19:11–12; 14:19–20; 9:33–35; 36:42; 20:8–12; 28:3–6, 8. This proves clearly that divine healing is a redemption blessing for the entire Holy Spirit dispensation.

Q. But we are taught that it was only for the beginning of the gospel dispensation. How about that?

A. The Bible does not teach any such doctrine.

Q. But it does teach that *"when that which is perfect is come, then that which is in part shall be done away"* (1 Cor. 13:10). How about this?

A. This Scripture has no reference to divine healing or any of the redemption blessings, that they shall be done away with in this dispensation. If there ever has been a time in this dispensation when it could have been said with reference to the full possession and manifestation of the gospel blessings, that *"that which is perfect is come,"* it was when the Holy Spirit came at Pentecost. But after this we see mighty works of salvation and healing, and they were in no sense done away with, but were greatly increased. So you see the "done away with" argument has no scriptural basis whatever. As long as the dispensation of grace shall last, so long shall the benefits of grace be extended to *"whosoever will"* (Rev. 22:17).

Q. Well, then, when was divine healing done away?

A. In the design of God it was never done away.

Q. Do you mean to say that it was perpetuated in the primitive church?

A. Certainly it was. History shows that for several centuries there was no other means of healing practiced in the church.

Q. But what after that?

A. Just what crowded out all other gospel truths—the superstitions and unbelief of the apostasy. But, thank God, the darkness is past and *"the Sun of righteousness...with healing in His wings"* (Mal. 4:2) is shining salvation and health to all who will forsake all their old doctrines creeds and superstitions and get back upon the old apostolic foundation, the Word of God.

Q. But how may I know that it is still God's will to heal?

A. Just as you may know that it is His will to save—by His Word. His Word is His will.

Q. But it may be His will not to heal me.

A. You must go outside of God's Word to find standing ground for such a conclusion, for there is nothing inside of the Bible about healing but what corresponds with our blessed text: *"Himself took our infirmities and bare our sicknesses."* Most people who argue that it might not be God's will to heal them are at the same time taking medicine and employing every possible human agency to get well. Why be so inconsistent? Why fight against God's will? If it is His will for you not to get well, then die. Stop fighting against God.

Q. But doesn't sickness come from God as a blessing?

A. No. It never comes from God except in a permissive sense, the same as a temptation comes to us; and sickness is never a blessing to us except as any other temptation or trial may be considered a blessing. The blessing is in the deliverance and healing. Every person who has ever experienced the healing touch of God knows what a blessing to the soul comes with it. Sickness is an abnormal condition of the body and cannot be a blessing from God.

Q. If it does not come from God, then where does it come from?

A. It comes from the devil and was always dealt with by Jesus in His earthly ministry as a work of the devil. The Word of God plainly teaches us that the devil is the author of disease. Read John 2:7; Luke 3:16; Acts 1:38.

Q. But aren't there some other Scriptures that teach us that sickness comes from God?

A. Only in a permissive sense.

Q. Does the Bible teach us that God intends to be the Healer of His people without the use of medicine?

A. Yes. It nowhere commands the use of medicine with prayer and faith.

Q. But how about Hezekiah's figs, the blind man's clay, and Timothy's wine?

A. It is true Isaiah told Hezekiah to take a lump of figs, but this has nothing to do with the New Testament means of healing. Also it is very evident that the figs did not heal him; but God said, *"I will heal thee"* (2 Kings 20:5). Jesus did not use the clay on the eyes of the blind man for any curative power, for He commanded the man at once to go and wash it off. No one has heard of blindness from birth being healed by the use of clay as a medicine before or since then. It is evident that the spittle and clay were used by Jesus as a requirement of submission and obedience from the blind man. The thought must have been repulsive and humiliating to him as the clay was applied to his eyes, but, like Naaman, he submitted and obeyed and received the blessing unspeakable of healing. Wine was recommended to Timothy as an article of diet and would not be objectionable today, in its proper use, under similar circumstances.

Q. Aren't medicines recognized in the Word of God?

A. Yes. Let us read how it recognizes them. *"Thou hast no healing medicines"* (Jer. 30:13). *"In vain shalt thou use many medicines"* (Jer. 46:11). *"A merry heart doeth good like medicine* [margin, *to a medicine*, showing that the merry heart is better than the medicine]*"* (Prov. 17:22). *"And the fruit thereof shall be for meat, and the leaf thereof for medicine"* (Ezek. 47:12). This latter reference does not mean any material remedy but is prophetic of the Tree of Life and divine healing. (See Revelation 22.2.) Thus we see the Word of God places no intrinsic value upon medicine.

Q. Is not the ministry of physicians for the body designed of God, the same as the ministry of the Gospel for the soul?

A. No. The greater portion of the physicians of the land are ungodly people; many of them are professed infidels and were never designed of God to administer drugs and poisons to anyone, much less to the people of God, whose bodies are the sacred temples of the Holy Spirit. The true ministers of the Gospel are the ministers for soul and body. *"And they departed, and went through the towns, preaching the Gospel, and healing everywhere"* (Luke 9:6). *"And they went forth, and preached everywhere, the Lord working with them, and confirming his word with signs following"* (Mark 16:20).

Q. But is not the ministry of physicians recognized in the Bible?

A. Yes. Let us read how it recognizes them. *"But ye are forgers of lies, ye are all physicians of no value"* (Job 13:4). *"And Asa in the thirty and ninth year of his reign was diseased in his feet, until his disease was exceeding great; yet in his disease he sought not to the Lord, but to the physicians"* (2 Chron. 16:12). *"And had suffered many things of many physicians, and had spent all that she had, and was nothing bettered, but rather grew worse"* (Mark 5:26). These Scriptures show that the Bible gives no very favorable recognition of physicians.

Q. Wasn't anointing with oil the mode of doctoring in Bible times?

A. No. While some kinds of oil may have some medical value for some kinds of diseases, it was not at all designed for any such use in connection with the prayer of faith in healing the sick. If anointing was the mode of doctoring, the church would have had no need of instruction in this respect, for it would have been a common practice everywhere by the doctors. Had this been the mind of the apostle, then he would have assigned the work of anointing to the doctors. "Elders are not masseurs."

33

GIFTS FOR MEN

Thou hast ascended on high, thou hast led captivity captive: thou hast received gifts for men; yea for the rebellious also, that the Lord might dwell among them. (Ps. 68:18)

After all the life of Jesus, after all His mighty signs and wonders and miracles, *"Behold the man!"* (John 19:5). *"Never man spake like this man"* (John 7:46). *"What manner of man is this, that even the winds and the sea obey him?"* (Matt. 8:27).

If He had stopped short at Calvary or at going down into the cold grave, His work would have been a failure. Many people look only at the dead Savior. They have only a dead religion of form and of works. They have no life or power. Remember Jesus brought life and immortality to light, to us, through the Resurrection. No, the grave could not hold Him, though all hell was up in arms to hold Him cold in death. A hundred or more armed soldiers stood around His grave for fear that His disciples would steal His lifeless body away. They also sealed the sepulcher with the governor's seal, and it was death to break that seal.

A mighty battle was fought. All the armies of heaven were engaged with the hosts of hell, in fierce array, around the cave tomb where the mangled body of

Jesus, our crucified Lord, lay cold in death. Hear the demons, "We have got Him, and we will hold Him captive. Where is your Prince? Where is your King?" But, listen! The battle turns. Victory is near. Help is coming. The Lord God is coming Himself, with His great angel who rolls back the stone from the sepulcher and sits upon it. His countenance was like lightning, his raiment white as snow, and the keepers quaked in fear of him. They fell and lay as dead men. God, with His mighty presence, sent a great earthquake, and with a great shout over death and hell and the grave, we see the Conqueror come forth, holding the keys to unlock the prison house of the dead.

We see the women last at the cross, the first at the grave. The angel said, *"Fear not, for I know that ye seek Jesus, which was crucified. He is not here: for he is risen, as he said. Come, see the place where the Lord lay. Go quickly, and tell his disciples that he is risen from the dead"* (Matt. 28:5–7).

As they went with great joy, Jesus met them, saying, "Fear not, but go and tell my brethren that I will meet them in Galilee."

The women were commanded by the angels, and later by the Lord Himself, to preach the first news of the Resurrection.

No, He is not dead. The Lord is risen indeed. Oh, praise God for a living Christ, a living church, and our soon-coming King and Lord!

The graves were opened, and many of the bodies of the saints who slept in their graves arose and came out after His resurrection, and went into the city, and appeared to many (Matt. 27:52–53).

The Jewish church had forsaken the Lord, and He had taken His Spirit from her. For about four hundred years she was in darkness. There were no prophets, no priests, and no communication from heaven until the birth of John the Baptist and Christ's birth were announced.

It says, *"Many...of the saints"* (Matt. 27:52). *Many* would mean thousands or more, and we have every reason to believe that most of those saints were the prophets and priests. Abraham, Isaac, Jacob, and Joseph; and those holy men of old, who spoke as they were moved by the Holy Spirit, including John the Baptist, who had lately been murdered for Jesus' sake.

Oh, praise God for the resurrection of these mighty men of old! Their bodies came up, and their spirits were united to them. They were living men, breathing and walking, and their bodies were free from corruptions. See them going through the streets of Jerusalem, going from one place to another and making themselves known.

Oh, praise God for the resurrection of our bodies and that we shall know each other!

Yes, the devil held their bodies captive for hundreds of years in the grave. But see the mighty Conqueror break the chains, take them captive from the devil and from the power of the grave, and, leading *"captivity captive"* (Eph. 4:8), take them away to some other world, where no doubt God is using them in some great way for His glory.

He did not take them to heaven when He went, for no one had ascended to heaven. Those who are raised at His coming will be the first fruits of the Resurrection. The spirits of the saints since Pentecost have gone to be with Christ. Paul said, "I know and am confident that when I am absent from the body, I shall be present with the Lord" (2 Cor. 5:8).

"He ascended up on high...and gave gifts unto men" (Eph. 4:8). Yea, to the rebels also. Jesus did not have all power until after God raised Him from the dead. No one could have the gift of God, eternal life, until after he was born of the Spirit.

Jesus has all power. He was raised up with all power. The Holy Spirit was with the disciples, but Jesus said, "He shall be in you." When they were all together, Jesus met with them, and He opened their spiritual minds. He breathed on them and said, *"Receive ye the Holy Ghost"* (John 20:22). They received Him and became partakers of the divine nature. They received the gift of God, were enlightened, and cried out, *"My Lord and my God"* (v. 28). No one ever had that experience before that time. They were sons of God by the new birth. It was the gift of God, eternal life, *"Yea, for the rebellious also"* (Ps. 68:18). This is the most important of all gifts, for without this gift you can never get inside the pearly gates.

When the sinner stops his rebellion and repents, God gives him faith to accept Christ. God gives him power to become a son of God, who is born, not of man nor of the will of men, nor of flesh and blood, but by the power of God. He is then no longer a rebel, but a son, for he has received the gift of God and has been born of the spiritual family of God. His name has been written in the family record by the finger of God, and it has been said, *"This man was born in [Zion]"* (Ps. 87:5). He has the finished work on Calvary for sin and uncleanness, and he is now a child of God, ready for any or all the gifts of the Pentecostal baptism and power. He is God's man.

Jesus received gifts for men. When Jesus was giving His last blessing on the mountain, before going up to heaven, He said to them, "Wait at Jerusalem until you are endued with power from on high. You shall receive power when the Holy Spirit has come upon you. You shall then be witnesses of Me. All power is given unto Me in heaven and in earth. Go into all the world and preach the Gospel to everyone. These signs shall follow those who believe on Me; these are some of the gifts that I will give to men: *'In my name shall they cast out devils; they shall speak with new tongues; they shall take up serpents; and if they drink any deadly thing, it shall not hurt them; they shall lay hands on the sick, and they shall recover'* (Mark 16:17–18)." (See Luke 24:49; Acts 1:8; Matthew 28:18–19.)

These were the last words our Savior spoke on earth before He was taken up in a visible manner out of their sight. After that they got the promised baptism and greatest gift; they went forth preaching the Word everywhere, the Lord working with them, confirming the Word with the signs following.

They could not see the Lord in person like in days past, but saw the visible signs of His invisible presence.

These signs and gifts could be seen and heard with the natural eye and ear. Jesus was with them, with all gifts and signs, and miracles, and diverse operations of the Spirit. With these He confirmed and put His seal on the truth, and on their preaching.

At Pentecost He sent the promise of the Father. The Holy Spirit came as a rushing wind and sat on all their heads as cloven tongues of fire. These cloven tongues were a sign of the new tongues; they were tongues of fire and of the Spirit, for they were all filled with the Spirit and began to speak as the Spirit gave them utterance.

It was the time of the great Jewish feast, and all the Jewish nations under heaven were gathered there, and they saw and heard the wonderful display of the Holy Spirit, the gifts, and the glory of God.

They were amazed, saying, *"How hear we every man in our own tongue, wherein we were born?"* (Acts 2:8). Jesus had sent gifts down for men and women. The Holy Spirit had come to stay. He was given now without measure.

God sent Peter down to Caesarea to hold a revival among the Gentiles. While he was preaching, the Holy Spirit fell on those who heard the Word, for they spoke with tongues and magnified God.

The Holy Spirit was poured out with all the gifts on the Gentile nations, just the same as at Pentecost on the Jews. *"For the promise is unto you, and to your children, and to all that are afar off, even as many as the Lord our God shall call"* (Acts 2:39). Oh, praise God, beloved, that includes you and me!

Jesus sent these gifts with all the Pentecostal power and glory. Our bodies are God's powerhouses; they are the channels for the Holy Spirit to flow out of like *"rivers of living water"* (John 7:38). *"That the Lord might dwell among them"* (Ps. 68:18). This is the sign to the lost world that God is with us, the signs of His invisible presence. We are a people to be wondered at. "Here, Father, am I, and the children whom You gave to Me" (See Isaiah 8:18; John 17.) We are for signs and wonders in Israel from the Lord of hosts, who dwells in Zion—down here, not in heaven.

"He led captivity captive and gave gifts unto men....He gave some, apostles; and some, prophets; and some, evangelists; and some, pastors and teachers" (Eph. 4:8, 11). These imply and include all the gifts and workings of the Holy Spirit.

Why did He send this power and gifts to men, to His brothers, and to the church? He says, *"For the perfecting of the saints, for the work of the ministry, for the edifying of the body of Christ"* (v. 12); to make the saints, God's men, perfect; to lead them in the same Pentecostal power and gifts.

Ministers need it, and they must have the seal of the Holy Spirit with all these signs and gifts to encourage them. They are the visible signs to the world—and seals to them—that God is with them, working together with them, confirming the Word with visible signs.

When the disciples were put into prison and their lives were threatened on account of the great power with them in healing and miracles, they were forbidden to preach in the name of Jesus, for others saw the power came through His name.

They came together, and they knew it was the power of God that caused all their persecution. They knew if they had a form of religion, and denied the power, that they would have no more trouble. But, beloved, they said, "We will be true to God. We will preach the Word if we die." Then they prayed to the Lord, saying,

"Lord, behold their threatenings; and grant unto thy servants, that with all boldness they may speak thy word, by stretching forth thine hand to heal; and grant that signs and wonders may be done by the name of thy holy child Jesus" (Acts 4:29–30).

You see, these ministers needed power to give them boldness to stand up for Jesus, to preach all the words of this life.

When they preached, they knew they must see the signs in the meeting of the presence of the invisible Christ, who will be present to confirm the Word and their message. Jesus had said, *"I am with you alway, even unto the end of the world"* (Matt. 28:20). Then, like Peter, they could say to those present, "This that you see and hear and feel, it is the promise of the Father, it is the Holy Spirit."

The Son was pleased with their prayer and with their faith and courage, and the place was shaken—the building where they were assembled—and they were all filled with the Holy Spirit and spoke the Word with boldness.

Beloved, see, this was a greater baptism. They needed it to prepare them for the work they had to do. After this, they had greater success. God did mighty signs and wonders at the hands of the apostles; great fear fell on all the church and on all who heard and saw these things. Multitudes of men and women came flocking to Christ and were added to the Lord.

Multitudes means thousands. They came from Jerusalem and all the cities round about, bringing their sick folk in beds and cots, placing them along the streets, so that the shadow of Peter as he passed by might overshadow them. You see that the power went forth from their bodies, as when Paul laid handkerchiefs on his body and sent them to the sick, and the devils or disease went out, and they were healed.

Oh, praise God, I am a witness to these things. We see the same thing today: some of the greatest miracles of healing and salvation I have ever seen have been done in the same way, hundreds of miles away. He gave gifts to men.

Read carefully the twelfth chapter of the first epistle to the Corinthians. Paul shows that the church is in possession of all the gifts, power, calling and work of the Holy Spirit, and that they are in the body of Christ, His church.

Oh, beloved, we ought to come up to this in these last days, when the bride is making herself ready. He says He does not want us to be ignorant concerning spiritual gifts: *"Covet earnestly the best gifts"* (1 Cor. 12:31), *"Follow after charity [love], and desire spiritual gifts"* (1 Cor. 14:1), for God has set them in the church.

Gifts are also for the rebellious. Thank God, the sinner no longer needs to be rebellious, but to fall at His feet and settle the old account. He says He has a gift for you: *"The gift of God is eternal life"* (Rom. 6:23), and then you are God's man, and no longer a stranger or foreigner, but have been brought near by the blood of Christ. Through Him we will have access by one Spirit unto the Father. You are a citizen with the saints and of the household of God; you are lively stones in the building that is being fitly framed together, a holy temple in the Lord.

Beloved, you are a son and an heir to all the Pentecostal blessings, gifts, and power. Press your claim at the court of heaven.

Seek the baptism of the Holy Spirit and power. You can be a pillar in the temple of God—in, to go out no more. Be among the wise who shall know of the Lord's coming, among the wise who shall shine as the brightness of the firmament.

Let all who read this take warning: He who knows the Lord's will but does not do it shall be beaten with many stripes (Luke 12:47).

Amazing Grace

Amazing grace, how sweet the sound!
That saved a wretch like me!
I once was lost but now am found,
Was blind but now I see.

'Twas grace that taught my heart to fear,
And grace my fears relieved;
How precious did that grace appear,
The hour I first believed!

Through many dangers, toils, and snares
I have already come;
'Tis grace has brought me safe thus far,
And grace will lead me home.

The Lord has promised good to me
His Word my hope secures;
He will my shield and portion be,
As long as life endures.

Yes, when this flesh and heart shall fail,
And mortal life shall cease,
I shall possess within the vail,
A life of joy and peace.

34

WOMEN'S RIGHTS IN THE GOSPEL

And when the day of Pentecost was fully come, they were all with one accord in one place. (Acts 2:1)

And it shall come to pass in the last days, saith God, I will pour out of my Spirit upon all flesh; and your sons and your daughters shall prophesy, and your young men shall see visions, and your old men shall dream dreams.
(Acts 2:17; Joel 2:28)

And suddenly there came a sound from heaven as of a rushing mighty wind, and it filled all the house where they were sitting. And there appeared unto them cloven tongues like as of fire, and it sat upon each of them. And they were all filled with the Holy Spirit, and began to speak with other tongues, as the Spirit gave them utterance. (Acts 2:2–4)

There was a wonderful excitement; the people came rushing in great multitudes from the city to see what was the matter. They saw these men and women, with their faces shining with the glory of God, all preaching at once, all anxious to tell what God had done for them and a dying world. Conviction went like daggers to their hearts. And, just as it is today, when the power of God is manifest, instead of yielding, they cried out, "Too much excitement," and began to fight against God. They said, "These people are mad, are drunken with new wine," and mocked them.

Peter got up to defend the cause of Christ. He referred to Joel:

And it shall come to pass in the last days, saith God, I will pour out of my Spirit upon all flesh: and your sons and your daughters shall prophesy, and your young men shall see visions, and your old men shall dream dreams: and on my servants and on my handmaidens I will pour out in those days of my Spirit; and they shall prophesy. (Acts 2:17–18)

Both Paul and Luke spoke as if it were very common for women to preach and prophesy: "*Every woman that prayeth or prophesieth with her head uncovered dishonoreth her head*" (1 Cor. 11:5). "*The same man had four daughters, virgins, which did prophesy*" (Acts 21:9).

Paul worked with the women in the Gospel more than any of the apostles; Priscilla and Phebe traveled with Paul preaching and building up the churches (Acts 18:2, 18, 26; Rom. 16). He and Phebe had been holding revivals together; now she was called to the city of Rome; Paul couldn't go with her, but he was very careful of her reputation and that she was treated with respect. He wrote a letter of recommendation:

I commend unto you Phebe, our sister, which is a servant of the church [which signifies a minister of the church] *at Cenchrea, that ye receive her in the Lord as becometh saints and that ye assist her in whatsoever business she hath need of you, for she has been a succourer of many and of myself also.* (Rom. 16:1–2)

This shows that she had authority to do business in the churches and that she had been successful in winning souls to Christ. He was not ashamed to say she had encouraged him. He spoke in the highest praise of a number of sisters who had been faithful workers in the work of the Lord, who had risked their lives in the effort to save souls. Not he alone, but all the churches of the Gentiles sent their thanks.

Paul said, *"Let your women keep silent in the churches"* (1 Cor. 14:34).[1] So said the law. We are not under law but under grace. *"And if they will learn anything, let them ask of their husbands at home"* (v. 35). What will those who have no husbands do? Do you suppose they will remain in ignorance and be lost? And if some women had to depend on their husbands for knowledge, they would die in ignorance.

Paul referred to contentions in the churches. Paul said you had better not marry. How many agree with Paul? How many obey? He was referring to contentions in the churches, that it is a shame to bring up questions and have jangling in the house of God. He wrote to the brothers, *"I hear that there be divisions among you, and I partly believe it"* (1 Cor. 11:18).

"Help those women which labored with me in the gospel, with Clement also, and with other my fellow laborers whose names are in the book of life" (Phil. 4:3). Several women in the Bible were prophetesses. *"Huldah, the prophetess, the wife of Shallum …dwelt in Jerusalem in the college, and they communed with her, and she said unto them, Thus saith the Lord God of Israel"* (2 Kings 22:14–15). In Exodus 15:20, Miriam is referred to as a prophetess. *"I sent before thee, Moses, Aaron, and Miriam"* (Mic. 6:4).

"Deborah, a prophetess, the wife of Lapidoth she judged Israel at that time" (Judg. 4:4). See the responsible position that God gave her, to sit and judge the hosts of the children of Israel. The children of Israel had sinned, and God would not fight their battles. For twenty years the nations arose against them and defied them to come out to battle. Barak did not dare to meet the enemy unless Deborah led the caravan. This brave woman, ever ready to defend the cause of God, said, *"I will surely go"* (v. 9). God's people must not be taken by the enemy. Oh, no; call out the armies of the Lord. Sisera's mighty host is gathering. Every soldier to his post. See the brave woman riding with Barak, the commander, at the head of the army, cheering on the hosts to victory, shouting victory as she led on the armies, sweeping through the enemy ranks, carrying death and destruction, until the king leaped from his chariot and fled for his life, but was captured and killed by a woman. Every man was put to the sword; not one was left to tell of the defeat.

The mother of Sisera looked out the window for the return of the king, her son, from the battle and cried, *"Why is his chariot so long in coming? Why tarry the wheels of his chariots?"* (Judg. 5:28). While she was weeping for her son's return,

---

1. Pastor A. A. Boddy, of Sunderland, England, has in these days heard women in Palestine asking questions at a service; Paul also referred to this kind of disturbance.

he was lying cold in death in the tent where he has been captured and killed by a woman.

Queen Esther interceded at the king's court, and the sad decree of the king was reversed, so that her life and the life of the Jewish nation are saved. (See Esther 1–10.)

Paul said that there is no difference, but that male and female are one in Christ Jesus (Gal. 3:28). Let us take Jesus for our pattern and example, and see no man, save Jesus only.

Women were called and commissioned by the angel sent from heaven and by the Lord Jesus Christ to preach the Gospel (Matt. 28:5–10).

The cowardly disciples had forsaken the Savior and fled. Peter denied the Savior and swore he never knew Him, but many women followed Him and stood by the cross and went to the sepulchre and saw the body laid away; the great stone was rolled against the entrance (Matt. 27:55–61). These women went home sad and brokenhearted, but they returned to pay a last tribute to their dear friend. They spent the night preparing spices to embalm the body of their Lord. They came to the sepulchre, as it was coming daylight. The grave was empty. The Lord was not there. As they stood weeping, two angels stood by them and said:

> *Fear not ye: for I know that ye seek Jesus, which was crucified. He is not here: for he is risen, as he said. Come, see the place where the Lord lay. And go quickly, and tell his disciples that he is risen from the dead; and, behold, he goeth before you into Galilee; there shall ye see him; lo, I have told you.*
> (Matt. 28:5–7)

They started at once with joy and rejoicing. They could not walk fast enough; they ran to hunt up the brothers to tell the good news. As they were going, Jesus met them, and they fell at His feet and worshiped Him. He said: "*Be not afraid: go tell my brethren that they go into Galilee, and there shall they see me*" (v. 10). It was not only the twelve who were to tell the good news. There were several hundred brothers, yes, thousands of followers at this time. They never thought of bloodthirsty soldiers who had put their Master to death and were seeking for His friends who would dare to defend Him.

Observe the wonderful mission that Jesus had entrusted to these weak women: to preach the first resurrection sermon, to risk their lives in gathering together the followers of Christ where the wonderful meeting was to be held. But just like many today, they would not believe. Thomas said, "I will not believe except I see the nail prints in His hands and the wound in His side" (John 20:25).

In the midst of all these discouragements, they went on with the work and had grand success. Jesus met with and preached to them; they were all made to rejoice. They were called by angels and the Lord from glory, and sent to preach the Gospel. The names of four women were given, and there were many others.

God is calling the Marys and the Marthas today all over our land to work in various places in the vineyard of the Lord. God grant that they may respond and say, *"Lord, here am I; send me"* (Isa. 6:8). This call was made after Christ had risen.

"In the last days...I will pour out of my Spirit" (Acts 2:17) refers in a special manner to these last days in which we are now living. God is promising great blessings and power to qualify His handmaidens for the last great harvest just before the notable Day of the Lord comes. We must first be baptized into Christ by the one Spirit—that is, to be born of the Spirit—then we ought to be anointed with power and wisdom. The Spirit needs to be poured out like oil on our heads to give us knowledge of the deep things of God. The Lord says we shall prophesy.

Paul said, *"Desire spiritual gifts, but rather that ye may prophesy"* (1 Cor. 14:1). It makes no difference how many gifts we have, if we have not the gift of talking and teaching, it will not avail us much. The Lord has promised this greatest gift to His handmaidens and daughters. Paul explained what it is to prophesy: *"He that prophesieth speaketh unto men to edification, and exhortation, and comfort... He that prophesieth, edifieth the church."* (vv. 3–4). No one can talk for God only by the enlightening power of the Holy Spirit. Moses said, *"Would God that all the Lord's people were prophets, and that the Lord would put his Spirit upon them"* (Num. 11:29).

While Jesus sat at Jacob's well to rest, there was a poor woman, one who was living in sin, who came to the well to get water. Although she had fallen very low and was despised by her friends, so that she had no one to lift her up and tell her of a better way, Jesus came to seek the lost, to lift up the fallen.

God help us to follow His example; if they feel that their feet are slipping into the pit of hell, Jesus is a mighty Savior. He can lift them up and make them children of a King.

216 ⌐ *Maria Woodworth-Etter: Collected Works*

Jesus preached salvation; the woman was converted; she left her pitcher and took the well of salvation with her, and running to the city, went up one street and down another, with her face shining with the glory of God. Perhaps the people would have scorned her an hour before; now they saw and felt the change. "Look what He has done for me. He will do the same for you."

The people left their stores, their places of business, left their parlors and kitchens, and came out in great multitudes to see the Savior of the world. There was a great revival there at the well. Jesus went into the city and stayed two days. The wave of salvation went on and on. This was the result of one sermon by a weak woman. (See John 4:5–42.) Many were converted and made to rejoice in a Savior's love by the preaching of the woman who said, *"He told me all things that ever I did"* (John 4:39). They came to her and said, "We know now for ourselves," and, like the Queen of Sheba, said, *"The half was not told"* (1 Kings 10:7).

My dear sister in Christ, as you read these words, may the Spirit of God come upon you and make you willing to do the work the Lord has assigned to you. It is high time for women to let their lights shine, to bring out their talents that have been hidden away rusting, to use them for the glory of God, and to do with all their might what their hands find to do, trusting God for strength, for He has said, *"I will never leave thee, nor forsake thee"* (Heb. 13:5).

Oh, the fields are white, for the harvest is great and ripe, and it is ready for the Gospel sickle! Where are the laborers to gather the golden grain into the Master's garner?

The world is dying, the grave is filling, hell is boasting; it will all be over soon.

God left the glorious work of saving souls in the hands of the church. What is the church composed of? Men, women, and children. We are putting up a building of God. Everyone has a part in this building; if we cannot be a pillar or cornerstone, let us be a spike or a nail or a brick; let us not despise the day of small things. Whatever we do for Jesus, with the right motive, is precious in His sight. God's church is a workshop; no idlers are allowed there. There should be notices posted, "To work, to work. Everyone at his post." When Satan tempts us, you and I, like Nehemiah, should say, *"'I am doing a great work, so that I cannot come down'* (Neh. 6:3). I am commissioned by the King of Heaven to work for Him." The work is great, and the time is short. He offers a great reward. Like the blind man, we will tell what God has done for us: *"Whereas I was blind, now I see"* (John 9:25).

"The Spirit and the bride say, come. And let him that heareth say, Come....And whosoever will, let him take the water of life freely" (Rev. 22:17).

If, like David, we have been taken away from that horrible pit over which we were hanging by the thread of life; if our feet have been taken out of the mire and clay; if the chains of Satan that were around us, like brass and iron, have been broken; if our feet have been set on solid rock and a new song put into our mouths; if we have been adopted into the family of God, of which part are in heaven and part on earth; if our names are written in the Book of Life, then we have the gift of eternal life, and we are heirs to the bank of heaven, to an eternal inheritance, to a mansion in the golden city, to a robe and a crown. We are sons and daughters of the Most High God. Should we not honor our high calling and do all we can to save those who sit in the valley and shadow of death?

Let us not plead weakness; God will use the weak things of this world for His glory. (See 1 Corinthians 1:26–27.) When He wanted to introduce His glorious Gospel to a dying world, He did not go to the Jewish Sanhedrin and select the wise and mighty; He went along the Sea of Galilee and chose twelve ignorant men and said to them, *"Follow me, and I will make you fishers of men"* (Matt. 4:19). They started in the strength of God, setting up the kingdom of our Lord Jesus. They were led on by the Mighty Conqueror, and today He sways His scepter from the rivers to the ends of the earth.

Oh, hear the Master calling for soldiers! He says He will lead us on to victory. Oh, who will respond to the call? Who will place his name on the heavenly roll? Who will enlist in the war and help to conquer the mighty foe? Who will help to beat back the powers of darkness? He does not ask you to die, but to live forever. He will give a glorious bounty—eternal life.

Let us work for rewards. We shall be rewarded according to our work. *"They that turn many to righteousness* [shall shine] *as the stars for ever and ever"* (Dan. 12:3). We do not want to have starless crowns. Oh, let us win stars for the Master's glory.

"Blessed are they that mourn; for they shall be comforted" (Matt. 5:4). If we weep and mourn now on account of poor sinners, we shall laugh through all eternity. Oh, let us work now, and by and by our weeping will be over. We shall come rejoicing, bringing in the sheaves. We can say, "Here am I, Father, and the children Thou hast given me." (See John 17:11, 24.)

A child was dying. "Father," said she, "I have come to the river and am waiting for the ferrymen to take me over." "Does it seem dark and cold, my child?" "Oh, no, there is no darkness here! The river is covered with solid silver. The boats, they are solid light. I am not afraid of the ferrymen. Oh, I see over the river! There is a great and beautiful city, all filled with light. The angels are making music. Oh, I see the most beautiful form! He beckons me to come. Oh! I know who it is—it is blessed Jesus. He has taken me in His bosom." And thus she passed over the river of death, made like a silver stream by the presence of her Redeemer.

35

VISIONS AND TRANCES

Where there is no vision the people perish.　　　　(Proverbs 29:18)

This fact has been proven all through the Bible. When the people of God were true and faithful, the Lord made known His presence by visible signs and revealed Himself and many things to them in visions.

Then they always prospered in every way. The fear of God fell upon the heathen nations; they fled before them and cried out, *"O Lord God of Israel, there is no God like thee"* (2 Chr. 6:14); and God's cause was glorified in the earth.

But when they were backsliders and disobedient, God hid His face. There were no visions, and the people perished in every way. They went on from one sin to another, substituting form and solemn feast and the outward, and offering polluted sacrifices and trusting to human wisdom and works, instead of the power and Spirit of God.

Then He took away His Spirit and visions and signs of His presence. They were left in darkness over three hundred years, until Christ came, and then they did not know Him. They crucified the Lord of Glory and turned loose a murderer on helpless women and children. Nearly the whole Jewish nation perished. All this happened because they would not be led of the Spirit of God.

When the new and living way was ushered in, the Lord gave many visions to show that Christ had come: that the Son of God was on earth; that no one need perish; that whosoever would be born of the Spirit, Christ would come and dwell in them, and abide with them forever, and manifest and reveal Himself to them through the Holy Spirit.

The Holy Spirit would glorify Him by revealing the things of God to us and by showing us things to come.

On the Day of Pentecost when the Holy Spirit was seen, heard, and felt, thousands were brought into the spiritual kingdom of God. Peter stood up in a blaze of Holy Spirit power and glory, and said when God poured out His Spirit on His sons and daughters, they would see visions and dream dreams and prophesy. He told them that these signs would be sure to follow the outpourings of the Spirit.

The Lord said to Miriam, *"If there is a prophet among you, I, the Lord, will make myself known unto him in a vision and speak to him in a dream"* (Num. 12:6). Moses said, *"Would God that all the Lord's people were prophets, and that the Lord would put his Spirit upon them"* (Num. 11:29).

Peter said that when we have the Spirit of God, we will all prophesy. Having visions is one of the signs that we have the Spirit.

The Lord says if we are prophets, He will make Himself known to us in visions (Num. 12:6). The heathen, or Gentiles, were perishing; they knew nothing of the religion of Jesus.

God used two visions to bring about a great revival, where the whole congregation was converted and filled with the glory of God. This was the first Holy Spirit revival among the heathen. It was a sample of all that was to follow. When the people saw the visible signs of the presence of God in their midst, and He revealed Himself to them, everyone felt they were in the presence of God, and sinners came rushing to the loving arms of Christ and were saved from the awful doom that awaits the unsaved.

"Where there is no vision the people perish." Those who are opposing the demonstration of the Spirit today say we do not need these things, that we are progressing with the age, that we want an intellectual religion, that we must explain and present the Word from a human standpoint in a scientific way.

In these last days, the masses of so-called religious teachers belong to the class of whom Paul said that they have a form of godliness but deny the power. From such, turn away. They will not endure sound doctrine and will turn the people away from the truth. (See 2 Timothy 3:5–6.)

These false teachers are in a worse condition than the Jews were. They are sinning against much greater light. They are willingly blind and are teaching their followers to hide behind a refuge of lies, trusting to doctrines and traditions of men.

"In vain do they worship me" (Mark 7:7), says the Lord. The judgments of God in the most awful way are coming upon the false church.

We might say they did not need these visions in the revival at Corinth. Why didn't the Lord call all the apostles and the thousands of holy men and women who were filled with the Holy Spirit together and let them do the work? No, He was going to show them and us that it is not by human power, wisdom, or a great multitude, but by His power and Spirit that the people must be saved. They knew nothing about the great work until it was over, and the waves of salvation swept all over the country until they reached the apostles.

It was four days from the time of Cornelius' vision until Peter came with six Jewish brothers. The news of the wonderful vision, and that such a servant of God was coming to lead them to Christ, spread. They believed that God had been in their midst and was coming in great power to save. They were convinced and convicted, and left all their work and came together. They were just waiting for the kingdom of heaven to come in their hearts with power and glory.

Some say Peter did all this mighty work. God did it all through the Holy Spirit. Peter only preached one sermon. He preached that repentance and faith in a living, risen Christ would bring a present salvation and a living Christ in their hearts to abide with them forever.

The ways and wisdom of God are foolishness to the unsaved, *"but God has revealed them unto us* [His chosen ones] *by his Spirit:...yea, the deep things of God"* (1 Cor. 2:10). Oh, praise the Lord for the wisdom and knowledge, the fellowship and presence, of the Spirit who lives and walks with us continually!

Stephen was not an apostle, but he was full of faith and the Holy Spirit, and we all are commanded to be filled with the same power. He did great miracles among the people. When he so nobly defended the risen Christ, fearless of losing his life, his false accusers looked on his face and said it looked like the face of an angel.

The pure Gospel, accompanied by the power of the Holy Spirit, cut the religious hierarchy to the heart. They would not accept it, and they gnashed upon him with their teeth (Acts 7:54).

> *But he, being full of the Holy Ghost, looked up stedfastly into heaven and saw the glory of God, and Jesus standing on the right hand of God. And said, Behold, I see the heavens opened and the Son of man standing at the right hand of God.* (Acts 7:55–56)

Saul, who was one of the best scholars of his day and had a polished form of religion, would not believe in or accept visions or visible demonstrations of the power of God; so when he saw the glory of God and heard Stephen tell the wonderful vision he had seen, when the howling mob gathered around, Saul helped them on and consented to his death.

Now the great persecution commenced. Saul, like a blood-hound who had got the smell of blood, followed the trail, filling the prisons and putting the saints to death (Acts 8:3; 26:10–11).

While on his way to Damascus to take the saints from prison to put them to death, about noon, when the sun was shining in all its strength, this man who did not believe in the visible power of God, said he saw a light from heaven above the brightness of the sun, *"shining round about me and them which journeyed with me"* (Acts 26:13).

He and all of his party were struck to the earth as dead men. There was no loud praying or singing or religious excitement to put these strong men in that condition. God had sent a shock from the battery of heaven.

Saul, who had hated demonstrations of the Spirit, saw at once he was lost and on the way to hell. While lying under the power of the Holy Spirit, the Lord showed him that he must preach the Gospel and that wherever he went he must tell about all he had seen and heard and things that the Lord would show to him in the future. Jesus appeared to him then and talked to him face-to-face, and many times after in vision.

The Lord used three visions to bring about the conversion of Saul, one of the brightest scholars of the Jewish church. He was under deep conviction, neither ate nor drank for three days and nights. He counted the cost. When he accepted Christ, he was filled with the Holy Spirit. The first thing he did was to preach a living Christ and to throw open the prisons and stop the awful persecution and show the despised followers of Jesus that he was their friend and brother. The churches all had rest, and the waves of salvation swept over all the land.

See the glorious results to the church and the world, all brought about by three visions.

"Where there is no vision the people perish."

Paul never doubted the power of God nor any demonstration. He knew more about the personality of the Holy Spirit and His many offices, gifts, visions, revelations, diverse operations, leadings, teachings, and power, and he taught more about these things than all the rest of the apostles. He proved clearly that all this power would be for the people of God forever.

The book of Revelation is the most wonderful of all in the Bible. Christ appeared to John in person and gave him one vision after another. He showed him the heavenly city, the great city, the city of gold, and the jasper walls. The city lies four square—fifteen hundred miles high, as long and wide as it was high. He was told about the climate, the inhabitants, and their occupation. He had visions of the Great Judgment Day, of the lake of fire and brimstone, and of all the lost that were swept into it. The Lord told him to write all that he saw and heard and show it to the churches, and they were to show it to the world.

The prophet said the time would come when, if anyone had a vision, he would be ashamed to tell it; that parents would renounce their prophetic children. (See Zechariah 13:3–5.) That time is here. The masses of church leaders look upon everything supernatural as a disgrace and cry out, "Hypnotism, excitement, drunkenness," or some other power. Just like the Jews, progressing with the age, they are satisfied with dead form.

The churches are filled with unconverted people. *"Where there [are] no vision[s] the people perish."* If there is not power enough for visions, there is not enough to save a soul.

The gift of visions was especially promised in the last days:

And it shall come to pass in the last days, saith God, I will pour out my Spirit upon all flesh: and your sons and your daughters shall prophesy, and your young men shall see visions, and your old men shall dream dreams; And on my servants and on my handmaidens I will pour out in those days of my Spirit; and they shall prophesy. (Acts 2:17–18)

Thank the Lord, those days are here, and God is revealing Himself to those who come to Him in the right way in special gifts, in healing all manner of diseases, in all the fullness of the Holy Spirit power. Hundreds are having wonderful visions, and wherever these signs follow the Word, all classes flock to Christ.

Dr. Talmage went into the Brooklyn Tabernacle one Sunday morning and said to his congregation: "I have been to heaven; I have just got back and will tell you what I saw." The first one he met in heaven was his mother, who had been dead thirty-two years. He knew her and talked to her. He saw many he knew while here on earth, and many were made known to him whom he had never known. He saw white horses hitched to golden chariots standing at the doors of mansions and others driving through the streets.

Many noted men and women, and all classes of the children of God, are bringing messages from heaven to earth. These things, with many other signs of the times, show us the Lord is coming soon for His saints and to punish a lost world. The Lord help those who profess to love Him to have enough of His Spirit and to know the power of God!

"Where there [are] no vision[s] the people perish."

Paul said that while he was praying in the temple, he fell into a trance (Acts 22:17). Paul also said he would come to revelations and visions of the Lord. He was carried away to the third heaven. Whether in the body or out of the body he could not tell, but God knew. He heard and saw wonderful things. (See 2 Corinthians 12:1–4.)

That was a wonderful experience. He could not tell whether he was carried away soul and body, or whether his spirit left the body for a while. But he was conscious of being carried away and knew it was the power of God. Paul said when the church came together, if anyone had a revelation, to tell it (1 Cor. 14:26).

36

THE SECOND COMING
OF CHRIST

For this we say unto you by the Word of the Lord, that we which are alive and remain unto the coming of the Lord shall not precede them which are asleep. For the Lord himself shall descend from heaven with a shout, with the voice of the archangel, and with the trump of God; and the dead in Christ shall rise first. Then we which are alive and remain shall be caught up together with them in the clouds, to meet the Lord in the air; and so shall we ever be with the Lord. (1 Thess. 4:15–17)

The Lord Jesus shall be revealed from heaven with his mighty angels. In flaming fire taking vengeance on them that know not God, and that obey not the Gospel of our Lord Jesus Christ. Who shall be punished with everlasting destruction from the presence of the Lord, and from the glory of his power. (2 Thess. 1:7–9)

But the rest of the dead lived not again until the thousand years were finished. This is the first resurrection. (Rev. 20:5)

And then shall all the tribes of the earth mourn and they shall see the Son of man coming in the clouds of heaven with power and great glory.

(Matt. 24:30)

But when ye shall see the abomination of desolation, spoken of by Daniel the prophet, standing where it ought not, (let him that readeth understand).

(Mark 13:14)

Blessed and holy is he that hath part in the first resurrection; on such the second hath no power, but they shall be priests of God and of Christ, and shall reign with him a thousand years.

(Rev. 20:6)

The subject of the Resurrection is grand and glorious to contemplate; it should be taught and explained in all our churches; it is the hope of the church; it was the theme of prophets' and apostles' preaching.

The Resurrection and Atonement are the keynotes of the New Testament.

We believe we are living in the last days, that the coming of the Lord draws near.

Wars and Rumors of Wars

A prophetic conference met in New York in November, 1878. There were one hundred and forty bishops and ministers from the different states and across the waters to compare the prophecies referring to the coming of Christ. They concluded that Daniel's "seventy weeks" had about expired.

Daniel spoke of many things that the angel revealed to him that should take place before the coming of Christ that have already come to pass. He spoke of the loss of life and property by fire and floods. Whole towns have been swept away; thousands and thousands of families have been left homeless and without a penny by these destroying elements. The last year was called the black year, aptly named because over two hundred thousand were swept into eternity by accidents and pestilence and over one hundred thousand were swallowed up in a terrible earthquake. *"So likewise ye, when ye shall see all these things, know that it is near, even at the doors"* (Matt. 24:33).

And as he sat upon the mount of Olives, the disciples came unto him privately, saying, Tell us, when shall these things be? and what shall be the sign of thy coming, and of the end of the world? And Jesus answered and said unto them, Take heed that no man deceive you. For many shall come in my name, saying, I am Christ; and shall deceive many. (Matt. 24:3–5)

It is said there are thirty-two persons in the world today claiming to be the Christ and each of these have a large following. Perhaps the most notable of them all is a Persian, Abdul Baha, whose home is in the Valley of Akka, and who is the founder of the Baha'i Movement, a false system of religion which has spread over the United States during the past few years and which has caused many of our best educated and cultured men and women to worship at his shrine.

Some of our wealthiest people in New York and Boston have made special trips to Persia for the sole purpose of obtaining an interview with this false Christ, and they have brought back to the United States teachers and followers of this cult and have furnished the means for promulgating the creed until the Baha'i Movement has swept across our country, and today is to be found in all of the larger cities, and has a following of twelve million people.

"And ye shall hear of wars and rumors of wars: see that ye be not troubled: for all these things must come to pass" (Matt. 24:6).

From the time of our own Civil War, which drenched our land in blood, almost every country has been plunged into the horrors of war. The great conflict between China and Japan in 1895 was followed by the Spanish-American War in 1898. Scarcely had the war-clouds between us and Spain rolled away, when the world was reading the details of another bloody strife, this time between Great Britain and the Boers, and for three years South Africa was deluged in awful carnage.

Just two years later occurred the Russo-Japanese War, which was the bloodiest of all recent conflicts. (Preached years since.)

When we realize that within the past twelve years, eight of the great nations of the earth have been engaged in the awful holocaust of war, and that each conflict has increased in intensity and loss of life, one is made to ask with deepest solemnity: What will the end be? (Think of conditions *now* in 1916.)

The powers of the world today are outwardly at peace, but more than once the rumblings of war have been heard on the Eastern continent and might have broken forth, except for the fact that strong internal forces of revolution are at work in Russia, Turkey, and China. Communism, nihilism, and socialism are threatening the foundations of the strongest thrones, and not a crowned head today is safe from the assassin's bullet.

For nation shall rise against nation, and kingdom against kingdom: and there shall be famines, and pestilences, and earthquakes in divers places. All these are the beginning of sorrows. (Matt. 24:7–8)

Earthquakes

"There shall be...earthquakes in divers places" (v. 7). On the subject of earthquakes, we find that during the past twenty-five years practically every country has been visited one or more times by a great convulsion of nature, and those that have been disastrous to life and property have been increasing at an alarming rate.

In 1899 six villages were destroyed and seven others damaged by an earthquake in Russia, in which one thousand people lost their lives. In the same year in Asia Minor, over sixteen hundred deaths occurred from the same cause, while many others were injured.

Most of us can recall the earthquake in South Carolina in which three-fourths of the city of Charleston was destroyed and about one hundred people perished. This same seismic disturbance traveled across the Atlantic and visited France and Italy, with two thousand people perishing in the latter country.

Let me give you the awful destruction of life and property through earthquakes and volcanic eruptions for just one year, 1892: In Turkestan, there were ten thousand deaths and fifteen thousand houses destroyed; and at another time during the same year, there were nearly seven hundred deaths and one thousand injured. On the Island of St. Vincent, two thousand people perished through a volcanic eruption. We all remember quite vividly the eruption of Mount Pelee, which resulted in the destruction of Martinique, where two thousand people were swept into eternity, and large numbers injured. And all this in one year! What an awful record!

In the first three years of the present century, there were forty-eight earthquakes. Allowing the same number for each successive three years, should the world remain, we would have the amazing record of sixteen hundred earthquakes for this century.

The chariots shall be with flaming torches in the day of his preparation....The chariots shall rage in the streets, they shall jostle one against another in the broad ways; they shall seem like torches, they shall run like the lightnings.

(Nah. 2:3–4)

Automobiles—we have had them now for almost fifteen years, and we become so familiar with these big, awkward chariots with their immense lights constantly passing to and fro in our streets, jostling one against another and running like lightning, that we have forgotten that they are only another fulfillment of God's prophecy for the last days. *"Shut up the words and seal the book, even until the time of the end: many shall run to and fro, and knowledge shall be increased"* (Dan. 12:4).

Today, when an event of any note occurs, it is flashed around the world in thirty minutes, so we can readily see the wonderful strides knowledge has made within the past few years, thus fulfilling Daniel's prophetic vision.

The first steam locomotive ever seen in the old Garden of Eden is today puffing noisily back and forth, hauling material to construct a mighty dam, which shall create a new channel for the river Euphrates, and thereby irrigate Mesopotamia, the land originally given to Abraham, and which is today being resettled through the Zionistic Society.

And Knowledge Shall Be Increased

When we stop to consider that we have gone from ox carts to flying machines in one generation, and that we have gone from no means of communication except letter and stagecoach to the immense public press, the telephone, and telegraph with their ceaseless streams of news and information, and which cover the earth with their ever increasing circulation like falling leaves from some mighty tree of knowledge, we can readily see the fulfillment of Daniel's prophecy.

Air Ships

The air ships of today that are to be seen flying about the country in different nations are another sign of the last days. The prophet Isaiah looked down through the centuries and saw the air ships of these last days and was made to inquire, *"Who are these that fly as a cloud and as the doves to their windows?"* (Isa. 60:8).

The angel told Daniel to seal up these prophecies until the time of the end, in the day of his preparation. The signs of the coming of Christ, spoken of by Daniel, Nahum, and others, have been sealed through all ages until the last fifty years.

Today the cars run over and under the river. *"The gates of the rivers shall be opened"* (Nah. 2:6). *"The chariots shall rage in the streets, they shall jostle one against another in the broad ways"* (v. 4). The Lord said: *"When ye see these things come to pass, know ye that the kingdom of God is nigh at hand. Verily I say unto you, This generation shall not pass away, till all be fulfilled"* (Luke 21:31–32).

These chariots or coaches should run in the day of His preparation. (See Nahum 2:3–5.) These things are to take place in the end of the harvest, the time we are now living in, when the last call is being given, the summons just before the Gentile age closes. These cars were not to run over all the land, but they were to reach Jerusalem, and the Jews were to see these signs of His preparation in Palestine, to enable them to know the end of the dispensation and the coming of Christ was near. The cars are now running from Joppa to Jerusalem. The electric cars are also said to be running there, and sewerage and all modern improvements are now seen. Every car or train that passes there is speaking to them, and to us, in tones of thunder, as a warning voice from God saying, "The harvest will soon be passed and the summer ended. The preparation days are closing. Christ is coming; go out to meet Him."

Jesus cursed the fig tree and the Jewish nation in Palestine. The rain and dew were taken away from the land; it became a barren waste and has been for two thousand years. The Lord told them when they, the Jews, or anyone, would see the fig tree again bearing, and the latter rains and dew in Palestine, they would know the coming of the Son of man was near, even at their door.

Dear readers, these signs are seen today by all who visit the Holy Land. For several years God has been sending the rains and dew, the fig trees are bearing, and many other kinds of fruit. The flowers are blooming. The Jews are going back by the thousands. This is one of the strongest signs. Oh, praise the Lord that we are living in the close of this last generation and are permitted to give the household of faith their portion in this, His due season! At this same time He promised to pour out His Spirit and give us the rains of spiritual power; that Christ, the Chief Reaper, would be with us in a cloud of glory and the Holy Spirit power to reap the harvest and gather in the wheat. Thank God we will have the pleasure of being one of the reapers.

He says to us, *"Watch ye therefore, and pray always, that ye may be accounted worthy to escape all these things that shall come to pass, and to stand before the Son of man"* (Luke 21:36).

The angels who are now holding back the powers of darkness will soon be commanded to let loose the four winds of God's wrath. This awful time of trouble will last some years. We think about three and one-half years. Then Christ will come back with His bride to begin the millennium reign of one thousand years, when the Jews will accept Christ.

"The residue of men might seek after the Lord" (Acts 15:17). The judgments will last one thousand years. One day with the Lord is as a thousand years. The six days are about passed, or six thousand years. The last or seventh is now about coming in. The saints will sit with Christ to judge the nations and angels all through this Judgment Day. *"Do ye not know that the saints shall judge the world?"* (Acts 15:17). The Lord is preparing His little flock now for this work. Reader, will you be among that number?

Jesus, in speaking of the signs of the last days, said:

Behold the fig tree, and all the trees; when they now shoot forth, ye see and know of your own selves that summer is now nigh at hand. So likewise ye, when ye see these things come to pass, know ye that the kingdom of God is nigh at hand. (Luke 21:29–31)

And this gospel of the kingdom shall be preached in all the world for a witness unto all nations; and then shall the end come. (Matt. 24:14)

Our missionaries tell us the Gospel has been sent into all the habitable parts of the earth, so today the power of the holy people is scattered over the earth. In every nation and kindred, tribe and tongue, there are those who are witnesses that Jesus has power on earth to forgive sins. So today the knowledge of the Lord covers the whole earth—a theoretical knowledge at least.

The Lion of the tribe of Judah has prevailed. The Mighty Conqueror is marching on from one victory to another. Today He wields His scepter *"from the river unto the ends of the earth"* (Ps. 72:8). Today He is reigning in the hearts of His people all over our land.

Beloved in the Lord, cheer up; the end, and your redemption, draws near, much nearer than when we first believed. Some, even ministers, pray for the time to hasten when the whole world will be converted. That is contrary to the teachings of the Word of God. Jesus said the people will wax worse and worse and do more wickedly. As in the days of Noah, they ate, drank, married, and went on in their wickedness, until the very day that the floods came and swept them all away; as in the days of Lot, they bought and sold, built and mocked at God's messengers, and although God sent angels to warn them, only eight were saved from the storm of fire and brimstone; so it shall be at the coming of the Son of Man (Luke 17:26–30).

Jesus said that time will not come except there will be a falling away in the churches. False teachers will rise up, *"having the form of godliness, but denying the power thereof: from such turn away"* (2 Tim. 3:5). There are hundreds of such teachers today. They are blind leaders of the blind. They are going down to hell together. This is a visible sign of the coming of Christ.

Since the last war, our churches have been decreasing in spiritual power and growing rich in fine houses, swelling the membership, but making little effort to get the people converted, taking in members without conversion—dead weights.

Jesus will send His angels to gather the wheat from the tares; God help us, dear friends, to be among the wheat.

"The sun shall be darkened, and the moon shall not give her light, and the stars of heaven shall fall" (Mark 13:24–25). These signs have been remarkably fulfilled. Thousands are living who saw the grand display of celestial fireworks, when the heavens and earth were covered with fireballs; people thought the Day of Judgment had come; a wonderful excitement prevailed; men, women, and children were crying for mercy; some took their own lives, and others became insane.

Many remember when the sun was darkened, it began to grow dark at ten, and at twelve it was so dark the lanterns were lit, the fowls went to roost, the frogs began to peep, the cattle came lowing into the barnyards, the moon was full, yet it was so dark one could not discern white paper from black velvet, and it lasted fourteen hours. *"Verily I say unto you, This generation shall not pass away, till all be fulfilled"* (Luke 21:32). This generation that has seen all these things shall live to see Christ coming; every prophecy is being fulfilled except those that shall take place at His coming.

Also, in a spiritual sense, the Sun of righteousness has gone down, or out of, most of all the churches. The moonlight is very pale; black, spiritual darkness is settling down all over the land; it is so thick that it can be felt. The old Serpent is dragging down many bright lights or stars.

Many bright lights are going out in awful darkness. We see those who seemed to be the best established, whom we thought would suffer almost anything for Christ's honor and glory, compromising with those who have no power, only a form. *"From such,"* the Lord said, *"turn away"* (2 Tim. 3:5). Many others go off in fanaticism, accepting delusions, that they might be damned. There never was such a time.

Fanatical teachers are swarming like bees in the large cities and going about to every place deceiving and being deceived, and if it were possible, they would deceive the very elect.

The perilous times are here. They will not endure the faith of the glorious Gospel of our Christ. Neither will they tolerate it much longer; they try to crush it out in every way.

The Lord said to work while it is day, for the night will come when no man can work (John 9:4). *"Having done all...stand"* (Eph. 6:13).

We are going through that time now, the spiritual famine is on us, but the Lord said He would sustain us in that time and care for those that trust Him.

We see the Laodicean church is being spewed out of His mouth. His Spirit is withdrawn from them; the next call will be to judgment.

Most of the salt of the professors of religion has lost its saving qualities. It is only a little flock that is holding the angels in check, and the world from awful rack and ruin. The servants of God will all soon be sealed, then the Lord will take His bride, the lights of the world, out. She is as fair as the morn, as bright as the sun, and as terrible as an army with banners.

Christ is a perfect Savior; He came to restore all that was lost in Adam's fall. When Adam fell, he lost his holy nature; sickness and death came to the body. If Christ could not restore soul and body, he would not be a perfect Savior. The believer's soul is made perfect in this life, pure and white; the body will be subject to disease until the coming of Christ.

At the Crucifixion of Christ, "*the graves were opened; and many bodies of the saints which slept arose, and came out of the graves after his resurrection, and went into the holy city, and appeared unto many*" (Matt. 27:52–53).

Paul wrote, "[He] *shall change our vile body, that it may be fashioned like unto his glorious body*" (Phil. 3:21). The last enemy that Christ will conquer is death; the time is coming when those who are in their graves shall hear His voice "*and shall come forth; they that have done good, unto the resurrection of life; and they that have done evil, unto the resurrection of damnation*" (John 5:29) in the image of the devil, their father.

Elijah went to heaven in a golden chariot, soul and body. Enoch went up in a whirlwind. Christ took the same body to heaven that was nailed to the cross and was laid in the grave.

Paul spoke of being perfect in one sense and not in another: he was already perfect in heart, but, "*if by any means I might attain unto the resurrection of the dead*" (Phil. 3:11), when he would be perfect, his soul and body united. When the saints are "*clothed upon*" (2 Cor. 5:4) with immortality, then they will shout victory over death, hell, and the grave.

When He says, "*Surely I come quickly,*" He expects to hear a hearty response from everyone who is true to Him, "*Even so, come, Lord Jesus*" (Rev. 22:20). God's true children are ready, watching morning, noon, and night for the coming of the Bridegroom, in the hour of death or in the clouds; they have lamps trimmed and burning; they are making every effort to gather in their friends and neighbors, before the storm of God's wrath bursts in awful fury on a lost and ruined world.

Soon the herald will shout, "*Behold, the bridegroom cometh; go ye out to meet him*" (Matt. 25:6). What a sight will burst on our enraptured vision as we see the King of Heaven coming! The Bridegroom, in His royal robes, with all the glory of the heavenly world and His golden chariot, with all the shining angels to escort the bride, the Lamb's wife to the golden city, the New Jerusalem, with the spirits of the saints coming back for their bodies. Oh, grave, give us our bodies! The Mighty Conqueror unlocks the grave, and, with a shout that penetrates the caverns of the sainted dead, the graves fly open, the sleeping saints come forth from dusty beds, set free from all the effects of sin. Old age, gray hairs, withered limbs, deformities, death, disease, are all the effects of sin. Jesus came to save us from the curse of sin, to restore all that was lost by the Fall.

Jesus died in the prime of life, in the strength and vigor of manhood. We will be like Him; these vile bodies shall be changed and made like unto the glorious

Son of God (Phil. 3:21), not that we shall be unclothed, but clothed upon with immortality (2 Cor. 5:4).

Oh, what a happy meeting that will be! Whole families and friends will rise up from the old churchyards and clasp each other in a long embrace, which will last forever; mothers and children shall meet, husbands and wives, brothers and sisters, friends and neighbors, pastors and flocks.

Those who are alive will be changed in a moment, set free from the effects of sin, and be clothed with the glory of heaven. Then a mighty shout of victory will go up from the millions of saints: *"Oh death, where is thy sting? Oh grave, where is thy victory?...But thanks be to God, which giveth us the victory* [over death, hell, and the grave] *through our Lord Jesus Christ"* (1 Cor. 15:55, 57).

Oh, the Rapture, as we shall march through the streets of pure gold! We shall raise our voices, which shall sound like rushing waters, like mighty thunders, in singing glory to the Lamb, unto him who has bought us and *"loved us and washed us from our sins in His own blood"* (Rev. 1:5). With harps and palm boughs in our hands and crowns on our heads—Jesus will place the shining crowns with His own hands upon our heads—then we shall march through the streets of the city, with all the music of the hosts of heaven, saying, *"Alleluia: for the Lord God omnipotent reigneth. Let us be glad and rejoice and give honour to him: for the marriage of the Lamb is come, and his wife hath made herself ready"* (Rev. 19:6–7).

Jesus will lead us to the Great White Throne and say, "Father, 'behold I and the children which [thou] hath given me' " (Heb. 2:13). We will prostrate ourselves before the throne and cast our crowns at His feet saying, *"Holy, holy, holy, is the Lord of hosts"* (Isa. 6:3). *"Worthy is the Lamb that was slain to receive power, and riches, and wisdom, and strength, and honour, and glory, and blessing"* (Rev. 5:12).

We shall all sit down to the marriage supper of the Lamb. Oh, what a company—apostles, martyrs, fathers, mothers, children, friends and neighbors, brothers and sisters in the Lord, ministers and converts! Oh, what a reunion, what a gathering that will be, as we look along the table at the bright and shining faces! Then to behold the dear Savior smiling on His children! Dear friends, will you be there?

37

PREPARE FOR WAR: MARSHALING OF THE NATIONS

For, behold, in those days, and in that time, when I shall bring again the captivity of Judah and Jerusalem, I will also gather all nations, and will bring them into the Valley of Jehoshaphat....Proclaim ye this among the Gentiles; prepare for war, wake up the mighty men, let all the men of war draw near; let them come up: beat your plowshares into swords, and your pruning hooks into spears: let the weak say, I am strong (Joel 3:1–2, 9–10)

But in the last days it shall come to pass, that the mountain of the house of the LORD shall be established on the top of the mountains, and it shall be exalted above the hills; and people shall flow into it. And many nations shall come, and say Come, and let us go up to the mountain of the LORD, and to the house of the God of Jacob; and he will teach us of his ways, and we will walk in his paths; for the law shall go forth of Zion, and the word of the LORD from Jerusalem. And he shall judge among many people, and rebuke strong nations afar off; and they shall beat their swords into plowshares, and their spears into

236

pruning hooks: nation shall not lift up a sword against nation, neither shall they learn war any more. But they shall sit every man under his vine and his fig tree; and none shall make them afraid: for the mouth of the LORD of hosts hath spoken it. (Mic. 4:1–4)

These two quotations from Joel and Micah sound a little contradictory. I have heard people say so. But the statements refer to two different parties and times.

The first, *"Beat your plowshares into swords, and your pruning hooks into spears,"* means, "Get ready for battle," and it refers to this present time, a time of war.

The second, *"Beat your swords into plowshares, and your spears into pruning hooks,"* means, "Get ready for a time of great farming."

The one calls us to prepare for the greatest battle the world has ever heard of; the other refers to the time when war shall be no more.

The first text in this chapter, *"Prepare for war, wake up the mighty men, let all the men of war draw near* [let the nations gather together for battle]" refers to this time of the end that we are now living in, when the Gentile time is full or closing.

You see the awful slaughter, massacre, deadly hatred, causing them to kill and destroy each other. God has risen up like a mighty Man of war. He will roar and shout out from Jerusalem until all nations are gathered in deadly combat, until the blood flows like a river.

In the text in Joel, the call is primarily to the Holy Land, where the great battle of God Almighty will be fought. The battle of the great Day of God while the angel is standing in the sun, calling all the fowls of the air to come to the supper of the Great God, to eat the flesh of all the mighty men, the great men of the world, and the rich men. They are invited to eat and drink the blood and get fat on the flesh, on the carcasses of kings and princes of the world, who will soon fall in the notable Day of the Lord.

The Lord will awake and shout out as a Man of war. He will roar out of Zion and will utter His voice from Jerusalem. The heavens will shake and the earth, when the nations are gathering for this great battle with the Lamb and His army from heaven.

John wrote,

I saw heaven opened, and behold a white horse; and he that sat upon him.... His eyes were as a flame of fire, and on his head were many crowns....He was clothed in a vesture dipped in blood. ...The armies which were in heaven followed Him on white horses, clothed in white linen, white and clean.

(Rev. 19:11–14)

Oh, praise the Lord! The saints have been translated to heaven. The marriage of the Lamb and His bride has taken place, with shouting and hallelujahs that have shaken all heaven and earth. The great marriage supper, with all its grandeur and glory and greatness is over. And they have been with the Lord executing judgments on the earth during the awful Tribulation.

Now the cup of wickedness is full. They have defied the God of heaven long enough. He has stood up in His wrath. All nations of the earth are gathering to the Valley of Jehoshaphat.

The Lord of Lords and King of Kings, with all His armies of heaven, comes riding in triumph, down through the skies. Enoch saw the Lord coming with ten thousand of His saints. The Antichrist has gathered his army and is about to destroy God's children. They will gather all their armies together against Jerusalem to fight, but then the Lord comes from heaven and fights this great battle. The saints do not have to fight: the Lord Himself does the fighting.

Then the millennial kingdom is set up, and Satan will be chained for a thousand years. During that time, the curse and its effects, including all weeds, thistles, and whatever would produce disease, etc., have been taken away. "*They shall not hurt nor destroy in all my holy mountain*" (Isa. 11:9). The time is coming when they shall cease to make war, and the devil is taken out of the hearts of the people.

Today they are just like wild beasts thirsting for each others' blood. They are burying the living and the dead together. Pestilence also has already began its deadly havoc.

Did you ever hear of a great war breaking out so quickly? For years past the most talented men have been inventing to see who could get the most deadly weapons.

God has been holding back the tidal waves and the other destructive forces. His angel has shouted back, "Wait until the servants of God are sealed with the seal of God."

The division of the book of Joel into chapters is bad. The first verses of the third chapter are a continuation of the last verses of the second chapter and should not be divided from them. *"It shall come to pass afterward, that I will pour out my spirit"* (Joel 2:28), baptize with the Holy Spirit, and scatter the power of the holy people.

God says, "I will rise up in My wrath in that day. When My judgments are in the earth, some will repent. In the last days I will pour out My Spirit." God says, "Wake up the heathen." God is sealing His saints, but that sealing time is pretty nearly over.

That they speak in new tongues is a sign that the Lord is coming.

The power of *"the sheep* [holy people] *shall be scattered"* (Mark 14:27). These are they who are clay in the Potter's hand. They are just clay, having no control of themselves at all. God Almighty speaks through them, *"With stammering lips and another tongue will he speak to this people"* (Isa. 28:11).

Proclaim and tell it to the people. Blow the trumpet. Sound the alarm in the holy mountain. What is the danger? The Day of the Lord is coming; it is near at hand.

God's people are blowing the trumpet. They are sounding the alarm in Zion. What is the signal of danger? The great Day of the Lord is near.

It is time for the saints to get this knowledge if they do not already know it. How can we give the signal if we do not know? How could we warn the people of danger?

If they escape when the sword is coming, good. But warn them anyhow. If we do not warn them, their blood will be on our hands. Wake up the heathen. Call up your mighty men. Call the soldiers into line. Get them ready. Get the weapons of war ready for the world's great conflict. There never has been anything like it, nor ever will be again.

There will be a scarcity of steel. They cannot make enough of it. The nations are all the time building new warships and manufacturing so many deadly weapons. It takes a good deal of steel to make these warships, such monster vessels. Each nation is trying to build the largest ships and invent the most deadly weapons.

Still, they are crying, *"Peace, peace; when there is no peace"* (Jer. 6:14). Right in the midst of this false peace and security, death and war and destruction have come like a whirlwind.

There is a lack of steel. Where are they going to get it? Pretty soon they will not be able to meet the demand for it. Then men will be hunting around in the farmyards, old barns, stables, and sheds, everywhere for old plowshares and pruning hooks for everything that they can beat into swords and spears to kill their neighbors with.

The time is coming in this glorious America when parties and factions will rise up—labor against capital, and other parties and factions. There will be no safety to him who goes out or goes in. And at that time they will not be able to buy or sell unless they have the mark of the beast. It will be death, and to have the mark of the beast will mean the second death. There will be no safety or hiding place to him who goes out or in: *"As if a man did flee from a lion, and a bear met him; or went into the house, and leaned his hand on the wall, and a serpent bit him"* (Amos 5:19).

It is implied that the land will be infested with poisonous serpents, reptiles, and insects, and they will be turned loose among the people, with their deadly power to bite, sting, and destroy.

So, if you run away from the sword and pestilence and try to hide in the house, you will lay your hand on the wall and be bitten by a deadly serpent. There will be no safety to him who goes in or out.

There will be awful, deadly hatred among the people, and they will be banded together hand in hand, and they will make weapons of steel with which to kill and destroy one another.

I read not long ago that the powers were crying out because of the scarcity of steel. Your neighbor will be hunting round for a piece of old steel to kill his neighbor with.

In Europe now they are calling out young men and boys to fight and to be destroyed.

It is time to wake up from the sleep of death and call on God to give you life.

According to the Word of God and the signs of the times, we are now living in the commencement of these awful times, when many who read these lines will see a great deal more than I have written. You and your children will go down in death or go through this dreadful time of trouble such as never has been nor ever will be again.

Many of the best Bible students say that the eleventh chapter of Daniel refers to the Sultan, or ruling powers of Turkey: *"He shall plant the tabernacles of his palace between the seas in the glorious holy mountain; yet he shall come to his end, and none shall help him"* (Dan. 11:45).

And they think that the book of Obadiah also refers to him.

The passage in Daniel does not refer to the Antichrist, for he will not be revealed or take his power until after the hinderer is taken away, until Christ takes out a people for His name from among the Gentiles, until He comes and takes His bride.

He will come to his end in the time of the end; and at that time Michael, the great prince, will stand up for his people; and all will be delivered whose names are written in the Book of Life, and the wise, who know these things, will shine as the brightness of the firmament.

The way the war is raging against Turkey, it looks as if she might lose her capital, Constantinople, and be compelled to leave her headquarters almost any day. How natural it would be for her to transfer her government to the Holy Land, of which she still has control, in haste; she could occupy almost any building for that purpose.

It is reported that the Turks are building a large palace, or building, and they are keeping it quiet and will not tell anyone what it is for.

"He shall plant the tabernacles of his palace between the seas, in the glorious holy mountain; yet he shall come to his end and none shall help him."

But he will not stay there very long; little by little, he will go down until he is entirely destroyed.

The Holy Land was to be trodden down by the Gentiles until the time of the end. Then and at that time, Christ will come. The Jews will flock to Jerusalem and again possess the Holy Land.

Most of those that have gone through the Tribulation will have had enough, and they will be ready to listen to the voice of that prophet.

If the angels are loosed, it will not be long before we take our flight. When these things begin to come fast, we will soon be taken out of the world. The worst trouble will come after the saints are taken out. The Antichrist will deny the blessed Christ and cause people to take his mark or to be put to death. Those who do not go with Christ will have to go through this or go down in it.

Jesus comes to take a people out for His name, for His bride. He comes and takes her away to the heavens. The great marriage supper takes place, after which they will be sitting with Christ on His throne and helping to execute judgment during this awful Tribulation.

Look at the awful death and carnage and destruction if you do not go up with the bridal company.

Those who go up when Christ comes are the Lamb's bride. He returns to build up the waste places of Jerusalem. All the soil will be fertile then, and the people will not need to do much work. It will be like a holy camp meeting all the time during the millennial age.

The first time Jesus comes, none see Him but the bride. The world hates her and cares nothing for her, and Jesus is going to take her away.

Christ will come as quickly as the lightning flashes from the East to the West; just that quick He will snatch His bridal company away while the world sleeps in a drunken stupor.

But the next time He comes, all will know it. *"Every knee shall bow to me, and every tongue shall confess to God"* (Rom. 14:11). Every eye will see Him, and every slanderous tongue will have to confess before the world that these were God's chosen vessels.

This honor belongs to the saints. They will have to confess that we were right and that they were wrong. God is very proud of His bride. Children of God now deny themselves many of the things of the world, but we are heirs of the kingdom, though many of us are poor in this world and having hard times. There is going to be a change in this old world. God is calling you to behold. Don't go a step further. Don't step over the mangled body of Christ any more, or it may be the last time.

The first time the bride will be caught away; the second time she will come riding on white horses. Jesus will stand on Mount Olivet, and they who pierced Him will see Him. You know now down in your hearts that Jesus is the Christ, that we are people in earnest, that we hear something more than natural men hear. That wisdom we get from God who gives liberally. That has been my prayer more than anything else, "Give me wisdom." Almost a blind man can see if he looks at the signs of the times.

Daniel says the wise shall know when the Lord comes.

You may say, "I don't believe." You don't want to believe, and that day will overtake you as a thief in the night. None of the wicked will understand the signs of Jesus' coming. You who are children of the light will know and that day will not overtake you unexpectedly. God gave Daniel a picture of the lost world, none of whom should know when He comes.

Who are the wise? Those who know the time of the Lord's coming. *"They that be wise shall shine as the brightness of the firmament; and they that turn many to righteousness as the stars for ever and ever"* (Dan. 12:3).

Don't be looking to the grave. Look, for behold He comes. Oh, glory to God in the highest! Come, O Redeemer, come quickly.

Addenda

World's Great War Tragedy Is Filled with Bloody Scenes

"Every man in a French force penetrating Ft. Douaumont was killed in a German charge.

"Men are fighting in dark, underground tunnels, using hand searchlights and knives and bombs.

"Hundreds of French and Germans have been buried alive in the wrecking of underground works by shell fire.

"Scores have gone insane from the lust of the horrible butchery.

"Surgeons, amputating arms and legs without anesthetics, report wounded French and Germans continuing the struggle with knives though unable to stand.

"A French captain reported 7,000 dead heaped along a 700-yard front."

—Extract from *Daily Paper*, U.S.A., 1916

May, 1916

"Preparedness" the Cry of the Hour in New York

The civilians in the mammoth preparedness demonstration in New York last Saturday are shown passing the New York Public Library. An idea of its magnitude may be gained when it is remembered that the marching columns composed of twenty men abreast extended for twenty miles.

Marshaling of the Nations

"By common consent, the European war was written down from its very beginning as the greatest titanic struggle ever waged by man; such a marshaling of the nations was never before seen on earth.

"After eighteen months' conflict, President Wilson said in an address at Cleveland, Ohio, January 29, 1916: 'While a year ago it seemed impossible that a struggle upon such a large scale should last a whole year, it has now lasted a year and a half, and the end is not yet in sight.'"

—*Washington Post*, January 30, 1916

The Toll of War

"The blackest eighteen months known to the modern world! The net result has been 2,990,000 men in the very prime of life killed, more than 2,200,000 made prisoners, and more than 9,830,000 wounded."

—*International News Service*

"'So over the whole world is heard the sound of the trumpet and of the alarm of war, and two-thirds of the world is at war. I know that daily we are treading amidst the most intricate dangers, that the world is on fire and sparks are likely to drop anywhere,' President Wilson said."

—*Washington Post*, January 30, 1916

This time is foretold in the prophecies of Joel 3:9, 14; Revelation 11:18; Jeremiah 25, 31:33. Two things are plainly seen in these Scriptures. First, that when the Day of the Lord is near, the nations of the world will be making gigantic preparations for war.

"Prepare war, wake up the mighty men, let all the men of war draw near; let them come up: Beat your plowshares into swords, and your pruninghooks into spears: let the weak say, I am strong" (Joel 3:9–10). If this had been written by a present-day observer of events, it could not have described the international situation more accurately.

Armageddon

The last conflict of the nations, or the European conflict, terrible and far-reaching as it is, is not the Armageddon of the nations of which the Scriptures tell us, but it surely is a forerunner of the last great clash of the world empires.

38

THE POWER OF PENTECOST

A few words about the wonderful work of God in San Antonio, Texas. The power often came like on Pentecost. The people were tossed about by the power of God as if by a windstorm, and they seemed light as a feather. Their faces shone and were looking up to heaven, like Stephen, seeing visions of Jews sitting on the right hand of God. God revealed Himself in many wonderful ways, as Jesus said He would, and showed us *"things to come"* (John 16:13). The last night of the meeting, the power filled the house from the opening until late at night, so that we could hardly close at all. It seemed that the Lord took hold of everyone who came into the house. Sinners were struck with deep conviction; they began to weep and rush to the altar. The whole house was soon one altar, souls weeping their way to Christ in all parts of the house. Many received the baptism of the Holy Spirit standing or walking around. Several soldiers were saved, got the baptism, and then got on benches or pulpit and began to preach and prophesy, speaking like the voice of God in other tongues; some interpreting, telling the wonderful works of God; little children were preaching and prophesying. I really felt as if we were going to be taken up in the Rapture.

Dear Brother Fred Lohman, the minister, was filled with God. He was a noble soldier, stood so nobly by and helped to push the battle on to the gates of victory. People talked much about going to heaven. I want to bring heaven down.

A bishop of the Church of England and his wife, who had been attending the meetings, came in, got halfway up to the pulpit, were struck with the power of God, and were held in the aisle, standing amazed at the wonderful display of the presence of God. Ministers all stood like the priests of old; they could not move or work, for the glory and presence of God filled the house of the Lord.

I felt we could not stand it much longer.

God Visiting San Antonio With Mighty Power

(Published by the *"Word and Witness"* at Malvern, Arkansas)

It has pleased our heavenly Father to grant us a gracious time of refreshing in this city during the past six weeks. Sister Etter has preached the old time Gospel, not with enticing words of man's wisdom, but in the power and demonstration of the Spirit. She has utterly ignored the "Creeds, Theories, and Dogmas of Men," and held high the "Bloodstained Banner of King Emmanuel," pointing to the bleeding victim of Golgotha as the only hope of the race.

From the first, God set His seal on the work, "confirming the word with signs and wonders in the name of Jesus." Sinners have been gloriously saved, the sick healed, the deaf have received hearing, the lame have been made to walk, and many have received the gift of the Holy Spirit, speaking with tongues as the Spirit gave them utterance.

Some Healing Miracles

A Spanish lady, a Catholic, seventy-nine years of age, all crippled up with paralysis, came into the meeting, and was saved, healed, and filled with the glory of God; her face shining like an angel as she stood on the altar praising God with uplifted hands for saving her soul and healing her body. A man, eighty years old, his form all bent with rheumatism for years, a great sinner (a Catholic), came into the meeting, heard the singing, saw the shining faces, felt the mighty power of God, fell down at the altar under awful conviction, got saved and healed, threw down his stick, and ran up and down the aisle shouting the praises of God.

An aged man, a precious saint of God, living in this city, who for years has been an invalid, suffering from a fall, unable to come to the meetings, but was brought in a buggy, was prayed for, and God touched him. Now, using his own terms, he "can walk like a man." Many miracles have been performed in Jesus' name. People have been healed of cancer, tumor, catarrh, rheumatism, diabetes, consumption, sore eyes, and eating sores. Lame limbs have been made whole, and deaf ears have been opened.

One lady, from all appearances dying with heart failure, was snatched from the very jaws of death. Her form was cold and limp, her eyes glassy, and the death stamp stood on her brow. She had bidden all good-bye and was sinking fast when Sister Etter reached her. But, glory be to God, when our sister rebuked "the grim monster," commanding him to loosen his grip, and calling to the departing one to come back, she rallied and came forth in the strength of Israel's God. Now for over a week she has been in the meeting, shouting and praising God.

Other Signs of God's Mighty Presence

Besides the mighty miracles of healing, God has shown many other signs of His mighty presence and the soon coming of the Lord. In many ways the Holy Spirit has signified that we were near the end. Sometimes during the preaching, God's power would settle down on the saints until some were melted to tears; others saw wonderful visions of His coming glory. Sometimes Sister Etter was held like a statue, unable to utter a word. Other times she stood weeping over the people, while the power of God swept over all like the tide of a great ocean.

Around the altar, souls saw visions of Him who is walking today among the candlesticks, holding "*the seven stars in His right hand*" (Rev. 2:1). Numbers seem to hear that "*voice as the sound of many waters*" (Rev. 1:15) and like John fell at His feet as dead. The unsaved, beholding the shining faces of those lying as dead men in the presence of God, wept and said, "These are strange things."

Many saw visions of Jesus coming in the clouds of heaven with power and great glory. Sometimes the Spirit would move like a gentle breeze, fanning every soul with the breath of heaven, then send torrents of weeping over the lost until it seemed to some that the very shades of the dark "tribulation" cloud was casting a shadow all around us. One morning while the Spirit was dealing with the saints in a marvelous way, suddenly a sister began to speak in a tongue unknown to anyone present, but seemed to be calling us forth to battle. At this same time several in the Spirit were hearing the tramp, tramp of a mighty army, and two saw the mighty army of heaven riding forth on white horses. Then the lady who had been speaking in tongues began giving a shout of victory, and victory was felt in many hearts, which was taken up by the saints while the power and Spirit of God settled down upon us until it seemed the whole place was lit up with the glory and presence of God.

God is wonderfully using our sister in gathering together the saints in unity, shedding forth the mighty truths of the Pentecostal baptism, showing forth the mighty power of God in this end of the age, helping the bride to make herself ready for the coming of the Bridegroom.

—Fred Lohman
San Antonio, Texas

God Working in Many Lives

Shouting the Victory

God set His seal on the very first service in a blessed way. From the first, souls have been saved, some baptized, and bodies healed. There have been some real miracles of healing. One woman came all the way from Oklahoma in a wagon. She had not walked for years, but after Mrs. Etter prayed for her and rebuked the spirit of infirmity in Jesus' name, commanding her to rise up and walk, she rose up, walking and praising God.

Another lady came from Chicago and was healed of consumption, and is in the meeting every night giving glory to God for His mighty power to save and to heal. Another lady about seventy years of age came to the meetings, having spent much and suffered much of many physicians. She was having hemorrhages of the lungs, was prayed for, and has been shouting the victory ever since, and can breathe and talk and shout like other folks. This morning she was in the meeting and walked up and down before the altar, praising God for having given her perfect soundness of lungs.

A civil engineer, who had not heard a word or sound for more than four years, his eardrum having been destroyed by an abscess, when he was prayed for and in the name of Jesus commanded to receive his hearing, immediately received his hearing. He was prayed for last Sunday night a week ago, and last Sunday night he was in the meeting and testified that he could hear perfectly.

A brother, a preacher, whose right ear has been closed for eighteen years from the use of strong drugs, was made to hear clearly out of the dead ear today, through Jesus.

People are here from Canada, Georgia, South Carolina, Oklahoma, Arkansas, and from many Texas cities. Some are inquiring from afar off, and others are coming. Interest is growing, and we are expecting great things from God. Bad weather has hindered the crowds, but many good people are coming who before would not attend Pentecostal meetings.

—Fred Lohman

Thousands Saved, Healed, and Baptized

After closing the meeting at San Antonio, Texas, my husband and I started on the long journey to California. We arrived in Oakland, where, twenty-six years before, I went with a sickly husband, two young girls, and a janitor. We were entire strangers. We had one large and six small tents in the rainy season, when all campers had taken their tents and left. There was scarcely a ray of hope or anyone to look to but the Lord. A few saints came out to see what was going on in the tent. They soon found out that God was working in a mighty way. Some of the most influential men and women of the city, among them George Montgomery, Dr. Smith and his wife, and Lawyer Tripp, lifted the financial burden off us. And others also came as they were able. Many thousands were saved, healed, and baptized in the Holy Spirit.

I remembered how the Lord had shown me at that time the great earthquake that was coming on San Francisco, Oakland, and adjoining towns, and that I would live to work over the ruins. Now, after all these years, I saw that prophecy fulfilled.

Dear Brother and Sister Montgomery kindly insisted on us stopping at their beautiful home of peace at Beulah Heights for a week of rest before commencing meeting in San Jose. But when the dear saints knew we were coming, they insisted on having a meeting if only for a week. We had a great desire to meet the dear ones after so many years, so we stayed one night with Sister Montgomery, then held services five days in the theater in Oakland. It was a time of rejoicing, meeting many who had been saved, healed, and saved from the grave. Brother and Sister Montgomery and Dr. Smith and his wife were greatly used of the Lord. All were surprised to see such an outpouring of the Spirit in so short a time, so many healed, saved, and filled with the Spirit.

Filled With Delight

(Copied from *Triumphs of Faith*)

We had the privilege of attending all of Mrs. Etter's meetings in Oakland during her six days' stay in this city. The meetings were held in Castle Hall, 387 Twelfth Street, a comfortable, well ventilated hall, seating several hundred. The services were well attended. Mrs. Etter gave Bible addresses on the New Birth, A Victorious Life in Christ, the Double Cure—or Healing for Soul and Body—the Coming of the Lord, and kindred topics. Often for more than an hour at a time, she would give teachings from the Word of God, and the power of God would so hold the audience from beginning to end that scarcely a person would leave before the close.

The altar services were remarkable, large numbers crowding forward for spiritual blessings and bodily healing. So many desired healing that it was impossible for Mrs. Etter to pray personally with each one, but she laid her hands on a large number at nearly every altar service and prayed the prayer of faith for them. Many of these seemed very ill, and we often noticed a great change in their outward appearance after prayer had been offered for them. We also heard many say that they had been wonderfully relieved from suffering. It was quite marvelous at times to note the different expression on each face as the light of God came into the soul through some teaching given at the moment by Mrs. Etter.

Quite a number of these suffering ones came from a distance, returning home after prayer had been offered, and so we did not see them again.

We conversed with a young woman who was instantly healed of deafness. She said she had been partially deaf for fifteen years, and very deaf for three years. She heard me as I conversed with her in an ordinary tone, and she seemed very happy and full of praise. Mrs. Etter had commanded the deaf demon to come out of her ears, in the name of Jesus.

A man whom we knew was healed of deafness, with which he had been afflicted for more than fifty years. He thought I must be shouting at him when I talked in an ordinary tone. He was delighted that he could hear people conversing as he passed them on the street. One little boy, who was afflicted with a cleft palate and could not talk intelligibly, was prayed with and could talk plainly afterwards, greatly to his delight.

There were many other workers at the altar, and the sick people who could not get near Mrs. Etter were often prayed with by these brothers and sisters.

Many testified that they were healed. The power of God was so manifest in the altar services that it seemed very easy to lead souls to Christ and to see them receive Him with great simplicity. Others received the Pentecostal baptism.

Sometimes a wonderful wave of praise and joy would strike the audience, and many faces would shine with heavenly rapture. On one occasion there was a marvelous heavenly anthem, in which many voices joined. One lady, who was herself quite a musician, but who had never heard anything of the kind, said afterwards to me with surprise and pleasure, "I think some angels must have been helping."

Since I began to write this article, a lady (almost a stranger to me) said over the phone: "I never expect to be as near heaven again while on earth, as I was in those meetings." And then she added about Mrs. Etter, "How wonderful she was in always pointing us to Jesus and never letting anyone get their eyes on her!" Yes, praise God, that was true. She begged the Christians to hold her up in prayer, while she preached.

Praise the Lord for the privilege of looking into the faces and taking the hand of fellowship of so many of the redeemed of the Lord. The power of the Lord was wonderful in leading the believers out into the baptism of the Holy Spirit, and clearing up experiences, and to heal the sick. Multitudes went forth to publish the Word with power and gifts as never before.

—Mrs. C. J. Montgomery
Editor, *Triumphs of Faith*

39

WORLDWIDE CAMP MEETING AT LOS ANGELES

Mighty Signs and Miracles

While holding meetings at Dallas, Texas, Brother Scott came from California to attend the meeting. God gave him a vision, showed him that I was to go to California to take charge of a great camp meeting, and he was to make all the arrangements. Brother Bosworth was asked to attend also, but he never promised to go.

I told him the Lord had given me a special call to gather the saints together, and I was making arrangements to have a worldwide camp meeting, but when we prayed about the matter, we all felt what the Lord was calling me to do, and that the worldwide camp meeting was to be held at Los Angeles, California.

Brother Scott started home, advertising the meeting all along the way, and all over the country, telling that I would be there. They succeeded in a marvelous way in making all the arrangements, in getting and preparing the tents, and everything connected with the temporal management, good light, and everything for our comfort. Dear Brother Studd assisted in all the arrangements, both brothers making every sacrifice to make things convenient and comfortable.

Thousands gathered from all over the state, some from foreign lands, and we believe it was the largest gathering of saints in the last days. The President, Brother Scott, stated that two hundred ministers were on the platform, sitting in fellowship and love. The Lord was present, showing His approval of the Word with mighty signs and miracles, especially in healing and baptizing with the Holy Spirit and fire. The slaying power was also greatly manifested, and many were struck down with the power.

Some had visions and revelations. It was stated by reliable ministers that two thousand individuals were prayed for by the laying on of hands. Many ministers and evangelists received great power and gifts by the laying on of my hands. These all went forth with great faith, expecting to have power over unclean spirits and devils, to cast out and to cure diseases. I have since heard from many of these good reports of their work; also, testimonies from many who were wonderfully healed.

Multitudes are carrying the news over land and sea, telling what they saw, felt, and heard. Oh, God, keep them going on and on, until we all meet in the Rapture.

Many Miracles

The worldwide camp meeting was no doubt the largest gathering of baptized saints in these last days. I had full control of the ten o'clock meetings, which would have lasted all day and night, for the power of God was poured out so wonderfully, but I had to close at two o'clock for other services. It was announced everywhere that I was to have charge of the spiritual part of the meeting, so the people came from mostly every state and place to see me and be healed. At the call for the sick and seekers to come forward, they rushed by scores and hundreds, all trying to get into the pool. Hundreds were healed soul and body. One day the "Cloud of Glory" had covered us; the Lord had worked many miracles. The blind saw, the lame walked, the dying got up and walked. Others sang in the Spirit. Visions and messages in tongues were given. People were saved and healed all around. I had to stop for the two o'clock meeting. As they led me to the steps that went off the large platform, I stopped and looked at the many hungry, anxious souls; then the power of God came on me; I raised my hands to heaven and stood there as the Holy Spirit swept over the multitude. I said, "The Lord is going to save a lot of you dear people just now. All who want to be saved just now, while I stand here and sprinkle the blood of Jesus on you, by living faith, come forward." There was a rush from all directions to the platform. They began to weep and shout and scores were converted, without getting on their knees, except those who fell down under the almighty power of God. No one there ever saw anything like it. If I could have had charge of the meeting until the evening, I am sure hundreds more would have been converted, but I had to give way for a different meeting.

Another day as I came off the platform, many who could not get near while I was praying for the sick stood, looking so sad, crowding around me as near as they could, trying to touch my hands or speak. I stopped to look at them. The power fell on me and swept over them. I raised my hands and told them all to look to Jesus, to look up, to lift their hands and faces to God; that I would sprinkle the blood of the Lamb over them and that they would all be healed. Oh, glory to God! The healing power swept over. Many miracles of healings were wrought; people were saved and baptized.

Now, about two years after, in our convention in Los Angeles, I heard many wonderful testimonies of those who were healed in the worldwide camp meeting. Two marvelous cases said they were healed the day that I was standing on the steps of the platform.

Healed of a Tumor

A Miss Gertrude Berry, of 510 East Thirty-third Street, Los Angeles, testified that she was one of those who were healed that day. She had a large tumor, so that she weighed over three hundred pounds. In a short time the tumor disappeared, and her weight was reduced nearly one hundred pounds. Her brother, who was a physician in a hospital at San Francisco, got uneasy and was under the impression she had Bright's disease. He examined her urine and found traces of tumors disappearing in it, which left her body. She is now well in body, and God is using her for His glory in the missions in Los Angeles.

The last day of my stay at the worldwide meeting, they gave me the afternoon meeting and night. All the honest in heart said that they never saw or felt the power of the Lord and His presence as it was there manifested.

Hundreds were healed; hundreds were saved and reclaimed or baptized in the Holy Spirit; hundreds received power for service or gifts or had their gifts stirred up as never before. I have held meetings in about twenty states. I have heard many strong testimonies of those who were healed and heard them tell of the wonderful things that they saw and heard in the worldwide camp meeting in Los Angeles, California.

I have had many calls to go back. I went back last October, 1915, at the call of Brother Garr and many others. At this time we held a large convention again, where God did mighty miracles. It was a great pleasure to meet so many of the saints whom I met in the great meeting over two years ago. Eternity alone will tell the results of that great meeting.

Sinners Convicted, Diseases Cured, People Healed

"The power of God to heal was miraculous. Sick were brought from far and near, and multitudes were touched by the power of God through the instrumentality of His humble servant, Sister Etter, whose simple faith brought deliverance to many. The lame walked, the blind received their sight, the deaf heard. Cancers were cured, tumors and tape worms passed away, and dropsy and consumptives healed.

"While there were many whose lack of faith hindered them from being healed, yet those who were healed were most remarkable. On one occasion, many were healed as Sister Etter raised her hands toward heaven, while she was leaving the tent.

"One afternoon such conviction fell on the sinners that many ran to the platform and were saved at once. It was a scene seldom, if ever, witnessed anywhere. There were times that the big tent resembled a battlefield on account of the many who were slain by the power of God. At times the power fell like rain, and the heavenly anthems filled the atmosphere."

A Wonderful Healing

April 21, 1913

Healed of Tumor, Bright's Disease, Dropsy, and Bad Heart Trouble

I want to praise the Lord Jesus Christ for the wonderful healing I have received of the above diseases in answer to prayer, and also in opening the way before me and bringing me to the Pentecostal worldwide camp meeting at Los Angeles, California. I came from Portland in the last stages of Bright's disease. I had to wear a large, loose wrapper most of the time, my body being swollen far beyond normal size. Quarts of water were hanging from my bowels, and my heart would scarcely act. Doctors told my son I might not live to cross the bar of the river at Astoria, but God said, *"As they went, they were cleansed"* (Luke 17:14). My burial clothes were brought with me, but I was prayed for and immediately healed. When Sister Etter laid hands on me and began to pray, my whole body quivered under the mighty power of God. The water sacks broke from my head down, and the water broke through the skin and trickled down until my clothing was drenched. My size was instantly reduced in sight of hundreds of people. I could afterwards lie down with perfect ease and put on my ordinary clothes with comfort. Oh, I can never praise His holy name enough! Seven days afterward, the tumor passed away in pieces, and I have been kept through the power of God ever since, a living witness to the truth that *"Jesus Christ [is] the same yesterday, and to day, and for ever"* (Heb. 13:8). Blessed be His righteous name. After having preached this blessed Gospel of salvation on this continent for many years, proving many times His power to heal the sick, and receiving the blessed Pentecostal baptism of the Holy Spirit, God is now calling my husband and me to the land of Egypt, and we are expecting to sail, God willing, this fall.

—Mrs. Elizabeth D. Van Horn,
Home address: Milwaukee, Oregon
Foreign address: Cairo, Egypt, after November 1, 1913

Note: This dear sister, with her husband, sold everything and sailed for Egypt. God has wonderfully used them in that dark land. They are both still in the battlefield.

Wonderful Testimony on Healing

Two years ago I went to Los Angeles for my health, and being there one year, a neighbor of mine told me of healing in Jesus. She said that she knew a place where I could go and get healed. So I went to Sixtieth and Pasadena to Mrs. Etter's meetings in a large tent. I saw wonderful miracles done through Sister Etter by Jesus. People were healed instantly; cancers and consumptives were healed; the lame walked, and the blind were made to see. I said that if it is for me, Lord, take me in and save my soul, baptize me in the Holy Spirit, and heal my body. I was paralyzed in both knees, could not walk for three years, and my spine was afflicted with consumption, and my eyes were affected, having to wear glasses for seven years. When Sister Etter prayed for me, I found that the Lord had wonderfully healed, saved, and baptized me. My eyes were restored to me, and I sat on my glasses and broke them in pieces. I praise and thank Him for giving me new life in spirit, soul, and body. This was on the twenty-fifth day of April, one year ago. I have not had a pain or an ache in my body since. I am just like a newborn baby.

The best of all is that after I was so wonderfully healed, my husband, who is a German-Jew, was convinced that it was of God. For three years he massaged my body with alcohol and liniments, and he said, "I thank God that He can do the same for me." He suffered with kidney and stomach trouble. He said, "I am going to ask the Lord to heal me, too." He got down on his knees the same day and had Sister Etter pray for him, and he was healed, too. The next day he went to the tent and asked the Lord to save him, and the dear Lord did. Four months later the Lord wonderfully baptized him in the Holy Spirit. He wrote home to his parents in Germany and told them that the Lord had saved, healed, and baptized him, and they were greatly convicted and believed it was God's work. His father sent for a German New Testament. We forwarded one and wrote down a number of Scriptures for them to read. His sick sister was healed by reading it. My brother-in-law is a German rabbi, and he was convicted and I believe the Lord is bringing the whole family in. Now, beloved, this miracle the Lord did in our family is through Sister Etter's prayers. She is a true child of God, and when the Lord works through her, we are healed. I believe it with all my heart and soul. God bless you all, and give your hearts to Jesus, and let Him have His way in your hearts. I praise and thank Him for the rest He gives in my soul and heart.

—*Mr. and Mrs. Victoria Freimark*
1212 Sanborn Avenue, Los Angeles, California

Broken Parts Restored

It is now nearly three years since the wonderful meeting in Los Angeles. We have many testimonies of those that God healed in the meeting and they went forth in all directions telling how the Lord healed and filled them with love and power.

Brother Scott was the president of the meeting in 1913; he was used of the Lord to call the people together and to ask me to take charge of the meeting. He came forward two or three times in the meeting in Los Angeles, 1916, and said he wanted to testify of the Lord's healing him of double rupture, in the world-wide meeting three years ago. He had suffered many years and very often in a dangerous way. While in this meeting, he was seriously hurt in some way, and for a while it appeared that he would die or have to be operated on. He said that when we laid hands on him and prayed, he was instantly healed, that the broken parts became natural, and he never wore a truss again; he was perfectly healed in every way.

Blood Poisoning Healed

Brother Anderson came from Portland, Oregon. He did not have much faith or knowledge in divine healing. But Sister Van Horn also came from Portland in a dying condition, and we knew they had brought her burial clothes with her. When he knew she was healed, he began to think there might be some hopes for him: every earthly hope was gone. He had blood poisoning and was covered with ugly running and eating sores, some nearly as large as his hand. He was a nervous wreck, and he could not sleep, and it was affecting his brain. He asked me if there was any hope for him, and I told him if he would give his restored life to be used to the glory of God, the Lord would heal him right now. He said, "I will." I prayed for his soul and body and sprinkled the blood of Jesus all over him, by a living faith. Bless God, the blood worked: I laid hands on him, rebuked the poison, and cast out the unclean spirits; the plague was stayed, and the blood was cleansed.

The power of God struck him, and he fell and lay like a dead man. I left him lying there, but praise the Lord, the next morning his sores were all gone. Not even a scar of those rotten sores remained. Where great raw sores had been on his hands and arms, his flesh was like a little child's. All could see that the Lord had wrought a miracle. This was in Los Angeles, and in our meeting at Long Hill,

Connecticut a while later, a brother rose in the back of the tent (it was Brother Anderson). He had just arrived on the grounds. He was full of the Holy Spirit, and his face was shining as he told how God had sent him across the continent to testify how the Lord had undertaken for him and did not let him go down to the grave and premature death, but had made him every whit whole and sent him out to tell what great things God had done for him, to preach the glad tidings of salvation for soul and body and that Jesus was coming soon.

I heard this brother testify in Chicago and Philadelphia, many months after, and he was perfectly healthy and giving God the glory.

Healed of Rheumatism

Dear Brother Studd was taken sick with sciatic rheumatism and other diseases of the nerves. His suffering was very great. It appeared he would surely die, and he continued to get worse, although many prayed for and with him. The hope was to bring him to the tent, and when they did bring him, he looked like a dead man. I told him to cheer up; he would not die but live to glorify God. (See Psalm 118:17.) We prayed for him with the laying on of hands, and he was soon walking around praising the Lord and helping me pray for others.

40

GLORIOUS WORSHIP
AND PRAISE

Most of the saints in the camp meeting at Los Angeles knew the sad and awful suffering endured by my dear husband. I started with two nurses to help care for him on the long journey from the Pacific to the Atlantic and away up to Long Hill, Connecticut, near Bridgeport. When we arrived there, my husband was almost dead, but I was much better. It was hard for me to travel with the best of care, but now our minds were on and for him; he could only rest for a few minutes at a time; every move he made moved me.

I expected to go at once to Long Hill, where the manager of the meetings had promised to have everything ready for our entertainment and everything ready for the meeting and arrangements to sleep and feed the multitudes. But to my surprise, he placed us off with some mission people, who did not have any confidence in him and would not help him in the least. We were left there about a week, and we won the love of them so they went to the meeting and helped me in many ways. I went out to the grounds several miles from Bridgeport, hoping to find everything ready, but could not even find a place to board and pay my board. The camp was quite a distance from the town; there was no boarding house, no place for the people to sleep. Finally a woman took me in, but she had no room for my dear husband. And now the saints began to come from all parts, the first party of about five from Canada; they, confounded, said to me, "What will you do; you cannot stand this and have a meeting under these conditions?" I answered, saying, "The meeting is advertised all over the country, and people are coming from everywhere, expecting to meet me, for it is announced that I am to have full charge of the services. So I will stay right here until the saints gather in, and see what can be done then. We must have a meeting at Long Hill." I said. "We must be brave; you must come to our help."

Soon a sister came from New York with a committee to have me go there next to hold a camp at some noted place. I told them that Long Hill was all I could think of then and wanted her to help in the meeting there. She said the Lord had shown her I needed help, and she came prepared. They at once took hold and ordered a lot of tents and arranged for a restaurant tent. A few were so disgusted that they went back home, but quite a number remained and stood by me, and the building went up because we *"had a mind to work"* (Neh. 4:6). Some old saints who had everything nice at home, carried hay and made beds of it. I saw an old, white-haired couple fixing up a bed of hay just across from where I was staying; it was raining and everything was damp and wet. I wept and praised the Lord that we were willing to endure hardship for Christ's sake. I shouted and told them, "God is coming in great power and glory in the meetings."

I had to leave my dear husband nearly a week in the city before I could get a room. I had won the confidence of the woman, and she gave me her parlor downstairs, fixing things as comfortable as she could. When they brought him out, a band of saints went to meet him at the train. I was unable to go, but he had worried so about the condition of things and being separated from me that he was delirious. He paid no attention to those dear ones who went to welcome him. He did not even know me when he got to the house. I thought I would die right there, but I had no time to die or complain! The battle was on.

The Lord's hosts were gathering from the East and the West, North and South to the help of the Lord against the mighty. The captain of the Lord's hosts was there to lead on the fight and give us the greatest victory of the age. All the trials and hardships and self-denials we all went through with such sweetness and patience brought us together in such confidence and love and fellowship that we all felt it was a privilege to be real soldiers for Jesus and enduring hardness for Christ's sake. This is the reason why the fire of the Lord was seen every night in and over the camp and the cloud of glory was over the camp continually. Many times the tent was filled with the glory of the Lord. Read carefully the description given by our brother from Ottawa, Canada, the editor and publisher; also that given by dear Sister Sisson. There was no fanaticism, no excitement, but when all was solemn and quiet, waves of glory swept over the congregation like wind. Resurrection, power, and lightness went through them, and they were lifted off their feet and would begin to dance in the Spirit in all parts of the tent. Young men and maidens, old men and virgins, all with closed eyes, many playing invisible instruments. Some of the brightest, most talented, and highly educated ministers were made to join in the holy dance—fourteen at once. Some of them gave wonderful messages. Many times these ministers would fall like dead men, among them was Brother A. Frazer and a brother from Canada. Many times the glory of the Lord was so great we felt that the Lord was coming to catch us away, and we were going to be translated. In all writings, I only tell a very little of the great trials and hardships I have to endure in every place. There are iron doors and great walls to go through and break down, but the Lord has laid it on me to send out to the world what I have written about Long Hill camp. And He will greatly bless all who read this in the Spirit of the Lord.

The Days of Miracles Have Not Passed

Many Wonders in Line with God's Word

(Taken from *The Herald of Truth*)

We often hear the question asked, "Have the days of miracles passed?" and the answer usually given by many of the Lord's people is an emphatic, "Yes." If all who are inclined to believe this could have been where I have been permitted to be during the past few weeks, and could have heard and seen what it has been my privilege to hear and see, they would—if honest in their souls before God—have to acknowledge that they were all wrong and that God had not forsaken this earth in the area of working miracles, but was again visiting His people with true old-time, Pentecostal power, even as He promised would be the case in the prophecy of Joel, as quoted by the apostle Peter on the Day of Pentecost.

It pleased the Lord to open the way for the editor to attend the camp meeting that is still in progress at Long Hill, Connecticut. I went there not only to investigate, but to see with my own eyes if all that had been reported about the Dallas and Los Angeles meetings was true. I went there fully prepared to either accept what I saw and heard if it proved to be in line with the God's Word, or to utterly reject it if I found that things did not agree with that divine oracle.

I attended every regular meeting that was held during that time, and I was also in nearly every meeting that was held outside of the regular meeting hours. In fact, I was on the platform in every meeting, helping in the meeting, and was therefore not more than two to five feet from where the events took place, which I am about to describe, as far as I am able to, for no tongue could fully describe some of the scenes that I witnessed during those very eventful days.

There is absolutely no use for any of my brothers to tell me that I was blinded by the enemy and mistaken in what I saw. If faultfinders and unbelieving, opposing brothers could have the privilege to listen for a few minutes to the wonderful heavenly anthem sung by those precious saints of God while under the power of the Holy Spirit, they would have to close their mouths in shame and report, "Truly God is among these people." Such ravishing heavenly music no human ear ever listened to since the days of the apostles, until it was again sung among these dear saints in different parts of the land during the past few years. I have often heard of it, but my own ears were never privileged to listen to it until on the evening of Lord's Day, June 8, and it seems to me that wonderful sound will never leave my ears.

Heavenly Music

Let me try to describe it for the benefit of those that have never heard this glorious music. The meeting was in progress and the power of the Holy Spirit was resting upon us in a wonderful way. There was flowing from the hearts of the precious saints a stream of worship and praise of the most intense description—something that I never saw anywhere else or in any meeting that I ever attended. I have seen love and worship flowing out to the Lord in many meetings in the past, but never before have I witnessed and experienced such intense worship and praise as I witnessed and experienced not only in our assembly at Ottawa, Canada, but also at the convention at Long Hill.

Suddenly there fell upon my ear—for the sound, strange to say, all seemed to pour into my right ear—a song of the most wonderful description. It did not at all appear like human voices, but seemed much more like the tones of some wonderful instrument of music such as human ears never before heard. It began on the right side of the audience and rolled from there over the entire company of baptized saints in a volume of sounds resembling in its rising and falling, its rolling and sinking, its swelling and receding character, the rolling waves of the ocean when being acted upon by the wonderful force which produces the tides. The nearest thing to which I can compare it is a complete band of skillful Italian violinists playing the most sacred music that could be imagined, combined with the mellow tones of a pipe organ; yet this is but a very poor description of what my ears heard.

Sometimes the sounds would rise to the highest possible pitch for human voices to utter, on the one hand, while at the same time in the company that went down to the lowest notes that could be sounded on a good organ. It was not simply the singing of four parts of music such as we do when we sing hymns, for, according to the notes we listen to, there is no telling how many parts are being sung, and it seemed to me there must have been scores of them. Such blending of tones, such perfect harmony of sounds, such musical strains, my ears never before heard, and I never expect to hear it again in this world under any other circumstances, not even from the most perfect band of music that human ingenuity can provide. Yet all these sounds were produced by a company of people who had that day gathered from all over the continent of North America, very few of whom had ever seen each other.

It would be just as impossible for men to train that company of people to sing the heavenly anthem as it would be to pull the sun down out of the sky, and yet there they were, singing it in the most perfect harmony that mortal ears ever listened to. It filled me with such holy awe, worship, and praise to the Lord that before I was able to realize the fact fully, the Holy Spirit led me to join in that heavenly song of praise with the rest. Glory and honor and worship be given to Him forever.

My ears have been permitted to hear and my own voice has been allowed to join the heavenly anthem that none but the redeemed and baptized saints can sing. It has so ravished my heart with His beauty and the glory that awaits all who suffer persecution for His dear name's sake that all reproaches now seem as only a passing breath that can scarcely move a feather.

We were permitted to hear that glorious song twice, and sometimes three times a day; every day while I was there. As the saints got more and more in the

Spirit and in the presence of the Lord, the volume and power of that song was increased, until it often came forth with a perfect roar, which almost made one's breath quiver, just as when you stand beside a powerful church organ while the lowest notes are being struck.

A professor of music was on the grounds, and I asked him to write in my notebook his description of this heavenly anthem. This is what he wrote: "The heavenly anthem seems to be a beautiful harmony of florid counterpoints." He also said that there were very few professors of music who have the ability to write it, and if it were written, none but those who have been baptized with the Holy Spirit can sing it. We had ample proof of this at the camp meeting. Some tried to join in it who were not in the Spirit, and at once there was a decided, grating discord in the precious music.

This anthem is surely what the apostle referred to when he said, "*Sing with the spirit, and…with the understanding also*" (1 Cor. 14:15). I will now turn my attention to other things that took place right under my eyes.

One Hundred and Fifty Healed

During the two weeks I remained on the grounds, I believe not less than one hundred and fifty people were healed. We saw just as wonderful cases of healing take place as were ever wrought by the apostles. The person used of the Lord to perform these wonderful miracles was a woman named Mrs. Woodworth-Etter.

I can say I have heard from her lips a stream of the most precious truths I ever listened to anywhere or from anyone, and I never heard anyone who tried harder to exalt and honor the blessed Lord Jesus Christ. She is a humble, unassuming child of God, who is faithfully seeking to carry out the wonderful commission that He in His grace has committed to her hands. The main part of her work is the healing of the sick and all who are oppressed of the devil.

The meetings usually began with the singing of several precious hymns, followed by several earnest prayers, which was succeeded by an address that was intended to stir up the faith of those who were seeking healing for their diseases. When an invitation was given, the sick and suffering would rush forward—that is, those who were able to come of their own accord—while those who were not able to walk would be carried either on cots or chairs. At times the rush to get on the platform was so great that the sick had to be kept back by force, for they would have "swallowed up" the dear sister who was working with other sufferers so faithfully that one often wondered how she could stand the terrible strain. Indeed, she never could have done it if she were not kept by the mighty power of God, for she is now in her sixty-ninth year.

I saw people, who were suffering from almost every kind of disease known to the medical profession, come on the platform. In less than five minutes I saw these same people spring to their feet and rush back and forth on the platform, which was about fifty feet long, shouting and leaping and praising God. This often had the effect of setting us all leaping and shouting the praises of the Lord. If anyone says this was all excitement of the flesh, let them read the third chapter of Acts and tell me if it was mere excitement that made the lame man whom Peter and John healed rush into the temple, leaping and shouting the praises of the Lord.

I thought I was going to keep perfectly cool, but I soon found out that this was impossible. Anyone who could stand three feet from a man or woman who was suffering terribly, for example, with appendicitis, and in a few minutes see that same person spring to his feet and rush back and forth before that vast audience, leaping and shouting the praises of the Lord for the wonderful deliverance that He had so suddenly given, without being moved, must certainly be in a strange state of soul.

I am not ashamed to confess that I often literally danced for joy and shouted to the Lord as loud as anyone on the platform when I saw the Lord stretch forth His strong hand and rescue some dear suffering child of His from the power of the great enemy and set them free.

The following are a few of the cases that were healed right before my eyes. I talked with those people afterward and also heard them frequently giving their testimony before the assembled multitude.

The first case was that of a dear brother who went to the camp meeting with me from Ottawa, Canada. He was suffering terribly from kidney disease and lately had nearly succumbed several times to the violent attacks of the disease. He was the first one Mrs. Etter prayed for and laid her hands on, rebuking the demons who were afflicting him in the name of the Lord Jesus, commanding them to depart, and, through faith in the Lord Jesus Christ, he claimed he had complete deliverance.

The next case I will mention was that of a man who roomed in the same house as myself. He was affected with some kind of heart disease, which to a large extent hindered the use of his arms and legs. He could not walk in a straight line nor was he sure of his footing; when he fell down, which he did occasionally, he was unable to rise again without assistance. His mind was affected and he was in a sad condition. He was instantly healed and became as active on his feet as it was possible for a man to be of his weight, for he was a very heavy, fat man.

A lady who was not only the wife of a physician, but who also has a son in the same profession, came to the grounds so sorely afflicted with appendicitis that she was almost in a dying condition. Her son and other doctors had insisted on her going to the hospital to undergo an operation, and if I remember rightly, had kept her from every kind of food for forty-eight hours to prepare her for the operation. But she refused to have the knife used on her, and in spite of their protestations, she came to the campgrounds. I saw her when she arrived here. She came just as the meeting was about to close and after some pleadings with Mrs. Etter to pray for her, as Sister Etter was nearly exhausted, she laid hands on her and in the name of the Lord Jesus Christ commanded the demons that were oppressing her to depart. This lady was a very intelligent person and talked very fluently, and she rushed up and down the platform almost beside herself with joy, shouting and leaping and praising the Lord in such a wonderful way that it set all the people shouting and praising the Lord. She also pounded on her body over the appendix with her clenched fist, until it almost sounded like a drum, to show that all trace of the disease had departed. I never witnessed anything like it and never expect to again.

The next day a lady came on the grounds with the strangest disease I ever heard of. She could not allow anyone to touch her for fear they had previously handled something sweet, and because of this terrible phobia, she could not touch a doorknob to open a door. She also wore a pair of elbow-length gloves to protect her hands and arms from anything sweet for five years. Her hands and arms were as red as a piece of raw beefsteak from the constant scrubbing to keep them free of sweets, and if her husband kissed her, she would literally scour her face to get the sweetness off. I saw her as they gathered around the table, and the sugar was just in front of her, and it was like snakes to her. She turned away and began to weep.

No one could live with her, so her husband was forced to leave her. I saw her prayed for, and in two or three minutes completely delivered from the grasp of the enemy, and I heard her shouting and praising the Lord. A brother stepped up and asked her to shake hands with him, and this she readily did before the whole congregation, with her gloves off, a thing she would not have been able to do for many years previous to this. Her hands almost immediately regained their natural color, and it was a wonderful joy to see her going about among the people every day, rejoicing in her great deliverance. She wrote to her husband and told him the precious news, and I heard his answer read in which he expressed his great joy to learn that his dear wife had been delivered from the power of the enemy. (Weeks afterward, her testimony appeared in the paper showing that she was still healed.)

Another young girl was afflicted with curvature of the spine. She saw so many rushing forward to be healed that she despaired of ever being able to get on the platform, so she took her case to the Lord in her seat. By this time the power was so great in the meeting that some were not only receiving their baptism in the Holy Spirit in their seats, but also getting healed, and this was the case with this young girl. She was instantly healed and also received her baptism, and I heard her giving her testimony to that effect. She not only spoke in an unknown tongue for two and one-half hours, but also interpreted what she said. If this is not a miracle, there never was one.

Her companion, so very sick that she was almost fainting, was brought on the platform. She had severe stomach trouble. She was instantly healed and was so filled with the Holy Spirit while giving her testimony that she fell into the arms of those standing nearest her and had to be laid down, where she remained under the power for a long time.

All these cases took place, and a hundred more like them, right under my own eyes, and I cannot be in the least mistaken. I saw many cases of cancer, appendicitis, rheumatism, nervous afflictions of various kinds, paralysis, lameness, etc., healed in a wonderful way, but space forbids that I give any more in this edition, but I hope to be able to do so in the next, if the Lord wills. I myself felt the healing touch in a wonderful way, and know whereof I speak. Praise the Lord. Praise the Lord forever!

No, brothers, the days of miracles have not passed. The Lord's promise in His commission in Mark 16:15–18 is just as true today as it was when He uttered these words. Although so many are rejecting it as not being for us now, to those who do believe and accept His Word as meaning them, He is even now showing forth His wonderful power, not only to save souls and to heal their diseases, but also to baptize them in the Holy Spirit.

—*A. W. Otto*, Editor and Publisher, *The Herald of Truth*, Ottawa, Canada

Wonderful Miracles Wrought in Jesus' Name

(An open letter to the *Evangel* readers by an eyewitness,
worldwide camp meeting, Long Hill, Connecticut, June 19, 1913)

I want to give you a slight glimpse of what God is doing in the worldwide camp meeting at Long Hill, Connecticut. I was never privileged to be where the power of God was so manifestly poured out, with many baptized in the Holy Spirit and many speaking in tongues, and some powerful cases of salvation to sinners and reclamation of backsliders.

God is working on all lines, but particularly in the healing of the sick. The first two weeks there were three hundred and fifty prayed for. A missionary carefully tabulated the healings after investigation, and the following list is a part of that list: neuralgia, neurasthenia, scrofula, lameness, appendicitis, mysophobia, blindness, deafness, dropsy, tumors, goiter, hernia, grippe, catarrh, kidney trouble, heart disease, bronchial infections, bowel ailments, liver complaint, displaced vertebrae, curvature of the spine.

It is difficult to keep track of the healings since they multiply so rapidly. We are in the third week of the meeting, and the power of God is increasing all the time. There is a very large attendance of Pentecostal workers and great unity of the Spirit. A marked feature of the meeting is the strong, direct teaching of the Word, the absence of fanaticism, and the repudiation of errors that here and there have crept into Pentecostal work. God Himself is steadying the ark. Bless His precious name!

The unity of the Spirit in which He holds us all is most hallowed and deepened from hour to hour. The praises He pours into our hearts and puts through our lips are mighty, and on this volume of praise the Holy Spirit moves out to do His work. The high praises of God are a two-edged sword (Ps. 149:6). We are proving that the walls of the city (spiritual Zion) are salvation and her gates praise (Isa. 60:18). We enter into His courts by praise (Ps. 100:4). The enemy falls before the voice of the Holy Spirit praise (2 Chron. 20:21–23).

One dear drunken sinner was brought to meeting in an automobile. After prayer, he fell off into a drunken sleep under the altar. When he had slept off the effects of liquor, he arose and began to call on God. He was converted, baptized with the Holy Spirit, and healed that night. The next night he brought his wife, who was saved, and then followed their son's salvation.

A colored girl, the wall of whose abdomen burst thirteen years ago after an operation, and the contents of large intestines came constantly through the sides, had been in the hospital for a year and had several operations; she is now healed by the power of God.

A goiter of twenty-five years standing went down somewhat with the laying on of hands, and the healing is now accomplished. Mrs. Mead, fifteen years a cripple, rheumatism in one knee, varicose veins in her other leg, unable to bend knees for fifteen years, received immediate deliverance when prayed for.

One from Ellendale, Ontario, blind seven years from an accident in which one eye was destroyed and the other blinded, total blindness for two years, saw the sun for the first time after his baptism of the Holy Spirit. The baptism was accompanied by two large balls of fire and a small one, which entered the eye, from which he has since seen the sun and more and more of other objects daily. In this case the healing is gradual, as is the case with an Ottawa brother who had catarrh for thirty-eight years, derangement of intestines for fourteen years, and kidney trouble for four years.

I have given so much prominence in this letter to the healing work of God, hoping it will encourage poor sufferers everywhere to trust God for their healing. He is no respecter of persons and says, "*According to your faith be it unto you*" (Matt. 9:29). "*I am the* LORD *that healeth thee*" (Exod. 15:26).

To my own soul, the most wonderful feature of these meetings is the glorious Shechinah of God's presence. Often He comes in the hallelujah choir and with it a heavenly radiance on every Christian face that is truly indescribable, but a rich commentary of "*He shall fashion anew the body of our humiliation, that it may be conformed to the body of his glory*" (Phil. 3:21 RV).

It is truly remarkable how God sustains His honored servant, our beloved Sister Etter, who has charge of this camp. At sixty-nine years of age, God daily reinforces her strength in the use of the gift of healing, upholding her in arduous labors that, unsustained by God, the vigor of young manhood could not endure.

Later, there came into this morning's meeting an unconverted mother, bringing her unconverted daughter of seventeen years. The girl had come three hundred and fifty miles for blindness to be healed, having been stone-blind since the age of two years. While Sister Etter's hands were on her in prayer, sight was given, and it was most touching to see the mother and daughter weepingly embrace and gaze with joy upon one another. Now for the first time that she could remember, the girl saw her mother's face.

We are praising God that in so many instances the unconverted come to trust Jesus for healing. It would seem that they sometimes trust more than His saved people! Oh, the damnable shortage of faith among "His own." *"He came unto his own, and his own received him not"* (John 1:11). *"When the Son of man cometh, shall he find faith on the earth?"* (Luke 18:8).

Still later, another notable healing! A father came from a distance bringing his deaf and dumb boy, born so. He had been in an institution for education and had become so enraged and so filled with hatred that when the father brought him to the grounds, he was like a wild animal and had to be restrained by the father from breaking away and running to the woods. As soon as hands were laid on him in the name of Jesus, the demons came out, his face became sweet and lovely, the hearing came, and he is learning to talk. Glory to God! The spiritual tide is rising every hour.

June 27—I must add an appendix to my camp meeting letter, for God has broken forth in a most astonishing manner in the camp. Yesterday morning the presence and power of God came suddenly upon us. While in worship and adoration of Him, one fell to the floor under the "weight of glory." Then a clergyman came forth and gave a powerful message in tongues: he seemed not quite finished when he, too, was prostrated. Then with a kind of rushing sound came the power, and all over the house, people fell under it. I counted fourteen on the platform and all around it—impossible to say how many fell all over the place, the slain of the Lord were many. There followed a scene that beggars all description, as under the increasing light and power of God, His people worshipped Him, sometimes in the cooing of the Dove—the Holy Dove of God—the Holy Spirit bringing forth from the innermost depths of the being sweet love notes to Jesus.

The voices were many, for all in the tent seemed worshipping; the sound was one, the comingled sound of many waters. No drilled choir could have kept in such harmony and unity, with sweetest melody. The bandmaster was evidently the Holy Spirit. He can render music without rehearsals on a company of yielded instruments. Glory! The "Hallelujah Chorus" was varied by most solemn, searching, loving messages in tongues with interpretations.

Meantime many were having visions, some seeing Jesus riding on the white horse of power, some seeing troops of angels hovering over us. One saw blood everywhere and the red horse of war striding on. Crowds of sinners stood on the outskirts of the tent, looking on, giving their most respectful and solemn attention. Some of the messages were for them, but most were for the saints. Several came through at this time into their baptism.

This meeting began at nine A.M. and closed at one P.M. We reassembled at three P.M., when the power immediately came upon all more strongly than in the morning. Two gray-headed sinners pushed their way through the crowd and surrendered to Jesus. One businessman said, "I have locked up my place of business and come, a sin-sick soul. For days I have watched these meetings, seen the healings and the mighty power, and said, 'If this be the power of God, I dare not say a word against it.' Now I know it is the power of God." He and the other white-haired man were both gloriously saved, coming out into the light almost immediately; they then began to push on for their baptism.

Truly, apostolic days are upon us! Many hymns and songs of worship were given in tongues. People lying on their backs with closed eyes at a distance from one another would sing these hymns in the same tongue in perfect unison. These duets in tongues were often followed by the interpretation in song. Many of those who were healed were leaping and dancing under the power, reminding one of the scene in Jerusalem when the onlookers said, "*These men are full of new wine*" (Acts 2:13). Yes, "*This is that which was spoken by the prophet Joel…[of] the last days*" (vv. 15–16).

Truly, we are in the last of the last days. The shortness of the time until Jesus comes was emphasized again by the Spirit-filled saints and most tenderly, pleadingly, did the heavenly Dove, the Holy Spirit, speak in many languages for us to get oil and prepare for the heavenly Bridegroom. These messages were interpreted for us by others under the power. Surely we shall be without excuse if we are found without "oil in our vessels with our lamps" (Matt. 25:4) in these last days!

This meeting, of which I can give you clear idea, closed about six o'clock P.M. We soon reassembled, and the Spirit held us in His power until eleven P.M., the awe deepening upon us. The majesty and glory of God became so great we could hardly breathe. No one looked to his neighbor, but all felt as though in the immediate presence of God.

An immense crowd of the unsaved had gathered and stood many feet deep all around the densely packed tent. Pungent, tender, and solemn were the messages given them; in sacred pantomime (see Ezekiel 4:1–8 and 12:3–7, for example), was enacted the Crucifixion of our Lord for them, His coming crowned to receive the lost ones who would let Him save them now. No altar service was called, and the meeting closed in a deathlike stillness. We quietly made our way home, not caring to see or speak to anyone, the sinners likewise; not a sound was heard as they trooped down the hills to the cars. As we came out of the tent, we found *"the slain of the LORD"* (Isa. 66:16) lying all around.

"We have not followed cunningly devised fables, when we made known unto you the power and coming of the Lord Jesus Christ, but were eyewitnesses of His majesty" (2 Pet. 1:16). To His honor and glory, as we have been with Him in this holy mount.

—Elizabeth Sisson

Jesus Is Coming

Jesus is coming! Go herald the tidings
    Far over the land and the sea.
Jesus is coming to gather the ransomed
    Redeemed by His death on the tree.
Angels attending, the heavens descending,
    All language our joy will transcend,
When we shall see Him, the King, in His beauty,
    Our Bridegroom, Redeemer, and Friend.

Lift up your heads and rejoice, O ye righteous,
    Your perfect redemption is nigh.
Swiftly the darkness of midnight approaches,
    "He cometh!" shall sound from the sky.
Long has the battle been waged against evil
    By suffering saints here below;
Jesus is coming to banish our sorrow
    And lead us where tears never flow.

Come, dear Lord Jesus, Thy promise fulfilling;
    Come quickly our souls cry unto Thee.

Long has the world been enthralled by the tempter;
  The curse is on land and on sea.
Yet Thou shalt triumph, the nations subduing,
  The truth of the Word cannot fail.
God's wondrous glory like ocean deep billows,
  The earth's farthest bounds shall prevail.

CHORUS

Jesus is coming! Our Savior and Lover Divine!
Soon in His glory the ransomed of ages will shine.
  Ages on ages we'll reign with our King on His throne.
Wonderful story, we'll share in His glory—
  Redeemed by His mercy alone.

41

UNITY OF THE SAINTS

At the Stone Church, Chicago, 1913

I t was marvelous how God brought all the different Pentecostal missions together. I never permit any doctrinal points, no "isms," no antagonistic points, to be aired or brought up in my meetings; nothing but Christ, and Him crucified, and the Resurrection. They soon understand and get their eyes off one another, forget their ideas and differences, begin to love one another, and soon feel the need of getting deep in God. It was glorious to have so many ministers, evangelists, and workers from everywhere coming like little children to the feet of Jesus to be refilled for better service; the watchword was "Go forward." We all felt we must get deeper in God, the need of more power from on high; of special qualifications from the Lord, of gifts and wisdom and discerning of spirits. They became hungry for more of God. Their very flesh cried out for God. We prayed for hundreds of those ministers and workers with the laying on of hands, and the power of the Holy Spirit fell on all. Many fell and lay at the feet of Jesus, like the prophets and apostles of old. They had visions of heaven and saw things to come; they believed what the Lord Jesus had said of the Spirit of God: *"He will show you things to come"* (John 16:13). Many received gifts and special calls.

The conviction was so deep that scores of believers came out from the audience wanting the laying on of hands and prayer. There were too many. So the Lord showed me that if they all would come and stand before the pulpit, He would bless them. I told all hungry souls to gather around and give themselves to God for everything and anything: we would stand and sprinkle the blood of the everlasting covenant, the blood of the Lamb, on them, and then God would pour out His Spirit and give them blessing and gifts. I asked several of the most God-filled ministers to stand with me in faith and prayer. Oh, it was wonderful how the cloud of glory and power came down! Many staggered and fell; the power swept all over the house. This was something new; no one had ever seen anything like it. Many were saved and healed. Surely the power of the Lord was present to heal, save, and give gifts. He honored His Word and our faith. The Word must be demonstrated.

One morning when I entered the church it was crowded—gallery and all—as it usually was in every service. They were singing. As I stood by the pulpit looking over the people, the Lord drew my attention to the first seat to two old people who were cripples; neither could speak English very well. The Lord told me to tell her to get up. She said, "No, I can't walk." I commanded her with a strong voice to get up and walk, the Lord was making her whole. She made an effort to rise, and she found she was healed and began to walk; she threw up her arms and was going up the aisle praising God. She had been sick and lame for years. Then I spoke to the old German man and commanded him to arise and walk in the name of Jesus, for Christ had made him whole. The power fell on him, and he arose and walked out after the old lady, praising and blessing God. He said he had been lame for sixty years, since he was ten years old, as a result of an accident. The people began to shout. I looked across the aisle, and a young lady had risen, standing on two crutches. I shouted to her to drop her crutches and walk out, the Lord had made her whole. She left them and walked out in the aisle, crying and praising God. By this time, many people all over the house were crying or laughing. Then a young girl about fifteen, on crutches, walked out from the pew and dropped them and started up the aisle after the rest; they all walked round the church and out in the vestibule until all the people were shouting and praising and giving glory to God. One of the girls said she had gone on crutches for five years; the other one said she had walked on crutches for three years.

I write this to show the reader that it is God, not man, and it is *"not by might, nor by power, but by* [the Lord's] *spirit"* (Zech. 4:6). I never laid hands on these people and did not know them or touch one of them, but I had faith in God and obeyed Him. After two years now, a short time ago, while holding a meeting in San Francisco, California, Brother Argue told the large audience of this wonderful display of God's working in our midst. He said, "they were all miracles." This last message of the soon coming of Jesus must be demonstrated. No one present could doubt that the Lord was again visiting His people and that Pentecost had come again. God help the dear reader to take warning and get ready for the very soon coming of the Lord Jesus.

The Day of Visitation: The Lame Walk, the Blind See, the Deaf Hear

Supernatural Power of God Witnessed Daily
July 2–28, 1913

(Copied from *The Latter Rain Evangel*)

Chicago has just had the mightiest visitation of the supernatural she has ever known. God came down and walked in our midst, fulfilling the Word to Israel, *"I will bring it health and cure…and will reveal unto them abundance of peace and truth"* (Jer. 33:6).

Healing streams flowed like rivers, and many are rejoicing in miraculous deliverance of body and in the glory of God filling their souls. The month of July has passed into history with its record of hundreds saved and healed, while the faith of thousands has been quickened many times over.

As arranged, Mrs. M. B. Woodworth-Etter spent the month of July at the Stone Church. Pentecostal scenes as in apostolic days were daily enacted; the blind received their sight, the deaf heard, paralytics walked, rheumatics were delivered, broken-down nerves restored, and demons driven out, in all of which the name of the Lord was magnified.

From the beginning of these special meetings, faith was strong, and the hearts were open for blessings. The unbroken unity and blessed fellowship that had characterized the revival since March 20, with continuous showers of blessing, had prepared for the harvest, so there was nothing to do but to take the sickle and reap.

All Chicago learned of the mighty workings of God in our midst. The daily papers reported some of the meetings, and though they tried to caricature the proceedings and bring to ridicule the sacred things of God, yet even in this garbled form some truth was presented. "*Surely the wrath of man shall praise thee*" (Ps. 76:10) and since it was admitted that there were healings, the Lord doubtless used these reports to awaken hope in some despairing hearts. Even those who came out of mere curiosity were moved at witnessing the power of God manifested in deliverance to the afflicted.

At first, the meetings were advertised by posters at the elevated stations, but after some marked healings occurred, this was no longer necessary. People came by carloads on the electric; they came in automobiles, wheelchairs, and on foot from all directions. It was a touching spectacle, reminding one of the gospel narrative: "*And all the city was gathered together at the door*" (Mark 1:33).

Earnest interest on the part of the workers was not by any means confined to the Stone Church people or those most intimately connected with the work. It was not a Stone Church affair but catholic in its broadness. From all over the city, Pentecostal leaders and workers came and participated with as much interest as though the work was in their own missions.

All who came, even from a distance, threw themselves into the work of praying with the sick with much earnestness, showing in a marked way the growing spirit of unity. There was no building up of "my work," which naturally characterizes individual effort, but on every hand it was evidenced that all were unselfishly working in the interest of Christ's body, and missions and churches were forgotten in the united effort to get souls to God.

Not only Chicago Pentecostal saints, but also God's children in a radius of hundreds of miles have received a mighty impetus to faith in this series of meetings. Indeed, we believe it is no exaggeration to say that the faith of God's people here has made the most rapid strides of any in modern times—it has gone forward by leaps and bounds. Ministers who came disheartened and discouraged because of failure found themselves taking a fresh hold and praying for the sick with marked results.

God honored the faith of all, and people who had their eyes on Him received healing regardless of who prayed for them. One sick woman who came in mistook one of the sisters for Sister Etter and asked her prayers. The sick woman was immediately healed. We hope this will be an encouragement to some sufferers to whom Mrs. Etter cannot minister.

Healing flowed all through the church at different hours; not only in meetings but during the day, here and there, you would see groups of people praying for the sick, and hear shouts of glory from the suffering ones who were told that the lightning from heaven had touched their bodies. When the ministering brothers saw the marvelous way in which healing opened the door to people's hearts and led them to seek salvation, they felt they had neglected one of the mightiest weapons Jesus had given to His disciples. As one remarked, ministers have spent their time in explaining what certain passages in the Bible mean instead of demonstrating to the world that all power has been given to the church.

A man who had received a wonderful experience of salvation said, "I never saw or felt such power in a meeting in all my life. Although I was a sinner, I felt the power of God." It wasn't the preaching that led him to repentance so much as the manifestation of the power of God.

The revival, which lasted for six months and was at its peak through July, was not due to any distinctions in theology or to the setting forth of any particular doctrine or creed, but because we have been getting back to the simplicity of the Gospel with much prayer.

Results have proved that setting forth of minute doctrinal and theological distinctions is not only nonessential, but its absence is strongly conducive to the spirituality of the church of God and the success of its work. The absence of all controversy and the beautiful spirit of harmony that characterized these meetings were remarked by all, and at the close Sister Etter said, "Such perfect unity and harmony in meetings I have never known."

Hungry souls who came from a distance were overjoyed because of the spiritual blessing they received; many received the baptism of the Holy Spirit and rejoiced more over this than in their healing. The power of the Lord was so strongly present that those who had sought the baptism in vain for years were swept into the experience. We heard of one who had been to Los Angeles and traveled all over the country visiting conventions and camp meetings for years, who received the long coveted blessing in these meetings.

After the first two weeks, the auditorium would not hold the people who came, and we held the overflow meeting nightly in the vestry, which seats five hundred people, with Brother Kent White in charge. Those who assisted in the overflow meetings said there were equal blessings downstairs: there were some marked cases of salvation and healing and a large number received the Spirit's baptism. There were from thirteen hundred to fifteen hundred people in actual estimate in the building nightly, and large numbers turned away. On Sunday we held three double meetings.

When the Sunday afternoon meetings dismissed at five o'clock, people were already coming for the evening meetings, and by 5:30 on the evening of July 27 every seat in the main auditorium was filled. "You are a little late," said an usher to a newcomer at 4:30, "the meeting is just about to close." "Oh, I am here for the evening meeting" was the reply.

Healing of Goiter

One of the first healings was that of a Mrs. Pickerell, who, while she had believed in healing for the body for many years, had found her faith wanting, and seeing no real miracles being wrought today, had become discouraged. Last winter she read Mrs. Etter's book, *Acts of the Holy Spirit*, and new faith sprang up within her, so she was ready for the healing when she came. We give her own words:

"When I came here, I had a goiter. It was very large on the inside, and it was choking me so I could scarcely swallow food. It also affected my heart so that at times I could not hold anything in my hand, and I would have to be helped to a chair. The goiter is all gone on the inside, and almost gone on the outside. I had suffered with this goiter for twenty-nine years.

"While I was lying prostrate under the power of God, He also put a new lining in my bowels. I was made new, set free from everything. Seventeen years ago this trouble began. I had an operation, and the doctors cut out two inches of the inner lining of the intestines and also two inches of the muscles.

"I had not been able to stand on my feet without a support, and suffered constantly. My intestines had the web cut out, which fastened them together, and when I would lie down, I would have to use a pillow to lay them on, all the time suffering from a constant burning. Last night when I took off the support I had been wearing, I could walk around without any suffering.

"There was also a loose bone in my side that slipped out of place through the operations I had, and God put that back.

"Three months ago I saw Sister Etter in a vision and heard a voice, saying, 'When she lays hands on you, you will be healed.' Whenever I got discouraged and felt my faith wane, I would get out her book and read it, and my faith would rise."

Spinal Trouble Healed

Another remarkable healing during the first week was that of a Mrs. Dolan. She was in bed and was given up to die, had hurt her spine a year ago, and was unable to walk or even stand on her feet. She said:

"They took me out of bed to bring me to these meetings. I cried all the time they were getting me ready. They brought me in a wheelchair in a baggage car, along side of a corpse, but I didn't mind that; I was coming to be healed. I knew when Sister Etter prayed for me, I would be healed. I obeyed in everything she told me, and when she laid hands on me and commanded me to rise and walk, I did it in Jesus' name. I had spinal trouble and also suffered from my stomach; both were healed."

She was in such suffering that she could not be lifted out of her chair. The helpers had to carry her onto the platform, but after God touched her body in a wonderful way, she walked up and down the aisles, praising the Lord; the people joined with her in glorifying God.

She later testified to the restoration of her voice; she said that she had not been able to sing since April fifth but was now able to sing as well as she had ever done. She stayed during the entire series of meetings, was in attendance regularly, and sat through the strain of long meetings without suffering; she often testified to the miracles wrought in her body and demonstrated the fact that she was no longer helpless by running up and down the aisles, glorifying God.

On Monday morning, July 14, four people received the touch of God in their bodies while the song service was going on. All four of them walked either on canes or crutches. One woman had gotten hurt from getting off a streetcar three years ago; the ligaments of her limb had been torn, and when Mrs. Etter said to her, "Arise and walk," she shook her head—she couldn't.

Then Mrs. Etter said, "In the name of Jesus, you can do it," and she started off, walking without any assistance. A man sixty years old, crippled with rheumatism since he was ten years old, walked without his cane. Another, lame for a year, couldn't walk without her crutches but was able to walk up and down the aisles without assistance; the doctors had not been able to tell what was the matter with her, but she could not step on the ground with her foot. Another was a girl with hip disease; she walked without crutches and without a limp.

All four of these walked up and down the aisles to the strains of "There Is Wonder-Working Power in the Blood." The singing was interspersed with shouts of praising and much rejoicing from the audience. It was a most inspiring sight. We felt like the woman who testified a few nights before, when she said, "I came for the purpose of having an uplift in my faith, but when I saw that paralyzed man healed, I said, 'Lord, I do not need to pray for faith now. I have it.'"

⌣

A remarkable healing connected with a vision was given by a woman who was healed on July 7. She said:

"I want to praise God this morning for my healing. I know it was God who healed me. I had never been in a church like this. I was a Christian Scientist for five years and thought I had all there was to be had, but about a year and a half ago, in a vision I saw myself in another church than the one I attended. I didn't know anything about this faith, but I saw Mrs. Etter lay her hands on my stomach in which I had been suffering great distress. I didn't understand it at the time; I came in here one Sunday evening and heard the pastor say that we could have every promise in the Bible. I wasn't satisfied and determined I would have every promise in the Bible for my own; so I came again and was saved and received the baptism. Wednesday morning when I saw Mrs. Etter walk on the platform, I recognized her as the one I had seen in the vision a year and a half ago. I saw the rain falling, the latter rain, and I know the vision was of God. Today I am perfectly healed."

⌣

Friday, July 25, was a red-letter day for healing.

The ushers said that as many people had been turned away from the building as there were people inside. The hearts of the ushers almost failed them as they were compelled to refuse admittance to many who were sick and had traveled long distances, but for whom there was no room. They were not simply curiosity seekers but hungry in heart and afflicted in body. Many had spent all their money on doctors and were *"nothing bettered but rather grew worse"* (Mark 5:26). The reports of the healings had flown on the wings of the wind, and hope sprang up in hearts that had long since given up in despair. A street meeting was held from the overflow of the two meetings, but the crowd was too disappointed to be satisfied.

Oh, the sick and suffering multitudes! How often these days have we thought of the Bible scenes when the crowds pressed and thronged Jesus in case they might perhaps touch Him and be healed. As we looked on the faces, marred by suffering, and on the crooked, twisted bodies and limbs, we realized that many were in a far worse condition of soul. We thought of how the great tender heart of Him who had compassion on the multitudes must be yearning today over the millions on earth—the disease-smitten and the sin-marred—the great, burdened masses filled with sorrow and despair!

A Notable Healing

The rapidity with which faith grew and the great advance taken along this line can be shown by the following incident:

We had announced from the beginning there would be no meetings on Saturday; because of the three heavy services on Sunday, we felt the ministers needed the rest. But on Saturday night, July 26, there was a little impromptu meeting simply because the people came. On this particular evening, a woman came, not knowing there would be no public meeting. She walked with a cane, and as she got off the car at 37th Street and Indiana Avenue, a German woman, seeing she was crippled, said to her, "Where are you going?" She said, "I am going to the Stone Church to be healed." The German said, "There will not be any meeting tonight, but if you come in, we will pray for you." Scarcely had she entered the door when the Lord met her, and as a few earnest ones gathered around and prayed, she was healed. She had been affected for five years with rheumatism and a growth on her hip and was not able to bend her knees. She received complete deliverance, knelt down, and thanked the Lord, and ran back and forth without cane or any support. She had been to the Christian Scientists for a year, but they hadn't been able to help her. After her healing, she said she was going home and would throw away all her Christian Science literature.

There were a number of healings in the audience and around the altar without the laying on of hands. A woman suffering from neuralgia said she felt the acute pain, which she had had for several years, going out while she was sitting in the seat, meditating on the Lord. Often the workers at the altar, seeing the sick had faith to be healed, prayed for them without taking them to the platform, and they were healed.

Another who had been an invalid for fourteen years testified that the Lord had perfectly healed her body. She said:

"I was so sick that life was a burden, and many times I wished I would die during the night so I would not wake up in my misery. Now I am glad God saved my life. I had heart trouble, liver trouble, and a floating kidney. My nerves were so exhausted I went into hysterics. I was dead to the world many a time, but I praise God I can stand before this people today and say that He healed me."

Her husband, who had been an infidel, was saved through witnessing the mighty works of God. He said. "I used to curse Jesus for years, but I don't do it any more."

Speaking of his wife's healing, he said, "My wife said, 'My kidney is loose. I am going down there to have it put in place.' It was on the side like a big lump. The sister asked Jesus Christ to put that kidney back into place, and she said she could feel it move back just as though somebody pushed it." This man first heard of the work through a little tract handed him by a brother workman. When he read it, he said to his wife. "You go down there and get healed." She did, and they both got saved.

Healings of Deafness

A father came from Oklahoma, bringing with him two afflicted children; one never had the use of his limbs and never could talk, and the other, a girl twenty-two years of age, was born deaf and dumb. The deaf spirit was cast out, the power of God came down upon her, and she shouted and wept alternately. She was so overjoyed at being able to hear that she walked up and down the platform for half an hour, weeping and praising God.

When her father saw that she could hear, he wept for joy. When she was filled with the power of God, she told, in her simple way, partly with signs with which she had been accustomed to speak, how Jesus died for us, went down into the grave, arose, went to heaven, and opened her deaf ears. As we met her after that at subsequent meetings and in the corridors, her face beamed. God not only opened her ears but brought a wondrous salvation to her soul. She laughed and cried when she heard the music and the singing for the first time.

A few days later, she called her father's attention to the fact that with both ears she heard the piano that was being played in the flat above. She could repeat words after you quite plainly, but her ears will have to become accustomed to sound, and she will have to be taught to speak just as a baby learns to talk.

The little boy also received some blessing, and for the first time in his life was able to raise his arms.

⌒

A deaf boy nine years of age, so born, received perfect healing one Sunday morning. A lady meeting him the next night stood behind him and said in a low voice, "God is love;" at once he repeated the words after her. When he received his hearing, he danced up and down for joy, and the tears streamed down his face.

⌒

A man brought his wife four hundred miles to the meetings; she had been partially deaf for thirteen years. He said they could now sit in a room and hold an ordinary conversation, and she had no difficulty in hearing him—something she had not been able to do for years.

⌒

A woman received her hearing while listening to the sermon. She felt she wanted to hear the sermon, and while sitting in the audience, with her heart uplifted to God, suddenly her ears were opened, and she heard the entire service. She came out of the meeting with a shining face, saying, "I heard the sermon perfectly."

⌒

A mother brought her daughter from Danville, Illinois, who was stone-deaf in one ear for three years. Some years previously she had typhoid fever, and it settled in her ear. When she went to a physician, he told her that the trouble was in the mastoid bone and that there were three complications, any one of which was dangerous. She had been to the hospital and had a growth taken out of her ear, but got no relief. The doctor said she could not live unless she was operated on and the pus taken away, for if it went to the brain it would be instant death; even with the operation there was only one chance in a hundred of her recovering. He said her eardrum was destroyed. He closed up her good ear to keep her from hearing, then used an ear trumpet in the deaf ear and shouted so he could be heard a half block away, but she couldn't hear. She told the physician she was coming to Chicago to be healed, and he told her she could travel the world over and not get her hearing restored. God opened her ear instantly, and she heard in the ear where the eardrum had been destroyed.

The mother was healed of heart trouble. She said the doctor called it *angina pectoralis*, and that if anyone had an attack of that, he had better be ready to go at any moment. The morning she was healed she had such a bad attack that they thought she was dead; a lump came into her throat so that she could hardly get her breath and nearly choked.

The mother also said that three years ago she was healed of blindness when three doctors had given her up. She could not see to read at all and went to a little mission in Danville where they prayed for her, so that she can now read the smallest print without glasses.

Healing of Partial Blindness

A colored woman who had been blind for six years came up for prayer. Soon we heard her scream out, "Oh, I see! I see! I see all your faces! Oh, praise the Lord!" Immediately the people were on their feet, rising in honor to Him who had touched those sightless eyes. She often came back after that and testified to daily improvement in her eyes. She said a few days later, "When I went to the chair for prayer, I could not see anybody. I tried to see Mrs. Etter, but couldn't. My right eye was entirely blind, and I hadn't been able to see much out of the left eye. I can see all over the church this morning. I made up my mind not to go out of this church until I was healed, and I told God so." Later she said she could see to read and write her own letters.

Ruptures Healed

Mrs. Floyd Reeves was healed of a double hernia she had suffered from for eight years.

A man said, "The Lord healed me last night of a rupture of twenty-three years' standing."

A minister who said he was in a backslidden condition came for healing of a rupture. He asked Mrs. Etter if he should take off his truss, and she said, "Not until the Lord tells you to." The next day, while sitting in the church, he felt a peculiar sensation in the region of the rupture and realized it was healing. He immediately took off his truss and afterwards testified to being perfectly healed.

On July 24, a Roman Catholic came and sat down in the chair where the brothers were praying for the sick and said he wanted to be saved. In the evening he came back and was healed of a rupture.

Miscellaneous Healings

One of our Stone Church people has been conducting a little Bible class in a Methodist Church on the outskirts of the city, and those to whom she has been ministering have gotten hungry for more of God in their lives, so they have been coming up to the special meetings, with the result that five have received the baptism in the Holy Spirit and several have been healed. One woman said to another, "A man up there says there is a bunch of grapes for each one of us. I am going up to get my bunch." She came and received the baptism in the Holy Spirit.

⌒

A woman testified several times to a healing of cancer of the breast. She said her breast was so sore it could not he touched without pain, and she was frightened when Mrs. Etter slapped the place where the cancer had been, but found it didn't hurt her a particle. The Lord had taken away all the pain, and she believes she is healed.

⌒

Another woman gave this remarkable testimony a week after she was healed:

"I want to praise the Lord for healing me a week ago Friday. I had a tumor in my head, kidney trouble, dropsy, indigestion, and a stroke of paralysis that drew my face to one side. I had everything imaginable and couldn't walk a block without somebody helping me. I had been in this condition since the twentieth of September. I was healed at once, and now can walk anywhere and as fast as anybody.

⌒

A lady brought a little Jewish girl whose leg was four inches short from hip disease. Some of the brothers prayed for her, and her limb was lengthened so her feet measured even.

Mr. Keyes of Zion City, Illinois, said, "I praise God a week ago last Monday morning I was healed of rheumatism I had for eight years and of catarrh that I had for three years. When Sister Etter and one of the brothers prayed for me, the power of God fell, and it was done. It only took about three minutes of their time."

Mr. H. W. Judd, also of Zion City, said, "For sixteen years I have been trusting the Lord as my Healer. Two years ago my little girl had an earache, and while we prayed for her, we didn't seem to get an answer; so I took a little piece of cotton, dipped it in some hot olive oil, and put it in her ear to quiet her, and she lost her hearing in that ear. It displeased the Lord. I brought her here today, and Sister Etter laid hands on her in the name of Jesus, and I say to the glory of God that little child has her hearing. I tested it this afternoon on the streetcar. I talked quietly to her, and she said she could hear me."

⌒

A young woman, who had been suffering from stomach trouble so severe it had affected her nerves and she had to walk the floor, came for healing. She had been treated by specialists and had gone to New York for medical treatment, but she had failed to receive help. She had been able to eat only clear soups and bread and tea, but after prayer she went home hungry. She ate a sandwich as soon as she reached home, and that night sat down and ate a boiled dinner, which she said contained all the vegetables in the market. She went to bed and slept soundly all night. She woke up in the morning feeling as fresh as a babe. The resurrection life of Jesus had made her a new creature.

⌒

The following testimonies are some of the grateful words that fell from the lips of those who had been blessed:

"I praise God for what my poor eyes have seen and my poor soul has felt, for the healing of my body and my eyes, and for baptizing me in His Holy Spirit. I came over two hundred miles for this blessing."

"I had a complication of diseases. I was in a hospital seven weeks and operated upon. The doctors told my father I never would get well, but I came here, and Jesus healed me."

"I praise God for healing me at home. I was sick, and I did just as Sister Etter told us to do, clapped my hands and praised the Lord, and He healed me."

The crowd was so great, and when the altar call was given there was such a rush, we had to have some system or it would have been impossible to keep the people within bounds. They pressed forward with tears in their eyes to get to the platform for prayer, some almost in despair for fear they would not be prayed for. We made rules, but they were often broken by the people in their desperation. A colored woman gave this characteristic testimony:

"I have reason to praise God. He saved me, soul and body. I was given up to die because of heart trouble. I could hardly get my breath. I thank God He led me right here. There was a crowd at the altar praying, but I made my way right through and walked up on the rostrum without being asked. I did not know it was against the rules, but Jesus had me by the hand. Glory to God, I am a living witness to His power to heal! After my healing, I went downstairs where the seekers for the baptism are, and I said, 'I don't want that thing called tongues.' But God held me over until I sought Him and He filled me. I have been an old-time Methodist."

⌒

Some amusing incidents occurred, but we were made to feel over and over that the Gospel of healing touches hearts as nothing else does; no amount of reasoning or preaching theories or denouncing people's sins, convinces the world that God lives and moves on earth today as does the fact that the blind see, the deaf hear, and the paralyzed walk. A woman came to one of the ushers and asked, "Will this healing continue all the time?" He said, "Yes," he thought it would. Then she said, "I have just been healed of three ruptures that I have had for eight years, and I am going to be one of your regular customers."

Some men passed two girls walking on the street, and one man remarked to the other, "Those girls go to the 'Glory of God' church." When the Lord delivers a body that has been racked with agony for ten and twenty years, who would not shout His praises? And if we did not praise God with them, the very stones would cry out (Luke 19:40). Men go to a political rally and cheer and clap their hands, making a noise that is positively deafening; baseball enthusiasts shout over their champion until they are hoarse, and no one is disturbed over it; rather, the world encourages hilarity on the part of its devotees. Have not the children of the Lord a right to shout and sing when their King comes into their midst? Let none think it strange that we greet the King of Glory with applause when He condescends to walk among us, breaking chains and setting captives free, loosing those whom Satan has bound for many years!

⌒

For the most part there was deep reverence on the part of the spectators; even the curious were respectful, but occasionally there was a skeptical person in the crowd. A young man came into the meeting one night and, during the prayer service, mocked and made light of the scene before him. Going home that night, he was struck by an automobile about two blocks from the church and was seriously hurt—his leg was broken. He sent word to us to pray for him!

Mrs. Etter closed her ministry Sunday night, July 27, but the meetings have continued with much blessing. All day Monday the people came together in little groups for prayer, and streams of healing flowed. On Monday night, as the brothers prayed, the power of God was present to heal. One old colored woman, when the shock from heaven's battery struck her, jumped up and exclaimed, "Oh, praise the Lord! I didn't expect it! I didn't expect it!" and ran down the aisle praising the Lord.

When the sick came seeking deliverance, if they obeyed instructions and praised the Lord, even though they did not feel like it, they generally received blessing. Mrs. Etter always called on the sick ones who had been prayed for to raise their hands and praise the Lord, and when they did, with heart and soul open to God, He met them. Brother Kinne gave some valuable instruction to people seeking healing, which we believe will be helpful to others who are suffering:

"It is not only that you should get your mouth open to praise the Lord, but more so that He wants your whole being set free to praise Him. These mouths belong to Him and so do these bodies. He wants to heal them and glorify Himself in you. The first thing is to get your soul and body full of the glory of God. The more you praise the Lord, the more the resurrection life of Jesus comes in. It is not your old strength that comes back; it is the resurrection life of Jesus flowing into your body. The old strength doesn't have time to come back. It is the same resurrection life that came into Lazarus when he rose from the tomb. When in your homes, in place of giving way to temptations of doubt and discouragement, walk through your rooms and praise the Lord, and every step you take will cause your faith to grow and the glory of God to increase within you."

Sister Etter emphasized the fact that the sick should first of all get a touch from God in their souls. She inspired them to look up and believe for a real shock from the skies to go through them, and often she said that unless the Lord met them in spirit, nothing would be accomplished. She endeavored to get the sick to get hold of God for themselves by actual faith and contact with Him, so that they might indeed touch Him and be made whole.

Hindrances to Healing

While there are many people who are prayed with who are not healed, we know that it is God's will to heal because Jesus *"took our infirmities and bare our sicknesses"* (Matt. 8:17) on the cross. People must be willing to meet God's conditions. We know unbelief stops God. Covenant breakers and those who have drawn back and refused to walk in the light may find God withholding healing until these evils are corrected. Then there are those who, like Job, find their healing delayed. They are conscious God's hand is on them and a great transforming work is going on in them, perfecting patience, endurance, and victory that glorifies God in the fire. In delay, their faith may grow strong, their obedience be made full, and a triumphant testimony to healing soon be given them. God has many such witnesses.

There were many striking and wonderful miracles of healing, but there were other cases in which the healing was but partially realized. We are constrained to believe that in both classes there are some who did not retain their healing, but this does not disprove that a supernatural work was wrought in many at the time they were prayed for. Some failed to return for teaching and, as Christ tells in His parable of the sower, *"Because they had no root, they withered away"* (Matt. 13:6). When a soul comes to God for salvation and then goes back among his worldly associates, he is in great danger of losing his precious inheritance in Christ. *"The cares of this world...choke the word, and it becometh unfruitful"* (Mark 4:19). It is the same with healing. Even though there has been a mighty inflow of the resurrection life of Jesus, if the person is resting in his feelings for the validity of his healing, he goes under at the first breath of testing. Those who are not deeply grounded in the Word and are surrounded by worldly, unbelieving associates are in grave danger of backsliding from any experience they may have in God, whether salvation, healing, or the baptism. It is especially incumbent on those who have just been healed to surround themselves with spiritual influences and mingle with those who are strong in faith.

We could fill the paper with testimonies of healings that have stood the test of years, but our present purpose is to show what God is doing in our midst today, for the encouragement of those who have need of healing and help. We cannot refrain, however, from giving a short testimony from our beloved Brother Graves, whose miraculous healing has stood the test of twenty years:

"When I think of those long twenty years of epilepsy that I passed through, listening to the teaching that the day of miracles was past, it doesn't seem possible that I stand before you today, for I never expected to be well again. I had over three hundred attacks; I have fallen under horses' feet and through scaffolding, and yet I lived to be fifty-seven years old yesterday.

"With all the quarts and gallons of medicine I took, there came a time when I put them all away; when Jesus said to the spirit of epilepsy, '*Come out of him, and enter no more into him*' (Mark 9:25). This blessed teaching we are having today is the teaching that brought me deliverance: '*Jesus Christ, the same yesterday, and to day, and for ever*' (Heb. 13:8). I thank God for the dear brother who held that up before me day after day, and day after day, until it was made real in my life. My healing has stood these twenty years. What are we going to do with the teaching that the day of miracles is past in the face of such testimonies?"

⌒

"Unto Him that loved us, and washed us from our sins by His blood; and hath made us kings and priests unto God and His Father; to Him be glory and dominion forever and ever. Amen."

—*Anna C. Reiff*

Note: Reports of this work were published in England. (A.E.S.)

Neglect Not the Gift That is in Thee

Mrs. M. B. Woodworth-Etter in the Stone Church, July 17, 1913

(Copied from *The Latter Rain Evangel*)

Note: One of the most deeply solemn meetings was that in which seventy elders, evangelists, and helpers had hands laid on them that they might receive a fresh anointing of the Spirit and have more power in their ministry. A holy hush fell on all, and the slaying power of the Lord was strongly manifested. One after another they were prostrated under the power until the large platform looked like a battlefield.

Then came a cry from those who worked in hospitals and visited the sick, that they might have more power to bring blessings to the suffering, and Sister Etter and several of the brothers prayed for nearly fifty. Again, as other ministers and workers came in at the close of the month's meetings, there was another service of this nature on Sunday, July 27, in which fifty more were prayed for. All present were deeply affected by seeing the mighty power of God resting upon His workers. The faces of many were wet with tears as they looked upon the scene.

On July 17, before giving a talk to the ministers and Christian workers, Sister Etter made a few introductory remarks in which she said she was not sending them out with license to preach, but that she did believe there were gifts lying dormant in many and that she thought part of her mission was to stir up the gifts in her brothers. She said: "I have no authority to send you out. My prayer is that God will give you authority. We can be of the same mind and same Spirit though separate a thousand miles. God has wonderfully blessed me by imparting gifts, and many have received the baptism when I laid hands on them. You are going out with a courage you never had before. We don't want to be a hissing or a reproach. We don't want to run ahead of the Lord or lag behind. Let us get deep in the Spirit, so the power will come on us this morning."

Brother Argue spoke of the fresh anointing that had come to many at the Los Angeles camp meeting through a similar service, and also emphasized the fact that these ministers who were about to be prayed for by the laying on of hands were not being sent out by Sister Etter or to claim any authority from her or the Stone Church, but that they might go away from this service with more power, a new courage, and a stronger faith. He spoke of the great need of wisdom and that some had not exercised wisdom and had gone out claiming authority from certain missions because hands had been laid on them at that place.

Everyone was committed to God and made to feel his responsibility to God. Many other valuable instructions were given fitting the hour, but lack of space forbids us recording them further. We give below the address given by Mrs. Etter. All felt the hush of the presence of the Lord, and it was a time of real solemnity to many hearts.

Instructions to Ministers and Christian Workers

"And this Gospel of the kingdom shall be preached in all the world for a witness... and then shall the end come" (Matt. 24:14).

"The Holy Ghost said, Separate me Barnabas and Saul for the work whereunto I have called them" (Acts 13:2). They had been called and were working, but now they were to be set apart in a special way. The Holy Spirit has to call you and qualify you.

Jesus Christ has to send you forth.

"And when they had fasted and prayed, and laid their hands on them, they sent them away. So they, being sent forth by the Holy Ghost, departed" (Acts 13:3–4). Has God sent you? The Holy Spirit has to qualify you. Our laying on of hands will do no good unless the Holy Spirit comes in to work mightily. The Holy Spirit said, *"Separate."* These men had been called and chosen, chosen for the special work to which they had already been called.

Now in the tenth chapter of Luke, we read that the Lord appointed the seventy and sent them forth two by two before His face. He said, *"Behold, I send you forth as lambs"* (v. 2)—let us remain lambs, and not become wolves to bite and snatch and tear and antagonize everybody. *"Behold, I send you forth as lambs among wolves"*—but remember, the wolves won't devour you. *"Carry neither purse nor scrip"* (v. 4)—don't be overanxious about anything.

"Behold, I give unto you power to tread on serpents and scorpions, and over all the power of the enemy: and nothing shall by any means hurt you" (v. 19). Then He told them not to rejoice because they had power over the spirits but rather rejoice that they are children of God. Don't be puffed up by the miracles, don't get your eyes on them, but keep your eyes on Jesus. You are not saved by miracles. You are saved and kept by the power of God. The miracles are the work of the Holy Spirit. You will get a reward for the works of the Holy Spirit that are wrought through you; they are going to make your crown, but they will never save you.

If a hundred thousand people were healed through my prayers every day, I could not pin my salvation to that. We are not saved by works, but through faith in Jesus, through living, constant faith and prayer. We are kept by the power of God. The works are thrown in, and there will be a great reward for them; our crown will be all the brighter.

Like Days of Old

Now in Moses' day, the work was as great as it is now, and the time came when the force of workers had to be enlarged. The Lord told Moses to select seventy men of good report, elders of the people, and bring them together to the tent of meeting that He might take of the Spirit that was upon Moses and put it upon them.

He said that they should be used in the same way as Moses; and so it was, the Spirit that rested on Moses came upon the seventy, and they all began to prophesy. Then they were sent out to work. When the Spirit of God comes on you, you are not going to sit around idly and do nothing. And the Spirit fell upon two men who had stayed in the camp. They had not been brought into the tent by Moses, yet the Spirit fell upon them.

That made some feel jealous, and you will find the same spirit today—jealousy of those who are being blessed. Are you jealous for the cause or jealous for yourself? It wasn't for God's glory Joshua asked Moses to forbid the prophesying of these men. Thank God for Moses' answer: *"Would God that all the* LORD's *people were prophets, and that the* LORD *would put his spirit upon them"* (Num. 11:29).

You must have the Spirit resting upon you if you are to do anything for God, either at home or abroad. You are not fit for work unless you have Him, and those who serve at home must have Him the same as those who go to China or Africa.

God is not calling everyone to the foreign field, but God is calling everyone in some way. Many whom God has not called make the mistake of going out, and many spend all their time running around to camp meetings. Let us make every place a tent of meeting with the Lord, and the Spirit may fall on us as on Eldad and Medad, who were not called to the tent of meeting. If you are not called to the foreign field, get to work in the place in which God does call you to labor. If you cannot get victory for God, you are not called. The hardest place God sends you to is just the place where He is going to give the greatest victory. But if you don't have the Spirit and His power to energize you, you will be stranded.

God expects us to be qualified by the Spirit resting upon us even more in these last days than in the time of Moses. The seventy whom Christ sent out had power, and how much more should we have power now that Christ is glorified? So we are expected to do all these great things set forth in the last chapter of Mark. Now in the twenty-fourth chapter of Matthew, it says this Gospel of the kingdom shall be preached to all nations as a witness, and then shall the end come. Friends, you and I cannot go out and preach as we used to do. Many sermons that God wonderfully blessed in the past I cannot preach now. I used to preach hellfire until you could nearly see the fire, and it took effect then, but the call today is for a different ministry.

It is not so much in the might of preaching but in the demonstration of the Spirit. Sinners are more hard-hearted than they used to be. You can preach hell until they see the blaze, and yet they will stand and look you calmly in the face; but let them see the mighty power of God manifested, and they are convicted. The disciples came to Jesus privately and asked Him what should be the sign of His coming and of the end of the world, and He answered these questions. The same questions are being asked today: "How will people know when He is coming back again? And then what will be the sign of the end when the great tribulation is over?"

Now, we are given signs that we may know Jesus is coming soon. He goes on to tell many things that will happen by which we may know. He says this Gospel must be preached all over the world as a witness and then shall the end come. This is our business, to sound the midnight cry, to herald the King.

It is our mission to blow the trumpet in Zion among the saints, for the Day of the Lord is at hand. It is near, even at the door. Jesus says in the same chapter, "Now learn a parable of the fig tree; When his branch is yet tender, and putteth forth leaves, ye know that summer is nigh: so likewise ye, when ye shall see all these things, know that it is near, even at the doors" (Matt. 24:32–33).

He had just been saying that the Lord would send forth His angels with a great sound of the trumpet to gather together the elect from the four winds. These are not actual angels but God's servants. The Greek word translated *angel* means messenger. You see the herald is going forth giving this last message of the kingdom, having power in the Holy Spirit, signs and wonders following; then know that the coming of the Lord is near at hand.

The Lord has given me a special mission to bring about a spirit of unity and love, and God is raising up people in every land who are reaching out after more of God and saying, "Come and help us. We want the spirit of love. We want the signs and wonders."

The Lord showed me last night, as I lay awake most of the night, to gather together the ministers as far as I could, that we might see eye to eye, preach the same Gospel, and have the same signs following. The Word is going forth, and the multitude is going to take it up and publish it everywhere—this Gospel of the kingdom, our last commission. So you see the saints going out to give this last message, telling the people that Jesus is coming soon.

Our Lord told us as it was in the days of Noah so shall it be in our day. While the great mass of people are busy with the affairs of this life, a little band like Noah and his family are preparing to be hidden away in Christ from the disaster that will come upon the world. And we are told in the *"time of the end"* (Dan. 11:35), the book of Daniel will be read and understood.

Daniel had called upon God to show him the future, and he was given a vision of great things taking place; but the Lord said, "It is not for this people, Daniel. It is for the people you ask about in the 'time of the end.' Seal up the book; they won't know anything about it now." (See Daniel 12:4–9.)

The book of Daniel is for our time, and God is now opening His Word. The light of heaven is shining upon us; God is unveiling it to us. He is giving us light on these things as never before. He says positively, "*The wise shall understand*" (v. 10). We are going to know before Jesus comes. Nearly everyone who is carried away in a vision gets the message, "Jesus is coming soon. Tell the people to be ready."

God expects us as ambassadors, as teachers, as messengers of His kingdom, to blow the trumpet that sounds the alarm to those who are not ready for His coming. He expects us to prove by His Word and by the signs and wonders following our ministry that Jesus is coming soon. His ambassadors must stop all contention; all hair-splitting theories must be dropped; this hobby and that hobby with continual harping on "finished work" or "sanctification," which antagonizes the saints, must be put away.

We are going out to lift up Jesus. Not many sinners come in by our preaching red-hot judgment these days. Paul says preaching has to be "*in demonstration of the Spirit and of power*" (1 Cor. 2:4). The Holy Spirit bears witness with signs and miracles; unless these attend our ministry, we cannot succeed.

There are scores and hundreds getting saved. They come from all parts of the country to get healed. The ministry of healing brings people more than anything else, and if you can lay hands on the sick and they recover, you will not have to preach to empty seats. You "produce the goods" of heaven, and people want the goods. Let the Word go forth in demonstration and power so people can see what God has for them. There will be no failure in your ministry when they see the power of the Lord present to heal.

The main thing to keep before the people is the near coming of Jesus. We are not to set the day—God forbid; but the saints will know as the day draws near. We can tell by the signs that it is near. God expects you to preach as one having authority. This is a generation that will go up without dying. Christ looked down the age to our day and saw the whole world in unbelief, men fainting and their hearts failing them for fear of the things that were coming upon the earth; and Daniel prophesied and said the wicked should grow worse and worse, and none of the wicked should understand, but the wise would understand.

Then the Lord gave Daniel another picture. He saw on the land and on the sea, here and there, messengers blowing trumpets, hailing each other as they pass along. For years back whenever I met a child of God, my greeting has been, "*Watchman, what of the night?*" (Isa. 2:11), and from those who have much of the Spirit of God, the answer comes, "*The morning cometh*" (v. 12). But the night is here, too. We have to preach that.

We know the darkness of hell is spreading over this earth and it will soon be a fearful scene, a regular deluge of blood. We have to sound the alarm and give the message that the King is coming. Some will be accounted worthy to escape all these things and stand before the Son of Man.

There is loving unity here. So far as I can tell, there is not a dissenting voice. There is not much wild fire. God will not permit it, and no one dares to chime in saying, "I am a dove," when he is a raven. No one dares to join us except to magnify God. Those just starting in the life of the Spirit will run off in the flesh more or less, but if they are honest, they will recover themselves and fall into their places. There is room for everything in the meeting but the devil. We don't want to give him a place. I haven't heard any hobby aired here. Christ finished the work on Calvary, the wonderful plan of salvation, but I do not consider the great work of the baptism was finished until after He went to glory, because the Holy Spirit could not be poured forth until after His Ascension.

That brings us into the heavenly places and leads us on in the way. There are powers and gifts and greater gifts; we are to go on from glory to glory. God didn't send us out to ride hobbies, to hold up this term or that term, but to hold up Jesus. He didn't send us out to tear down churches.

When Christ sent out His workers, He said, "If you go to a city, don't go gadding about. Abide in one place, be much in prayer, and don't be worried about the money not coming in, for the laborer is worthy of his hire." Give yourself wholly to your ministry. If you are in the will of God, He will provide for you. And eat such things as are set before you; don't have some fit about diet. Don't say, "I don't eat this," or "I don't eat that." If you don't eat it, let it alone, but don't air your opinion about it. (See Luke 10:2–9.) The Lord says, "*He that receiveth whomsoever I send receiveth me*" (John 13:20), and we want to represent Him worthily.

As for forbidding to marry or having spiritual affinities—shun such things as you would a deadly viper. But you don't need to talk about these things. Just hold up Jesus. God doesn't want you to be personal about these sins. Let Jesus have the preeminence.

The more He is held up, the deeper people get in love with Him, and the quicker they will drop everything else. So let us hold up Jesus and herald the coming of the King. Show them the great danger of the Tribulation. Preach Jesus and hold unto God until the signs follow. There is something wrong unless they do follow. Don't wait until you have any special gift. Believe you can do it, and it will be done. Not only send forth the prayer, but also look to God for courage, command the devil to go, and you will see victory perched on your banner.

People are affected every day by seeing the wonderful miracles. There are different degrees in heavenly places; there are the moon and the sun and the stars. The time has come when we have to be something more than the moon. We have to be as the sun. *"They that be wise shall shine as the brightness of the firmament"* (Dan. 12:3).

Don't denounce churches. Don't denounce the Catholics. Catholics won't come in for fear you will denounce them. I never mention Catholics. I never denounce any particular church. We can show the signs of the formalist in a general way, and they can see they have been fed on chaff, and they know they are frozen to death and will want to get alive.

Let us hold up Jesus, and if we do that, these antagonistic spirits will be put to shame. They will find themselves lacking. If you blow the trumpet, show the people a supernatural God, and give them the light on what is coming in the millennial age—that they will be kings and priests—they will realize that the King is in our midst in power and might and glory. Anyone who will call upon God in the right way shall be saved. He is pouring out His Spirit upon the sons and daughters. There is a special ministry for women in these days.

The sign that brought the people together when the five thousand were converted (see Acts 3:1–4:4), and there would have probably been ten thousand if the meeting hadn't been broken up. Five thousand as the result of this one man being healed, and for that healing the disciples preached the mighty works of God. So the great revivals all through the New Testament were the result of somebody getting healed. For example, Aeneas was eight years afflicted with palsy, but everyone in the surrounding towns who saw him healed and whole turned to the Lord. (See Acts 9:33–35.) A man we prayed for the other day was probably in a worse condition than Aeneas. He could not bend himself, could not open his mouth, could not even move his eye or his head. Soon he was able to stand on his feet; he had been carried in and while we were singing, he ran down the aisle and down the stairs, without taking hold of the banister, and down the street. All who saw him glorified God as the people did when Aeneas was healed. There are scores who get saved and healed, so you will always have the miraculous if the signs follow. God is going to draw in such as can be saved to see the mighty works.

Paul said to Timothy, "*Stir up the gift of God, which is in thee*" (2 Tim. 1:6). If there is any gift God is showing you that you ought to have, you can receive it by the laying on of hands. It is not so much what you say about the baptism and the Holy Spirit, but what they see you have. We can talk until we are hoarse, and they won't be convinced, but the power of God convinces them. Don't wait for manifestations before you go forth and do something. When you are weakest, then you are strong. Let us go out and work miracles. Then the people will glorify God.

Be Patient: His Coming Draweth Nigh
Present-Day Conditions Portrayed in Prophecy

(A. H. Argue, in the Stone Church, July 24, 1913)

I feel in my innermost soul that God is revealing Himself to me in a deeper sense, ever since my coming to Chicago. God, of a truth, is moving here—moving on the hearts of the people in a very special way. Sister Etter spoke a moment ago about visitations of God in revelations and dreams. He surely is visiting His people in many ways—in dreams, visions, and revelations. While in California, I had a dream of a terrible disaster. I saw people swallowed up one after another in a great flood. Only a few days afterward, I received a newspaper telling of the terrible calamity in Ohio, and this dream was forcibly brought to mind. I had felt at the time it was a warning of coming disaster.

God is not only speaking to the hearts of His people in these days, but He is confirming His Word by signs and wonders in our midst. Those who have charge of the work here could not sit down and map out a plan for God to work by; we could not reproduce this meeting if we should try. But God has graciously heard the prayers that have ascended from His little ones, and as they have gathered here, He has come forth in power and is really shaking the city.

He is reaching the world through these meetings. I truly believe that before He is through with this work, He will send men and women forth to different quarters of the globe with more faith in God and more filled with the Spirit than ever before, that they may speak His Word with authority and that signs and wonders follow their ministry.

I love to see these precious brothers here working side by side, and I feel in my own soul that God is dropping down faith and giving fresh courage, enabling us to go forth in the power of the Spirit and believe for greater things than we have yet seen. I want to read to you 1 Timothy 4:14: *"Neglect not the gift that is in thee, which was given thee by prophecy, with the laying on of the hands of the presbytery"*—that is, the elders, those who have the ministry. We have read this and reread it, but only as it comes as a revelation from heaven to our own souls does it become a living truth to us.

This injunction has largely been a dead letter to us, but God is bringing us to the place where it is a living truth. Many of God's children here have been inspired, the gifts have been stirred up, and we truly are believing for great things. I am convinced that God is moving us on step by step and that, as we deepen in the Spirit, these truths more and more will become living, bright realities to us and give us a real hold on God for His mighty power to be manifested.

When I go downstairs where they are praying with seekers and inquire, "How many have received the baptism today?" the answer usually is ten, twelve, or fifteen. One brother, whom I believe is a real good authority, said there were forty baptisms in the Holy Spirit in three days last week. He says he notices how easily and quickly they come through into the blessed experience because of the mighty power of God that is present. The spiritual tide is a high tide, and it is not as in the past when there has often been a long, hard struggle in prayer to bring people through into the baptism and that when they got it, there wasn't much of an overflow.

Now they come through filled with the Holy Spirit and speaking freely in tongues. God is dealing with His people in such a way that they will go forward, strengthened and deepened in greater measure than at any time since the Pentecostal movement came into existence. I believe we are now moving forward to a deeper life in God and will be better equipped for the work than ever before.

This has not been brought about by man but by the Lord Himself who *"worketh all things after the counsel of his own will"* (Eph. 1:11). And now that we have had this visitation of God, now that we have heard Him speak in revelations and visions and show Himself in signs and miracles, it behooves us not to limit God.

The devil would like to keep us back, but we are children of the day and as we draw nigh to God, He will increasingly reveal Himself to us. Let us not only talk about these things, but also do them in the name of the Lord.

The Lame Walk; Cancerous Sores Healed

Several days ago a lady was brought to the platform in a chair. She said she could not bear to be moved into the chair that others were being prayed for in. After prayer and some effort with her, which did not appear to be doing much good, Mrs. Etter, with authority in the name of Jesus, commanded her to rise and walk. She did so and was soon walking very well. She testifies in the meetings and goes about apparently as supple as others.

An old lady was afflicted with two cancerous or poisonous sores. One of these was nearly the size of a silver dollar, located above the right temple in the edge of the hair, the other on her side near the heart.

Several days after she was prayed for, neither of them was sore or had seeped a particle, although they often oozed so badly that they filled several handkerchiefs at a time. The first night she went to bed, forgetting to bandage her head as she always did, but there was no blood.

The Impartation of Gifts

The attendance was large and increasing. Many Pentecostal ministers and workers were present. At two morning services Mrs. Etter, assisted by brothers, laid hands on more than one hundred ministers and workers for a deeper endowment of power and the reception of gifts of the Spirit. These were two of the most powerful services in the series. The imposition of hands was preceded by instructive teaching as to being sound and sensible and avoiding foolish and fanatical extremes and the preaching of hobbies and doctrines that tend to division. They were told to preach Christ and the Resurrection and to leave alone such questions as forbidding to eat meats and abstinence from marriage. If you have faith that you ought not to eat meats, keep it to yourself. Marriage is honorable.

Do not be personal, and single out this church or that lodge, but hold up Jesus, and people will drop those things that are wrong, for the Spirit will show them. It was asserted we are not yet up to the fullness of the former rain, and that when the latter rain comes, it will exceed anything we have seen. This was confirmed by powerful messages of prophetic interpretations. The plaintive notes of the Dove were heard as a warning that the storm of wrath and the Tribulation is soon to break on this poor, sin-cursed earth. We were warned under the Spirit of prophecy to awake and seek shelter from the storm. I was told that there were many crooked and wrong spirits coming to the meeting. A brother said to his wife, "They are all here." But they were silent, chained down by the power of the Spirit. The croak of the frog and chatter of the raven could not join in the heavenly chorus and the notes of the Dove.

In the last service of prayer for ministers and workers, about fifty were prayed for, most of whom were prostrated under the Spirit. Some testified to having been very greatly helped and anointed. One of the best testimonials was the fact that numbers of ministers and workers were praying for the sick of all classes with gracious success. The numbers were far too many for one to pray for. Sometimes nearly two hundred were prayed for in one service. After having laid hands on as many as she could at this ministerial service, there were still perhaps one hundred and fifty waiting. She had them stand before the platform and requested the ministers to join with her, stretching their hands over the people, while she prayed for them all together.

She then requested some of the brothers to lay hands on the people. Most of those who were touched by the hands fell to the floor. It seemed like taking a sword and cutting them down, the power of God was so mightily upon us.

Every Pentecostal convention has its distinguishing features. The one thing that stood out most prominently in this one was the impartation of gifts of healings and faith for their exercise. This was accomplished through teaching, practical demonstration, by example before the whole congregation, through prayer, and by the laying on of hands. They were then put to work praying for the sick on the platform.

As many as four or six groups of workers prayed for as many sick ones at the same time. It is much to be able to do the mighty works by faith, but a still more blessed ministry to succeed in stirring up the gifts in others and arousing them to battle. Many will, we feel sure, go forth from this meeting to cast out demons, heal the sick, and work the mighty works of the coming King. There has been for some time a prophecy in the hearts of many of the more spiritual of God's saints that a greater and mightier revival than the world has yet seen is soon coming.

"And this gospel of the kingdom shall be preached in all the world for a witness unto all nations; and then shall the end come" (Matt. 24:14).

—Seeley D. Kinne

Eyewitness to Events

We are sending this August *Evangel* into all the world as a witness to the supernatural working of the Holy Spirit in these days. We were eyewitnesses to the events recorded in its pages and much care has been taken to give accurate accounts of healing and other manifestations of divine power. The testimonies are given as they fell from the lips of the witnesses. We believe that the record of this great Chicago meeting, and the testimonies of healings wrought, will build up and inspire present-day faith throughout the world as it never has been done before. Never in any single month's meetings have we seen such a record, and we feel God has been giving an object lesson for His saints throughout the world.

—Lydia Piper

Beautiful Threads of Gold

Weaving them into a work-a-day life,
　Beautiful threads of gold,
Weaving them in with the toil and strife,
　And yet the hands that hold,
Fashion them out into patterns rare,
　Beautiful threads so new and fair;
Soon the Master will find them there,
　In beautiful threads of gold.
Weaving them in with a patient hand,
　Beautiful threads of gold,
Filling them in as the artist planned
　Who laid life's somber fold;
Weaving them in with the homeliest cares,
　Over some burden another bears,
Glad the Master Weaver spares
　Some beautiful threads of gold.

Weaving them in with our hopes and fears,
    Beautiful threads of gold,
Brighter the thread of the gold appears,
    As when life's web grows old;
Weaving them in with a smile and song,
    Wonderful threads so fine and strong,
Under the good and over the wrong,
    Some beautiful threads of gold.

Weaving them in with a watchful eye,
    Beautiful threads of gold,
Shining across where the shadows lie,
    With life's web all unrolled;
Weaving them in with the Master's call,
    Let the bright threads of the shuttle fall,
Angels will come to gather them all,
    Life's beautiful threads of gold.

42

VINDICATION FROM FALSE CHARGES

The meetings at Montwait, Massachusetts, were held at the great Coliseum on the Chautauqua grounds. It was said to be the greatest battle against sin and science (so-called) ever fought in the state, but Jesus was the victor. That whole part of the country was stirred for or against religion. All the noted papers in Boston, twenty miles distant, sent reporters to write us up and to take our pictures and photos of those who were slain under the power of God and of the crowd of seekers at the altar. They also wrote up the work in a general way. They wrote it up straight, so that the people all over in the different states heard of the great revival at Montwait.

We had a sunrise meeting, one at seven, one at nine, another at two in the afternoon, and at seven in the evening. Thousands attended the meetings. The miracles were as great as in the days of Christ and the apostles. The fear of God came on the people as they saw the sick, who were carried in on beds, dying, rise up and shout praises to God and walk and run. They saw them leap and dance. Many fell and lay like dead men and women.

One morning as I left the meeting, I counted the slain of the Lord. There were fifty-eight men and women lying around like a great battlefield. As I walked out, men and women were lying nearly at the edge of the entrance of the pavilion or building. The whole place seemed like holy ground.

Persecution and Arrest Follows

Through our arrest at Montwait, all the New England people were stirred up about the apostolic meetings; many calls came to us from the largest cities. They offered us the largest theater in Boston and said they were hungry to know more of this faith and power. Hundreds were saved and filled with the Holy Spirit at the same time, as hands were laid on them and they were prayed for. The glory of the Lord was so marvelous, they were prostrated; many lay for hours under the power. Some had visions and revelations, and many came through speaking in tongues and interpreting.

Some rose from the chair after being prayed for, shouting, praising God, and speaking in a new tongue. Brother Otis stood by nobly and conducted a sunrise prayer meeting every morning. The presence of the Lord was seen and felt in a marvelous way. At the close of the prayer meeting on Mount Pisgah, the people gathered in the large tabernacle at nine A.M. for another prayer meeting at ten o'clock. I took charge.

The heavenly choir was manifested many times, and it was most glorious. There was not a discord or contention in the whole month's meetings. We must *"see eye to eye"* (Isa. 52:8) before the Lord brings in Zion, before the manifestations of the sons of God. Thus God is doing His strong work convincing the people, that we are in the last days by pouring out His Spirit just before the notable day—the Second Coming of the Lord.

Notable Healings

A young man was brought to the altar all drawn out of shape, twisting and jerking like a snake. It took four men to hold him, for he had been in this condition all his life. In less than a half hour from the time he was prayed for, he was standing straight with both hands up, clothed and in his right mind.

A woman from Boston was carried to the platform on a cot; she was more dead than alive. She was soon walking and praising the Lord for His wonderful healing power and the blessing she had received in her soul. She ate a hearty dinner and was on the platform to testify to her healing in the afternoon.

Troubles Cured

(From *The Christian Worker*)

Large numbers of people have been healed during the month of August; also very many have received the baptism. People received the baptism in some cases, while being prayed for in the chair for healing, and spoke in other tongues. Some fell under the power before reaching the chair. Many were healed of nervous troubles. Eyes were healed. One testified to never having been able to tell one person from another on the platform, but now he can see each face clearly.

The cook was cooked in the cook room one day; in other words he was terribly burned on the arm and face, the result of pouring oil on the fire. He was prayed for and healed so that the pain was taken right away, and he was able to go right back into the kitchen and work over the hot stove.

Miscellaneous

A sister came to Montwait on money she had saved for funeral expenses, but God healed her, and she proved a lively corpse.

A young woman who had been afflicted from childhood, and when she came here had not been out of bed in seventeen weeks, was perfectly healed.

A sister was healed of a tumor which kept growing smaller and smaller every day.

On one Sunday, seven little girls were under the power for a long time, and several came through speaking in tongues. One of them prophesied at length, the burden of her message being, "Jesus is coming soon; get ready, get ready, get ready!" She had a vision of Jesus and saw Him coming on a cloud and saw those who were left. The Spirit said through her, "It is too late, too late; you can't go, you can't go!"

One sister looked out at midnight and saw two balls of fire in the auditorium, going back and forth. This continued a long time. Other supernatural sights were seen at different times.

Some of the saints from the West and South have made sacrifices to get to this meeting. One brother and his wife pawned his watch to get here.

We have been having sunrise prayer meetings since June at Mount Pisgah, with blessed results. Some have received the baptism of the Holy Spirit in these early meetings, among whom is a preacher from Boston.

Divine Healing a Sign of the Lord's Coming

Powerful Blessings

Among the many signs so rapidly fulfilling and heralding the coming of the Lord, none is more conspicuous than the increase of supernatural, physical healing among God's people. About twenty-four hundred years ago, Jehovah, by the mouth of Malachi, uttered the promise: *"Unto you that fear my name shall the Sun of righteousness arise with healing in his wings* [or in Hebrew, beams]; *and ye shall go forth, and grow up as calves of the stall"* (Mal. 4:2).

A measurable fulfillment of the prophecy was recognized in the life and work of Jesus on earth where healing virtue flowed from him on every side. As Zacharias, filled with the Holy Spirit, said, *"The dayspring* [sun rise, margin] *from on high hath visited us"* (Luke 1:78). But there are successive fulfillments in God's prophetic utterances, and the full fulfillment of this Word was to be in connection with *"the day cometh that shall burn as an oven; when all the proud, yea, and all that do wickedly, shall be stubble"* (Mal. 4:1).

Thus the sunrise of our blessed Jesus in divine healing, heralding His return, began markedly about forty years ago in the days of Dorethea Truedel in Germany, and afterwards Dr. Cullis and others in the United States, England, and elsewhere.

We know sunrise has several stages, or there is a progression from the daybreak to the full effulgence of the body of the sun. The coming sun first breaks the midnight darkness, but as it pushes on its way, its bright beams herald its coming with more and more powerful radiance until the sun itself appears; exactly so has been the history of the return to the earth of our blessed Lord.

The healing beams of this blessed Sun of Righteousness have not this time been confined to the little land of Palestine, but they have extended to every part of the known earth, to the islands of the sea, Philippines, Sandwich, etc., as far as the light has penetrated through missionaries in Africa, India, Russia, China, Japan, Korea, South America, etc.

Even the dead here and there are brought back to life through faith in His name. Fuller and fuller has become the outworking of this prophecy as Jesus' approach draws still nearer, until we have seen it in altogether a new way of late in Long Hill camp, Chicago revival, and now in Montwait. Wholesale healings on every side, under the drenching power of the spiritual presence of the Lord Jesus!

Along with these powerful bearings comes the further fulfillment of Malachi 4:2: *"Ye shall go forth, and grow up as calves of the stall,"* or as the Hebrew has been more closely rendered, "Ye shall leap and dance as young calves."

Perhaps all who read this article have seen the joy of life in the young calf. Almost instantly they are dropped, they begin to move, and presently to leap and bound with the exuberance of life. Similarly the resurrection life of their Lord is now taking possession of His people, as the healing beams of the coming Sun touch them. They leap and dance on the platform and in worship and adoration in the exuberance of His life coursing through their veins, yes, through their whole beings! Surely with the healing beams coming so powerfully upon His people, we must know that the body of this Sun of Righteousness will soon appear!

As first, Judah and then Israel, with one consent, drew together to make David king, so now King David's greatest Son is being drawn unto by hungry people who are seeking in their hearts to make Jesus King, and to one another they are "speaking the words of bringing back the King." Oh, beloved, even now He is riding in, in power upon the chariots of His willing-hearted people, for theirs is a spiritual form of the second coming which precedes the open, literal coming!

One slain under the power of the Holy Spirit, lying on the floor, saw a bright path into the opened heaven, and riding down upon that glory pathway came her adorable Lord, where to her astonishment a bright shining company drew to Him. He went right into that circle and was seen no more in person, the company absorbing Him and His. Unutterable radiance began to shine forth through them, His life, His preaching, His acts, radiating from that glorious company, and she was made to know that *"He shall come to be glorified in His saints, and to be admired in all them that believe"* (2 Thess. 1:10) before He comes for that radiant company.

Persecution

Apostolic faith, producing results such as the healing of the sick and other demonstrations of God's mighty power, naturally results in apostolic persecutions.

On August 18, 1913, Mrs. M. B. W. Etter and her colaborers Earl W. Clark and Cyrus B. Fockler were arrested and hailed before the police court of

Framingham, Massachusetts, for obtaining money under false presences. This arrest resulted in a trial that lasted for four days, during which about thirty-five witnesses clearly testified of their remarkable healings, etc., and to the falsity of the charges in the complaint. At this date, August 29, the case was closed before the judge, who has taken until next Tuesday, September 2, to give his decision.[2] Being confident in our God of perfect victory, we rejoice in this privilege of suffering some shame for Jesus' sake.

—Mrs. M. B. Woodworth-Etter,
Earl W. Clark,
Cyrus B. Fockler

Testimony of Mrs. M. B. Woodworth-Etter, Given on Witness Stand

Q. Where were you born?

A. New Lisbon, Ohio.

Q. Your age?

A. Sixty-nine last July.

Q. When did you begin your ministry?

A. About thirty-five years ago.

Q. Previous to that time?

A. At home with my family.

Q. What did your family consist of?

A. Husband and six children. My first husband and all the children except the oldest are dead.

Q. What was the occasion of your beginning to preach the Gospel?

(Objection raised by the prosecuting attorney.) Permission finally given by the judge to proceed, and Sister Etter gave a brief outline of God's dealings with her, from the time of her conversion at the age of thirteen down to the present time; with the description of many different meetings held.

Questions were then asked by Attorney Nash as follows:

---

2. On Sept. 2, the judge dismissed the case. The charges proved to be false.

Q. In what cities and towns have you held meetings?

A. I could not begin to remember: Louisville, Springfield, St. Louis, Cleveland, Oakland, Los Angeles, Memphis, Dallas, and Chicago.

Q. About how many years?

A. About thirty-five.

Q. Do you remember the first occasion when any of the prostrations occurred?

A. Yes, in the first meeting after we went West.

Q. How long ago?

A. About thirty-two years.

Q. Have these continued to occur since that time?

A. Yes, the power has been always displayed.

Q. The power has fallen upon the people?

A. Yes.

Q. Do you remember as to the number?

A. In large meetings like St. Louis, where we were five months, thousands. People said there were hundreds struck down outside—hundreds I never saw; they were struck down fifty and a hundred miles away.

Q. How did you know this?

A. Through their own testimony and that of their friends.

Q. Have you seen people fall under the power of God?

A. Yes, I have seen them struck down as if by lightning.

Q. Have you ever studied hypnotism?

A. No.

Q. Have you ever practiced it?

A. No.

Q. Have you ever seen it practiced?

A. I never have.

Q. Tell us what you know about it.

A. On account of the power in the meetings, hypnotists have come in to investigate. They investigated me when I lay under the power seven hours. Hypnotists have been in the meetings for days, sometimes, when I did not know it, and they have investigated people. Many of them have been honest enough to come to me in private, and also in public, and say the power was altogether different from hypnotic power; and some said, "If there is a God, this is of God."

Q. Is there any difference between the meetings at Montwait and other meetings you have held?

A. Since I have been with the Pentecostal people, there has been more of a noisy exhibition in praising the Lord than when I was alone. I tell them to lift up holy hands; I say, "Do you know you are a child of God?" I ask, "Do you know you have been healed of one or more diseases by the Lord Jesus Christ?" I have always done that. In Chicago, a minister from Canada requested everyone to clap their hands together and make a joyful noise. It was scriptural, and I allowed it. The only thing we could do the night the mob came was to stand up, clap our hands, and shout to the Lord.

Q. Have you heard anyone say you were able to cure cancer?

A. Never, but they charged that against me in this place.

Q. Have you yourself ever said, "I have healed"?

A. No, God forbid.

Q. Have you ever said you had any special power?

A. No, I have not.

Q. Do you believe anyone has been healed by you?

A. No, nor saved.

Q. Do you believe people who have asked for healing in the meeting have been led to do so by observation or by testimony?

A. I should say they had—thousands of them.

Q. You published a book?

A. Yes.

Q. When did you publish your first volume?

A. I think I had not been in the West more than a year; I had been ill and was healed, and I published this little book telling about this. I did not preach healing, but I said I had been healed, and I believe God could heal.

Q. When was the first testimony given by anyone who claimed that, through Christ, he had been healed at your meetings?

A. Several came, and they said some way God helped them. I did not know anything about it, only when I started West.

Q. Since that time, have you prayed with people? And have they given testimony that they have been healed?

A. Yes.

Q. Can you give a particular case?

A. Doctor Dagget, near Kokomo, Indiana, is the first man I remember laying hands on.

Q. How long ago?

A. When I first went West.

Q. Have you held meetings at Montwait during August?

A. Yes.

Q. Similar to the ones you have held formally?

A. In many ways.

Q. Have Mr. Clark and Mr. Fockler been with you before Montwait?

A. Mr. Clark only met me at Chicago and came with me.

Q. Who was with you at Long Hill?

A. Ministers of different denominations.

Q. Did you have any particular assistance?

A. Only myself and husband and a man and his wife, who cared for my husband.

Q. Where is your husband?

A. He is at Montwait.

Q. He has not been here?

A. No, but he would be glad to be here.

Cross-questioning by the prosecuting attorney:

Q. You have held meetings in a great many cities?

A. Some of the largest in the country.

Q. At St. Louis?

A. A number of times, once for five months.

Q. At Los Angeles?

A. Yes.

Q. At these meetings scoffers, skeptics, and others who came and created disturbance were converted?

A. Yes.

Q. Have you had disturbance by the outside element in other meetings?

A. A little, but always had protection, and it was stopped right away.

Q. In St. Louis?

A. For a little while.

Q. In Ohio?

A. No.

Q. Nothing with the authorities?

A. Not that I remember; a little in St. Louis, at first. That was not in connection with the method of carrying on the meetings.

Q. Los Angeles?

A. A little from the outside element, but nothing from the meeting.

Q. If you have had trouble before, the experience at Montwait is nothing new?

A. Yes, we never had rotten eggs before nor ever were arrested.

Q. While you are conducting meetings, the outside element makes the trouble?

A. Yes.

Q. Was it necessary to call the police at Los Angeles?

A. No.

Q. Did you shorten your time?

A. No.

Q. Have you the correspondence that passed between you and Mr. Otis in regard to your coming here?

A. I have not; my husband did what was done.

Q. Have you that?

A. No.

Q. Is that correspondence in your husband's possession?

A. We never kept copies except it be of typewritten letters; these were by hand.

Q. The rest of the arrangements were verbal?

A. Yes.

Q. At Long Hill?

A. Yes.

Q. Have you the card given in by the man treated for some skin disease; rumor said he had been cured?

A. I have not a single card myself.

Q. You remember the case to which I refer?

A. Yes.

Q. What did it say on the card?

A. I never looked at that.

Q. What, if anything did he say to you?

A. As nearly as I can remember, it was a boil; he had some skin disease; I do not think the boy said anything; I don't know who brought him; I noticed he had a very dark complexion, but no breaking out on his face. His hands had been broken out, looked like blood poison. I prayed for him.

Q. You prayed for him?

A. And asked God to rebuke the disease and heal him in Jesus' name.

Q. Did he become prostrate?

A. No.

Q. Did he go from the platform himself?

A. Yes, with his friends.

Q. Did you make any announcements to the public?

A. I think I said he had a skin disease, something like leprosy. I did not say it was; afterwards I found out they said it was a syphilitic case. People knew, where they lived. Then I corrected it.

Q. Your statement was, the boy had been treated and healed?

A. I believe he would get well of that disease.

Q. It was told you by the boy, or those with him, that he had leprosy?

A. They did not say so.

Q. Had you seen him before?

A. Never, nor afterward.

Q. Did you make an examination?

A. Never.

Q. Have you made any inquiry about what it said on the card?

A. I do not think we have the card.

Q. Regarding the woman who had a hemorrhage?

A. One Sunday morning, when there was a large congregation, they told me a woman was dying or dead. I went back, and when I saw her, I thought she was dead. I had never seen her before. Someone said she had had a hemorrhage. I prayed for her and asked her to open her eyes. The hemorrhage had stopped, and she wanted to be brought up in front. I wanted her to leave the meeting, but people do not always do what I say. They laid her in the straw, and I went on with the meeting. I heard her moaning, and I went down and told them to take her out and call a doctor, but they did not. The second time I told them they must.

The day they arrested me when the chief came in and asked for me, she heard him, and the fright started the hemorrhage. I went away, and when I came back, they told me she was nearly dead. I went in; sent for a physician. Someone went out and met Mr. Otis, and he came in, and I said I had sent for the doctor. In a few minutes he came. Now, she is out and around.

She is in the same house with me, and I see her nearly every day. She was never prayed for on the platform.

Q. You said you had never had any trouble with the authorities?

A. Never arrested until here.

Testimonies Under Oath

(Editorial from *Word and Witness*)

Malvern, Arkansas, October 20, 1913

Some doubting Thomases have claimed that testimonies to modern divine healing are not genuine, but forged by advocates of divine healing. During the month of August, 1913, at Montwait, South Framingham, Massachusetts, Mrs. M. B. Woodworth-Etter, C. B. Fockler, and Earl W. Clark were arrested and brought into court before Judge Kingbury on the grounds that the healings claimed in their meetings were not real healings, and that therefore to receive public collections to continue such ministries defrauded the public and was obtaining money under false pretenses. Hence it was up to these three defendants to prove in open court with the chief of police, the prosecuting attorney, three doctors, and two preachers opposing them, that beyond all dispute, people were being healed of bodily diseases by the Lord in these meetings, or be convicted and go to the penitentiary as defrauders.

On August 27, they began to put witnesses on the stand. Bear in mind that every person was under oath and would have been prosecuted for perjury if he or she had sworn falsely. You will find these testimonies in the daily papers, the *Framingham Evening News*, August 27 to 29, the Boston dailies, and others of the same date. They are recorded here as given to reporters in the court.

Fresh Anointing

Miss Eaton of Bloomfield, New Jersey, was the first witness called by Attorney Nash. She testified that for sixteen years she had served in the missionary field in India, and there were meetings similar to those at Montwait all over the world. She has known Mrs. Etter for two years and has always heard her give God the glory for the healings.

She characterized the physical healings at Montwait as a fresh anointing of the flesh from God. She had seen with her own eyes many healings and prostrations elsewhere; she meant a state of mind that was not unconscious.

Healed through Prayer

Mrs. L. N. Harris, of Atlanta, Georgia, said she had attended most of the meetings, that she was one of the Pentecostal people, and had been in attendance for six years. When she approached the platform at Montwait, she was prayed for. She was afflicted with rheumatism and a blind eye, caused by spinal meningitis twenty years ago. "When I came to, the dead nerve began to jump, and the dead nerve was healed, and my rheumatism was gone. I feel now like a sixteen-year-old girl. I knew all that was going on while I was stretched on the platform. I never heard the defendants claim credit for curing. If I had heard such a thing, I would have been home in Atlanta, Georgia."

The Devil Rebuked

Mrs. Florence Johnson of Chelsea, Massachusetts, was the next witness called. She has for four years been a member of the Pentecostal people and has attended meetings in Boston. She said, "Brother Earl Clark rebuked the devil, and my knee that I could not use for years was made well. I have never heard these people claim to cure; they say God can heal. I had a little girl eight years old instantly healed of bronchial and nervous troubles." The little girl herself then stood up and praised God she was healed.

Visions

Lillie Walker, an Evangelist of Chelsea, Massachusetts, said, "I saw a vision, the hand of God bleeding and the blood running down on me. I saw the skeleton of death. I have been healed of catarrh and weak eyes. I was put under the power. I was not unconscious."

Instantly Healed

Mrs. Elizabeth A. Davis, of St. Thomas, Ontario, Canada, testified: "I suffered from neuralgia and an ulcerated tooth, and the Lord, through Mrs. Etter, instantly healed me."

A Weak Lung Cured

Ethel Lewis of Petersburg, New York, testified that, on being prayed for, she had felt none of the feelings others had testified to, "but I received spiritual and physical healing by the laying on of hands. A weak lung was cured. I know it because I'm a trained nurse."

"A Good Work"

Mary Thomas, for thirty years a resident of Montwait, is not a member of the Pentecostal rank, but felt these people are doing a good work. "This arm I have not raised for twenty years. Since the coming of these people I can now raise my arm as high (raising her arm high up to illustrate) as this."

Healed of Heart Trouble

She testified: "I have been in a bad condition, broken down for five years. I had been to three physicians. I had neuritis and valvular heart trouble, and my husband had to turn me off my back in bed at nights. I have been perfectly healed at Montwait."

The above and many more can be found in the *Framingham Evening News* of August 28. We now give a few from *The Boston Herald* of August 27, of the sworn testimonies to divine healing. After hearing more than a dozen witnesses testify that they had been miraculously cured of long-standing ills through the laying on of hands of the Pentecostal disciples, Judge Kingsbury continued the trial until tomorrow.

Baptist Pastor's Wife

Seventeen-year Illness Cured

Mrs. Peck, whose husband is pastor of the Baptist Church at Petersburg, New York, testified that she had been cured of an illness of seventeen years standing, as a result of attending the Montwait meetings. She said she had never heard any of the defendants ask for money in exchange for cures.

Was Physical Wreck

Mrs. Carrie F. Craigan, of 563 Chestnut Street, Lynn, Massachusetts, testified: "I have been in evangelistic work many years and have been cured at Montwait of heart trouble, tumors, rheumatism, kidney and bladder trouble. I was a physical wreck when I came here, and had not been able to wear a corset for years."

Healed of Depression

Robert G. Lake, of New York City, says: "I am an undertaker, director of the First National Bank in my home city, and have been a member of the Methodist Church for the past twenty-eight years. I have been a mental sufferer for the past three months. My wife and I came to Montwait out of curiosity, and I have been wonderfully cured of mental depression, and my wife has been relieved of a physical ailment of twenty years standing. For twenty years she suffered from varicose veins and had to wear an elastic stocking, but now I believe she has been miraculously healed by God since coming to Montwait. If this is hypnotism, I would like to be hypnotized all my life. I would be a coward not to stand up and say what God has done in my case." He added: "My mental state was such that my heartbroken wife thought I had ceased to love her and was about to separate from me, yet the sky above seemed of hard brass, and I could get no help until I came to Montwait."

Many unimpeachable testimonies were given for which we have no space; but these ought to satisfy any fair-minded inquirer that God is healing people today, and that their testimonies are genuine beyond all doubt. They satisfied Judge Kingsbury, for on September 2, 1913, in district court, he found the defendants not guilty and dismissed the case. The silly claims of unbelievers that people were not healed were disproved by scores of living witnesses under oath and forever set to rest.

Wonderful Healing

(Copied from *Word and Work*)

Testimony of Miss Jessie Van Dusen of Knoxville, Pennsylvania, Tiago County, given in the tabernacle during C. B. Fockler's address, Sunday evening, August 24, 1913.

I am glad to testify tonight to the healing power of Jesus. Three years ago I was injured in an accident, and from that time I had serious attacks of pain in my back and stomach. About two years ago they became more frequent, so I had to go to bed and then to the hospital.

A year and a half ago I was taken to another hospital. Ddoctors operated and operated and tried to find where the trouble was, but I was taken home in a few weeks in the same condition. About a year ago in the hospital in Philadelphia, I asked the doctor if I ever would be strong again. He did not give me any encouragement, and I was in bed almost all winter. I could not see anyone and suffered intense agony in my back. In March, the pressure went into my hip, and the hip would not work; I would fall to the ground. Then it went to the ankle, and I could not use my foot. I was terribly ill. I had two doctors, but they said they could not do anything at all. I was taken to the University Hospital in Philadelphia, but the doctor would not operate on account of my weak heart. They fixed up an iron brace for me that came around the hip and up the back. They told me if I got stronger, they would operate, but said they could do nothing to relieve me of pain.

I was given morphine, and this was worse than the pain. I said I would rather stand the pain than the aftereffects of the drug. When I went home from the University Hospital the middle of May, it was the last time I was out of the house. I could walk a little on the level, but could not step down or up.

During these eighteen weeks, I gradually grew worse in my spine, then my head. Sometimes I was delirious, not knowing my own people or the family physician. The agony of that time can only be known to one who has gone through it. I was blistered at the base of my brain to give me a little relief. About two weeks ago someone brought Sister Etter's book to the house. I knew God, and I said, "If He can heal others, why not me?" I looked up to God and said, "If you want me to go to Montwait, You will have to give me the means," as I had used all my money on doctors and hospitals. The sister who brought the book told me the Pentecostal people wanted to pay my expenses if I could go. My sisters did not believe this way, but were willing to have me come here; they had done everything they could, and I was growing worse every day. I was afraid to ask the physician if I could go three or four hundred miles, but I asked him if I could go six miles to a friend. He finally said if I had a strong hypodermic before I started, perhaps I could go. He said he would come and give it, but he did not come, and I started without it.

I went six miles the first day. The next place I was very bad, and a physician was called, but we started the next morning by faith in God and came on to Geneva. I had another attack; at Syracuse a week ago, I was unconscious and did not realize anything for a long time. At the station they called a trained nurse and a physician, and he said the only way I could go on was to get a cot and be carried on that. I arrived at South Framingham on Saturday, but was too sick to be brought to Montwait. I had got my eyes off God and onto my feelings. Some of the party came here to Montwait, and when they told me how God was working, it gave me new life, and I said, "I will go this afternoon."

I was brought in an automobile and carried to the platform in a chair. I had not been able to stand any noise or talking for fifteen months, but I was not a bit frightened. I wanted Jesus to heal me, and I wanted Him. As I sat in the chair, almost before hands were laid on me for healing, the power came all through me, and I was laid out by the mighty power of God, and He talked to me. He let me see the cross of Jesus and the blood shed on Calvary, and I knew it was for my body as well as my soul. He told me I was every whit whole. In South Framingham, I stayed at the Standish Hotel, and Mrs. Gold said to me, "If you go there and are healed, I shall know it is of God." I have been back there, walked to the train, to the hotel and upstairs. I am healed, and without money and without price. I never had any conversation with Sister Etter, never shook hands with her, never paid her a dollar.

Convinced

I came to Montwait as Miss Jesse Van Dusen's nurse, having prejudice against the Pentecostal people. It never occurred to me that I would be affected in the least by the meetings, because I thought I was already established in the Lord and that the Pentecostal people were in error. I went to the meeting Saturday afternoon and became so stirred up that I left. In the night service, during the singing by the heavenly choir, I was convinced that it was of God. I became so anxious to have Miss Van Dusen healed that I promised her that I would seek more of God if she would go for healing. After I saw that she was healed, I felt I must keep my promise. Although I always wanted God to manifest Himself through me in a very quiet way, after I yielded myself to Him, His power came upon me, and I lay under it for an hour. The preciousness of that hour can never be fully explained. I do praise God for taking out all prejudice and making me willing to let Him have His way.

—*Florence Olive Cargill*
Knoxville, Pennsylvania

Testimony of a Doctor, as Given on the Witness Stand

(From *Word and Work*)

Dr. Mulford said, "I have practiced in Cleveland, Philadelphia, and as a missionary in India, going out independently as a medical missionary. I came in touch with the Pentecostal people while in India and became a believer in their work.

"I came to Montwait because I wanted to attend a Pentecostal camp meeting. I have observed what has taken place on the platform, and I should say there was no hypnotism practiced on the platform; my reason for so thinking is that the people were not in the condition hypnotized persons would be in. I was on the platform in the chair. I was told by someone (I do not know who) that I must praise the Lord for all He had done and all He would do; then two or three persons laid hands on my head and shoulders, I do not recall the words that were said. Before I went on the platform, I was suffering much indeed; afterwards, when I went home I was entirely healed, spiritually, mentally, and physically."

Note: I knew this doctor quite well at Rochester, New York State, 1915.

—Elder A. E. Sidford

Cancer Healed

I went to Montwait to be healed of a very bad cancer in my face. The doctors said there was no hope for me. Now I am healed, for Jesus has healed me. All praise and glory to His name.

—Adelia Robinson
Brentwood, New Hampshire

Healed of Ulceration and Neuralgia

I suffered from ulceration and neuralgia in the right side of my face and around the right eye for a long time. The first time I was ministered to in the Etter meetings at Montwait, there seemed to be only partial, if any deliverance in the feeling. The second time, I crossed the word "ailments" on the card and wrote, "I desire the baptism of the Holy Spirit more than anything else."

When ministered to, one of the brothers asked, "What ailment?" I replied, "Strike that out. I desire the baptism of the Holy Spirit with all it involves, more than anything beside." They prayed, and among other petitions I remember this: "Lord, rebuke every weakness in this woman's body." Since then the right side of the face and right eye have been free, and better still, I have the assurance of faith that the baptism in the Holy Spirit and fire is mine. Praise the Lord! He is faithful who has promised. Glory to His Name.

—*Lucy D. Harrington*

Testimonies Under Oath

(From *The Bridegroom Messenger*)

Satan, the enemy of Jesus Christ and His power, surely overreached himself when he caused the chief of police of South Framingham, Massachusetts, to issue warrants for the arrest of Mrs. M. B. Woodworth-Etter and her colaborers, Cyrus B. Fockler and Earl W. Clark, for obtaining money under false pretenses. The prosecuting attorney stated, "That the whole trend of the complaint was the pretense of these parties affecting cures" of all kinds of sicknesses and diseases. This arrest gave a glorious opportunity to put upon the witness stand about thirty witnesses, who, under oath, told how they had been spiritually blessed and healed. These witnesses came from many walks of life.

Ministers, doctors, missionaries, nurses, schoolteachers, a dramatist, and a banker—old, middle aged, and young—all told of the wonderful power of God, how it surged through their spirits and bodies when in the name of Jesus Christ hands were laid upon them, and the demons and diseases were rebuked, some falling prostrate under the power of God, others leaping and praising God in a loud voice. The purpose of this article, however, is not so much to speak about the court trial and the victory that was won by the judge deciding in favor of the defendants and against the chief of police and his fellows, as it is to bring before the readers the fact that these people were healed, some being real miracles of healing.

One woman was healed of cancer, and others who were pronounced hopeless by the physicians. These persons of their own volition, under oath, gave testimony to the same. Some criticisms and whisperings have been heard concerning the methods by which these blessed results are obtained, some also doubted concerning healings reported in these meetings. This perhaps is due to several causes, one being because some came more desirous to be healed than to worship God, often having in their hearts some hidden iniquity, which God sees and which hinders them from being healed; these and their friends, of course, give an adverse report.

Why Some Go Back

Then there are occasionally some who testify to healing and soon afterwards, when tempted, backslide from their healing, just like many professing conversion and others professing the baptism backslide. Yet we do not hear such harsh criticism concerning the latter as we do the former; all ministers and workers continue to urge men to become converted and baptized in the Spirit and warn them against backsliding. Why not do the same in reference to the healing of the body? What is wrong with this method? Did not Jesus give us to understand that all this was likely to occur, when He said, *"Sin no more, lest a worse thing come unto thee"* (John 5:14)?

Then there may be here and there an isolated case of some enthusiast who declares he is healed and gives testimony to that effect, gladly offering to have it published, yet soon afterwards speaks of only having "taken it by faith."

Concerning all such, and any other apparent failures of any kind, we express our deepest regrets, and we would urge all who write to be sure that the persons written about do not belong to any of the above classes. There are hundreds of perfect healings in these meetings everywhere; persons like these sworn witnesses of Montwait, Massachusetts, who would under oath testify to the mighty power of God that came upon them, when in the name of Jesus Christ the evil spirits and diseases were rebuked and hands laid on them, according to the command of Jesus.

About Methods of Healing

And now a few words on the whisperings concerning the methods used in these meetings. Is it wrong to have a person for convenience sake come upon the platform because of the great throng around the altar? Is it wrong to ask him if his soul is right with God? Is it wrong to tell him to surrender himself fully to Jesus and to expect Him to free him from all their diseases?

Is it wrong, like Peter and John, to fasten our eyes upon them and command them to look on us, and then in the name of Jesus Christ command them to rise up and walk, taking them by the hand and helping them up? Is it wrong to say, like Peter, *"Aeneas, Jesus Christ maketh thee whole"* (Acts 9:34)?

Is it wrong, like Paul, to steadfastly look upon one and thereby perceive whether they have faith to be healed or not? Is it wrong to command in a loud voice for them to stand upright on their feet? Is it wrong to do as Paul did, coming to one possessed with a wrong spirit, and command it in the name of Jesus Christ to come out of them? Is it wrong for the people to sing and unitedly praise God and be filled with great joy?

Is it wrong, as when Solomon dedicated the temple, to have a great crowd of priests (ministers) and many singers and instruments of music, all making one mighty sound of praise so that the whole house was filled with the glory of the Lord, so that the priest could not minister for the glory of the Lord (see 1 Kings 8:11), and all the people fell upon their faces on the ground?

And last, is it wrong to urge the person being ministered to, to act on his faith by telling him to clap his hands and praise the Lord? No, truly, no! I believe there can only be one answer to all the above questions and that is, that it is not wrong but is right, and therefore, these methods are encouraging faith in God with the persons being ministered to and to others desiring ministry.

If the methods employed in these meetings are wrong, then Solomon's methods in the dedication of the temple were wrong, and he himself a great deceiver. Then Peter and John and Paul were wrong in their methods, and Jesus also, for He told them to "look up," to "stretch forth their hand," and in many other ways encouraged them to act in faith.

Nonsense! Why all this doubting and murmuring about methods and this power? They may not be according to some persons sedate methods, but God honors and blesses them, and hundreds are being saved and healed and baptized in the Holy Spirit in these meetings. Let all cease from murmuring lest we fall into the same manner of unbelief. *"Neither murmur ye, as some of them also murmured, and were destroyed of the destroyer"* (1 Cor. 10:10).

—*Cyrus B. Fockler*

Under the Power of the Holy Ghost

Testimony of Florence Johnson Given on the Witness Stand

I have been connected with the Pentecostal movement for about four years. Previous to that I was a member of the Methodist Church. Have attended

Pentecostal meetings in Boston. I have been on the platform at Montwait and was healed there. Sister Etter asked for anyone who wanted to be healed to come forward, and I went up and sat in the chair. I had not been able to move my knee for over a year. Brother Clark rebuked the devil; they prayed; I prayed and praised God. I was laid out under the power; when I came to, I could walk and haven't had a bit of pain since.

Yes, I have seen exhibitions of hypnotism when I was a young girl. I think I was put under hypnotic power, and it was altogether different from this. They looked you right in the eye; here, I had my eyes closed.

Yes, I know of others beside myself who have been benefited at these meetings. There was a little girl, eight years old, healed of bronchitis and nervous trouble; she was healed instantly. She went under the power and came out speaking in tongues. No, I did not understand what she said. She was under the power of the Holy Spirit. I have heard others talk in tongues and have talked myself. No, I did not understand what I said; no one knows, unless it is interpreted; or sometimes, someone is present who knows the language and can interpret it. No, Sister Etter cannot understand it unless God gives her the interpretation.

Epileptic Cured

Testimony of Mrs. Eva Harris, Given on the Witness Stand

In reply to questions, Mrs. Harris stated: I intended to send my daughter to Montwait with a friend. She has been afflicted with epilepsy for years; I did not intend to come myself, but I felt that I needed spiritual help; I decided for spiritual instruction and received it. My daughter has been afflicted with epilepsy since she was eleven months old. She is a different child since coming to Montwait; she did not even remember coming. Now she is almost in a normal condition. I was present when she went on the platform and answered for her. Several laid hands on her. I was so anxious I did not notice, but I think they all placed their hands upon her. I do not think I would care to have her placed on the stand, but she is at Montwait. I think any physician would say it might be injurious for her to be placed on the stand, it might be a strain on her mental capacity. She has been treated by Dr. Mills of Philadelphia, Dr. Stuart of Atlantic City, and by Dr. Jackson of Albion, until recently. I think excitement is likely to have a bad effect on her, although she has not been affected at Montwait. I do not claim instantaneous healing. God does not always heal instantly. I am sure she is healed and is improving; her face was perfectly blank when she came here. She was treated on the platform in the chair; I do not think she lost consciousness at all. She said she knew we were with her; she was carried away, and I was beside her; she lay probably half an hour and then walked home. I have not had a doctor examine her since. I did not think it was necessary. It is not Mrs. Etter I am trusting in; it is God.

The Baptism of Power
August 14, 1913

After some hearty singing and devout prayers, Mrs. Etter asked that all who had been called to be preachers, workers, evangelists, and missionaries should separate themselves from the congregation. The large platform was cleared for them, and about one hundred filled it. Mrs. Etter asked the people to pray that these disciples might all be baptized with the Holy Spirit and fire before they went out to the work. Mrs. Etter said that at Chicago she had laid her hands on two hundred ministers for the baptism of power, and great is the multitude that is going to publish the Gospel. They want the signs in all parts of the earth, and many hundreds of handkerchiefs are being sent out, Mrs. Etter said, to those we cannot reach.

Mrs. Etter and the elders then laid hands on the heads of each candidate for the ministry, and Mrs. Etter said, *"Receive ye the Holy Ghost"* (John 20:22), and imparted to each disciple the power to heal the sick and cast out devils. Mrs. Etter believes that the command of the disciples, whom Jesus sent out two by two, is just as binding upon His disciples of today, and that the signs He promised them should follow their preaching the Gospel will follow our preaching, if we really believe and meet God's conditions of faith and obedience.

She referred to Elijah's faith and Elisha's striking the river with the mantle when the waters parted, to let him pass over dry-shod. Strike the mantle every time, and remove every obstacle to God's work. Mrs. Etter told them God never gives us courage today for tomorrow's work. Jesus commanded Lazarus to come forth. "In My name," Jesus said, "you shall cast out devils, and you shall lay hands on the sick and they shall recover." (See Mark 16:17.) Mrs. Etter said that God is a match for anyone. He uses a poor worm of the dust like me, who feels as if I could crawl out of sight under the altar. Then she talked of Paul wanting to visit the baptized people so he could impart special gifts to them by the laying on of hands. Then she said to the candidates that Holy Spirit power gives courage and authority; therefore, get the fullness of the Spirit.

Mrs. Etter declared we live in the last times. We have to preach the Gospel of the coming King, in the Holy Spirit power. We are the messengers to blow the Gospel trumpets and make sinners tremble. The Day of the Lord is at hand, even at the door. The question is asked. Why are not all healed? For the same reason that Jesus could do no greater works in Nazareth, I suppose. Some people do not believe they can be healed, and the Bible says. *"Without faith it is impossible to please* [God]" (Heb. 11:6). *"Let not that* [doubting, wavering] *man think he shall receive any thing of the Lord"* (James 1:7).

—*Mrs. E. W. Pitblado*
South Framingham, Massachusetts

43

DISEASED MADE WHOLE

God was with us in power to save and heal. Many ministers and workers were present from many states. The Word was spoken with power and great was the multitude that gathered up and carried the baskets full to give out to hungry souls. Many miracles of healings were performed.

One, a girl who was hopelessly blind, was saved and got instantly healed. When we laid hands on her and prayed for her sight, it was perfectly restored. Her mother was taken there, a hopeless cripple with many diseases, nearly insane. She thought that she had committed the unpardonable sin. She was saved, healed, made perfectly whole, and received the baptism of the Holy Spirit. She then went from Arkansas to California, telling all along the way what God had done for her. After two years, I met them again in San Francisco, California, both full of the Spirit and always ready to tell the large audiences how wonderfully God had healed them. The young sister who received her sight had the loveliest pair of blue eyes you ever saw; large, with long lashes. It surely was a great miracle.

A saloonkeeper in the city bought one of my books, *Acts of the Holy Spirit*, and took it to his wife. She had taken very sick. While sitting by and waiting on her, he began to read the book. He got convicted, was converted, and soon sold out his two saloons and went to Moody's Bible School in Chicago, and is now preaching the Gospel. This is just a little of what God did in the Hot Springs meeting.

I could write a good-sized book from every meeting that we held, telling what God has wrought, but write just a little here that you may know that there is a God in Israel.

—*Mrs. Woodworth-Etter*

More Good Work

(From *Word and Work*)

The good work goes on, praise God! One night a man, blind for twenty-five years, was healed. He had been pronounced incurable by specialists. God sent him here from Des Moines, Iowa, to receive his sight. Others are being healed.

God Stretching His Hand to Heal

Revival Spreading throughout the City

Hot Springs, Arkansas

In the providence of God, our beloved sister, Mrs. M. B. Woodworth-Etter, and Brothers Earl W. Clark and C. B. Fockler have come to Hot Springs, Arkansas. The meeting is being conducted in the auditorium in Whittington Park, a very beautiful place, and a blessed revival is spreading throughout the city. More than one hundred campers came from the Malvern Camp to attend this meeting. Visitors have come from almost every state in the South and some from the northern states. Most of them have come to be healed. In the first night of the meeting, the first two who were prayed for fell under the power immediately after prayer, and the next day testified that God had healed them. Many have since been greatly blessed of the Lord and testify to healing.

One woman, sixty-seven years old, was instantly healed of deafness of thirty-five years standing. She could hear even a low-toned conversation. (The writer was standing by her side when prayed for and witnessed the deliverance with his own eyes.)

Mrs. Ruth Webster said: "For the glory of God, I want to tell of my healing. I came to Malvern and on to Hot Springs to be in the meeting. While at Malvern, prayer was offered with laying on of hands in Jesus' name, and through His stripes I was made whole. I was healed of two fibroid tumors and stomach trouble. Inside of a week I was reduced six inches around the waist and three inches around the hips and abdomen, besides realizing a great change inside the body. Just like Jesus! Praise His dear name! I am saved, filled, healed, and looking for Jesus' soon coming."

Mrs. Minnie McHargue, from Missouri, said: "I came to Hot Springs on the twenty-fifth of September, and on the twenty-eighth of September the Lord healed my body of tuberculosis of the left kidney and throat trouble. He also gave me my voice."

Singing in the Spirit, the heavenly anthem, the song that none but the redeemed can sing, is a frequent and very beautiful manifestation of the Holy Spirit. This is generally followed by beautiful messages from the Lord through prophecy and tongues and interpretations. One very blessed feature of the meeting is the love and unity manifested among the saints.

—D. C. O. Opperman

Jehovah Still Working

November 20, 1913

There have been several remarkable cases of healing lately. A woman, with scrofula from childhood, came from St. Joseph, Missouri, and was healed the same day. A man from Hot Springs was wonderfully saved and healed of rheumatism of years standing last Sunday. Also, a girl, a graduate of the state deaf-and-dumb school, was healed of deafness and could hear clearly.

We have moved the meetings from the park to the Opera House downtown. The interest is increasing.

—Howard A. Goss
Hot Springs, Arkansas

"I Am the Lord that Healeth Thee"

The Testimonies of Two Women Who Were Miraculously Healed by the Lord in the Revival at Hot Springs, Arkansas

(Copied from *The Christian Evangel*)

"And they went forth, and preached every where, the Lord working with them, and confirming the word with signs following" (Mark 16:20).

Thirty years ago there were scarcely any witnesses to the healing virtue of the Lord Jesus Christ. Those who did press through and touch the hem of His garment were so filled with holy boldness that, in spite of great opposition, the glad tidings of deliverance for the body as well as the soul through the reconciliation of Christ spread abroad. Those in opposition were gradually shamed into silence, and thousands both in this and other lands have come into the knowledge of Christ, the Healer of all their diseases and the Savior of their souls.

During the past few years the power of God in the healing of the sick has been brought before the world in a more aggressive manner than ever before. Great meetings have been held in which the healing of the sick was a prominent feature, thousands of lives being touched, and many being converted through the manifestations of the power of God on their own bodies, or else on the bodies of their friends. Prominent among these are the meetings of Mrs. M. B. Woodworth-Etter in Dallas, Texas; Long Hill, Connecticut; Chicago, Illinois; Montwait, Massachusetts; and Hot Springs, Arkansas.

I was converted seventeen years ago, but praise the Lord, He baptized me in the Holy Spirit and fire, and I am now healthy and happy, eat and sleep well, and never get tired of running to and fro, telling of the wonderful works of Jesus. Bless His holy name.

—*Mrs. Preston Roberts*

Healed of Rheumatism and Bowel Trouble

Hot Springs, Arkansas, November 27, 1913

I was healed of afflictions of four years' standing. Had rheumatism and could hardly get around with the aid of a crutch and cane, and was all doubled up with pain so that I could not go up and down stairs at all and was unable to do my own housework. I had an operation performed for bowel trouble, and during the operation one of the muscles of the stomach was severed so that I had no control over my bowels at all. But, thank the Lord, I was made every whit whole when hands were laid on me in Sister Etter's meeting. How wonderful are the works of God. I want to tell everyone I meet of my healing, for now I can run up and down stairs, wash, iron, or anything there is to be done about the house. The greatest miracle is that God has joined together the severed muscle, and I now have perfect control of my bowels. Praise His precious name!

—Mrs. Barnett

Note: The sister gave this testimony on the above date and demonstrated her healing by running up and down the aisle, shouting and praising the Lord. She received her healing in the first part of the meeting, about three months previous, and is still shouting His praises.

The Lasting Influence of the Meeting

(These testimonies especially reported for
The Christian Evangel by Earl W. Clark)

When we left, the whole city was stirred by the mighty power of God. The meetings continued in power and demonstration of the Spirit; many were saved and healed and baptized in the Holy Spirit, for the hall in which we held meetings had been secured for six months, and Brother Fockler was left in charge until Christmas. One of the lasting results of the meeting was the donation from a sister of five thousand dollars with which to erect a tabernacle for the Pentecostal work. Brother Opperman is in charge of the Hot Springs work and is opening a Bible school.

Hope for Sinners

O sinner, friend, wouldst thou be free
From thy passion, thy pride, and thy sin?
Throw open the door of thy heart
And let the dear Savior come in.

CHORUS

Are you coming? Yes, I'm coming,
   I am coming home to Thee,
For I hear the Savior calling,
   And there's hope for even me.

Come down from your self-pleasing life,
   Its ambitions, follies, and its cares,
For what price would you barter your soul
   And be outside the City up there!

Come down from your works, to gain heaven,
   Your empty profession and creed,
Your goodness or wisdom in self,
   Your schemes to make money through greed.

Come down as Zacchaeus came down.
   From your self-exaltation today,
For salvation comes down to the lost,
   And my Savior will never say nay.

See yon tree upon Calvary's mount,
   Where salvation was finished for you?
Praise God through the blood of the Lamb,
   It leaves us no climbing to do.

44

WONDERFUL HEALING

T (Copied from *The Way of Faith*, December 18, 1913)

he Lord is wonderfully working here in Memphis, beginning with the first meeting, a week ago Sunday. His Spirit was poured out in a striking way, healing many sick ones. He blesses Sister Etter, giving out the Word. Her mission is to call God's people together. They are coming from many states, as they do to all her meetings. There are people here who were healed a year ago in the Dallas meeting. Also a sister who was healed in the San Antonio meeting. Here is her testimony:

"Though it has been nearly a year since I was healed, my testimony has never been printed in any paper, but feeling it is my duty to God and man, I now send it. In the fall of 1912, a hard lump appeared in both my breasts. My home physician treated me for several weeks, and the lumps kept getting larger, and the swelling around them kept spreading out on my body and arms. He sent me to a specialist at Winona, Mississippi, and after examination he pronounced my trouble cancer, and wrote my home physician, and sent the letter by me, and he read the letter to us at home when I gave it to him. It said, 'I find Miss Ray to be suffering from malignant cancer in both breasts, etc., and I have advised her that her only hope of cure is an immediate surgical operation.' This was in October, and I put off the operation until June 18, 1913, and went to Sister Etter at San Antonio, Texas, and she laid her hands on me and prayed. The lumps and swelling went, and I was healed. I have been praising God ever since."

—*Miss Carrie Ray*

The Sick and the Lame Healed in Jesus' Name

Grace and Truth Assembly, Memphis, December 8, 1913

God has been mightily in our midst during the past week, showing Himself mighty to deliver from sin and sickness, and baptizing in the Holy Spirit. Crowds have been coming. The sick and the lame have been brought and have been healed in Jesus' name. Sunday morning a woman from another state was brought in, being carried by two. Before she got to the platform the power fell upon her, and she began to leap and praise God, healed and full of joy.

Many handkerchiefs[3] have been prayed over and sent out, and reports are coming in that the ones they were sent to were healed. Many are here from a distance, and others write they are coming.

Those Divided are Coming Together

(Copied from *The Christian Evangel*)

"Praise God, from whom all blessings flow." Surely the Lord is good. We trust the readers of *The Christian Evangel* will pray much for us and that the Lord will guide us. We started on our southern tour, expecting to spend from fifteen to thirty days in a place. We came here last Friday and opened our meeting Sunday, November 29. The attendance was good, and such a lovely spirit in the meetings. The meeting opened with such gracious healings. Sister Etter has great liberty in preaching, and as she laid hands on them, nearly everyone jumped and leaped and praised the Lord for their healing. All the saints were helping with uplifted hands, praying and believing for victory, which was very marked. Some were saved, and others baptized.

---

3. Those who do not understand the ministry of hankerchiefs need to read Acts 19:11–12. God has wonderfully used them of recent years, with "signs and wonders following."

The saints of the community, who were much divided, came together. Every difference was laid at Jesus' feet. All made a new start, determined to see and know nothing but Christ and Resurrection. They were all built up in the holy faith. The result was a wonderful outpouring of the Spirit.

45

TESTIMONY OF A MEDICAL DOCTOR

Woodworth-Etter Meeting

(Copied from the Meridian, Mississippi, *Star*)

Beginning New Year's night, at the gospel tent on Sixth Avenue, East End car line, with services held at 2 p.m. and 7:30 p.m. daily, the meetings have been a great success from the first service. The prominent figure in the meeting is Mrs. M. B. Woodworth-Etter of Indianapolis, Indiana, with thirty-five years' evangelistic experience. Thousands are reported to have received healings from the Lord through her ministry. Some fifteen or twenty persons have already testified to having been healed at this meeting, of diseases varying from neuralgia to Bright's disease and cancer. The tent is filled nightly with respectful and attentive audiences from the city and from out of town, from a distance of three hundred miles or less.

Among the number of persons prayed for, with the laying on of hands, was a daughter of a prominent physician and surgeon from northwest Alabama. She was unable to walk on account of a stiffened knee from rheumatism, after medical skill had been exhausted, her father testifying to her condition. Mrs. Etter is one of the most level-headed, matter-of-fact, discreet, and courageous women. Nothing is said or done by her that reflects unfavorably on other denominations or upon the physicians.

Numbers Healed While Sitting in Their Seats at Meridian, Mississippi

Multiple Blessings

(From *Christian Evangel*, January 17, 1914)

Truly the Lord is good, and His mercy endures forever. He is blessing us here in a marvelous way. While we are just beginning the meeting, yet the power of God is so manifest that numbers have been healed while sitting in their seats. The power of God is also falling on the people, and sinners are being saved in their homes.

Last Tuesday, a prominent physician from Alabama brought his daughter for healing. He is a doctor and surgeon and has taken his daughter to the best physicians in the country. She has been operated upon eight times. She has taken fifteen different anesthetics and has suffered the loss of one limb. Her remaining limb was all crooked with rheumatism. When prayed for, almost immediately the crooked limb straightened out, she raised her eyes to heaven, and with tears in her eyes, began shouting, "I am healed! It is straight! It is straight!" Nearly everyone in the tent was in tears, and there was a good crowd for an afternoon meeting. The doctor was so pleased and testified; he wanted all that the Lord had for him. At the night service he was down at the altar, seeking his baptism.

I want to thank those who are making it possible for us to send Sister Etter's book to the foreign fields. Fifteen books will go out this week. We are getting testimonies now from those we have already sent, of the blessings they are bringing to those receiving.

I am certain it will be a wonderful way to reach the heathen through divine healing, so continue to pray that the Lord will send us money to send the book out until every foreign missionary shall have received a copy.

Great Interest in Revival

(Copied from *The Christian Evangel*, January 31, 1914)

The interest in the meetings continues without a lull. A number have testified to having attended Moody and Sankey meetings, Sam Jones' meetings, all the big meetings that have been held here for the past twenty-five years, but never have they seen one to equal Sister Etter's meeting. Crowds throng the outside of the tent every night, and tomorrow they will add tent space enough to hold four hundred more people.

The Lord has marvelously healed many during the meeting. A very wonderful healing was that of a cotton buyer, well-known in Meridian, who had rheumatism for twenty-nine years and a bad case of pellagra for four years, and who was instantly healed when prayer was offered for him. He had been to the best physicians in the country without any permanent results, but when he came to the Great Physician, He healed him. Many are coming from surrounding states. Yesterday a man arrived from the state of Washington. His fare was seventy-four dollars. He came for the baptism of the Holy Spirit and healing.

Prayers of Faith for the Sick

All Glory to the Great Physician
By Earl W. Clark

We began our meeting here, on New Year's Day, 1914. The friends had provided a tent with a seating capacity of six to seven hundred people, just ten minutes' ride on the car from the center of the city, which made it convenient for everyone. The Lord very blessedly worked, filling the tent from the very beginning and manifesting His mighty power by healing the sick, as the prayer of faith was offered by Sister Etter, hands were laid on, and the demons cast out. At our very first meeting, a sister, Mrs. Mary E. Mills of Waterproof, Louisiana, received a wonderful healing. She gave the following testimony many times during the meeting and is still here to tell it:

"The first night of the meeting, January first, I went to the altar in a backslidden condition, to get right with God and be healed. I had a terrible stomach trouble, something like cancer of the stomach, for at times I had such pain in that part of my body that I could not stand to have the bedclothes on my stomach. The doctor did not advise me to start on the journey of three hundred miles to this meeting, as he was afraid I would die on the way, but I came and was compelled to take some medicine as a stimulant on the journey. I came in faith believing, and when I knew I was reclaimed by God and my soul was pure and holy, I went upon the platform for healing. Praise the Lord, I received healing almost instantly, whereas before I could not bear the weight of a blanket or my hand upon my stomach, I can pound it now, and I am perfectly healed. Glory to God! He is the Great Physician!"

Dr. Tucker of this city says that the Pentecostal people are the cleanest set of people he has ever mingled with; that he didn't smelt the odor of tobacco, snuff, or whiskey about any of them; that none of them ever went to movies, which was a great deal more than he could say of many others; and that, in a plain statement, they were the cleanest people, from the preacher up. He also told of being healed of throat and lung trouble, which he had for some time. Every time there would be rain, he said, his throat would be in a terrible condition, but since he had been prayed for, he has passed through several rainy periods and not felt the effects of it as formerly.

He was also prayed for by Sister Etter for something like a tumor and testified that it seemed to be greatly diminished. Praise God for healing power!

A baby was brought three hundred miles to be healed of water on the brain, its head being more than twice the normal size; it was a sight to behold. It was prayed for and its mother, who attends the meetings regularly, testifies that the child's head has been reduced a half-inch and that the child is gaining strength in other ways.

Mrs. Charles Woods, a resident of this city, was healed of Bright's disease while sitting in her seat. Glory to God! This was in the evening. The next morning a pain passed through her back, and the devil tried to tell her that she was not healed, but she rebuked the pain in the name of the Lord and now has no pains. We have a wonderful Savior!

A Fourteen-Year-Old Boy Healed

One of the brightest and best cases of healing is that of little Charlie Owen, Meridian, Mississippi, fourteen years old, who had been sick with rheumatism almost all his life and was known by the doctors as a bleeder. His physicians pronounced him incurable. He could not even play. When he was brought up to the platform to be prayed for, he could hardly walk. His father nearly carried him, and he looked so white, almost like a corpse. Glory to God, after being prayed for, he was instantly healed and walked down from the platform as well as anyone there. He says the doctors said they could not heal him, so he put his entire faith in God and was healed immediately. The color has returned to his cheeks, and he is a regular attendant at the meetings and never fails to testify to God's healing and saving power. He is a wonderful little missionary for Jesus. After his healing, his mother was healed, his father saved and healed, and his brother and sister healed. The family members are at the meetings every night. The father is a railroad engineer and will be very helpful in the Lord's work. Here is the boy's testimony:

I will be fourteen years old in May, 1914. I have been what the doctor called a "natural bleeder" all my life and have had rheumatism since I was about five years old. At times it would seem as though I would go into convulsions from the pain. I would have to take morphine, aspirin, cocaine, and all kinds of opiates for ease and had to have Mamma heat hot irons and bricks to put in bed with me to try and get some sleep. Sometimes I could not lie down at all.

But I went to Sister Etter's meeting here in January, and she laid hands on me and prayed, and, praise the dear Lord, I was healed. I have had a tooth pulled since, and I didn't bleed any more than anyone else would have. The Lord has also saved my soul and baptized me with the Holy Spirit. I am living on the "hallelujah side."

—*Charlie F. Owen*
823 B Street, Meridian, Mississippi

From Charlie's Mother

The Lord has healed the entire family during this meeting and Jesus has come in our home to dwell. Praise the Lord.

—*Mrs. Dan L. Owen*
823 B Street, Meridian, Mississippi

Wonderfully Healed of Bright's Disease

February 4, 1914

Dear Readers of the *Christian Evangel:*

I want to praise God for wonderfully healing me of kidney trouble and nervousness. I have suffered with kidney trouble for four years and have almost been a nervous wreck for ten years. I could scarcely sleep at night, and my back was weak and pained me continually. A doctor here, in Meridian, Mississippi, treated me for three years and said he could only give me temporary relief.

But, glory to God, I can never praise Him enough. He healed me January second here in Sister Etter's meeting. This is February fourth, and I am still healed and sleep well. Glory to Jesus! He also healed me of acute indigestion last June and baptized me in the Holy Spirit. Glory be to His name.

—*Mrs. M. L. Whitlock*
2051 26th Avenue and B Street, Meridian, Mississippi

Note: Miss Olga Carlson, 509 23rd Avenue, Meridian, Mississippi, in writing to us about the above case, did not give any particulars, but said, "It is a wonderful cure."

Following the Lord's Leading

We closed the meeting at Meridian, Mississippi, with victory in our souls. The family where we stayed is a beautiful Christian family and did all they could to entertain us and carry their share of the burden. When the hour arrived for us to leave, a number of saints gathered at the station to bid us farewell; tears of joy and sorrow were mingled together, sorrow because of our departure and joy because the time was fast approaching when we should part no more, but could be with Jesus forever. As the train pulled out of the station to go to Alabama, to the right stood a freight train in which was an engineer who had been saved with nearly all his household, and many of the family wonderfully healed.

At Birmingham, we enjoyed a much-needed rest with our relatives. When the saints of the city learned we were in their midst, they longed for us to come out to their various assemblies to hold meetings for them. One young man followed us all the way from Florida to see and to speak to us and be in our meetings. Among the outside calls we received while in Birmingham to hold meetings in various communities was one from Warrior, Alabama, a little place about fifteen or twenty miles out of the city. The saints there sent a delegation, begging us to come out to their place and to hold at least a few meetings. They were a good, eager-looking band of saints, and we felt that the Lord's hand was in it, and therefore it was our duty to go and hold a few meetings.

A Very Remarkable Incident

We went out on Saturday and came back Monday. When we reached Warrior, we were met by a host of saints, who all welcomed us to their town. One of the first to meet us at the station was Dr. J. W. Abbot, an old man of eighty years. About eight months previously, he had sent us a handkerchief to be prayed over, for an awful cancer that he had on his stomach. He had been battling with this cancer for some time, availing himself of the best aid medical science could give, but all without success. Even before the handkerchief reached him, God gave him the witness that he was healed, but he was afraid to eat a good, hearty meal yet. When the letter reached him a few days later, it had these words in it, "You can eat anything; it will not hurt you." At this his faith took a new hold on God. He began to eat hearty meals and has been a well man ever since; his cancer is gone. As he shook hands with us at the station, giving his testimony before the rest of the saints of what the Lord had done for him, he handed us a slip of paper. On it was an order for fifty copies of our book entitled *Acts of the Holy Spirit*, which he purchased to distribute among the people of the neighborhood.

During our short stay in Warrior, numbers were saved, healed, and baptized in the Holy Spirit. The saints came from near and far to attend these meetings. The Spirit of God came down in mighty power upon them, sometimes so strong on some that they danced in the Spirit, while others broke down before God and wept, making their way through to God.

In the home where we were entertained, numbers of saints would often gather together, and we spent much time singing praises to our Savior. In a number of these gatherings the power of God came on nearly all of those assembled. As many as three or four were speaking in other tongues, talking one to another under the influence of the Holy Spirit. At such times the whole room was always surcharged with the power of God.

46

"ENLARGE THE PLACE OF THY TENT"

Slight Earthquake Shakes City, Then Shaken by A Mighty Revival: Many People Healed, Saved, and Baptized

On the fifth day of March, 1914, Mr. Etter and myself (he then doing quite poorly), with two young men who were just branching into the Christian warfare, boarded the train for our field of labor in the city of Atlanta. The battle from a human standpoint promised to be a hard one, but we looked to Jesus, from whom we have received our commission. In His strength we went forward, knowing that as we did this, we would win a great victory for Him, which would result in bringing many souls into the kingdom. I had hoped that the Lord would send us at least one good Spirit-filled minister on whom I could depend a little to stand by my side, but no one seemed to be in sight, and no one was sent by God. In the meantime God showed me plainly that I was to look to Him entirely for the help and strength needed when the battle commenced, and that later He would send the help that I needed.

One thing that made the battle hard in Atlanta was the division of God's people into many factions. A number of the saints desired us to come a few months later, when they were going to have their large tabernacle ready for us; some seemed to pull one way and some another. A businessman of the city, Mr. C. H. Burge, has had a little mission for years and the worshippers there call themselves "The Gideon Band." These people later showed themselves worthy of the name. They sent a representative to Meridian while we were there and gave us an invitation to come to Atlanta. We felt that God's hand was in this invitation and so accepted it, provided that the way would be opened. When Brother Burge's representative reached home, he gathered together all the saints who could be interested in the prospect of having a great revival if I could come to their city.

It was to be a union meeting; no special doctrine was to be preached. Jesus and the cross were to be upheld as the need of sinners. It was to be a meeting for everyone, no matter to what creed or "ism" they belonged or whether they belonged to any at all. They formed a committee that was to look after the business and financial part. On this committee were men and women of various denominations. There were people on it from the various Pentecostal missions, from the Gideon mission, those who belonged to the Holiness movement, those connected with the Methodist and Baptist churches, etc.

A Glimpse of Battle Given by Vision

A short time before the meeting began, one of the workers had a vision in which he was in a place where about four or five feet of snow fell during the night. The next morning there was a struggle with all the people to get through the snow so they could go about their business. The roads were all blocked so that it seemed impossible for anyone to get through. Everyone seemed to be afraid to risk going any farther than their own premises in way of opening the road. The people seemed to be waiting for someone to come along and open the way. As they were in a great state of expectation, suddenly a one-horse cutter came along with a single individual in it; the occupant was a lady; this cutter worked its way right through the snow. Then quite a number of vehicles could be seen, all following this one-horse cutter. All kinds of traffic were soon carried on over this road, and the people seemed to be happy because someone had ventured to break through the snow and open the way. At this point he woke up and found it to be a vision. This took place just a few days before we started the meeting in the large and beautiful city of Atlanta, where God did such marvelous work for the sick and the afflicted in the body as well as the soul.

We had not been in the city more than one hour when the city was struck by an earthquake severe enough to throw dishes down from shelves in many homes. It was felt in many places, but the city seismograph did not register it. I and many others felt that it was the voice of God, thundering and warning the people that He was coming in great power and that awful judgments were soon coming on the world, that we were to get ready for the soon coming of Christ. We commenced on a Sunday morning with a large crowd. While I was preaching my first sermon, they carried a woman who was dying with consumption in on a cot. She was not in her regular dress but had on only a short gown, and she seemed to be choking to death. I could not stand it. I left the pulpit and went to her. She was dying and not even saved, burning with fever. I laid my hands on her and covered her with the blood of the Lamb of God. She quieted down, the fever left her, and she began at once to praise God and got off the bed just as she was, in her short gown, and walked back and forth before them all, shouting and praising the Lord. I went back and finished my sermon. In the afternoon she was on the platform, singing with the rest. Someone asked me if I knew what had become of the woman who was healed in the morning meeting. I said that I did not and that I had not seen her since. Someone said, "Why, she sits there on the platform!" She came forward nicely dressed and singing like the rest.

The report was soon circulated that wonderful things were being performed in the Old Baptist Tabernacle down on Luckie Street. During the day the interest increased until many were turned away for lack of seating room. It was estimated that in one night from one to two thousand people were turned away, the doors, aisles, and windows were packed with people listening to the Gospel being preached and watching the Spirit being demonstrated. People always manifested a great interest when the sick were being prayed for. They were not accustomed to seeing the sick being healed in the old Bible way and having the signs follow after believers, as spoken of in the last chapter of Mark. One of Atlanta's leading surgeons and physicians testified continually that in this meeting, case after case came on the platform for which medical science could do absolutely nothing in the way of curing them. This doctor himself (Dr. Bowen) was healed in the meeting after the physicians had given him up to die. At the close of the meeting, he and his wife were seeking their baptism in the Holy Spirit and preparing themselves to do missionary work the remainder of their lives.

Many neighborhoods outside of the city were greatly benefited by the meeting. Besides preaching and healing the sick, the Spirit manifested Himself in a new way, through the most consecrated ones dancing like David of old, both on the platform and in the audience. Little children, young men and women, and gray-haired men and women, all at one time could be seen dancing, being swayed to and fro as the Spirit moved them. Some, while being used so mightily by the Spirit in this way, would be prostrated and fall as dead and receive visions and revelations from God. Such a demonstration of the Spirit generally brought awe and conviction on sinners. They saw a supernatural power at work, and the more they investigated, the more this conviction deepened, until they gave their hearts to God.

Ten Mutes Healed

Among the miracles of healing in the first Atlanta meeting were about ten mutes, some who were born deaf and dumb. Among them was a lady who was healed and converted at the same time. She spoke several words of praise right away; her whole body became light with resurrection power. She began to dance back and forth right away and went to the piano and heard the music for the first time in her life. She was much affected and began to keep time with the music. Soon after she brought a friend with her who was born deaf and dumb. They were sitting together. The Holy Spirit took possession of a minister; he spoke several languages and danced and sang in the Spirit, and then he "spoke" the message in sign language. The message was to the deaf-and-dumb woman. God took hold of her, and her friend brought her to the altar. In a few minutes she was saved and could talk and hear. They both began praising the Lord and danced. They both went to the piano and cried and showed the audience that it was like getting into a new world. Oh, glory to God for His wonderful works! Let all the people praise Him. These things always move the audience to tears and shouts of praise.

A Jew Understands Message in Tongues

The same young minister, one of my workers, who traveled with me in another meeting, was speaking in other tongues. A Jew was in the congregation, and God talked through him to the Jew. The power of God struck the Jew so that he fell to the floor, like Paul, in a trance. Jesus appeared to him. When he came out, he was converted and filled with the Spirit. He arose and began to preach with great power and said the message was for him, speaking in the Hebrew language. He said the Lord appeared to him, and he was taken all through the Crucifixion. I never heard anyone before or since make Christ so real, showing up the tragedy of Calvary with so much power and eloquence, magnifying the name of Jesus. No one who saw and heard him could doubt that Jesus is the Messiah, the Son of God.

A Telegram Comes for Prayer

One night about the time I commenced to preach to a very large audience, a messenger boy came and handed me a telegram, which said that George Montgomery, the husband of Carrie Judd Montgomery, was dying with double pneumonia, and asked us to pray for him. I was well acquainted with the dear brother and felt that we could not spare him, that it would be for God's glory to raise him up.

I asked the saints to unite in faith while I prayed for him; I prayed aloud and received the witness that he was healed. I told the people we had victory, our prayers were heard, the plague was stayed, and the Lord would raise him up, and he would go to the camp meeting and glorify God.

This was Saturday night about nine o'clock when we prayed. Over in California the loved ones were watching every minute (all earthly hopes were gone) to see him pass away, and across the continent the Lord heard our cry and gave the witness that he was healed.

To the surprise of all, he rose up the next morning, dressed, walked to the dining room, and ate heartily. He is continuing to gain strength daily; praise the Lord for the great mercy in raising him up.

Many who read this will have heard about his long, serious illness and wonderful healing. Sister Montgomery had it published far and near, but she never knew how the Lord gave us faith and the witness that He had heard our prayers thousands of miles away, and gave me courage to tell the great company that he was healed and that we would soon hear from him. Oh, praise God! While we call on Him, He will answer. It is now two years since, and a few months ago while holding a meeting in San Francisco, he and Sister Montgomery were a great help in the revival there. Oh, how I praise the Lord for saving his life and that he was strong in faith and courage, going on together in the "good old way."

Physician and Surgeon Healed of Fractured Skull and Broken Limb

I was healed in Sister Etter's meeting on April 9, 1914, of an injury that I received in a wreck four years ago. My horse ran away with me, and I was thrown from my buggy and sustained severe injuries as follows: fractured cranium (skull), fracture of the lower third of the right fibula (or small bone), and injured internally where I was kicked over the heart, all of which left me a physical wreck. My heart was enlarged, had bad circulation, so much so that my skin was blue from mixed circulation, and I knew I could not live long. I was treated by the best doctors in our city. They held out no hopes for me, but all said that I would have to die, and that at an early date.

Just at that time I heard by chance of Sister Etter's meeting at the old Broughton Tabernacle on Luckie Street, and I went to see if Sister Etter could do anything for me. I heard her preach on divine healing, but I could understand very little of it; but I decided that I would try it anyway, as that was the last chance for me. So I went up for prayer, and Sister Etter laid hands on me and prayed that I might be made well, and I was healed instantly. That has been two years ago, and I am still healed today. Glory to Jesus!

I want to mention very briefly a few other healings I saw. I suppose I saw over one hundred healed of incurable diseases, such as we doctors can do nothing for: consumption, pellagra, Bright's disease, cancer, paralysis, blindness, and valvular heart trouble (or regurgitation of the blood). I saw these diseases healed two years ago, and all of them whom I am personally acquainted with are healed today. I will also mention two children I saw healed. One eighteen months old, who was born blind and seemed to have no marks of human intelligence, was badly deformed and had curvature of the spine so badly that the backbone was curved in such a manner as to be much higher than the shoulders. When Sister Etter prayed for it, the eyes received sight, the human intelligence came in, that awful curvature of the spine straightened out, the baby stood on its feet and smiled for the first time in its life, so the father and mother said, and, of course, they shouted and praised God. The other was a baby fifteen months old, a Methodist minister's baby, who was born blind and received its sight under Sister Etter's prayers. Could write a large book on the healing I saw in Sister Etter's meeting in the city of Atlanta in the nine weeks she was here in 1914.

Dear Sister, you may use this any way the dear Lord may direct, as I herewith give my consent for it to be used to the glory of God.

I am all for Jesus,
—*John H. Bowen*

P. S.: I neglected to say I am a physician and surgeon in the city of Atlanta, and am well known in many of our southern states, having practiced my profession twenty-one years and am still in the practice.

Yours, *J. H. B.*

"*Divine Healing*"

(Copied from the Daily Papers of Atlanta, Georgia)

Pastor Says Mrs. Etter Is Supported by Authority of the Bible

During his services Sunday morning, at Moore Memorial Church, Dr. Holderby referred to Mrs. Etter, who is conducting what she calls "divine healing" services at the old Broughton Tabernacle, having been asked by a number of people both in and out of the church to express his opinion of the teaching and methods of Mrs. Etter, who claims that God can heal the sick. "I have no hesitancy in giving my views," said Dr. Holderby. "I have not attended any of Mrs. Etter's services; but from what I am told as to her doctrine in the matter of God's power to heal the sick, she certainly has behind her the authority of the Bible and is therefore right. I never criticize anyone whose object is to do good, although I may not endorse all their ideals and methods. The doctrine of divine healing or healing by faith is certainly taught by Jesus Himself, and He gave command to His early church to preach the Gospel of the kingdom and to heal the sick. (See Matthew 9:35; 24:14.) And this the disciples did by the power of Christ. But the church seems to have lost the power because she repudiates the doctrine. The doctrine has become a 'dead letter.' Will the church ever regain her lost power? Yes, when she has faith. But this question of divine healing is very unpopular with the church today. The man who preaches it is regarded as an idiot or a fanatic. If the preacher is not prepared to lose his job, he had better not preach the doctrine of divine healing."

Note: What a comment this is on the lack of faith today!

Report of the President of the Executive Committee and His Associates

A testimony to the permanency of the work and healings

Note: Brother C. H. Burge is President also of the Local Camp of "The Gideons" or Christian Commercial Travelers' Association of America, whose main object is winning businessmen to Jesus Christ.

Atlanta, Georgia, June 27, 1914

To Whom It May Concern:

We, the undersigned members of the Executive Committee, and workers in charge of the Etter meetings, held in the city of Atlanta, Georgia, from March 8 to May 10, 1914, conducted by Mrs. M. B. Woodworth-Etter, of Indianapolis, Indiana, wish to, unsolicited, put our unqualified endorsement upon the work. While Mrs. Etter was here, many were saved, and hundreds and hundreds were most marvelously healed of nearly every disease known to science; many that had been declared hopeless and sent back from sanitariums to their homes were brought to these meetings, and by the laying on of hands by Sister Etter, were healed, and in many cases, instantly.

Atlanta has never been so wonderfully blessed in her history. Thousands were lifted up to a higher plane, and their faith increased by seeing the miracles performed; in fact, it was a most wonderful visitation of God.

We had heard so much from a certain source that the people would not retain their healings that we have delayed giving this endorsement of Mrs. Etter's work, but now we unhesitatingly say that we do not know, of the many hundreds that were healed in Atlanta, a single one that has not retained the healing. Many have increased in health and strength; and we have heard from many that had come from other cities and towns all over the United States to Atlanta to get healed and have gone back home, and they are still healed.

Any city or town that wishes to get someone that knows God in His fullness to come to hold a meeting might go all over the world and not find anyone that stirs the hearts of the people as Mrs. Etter. We might add that we were twice forced to enlarge the building in which the meetings were held; even after that, many nights we had to turn many hundreds away who were clamoring for admittance.

It is the desire of the many thousands who were saved under Mrs. Etter's ministry to have her come back in October and to hold meetings indefinitely. The work has gone on since Mrs. Etter left, services being held twice every day, conducted by Reverend C. B. Fockler.

—(Signed) *C. H. Burge* (Chairman), *Stella Murry,*
Thomas Bedford, Mrs. J. P. Eve, Charles Du Bose,
M. P. Askew, C. H. Hatcher

The Revival in Atlanta

Many Reported Saved and Healed, May 17, 1914

(Copied from *The Christian Evangel*)

New additions have again been made to accommodate the crowds that fill the tabernacle night after night. The day meetings are also largely attended. God is surely in the midst of His people. The mourners' bench is filled at every service—sinners seeking salvation, believers the baptism, and suffering humanity being relieved. A prominent citizen and surgeon of our city, who was injured in a wreck three years ago, beyond the help of the finest medical skill, found Jesus, and his body was made whole. He is seeking the baptism and testifies to this miraculous healing, witnessing on the platform. One feature of the meeting is that so many church members are seeking the baptism. One night, eight from one of our largest churches were at the altar at one time seeking. All kinds of diseases are being healed, including deaf mutes. People are coming from Oklahoma, Texas, Delaware, and Alabama, North and South Carolina, Tennessee, and other states. Sister Etter has presented Pentecost to the city of Atlanta in such a way as to take away the prejudice, and many are seeking God.

—(Signed) *Mrs. L. N. Harris,*
Chairman of Ladies' Committee on Arrangements

Further News of the Revival

One strong factor in drawing these people to the meetings is that they see the Gospel demonstrated, as of old, with *"signs following"* (Mark 16:20). The Lord

Himself is stretching forth His hand to heal, and signs and wonders are being done in the name of Jesus.

Some of the first signs that followed the Word here in Atlanta were a number of consumptives who were far beyond medical reach. These, after the demon had been cast out and the disease rebuked, walked and praised God, and began to mend from that very hour. Since then God has done many wonderful things in the way of displaying His power to convince even the hardest sinner of the reality of the Gospel and in supplying the sinner's need for both soul and body. It has stirred the people of Atlanta to such an extent that businessmen can be seen talking, while at business, about what is going on in the old Baptist Tabernacle down on Luckie Street. Some of Atlanta's leading men are being reached. One remarkable case is that of a little school boy, ten years old, who was blind in one eye ever since he was thirteen months old. After prayer, his sight was restored to such a degree that he could see out of it just about as good as the other.

The same evening a woman came in from an outside place with a little child a year old in her arms. The child's spine was useless; it could not sit up. Its mind also was affected; no one could draw its attention. It also was blind in one eye. After prayer it received strength in its spine, sat up straight, grasped hold of everything that it could get hold of, showed intelligence with a smile on its face, and also showed by every test that its sight was restored. The mother during this time was shedding tears and flowing over with praise to God.

A Reverend D. T. Cain, of Westminster, South Carolina, wrote for information about his case. He stated that he had been totally blind for nearly a year and spent his means on the physicians; he heard of the wonderful works that God was doing in Atlanta. He came as a last resort to receive back his sight. After prayer, his eyes were opened, so that he could see to read signs on the street. On the way home he testified to many on the train, and after reaching home began to preach again. About a dozen or more people gave testimonies to the fact that they personally knew Mr. Cain and that his testimony was correct.

Under the date of July 9, 1914, we received the following letter:

Brother D. T. Cain, a minister of Westminster, S. C., came to your meetings in Atlanta, Georgia, a few months ago, and was most marvelously healed of blindness and other disease. Praise the Lord. He left Westminster blind and suffering, came back seeing everybody. As soon as he came back home, he was met by a crowd at the depot. Oh, how he did praise the Lord! I heard all about this wonderful, wonderful healing.

A home missionary,
—Mrs. E. J. Harrison
Lando, S. C.

A telegram was received from a man in Colorado who wished to know how long the meetings would continue. He wanted to be healed and also to receive his baptism of the Holy Spirit. He came, got his baptism, and came out speaking in the German language. Some of these messages in tongues, spoken when under the influence of the Spirit, have been in Hebrew, and understood by some in the audience. As the result many Hebrews have been converted already, and also many healed. These are only a few of the scores of the miracles that are being performed by the power of God. Time and space forbid to mention any more.

The Atlanta Georgian News gives the names and accounts of healing of the following: Mrs. Aler, a blind woman. After being prayed for, she said, "Why, why, why, I can see! Look! I see the light!" The paper states that this is only one of a hundred cures affected during the three weeks that Sister Etter has been here.

Wonderfully Delivered from Lockjaw

(Healing of Margaret Daniels at the Etter meetings
in Atlanta, Georgia)

I desire to give my testimony to the glory of God and His dear Son, who bore our sicknesses and infirmities on the cross as well as our sins. Some weeks ago, while at my home in Wilmington, Delaware, after having the nerves of two teeth taken out by a dentist, symptoms of lockjaw began to develop, and the suffering I endured at times was almost unbearable. But through the prayer of faith and trusting God's promises, I had deliverance many times, but not complete victory. The awful pain and agony would return with redoubled force. Then again the "fight of faith" would bring victory to the extent that Satan was unable to lock my jaws.

While suffering thus, the Lord asked me if I would go to Atlanta and be a witness for Him. I told the Lord if He would open the way for me, I would go to Atlanta and have Mrs. Etter lay hands upon me and pray for my healing, and then be a witness for Him. The Lord provided the means almost immediately and made His way plain before my face.

I also had been a sufferer for eighteen years from terrible headaches caused by the roots of a tumor being cut away from five nerves of the brain and the nerve of the left eye. These headaches always prostrated me and brought on other complications. During those years the Lord gave many deliverances in answer to believing prayer, enabling me to go forth in His service, traveling thousands of miles, proving His grace to be sufficient.

On Sunday afternoon, March 8, the first day of the meetings held in Atlanta by Mrs. Etter, in the old tabernacle at Luckie Street and Tabernacle Place, hands were laid upon my head and jaws, and I was immediately healed by the Lord. Praise His name! It is wonderful! The resurrection life flows through my entire being. Glory to Jesus for such a marvelous deliverance and perfect healing.

—*Margaret Daniels*

Other Testimonies of Healing

Avoca, New York, June 4, 1914

Dear Precious Sister:

Please send a handkerchief over which you have prayed. *We have had marvelous results in using these for the sick.* I need this for myself; please pray for my body. I have your book, and I am praising God for a Pentecostal experience. Awaiting His coming,

—*Ersula Gledhill*
626 Stonewall Street, Dawson, Georgia, May 6, 1914

Mrs. Etter:

My child that I carried to you for prayer the night I left to come home, that the doctor had given up, he is now able to walk about. Hoping that you are having success in your work in the healing of the sick,

I am, truly,
—*Mrs. J. A. Perrin*

Laurel, Maryland, Oak Crest, May 19, 1914

My Dear Sister Etter—Beloved in the Lord:

I have delayed writing to you until I could say that there was not a vestige of the cancer left.

I praise God for your ministry on my behalf. He is getting much glory from my healing. The faith of many has been greatly strengthened through it, and words fail to tell what it has meant to me.

May the God of all grace pour out His richest blessings upon you is my constant prayer.

Your sister in the fellowship of the Spirit and the love of Jesus,
—*Mrs. Ellen M. Winter*

77 Brotherton Street, Atlanta, Georgia, May 10, 1914

Dear Sister Etter:

I wish to write my testimony for the glory of God. For years I was a sufferer from many diseases, spent hundreds of dollars for doctors, but never derived any benefit. I had indigestion in its worst form and would nearly die with what I thought was heart trouble after eating—had the very best specialist, but only temporary relief.

I also had rheumatism, was in a terrible condition, my limbs all swollen and drawn until I could not walk, and kidney trouble of several years standing, also other troubles—and all these twelve years of suffering. I could get no cure until I came to Sister Etter's meeting in Atlanta, and she laid hands on me and rebuked these diseases in Jesus' name. I believed that Jesus would heal me right then, and glory to His precious name—He instantly healed me of all those diseases, and I knew it, because the power of the blessed Holy Spirit came upon me, and I could feel the diseases going out of my body and the new life of Jesus Christ coming in. The feeling I shall never forget, for fully three hours after I left the meeting and I went home, I could still feel the healing power, and, praise His dear name, I have not had the slightest symptom of an ache or a pain since; all glory and praise be unto our God forever and ever.

Yours in His love,
—*Mrs. Mary N. Wheeler*

243 E. Georgia Avenue, Atlanta, Georgia

Dear Sister Etter:

Your meeting here has been such a glorious blessing to me of both soul and body. The Lord has healed me of Bright's disease and extreme nervousness.

I have been treated for years by the best physicians and have been told by them that I was liable to die any time. But glory to God I am well and expect to remain so by the blood of Jesus.

—*Mrs. H. P. Swilling*

Received Baptism and Came Under the Power of the Holy Spirit

I had been saved only a week, when on a Sunday afternoon, I was tarrying at one of the sister's homes, for a certain one of them to receive the baptism. I had only heard it preached once and knew very little about it. I wanted all the Lord had for me, and I hadn't been praying three minutes until I began swaying under the power of God. I had just told Him everything I had was on the altar, even husband and baby, and I wanted all He had for me. I knew it was the power of God and did not resist, but gave up completely.

They laid me on the floor. My body began to rock, and my hands were waving in the air. I was all the time praising Jesus and felt myself going up. They told me afterwards that my body raised until they could see the light under it.[4] I was between the window and the rest of them, about ten in number. The Holy Spirit came in singing in two or three unknown tongues. The people said one was Chinese, but did not know the others. I knew in my mind that I was singing, but could not sing it in English; later on I interpreted it in our language. Oh, such glory was around me until I thought I was almost in heaven, everything was so bright! I was singing the praises of God for two hours and a half, and never had my arms down during the time. They felt as light as the air. Afterward I was so strong I felt I could move a house, and my arms never had a particle of soreness in them after being held up that length of time. It was the power of God that kept them, and that keeps me daily. Oh, praise Him forever!

—*Mrs. Pearl Hopkins*
412 Williams Street, Jacksonville, Illinois

Baptized and Healed

A woman (Phillips, by name) was carried into the meeting on a cot, sick with pleurisy and consumption. When prayed for, she was delivered and received the baptism of the Holy Spirit. A few days later she sang and played in the Spirit

---

4. See also testimony of Brother A. W. Frodsham at Petosky, Chapter 48.

(demonstrated playing a harp) in such a way that the people were awestruck by the workings of the Spirit.

Mr. Walter Decker of Hempstead, New York, a young man traveling with The Dramatic Stock Company, was in a providential way drawn to the meeting. He soon was convicted that God was working and found his way to the mourners' bench, gave his heart to God, and shortly afterwards was speaking in another language as the Spirit gave him utterance, happy in Jesus. He went back home to tell the good news to his friends and relatives.

Mr. William Evans, 69 Grape Street, was totally blind for two years and also lame. They brought him in, he having to use two sticks. The doctors told him that there was not a chance for him to recover. When prayed for, the power of God struck him and healed him instantly, and he got up shouting the praises of God for his deliverance.

Mr. W. S. Napier, General Baggage Agent, of Houston, Texas, came to these meetings with creeping paralysis. He had been treated by the finest of specialists of Houston, Texas, and New Orleans, Louisiana, and was in such a condition that he would stagger; he had been unable to dress himself for about five months. He also had chronic stomach trouble. His doctors had dieted him, and he could eat but very little, and they gave him no hope whatever that he would recover. After prayer, his color changed, and he began to mend immediately. In a short time he could dress alone, could walk for blocks, feeling limber as a little schoolboy. In a few days' time he went home a happy man. This man had been for years a deacon of the First Baptist church of his city.

Richard C. Alewine, 424 Windsor Street, is a little boy eleven years old. He suffered with soft bones and had to walk on crutches. The doctors had operated on him eight times but held out no hopes for him whatever. They told him finally that he would have to die. He testifies that he heard about the Etter meetings and decided to come. He was prayed for and told by Sister Etter to throw away the crutches and never use them again. He did so and has never used them since.

Born Blind

On the night of the fourth of May, Mrs. G. L. Hickman, 68 Jones Avenue, brought in her little baby who was six months old, born blind. While being prayed for, its eyes opened so that he could see. A noted physician and surgeon was there to examine his eyes after they were opened, and testifies to the fact that he could see. The next day his father also gave positive testimony that he could see.

Ruskie Ramsey, East Point, Georgia, was healed of leakage of the heart. She had not been able to lie down for six months; she had also suffered from nervous prostration for some months.

Ralph Hammond of Atlanta, a boy eleven years old, was paralyzed in his arm, and his hand was drawn up. He also suffered with nervous fits and could not go to school on account of his nervous condition. He tells now with gladness that Jesus perfectly healed him, and he now goes to school.

Mrs. Ella Smith, of Tilton, Georgia, was deaf and dumb. After being prayed for by Sister Etter, she said she could hear the piano.

Mrs. Hart Baldwin, R.F.D. No. 2, Sandusky, Michigan, wrote: "Last February I wrote you requesting prayer and an anointed handkerchief for a rupture from which I was suffering greatly. I received the handkerchief and applied it in the name of Jesus, and, praise His name, He healed me instantly of the rupture. I have not seen or felt it since."

Nigie L. Lofron, of 20 Mason Avenue, a little girl who was born deaf and dumb, was instantly healed March 11 at the evening service when Mrs. Etter commanded the deaf-and-dumb spirit to depart in the name of Jesus. Before Mrs. Etter began to lay hands on the child, she was frightened and began to cry. When she was healed, she put her arms around her neck and kissed her. The child's father said he had tried specialists for years, but they could do nothing for her.

One day an elderly man said he had driven four hundred miles to get to the meetings. The lower part of his body was paralyzed so that his limbs were lifeless, and his arm also was withered. It took three men to carry him onto the platform. When he was told to raise his foot, he made an effort but could not. He was then told to do so in the name of Jesus, and he tried again, and the foot moved a little; when he tried again, the limb moved more; he struggled and soon got the victory, and in a short time he walked the platform shouting and praising God. About a month later, testimony was sent in that his arm had filled in nicely and that he was well.

Work Among the People

In the city of Atlanta—as is common in the South—the white and colored races do not worship together. From the first of the meeting, some of the colored brothers ventured to attend the services, sitting in the rear, alone. This was permitted for a time because it seemed impossible to turn them away. These friends soon spread the news in the colored settlements, telling how God worked, that the power was being demonstrated, and signs and wonders followed, as of old when Christ was on earth. As a result of this, the colored folks came and occupied so many seats as to crowd out the white people. They now begged Sister Etter to come to some of their large churches and hold a few meetings for them. She felt constrained to go to them as they were prohibited from attending the regular services in large numbers. They stood around the outside on many occasions with the sick and waited until the service was dismissed, just to have Sister Etter say a word or lay her hand on them and pray while she was passing by. In nearly every case of this kind, they received instant healing, jumping to their feet, praising God, and leaping and shouting for joy.

Arrangements were made to give them a meeting a week in various churches of the city. They would come together in large numbers in these gatherings, as they had secured the largest churches possible for the meetings, including Methodists, Baptists, and other creeds. In these meetings, when it came time for praying for the sick, it seemed almost impossible to hold back the throng, so many were anxiously awaiting to get into the pool and have the Living Water cleanse and heal them. The floor was at times covered with the slain of the Lord.

Limbs and Spine Straightened

A middle-aged man was carried in on crutches, having all his limbs drawn out of place. He had been in this condition for years, being a hopeless case from a medical standpoint. When he was prayed for, his limbs could be seen straightening out, and he walked out of the meeting carrying his crutches.

A young girl was prayed for; the power struck her and prostrated her on the floor. She had curvature of the spine and other diseases. The power came on her so strong that it straightened her spine immediately while she was lying on the floor. Those with cancers, consumption, and nervous troubles were healed, and all kinds of demons were cast out during these few meetings. Many calls from various parts of the city could not be met. Nevertheless, the people all praised God that Sister Etter had been permitted to come into their midst and for what had been done for the colored people.

The Awesome Power of the Spirit

One feature of the meetings that held both saint and sinner awestruck was the way the Spirit manifested Himself through the heavenly choir. The Spirit operated much in this way from the beginning of the meeting until the end. Some of those whom the Spirit would use in this way were also prostrated and saw visions from God. When the Spirit operates in this way, deep conviction comes on the people. As the prophet said, *"Then shall the virgin rejoice in the dance, both young men and old together"* (Jer. 31:13). There were often seen dancing on the platform around the pulpit and near the front, from fifteen to twenty people or more at one time, with eyes closed, and never jostling against each other or falling off the edge of the platform. Many times some would stop and give a wonderful message in tongues loudly and fluently.

The Spirit of fear fell on the large audience. They knew there was a God in Israel who was putting a seal on His mighty signs and wonders. They were convinced that the same power that laid them down as dead, raised them up and made them dance so gracefully, and took hold of their vocal organs and made their tongues like *"the pen of a ready writer"* (Ps. 45:1), speaking the wonderful works and wisdom of God. Many languages were spoken and interpreted. They were given to know what language was spoken, sometimes by a minister or a stranger in the congregation. Sometimes little boys or girls, five years or more, would hold the people still as death, while they preached in tongues and interpreted, or in English, or while they danced, convincing the people that it was the Holy Spirit working through them. Many times unseen instruments were heard in the audience, mingled with the heavenly choir. A holy awe held the people. Many wept. All classes rushed to the altar in every meeting. All kinds of sick people and sinners, also helpless men and women with children, waited to be put in the pool.

On the last Sunday that Sister Etter and her workers were in Atlanta, the Lord's Supper was administered. This certainly was the great day of the feast. Nearly two hundred and fifty of the saints, newborn babes and older ones, came forward and partook of the bread and wine. Many came for the first time, and strong men wept like little children.

Detective Converted

A detective of the city, whose duty it was to spy out law-breakers, found himself to be a lawbreaker and a rebel against the powers that are on high; weeping like a little child, he made his way through to God.

At a late hour of the night, hundreds filed up in line to bid Sister Etter and her workers good-bye, giving them a hearty invitation to come back in the fall.

47

CONQUERING THE DEMON OF DEATH

On the way north from Atlanta, we stopped at London, Kentucky, and held a few meetings. The leader, Dr. G. F. Lucas, a noble-hearted dentist, had one case in mind, thinking that if that one individual got healed, he would feel himself amply repaid for giving the invitation to stop off at London. His case was a middle-aged man who was born deaf and dumb. When he was prayed for, his tongue was loosened and his ears opened, and he began at once to sound praises to God. He commenced learning words, and in a short time he could pronounce some of them after anyone. The assembly praised God for what they saw in the way of healing the sick, realizing in a new way that God's power is really the same today as of old, if the conditions are met. Two or three others who had been mutes since childhood were also delivered. An old, gray-haired man, who had been deaf since the Civil War, whose eardrum was destroyed in one ear and the doctor told him he could never hear out of it again, was prayed for and heard the birds singing with his lately deaf ear on the way home from the service.

God did wonders for this little assembly. A neighboring woman at the house where we were staying had a little child about a year old. This child had been deformed from its birth and had a very irritable spirit, so that the mother had to carry and nurse the child day and night. She brought her child to the house where we stayed to be prayed for. We readily saw that the child was possessed of a demon, which was cast out in the name of Jesus, and from that very hour the child began to mend. In a few days the child was normal and quiet. The mother praised God for delivering her child. At the close of this meeting we felt led to go to Indianapolis and rest before we began the battle at Petoskey, Michigan, where meetings were billed for the month of July.

Testimonies
Death Demon Conquered

London, Kentucky, May, 1914

Praise God for saving me and baptizing me with the blessed Holy Spirit and for what He is doing at this place.

Last Friday morning I was very sick. I did not know what was the matter, but I said I was going to church in the strength of Jesus, and then I fainted. On the way one of God's children laid his hands on my head and prayed, and I went on. The sickness increased. I could not see and could not talk. Then I became unconscious. People said I was dead: my pulse ceased to beat, and health was gone; my eyes and jaws were set. When I recovered consciousness, Sister Etter was standing over me, rebuking the demon of death. It seemed to me the smile of heaven was on her face, and such peace. I felt as if I was in the arms of Jesus.

She said, "You were poisoned." Every symptom was of poison.

"The works that I do shall he do also" (John 14:12).

—Mrs. J. C. Brewer

Note: A number of adult men and women testified that Sister Brewer was dead. They told the people that Sister Brewer was dead and that God raised her up when Sister Etter rebuked the monster death and commanded her to rise up.

London, Kentucky, May, 1914

I feel it would be to the glory of God for me to testify to the healing of my body. I have been suffering very severely from catarrh for years, and also from rheumatism, which I have had for four years.

Sister Etter laid her hands on me and prayed; then I felt the healing virtue of Jesus go through my body.

I also witness to the case of Mrs. J. C. Brewer. I laid my hands on her, and I believe she was really dead.

—*Rosa Green*

London, Kentucky, May, 1914

On May 13th, during Sister Etter's meeting at London, Kentucky, I was healed. I feel it would be to the glory of God for me to tell it. I have been healed of rheumatism, which I have had very seriously for two years, and also healed of female trouble.

I also witness to the healing of Mrs. J. C. Brewer. I saw her struggling in death, and I saw Sister Etter rebuking the demon of death. She had a very severe battle but soon was brought to life again. Oh, the wonderful works of God that were done through Sister Etter while holding the meeting in London!

—*Ella Freeman*

He's Real to Me

My Father God is real to me;
In Christ revealed His heart I see.
I am His child, a princely heir;
In royal rights with Christ I share.

CHORUS

He's real to me, He's real to me;
My Father God is real to me;
My soul demands reality;
My Father God is real to me.

My Savior's name is real to me;
In battle gives me victory;
It breaks the rule of Satan's host,
Restores the pow'r of Pentecost.

The Spirit's real, His mighty power
Protects me in temptation's hour;
In perfect light He guideth me,
And makes Himself Reality.

The Word is real, O soul, rejoice!
It is my blessed Savior's voice!
It tells me of His constant love,
That intercedes for me above.

His promise is so real to me;
He's coming in reality;
When I shall see His blessed face,
And praise Him for His matchless grace.

O soul, He will be real to thee
If thou but claim reality;
Be real thyself in ev'ry part,
Reality will fill thy heart.

48

ANGELIC MUSIC

The meeting at Petoskey, Michigan, was great in many ways, from first to last. It is a summer resort. The meetings at this place were not advertised long before the large, beautiful tent was put up, with many small ones. There were no streetcars; everybody had to walk from the main part of the town. This was much against the start of the meetings, but the power soon fell, and God drew the people.

This meeting was noted for sinners coming to Christ. In the first service, several old people and some very prominent citizens were brightly converted. There were some great healings—great miracles the people called it—some were also struck down by the power of God. It was soon spread about that God was visiting the place. The interest increased at every service; these old men and women testified with bright faces and ringing voices, praising God that their names were written in heaven. Many of these received the "double cure"—they were made whole of all their diseases and received the resurrection life.

Ministers, evangelists, workers, and all classes came from many states and were healed. Many were baptized with the Holy Spirit and received gifts of the Spirit and fresh anointings. They also got the gifts stirred up and went forth from the meetings to publish the Word and tell what great things God had done.

We have heard many wonderful reports of good works from those who scattered the holy fire.

The heavenly choir was glorious. It was as if heaven had come down and the angelic choir had joined in with the redeemed of the Lord, having many invisible instruments. The large platform was filled with baptized saints, with their bright faces looking up to God, holding up holy hands. Bright lights were often seen over them. Jesus was seen by many of them standing or walking in their midst. Musical instruments (spiritual) were heard away back to the rear of the tent. A thousand or more were present. A holy stillness and a spirit of awe settled over the audience; they knew that God was in the midst. Two or three different times I asked the people to answer me honestly, in the fear of God, if they heard different instruments of music from the platform. The sounds were not given on instruments but by the Spirit. I knew they had heard it. I asked all who had heard the heavenly music or instruments to rise in the presence of God. Men and women rose up here and there, clear to the back of the tent. The prophet said God would in these last days bring heaven down to validate His Word. He would visit us with celestial fireworks like on the Day of Pentecost. They would see, hear, and feel the Holy Spirit work His work, His strange work. Once, when the power of God was wonderfully present, I heard a sister's music; looking round I saw a sister (an evangelist) with eyes uplifted to heaven, her face shining, playing the harp in the Spirit. She said the glory of the Lord covered her, and the Lord placed a golden harp in her hands. Her fingers began to play, bringing forth the heavenly sound. Several others were playing on different instruments, sending out heavenly music.

I felt like I often do at such times, that we were going to be translated. Then came forth strong messages in other languages, God thundering forth from the light of His glory, through lips of clay as if they were a telephone, warning the people to prepare to meet their God, that Jesus was coming soon. They were prophesying, telling of the awful things that are coming on the earth, the judgments of God; warning the saints to go forth quickly and warn the people, to gather His chosen ones together, and to prepare for His coming.

As a result of these meetings, there were over sixty baptized in the river soon after we left. The procession of people was said to have been over half a mile long. The power of God fell on the multitude as they saw this wonderful sight, saying, "We never saw anything like this, or after this fashion." Most of the candidates came out of the water shouting and praising God. Several were struck down by the power while in the water, so that they had to wait on them before they could baptize them. Some again were struck to the ground before they went down in the water. Some were healed while they were baptized; on others the power of God came forth speaking in other languages. Oh, praise the Lord, this is the way He does if He leads or has control!

A Remarkable Experience

Among the many healed was Sister Marguerite Black from Oberlin, Ohio. They sent word to me that she was coming, to look for her, for they were afraid that she would not live to get there. She got hurt in a wreck and was paralyzed. Her spine was hurt. Her kneecap was dislocated or broken. She had a running abscess and had cataracts on both eyes—nearly blind. We went to her at once. When she was brought in, more dead than alive (hope had kept her alive), she said that she knew if she could live to get there, that when I would lay hands on her, she would be healed. It was as she expected. In a few minutes she was straightened out, clapped her hands and stood on both feet, putting her weight on the lame, sore knee and began to praise the Lord, running and leaping for joy. She told us how awfully helpless she had been, that she could not walk or help herself, her mind being gone part of the time from her spinal trouble. The cataracts fell from her eyes; that day she stayed all through the meeting. People had great faith in her healing. I did not know that I had ever seen her before, but she had been carried into the St. Louis meeting fourteen years before, a helpless, paralyzed cripple. When I laid hands on her and prayed, she was healed and saved, until she got hurt in a wreck. She knew that if she could only reach me, she would live to praise and give God glory. She was greatly used of God.

God gave her the gift of prophecy. She was in Galveston, Texas, before the flood. God showed her the awful tidal wave that was coming and the great destruction. He told her to warn the people. She obeyed God and began to go here and there, wherever the Lord led her to go. Some believed; others mocked. Her sister had a large family, was rich, and had much property. She got angry at her and called her a crazy fool. So Sister Black left the city. In two weeks the tidal wave came. The dreadful loss in life and property is now common knowledge. Her sister lost all, and nearly her life and the lives of her family.

Also at St. Louis, the Lord showed her about the great cyclone that was coming with awful destruction and that she was to warn the people. She continued until the last moment to warn and urge the people to seek the Lord. She was permitted to stay and go through the cyclone. The day the storm came, she was weeping nearly all morning. The lady with whom she stayed asked what was troubling her. She told of the coming storm and said she felt that she must tell it. She next went to the door for something and came running back with a white face saying: "My God, the cyclone is coming! It is here sure enough." God wonderfully saved her so that she was not hurt. The Word says, *"He will show you things to come"* (John 16:13).

The Spirit of prophecy has been in my work from the beginning. Almost every great calamity has been shown and prophesied before it came. The Lord is showing many things now that are coming on the earth. The only safe place is to be hid away in Christ. Dear reader, make haste; get ready to meet your God. *"Behold, he cometh"* (Rev. 1:7); go out to meet Him! *"Despise not prophesyings"* (1 Thess. 5:20).

Cancers Healed

A woman was taken to a Chicago hospital. The doctors made an examination; they made two incisions and found she had two deadly cancers that could not be cut out. They said she would die in the operation. He sewed up the incisions and told them to take her home, that she would die. In this condition they brought her to Petoskey, Michigan. She was not saved. I told her if God did not heal her, she would soon pass away. I said that she had better get saved, but that the Lord could heal her as quickly as He could save her. I told her that if she would give her life to God and promise to serve and glorify Him and tell what great things He had done in making her whole, soul and body, He would heal her and add months and days to her life. She was deeply convicted. We prayed and laid hands on her *"in the name of Jesus"* (Acts 16:18) and commanded the cancer demons and all the power of Satan to come out.

The burden of sin and disease rolled away. She sprang up leaping, shouting, and praising God. You would have thought all the stitches the doctors had taken would break loose. She was perfectly whole from that hour and soon got her wonderful baptism of the Holy Spirit. Her testimony and work had a great, convincing effect on all who saw her.

About six months after, she attended our convention in Chicago. She had become so large, had gained thirty or more pounds. Again about eight months after, we held another convention in another part of Chicago. Again she came to the help of the Lord, well and filled with God, having gained by this time nearly fifty pounds. Her very appearance convinced all who saw her, and almost all who heard her wonderful testimony were convinced that Christ is *"the same...to day"* (Heb. 13:8).

She had her testimony printed and sent out everywhere. One was taken to a lady who was dying in the hospital with cancer. They were looking for her death any time. We were holding our third convention or revival in Chicago, when she heard of this wonderful cure. She wanted them to bring her to the meeting. They brought her in an auto and carried her in near the close of the meeting. They said she was so low that she could not stay, that I must see her at once. We found her a mere skeleton. Her nerves were a wreck. Her whole body was full of poison and disease from the cancer, but there is nothing too hard for the Lord. She was healed soul and body and arose, walked, shouted, and praised the Lord, who was ready to undertake for her. God did not let her go down to the grave before her time to become food for the worms, but to live to honor and to praise His great name.

A day or two after, she came walking into the meeting, anxious to show what great things the Lord had done.

The Spirit Convicts

(From *Word and Work*)

The camp meeting held by Sister M. B. W. Etter during the month of July was in a big tent that overlooked the city. The following was sent to us:

A spirit of conviction was on the people. God demonstrated His power in such a way that sinners were awestruck and under deep conviction and knew that they must sooner or later give their hearts to God. A lady gave testimony that her husband was sick in bed trying to fight off conviction. This is the condition of many souls who came to the meeting. Saved people who were members of churches made inquiries about receiving the Holy Spirit; some of these got it and came out speaking in other tongues. Many of these people believed that they had the baptism before, but saw now that they were mistaken. Sinners were seeking salvation, saved people the baptism, and others the Lord for their bodies.

God marvelously healed many. Joseph Walker, a farmer living near Niles, Michigan, who has for some time suffered from a stroke of paralysis so that he could hardly walk, testified that he had to drag his foot along. When he was prayed for, he felt the power of God shoot through his body like an electric current. He jumped on his feet and started to walk. He is a man of seventy years. To prove to the audience that his healing was genuine, he ran like a little boy of twelve years along the rostrum, in full view of the audience.

A Minister's Testimony

Mr. A. W. Frodsham, of Fergus, Ontario, Canada, wrote: "I intended to pay a short visit of twenty-four hours to the Pentecostal camp meetings at Petoskey, Michigan, but received such blessings that I stayed four days. I have been in Pentecostal work for some time in Bournemouth, England, but before returning to Canada, I became very weak in my body and felt I would like to have prayers for my body. The spiritual blessings that I received were greater than the physical ones. I had a deafness in one ear and had a peculiar disease in my teeth called Riggs disease that made them very loose and caused very offensive breath, as well as stomach trouble. The Lord wonderfully healed me when Sister Etter laid her hands on me and prayed for me. The teeth tightened up in a wonderful way. I also had her lay hands to anoint for special service for the Lord, and for the resurrection life of Christ. Surely the Lord met me. Praise Him. The Spirit worked my arms until at length I was lifted right off my seat several feet in the air. To me it is a clear token of translation power. The Spirit led me to dance, a thing I had never learned to do, and as a former elder of the Presbyterian church, I was against it in social life. To those who witnessed it, it was most graceful. Later Sister Etter gave a beautiful talk on dancing from a scriptural standpoint. She told how the devil had taken it away and had used it for his own purposes. I feel that the Lord has given me a new baptism, as it were, which leads one to a fuller devotion and consecration to Him. All glory to the Lamb!"

Fred W. Adams, of Wichita, Kansas, gave this testimony: "I came over eleven hundred miles to attend these meetings and get healing for both body and soul. For nineteen years I had been affected with something like rheumatism, the effect that the grippe left on me. I also had stomach trouble and other diseases. I have been at Hot Springs and other springs, but I did not get healed. I have used medicine nearly half the time. Now, since hands were laid on me and prayers said for me, I am getting healing for the body and also got salvation for my soul. Praise to God forever!"

One night a woman was struck down under the power of God. Her husband got under conviction and wanted to do away with himself. As he gazed at her for some time, his heart broke down, and he soon wept his way through at the altar. His wife also came out with a bright experience in Christ.

Mr. Arthur Jones, of 224 State Street, has had tuberculosis for three years. He has been treated by various doctors, but to no avail. He had heard about the meeting going on in Petoskey. He came one evening to see if he could get healing for his body. The way did not seem to open for him to get prayed for while the meeting was going on. The meeting closed, with a great desire still in his heart to be prayed for. As a last resort, he worked his way up to the platform to have hands laid on him. When he got to the platform, he was in an exhausted condition, panting for breath. Sister Etter met him on the steps of the platform just as she was going to leave. He was prayed for, the disease was rebuked, and he was healed immediately. He could take a long breath, throw back his arms, and hit his breast hard with a fist, without suffering any inconvenience. He went home that night without suffering anything. Coming to the meeting, he coughed and panted for breath. The next night he sang on the platform with the rest of the saints. Ten minutes after he was prayed for, he shouted with a strong voice saying, "I am healed and saved." He pounded his lungs to show the people that his healing was complete. Both father and mother stood by and gave witness that all was true, tears running down their cheeks as they did so. They told how the doctors had for months expected him to die. Now he stood before them a well young man.

A lady who was almost dead with the same disease got healed, saved, and now sings in the choir. Another one about fifty years old, in the last stage of tuberculosis, was put in the chair. In a few minutes after she was prayed for, she was walking the platform shouting, "I am healed and saved." This is the way the Lord works if the people come and do what they are told. Glory to God for such a Savior!

Mrs. J. R. Callihan, 127 Champion Street, Battle Creek, Michigan, gave this testimony: "I was healed in Sister Etter's meeting in Petoskey, Michigan, of a complication of diseases, of which I suffered continually for three and a half years: chronic stomach trouble, bowel trouble, neuritis, uterine trouble, and nerve exhaustion. I doctored steadily for three years, until the doctors refused to give me more medicine. Then was the time that I decided to come to these meetings and give my soul and body to God, my Creator. Glory to God! He not only healed me, but He also baptized me with the Holy Spirit and gave me the love of Jesus, which is joy and peace and resurrection life. Oh, that all men would know the power of God through His Son Jesus![5]

Miraculous Healings at the M. B. Woodworth-Etter Pentecostal Camp Meeting, July, 1914

(From a report published by Local Helpers)

And said, If thou wilt diligently hearken to the voice of the LORD thy God, and wilt do that which is right in his sight, and wilt give ear to his command-ments, and keep all his statutes, I will put none of these diseases upon thee, which I have brought upon the Egyptians: for I am the LORD that healeth thee. (Exod. 15:26)

Surely he hath borne our griefs, and carried our sorrows: yet we did esteem him stricken, smitten of God, and afflicted. (Isa. 53:4)

He cast out the spirits with his word, and healed all that were sick: that it might be fulfilled which was spoken by Esaias the prophet, saying, Himself took our infirmities, and bare our sicknesses. (Matt. 8:16–17)

And these signs shall follow them that believe; In my name shall they cast out devils; they shall speak with new tongues; they shall take up serpents; and if they drink any deadly thing, it shall not hurt them; they shall lay hands on the sick, and they shall recover. (Mark 16:17–18)

The signers to the following testimonials, with grateful hearts to the Lord for the wonderful things He has done for them, gladly tell their experiences for the praise of His dear name:

I was born blind in my left eye. I could only see daylight, could tell when it was day or night, or some large object, but could not tell what it was. But God wonderfully gave me sight. Now I can see to tell time on my watch. Glory to Jesus, He healed me in less than five minutes.

—*Mrs. John Ditton*, Detroit, Michigan

---

5. I met this sister at Battle Creek, May, 1915; wonderfully well—*A. E. Sidford*, Minister

Healed of Hay Fever, Asthma, and Heart Trouble

I am healed of asthma of twenty-five years' standing, hay fever of fifteen years, and heart trouble of four years. I had to have four hypodermic injections to be able to get here to the meetings. Sister Etter prayed for me, and the pain left instantly. Now I am able to walk miles without fatigue. Praise the Lord for this wonderful relief to my once afflicted body.

—*Mrs. E. G. Richards*, Evanston, Illinois, 1914

(From a report published by Local Helpers)

March 28, 1916

Dear Mrs. Miller, Petoskey, Michigan:

No doubt you will be surprised to hear that the wonderful healing which I received at the Etter meeting in Petoskey, July, 1914, still is with me—healed of asthma, hay fever, and heart trouble. Praise God, He has made me whole, and I have enjoyed the blessing of good health ever since and gained wonderfully in flesh. I am a marvel to my friends, those who used to see me suffer all the time. Glory to Jesus! Praise His holy name forever!

Your sister in Christ,

—*Mrs. E. G. Richards*, 2347 Ridge Avenue, Evanston, Illinois

In January, 1913, I was taken with hemorrhages until I was so weak I could hardly walk about the house. I went to a doctor, who told me I must hurry to a hospital and have an operation, for I might die at any moment. I was operated on by the famous Mayo brothers of Rochester, Minnesota, considered to be the world's best; they relieved me for a time. By April 30, 1914, the hemorrhages became much worse than before. By midnight I lay as one dead and remained so the greater part of the next day. After six weeks' time, I could sit up and gained strength until I was able to come to this meeting.

Sister Etter prayed for me, as I was arriving in an almost helpless condition, and I received instant relief; I am perfectly healed and able to sleep at night, which I had not done for a long time. I am now rejoicing in the Lord. Praise be to His dear name!

—*Mrs. F. E. Leonhard*, Pellston, Michigan

I had tuberculosis of the lungs in the second stage, my strength was almost gone, I knew there was no earthly hope for me. For a year I was unable to do work of any kind. I was engaged in city mission work and felt sure that the Lord would heal me for His glory. Bless God, when I came to Him and stepped out on the promise, He took every trace of disease away. I can sing as long as I wish and not cough. God took the disease and everything that went with it. Hallelujah! I am gaining in flesh and getting stronger every day; I expect to go to work for Jesus again soon. I do praise God that Sister Etter and her workers came this way.

—*Lennora Annabell*, Petoskey, Michigan

I want to praise the Lord for my healing. I wore glasses for twenty-five years. Now I can see to read without them and have no pain. I give Jesus all the glory.

—*Mrs. Hattie Goslow*, Gaylord, Michigan

I received an injury on my knee about two years ago that resulted in tuberculosis of the bone and made me so lame that I had to be carried up and down stairs and to and from the table. The doctor said the leg would have to be amputated. But praise the Lord, through His healing power the leg is perfectly well, and I can now run and exercise without pain. How good Jesus is even to His children if we but trust Him.

—*Arthur L. Peffer*, Petoskey, Michigan

For seven years I was badly crippled with paralysis and heart trouble, unable to walk except with a cane and the aid of someone at my side. Praise God, through faith in Him I am perfectly healed; though seventy-four years old, I can now walk around with ease and without the assistance of anyone.

—*Edward Annabel*, Petoskey, Michigan

I want to praise Jesus for His mighty healing power in delivering me from epileptic fits which I had been afflicted with for over fifteen years.

—*Harry Shannon*, White Cloud, Michigan

I have been a great sufferer from goiter all my life. I tried many doctors with but little help; but by faith in God and Jesus' power through Mrs. Etter, I was healed. I praise God for His love to me.

—*Harriet L. Gray*, Petoskey, Michigan

Dear friends, I praise God that through the shed blood of Jesus Christ I was healed of liver trouble, tuberculosis of the lungs, and stomach and kidney trouble. I am fully healed. Praise the Lord!

—*Arthur Jones*, 224 State Street, Petoskey, Michigan

I have had leakage of the heart for over a year; I have doctored with six doctors and they all said I would never be any better. Sister Etter laid hands on me and prayed, and God healed me; for this I praise Him. I am sixty-eight years old, doing all my work. I feel no return of the disease.

—*Mrs. E. Annabel*, 1028 Jefferson Avenue, Petoskey, Michigan

We, the undersigned, heartily corroborate the healings herein related, the truthfulness thereof having been evidenced before our eyes. We appeal to you, suffering reader, to press this tract with the sweet consolation it brings to your heart, stand on the blessed promises contained in the Scriptures that cannot fail, vow to give God the praise, and the Lord will manifest His power in your behalf. (See Mark 16:16–17; John 14:12; and Acts 19:12.)

—*E. A. Blocher*, Carrington, N. Dakota
C. R. Orsburn, Traverse City, Michigan
Mrs. Ida Tribbett, 306 E. West Street, Sturgis, Michigan
Mrs. W. C. Hoover, Valparaiso, Chile, South America
Mrs. J. L. Bradberry, 3616 Prairie Avenue, Chicago
Wesley Wartenbe, Petoskey, Michigan

"*And he saith unto me, Write, Blessed are they which are called unto the marriage supper of the Lamb*" (Rev. 19:9). "*And the Spirit and the bride say, Come*" (Rev. 22:17).

Mrs. P. J. Howard, Petoskey, Michigan, a prominent worker in the Methodist Church, wrote these words: "Yes, I attended the Pentecostal meetings held in Petoskey during July. I went there prejudiced, but went away saying, '*I will follow thee whithersoever thou goest*' (Matt. 8:19). The presence of the Holy Spirit was there from the beginning to the end, and the slain of the Lord were many. We saw, heard, and felt that it was now even as it was in the days of Christ when they tarried in the flesh. Praise the Lord. The blind receive their sight, the lame walk, the lepers are cleansed, the deaf hear, the dead are raised up, and the poor have the Gospel preached to them. Glory to God! May the Pentecostal power speedily fill the whole earth!"

One brother who came from southern Michigan wrote these words: "While I was sitting in the big tent and Sister Etter was speaking to the people, the Spirit of God fell on her so that she was transfixed as a statue of marble for three or four minutes. I closed my eyes. Soon the Spirit fell on me and filled me to overflowing. When I opened my eyes, I saw the west end of the tent as if it was lined with pure gold. This lasted for some time and was the most beautiful scene that I ever witnessed."

One morning an Indian woman, who got saved a short time before, received her baptism and came out speaking in a new tongue. Her daughter got saved; she could not speak well in their native Indian language. When she got her baptism, she began at once to speak her language fluently (her mother said), this being done under the inspiration of the Spirit. Both mother and daughter immediately told the people that they got a call from the Spirit to go to their people and preach the good news of the kingdom to them. The daughter gave a heartrending exhortation to the audience to give their entire lives to Jesus, who had done so much for them. These were some of her words: "Oh, come! Oh, come! God wants you. God is calling you. People won't always stand by you, but God will. Oh, it is so sweet; He stretches His arms out to you. Come today. Jesus is always willing. He is so sweet. There is no real pleasure in this world." She exhorted like this in the Spirit for some minutes. This young woman testified that she was just getting ready to go on the stage, wishing to take her mother along. She feared a little to come to the meeting, thinking that probably she would change her plans; praise God, she did change her plans. The Spirit of God got her under deep conviction, then saved and baptized her, then gave a message in tongues with the interpretation.

Visions

Miss Esther Pratt, a young woman of Petoskey, Michigan, was saved and baptized in the Spirit in these meetings. While lying under the power of the Spirit she got a vision. She first saw a black cloud, then a white one, and then a blue one. These all passed away, and then she saw Jesus in His majesty sitting on the throne with the angels around Him. He reached His hand out, saying, "I am coming soon. Go and tell the people that I am coming soon." Everything seemed to be bright with the glory of heaven, when suddenly she was aware that she was speaking in another language.

The power of God has been manifested so strong at times in these meetings that some of the saints were held like statues under the power. Once while the power held Sister Etter in this condition for a long time, the power began to fall all over the meeting; people began to go down in various places around the altar. During this period a dear brother got a vision in which he saw the tent around the altar all ablaze with the glory of God. It was all lit up like burning gold with the bright light from heaven. The God of the heavens is surely in the midst of this work. The same day in the evening, when the meeting was about to close, a young woman got in the chair to be prayed over for the healing of her body. While she was being prayed for, the power struck her, and with it came a burden for her girlfriend who was seeking at the altar. She made a rush for her, embraced her, and helped her. The power immediately came on her friend and prostrated her, giving her, too, a glorious experience in God.

The meetings began to increase in number and interest from the very start. Already a number of ministers are among the seekers. Some of the churches are opening their doors and wish to have their members attend the meetings and get all the good from them that they can. One minister began to oppose the work, but soon found that his members were of a different frame of mind. They began to attend the meetings quite regularly, and one by one they fell in line with the work. Some soon received the baptism of the Holy Spirit and came out speaking in another tongue. Others were getting saved and healed. Since then various members of the board of that church extended an invitation to the Pentecostal people to use, free of charge, a nice basement of the church to conduct meetings after the camp meeting closes.

Testimony of the Outpouring of the Holy Ghost

Petoskey, December 3

We are praising God today for the wonderful work that has been done in Petoskey since July first, the beginning of our camp meeting. The large tent, which holds over two thousand people, was filled to overflowing several times. A great many came from long distances. There were at least one hundred and fifty who were saved and about the same number baptized in the Spirit. Forty were baptized in water, and others are waiting until the next baptismal services.

The outpouring of the Holy Spirit was marvelous and refreshing to the saints and in reclaiming backsliders and bringing sinners to repentance. Many were slain by the mighty power of God; many times there were twenty or more under the power at the altar. Many came through speaking in tongues, the Holy Spirit often giving the person the interpretation that "Jesus is coming soon; be ready to meet Him." The music by the heavenly choir was wonderful, the power of the Holy Spirit taking control in producing "The Song of the Dove" and the tones of various musical instruments, all of which were produced by the power of the Holy Spirit taking control of the vocal organs.

The ministers of the different denominations were in attendance, some taking part in the worship. People of many different nationalities came from all over the United States and Canada. A number of Indians were present, and some were converted, healed, and baptized in the Holy Spirit, speaking in another language fluently.

In making mention of the healing of the son of Brother Day, the whole family had faith to believe when Sister Etter ministered to the father's right eye, which had been blind for thirty years, and his eye was perfectly restored. After that they all had faith to believe God's promises. The whole family of five have all been converted, healed, and received their baptism.

Oh, we do praise God for this camp meeting and that Sister Etter ever came this way. It awakened many drowsy, sleepy, sleeping Christians. The blessings cannot be estimated that brought whole families to the Lord, among whom were drunkards, very hard cases to reach. They are all proving faithful yet. We have an average attendance at our prayer meetings of seventy. There is a great interest awakened, and it is increasing.

—*Mr. and Mrs. D. D. Miller*

In the Great Triumphant Morning

In the great triumphant morning,
When we hear the Bridegroom cry,
    And the dead in Christ shall rise;
We'll be changed to life immortal
In the twinkling of an eye,
    And meet Jesus in the skies.

REFRAIN

We shall all rise to meet Him, we shall all go to greet Him,
    In the morning when the dead in Christ shall rise;
We shall all rise to meet Him, we shall all go to greet Him,

And shall have the marriage supper in the skies.
In the great triumphant morning,
What a happy time 'twill be,
    When the dead in Christ shall rise;
When the Lord descends in glory,
Sets His waiting children free,
    And we meet Him in the skies.

In the great triumphant morning,
When the harvest is complete,
    And the dead in Christ shall rise;
We'll be crowned with life immortal,
Christ and all the loved ones meet,
    In the Rapture in the skies.

In the great triumphant morning,
All the kingdoms we'll possess,
    Then the dead in Christ shall rise;
Reign as kings and priests eternal,
Under Christ forever blest,
    After meeting in the skies.

49

"O DEATH, WHERE IS THY STING?"

We went to Philadelphia, Pennsylvania, at the call of Brother William Anderson and a few saints. There were many missions in the city, but not two united. Only a few were willing to stand with Brother Anderson, but the few put their whole energy with their money in the work. The Lord was in the move; the building went up. We found a nice tent at the end of the car line, with many small ones, and a fine tent for meals. Also, we found a nice home, well furnished, for myself and workers, with a sister there to cook and care for us. They gave us a warm welcome, and dear brother Anderson stood so nobly by us all through the meeting and helped to push the battle to the gate.

We would not permit any antagonistic spirit to come in, or any doctrines aired that would cause strife or division. The spirit of love was felt; they began to come from all the missions and felt that they were one in Christ Jesus. All felt their need of getting deeper in God. As the great crowds continued to increase, the presence of God was seen and felt by all. As the Word was preached with power, God demonstrated *"with signs and wonders, and with divers miracles"* (Heb. 2:4), until the sinners trembled and cried out, *"What must I do to be saved?"* (Acts 16:30).

Multitudes of men and women were healed and turned to the Lord. Many were baptized with the Holy Spirit and gave strong messages in other tongues as the Spirit gave utterance.

God wonderfully used Pastor Anderson in tones of thunder, sounding like the voice of God. It was, for God said that in the last days *"with stammering lips and another tongue* [He would] *speak to this people,"* but for all that, some will not hear and believe (Isa. 28:11–12). Then the interpretation was given. Old men, women, and children spoke in languages, preaching and prophesying, singing new songs— the words of which had never before been heard—magnifying and praising the Lord. Many of all classes joined the holy dance, or joy dance, filled with the resurrection life and lightness, dancing with closed eyes, faces bright and shining, sometimes playing with unseen instruments, singing and dancing to their own music.

Bright lights were at times seen over the pulpit and over various people. The Lord was using a brother in other tongues, prophesying and interpreting. A Methodist minister sitting in the congregation came forward and said that he saw an angel standing by the brother all the time while the brother was talking. He was very much affected and said he had to come forward and tell what he had seen. Nearly all classes were convinced and convicted. Policemen and streetcar conductors took a great interest. I do not know how many were saved and healed.

Our last meeting was on Labor Day. We had a special meeting on that day to pray for ministers, evangelists, and workers for the baptism, fresh anointings, and power for service for the stirring up of gifts, and new gifts to be imparted by the laying on of hands. We had three meetings. The large tent was crowded with people standing all around; though so crowded, we had the best of order. Everybody was interested and wanted to see and hear or get some special blessing. The glory of the Lord was like a cloud; it swept over and over the place. We placed chairs on the platform; those who wanted special prayer and laying on of hands sat in the chairs. The power of God fell on everyone. They all got filled with resurrection life, leaped, danced, and shouted praises to God. Most of them fell and lay in green pastures. Scores of men and women were lying all around as if dead. Strong men and women were weeping, both in and outside of the tent.

While we were holding a meeting in Chicago some months later, a minister, speaking of this meeting in Philadelphia, said the last day—Labor Day—he counted one hundred and fifty that were struck down that day by the power of God. Surely the slain of the Lord were many. The work spread far and near. New missions sprung up as a result of this meeting in Philadelphia. Now, after nearly two years, I have a pressing call from the same minister to hold meetings. He has a strong assembly in another part of the city that came from that meeting. Praise God the work is going on.

Wonderful Blessings

A Number Saved and Baptized

The work that the Lord did here through Sister Etter was more than a natural man could understand. There were many wonderful works of healing wrought by the power of God. Many were saved from sin and others were baptized with the Holy Spirit, with the same outward sign as recorded in Acts 2–4 of speaking in other tongues as the Spirit of God gave utterance.

Two young girls got saved and baptized with the Holy Spirit, and God has since wonderfully manifested His power in their home, in so much that their four sisters and their father have since been saved, the four sisters and their mother having also received the baptism of the Holy Spirit. Through meetings held in their home a number have since been saved and baptized. The meetings are still going on, and God is still continuing to bless. Glory be to His holy name!

Many people, whom God has since used to be a blessing to many others, came to the camp meeting from other towns and cities and were wonderfully blessed, several of them receiving the baptism of the Holy Spirit.

Yours in the Master's service,
—William Anderson

Many Healed as God Has Confirmed His Word

The Holy Spirit Is Working

The Pentecostal camp meeting opened on August 1, 1914, with Sister M. B. Woodworth-Etter in charge.

Many have been built up in biblical faith and love in the Holy Spirit. The Gospel of Jesus was proclaimed, not only in word, *"but in demonstration of the Holy Spirit and of power"* (1 Cor. 2:4). God has confirmed His Word with many signs, manifesting His holy presence in mighty power.

388 ᓚ Maria Woodworth-Etter: Collected Works

The outpouring of the Holy Spirit was marvelous to behold. How true the prophecy: *"I will pour out of my Spirit upon all flesh"* (Acts 2:17). It has been very refreshing to the saints, strengthening their faith and begetting in their hearts a hunger for the deeper things of God, reclaiming backsliders, and bringing repentance and salvation to sinners. Many were baptized in the Holy Spirit and speaking with new tongues as the Spirit gave them utterance (v. 4).

A man came two hundred miles to be healed of locomotor ataxia. He had to be helped to the camp by two men, but when the Lord touched him, he threw away his cane and walked alone. Another man was perfectly healed from a rupture after wearing a truss for twenty years.

The signers to the following testimonials, with grateful hearts to the Lord for the wonderful things He has done for them, gladly tell their experiences for the praise of His dear name:

I praise God for His healing power. He healed me of a goiter, which I have had all my life, born with it. When Sister Etter laid her hands on me, I felt the healing power go through me, and the goiter is disappearing rapidly. Praise God!

—*Mr. Paul De Meurers*, Philadelphia, Pennsylvania

I had a stroke last Easter, and my whole one side has been paralyzed since. At first I did not like the method Mrs. Etter used in dealing with the sick, but I grew worse and worse. It came to me that I had my last chance to get well, so I went forward. Sister Etter laid hands on me, and I felt the power of God go through me, and before I believed it, I was dancing. Praise God!

—*Mrs. Dennison*, Woodbury, New Jersey

Nine years ago I met with an accident, and I was left with spinal meningitis and muscular rheumatism, having to use a cane; also my eyes were affected. I came here on Wednesday night, and when Sister Etter laid hands on me, I was healed. I am a Catholic and was praying for nine days for money for a spinal brace, so it was on the ninth day when I came here and was healed. A doctor, when he saw my healing, came out and was healed also.

—*Mrs. R. A. Arnal*, Philadelphia, Pennsylvania

It has been six years since I have suffered with this awful disease, having seventeen hemorrhages in five days. I consulted a specialist, who told me both lungs were gone and the throat was badly affected and nothing could be done.

Seeing it was hopeless, I went to the Lord about a month ago, after reading a Pentecostal paper. Then the way opened, and I came to this camp. Mrs. Etter laid her hands on me, and immediately I knew I was healed. Before, I could not move my arms without bringing on a hemorrhage, but now that is passed. Glory to Jesus!

—*John Ressler*, Gordonville, Pennsylvania

A Striking Testimony

After being a great sufferer for seven years and having undergone eight operations, none of which were successful, I gave up in despair, because an open sore in my side for four years caused me untold agony. This, the doctors said, would eventually result in cancer or consumption, causing death between the ages of thirty and forty years.

My sufferings and fears cannot be imagined. A specialist suggested another operation, and I was almost ready to yield to instruments again, when a dear Christian girl pointed me to the Great Physician. The Lord opened the way for me to attend meetings for divine healing conducted by Mrs. Etter in Philadelphia, Pennsylvania, during August. While there, I accepted healing by faith.

Mrs. Etter laid hands on me, and in the name of Jesus, the devil was cast from my body. All glory to God, for victory is mine through the precious blood of Jesus. Hallelujah!

My spiritual blessings can scarcely be described, for the power of God came upon me so mightily that I became unconscious for hours, and during that time I was carried to the Great White Throne. Oh, the joy of my soul! Hallelujah! There I wanted to stay, but in my vision Jesus lovingly commanded me to return and tell the suffering world what had been done for me so that others might know and believe. Glory to Jesus! He is just the same today as when He walked in Galilee—ever willing, ever able, to help those who put their trust in Him. Glory be to God for what He has done for me.

—*Nora Stuber*, 643 Locust Street, Reading, Pennsylvania

My Husband Passes Away

In the midst of this meeting, on a Sunday afternoon, while I was preaching, my husband, S. P. Etter, fell asleep in Jesus. I took a fast train to Indianapolis, laid him in the beautiful Crown Hill Cemetery, and got back to Philadelphia to continue the meeting the following Saturday night.

He passed away triumphant. At his request, "Jesus, Savior, Pilot Me" was sung. Waving his hands towards heaven and the saints, he passed over the tide.

50

OVERCOMING OBSTACLES

God Can Do Wonderful Works

Our Chicago meeting started on October 10, 1914 and is to continue one month or longer. It seems that we have never entered a battle before where the enemy had put up so many obstacles to prevent us from coming. These obstacles came at both ends, too. The dear saints who opened the way for us had their faith severely tested in overcoming these obstacles. I felt that God wanted me to go at this time and that He was going to do a marvelous work there. This was one reason why the enemy hindered like he did. However, we *"overcame him* [the enemy] *by the blood of the Lamb"* (Rev. 12:11), and the saints are all shouting victory.

The first meeting showed that God was well pleased to have this meeting go on at this time. Many of the saints were out, although the weather was unfavorable. Many of them were awe-struck by a cloud of glory that hovered all evening over the meeting. This cloud would come down at times until the saints felt the glory of the heavenly world. When the first meeting closed, the saints felt that it spelled victory, and all felt impressed that God is going to do a great work in Chicago at this time.

The meetings are going on well, three times a day ever since they started. The crowd is increasing continually, and the interest increases. Many have been healed already of various diseases, also saved and baptized. Some lay prostrated at the altar at the close of nearly every meeting. While the message was being delivered, the power struck some, and they went down under the power of God.

A number of saints are present who have been at our meeting at Petoskey, Michigan, and have been marvelously healed there. These are still shouting victory.

Some are here that have been healed in my meetings as long as nearly thirty years and are still shouting victory and have it, too.

Last night we had the greatest day of the feast yet. It seemed as if heaven had come down. Some danced, some shouted, "Glory! Glory!" with uplifted hands, praising God for His mighty presence among us. Others sang in the heavenly choir, God giving some heavenly instruments, which they played by faith. The meeting had a great effect on unbelievers, who are earnestly inquiring into the cause of the strange power that is manifesting itself in these meetings. The Spirit has also given us many messages in tongues, with interpretations, speaking mainly of the near approach of the Savior, and warning the saints to be prepared to meet Him and what is coming in the world.

Devils Cast Out

I feel it would be for the glory of God for me to tell how God so wonderfully delivered me from the power of Satan. For five years I was devil-possessed. During these five years, it was almost impossible for my own loved ones to live with me. I was so abusive and did everything that the devil wanted me to do. Many times I attempted to take my own life and sought the life of others, but God in His love and mercy kept His hand upon me and kept me from committing any rash deed.

I was taken to Sister Etter's meeting in Chicago and began to quiet down a little and felt that God was there, and began to feel my sins and awful condition. They tried to take me to the chair to be prayed for. Immediately I got angry and began to curse and swear, the devils taking full possession. It took five men to hold me.

Sister Etter began to rebuke the insane and all the other devils to come out. The power of Satan was broken. The devils came out screaming. The police came in to make arrests, thinking that someone was being killed or was crazy. The truth was, the insane demons had gone out. I was clothed in my right mind; my mind came back, clear and sound, the first time for five years. I began to praise the Lord for my wonderful deliverance and stepped forward near the pulpit filled with the glory of God and told the excited people what great things God had done. Many wept for joy. The police looked glad and were convinced something great had happened. I continued to attend the meeting until the last day. One day someone was telling about my deliverance. They then said that I was in the audience. Sister Etter called me to the platform. The Lord took all fear away and gave me boldness to stand before the multitude, a witness for Christ. They said that it was like in the days of Christ, surely a miracle has been wrought.

Truly my heart is melted in deep gratitude to God for all He has done for me. I praise Him for the joy of salvation that passes all understandings. Tongues cannot tell the joy and peace that I have in my soul. Hallelujah! Every longing of my soul is satisfied. I'm happy with Jesus alone. My life and all that I have is consecrated to Jesus for His service. My desire is to live a true, devoted life to God and let Him have His way with me. Hallelujah! I earnestly solicit the prayer of all the saints that God will keep me humble at the feet of Jesus.

This is the experience and testimony of,
—*Miss Goldie Howell*, 25th and Dearborn Streets, Chicago, Illinois

Many Pentecostal Meetings

Trials Do Not Discourage Sister Etter

(From *Water of Life*)

Englewood Gospel Tabernacle, W. Sixty-third Street,
October 10–November 10

Just three days before the meetings were announced to open, God wonderfully opened a place in the best location on the South Side. The problem of financing so large a campaign without any money in sight was another great mountain that was swept into the sea.

The physical weakness of our beloved sister, humanly speaking, would have forbidden her undertaking such an arduous campaign. Other trials would have discouraged both Sister Etter and those planning the campaign had not God wonderfully strengthened their faith and given assurance that He would "stand by," and surely the results of the meetings have borne tremendous testimony to the leadings of the Holy Spirit as well as to the miraculous operations of the Holy Spirit.

"Jesus is Coming Soon"

From the opening service, the keynote of the meetings has been "The Near Coming of Our Lord." In nearly every sermon, in frequent prophecies and warnings, in every message in other tongues interpreted, the message has rung out clear and strong: "Jesus is coming soon."

Sister Etter from the beginning made it very clear that she did not regard the ministry of healing her most important work. The burden that the Lord had laid upon her was to *"blow…the trumpet in Zion, and sound an alarm"* (Joel 2:1), and to call the saints together for the coming of the heavenly Bridegroom.

Leadership of the Holy Spirit

She has shown wonderful tact and wisdom in the conduct of all the meetings by avoiding and prohibiting disputations, by discerning the mind of the Spirit, so that the meetings never got into a rut or followed a set program. No two services were alike. It has been a wonderful demonstration of the unlimited resources of the Holy Spirit when His leadership is recognized. The thrilling moments and climaxes of the services were not managed by human ingenuity but were directed by the Spirit Himself, as He burst forth with diverse operations and supernatural acts.

Hundreds of sinners were drawn there nightly, notwithstanding the attractions of theaters and places of amusement on every side. The tabernacle, which seats eight hundred, was filled every night. Sunday nights hundreds were turned away. The day meetings at ten in the morning and two in the afternoon were also largely attended.

Sister Etter's Work Confirmed by Many Witnesses

Never has the public ministry and lifework of one of God's servants received fuller confirmation and endorsement than has the long ministry of Sister Etter during this campaign. There were scores and hundreds of visitors from out of the city whose united testimonies covered practically the entire public career of our sister: witnesses to healing, witnesses to salvation, witnesses to the baptism in the Holy Spirit. There were witnesses from that wonderful tent campaign in St. Louis twenty-five years ago; witnesses from revival meetings conducted in Ohio, Indiana, Illinois, for many years back; witnesses from Dallas, Texas; witnesses from Los Angeles, California; witnesses from Long Hill, Connecticut; scores of witnesses from the Stone Church, Chicago, who were permanently healed over a year ago; and many witnesses from the more recent campaigns at Petoskey, Michigan, and Philadelphia, Pennsylvania. These all bore testimony to the real and lasting work wrought by God through the instrumentality of His hand-maiden. It would seem as though God had planned that this meeting should be a complete and full vindication of the ministry to which He had called her many years ago.

The Word Opened

The criticism has sometimes been made that preaching and teaching from the Word does not have sufficient place in these meetings. In reporting this campaign, we are glad to note the prominence given to the teaching message.

Sister Etter was used in giving some of the most powerful messages to which we have ever listened. Truly the Word had free course. It ran and was glorified. Not only so, but every manifestation of the Holy Spirit was backed up by the Word.

Sinners Converted

Our friends who are out of sympathy with this work often bring the charge that few sinners are saved at Pentecostal meetings. This campaign alone would establish the fact that the preaching of the Word, which is confirmed *"both with signs and wonders, and with divers miracles and gifts of the Holy Ghost"* (Heb. 2:4), attracts throngs of sinners, brings deep conviction of sin, and leads to definite results in scriptural conversions.

No meetings held in Englewood in recent years have drawn the unsaved in such numbers. Hundreds have been present every night. The meetinghouse for once proved a greater attraction than the nearby theaters and billiard rooms. The miracles that they saw convinced them, where preaching alone would have failed. No records have been kept, but every day some have accepted Christ and have knelt with the seekers, and a number have been both saved and baptized in the Holy Spirit, while others have had the "double cure," as Sister Etter calls it, for both soul and body, and many have renewed the baptism in the Holy Spirit.

Seekers Baptized

A very moderate estimate of the number who *"were all filled with the Holy Ghost, and began to speak with other tongues, as the Spirit gave them utterance"* (Acts 2:4) would be over one hundred at the least. There have been seekers at every service and some have been baptized at nearly every service. Members of denominational churches, who had no knowledge of Pentecost, have been swept into this company of rejoicing saints.

The Sick Healed

While healing was not given chief emphasis in the meetings, nevertheless scores were healed from all manner of diseases. Deaf ears were opened; the dumb spoke; the lame leaped and walked and praised God; tumors and cancers were smitten by the sword of the Spirit in Jesus' name and withered; sufferers from heart disease, catarrh, organic diseases, functional disorders, insanity, apoplexy, fits, and all manner of diseases were healed by the power of God in Jesus' name. Many who were demon-possessed were set free. The evil spirits came forth at the word of command with loud cries and terrible screams.

Some were healed sitting in their seats, for *"the power of the Lord was present to heal"* (Luke 5:17). One sister who was stone-deaf for eighteen years in her left ear was healed without the laying on of hands as she sat listening to the message. A few testimonies to healing are given elsewhere in this issue.

Visions

Many visions have been given the saints. One saw the bride caught up to meet the Lord in the air. Another had a vision of angels, another had a vision of the all-searching eyes of God. Others had visions of heaven opened and the Rider on a white horse, while a number had visions of calamities. At one of the meetings, a sister ran violently about the room with arms uplifted. She had a vision of the Tribulation, and the Spirit made her run to portray the terror that will fall upon the people of the earth when they cry for the rocks and mountains to fall upon them (Rev. 6:16).

Several have had visions of destruction—the crumbling of high stone buildings, of flaming fire, of rushing water, of horses and men rushing through the streets, which they believed was warning of some calamity that will come to Chicago. One sister, a prophetess, who foretold the Galveston disaster and the St. Louis cyclone, has been so burdened at night with visions of disaster and has had such groanings in the Spirit that she could scarcely eat or sleep for days at a time. Another sister who was slain on the platform under the power of the Spirit saw a vision, which she afterward related as follows:

One of the Visions

"The Lord has shown me many wonderful things, but He showed me today in a vision the most wonderful things I have ever seen.

"I saw a halo of light around Sister Etter's head. I saw tongues of fire on the top of her head.

"I saw chariots on the battlements of heaven coming down.

"I saw rain falling on this whole congregation. Those of you who would have Jesus can have Him now.

"I saw Jesus standing with outstretched arms, waiting for you—to forgive you, to cleanse you, to heal you, to baptize you in the Holy Spirit and fire.

"I saw that there are some in this house who, if they do not accept Jesus Christ, if they do not accept this woman as a messenger of the Gospel of peace, are going to judgment. I saw that some of you here, if you reject the message, if you reject the Word, if you reject the Holy Spirit, are sealing your own doom.

"I saw, and God spoke to me as it were from heaven, and He said these words: 'Jesus is coming soon.'"

Messages in Other Tongues

At nearly every meeting, there have been one or more messages in other tongues that have been interpreted. The burden of these messages has been the near return of Jesus. They have taken either the form of warning to the unprepared or of joy and glory and rapt expectation to the saints who are ready. Following is one of the messages of warning, of which many were given with similar import:

Message of Warning

"He's coming soon! Jesus is coming soon! Oh, He's coming soon! Oh! Oh! Oh! Great destruction is coming on the people who do not believe! It is better that they were not born than to have heard and not listened to the voice of God to come unto Him. They will cry to the rocks, but they will not hear them.

"My anger will be upon them; I shall laugh at their calamities. I am sending forth My messengers far and wide. This is the last call to the world. Jesus is the Light of the World. He comes to catch His bride away. He will not tarry. Oh, those who have not the oil in their lamps, wake up! Can't you see My hand? I have sounded the trumpet! Can't you hear it? Oh, wake up! Wake up! I am coming soon! Can't you hear, I'm coming soon? Wake up!"

At one of our evening services, one of the workers under the anointing of the Spirit was seen suddenly to revolve his arm with great speed and power like the revolution of a flywheel, while great solemnity and awe rested upon the audience. Suddenly he spoke with great energy these words:

"Surely God is winding up the Gentile age! Surely God is winding up the Gentile age! Surely God is winding up the Gentile age! The sun is going down upon you. Flee to the Lamb! Flee to the Lamb! Sing praises unto God. Oh, turn to the Lord, for why will you die? Turn to the Lord, for why will you die? Oh, why will you die? Turn! Turn! Oh, why will you die? Oh, stiff-necked and hard of heart, resist not the Holy Spirit. Surely God is winding up the Gentile age!" (See Ezekiel 18:31 and 33:11.)

One of the messages for the saints, recorded in shorthand, was given at a Sunday morning service. Sister Etter had been preaching with great power. She asked all who believed that Jesus was coming soon to raise their hands. Hundreds of hands were raised. Then she asked all who knew He was coming soon to raise their hands. Then all who wanted Him to come soon to raise their hands. Then all who wanted Him to come to stand and give a wave offering. The Spirit fell upon the audience in floods of glory. The outbursts of praise and song were heavenly. Then this message was given in "other tongues" and interpreted by the Spirit through the same brother in alternate sentences of the unknown language and of English.

A Message in Hebrew

One of the most convicting messages as a sign to the unbelieving (1 Cor. 14:22), was given by one of the workers at an evening service when hundreds of sinners were present. There were three definite supernatural aspects to the message: first, it was a message in an "unknown tongue"; second, it was revealed to the brother that he was speaking in Hebrew; third, it was also revealed to him that he was speaking to a Jew sitting in the audience several rows back. He repeatedly said in Hebrew, "The Spirit is speaking to the Jewish brother sitting back there. Get up, and tell what has been said to you." But the man sat with his head down as though he were stunned. After much persuasion, he arose and said that the message was for him and that he understood it.

When the altar call was given, he went forward, apparently under the deepest conviction. His prayers and groanings had the tone of deep penitence. Presently when asked about his condition, he replied with radiant face: "Jesus is my Messiah. Messiah is here," pointing to his breast. Then he was asked whether the brother had spoken to him in Yiddish or Hebrew, and he replied that he had spoken to him in pure Hebrew. When asked what the message was, he replied, "You must come down and acknowledge Jesus to be your Messiah." This was repeated several times, he said.

Brother Howell, through whom the Lord gave the message, testified that he had never studied languages, knew nothing about Hebrew, and had never graduated from the grammar schools. Here, then, is indisputable evidence that the new tongue is a real language. It would take years of study to enable one to converse in Hebrew, which is a very difficult language, yet the Holy Spirit can miraculously use the vocal organs to speak the language with the perfect purity of a highly educated Hebrew.

The Heavenly Choir

Singing in the Spirit (1 Cor. 14:15) was one of the manifestations of frequent occurrence. Sometimes many joined with "other tongues" in the heavenly choir, which only the redeemed of the Lamb can sing. It would rise in bursts of praise like the sound of many waters or sink to the sweetness of the dove-note, and then rise again to greater heights like the incoming waves. It was indeed the heavenly Dove singing and calling for its mate. Untrained voices joined with a purity of tone and harmony surpassing that of expert vocalists. Such scenes recall vividly the loving conversation of the bride with the Bridegroom given in prophetic allegory in the Song of Solomon:

Rise, up, my love, my fair one, and come away.
For lo, the winter is past,
The rain is over and gone;
The flowers appear on the earth;
The time of the singing of birds is come,
And the voice of the turtle is heard in our land;
The fig tree putteth forth her green figs,
And the vines with the tender grape give a good smell.
Arise, my love, my fair one, and come away.

(Song of Solomon 2:10–13)

We have heard a brother sing a sacred hymn to God in other tongues, as a solo, in which the tone-placement, tone-purity, and tone-color were fully equal to that of grand opera singers, and yet he never had but the slightest training in singing.

Dancing in the Spirit

Among the *"strange act[s]"* (Isa. 28:21) that God is performing these last days are dancing and playing on musical instruments in the Spirit. These manifestations are not induced by suggestion or by imitation. It is true that some will occasionally step and hop about who are simply expressing their joy and praise in their own way, as all of us in former days have seen the saints, when they are blessed, jump and skip and run in holiness meetings. These fleshly manifestations cannot be regarded as sinful and certainly are not hypocritical. They are the human expression of feeling toward God under great blessing, just as demonstrations at a baseball or football game are the natural, human expression of feeling in that lower, carnal plane of joy.

But the real dancing under the power of the Spirit is altogether different. It is spontaneous. It comes without premeditation or choice. It lacks all human direction and control. It does not follow the two-step or waltz or any dance ever learned. The steps are controlled and directed by the Holy Spirit. The whole body is energized by the Spirit. The eyes are closed. The movements are wonderfully graceful and often rapid beyond all possibility of imitation. There are none of the attitudes or poses or familiar joining of partners, which characterize the ordinary dance.

Playing on "Harps of Gold"

Others have played upon invisible musical instruments with the apparent skill and dexterity of musicians. This experience is not less startling to the observer than to the one who is thus exercised, when suddenly his fingers are moved by an invisible power in which he has absolutely no part. One who has had the experience can testify to the supernatural aspect of this *"strange act,"* when the fingers are involuntarily reaching and stretching for chords of the harp, and when the pulling and straining of muscles and the loosening of the joints of the hands and fingers is similar to that induced by years of technical practice in our schools of music.

Some were seen to dance and sing with the accompaniment of invisible violins and harps that they were playing with great skill. Still others were representing heavenly instruments by inimitable sounds formed in the throat, which sounded like harps or bells to those present. It was all truly wonderful. Sister Etter declared that these are the last manifestations of the Spirit, who is training the bride to dance and sing in preparation for the wedding feast of the Lamb. This celebration is soon to take place and will surpass in glory and splendor and sumptuousness and singing and dancing and joy and music every marriage feast and every bridal chorus and every wedding march that the world has ever known. This description is given in Revelation:

> And I heard as it were the voice of a great multitude, and as the voice of many waters, and as the voice of mighty thunderings, saying, Alleluia: for the Lord God omnipotent reigneth. Let us be glad and rejoice, and give honour to him: for the marriage of the Lamb is come, and his wife hath made herself ready. And to her was granted that she should be arrayed in fine linen, clean and white: for the fine linen is the righteousness of saints. (Revelation 19:6–8)

In Appreciation

Sister Etter has been like a mother in the Lord. She has shown an interest in the work and carried the burden of the work to a degree that is seldom seen in evangelists who come and go. In the area of financial arrangements, she has shown a liberal and generous spirit, voluntarily releasing the committee from their full obligations and personally donating to the work a considerable sum of money that by arrangement belonged to her. We believe it is right that credit and appreciation should be shown where they are due.

Fallen Asleep in Jesus

Promotion of Brother S. P. Etter

"To Live Is Christ, and to Die Is Gain"

The decease of Mr. S. P. Etter, August 16, 1914, marked the end of three years of suffering and the liberation of his spirit from its tenement of clay at the ripe age of nearly seventy-two years. He is survived by his wife, Mrs. M. B. Woodworth-Etter, and by two daughters, Mrs. J. P. Begg, Birmingham, Alabama, and Mrs. Ida Eddy, Hot Springs, Arkansas.

At the time of his death, Sister Etter, to whom he was joined in marriage a little over thirteen years ago, was conducting a camp meeting at Philadelphia, Pennsylvania. At his urgent request, she had continued in the field where she carried both the burden of the work and the load of anxiety for his welfare. She was hurriedly summoned home to Indianapolis, where she laid him away, and then went back to carry on the Philadelphia campaign. Witnesses have testified in Chicago of the marvelous fortitude and grace with which she went through this trial and never faltered at her post.

Ever since their marriage, Mr. Etter has stood by the side of his wife in doing evangelistic work. He was brave, never faltering from duty, always ready for every emergency, doing hard manual labor as well as exhorting sinners to repent. The Lord wonderfully used him in singing at revivals and also in praying for the sick. Even after he had been taken sick, he united with his wife in praying over and anointing hundreds of handkerchiefs. Testimony after testimony came back from people who praised God for deliverance.

At the Dallas, Texas, meeting he was stricken with tuberculosis of the bone and stomach. He soon became helpless and had to be carried from place to place. The calls for labor were so many and urgent that they traveled under those unfavorable conditions over eleven thousand miles, preaching the Gospel, holding three meetings a day. They went practically all over the United States. Many times when Mrs. Etter went to the meeting after kissing him good-bye, she did not know whether she would find him alive when she returned. This was especially true in the meeting held in Atlanta, Georgia, from March 8 to May 10.

As the weather got warmer, he had a desire to get home and rest for a while, expecting that God would before long either deliver him entirely or take him home to glory. They reached home toward the end of May. He enjoyed his little home very much and had perfect victory in his soul.

Sister Etter had a great desire to be with him until the last, but together they had promised the saints at Petoskey, Michigan, and also at Philadelphia, Pennsylvania, to hold meetings for them. When time arrived to leave, he burst forth in strong exhortation urging through it all to be brave and courageous in the Lord's work, that the Lord's coming was drawing nigh. When out of the house his last words heard by his wife were these: "Go forward, God speed you on."

She trusted that God would spare him until she got back again, but felt perfectly resolved to God's will.

Soon after the meeting in Philadelphia started, he showed signs that God would take him to rest before long.

When asked whether Mrs. Etter should stop the work and come home, he said, "No, she must go on until the meeting closes at the end of the month."

Later on his nurse perceived that he was sinking rapidly.

A message was sent for his wife to come home at once. She took a fast train immediately, but before she could reach his bedside, he had passed to glory. He died peaceful and happy on the afternoon of Sunday, August 16.

Testimonies to Divine Healing

(From Water of Life)

Healed of Asthma, Catarrh, and Heart Failure

A Sufferer for Twelve Years and Given Up by the Doctors

I was walking down 63rd Street to Halsted, October 18, 1914. I thought the air would help me as I was suffering so much in breathing. In looking at the things on the street, I saw a large sign out on the front of a building, saying, "The

Woodworth-Etter Pentecostal Meeting." I thought I would see what was going on in there and so entered.

They were praying for the baptism of the Holy Spirit and for the healing of the body.

Now, I have been a sufferer for twelve years with asthma, catarrh, and heart failure. All the doctors told me that there was no help for me. I spent lots of money for my medicines, but they only relieved me for a few minutes. For ten years I have always carried morphine and Shiffman's asthma remedies in my handbag for relief in case I had an attack of these diseases while I was out. Sometimes I would be so bad that I would have to go to a drugstore for relief. For eight years I could not lie on my left side at night, and for five years could scarcely breathe through my nose. Now that was the state I was in when I came to this mission.

I found them praying for people there suffering from all kinds of sicknesses, but I got afraid of them. I thought they might be spiritualists. After I got home, I took my Bible and compared the Word of God with these meetings, and I saw that the healing was in accordance with the Word, so I went again several times. The following Saturday, I asked the little shepherd boy, as I called him (she refers to Brother Howell), to pray for me. He laid hands on me and in the name of Jesus commanded the diseases to depart. Thank God, I have not had to suffer since. I am praising God for the mission and those in charge and for all the dear helpers of our beloved Sister Etter. May God turn every saloon and drugstore into a Pentecostal Mission, to save the souls and heal the bodies of the people.

—*Mrs. L. E. Miller*
6330 Eggleston Avenue, Chicago; Illinois

Note: The sister who writes the above testimony has been blessed in soul as much as in body. Although of a naturally quiet disposition, she has been seen on more than one occasion since her healing dancing in the Spirit, full of joy unspeakable and full of glory.

Healed of Many Chronic Diseases

Had Floating Kidney for Nine Years

I praise God for what He did for me. For fourteen years I was sick with a complication of diseases. The doctor said I had heart trouble and female trouble.

My nerves were wrecked and, at times, I could not talk or move for a long time. For nine years I had a floating kidney and suffered from that very much. The doctor told me I could never get well without an operation. My heart was so weak that I had to take medicine to give me strength, but the more I took, the worse I got. I was going rapidly to my grave.

Oh, how I praise Jesus for His love to me! It is one year and five months since I was healed, and it is there to stay, for I have no trouble with it. Glory to Jesus! He made the operation without the knife. How I praise Him for it! Oh, glory to Jesus! Since then He has baptized me in the Holy Spirit, and I have talked in tongues. I praise God for His love. He keeps me day by day.

I also have a son twelve years old, whom the Lord has healed from tuberculosis of the spine and glands. His liver was enlarged; he had water on his stomach. The doctor said as soon as the water reached his heart, he would die. He was a great sufferer all his life. He could not run and play like other children, but had to sit down and rest often. I had many doctors. They all said that my son could not live. He was not in school for two years; he was just an invalid.

How I do praise Jesus for His mighty power to save and heal.

—*Mrs. Olof Smith*
1537 South Crawford Avenue, Chicago, Illinois

Healed of Tumor—Used an Anointed Tract

I had a tumor that the doctors said was six years old, and also heart trouble. They said there was no hope for me to recover. I heard of the wonderful outpouring of God's Spirit and the healing of the people in the apostolic meetings in Dallas, Texas, through a sister; she told me also of Sister Etter's gift of healing, and I sent word for her to pray for me, and she sent me an anointed tract. I placed it over the affected part and prayed for healing, and bless His holy name! He healed me one year and eight months ago, and I am still healed.

—*Mrs. A. V. Hawkins*
3661 Forest Avenue, Chicago, Illinois

Healed of Choking Goiter

About thirty-five years ago a goiter commenced growing in the side of my throat, and now for many years, because it was choking me, I had to sleep sitting up in bed. For three or four years I have suffered so with my stomach that I could not sleep most of the time. I was constantly taking medicine, which gave only temporary relief. I also had inflammatory rheumatism, which caused the muscles of my legs to draw in, resulting in stiffness of my knees so that I could not stoop over. When I sat down, I could hardly get up again. I went to Sister Etter's meetings, and she and others prayed for me, and Jesus made me whole.

I do praise my God for what He has done for me.

—*Mrs. Phoebe Tomkins*
4010 West Lake Street, Chicago, Illinois

Diseased Limb

A lady in England had a diseased limb and was in a terrible condition. She heard of the great work of God and sent us word about her suffering and that nothing could help her, and she asked us to pray for her and send her a handkerchief. We prayed and sent her a handkerchief, and it was not long until we received a letter from her, and it began with praises to God. She said when she got the handkerchief, the power of God came upon her, and she laid the handkerchief on her limb, which was almost rotten. She was healed completely. Hallelujah!

Insanity

Not long ago an insane woman in Germany was healed. She was the daughter of a Pentecostal man. She was possessed of demons and was worrying the life out of him. He wrote to me and said God had put it upon him to translate my book into German, but his daughter was driving him almost crazy, and unless something was done, he could not accomplish anything. I was very much concerned, as I wanted to see the book written in that language. Several of us prayed for him and for his daughter, and not long after, we received a letter saying that the devils had been cast out and the daughter was well.

—*Mrs. Woodworth-Etter*

The Call for Messengers

Christians, the Lord says, "Forward go to the harvest,
    Look and behold, the fields are waiting white;
I will be with you until your labors are ended."
    Soon, oh, soon, will fall the shades of night.

CHORUS
    The Spirit within says, "Forward go
    Be not afraid, my child, to sow,
    For I will go with you to the end—
    Speak boldly the Word, My truth defend."
Why should you live in ease while others perish?
    Ye who now in God's truth and grace abound;
Give to the world the Gospel of God's kingdom,
    List! The call for help the world around.

Brother, the harvest day will soon be ended,
    Then will the Master say to you, "Well done!"
That you may dwell with God and Christ forever,
    In His kingdom shine forth as the sun.

Brother, the Lord is needing Christian soldiers,
    Those who will dare to stand for truth and right;
Those who can demonstrate God's wondrous pow'r,
    Those who ne'er retreat will win the fight.

Lord, I will go and labor in the harvest,
    Gathering precious golden sheaves for Thee;
Sowing the needed Gospel seed, and reaping
    Souls for my labors then the hire shall be.

51

PERSONAL HEALING FOR SISTER ETTER

Sister Etter's Vision

Greetings to all the saints, in Jesus' name, at home and abroad. For the last three years my burdens and cares have been heavy. I traveled over eleven thousand miles, carrying and caring for my invalid husband. I carried him from the Atlantic to the Pacific, holding meetings three times a day in the large cities, and stayed at each city for a month or longer. With all the burdens that are connected with the work of the Lord, standing alone at times, caring for my husband day and night, then adding to all this the sorrow and bereavement of laying my husband to rest in August, while I was in the midst of a large campaign in Philadelphia, Pennsylvania, he urging me to go forward with the work to the very last. Passing through this heavy strain and laboring continually, I finally got very weak in my body. I only kept going through divine life and strength.

When I left home for our meeting in Chicago, they had to take me to the depot in an auto. I went, believing that God called me, and that He would hold me up through the meeting, which was to continue for one month or longer. The Lord wonderfully sustained me through the time that I had promised. In my weakened condition I contracted a severe cold one day, which soon developed into pneumonia. My colaborers and friends at once decided to take me away from the meeting home to Indianapolis, where I could rest. Following you will find the testimony of a skilled medical brother, Dr. Green, of the Martinsville sanitarium, Martinsville, Indiana, about my condition at this time:

Martinsville, Indiana, December 24, 1914

My dear Mrs. Etter:

I wish to testify that on the 20th of November, on 63rd Street in Chicago, at 10 A.M., I saw you in your room with a temperature of 102, pulse rate 100 and irregular, with prune juice expectoration, making a germ-cell pneumonia, and an engorged entire lobe of the left lung. Upon my advice you were removed in a drawing room car to Indianapolis on Wednesday evening, November 11. On the following evening, Friday, at 5:30, I visited you in your home, found a temperature of 100½, pulse rate 84, respiration 28, complete consolidation of whole lower lobe of left lung with tubular building. I again visited you on Tuesday morning, found temperature 100, pulse rate 84, expectorating with great difficulty, great quantities of prune juice loaded with pneumococci. I again visited you on a Friday afternoon, found temperature normal, pulse rate 84 and regular, lower lobe of lung clearing nicely, tongue clean, taking a sufficient quantity of milk and eggs, and having slept soundly during the night before. I again visited you on Monday following and found a complete crisis had been passed, lower lobe clearing up nicely, respiration 24, excessive sweating for two days, appetite good, sleeping well.

This result came to you through implicit faith in God's power to heal you. You took nothing but air, milk and eggs, and passed through what is ordinarily fatal in sixty per cent of persons seventy-two years of age.

Sincerely yours,
—E. V. Green, M.D.

When I was told of my condition, I began to praise the Lord. Soon the Lord appeared to me in a vision in a cloud of glory, sitting on a great white horse with a sword in His hand, showing me that He had conquered death and disease, and that I should go forth again in great power, that He would be with me. I praise

God, through the prayers of the saints that have gone up in my behalf, my life has been spared. Now He is calling me out in the work again. The Lord willing, I shall commence my next meeting in Tampa, Florida, some time between now and the beginning of February.

Martinsville, Indiana, December 5, 1914

My dear Mrs. Etter:

May the love of God, the Father, and the peace of our Lord and Savior, Jesus Christ, abide with you constantly from day to day, assuring to you that His life-giving current will continue in your life for many years yet to come in His service. This has been a wonderful victory for you. God's purposes can never be questioned. Be patient and do not do too many hours of work yet, until you have had time to regain your energy and strength again and repaired the injured lung perfectly. The meetings in Martinsville are progressing nicely.

With a most kind remembrance to your entire household, I remain,

Sincerely yours,
—E. V. Green, M.D.

When the time arrived for our meeting in Tampa, Florida, I was still very weak in my body, but strong in spirit and courage to get out in the battlefield again and let God fight the powers of darkness through my body. I said to myself, "Lord, I will not disappoint the dear people down there, though I perish on the way." God wonderfully sustained me on the trip and kept me well all through the meeting.

God came forth in a manifest way in this meeting. The power came on a little baptized girl about twelve years old, time and again, so that she would plead with strong, crying tears for sinners to give their lives to God. She spoke under the inspiration of the Spirit, many times for about half an hour, about the wonderful things of God, exhorting everyone to repent and seek more of God. The fruit of the exhortation of the Spirit through this child was always a rush to the altar seeking God. This little child was helpless to do or say much for Jesus if the Spirit did not come on her. There is no end to the way God can use us, if we are only clay and let the Potter use us.

Pastor's Report of Woodworth-Etter Meeting

God's Power is Remarkable

Yielding to God

Our Sister Etter came to us in the blessings of the Gospel, and the meetings are growing in power.

God met us the first night and set His approval on the meeting. We praise God for the way He blessed in this meeting. Many were healed and saved, also a number filled. There was a man kicked by a horse in the breast and was not able to do anything for months, and he came to the meeting, was prayed for, and God healed him, and he went to work next morning and has been working ever since.

One man was struck by a train a few years ago and has not been able to walk without a stick. Even then had to be helped up and down, but he was healed and can now walk and run and jump and praise God for healing. Another man was healed of rupture and took off his truss and ran over the house, jumping and praising God. Still another was healed of rupture and burned his truss. We are looking for God to do great things at this place. Let all the saints pray that God may have His way in these meetings. God is blessing Sister Etter.

We could tell of many such cases. The last day was the best of all. The power of God came down, and my wife began to play the piano under the power of God and continued for about one hour and a half. At the same time a brother fell back in a chair and began to play some unseen instrument and chorded with my wife while playing on the piano, and about four or five little girls were dancing with the music. It was a melting time.

Sister Etter has gone to Atlanta, Georgia, for a meeting. We pray God to bless her labors there. Let all that read this pray for the work in South Florida.

—*Pastor J. M. Rowe*

Eternal Fruit

Report by Pastor E. A. Blocher

The fact of Sister Etter being raised from a protracted sickness and almost helpless condition to come among us, and being so miraculously sustained for her labors, was in itself a manifestation of God's infinite grace and power.

People came to join in the campaign against Satan's kingdom of darkness from more than a dozen different states. (Foreign readers should note that such journeys often mean traveling equal to the whole length of England.)

The wonderful manner in which this handmaiden of the Lord expounded God's holy Word to the conviction of sinners, and portrayed God's wonderful love to mankind, constrained many to seek God with their whole heart. Many rejoiced *"with joy unspeakable and full of glory"* (1 Pet. 1:8). There were marked cases of healing from ailments of many years' standing. The heavenly choir was much participated in by the saints with exultant joy.

Other yielded souls were baptized in the mighty power of the Holy Spirit, giving messages of consolation to believing hearts. There were visions of the heavenlies and dancing in the Spirit for real joy of heart. The burden of intercessory prayer was another blessed working of the Holy Spirit.

Eternity alone will reveal the fruitage of these efforts of dear Sister Etter.

The Liberty Bell

Ring the liberty bell, sweet bell,
    The jubilee trumpet sounds;
Its silver tones in waves of joy,
    O'er heaven and earth abounds.

CHORUS

Ring the liberty bell, sweet bell,
    Ring the liberty bell!
For Jesus has risen to open the prison,
    And burst the bars of hell.

Ring the liberty bell, sweet bell,
    Some prodigal child's been found,
Who is saved from sins, so the joy begins,—
    Sweet music to all around!

Ring the liberty bell, sweet bell,
   With timbrels and dances sing;
For the horse and the rider are drowned in the sea,
   Victorious anthems ring!

Ring the liberty bell, sweet bell,
   For the Comforter's come in power,
To take control of each blood-washed soul,
   Who seeks for the heavenly shower.

Ring the liberty bell, sweet bell,
   Hark! the harpers sweetly play
On the glassy sea; 'tis the Jubilee,
   Of our God's eternal day.

52

LASTING HEALINGS

After One Year's Time, Old Converts Well and Happy

On our way home from Tampa, Florida, at the earnest call from the dear ones at Atlanta, we felt the Lord was calling, so we went and commenced a meeting in Brother Jackson's new hall, which was almost outside the city. We knew it would be hard for the people from the city to get there, especially the poor saints who would not have carfare to pay. Mr. Chapman and Mr. Alexander were holding a revival in the large tabernacle that was built for that purpose. The whole city had been canvassed; all churches and missions had promised to help them. I did not want to commence near them, as it would look like opposition. Not one in a thousand would have tried to start a revival under such conditions. No one had promised me a dollar. I stood responsible for rent and all expenses. I knew that many poor people could not attend the Chapman and Alexander meeting. I said we would start the meeting in Brother Jackson's hall and trust the Lord to draw the people. We shouted victory in Jesus' name and told the saints that the large hall would not hold the people, and it was so. Thousands attended the meeting; they could not all get in at times. Jesus says, "I, if I be lifted up from the earth, will draw all men unto me" (John 12:32).

Hundreds who had attended the year before, when we held a nine weeks' meeting in the large tabernacle, came. Ringing testimonies came from those who had been saved and baptized with the Holy Spirit or healed, from day to day. As many as sixty who had received these blessings testified in one day that they had been healed of all kinds of sicknesses and diseases and had been kept well in soul and body. Jesus said, *"Ye are my witnesses"* (Isa. 43:12), and *"In the mouth of two or three witnesses every word [shall] be established"* (Matt. 18:16). Jesus loves to hear the praises of the redeemed so well that He stopped a great procession while on earth to hear the testimony of one poor leper and the poor old woman who did not have a friend in the world. I am sure He stops the angel choir and the music in heaven to listen to these wonderful testimonies in Jackson's hall; for the eternal gates flew open and the tidal waves from the river of life, from before the throne of God, came sweeping in over the people like mighty, rushing waters, until the healing and life-giving power of God was felt by all in the building.

Some would weep, some shout, some were healed standing or sitting in their seats. One little boy, eight years old, gave messages in tongues, interpreted, danced, preached, and held the great crowd spellbound. He told them he had been saved and healed and baptized in the Holy Spirit when we were there the year before. He said all his family, sisters and brothers and parents—except one— had been saved, and he knew that one would be soon. Almost all the family had received the baptism in the Holy Spirit. We had wonderful music played upon the piano by those who were entirely controlled by the Spirit. Their whole bodies were charged and moved with the mighty power of the Holy Spirit. It had a great effect on the people; the instrument seemed full of the glory of God.

Dying, Now Filled With Resurrection Life

Sister Ida Ball, who had been saved and healed in the last stages of consumption, was there all through the meeting, and, filled with God, she was wonderfully used of the Lord. She is small and frail looking, very fair with golden hair. Whenever she came before the audience, she held the people spellbound; they said she looked like an angel. When the Lord took possession of her, she became light as a bird and would dance the holy dance, and her hair would fall around her face and shoulders like a veil. She sang new songs in other tongues that no one had ever heard before, and then sang them in English; she also gave wonderful messages in different languages and interpreted them. I took her with me through several conventions. God used her everywhere to convince one and all that God lives and moves in His own today.

Saved and Healed Through Getting a Book

April 3, 1915

Praise the Lord, I was healed in Sister Etter's meeting at the Old Broughton Tabernacle in Atlanta, Georgia, April 10, 1914. I had nervous prostration and leakage of the heart. It was through her book that I went to the meeting and was healed and saved. I was a nervous wreck and could not lie down to sleep; I had to sit up in a chair for months. The doctor said I must not exercise, that I must be still. I was taking four kinds of medicines all the time, but, praise the Lord, when Sister Etter laid her hands on me and prayed for me, the Lord healed me, and I am well and all right today. Glory to Jesus, I don't have to take medicine now, and I have three children who have not taken a dose of medicine since I was healed. Glory! Sister Etter's book has been worth more to my family and me than I can ever tell. It has been the means of all the family being saved and baptized with the Holy Spirit. Praise the Lord!

—*Mrs. J. F. Gossett*, Atlanta, Georgia

On the Battleground

(From *Word and Work*)

Sister Etter and her coworkers send greetings to all the saints.

Sister Etter, who was stricken down with pneumonia in her Chicago campaign last November, is right in the battlefront again, lifting up the banners of Jesus with old-time vigor and power. She fulfilled her engagement in Tampa, Florida, as was advertised, for a month or longer. God wonderfully blessed in the Tampa meeting; about twenty-five or more received their baptism; others got saved, and there were some marvelous cases of healings. The district in which the meetings were held was one in which people knew little or nothing about this way of worshipping God. There were only a few saints scattered abroad. Many foreigners, Cubans, Italians, French, lived in the neighborhood of the hall. God mightily stirred these people and reached some, saving and baptizing them, also healing some of incurable diseases. These people looked at Sister Etter as the woman whom Jesus sent into their midst. We believe that this meeting will be the means of starting a great work among the Cubans, which will go on until Jesus comes. Some of the workers are still carrying on the work in the neighborhood and continue to send back good reports.

During the midst of the Tampa campaign, Sister Etter got a telegram from her only daughter in Indianapolis, stating that she had a stroke of paralysis, making her absolutely helpless. We held on to God for her. While we had special prayer, the power came down on some of the saints. Some received visions in which they saw her out of bed. We praise God that He answered our prayer in raising her up. She is able to walk around now. Her case is a remarkable one. From a medical standpoint, she was a hopeless case. We praise God for the victory. After six weeks, we returned home and found her perfectly restored, serving us at the table.

Souls Seeking

For some time, many calls have been coming to us from Atlanta to hold another meeting in this city. We felt that now was the time, while we were on our way up north. We decided to come immediately after the time was up in Tampa, so we could stay a month or longer in Atlanta. We came here while Atlanta is having a great revival, the Chapman-Alexander revival. We knew nothing about this meeting when we promised the saints to come. God has set His seal on the work in our first meeting by letting His power come down in a mighty way. Every evening when the weather is at all favorable, the big hall is filled with people. They are under conviction all over the audience, readily yielding and giving their hearts to God when asked to. Some get saved in their seats. A man testified that he was under deep conviction. While the heavenly choir was making music in the Spirit, he got down and prayed to God. Suddenly the burden lifted, and the peace of Jesus filled his soul. He immediately began to seek his baptism.

One very encouraging feature about this meeting this time was to hear the many testimonies on healing. People all over the audience testified to being healed in our last meeting a year ago, and they are sound and well today. Among these are people who were afflicted with all kinds of incurable diseases and given up by the doctors. Today they have absolute victory.

Full of Resurrection Life

One young woman who had to be helped to the meeting a year ago, dying with tuberculosis, was prayed for. She immediately received resurrection life, got the victory, got her baptism, and felt led to go out in the field and labor for the Master. During the summer God wonderfully used her in bringing souls to God.

Now she is back in the meeting, full of praises and joy, a well, sound woman. God wonderfully uses her to give messages in tongues.

Another young woman, whom the doctors had given up because she was dying with tuberculosis a year ago, is in the meetings today, well and happy and praising God. Her doctors all said she had tuberculosis and held out no hope for her. She was prayed for last year and is a well woman today. Both these cases gained wonderfully in strength and weight during the year.

A prominent businessman testified that he knew of nine deaf and dumb persons who were delivered during the last campaign. Some of these were born deaf. While in Tampa, Florida, last month, a prominent minister from Atlanta came to the meeting one day and testified that a day or two before he left Atlanta for Florida, he spoke on a streetcar to one of these deaf and dumb mutes. She had learned to talk since she got delivered, and she talked freely to him.

Whole Family Gets Saved and Baptized Through Book

Another remarkable case is how nearly a whole family got saved and received their baptism in that meeting. The mother of this family was healed of a leakage of the heart after all medical aid failed. Her husband bought one of Mrs. Etter's books while the meetings were going on. His wife had to be propped up in bed and be fanned day and night, fearing that her heart might stop beating any time. When she saw the book, she scolded her husband for spending $1.50 on a book, because it was needed for so many other things. But she had some of the book read to her. When she heard and saw what God had done for others, faith sprang up in her heart. She believed that if she could only get down to the meeting, God would heal her. They took her down. She was prayed for and was instantly healed and converted. After a year, she is as sound as ever. The family is continually praising God.

Blind Eyes Still Open

A Methodist minister, Mr. Cain, of Westminster, South Carolina, came to the meeting last year, totally blind. He had been blind for nearly a year and exhausted nearly all his wealth trying to find a doctor or specialist who could restore his sight. He doctored in his hometown and sought the best physicians in Atlanta. With one accord, they all voiced the same idea—that the optical nerve was destroyed (dead) and that he could never see again. He wrote to Sister Etter about his condition. She advised him that there was hope for him, if he came believing. Another man escorted him to the city. When he was prayed for, his eyes opened up and he could see. He ran back and forth on the platform, praising God with tears flowing from his eyes. When he went home, he began to preach again. He was a man of influence. There were many people in the audience who knew him. Now after a year's lapse of time, while we are in the city again, a man testified that Reverend Cain has still got his sight and is about the Master's business. We praise God that He does heal today, and people stay healed, too.

Idiotic Baby Instantly Healed

One of the most remarkable cases of healing that took place a year ago was a little baby about two years old. A mother brought this child on the rostrum one evening to be prayed for and get healed. He had been idiotic from birth. Even his own mother could not draw his attention. His spine was useless and curved. He had cataracts on the eyes, one eye being totally blind, and he had other troubles also. A noted doctor and surgeon stood close by and paid special attention to these things. That these things were so had been proved by a number of witnesses, after a year's time. When the child was prayed for, it seems he shed off everything in the way of disease and imperfection from his little body and soon received strength in his spine and sat up. His spine also straightened. The cataracts left, and both eyes were healed. He got life and energy. A fan was held up to the child, and he grasped it and would not let go. His grasp was firm, and immediately the little one got busy watching what was going on around him. While this was going on, his mother walked back and forth on the platform, weeping for joy. After a year's time, two ladies heard the mother at a religious meeting one day testifying that her child got completely delivered in Sister Etter's meeting, and that he was perfectly well and happy today.

Still Healed

One of Atlanta's leading physicians and surgeons, Dr. Bowen, who was so marvelously healed a year ago, is still healed today. He was injured on his head and heart from a runaway. The doctors said he could not live. He knew it himself. His skull, at one place where he was injured, pressed heavily on the brain, affecting his mind. This spot could easily be felt and was soft and tender. Now it is all healed up and just like it was before. The power of God raised it and set it in its place. His heart also was completely healed. He said that when he was prayed for, he felt as if a gigantic hand took hold on the heart and pressed it back into its normal condition and made it beat naturally. He also had a fractured limb that God healed. He has complete victory over all those things today. He has watched many cases last year in the meeting that got healed, which he knew were hopeless cases. Today they are well. Tumors that were removed last year are still gone. Pellagra cases still have the victory. People who were taken off crutches are still off. Rheumatic sufferers still have complete deliverance. These people are here to testify and their testimony cannot be denied.

Healed of Cancer

While we have been back in the city again, God has been in our midst in a marvelous way. In one of our first meetings, a lady was prayed for who had a cancer on her breast. When prayed for, the power fell on her, and she was prostrated. Then in a semi-raised position, she prophesied, showing us about the serious times in which we live. When she got up, she pounded her breast, showing that all soreness was gone and the cancer was dead. Two weeks later she is still doing it. The work is done.

Healing Demonstrated on Sidewalk

One evening a woman, paralyzed from her waist down for some time, was helped on the rostrum to be prayed for. She was a sinner who sought salvation. When she was prayed for, healing and saving power struck her. She soon got on her feet and began to walk back and forth on the platform, praising God, shouting His praises with a loud voice. She had made light of the Pentecostal people and spoken hard things about them when this came on her. Now she praises God for deliverance and being one of them. On the street in the evening, sinners gathered about her and asked her to demonstrate to them that she was completely healed by running on the sidewalk. She did it. The boys then told her that anybody who would not believe that this was of God, would not believe, *"though one rose from the dead"* (Luke 16:31). This comes very near to being the truth.

Soldier Understands Part of Message in Tongues

One night a lady was brought in, dying with consumption. When she was prayed for, the power of God came on her, and she began to speak in other tongues. Back in the audience was a young man, a soldier of the army, who said that he understood part of the message, which was in French. This woman has since played a mouth harp in the Spirit, so plain and distinct that an expert could not have noticed that she did it without an instrument.

The heavenly choir comes forth in a strong way, like rolling water. The chanting can be heard all over the audience. With uplifted hands, the saints yield and let the Spirit play through and roll in and out of their bodies. This puts great conviction on sinners. Some of the saints play instruments and get visions while yielded to God in this way. Jesus was seen in the clouds. That His coming is very near is evident to every saint who is fully yielded. One night we could hardly close before eleven o'clock because the power was so great, and the Spirit worked in a marvelous way.

While God has greatly blessed the work among the white people during Sister Etter's stay in Atlanta a year ago, and now again, the colored people have not been neglected. Five or six meetings were held a year ago, in which all kinds of healings took place. Now we have already had a number of meetings among them. It is encouraging to hear the various testimonies on the healings of a year ago. Today they are well. In our meetings so far this year, God has healed everyone, with probably a few exceptions. When the power struck them, all traces of the diseases disappeared in a short time, in most cases. Some who were not saved got delivered and saved. Others came out speaking in tongues. The power was so strong and manifest at times that it struck them almost immediately when they sat in the chair. They would soon jump out of their chairs and praise God.

One sister, who had made a vow not to eat or drink until God would heal and save her, was paralyzed from the waist down. She had gone for four days without food or drink. She came to the meeting. When prayed for, the fire struck her, and she got saved and healed, so that she could walk back and forth. She opened her mouth, too, for the first time in four days, the saints said. We praise God, for His power is the same today.

—*A. D. Feick*

Miracles at Atlanta, Georgia

A seventy-five year old man testified he had been made deaf during the war by the explosion of a shell, but is healed and can hear.

A totally blind woman, while being prayed for, raised her hands and shouted, "Praise God! I can see my hands."

A pretty girl, born deaf and dumb, rose and danced on the rostrum, praising God, while her face shone with gladness and the glory of the Lord, as she said, "Praise God!" Next day, when another mute was healed, they danced together.

A year-old infant with spinal trouble had no use of its body; its head dropped every way; it had not mind enough to notice anything. After prayer it seemed every whit whole, sat upright, head erect, looking intelligent and pleased.

—*S. C. Johnson*, Evangelist

680 Glenn Street, Atlanta, Georgia

April 1915

Praise God for salvation through the blood of Jesus and the baptism of the Holy Spirit. Praise Him for speaking with other tongues, as the Spirit gave utterance.

God healed me of heart trouble and nervous prostration. Praise the Lord for permitting me to attend Sister M. B. Woodworth-Etter's meetings in Atlanta, Georgia, and witnessing the wonderful works of God, especially the extraordinary healings.

A beautiful, cultured, refined young girl came forward weeping. She said her sister—a Mrs. Carter—who lived in the best part of the town, was dying with appendicitis. Three of the best doctors of the town had given her up to die, but said they could keep her alive a little longer by an operation.

Prayer was offered immediately for God to stay the knife and rebuke the disease. We all had the witness that the work was done. One sister had a vision of the sick one in the hospital. Jesus walked up and laid His hand on the afflicted side and healed her. The girl was told to hurry home and not allow them to carry her to the hospital. They had already done so, but God answered prayer when they laid her upon the operating table. The power of God fell upon her. The doctors thought she had fainted and tried to revive her, but could not.

The power of the Spirit was upon her for ten or twelve hours. When she came to herself in the night, God told her she was healed. She desired to go home, but the nurse would not allow her to go. The next day she returned home, boarded the car, came to the meeting by herself, and told what great things the Lord had done for her. Praise His name! The Lord Jesus Christ is *"the same yesterday, and to day, and for ever"* (Heb. 13:8).

—*Mrs. A. M. Floyd*

Behold I Come

When I survey the wondrous theme
   Of Jesus coming for His own,
'Tis like the morning's rising beam,
   Calling to our heavenly home.

In these last days of darkened time
   When demons prowl with subtle power;
Our God is showing us the signs
   Of coming day, and nearing hour.

Awake, my soul! soar up above;
   Fix on that "hope" thy steadfast eye:
Soon shall we meet the Lord of love
   In clouds together in the sky.

There's comfort to the weary soul
   In that bright hope of nearing joy;
For ceaseless ages then shall roll,
   Where powers of hell no more annoy.

Come quickly, Jesus, for Thy bride
   Longs for thee, and that wondrous time
When seated with Thee, at Thy side,
   She'll reign with Thee, in heaven's clime.

53

MIRACULOUS TOUCHES OF GOD

After spending some time in waiting before the Lord to be sure that He wanted me to accept the earnest call from Brother Hall and the saints to go the third time to hold another convention in the wicked city of Chicago, when there were so many calls waiting for a date, to come to other states and cities, I was led to decide to go. Brother Hall came to my home in Indiana, and the Lord greatly blessed us in prayers, and I felt convinced the Lord was leading me to give Chicago one more warning to prepare to meet Him. The dear brother secured the largest church available in the city, and ministers and saints came from all over the city, and also from many other states.

Among those who assisted was Brother Frazer of the Stone Church. Sister Sisson, who has been much used and blessed of the Master, too, and has labored in foreign fields, also assisted me in several other states. May the Lord add days and months to her life and make her flourish, bearing much fruit in old age. Many messages and prophecies were given, both in English and "other tongues" of the soon coming of the Lord Jesus, and "the great Tribulation," and of the awful war that is now on, and many other things that have already come to pass now in less than a year.

Several had a vision of the dreadful calamity that came a few days after the meeting closed, when the pleasure boat capsized on Lake Michigan and hundreds of people lost their lives. They told again and again that a great calamity was at the door. It was told that some of those present who were mocking would go down. The strike, which came on before we left, was foretold: many got their last call of mercy. The next will be at the Judgment.

Jesus said, *"The works that I do in my Father's name, they bear witness of me,… But the Father that dwelleth in me, he doeth the works…But now they have no cloak for their sins…*[They stand guilty and naked before God]" (John 10:25; 14:10; 15:22).

All Glory to the Lord

"Marvellous are thy works, Lord God Almighty" (Rev. 15:3).

"That he may do his work, his strange work; and bring to pass his act, his strange act" (Isa. 28:21).

Surely we have seen these "strange works" and "strange acts."

Miracles were wrought daily. Multitudes heard the Word. Many believed, some doubted, some mocked, many were converted.

Cancers, tumors, rheumatism, deafness, many incurables were healed. People brought in on wheelchairs walked home.

Heavenly songs, dancing, falling under the power. Jesus, the King of Glory, was in our midst! His name honored. "Victory in Jesus' name." In Him,

—*Evangelist L. C. Hall*

Healed of Asthma When Baptized with the Holy Spirit

I was sick twelve years with asthma and other diseases, but God did so wonderfully heal me when He baptized me with His Holy Spirit, and about three years ago I had erysipelas in my leg. Many said I would have to have it taken off, but glory be to God, I knew He had put me here with two legs and was able to take me away with two, so I trusted God, and glory to God, He healed me. I just praise His matchless name.

Your brother in Christ,
—*C. Bowman*
Chicago, June 19, 1915

Healed of Locomotor Ataxia and Hemorrhoids

I have been afflicted with locomotor ataxia for twenty years. I am now fifty-four years old, the last six years unable to work at my trade and suffering with a pain in my back almost constantly. I live at the County Infirmary, and learning that Sister Etter was to be in Chicago, I came to the meeting on June 10, was prayed for, and all pain left me instantly, and also hemorrhoids that I was suffering from were healed. My knees were sore and weak. I can now pound my knees against a hard chair and stamp my feet. I am growing stronger every day, for which I praise and thank the Lord and give Him the glory.

—*George R. Hancock*
Chicago, Illinois, June 1915

Healed Two Years Ago of Rheumatism; Still Well

I was helplessly afflicted with rheumatism for eight weeks, confined to the bed all that time, taking all sorts of remedies, but receiving no practical benefit. When I was able to get out of bed, I had to go on crutches, expecting to be on them the rest of my life. Hearing of Mrs. Etter's meetings at the Stone Church two years ago, a lady took me over there, and after I was prayed for I was instantly healed and ran across the floor praising God, and I have not seen the crutches since. And now I take Jesus for my Healer.

—*Mrs. A. Miller*
June, 1915, Chicago, Illinois

Testimonials Given at Woodworth-Etter Meetings, Chicago

For the last seven months I have been afflicted with cancer and unable to take a step. Doctors told me I would never be well, and that my case was a hopeless one. My sufferings could not be described, and the cancer was eating my vitality and strength away.

I heard of a Mrs. Cantile, who had been healed of a double cancer in one of Sister Etter's meetings in Petoskey, Michigan, and that Sister Etter was now at the tabernacle. I came to the tabernacle in a hack, as I was unable to walk, and I was carried on a chair to the platform. Mrs. Etter rebuked the cancer and prayed for me, and I was healed, and immediately I was able to walk and jump like a young girl. Glory and praise to the Lord.

—*A Colored Lady*

Testimony of Healing and Salvation

When Mrs. Woodworth-Etter was in Muscatine in 1902, my mother was healed of a very bad case of heart trouble, consumption (her mother, one brother, and other relatives had died of it), and other troubles that she had. She was to be operated on, but they couldn't because of the condition of her heart. She doctored with one of the best doctors in Davenport (twenty-eight miles from Muscatine), but she grew worse. She also doctored in Muscatine. When she did not have long to live, she attended Sister Etter's meetings, who laid hands on her. She was instantly healed and saved. Praise God. She is strong today (June 8, 1915) and has no trace of consumption. Praise God. Through her healing, my father was convicted of sins, and the next year he was saved from smoking, chewing, drinking, and gambling, and sin, too. Praise God. My sister was saved and healed of a large neck in those meetings and is now a missionary in China. I myself was saved and healed of a swollen foot, which has never troubled me since. Praise God. Something over six years ago the Lord baptized our whole family with the Holy Spirit, as in olden times. Praise God.

—*C. E. Stieglitz*
Muscatine, Iowa

Healed of Tuberculosis and Adenoids

(Testimony of Gladys Allen, of Rio, Wisconsin.
Given by her aunt, Miss May Allen, at the Woodworth-Etter meeting
in Chicago, June, 1915.)

Gladys was always a delicate child, and when six years old she had bronchial pneumonia, from which she never recovered. A year later it had developed into tuberculosis.

Two years ago her father died of tuberculosis, and in October I took her to Colorado Springs to Dr. Zwan, one of the celebrated physicians in the country, so as to give her the best hospital treatment. She improved a great deal, but when brought home she gradually went back to the same condition. A year ago last February, I had Sister Etter pray for her, through the anointing of and prayer over a handkerchief, which was sent to the child, sixteen hundred miles away. After the handkerchief was applied, she immediately began to improve and had no more severe colds, and she is now perfectly well. Before taking her West, she was operated on for adenoids in the nose. On one side of the nose was a bony growth, which nearly closed up the nostril. One physician advised another operation to remove this growth, but instead I brought her to Sister Etter's meeting, and she was healed the same day we arrived. We praise and thank the Lord Jesus for His wonderful mercy and goodness to this child and give Him all the glory.

Healed of Many Diseases

I praise God for what He has done for me.

I was sick since my eighth year with epilepsy, and crippled and sent to one hospital for ten years. I also had spinal meningitis and typhoid fever, paralysis, and heart disease, and was all swollen with dropsy, was in the insane asylum and the poorhouse, given up as a hopeless case by so many doctors. But when I was brought to Sister Woodworth Etter's meeting after being crippled for eighteen years, God healed me. Oh, how I praise Him! I was healed the first time they carried me in, and I walked out rejoicing. Oh, I praise God! That was twenty-five years ago, and I have been working for the Lord ever since. Oh, how I thank God for all His blessings and that I was ever brought to Sister Etter's meetings! Praise the Lord.

—*Miss Lizzie Herty*
Monroe Street, Chicago, Illinois

Chronic Catarrh Healed

I was a terrible sufferer from chronic catarrh for twenty-eight years. It kept me spitting night and day. I was certainly a slave to it, and it was draining my life away. Brother Feick, one of Sister Etter's workers, laid hands on me, and I was instantly cured.

Words cannot express the feeling of relief from that terrible disease, for which I do praise God, and for the way He used His servant in delivering me.

I was also prayed for for a rupture. All is under the blood.

—*C. W. Griffin*, Moira, New York
Given at Chicago, Illinois, June, 1915

Striking Cancer Case

In August, 1913, I went under an operation and had some of the best doctors in Chicago, who found I had one cancer in my back, also one near my heart. They could not remove them. They sewed up the incision and said I had but a few days to live. I kept up through prayers and was steadily losing weight and strength until July, 1914, when I went to Petoskey, Michigan, and to Sister Etter's meetings. The third day I received the baptism of the Holy Spirit, and the same afternoon Sister Etter laid hands on me in the name of Jesus and demanded the unclean spirits to leave me, and I was healed. I am still happy in the Lord Jesus.

—Mrs. F. Cantile,
4618 West End Avenue
Chicago, Illinois

Mother Healed of Many Afflictions and Children Baptized with the Holy Spirit

About four years ago I was severely injured in the spine from heavy lifting and was confined to the bed, unable to walk. Hearing of Sister Etter's meetings at the Stone Church in Chicago two years ago, I was brought there in a wheelchair in the baggage car. I was so very low they did not think I was hardly able to get there. When Sister Etter laid hands on me and prayed, I was instantly healed by the Lord and walked all around the church.

In September, following my healing in the Stone Church, we had threshing machine men and straw presses; not being able to get sufficient help, I overworked and took dropsy and was brought down to near death. I called the children around me and told them they would have to help pray or they would soon have no mother, and five of them got saved and baptized in the Holy Spirit. During this severe sickness and trial, the great spiritual blessings and faith received in the meeting at the Stone Church were with me. A doctor said only a miracle could save me. When I saw death staring me in the face, I said, "Do I have to die and leave my husband and the children?" All at once it came to me, "I don't have to die, for Jesus is the Healer." The swelling from the dropsy went out of my chest and abdomen, and my heart became normal. Two places opened on my ankles, and the water ran out. From then on I got rapidly well.

Last fall, when Sister Etter was holding meetings at the 63rd Street Mission in Chicago, I was being prompted by the Spirit of God to come to Chicago and testify and give God the glory for the healing and baptism received in the Stone Church meetings, but it being very inconvenient to get there, and Satan suggesting difficulties, I failed to obey the leading of the Holy Spirit when I could have done so if I had made sufficient effort.

About seven or eight weeks ago, I was severely injured by a horse attempting to run away with me while driving home from a meeting in Zion City. The terrible strain of pulling on the horse injured my heart and spine. I grew continually worse, being confined to the bed and almost choking to death from the injured heart, suffering great pain in the heart, the beating of which shook my body and the whole bed. The injury to the spine affected the whole nervous system, being almost blind and deaf. Also I suffered severe pain on the top of the head and back of the neck. Dropsy again set in, and my whole body was bloated.

All the family and myself have felt that the Lord may have permitted this injury because of the disobedience of not coming to testify last fall. It was quite a humiliation to have to come to Chicago again in a wheelchair in a baggage car. I was so low I had to be carried from the house to the automobile to be taken to the station. We arrived at Sister Etter's meeting, May 23. The next day I was prayed for, and my heart and stomach were instantly healed. Several mornings later, I awoke with the head healed and have been walking around the church praising and thanking God, growing stronger every day.

I do thank and praise the Lord for His great mercy and love in delivering me from so great an affliction. My daughter Beatrice was injured in the back from lifting me, and she also has been healed by the Lord since coming to the meetings. To God be the glory!

—*Mrs. James Dolan*, June, 1915, Zion City, Illinois

Healed of Heart Disease and Dropsy

I was taken some months ago with heart disease and dropsy; was taken to the Cook County Hospital and was there three months. For a little while I got some better and was able to get on my feet; then I got worse again and was on my back three months, all swelled up with the dropsy. I was pronounced incurable and put in the incurable ward. Then a lady came with a tract on divine healing with the address of the Woodworth-Etter meetings. I prayed about it and was determined to go. Any man in health could have got to the place by walking in thirty minutes, but it took me three hours. I prayed all morning, and God gave me strength to get on my feet and to get to the meeting. When I was prayed for, my flesh instantly began to shrink, the dropsy disappeared, and my heart ceased bothering me. I can sleep at night, which I could not do before. I am growing stronger all the time. I can't express the thanksgiving and praise that is in my heart. I thank God nearly every minute in the day.

—*John A. Weaver,* June, 1915, Austin, Illinois

"I was sick with Bright's disease, dropsy, and kidney trouble for fourteen weeks; I was really dying and fell off in weight thirty-eight pounds in four weeks. Last Tuesday I came here, and when they laid on hands and prayed for me, I was healed and made every whit whole. Praise God for all He has done for me."

— *J. W. Gordon,* 1106 Monroe Street, Chicago, June 2, 1915

What a Joyful Meeting

Soon the King of Kings shall descend from heav'n,
    And we'll hear the trumpet sound,
Then the living saints, life eternal giv'n,
    Shall meet those who arise from the ground.

REFRAIN

What a joyful meeting, what a happy greeting.
    When we meet to part no more—
Then on plains of glory, we will sing life's story,
    And our blessed Savior's name we will adore.

When the trumpet sounds and the dead shall wake,
    And we rise to meet our King,
Of the wedding feast we shall all partake,
    And the songs of redemption we'll sing.

By the grace of God I am going through;
    Look for me in Paradise;

To my Savior's name I will e'er be true;
    Then I'll meet all the saved in the skies.

Sinner, come to Christ, let Him make you whole;
    Plunge beneath the cleansing flood;
With His Spirit filled, purified as gold,
    You can meet loved ones, washed in the blood.

54

"THINGS OF GOOD REPORT"

Where God So Wonderfully Blessed in a Revival Years Before

We were in St. Louis two weeks and held meetings twice a day. We had a glorious reunion with the dear saints who had been saved and healed and blessed in our former meetings in St. Louis, many from the noted Kerry Patch meeting twenty-seven years ago. They all came together in love and fellowship, praising God for sparing my life and theirs to meet together once more to build up the temple of the Lord. The convicting, saving, and healing power of the Lord was poured out on the meeting. Many received the baptism in the Holy Spirit, and sinners were slain by the mighty power of God. Many of the saints were led down in *"green pastures"* (Ps. 23:2), having visions, and *"things to come"* (John 16:13) were revealed with great demonstrations and diverse gifts and operations of the Spirit. The crowds could not get into the hall; part of them had to stand on the outside, and part of the time they were held still and looked on in amazement. Brother Bosworth of Texas was with us and assisted in the meeting, and many other ministers also. There was no discord to disturb at all. All felt at home and that heaven had come down and that the Lord of Hosts was present, *"confirming [His] word with signs following"* (Mark 16:20).

Brothers Bell and Flower and Sister Flower were also present and helped. The Lord gave some messages in other tongues with power, eloquently and fluently, through Sister Flower. She is a power in the hand of the Lord. She was wonderfully used in speaking in other tongues and in interpretations. Many others gave prophecies, messages, and warnings, telling the wonderful works of God and of awful judgments coming on the world. It is nearly a year since then, and many of the terrible things have already come to pass; many more will soon follow.

Some were in the holy dance with such grace and lightness, and the glory of the Lord shining in their faces and all over and around them. Everybody said that dear Sister Ball, who was healed of consumption in Atlanta the year before, looked like an angel. Her golden hair fell like a silken veil over her shoulders. She spoke in several different languages and sang songs that no one had ever heard before, some of them in English.

Many of my old friends from the other churches, who had been very much opposed to the "tongues movement," as they came and heard the preaching, saw the many signs, heard the testimonies, saw everything was done in God's order, according to the Word that was preached, and that there was no wildfire or fanaticism, contentions or rebuking, or bluffing one another, said that of a truth "Pentecost has come again," and that God was pouring out His Spirit. Brother Feick, who has been traveling with me for two years or more, was wonderfully used of the Lord in the holy dance, with closed eyes as they all do, with such lightness of limbs, and using his hands and whole body with power and grace, taking many steps that were never seen before. He was playing some invisible instrument and dancing to his own heavenly music. While all this was going on, the people were held spellbound. He is naturally very quiet, never went to a dance in his life, and never tried to dance. All felt that God was present, working His *"strange work"* and His *"strange act[s]"* (Isa. 28:21) in our midst.

If our time had been unlimited, we would have had another Kerry Patch revival, but we had to leave, hoping and believing that in the future God would answer our prayers and give the dear people of St. Louis another call.

One blind woman received her sight. Many are praising the Lord today for their healing and salvation in those meetings nearly two years ago.

Good Results Everywhere

(From the *Christian Evangel*)

Sister Etter has come to St. Louis, and we are indeed glad to have her with us. The meeting, which had been widely announced in Chicago at the Tabernacle, a red stone church on the corner of Ashland Boulevard and Ogden Avenue, was closed a week ahead of time on account of a streetcar strike, which hindered the people from getting out to meetings.

Sister Etter planned to be with the saints in St. Louis this week until June 26, and possibly a few days longer. The Assembly on Easton Avenue joined in with the Assembly on Olive Street, and the two assemblies are now cooperating to the best of their ability in helping on the cause of God and in upholding Sister Etter's hands as she preaches the Word and prays for the sick. There are many obstacles to be overcome, and this meeting is only a forerunner of another greater and longer meeting, which we trust will be held in St. Louis sometime in the future.

Already we have seen some good results as the sick have been prayed for and as sinners have wept their way through to Calvary. Some needed instruction has also been given that is going far to help the people in their desire to obey God and let the Holy Spirit have His way with them. Sister Etter is fearlessly declaring a full Gospel, and the Lord is graciously confirming the Word with signs following.

We received some blessed reports from the Chicago meeting. One brother wrote us that God was present in great power, saving, healing, and baptizing in the Holy Spirit. Brother Feick wrote, "A number of helpless invalids, who came to the meeting in wheelchairs, are now walking by themselves." It was reported that twenty states were represented and that the power of God was prostrating many of the saints daily, some of whom received marvelous visions.

J. W. Gordon, 1106 Monroe Street, Chicago, Illinois, testified that he had been healed of Bright's disease, dropsy, and kidney trouble, after he was dying, having lost thirty-eight pounds in weight. This testimony was confirmed by a brother who arose and said he had known Brother Gordon for seven years.

A woman who was brought into the meeting in a wheelchair testified to healing of palpitation of the heart and an injury to her back, which she received in a runaway accident nine weeks before. She said that it was all gone now, including severe stomach trouble, and that she hardly knows she has a stomach now.

55

THE FIRE FALLS
AT TOPEKA, KANSAS

Enemy Gets Stirred, People Blessed, a Great Victory Won

For two years Brother Foster and the saints had been calling me to Topeka to hold a convention. At last we felt that the Lord was leading, and so the last of July 1915, with several good workers, I landed in the beautiful city of Topeka. Many of my readers have read of the great meeting we had in that city twenty-seven years ago, when I went with two young girls and a janitor as strangers, at the invitation of one minister, and held meetings for nearly two months in the beautiful park. My large tent that held nearly eight thousand had been given to me in Oakland, California, was destroyed by a storm. Thousands came out and saw we were trying to continue in the grove. They went to work at once, raised money, and bought me a large new tent. Now, after all these years, I find myself again holding meetings in the large city park theater, with merry-go-rounds, dance halls, all kinds of sports and amusements around. The dear Lord Jesus said, *"And I, if I be lifted up,...will draw all men unto me"* (John 12:32). He is the great drawing power. As we preached the Word, giving Him the preeminence above all men and powers, the Lord was with us, confirming the Word with signs and wonders. They began to bring the sick on beds and crutches, the lame and the blind were seen running from their cots and beds, and the blind were made to see, the lame leaping and shouting. Sinners wept their way to Calvary and arose and praised the Lord, for they had found Him precious to their souls. Many times the places of amusement were empty, and the great theater was crowded and many could not get in. Many ministers of different faiths came from all parts on trains, in companies, bringing the sick with them.

All this was voiced abroad, and there was a great stir. The brothers had been having meetings in the city for years; they were not liked, and some had a prejudice against them. When they saw the great success, interest, and large crowds, they said, "We will stop this," so they began to look for something to accuse them of. They found a child at the altar lying under the power of God, and they passed a decree that if they found another child under sixteen at the altar, they would arrest the parents and close the meeting. A woman brought her son over a hundred miles to be healed. The doctors could not do anything for him, and the mother was also very badly diseased. They were both healed the first day.

Officer Grabs Boy from the Altar

That night the boy went with his mother to the altar to seek the baptism in the Holy Spirit. The police went from one end of the long altar to the other, which was filled with men and women. Down at the end they found this boy kneeling with his mother. They grabbed him up away from his mother, who tried to hold him, and took him to the police station. The next day they told the mother to send the boy home, and if he went back to the meeting, they would arrest them both and they would have to pay a fine. They were from another county and could have sued the city for heavy damages. After all this fright, the boy was perfectly healed. They told the leaders of the meeting that they must leave the grounds at once. We had many small tents, and we could not move in a minute. That night the crowds had gathered and they had said that they would turn out the lights at eight o'clock. Well, the lights went out, and we were left in darkness. A man at this time stepped forward and said that he had a lovely grove just across the way, and we could have it free of charge, and he would see what the city would do with him, and we could stay as long as we wanted to.

Pastor Arrested and Released

The officers were raging and arrested the leader, took him to the station, but he was soon bailed out. I expected them to take me next. I went through a martyrdom the next two or three days, looking continually to be arrested. Every day I carried a kimono and some little things I would need in jail. But they were not after me; they never spoke against me at all. If you follow the steps of Jesus closely, you will know how the martyrs of old suffered and were persecuted. The whole city was stirred, and everywhere they were either for or against the meeting. Oh, glory to God! Christ was the Victor. He was leading the hosts of the Lord. A large tent was secured at once, and the small ones were soon removed to a much better place than we had before. The crowds increased continually, also the interest. Many of the best citizens and church members who had taken no part or interest were very indignant at the way we had been treated and came out to see. The tent was crowded; people were standing packed all around the tent and so still that all could hear. The power of God came like a cloud and rested over the tent and grounds, and the fear of the Lord and the presence of God were felt by all. Everyone seemed to respect us, and ministers continued to come to the help of the Lord. Many who had never seen the *"mighty signs and wonders"* (Rom. 15:19) God is giving these last days saw the sick healed of the worst diseases, the deaf made to hear, the lame to walk, and the blind to see. They said it looked like the days of Christ in Galilee, and when they saw all classes—old men and women and little children—speaking in other languages and giving the true interpretations, all telling the wonderful works of God, they were confounded and said, "'*What meaneth this?*' (Acts 2:12). Surely we have seen strange things!"

Sister Oaks, a poor woman with three little children to care for, gave many strong messages on the campgrounds in *"other tongues"* (Acts 2:4) with a voice like thunder. She was very small and frail, and she would pray and sing in the Spirit in other tongues. She, with others, would join in the holy dance. They were so light that it seemed that they would float away. The holy fire spread far and near, and eternity alone will tell the mighty work God wrought in Topeka.

The Work Continues

Notes on the camp meeting held in Topeka, Kansas, during the month of August, 1915, by Sister Etter and workers, Brother and Sister Howell, Brother Feick, and Sister Ida Ball.

There were about three hundred people from many different states and from Canada in attendance.

Many, whose names we never learned, testified to healing. The power of God was wonderful. As songs of praise went up to God, the power fell and singing and dancing in the Spirit were features in almost every meeting.

Sister Etter is an illustration of the power of God upon one's life. Although she has reached the age of three score and ten, she is remarkably preserved. It seemed the Holy Spirit prompted all she said. Truly grace fell from her lips. Her prayer for God to "drop down something for the people to take away" was answered in every meeting.

Had not the enemy divided the saints in Topeka over a false doctrine, God could have worked even more blessedly than He did.

Many blessed messages in tongues and interpretation were given. Eternity alone will reveal the results of this meeting.

Healings

Mrs. Ella Tunnelly, a colored woman, North Tokepa, Kansas, was healed of a tumor of four or five years' standing and heart trouble. She had to walk with a crutch. When healed, she was able to jump. Her mother and sister were watching to catch her, for they couldn't understand the instantaneous healing she had received. She said, "I ain't tired. If I keep on feeling this way, I'll never die. I'm so glad I've come, I don't know what to do."

This precious sister was so filled with the Holy Spirit and the joy of God that she talked for about three-quarters of an hour, and the people listened, spellbound, for she spoke with the unction of the Holy Spirit.

Mrs. George H. Hough, Kansas City, Missouri, for four years troubled in her side from a dislocated rib caused from lifting a big piece of coal, was healed by the power of God.

Mrs. P. M. La Burge, Roosevelt, Oklahoma, testified to having been healed of consumption with which she had been troubled more or less for twenty-two years. While Sister Etter was praying for her, she told her to praise the Lord instead of coughing. Mrs. La Burge said, "Fifteen years ago, when my name was Agnes Ozman, I tarried for my baptism ten days here in Topeka, Kansas, with a number of others. I had been a missionary twelve years, and I saw there was more for me. My heart was so hungry. The power of prayer was mighty upon me. I did all I knew to do; I told the brother whom God was using in leading us out to lay hands on me that I might receive what there was for me. He did so, and I spoke in tongues. My heart was satisfied. I didn't know I would speak in tongues and couldn't speak in English for a while. I found it was scriptural. Some who understood Bohemian heard me speak in the Bohemian language in a mission. Not understanding God's dealings with me, I got into the flesh and was under a cloud spiritually, and was willing to lay down the baptism because of criticism and censure. I fasted three and one-half days, and the Lord gave me this Scripture: *"If a son shall ask bread of any of you that is a father, will he give him a stone?...how much more shall your heavenly Father give the Holy Spirit to them that ask him?"* (Luke 11:11, 13).

How blessedly He reveals Himself to us by His Spirit! *"Himself took our infirmities, and bare our sicknesses"* (Matt. 8:17).

Mrs. Stewart, of Beatrice, Nebraska, was healed of tuberculosis of glands of the neck. She couldn't raise her left arm. Her skin was almost yellow. She was healed instantly. All praise to Jesus.

Rebecca Templeton, a colored woman of North Topeka, crippled for nine years, had tried doctors and medicines and liniments of every kind and couldn't be cured. In fact, she tried every remedy anybody told her to. The Lord healed her.

Mrs. N. E. Porter, 1115 North Madison Street, received healing and the baptism of the Holy Spirit. The glory of God filled her soul, and she shouted and praised the Lord and talked in tongues. God also gave her the gift of interpretation.

Mrs. Brayfield had used no medicine for eight years. She was healed of rheumatism. She had lost the sight of one eye, but God is restoring sight. She praised the Lord for Sister Etter and her workers and those who labor for souls. She testified about a blind man receiving his sight since going home from the meetings and that his wife was healed when they prayed for her.

Mr. Schultz, Dearfield, Ohio, read Sister Etter's book and went to Chicago and was healed when given up by doctors. He and his wife came a thousand miles to attend the camp meeting. Mrs. Schultz received a healing from stiffness in her knees, from which she had suffered for years, while she was lying under the mighty power of God. She lay there for hours.

Mrs. Strommer, Montevidea, Minnesota, was brought in a dying condition with cancer of the stomach. She was reduced to a mere skeleton. She could not have lived but a few days longer, apparently. After being prayed for, she walked back and forth in front of the rostrum, praising God. She said she had a new life from God as soon as she was prayed for.

Reverend J. L. Bishop, Pomona, Kansas, was healed of hay fever and received his baptism with the Holy Spirit. He was a Congregationalist preacher.

Earl Rush, Cedar, Kansas, was healed of weak ankles. He walked four miles the next day after his healing. He was saved two years ago when he was a drunkard and addicted to the use of tobacco. He was healed of appendicitis then, too. His ankles had been weak from childhood.

Miss Louise Albach, Scranton, Kansas, praised God for what her eyes saw of the power of God in these meetings, for the liberty of the Spirit which she enjoyed, and for the divine touch she received when Sister Etter prayed for her. She was healed seventeen years ago of a tumor and nervous prostration and has not touched medicines since.

Miss Ada Gilbert, near Country Club, Topeka, Kansas, testified to God's healing power in restoring her sight. She had weak eyes as a child and had to give up schoolwork at the age of twelve. The mucous membranes of her eyelids were destroyed from the medicines she had used. She couldn't see well enough to go alone anywhere, but after seeking God earnestly and being prayed for, her sight began to return. She recognized colors, something she had not done for years. The power of God rested upon this dear sister during meetings, and her testimonies showed a deeper sinking into Jesus day after day. God gave her the assurance that her sight would be entirely restored.

Praise His Name

August 12, 1915

Greetings in Jesus' precious name. I just returned from the Topeka, Kansas, camp meeting, conducted by our beloved Sister M. B. Woodworth-Etter. Glory to God. The Lord is working in mighty power. Sinners weeping accept salvation, believers receiving the Holy Spirit as in Acts 2:4 and 19:6; the sick and afflicted shouting complete healing. Praise His holy name. Sick and afflicted from many states are there at the end of the first week, and almost every train brings others, coming for healing. I will give a short sketch below of what I witnessed:

Mrs. R. S. Paxton, Topeka, nervous prostration nine months, given up by five doctors, one specialist said the asylum was the only resort; instantly healed.

This is only one of the many marvelous works of God I beheld the short time I was there. Glory to God!

—*Andrew L. Turner*, Kiefer, Oklahoma

Verses by the Late Mr. Etter

When I was far away and lost,
    Oh, it was wonderful!
That I was saved at such a cost!—
    Oh, it was wonderful!

CHORUS

Oh, it was wonderful! Oh, it was wonderful!
That Jesus gave His life for me.
    Oh, it was wonderful.

My sins were all I had to bring—
    Oh, it was wonderful!
That I was made His love to sing.
    Oh, it was wonderful!

Jesus keeps me day by day—
    Oh, it is wonderful!
When I trust Him and obey,
    Oh, it is wonderful!

Sinner? Jesus calls for you—
    Oh, it is wonderful!

His blood was freely shed for you.
    Oh, it is wonderful!

Will you come to Him today?
    Oh, it is wonderful!
Will you not His Word obey?
    Oh, it is wonderful!

Hearken now to His command,
    Oh, it is wonderful!
Lest you at His judgment stand.
    Oh, it is wonderful!

56

CRIES FOR HELP

Revival is Needed

The work that God did at our meeting at Topeka, Kansas, began to spread far and near. Los Angeles, California, where we held the world-wide camp meeting just a few years before, was the next field of labor that we had promised.

In the meantime the saints at Colorado Springs, Colorado, learned that we were to pass through their city and that we had a little time left before our meeting in Los Angeles began. They sent in urgent requests to us, real Macedonian cries for us not to pass them by without giving them a meeting, and deal out to them the Bread of Life. Although I needed rest so badly, I felt that I could not pass by this needy field of labor, and we promised them a few weeks' meeting. When the saints received my assurance that I was coming, they at once began to cry to God for good weather. They had had rain almost every day for a long time, making it impossible to hold a meeting in a tent. God wonderfully heard and answered their prayers. The day the meeting started, it stopped raining and did not rain again until the day after we closed, except for one little shower, which lasted only a few minutes while the meeting was on. This little shower showed us how helpless we would have been had not God checked the rain, as the tent let the water through so that we had to use umbrellas.

God greatly blessed us while the meeting lasted. They all told us that it was a hard field of labor, little having been accomplished for God all summer. We found out that this was so, but nothing is too hard for God (Jer. 32:17) if we only trust Him and keep looking up to Him.

The meeting was not extensively advertised, as we came on short notice. Just a few days before we arrived, the minister, whose field of labor it was and whom we expected to stand right by us, got an urgent call to help in another field. This left us practically alone, but God was still with us.

The crowds were not so very large to begin with, but some very hungry, needy souls were present, who soon got filled with God. Some of the mightiest miracles were performed daily by the sword of the Spirit.

Miner's Consumption Healed

A man was dying with miner's consumption. The doctors gave him only a few months to live. His wife told him to go down to those meetings and see what could be done for him. He almost went in a rage at the thought of going to a religious meeting, especially down in that tent. But the disease was playing havoc with his body. He knew his time on earth was limited. He did decide to go down one day. He took a seat well up toward the front. Before the customary time for prayer for the sick arrived, the Spirit pointed this man out to me. I went down to him, a perfect stranger to me, and began to deal with and pray for him. It was not long before the power of God struck him like lightning. He threw off his coat and cried, "I am saved and healed." He began to demonstrate by pounding his lungs hard with his fist. He did this day after day, prayed, testified, and made himself very useful in the meeting. The change in him was marvelous. His appetite returned. His wife could hardly cook enough for him.

Deaf and Dumb Spirit Goes Out

I noticed a sweet woman about forty years of age look so earnestly at me day after day, well back in the audience. I asked myself the question, Why doesn't she praise the Lord or testify? She does not seem to say a word at any time. Later on, they brought her on the platform to be prayed for and told me she was deaf and dumb from birth. I understood it all then. We prayed for God to open the deaf ears and loosen the tongue, and in a short time she heard the music and began to rejoice with us. You never saw a sweeter and brighter face than hers when she heard and made sounds.

Various Diseases Go

One woman was brought in suffering so severely with appendicitis that she was in a screaming condition. She had been in a bad state for about six weeks. Nothing but an operation would have saved her life, outside of the power of God. When I prayed for her, the pain instantly left her, and she got saved. She got complete deliverance.

Many people were brought in on cots, suffering with all kinds of diseases. Sometimes the odor was offensive, but God touched and healed everyone, I believe. It was marvelous the way the sick and afflicted got up and walked in this meeting. God's power was present to heal.

Another woman was suffering with a complication of diseases, mostly hardening of the arteries. She had been helpless for some time; she was lying on a cot, waiting her turn when I laid hands on her and put the blood of Jesus over her. She immediately went to sleep, and when she woke up, she smiled and said that all pain was gone. She began to get happy and praise God for what He had done for her.

The interest and crowds increased as the people began to find out what God was doing in the tent. The power of God was being demonstrated as people were saved, healed, and baptized. Some of the saints came as far as forty miles from Pueblo, Colorado, in their autos, to be in the meeting. God greatly blessed them; some received their baptism and began to glorify God in other tongues.

Some prominent people attended this little meeting. Millionaires were among our company and sought God with us. All felt sorry that our time was so limited. Sinners told us, "You should not leave yet, as people are just beginning to find out what is taking place; in a short time if you stay, the tent won't hold the people." We felt this was true, but our next meeting made it necessary for us to move to our next field of labor out West.

Many books were scattered in this little place. On the day we left, one of my workers entered a little shoe shop to get his shoes repaired. On entering the man said to him, "You are having wonderful meetings down there in the tent." The answer was, "Yes, sir, we are." The man then said, "I got one of your books the other night, and here it is lying open right by me. I have read it halfway through already. My, it is wonderful the way the power of God is demonstrated. I believe this is what we all ought to have. My wife is a Presbyterian. She is very quiet. I know this baptism of the Holy Spirit is what we both need." Soon others who had practically the same thoughts in their hearts entered the shop. "We need more of God, too. You people pray for us."

Saints Get Blessed

The saints who came up from Pueblo, Colorado, gave us no rest until we promised them a few days' meeting at least. They said, "We will bring you to Pueblo in an auto, so it won't cost you a cent. Pueblo is on your way to Los Angeles." It seemed almost impossible to refuse. We promised them and had a nice trip to their city, seeing the beautiful country, although it was very hard on me.

God greatly blessed our little stay here with the precious saints. The power fell in a mighty way. I felt that if we could have stayed in this place for some time, a revival would have been the result. Some wonderful cases of healings took place. May God greatly bless their pastor and the dear family who so kindly took us into their home and provided for us.

Both the saints at Colorado Springs and Pueblo, Colorado, are calling us back to their field of labor for a regular campaign. I hope and pray that God will speedily open the way so that they will get their heart's desire.

Brother A. E. Raiford of Eufaula, Oklahoma, wrote under the date of April 1, 1916: "I saw people come there to be healed who were just about dead, and were healed and went away rejoicing. My remembrance of you will never be forgotten." This dear brother is out and out for God. The sights that he saw, how the sick were carried in and walked out, left a deep impression on him.

57

ANGELIC VISITATIONS

Much Work, Two Angels Visit the Place, Some Wonderful Healings

From the time I left the worldwide Camp Meeting in Los Angeles, I felt that the Lord would call me back and that my work was not finished in that city. From the time I left, I received calls from all over the state to go back. At last, through the earnest call of dear Brother G. Garr and many of the saints, and feeling sure that it was the Lord's wish, I accepted the call.

They rented a large garage, the largest building that could be secured, seating about two thousand people. October 1st was the date set for the opening. We had been laboring hard and steady from the time the Lord had raised me from what many believed to be my deathbed through His miraculous power, eight months before, when we started on the long journey to Tampa, Florida. In those eight months, we had held conventions in six states, the meetings lasting from two to six weeks at a time. I was very tired when we started on the long journey to California, but the Lord sustained me and kept me safely night and day for the month in Los Angeles.

We had many difficulties and trials and many things to contend with that greatly hindered the work so that the Lord could not have His way. The cloud of glory was always over the people, but many times when the Lord was ready to come forth in a mighty way, one or more would get in the way, and the cloud departed from the tabernacle. Oh, why is it that so many of the saints get in the way and try to steady the ark, when they ought to know that it is speedy death or barrenness to their souls and lives when they do it? The Spirit is grieved, which is why there is so little of the presence of the Lord felt and seen, and also why there are not great results in the salvation of souls. God cannot come forth with His wonderful working power in the baptism of the Holy Spirit, sealing the saints with the signs following.

Many Ministers Present

Many of the saints came from all over the other states and from all parts of California. Many of the most noted ministers, evangelists, and workers were present. Brother Eldridge and his wife of the Christian Alliance have been baptized in the Holy Spirit and spoke in other languages as the Spirit gave utterance. They are lovely saints and have power with God and the people. The dear sister had been miraculously healed several years before in Indianapolis, Indiana, when Brother Eldridge took my husband to their home. We laid on hands and prayed, and in a few days he brought her to our tent meeting. She looked fine, younger, and talked and praised the Lord, and said they were praying for her all over the world. Praise the Lord, I was glad to meet them again and see them so well and earnest for the glory of God. They were a great help in the meeting. Dear Brother Argue is a power in the pulpit. He did much to encourage and help in the great work in Los Angeles. Brothers Black and Collins, also Brother Garr and many others, stood nobly by the work and were a great help. Eternity will tell of their labor of love.

It was a lovely sight to look over the great sea of faces, day after day many of them bright with the glory of God. Waves of power swept over us many times until the whole audience was moved; the shouts of the redeemed went up like the roaring of the sea. Some laughed, many cried; some were converted, many reclaimed; some healed and baptized in the Spirit in their seats. The Lord was proving to them that it was not any man's or woman's power but it was His power. The heavenly music and choir was simply glorious. It was as though the angels of heaven came down and joined in with the saints of earth. Unseen instruments were often heard by both saints and sinners. It was what John the Revelator saw and heard—the waiting bride singing the "heavenly choir" song. Alleluia! It reached the throne, and it sounded like the rolling thunders or the roaring of the sea, saying, *"Let us be glad and rejoice,…for the marriage of the Lamb is come, and his wife* [is making] *herself ready"* (Rev. 19:7).

Sometimes the house was so filled with the glory of His presence that it felt as if we were going to be caught away in the Rapture and that we could not remain on earth. How true are the words of the prophet, in speaking of these last days, when Christ our Lord is so present with His people, that we *"are for signs and for wonders"* (Isa. 8:18) from the Lord of Hosts who dwells in Zion.

Run Over by Auto

Many were saved, reclaimed, and filled with God and baptized in the Spirit. All manner of sicknesses and diseases were healed, the lame walked, the deaf heard, the dumb spoke. All kinds of demons were cast out. Some who were said to be dying rose up and walked. A man who had been run over by an auto was brought in. He was hurt and bruised all over. They thought he was killed. Several of the brothers went with me into the office where he was, and it was apparently a hopeless case, but we told them if he were dead, God could raise him up. Praise the Lord! There is no case too hard for Him. We soon saw signs of life; we shouted victory. Before the night service was over, he was able, with a little help, to walk into the meeting. Hardened sinners who had seen the accident were convinced that God had saved the man's life through our prayers. As at all the other conventions or meetings, we can only tell a little of what God did. The following testimonies and reports speak for themselves:

Two Marvelous Healings

Brother and Sister Garr, with the help of several others, brought a woman who was dying with a cancer of the breast on a bed in an auto. She was swollen all over, her feet and arms were ready to burst, the swelling was circling around her heart, and she was smothering. They thought she would die on the way, but it was her last hope. The odor was so offensive they had to leave her in the rear of the hall, away from the crowd. The cancer was open, eating, and the discharge was awful. It made me sick; I nearly fainted as I looked at her. I said I would as soon pray for God to raise the dead as to pray for her, but the Lord gave me faith and strength to lay hands on her and say, "There is no case too hard for the Lord;

if you were dead, He could raise you up. Forget all about failures. (They had been praying for her all over the country.) We will rebuke the deadly cancer with all its effects, and the Lord will heal you right now."

We resisted the devils, and, as when Jesus commanded them of old, they fled. Praise the Lord! Although they had to leave, they tried to kill her as they went out, but new life came surging through her, and all suffering left. She could breathe well, the awful discharge was passing away, the swelling had gone down, and she went away praising God for deliverance. All who saw the change stood in awe; many wept or praised the Lord.

In a few days she was out walking around and soon was going to church, showing by her presence and testimony that God had wrought a great miracle.

Bad Case of Dropsy Healed

A woman was brought from Pasadena, California, in the last stages of dropsy. She had been operated on several times, and great quantities of water were taken, and they could do nothing more for her. She was swollen all over and had water sacks from head to foot. As we prayed for her, the healing power surged through her, and the water began to flow from her skin and kidneys and bladder, so they took her from the platform to the corner of the church. I went to her there; she was as wet as though she had been dipped in water. I told them to wrap her well, and they covered her in blankets and carried her home. In a short time she came back and told what great things God had done for her, and everyone could see it, too.

"Oh that all men would praise the LORD *for his goodness, and for his wonderful works to the children of men!"* (Ps. 107:8).

Yielding to Faith

Much Interest in the Meeting

The revival, which began October 3, at 1315 South Main Street, Los Angeles, California, has continued through the month of November with good interest manifested. Many strangers have come, and while listening to the Word preached, they were convinced and turned to the Lord. Sister Etter has been empowered to pray for the sick and afflicted, and the results have been marvelous and glorious.

Tumors, cancers, fevers, lameness, deafness, blindness, and many other things produced by the enemy have yielded to the *"prayer of faith"* (James 5:15), and the results are faith-inspiring indeed. One sister who was prayed over was relieved of a tumor that weighed one and three-quarters pounds and had seven or eight roots. Many things I could tell that I know happened in the meetings, but I will not mention more because of lack of space.

Visions are seen by the saints also. One young man, educated in Rome for the Catholic priesthood, has received the baptism, and the Lord sent a company of angels to visit him in his room. The audience was electrified as he related the story. It was not a vision either, but a reality, as he was wide awake and tried to awaken a friend who was beside him, until the angel told him not to do so. Then the angel told him of the war in Europe, and why it was, saying: "God has spoken to Europe with the Gospel of peace and mercy, and they had rejected it for years," and now He is speaking to them with the cannon's mouth; in a short time He is going to speak to the United States by the cannon, as they, too, have rejected the Gospel. Visions of angels and the white dove soaring in the meeting were seen, and those beholding were awed by these manifestations.

Messages of the soon coming of Jesus were abundant.

The saints, in general, are convinced that the Lord's coming is not far distant.

Yours in the precious name of Jesus, our Lord and Savior, High Priest and coming King,

—*A. G. Garr*
126 North Flower Street, Los Angeles, California

Missionary's Testimony

I have joy bells ringing in my heart over the wonderful manifestations of God's power in the meetings conducted by Sister Etter in Los Angeles during the months of her visit, having been in the work of Pentecost since it started. I have seen many mighty signs and wonders done in the name of Jesus, but I assure you that I saw cancers, tumors, and other diseases brought to these meetings and saw them going forth, healed, and singing under His mighty power. This is only a short testimony to confirm other testimonies already sent forth. I prayed with our precious sister over some of these cases. I only wished that God would endow others with the same word of authority to bring deliverance to the suffering. I have seen the blind prayed over and the sight restored in the case of a boy. Bless His holy name.

I was healed of fits, having had twenty-six in one day, when God healed me and saved me back in Boston years ago, and His work in and through me since would fill volumes. I had the privilege to meet our sister two years ago here, and I shall ever praise God for meeting one who looks in the natural as only a handful. But, oh, how mighty a weapon in the hands of our Christ! Yours in Jesus until He comes,

—*Thos. B. O'Reilly*, Missionary to South America
3344 East First Street, Los Angeles, California

Permanent Healing

I wish to add my testimony to God saving, healing, and baptizing people in this time of the outpouring of the "latter rain," when God is so marvelously working.

God truly blessed the work during the two months' campaign in Los Angeles. The power of God fell upon the people from the first and continued all through until the end.

At times wave after wave of glory came down and settled all over the people, so that it was hard for God's servants to minister by reason of the cloud. As of old, of one accord we all praised and thanked the Lord, for His mercy endures forever, and of His goodness there is no end.

Some marvelous messages of tongues were given and interpreted in English. This always has been inspiring, because the Spirit generally settled over the meeting after God came forth in this way. The power of God came down and blessed many of the people so that they gave way to their joy by dancing under the Spirit's power, like David of old.

In my experience in the work with Sister Etter, I have seen many insane healed and restored to their right mind. As many as seven people in one meeting, all born deaf and dumb, had their ears opened and their tongues loosened. Some of these I know talk in English today.

I know of cancerous cases, whom the doctors had opened but would not operate on because of their hopeless condition. When prayed for, they got saved, healed, and baptized, and are strong and happy today.

Let us, with one accord, magnify and praise God's name for His works unto the children of men these days.

—*August D. Feick*, Ayton, Ontario, Canada

A Truly Marvelous Case

I thank God that He ever led me to trust Him for the healing of my body. A year before I received the baptism of the Holy Spirit, which was November 20, 1910. He led me to trust Him for healing, and so many times I felt His healing power. For several years I had a large tumor on my arm, reaching over on my chest. It had become so large that I had trouble wearing my clothes. I would pull it back on my chest so it would not show through my sleeve. The poison from this tumor was in my chest, as large kernels were growing all over my chest. At times it would pain and ache until I would have to stop work. Three doctors examined it and advised an operation. But after I began to trust God for healing, I told them I would trust Him for the tumor also. So many times He would deliver me from other troubles, and I would cry out, "Oh, God, heal me of this tumor also!" When I started to trust God for healing, He knew I meant to go all the way. I would rather have died than to fail God and let the doctors cut it out.

When the worldwide camp meeting began in Los Angeles two and one-half years ago, we were living eighteen miles east of Los Angeles. Our post office address was Puente, and hearing how God was aiding Sister Etter in praying for others, I was anxious to go to the meeting and have her pray for me. I could not stay at the meetings all the time, but came in as often as I could. I tried every time to get to Sister Etter for prayer, but as there were always hundreds to be prayed for, I did not have any chance to get to the platform. As I did not think I would get back to the meeting again, I felt I must shake hands with Sister Etter once, so I stood at the end of the platform where she would pass by. I did not intend to ask her to pray for me because she looked so tired.

As she came by where I was standing, I took her by the hand. I can see now that God was running the whole affair. He knows how to work if we will only obey. I told her I wanted to shake hands, that I was afraid I could not get back any more, that I had a large tumor on my arm and chest and wanted to ask her to remember me some time in her prayer closet, that she looked so tired after praying with so many that I would not ask her to pray for me then. She said, "Dear, can't you come back?" When I told her I was afraid I could not, she laid her hand on my arm and for a moment I forgot myself and began to pray for her to ask God to give her strength. She smote the tumor in the name of Jesus, and I was filled and thrilled with the mighty power of God. Bless His name! I knew the work was done. At this time I weighed over three hundred pounds. The tumor and flesh began to pass away through the kidneys. It was wonderful.

My brother, who is a physician, was in San Francisco at this time, but a few months after this, he came home. When he saw the change in me, he began to inquire what it all meant. He was afraid I had Bright's disease. I told him, "No, it is the mighty power of God healing me." Being raised by a Christian mother, he knew God could heal, so he said, "If it is God, all right; if not, I want to know it." So, to satisfy him I gave him a sample of urine, and he sent it to the hospital in San Francisco where he had been working, and some of the best doctors there analyzed it and wrote him that his sister was in a favorable condition; that all they found in the urine were traces of tumors leaving my body and brain. My brother said, "Sister, I will agree with you that it is His divine hand." In one year I lost nearly one hundred pounds. How I praise Him for what He has done, and for Sister Etter, that she believes God!

—*Miss Gertrude Berry*
510 East 33rd Street, Los Angeles, California

A Visit of Two Angels

Los Angeles, California, October 15, 1915—Brother Edward Leroy Wiley of Gonzales, Monterey County, California, came four hundred miles to get the baptism with the Holy Spirit, as he heard of Sister Etter's meetings. God had reclaimed him three weeks before from a backslidden condition and had been filling him with such a hunger and thirst for more of God that a fear and chill would come over him at the thought of not coming, until he knew he must come to Los Angeles. He came to the meeting and tried to get his baptism with his head down in quiet, but that is never God's way, but when he held up his head and praised God with all his might for what He had already done, the glory fell. Hallelujah! He was under the power for some time, and the Holy Spirit spoke through him in two languages, giving one special message for these last days in the Turkish language. Brother Wiley's own sister tried to tell the people he knew no other language, and Brother Wiley turned to the sinners and tried to tell them in English that he could speak no other languages, but he spoke it in Turkish and cried to the sinner to come to God while He was calling and be filled with the

Holy Spirit (every word spoken in Turkish). Then he grabbed his sister and told her to get down on her knees and ask God to baptize her, and she got her baptism speaking in Turkish.

Brother John Riese, who understood every word spoken, fell on his face and cried to God to have mercy, for his heart was broken for these sinners who would not heed the voice of God. We want to say here that our Brother Riese is a well educated young man, born of Italian parents, educated to be a Roman Catholic priest, but he was converted from that church by reading the Bible, the Word of God. He speaks seven languages and served in the Italian-Turko war. He came to America for a sightseeing trip, but God baptized him with the Holy Spirit and fire, and keeps him here and uses him for His glory. Brother Riese gave the interpretation of the wonderful message spoken through Brother Wiley to those who remained at that late hour, but many had gone whom God wanted to hear the message, so Brother Riese went home. He went to bed and to sleep, and he was awakened by a voice and saw two angels standing by his bed. His room was in darkness, but a light filled the room, as the angels were bright and shining as the sun. They had long golden hair and beautiful wings, and each carried a golden palm. Even their hands and feet, fingernails and toenails were all shining with the same brightness, and their feet never touched the floor, but they stood on a level with his bed.

Brother Riese thought Jesus was surely coming and tried to awaken the brother who slept nearby, but he slept on. One of the angels spoke to him in such a tender voice of sweetness and said in English the same message that Brother Wiley had given in Turkish: "Go back and warn God's people to watch and pray, for the time is at hand of the coming of the Lord. Tell them to warn the American people that God is preaching to Europe at the cannon's mouth, because He spread His hands all day long to a rebellious people, speaking to them by the Spirit. Each nation claims its God to be the greatest, yet in reality they are mocking God. Tell the American people they are the last nation to receive the baptism of the Holy Spirit and to repent while the windows of heaven are open to pour out the Spirit on all flesh. Tell them the knowledge they profess came from the Nazarene, the Son of God, for their country before the Gospel came was evil and full of darkness; but even now men reject the wisdom of God, making themselves greater than God. A man will soon conquer Europe, and then God will preach to this nation at the mouth of the cannon, and those who are asleep (deceived) will remain asleep, and those who have their eyes on man will remain with man, and this country will also be conquered by the man of Europe; then Jesus will catch away His bride, and God will take away His Spirit from the earth, and those who are not filled with the Spirit, whose lamps are not trimmed and burning, will fall on that day. The time is at hand." The angels then disappeared softly, with smiles, through the wall. Brother Riese said all strength left him, and he seemed so small and helpless before these ministering servants from God.

Friend, you who are not in the ark of safety, this is certainly a warning to come to God and be filled with the Holy Spirit and be ready before it is too late.

Saints of God, take warning. Truly the time is short when God will send His angels down to earth to warn the people.

—*Grace Cochran Thomson,*
3026 Sixth Avenue

Some Results of the Two Angels' Visits

Six Saved, Several Baptized, through Reading the Account

In the November issue of *The Pentecostal Herald*, we gave an account of a visit of angels, which occurred in October 1915, during the Woodworth-Etter meetings in Los Angeles, as told by one Edward Leroy Wiley.

The following testimony is a direct result of reading the article:

"I want to praise God for what He did for me. I had gone some time before to the Pentecostal meetings and saw many praising and giving glory to God. My soul hungered for more of God, so I went to the altar and started to praise the Lord, and down came the power of God, but He did not finish His work of baptizing me. I kept seeking the Holy Spirit for five months, but had not gone to any Pentecostal meetings for some time. One day I was reading a copy of *The Pentecostal Herald* that was handed to me by Brother Nelson, and I found out that the Lord was coming soon by reading about a visit of angels. I beseeched God to baptize me with the Holy Spirit, and that night the Lord baptized me in my home, and I started to speak in tongues. At once I had a great desire for the salvation of my family. We were invited by Brother Nelson, who gave me the paper, to come to the Central Pentecostal Assembly at 1744 West Lake Street. When we came there, my husband, two brothers, and my sister were all wonderfully saved.

Praise God! Since then, the Lord baptized one of my brothers with the Holy Spirit, speaking in other tongues, and saved one of my step-brothers in his home. They are all tarrying for the baptism. Praise the Lord.

"I was a member of the Catholic church for twenty-nine years. After being baptized with the Holy Spirit, I went to my former priest for some reasons and because he forbade me to read God's Word. After a few questions, the power of God fell upon me, and I started to talk in tongues. The priest was alarmed and told me it was a miracle and to go the way God wanted me. He said he could see that I am on the right way. Glory be to God forever!"

—Mrs. Julia Wojewodzki
In the *Pentecostal Herald*

Note: The Editor has received several letters of testimony corroborating the story of the visit of angels referred to above, and requesting that we reprint it.

Stone Tumor Healed

Los Angeles, California, October 22, 1915—Mrs. Rosa Lopez, the wife of a Spanish Pentecostal preacher, had a stone tumor for seven years, but has been much worse the last four years, and from October 4th to the 9th she suffered intensely, so much so that her life was despaired of. Her husband thought she would surely die. She could not keep even water on her stomach, but would vomit incessantly.

The authorities requested him to take her to the county hospital to be operated on, but when he objected, they allowed him to take her to Dr. Yoakum's faith home October 9. However, the Lord spoke to Brother Lopez and told him to take her to Sister Etter's meeting, and he telephoned for her to pray that his wife would be able to get there.

Brother Lopez brought his wife to the meeting Saturday, October 9, and Sister Etter prayed for her at 8:30 p.m. When she commanded the devil to loosen his hold on her and said, "I take the sword of the Spirit and cut this evil tumor loose in the name of the Lord!" the tumor was immediately cut loose as if a surgeon's knife had been used. Both were filled with the power and went home and waited on God for full evidence. At 3:30 a.m. on Sunday, the stone tumor passed away, root and branch. Glory to God! And she didn't have to stay in bed to convalesce, as she would have done had a surgeon performed the operation. We have a wonderful Physician.

Brother Lopez will be glad to answer any inquiries concerning her case, as his heart is filled with praise unto God. He had no money and no hope but Jesus, and Jesus did not fail them.

He says, "Thanks be to God, who gives us the victory at all times through the blood of His own Son, our beloved Savior, Jesus Christ."

He says God gave him Psalm 34:1–4, and truly delivered him from all his troubles.

His address is Abundio L. Lopez, 130 North Vignes Street, Los Angeles, California.

A Vision and Testimony of Healings

Los Angeles, California, October 1915

I went to the Pentecostal meeting, and there I saw that they had something that I didn't have, and my soul hungered for their experience. I was sick, and I went to the altar and was prayed for, and the power of the Holy Spirit touched me, and I was healed immediately and began to talk in tongues. I had been on the operating table a few months before, and my doctor had informed me that another operation would be necessary before I could be well. He said it would have to be by the tenth of October, this year.

I had a tumor.

After suffering this way for two years, I came to Mrs. Etter to be prayed for. That was on October 10th. Four days later a tumor weighing one and three-quarters pounds, having seven large roots, passed away. I felt a slight pain, and where the tumor was there seems to be a cavity.

All Glory to God for This Marvelous Miracle!

I sent an anointed handkerchief to my mother, Mrs. J. J. Mason, St. Clair, Tennessee. She fell off a porch fifteen years ago, and a washing machine fell on her, which caused her to be an invalid ever since, as her limbs withered away. As soon as the 'kerchief touched her, she was immediately healed and is praising God for it all. This 'kerchief was then sent to Mrs. P. C. Phillips in Chicago, who had been crippled with rheumatism. She was also instantly healed and is praising God. The days of miracles are certainly not over!

When they prayed with me, the Spirit came upon me, and I saw many beautiful visions. He first showed me Jacob's ladder, and at the top of the golden stairs, I beheld two snow-white angels. Each had a beautiful harp in its hands, and Jesus took me by the hand and led me through the most beautiful flower garden I ever beheld. He also showed me numerous beautiful mansions. He took me with His twelve disciples, and we crossed the River Jordan. He showed us where He was nailed to the cross and told me how He suffered and paid the price of deliverance for all lost souls. I saw the Lamb slain, and the blood was put over the door and on the step. I want to praise God for His divine love and His great healing power.

I also had adenoids all my life so that I was never able to breathe through my nose; these disappeared. Then, in one of my ears I was deaf for many years. After prayer, my ear opened up so that I can hear better out of it than the other.

One of my children took spells (like epileptics do) all his life, from two to five a day. I took him up to be prayed for, and he has never taken one since, and he gained nearly twenty-five pounds from the time he was prayed for until the meetings closed.

—*Mrs. E. E. Parker*
5315 Lincoln Street, Los Angeles, California

Healed of a Tropical Disease

Mr. Carl L. Williams, of Monrovia, California, had been sick for one year following an operation. He was attacked last May, while living in Honolulu, by what the doctors called dengue fever, a tropical disease.

After he recovered, his wife's health necessitated her leaving him and returning to California. Shortly after her arrival there, she received word that Mr. Williams was very ill in Honolulu with what two doctors diagnosed as tubercular peritonitis.

They took three X-ray pictures of the abdomen and found a large lump behind the stomach. Some of the doctors (there were seven in all) were of the opinion that it was a cancerous sarcoma and absolutely incurable. He grew rapidly worse.

His wife received two cable messages that there was yet hope; then came a third, saying: "Lump immovable; doctors say he cannot sail; you come."

Two days later she sailed from San Francisco and arrived at Honolulu on October 26. Before starting, she wrote to Sister Etter, requesting prayer and begging her to remain in Los Angeles until she could bring her husband back from Honolulu. She had hope that if she could get him back and have prayer for him, he would be healed. At once, Mrs. Etter began to pray that he might be given strength to return to California.

Mrs. Williams found her husband in a hospital, having undergone an exploratory operation. The result of it was that the doctors found so many adhesions of the peritoneum that the lump could not possibly be removed. Two of the doctors still suggested that serum treatment might prove beneficial, but the majority said if it was cancer, there was absolutely no hope for his life. So, they left him for nine days on a cot in the hospital, and not one of them even looked in on him.

Then his wife arrived and took him out of the hospital to the house of missionary friends, Mr. and Mrs. H. J. Johns, who kindly offered their home and did everything in their power to make him comfortable. His wife nursed him there for more than three weeks, and then he was able to start for California. He stood the voyage fairly well, in answer to prayer, and was not seasick at all; but on the last day of their journey, between San Francisco and Los Angeles, the enemy fought hard for his life.

The pain in his back was excruciating, and he could not masticate or swallow his food, or even expectorate without intense pain. The next day (Thanksgiving Day, November 25), they were able to come to Mrs. Etter's afternoon meeting. Mr. Williams had to lie down until the close of the service, as his pain was so extreme. Then he was just able to sit in a chair on the platform, while Mrs. Etter prayed for him.

In a few moments, he was prostrate under the power of the Spirit of God. It was not long before he sprang up without any assistance and was able to stand perfectly straight, whereas before he had walked in a doubled-up condition. He walked from end to end of the platform, leaping and praising God that he was completely whole. He then testified in a clear voice to the assembled crowds, telling them how wonderfully the power of God had quickened every part of his body. In a few more moments, he was eating a raw apple with ease, finding no difficulty whatever in swallowing and praising the Lord at every mouthful.

Mr. Williams, who came from Honolulu and got healed, came back a few days afterwards and walked by his wife, helping her up on the platform and gave a marvelous testimony of his deliverance. He also demonstrated and showed the people how complete his deliverance has been. A person who did not know him would have hardly believed his eyes. His wife gave a marvelous testimony of how God came at last to their rescue, and how she was healed by the laying on of hands of God's servant.

Locomotor Ataxia

I thank God for healing my son in St. Louis of locomotor ataxia. When I heard of so many being healed through anointed handkerchiefs, I got Sister Etter to bless one for my son. He was saved and healed, and he gave up his drinking and smoking. We are praising God for His wonderful goodness to the children of men.

—*Mrs. S. E. Rogers*
720 Golden Avenue

Healing Power Present

A woman had not walked on her feet for sixty years; her limbs were drawn up so that the doctors wanted to cut them off. This was caused by spotted fever, which she had when she was very young; after prayer was offered for her, she walked back and forth and praised God with uplifted hands for her healing.

A young boy was brought to the meeting, being totally blind for some time. After he was prayed for and on the way home, they tested his eyes. He was asked whether he could read a sign spelling "Ford." He spelled it "F-e-r-d." When told it was wrong, he immediately looked again and said, "Ford!" The "o" looked much like an "e."

Mother and Son Healed

I want to praise God for what He has done for me. I suffered for eighteen months with stomach tumor, kidney, bladder, stomach, bowel, and liver trouble. I had excruciating pain. My disease was very complicated. Sister Etter prayed for me October 31, and God, for Christ's sake, completely healed me. How I do praise His holy name! After my healing, my little son said, "Mamma, I believe God will heal my finger." He had something like a string of warts all the way around his finger, and when he struck it against anything, there was much pain and bleeding. He put an anointed handkerchief around his finger. The next morning all the swelling was gone, and the following morning twenty dead roots had come out. We praise God that He sent Sister Etter to us, and to Him we give all the glory.

—Mrs. E. P. Lyman

I want to testify how God so wonderfully healed me. I was born in Richmond, Virginia, about ninety years ago, a slave to Betsy Kincade. I was sold to William Dansby. I have lived in Los Angeles for thirty years. About seven years ago, I was run over by a man on a bicycle and taken to the hospital. My shoulder was crushed down on my lungs. My arm was broken, and for seven years I had suffered misery. The doctor said I also had kidney trouble, and I suffered a great deal. I could not use my arm. Two weeks ago, I went to Sister Etter's meetings. She laid hands on me and prayed, and God wonderfully healed me and made me whole. I am praising and thanking Him.

—Malinda Dansby

All Praise to God

I was healed of heart trouble and deafness two and a half years ago at the camp meeting when Sister Etter prayed for me. I had come eleven hundred miles to be at that meeting. I have been praising God ever since. I came to attend the meetings at 1315 South Main Street and was run over by a motorcycle and carried into the convention hall in a dying condition. Sister Etter and the saints prayed for me. God healed my body and set me free. I do thank and praise Him.

—W. J. Adams

Testimonies of Healing

At the Woodworth-Etter Meetings, Los Angeles, California

I had inflammation of nerves in my limbs from my knees to my toes, making my cords just as stiff as could be for ten years or more. I also had a disease like dropsy and a rupture. I was prayed for by Sister Etter, and ever since I am healed, all limbered up, no stiffness. I can bend down to the floor, something that I could not do before.

—Mrs. S. E. Bughle
103 W. 14th Street, Los Angeles, California

We have received quite a number of testimonies and reports of how the Lord worked during the Los Angeles meetings, which for lack of space we are compelled to condense. One or more have been healed of the following diseases: stone tumor, consumption, epileptic fits, cancer, deafness, broken ankle, afflicted eyes for fifteen years, kidney trouble, spinal trouble, brain trouble, burning fever, soreness in lungs, appendicitis, chronic catarrh, stomach trouble, tuberculosis.

The latest report received is from Sister Smock, with whom the editor is personally acquainted, and who states that hundreds have been healed of which no record has been taken.

Bless the LORD, *O my soul: and all that is within me, bless his holy name. Bless the Lord, O my soul, and forget not all his benefits: who forgiveth all thine iniquities; who healeth all thy diseases.* (Ps. 103:1–3)

I want to thank Sister Etter and praise my God for healing my daughter. She had typhoid, which left her weak and with one leg short and with spinal trouble. God touched her. She went under the power and came out healed. How I thank Him. She is well and happy, praising God.

My son could not breathe or eat for two weeks and had a fever. Sister Etter prayed for him, and God healed. Oh, glory to His precious name!

—Mrs. Nellis
3027 Malabar Street

Healed of Cancer

I had a cancer on my right hip so large and so sore that I could not lie on that side. I went to four doctors, then I went to the hospital, where the doctors pronounced it cancer and were going to burn it out. I knew that I could not stand that, as I am seventy-seven years old, so my son-in-law brought me to the mission where Mrs. Etter prayed for me. The pain all left, and the fever went away. I was perfectly healed and feel ten years younger than before.

—Mrs. Margaret Dyer
5226 Los Angeles Street, Los Angeles, California

Healed of Spider Cancer and Chronic Catarrh

On the thirteenth day of October, 1915, I was healed in Sister Woodworth-Etter's meeting of the following afflictions: afflicted seven years with spider cancer and chronic catarrh of the bladder; also ulceration of the uterus; there were two small cancers in the neck of the bladder. I had been in bed ten months, given up by four doctors, and kept under the influence of the hypodermic needle.

—*Mrs. Sydney Buick*
1145 East 39th Street, Los Angeles

Healed of Heart Trouble

To the glory and honor of our heavenly Physician, I wish to add my testimony:

I have been living in constant fear of dropping dead from heart trouble. Several physicians have told me I was in this condition. Sunday, October 17, 1915, God healed me. As Sister Etter prayed for me, the power of God filled my body, and I was healed of this dreadful disease. My heart was paining me at the time, and the previous day I had nearly fallen twice from the leakage present. Glory to Jesus!

—*Mrs. William Warnholz*
425 East 2nd Street, Glendale

Healed of Tuberculosis

Beloved Saints:

In the fall and winter of 1912 and 1913 my friend, Mrs. O. C. Armstrong, became very ill, and it looked as though she would die with tuberculosis. The doctor ordered her to Los Angeles. She was living in Spokane, Washington. The Lord answered prayer, and her husband arranged for her to come South, presumably to stay with his mother. But upon arrival, it was not found convenient for her to stay there, so she took a tent at the camp meeting, which place she longed to be in.

She was very emaciated. Sister Etter prayed for her, and she was healed and has stayed healed.

She returned North, and her husband has taken her from one place to another through Oregon and Idaho, and she has had to wash and cook and sew for men, yet she still has the victory. To God be the glory!

—*Mrs. A. B. Hogan*
6306½ Elgin Street, Los Angeles

Bodies And Souls Being Delivered

(Report to the editor of *The Pentecostal Herald*)

Los Angeles, California, October 14, 1915

Dear Editor:

The meeting opened on October 2, in the evening, as a large company of saints gathered to welcome Sister Etter, and it was a time of great rejoicing and praising God for sparing her life. Sister Etter's message was direct and to the point: that God sent her forth to preach salvation from sin and the baptism with the Holy Spirit, that we must be born again and receive the power of the Holy Spirit in our bodies.

Christ came to destroy the works of the devil so that we might be free from sin and disease, glorifying God in our mortal bodies.

So many people want to be healed but don't want to give up their living in sinful pleasures; they don't want to give up their will to do the will of our God.

Sister Etter exhorted the people to humble themselves before God, and backsliders to come back to God and get cleaned up that He might heal them, body and soul.

Many responded to the call, and the long altar was soon filled on both sides, some for salvation and some for the baptism with the Holy Spirit. The meetings have increased in interest and attendance and, best of all, in the power of His might, many of God's children are being delivered from Satan's bonds.

One young woman of twenty-one years had never stood on her feet and could not turn over in bed. She yielded herself to God, and He saved her and touched her body. She testified the next day that she turned over six times that night and took eight steps alone.

A brother told me that one of his ears was totally deaf for twelve years. Sister Etter prayed for him, his ear was unstopped, and he could hear all right.

These are only a few cases, many being healed of all manner of diseases.

Yours for Christ,
—F. M. Langdon
1604 Griffith Avenue, Los Angeles

There's a Great Day Coming

There's a great day coming, a great day coming,
There's a great day coming by and by;
When the saints and the sinners shall be parted right and left—
Are you ready for that day to come?

CHORUS

Are you ready?
Are you ready?
Are you ready for the Judgment Day?
Are you ready?
Are you ready for the Judgment Day?

There's a bright day coming, a bright day coming,
There's a bright day coming by and by;
But its brightness shall only come to them that love the Lord—
Are you ready for that day to come?

There's a sad day coming, a sad day coming,
There's a sad day coming by and by;
When the sinner shall hear his doom, "Depart, I know ye not,"
Are you ready for that day to come?

58

TRYING BUT BLESSED TIMES

During Panama Exposition

While holding meetings in Los Angeles, we had many calls from all over the state, but no one gave us any encouragement to go to San Diego. They said no one seemed to have very much means, that it was a hard place with only a few saints, and that they were all divided on strange doctrines.

I said, "I think I am more needed there than any other place." God is all-powerful, and He always sends me to the hardest place, but He never has failed to go with me and has always came forth and led us on to glorious victory. I hear Him say, "Preach My Word, and I will be with you and bear witness of My presence and approval with signs and wonders." Well, praise His name, there was not an encouraging feature; we were up against a stone wall. The few saints made quite an effort and were willing to do anything to have victory for the Lord Jesus in that place, where they knew so little of the Spirit and power of God.

Brother Harlow did all he could, stood nobly by, and went on with the work after I left with good success.

The Lord was present in the first service to save and to heal.

As the saints and ministers came in from different places, they all began to get deeper in God. He came forth in many mighty signs, the most powerful messages in new tongues and other languages, many as on Mount Sinai when the trumpet sounded louder and stronger and the people in the camp trembled. They knew it was the voice of Jehovah.

So in the meeting at San Diego, the people knew that the Lord was speaking through lips of clay, warning and prophesying and showing the judgments of God that were being poured out, and more awful calamities that were coming soon and some that were right at the door.

These messages were interpreted in English in an intelligent and fluent manner so that the fear of God came on every meeting.

God also demonstrated in signs, showing forth the Word and by the Spirit that Jesus was coming soon. The doom of the foolish virgins was so clearly demonstrated that we felt as if we could almost see them shut out and hear the voice of God saying, "Too late, I know you not."

They were shown the great storm and flood that was at the door, and the awful suffering and the loss of life and property that came from the breaking of the dams.

The storm struck the city the day we left; we could hardly get to the train.

The Spirit of conviction went out in all directions, many were saved, and many more were inquiring, "*What must I do to be saved?*" (Acts 16:30). Some were filled with God and baptized in the Holy Spirit.

Many church members were saying, "We are convinced that God is working with you people and that He is visiting His people. We have long been too far away from God, below these precious blessings, and we will never stop until we get the baptism of the Holy Spirit."

The Lord performed many cures or healings, and all who saw them said that no one but God could open the eyes of the blind, make the lame rise up and walk from their beds, or throw away their crutches.

As they looked on the great work of God, the Spirit of the Lord swept over again and again. As in the days of Christ, scores rushed to the platform, everyone trying to be first to get in the pool.

The heavenly choir and the holy dance, with the shouts of the redeemed, made heaven ring.

As it always is, there were all classes of people begging us not to close.

We have had good reports of the work since leaving; it is still going on.

"And The Door Was Shut" (Matthew 25:10)

Remarkable Experiences

The Woodworth-Etter meetings held in the armory building in San Diego in connection with the Seventh Street Apostolic Faith Mission Assembly were quite successful.

There were marked demonstrations of the Spirit along the lines of messages in tongues and interpretations; also some very remarkable manifestations through the saints, as they were used of God to bring forth the Scriptures that apply definitely to these last days.

One of these I will mention briefly. The power of God came on one of the sisters in the back part of the hall. She came quickly to the front, taking off her hat, coat, and other loose articles of apparel as she went. (Stripping for the race: *"Let us lay aside every weight, and…run…the race that is set before us"* [Heb. 12:1].) She turned the pages of her Bible as she went rapidly. (Running with the vision: *"Write the vision,…that he may run that readeth it"* [Hab. 2:2].)

She went forward along the altar up to the gates (the narrow way), to a closed door at the farthest corner of the long hall. There she knocked on the door and continued knocking harder and harder, but she got no response. Then after a time, the truth seemed to dawn upon her mind—that she was shut out. Such a look of disappointment and dismay came over her face as she retraced her steps. Moving backward all the time, she kept her eyes fixed upon the shut door. When she came to the extreme farther corner of the room, she appeared to try to hide herself away.

Soon another saint was led under the power over the same route, hopping along, up to the door. She knocked over and over, harder and harder. She got down on her knees, begging and entreating and wailing, but *"the door was shut"* (Matt. 25:10). Such wailing as she retraced her steps, going all the way back on her knees.

The presence and power of God was so manifest at these clear demonstrations in the Spirit of just what is going to take place so soon in the lives of many professors. A holy awe filled the hall, sinners were convicted, and saints were made to humble themselves anew before God. Amen.

Space forbids further mention of many other remarkable experiences. I am enclosing a few articles kindly handed in by the saints for publication.

—W. F. Harlow
1467 B Street, San Diego, California

Visions Given of Coming Revival

(A witness of the meeting that was held here in December)

At different times, God gave others and me a vision of a revival here. Over four months ago, before anyone knew of Sister Etter coming to San Diego, He showed that many would attend the meetings and would be fed, and He would reveal Himself to little babes. During the meetings a little girl, about six years old, gave a message, pleading with sinners to come to Jesus, that He was soon coming. I am a witness that God called the meeting. He confirmed His Word in signs and demonstrations of the Holy Spirit and shouts of praise went up to our Father in heaven.

Your sister in Christ,
—Mrs. Rosa Winston
San Diego, California, January 11, 1916

Victorious Demonstrations of Power

To the saints at large, Greetings:

I wish to give my testimony as to how the Lord is answering prayer. First, I want to give God the glory for saving and healing me and baptizing me with the Holy Spirit and fire, with the Bible evidence following. I was afflicted five years with a so-called incurable disease—creeping paralysis. Five years ago I could not walk, but through the prayer of faith offered a short time ago, I have been walking for Him ever since. Praise His name!

I want to report victory in our meetings, which closed the first of the month and were led by our beloved Sister Woodworth-Etter. However, the victory had to be gained through persecution, for when the saints gathered together to worship, the devil came also, and the sound of the raven was heard in our midst. But the ear of the servant of God was tuned to the voice of the Holy Spirit and soon detected the counterfeit and rebuked it in the name of Jesus. Soon the voice of the dove came forth in such a wonderful manner that it silenced all the demonstrations of the enemy.

The most wonderful demonstration was that of a brother with locomotor ataxia for ten years. He was taking from five to seven grains of morphine and cocaine a day to silence the pain, and he had gotten to the place that the doctors said it would kill him if he did not quit, and it would kill him if he did. So it seemed a death proposition either way. So, when he got to the meeting and came in, he looked just like a dead man; but when Sister Etter laid hands on him in Jesus' name and commanded the drug demon to come out of him, it threw him on the floor and fought like a snake. Some thought he was dying, and apparently he died; but when the resurrection power struck him, he arose from the floor and walked back and forth across the platform, shouting and praising God, very much alive. The desire for the drug was taken away, and he has still got victory in his body. He gained over eighteen pounds in four weeks, and, contrary to man's wisdom, he is gaining every day. Glory! Oh, we have a wonderful God, and He is manifesting Himself in a marvelous way to His children. Pray for San Diego, that the Lord will have His way in the saving of many precious souls.

Yours for His service,
—*Brother B.*

Healed of Bright's Disease

Another very bad case, that of a little boy, who had Bright's disease; the doctors said he could live but a few days. He could not eat anything and was passing blood all the time. After Sister Etter prayed for him, he wanted something to eat right away, and he is gaining strength all the time.

—*Mrs. D. B. Harrison*

Unification

God gave us wonderful victory the last ten days or so of the meeting. Not a stone was left unturned to show His saints the great need of laying aside every doctrine and coming together in unity and love. Message after message came along that line, and God marvelously backed up His Word with demonstrations and signs, pointing out that we are very near the end of this age. One brother had a vision of handwriting on the wall as in Daniel 5:27. Others had visions of white horses and saints riding upon them, and balls of fire.

At the close of the meeting, many church people asked that the meetings be continued, saying they were just beginning to learn that God was there.

Many were healed, and many captives were set free and received help that they so much needed. We left them with happy faces, believing God had visited San Diego as perhaps never before.

—P. F. Kruse
San Francisco, California

59

FIGHTING THE GOOD FIGHT

The Battle at San Francisco, 1916. Revival Spreads

From San Diego we went to San Francisco. Brother Craig met us and took us to his Home of Faith. There we were made to feel at home, and everything was done for our comfort. Many saints came to the home, and we had blessed fellowship; the sweet peace of God was always present all over the house.

The meeting commenced with power. The saints had been praying much, and they made every sacrifice to push the battle through to victory. The Lord was present to confirm His Word with visible signs of His invisible presence. The people came and heard, saw and wondered. Fear and conviction fell day after day, and the people were made to say, "Surely God is in our midst." The altar was crowded daily; they came from all parts and were saved, healed, filled with God, and baptized in the Holy Spirit. When their friends saw what a change had taken place, many of them started at once to attend the meeting. The interest grew. People of all classes were saved, including Jews.

One afternoon as we entered the theater where our meeting was held, the minister met us at the door. He told us that they had brought a woman in an auto, that the last six dollars they had were given to him to bring her, and that he would not wait for the meeting. He placed the sick woman in the aisle nearest the entrance. It was a sad sight. The woman had two little children, and she had not walked alone for four years. She was afflicted with many diseases. Her husband was also badly diseased and discouraged. She knew it was her last chance, so she had faith as we pointed her to the loving Savior. As we prayed the prayer of faith and laid on hands, the unclean spirits left her, the healing virtue came and swept through and over her, and she knew she was healed. She stood up, walked, and shouted, "Glory to God!" Her husband began to praise the Lord, and he, too, was healed. She took up her child and walked out to the auto.

As I went forward to the platform, I saw them carry a woman who was helpless; she was from a hospital for incurables, had not stood or walked for seven years. I looked down at her and several other cripples. The Lord told me to rebuke her sickness and command her to get up and walk, that she was healed. The power of the Holy Spirit came on me, and I commanded her to arise and walk in the name of Jesus. She looked at me, then began to try to move, and then she stood up. I told her to walk out and come up those steps. Then I came down about three steps from the platform and caught her hand; then she walked up to and over the platform, like a girl. Those who brought her were frightened at first, thinking she was going to die, but when they realized she was really healed, they wept for joy and told how helpless she had been; she could not turn in bed for seven years.

Another lady, who had been lame for ten years, began to cry and said, "Well, if she can walk, I can, too." She arose and began to walk up and down; in less than twenty minutes, seven helpless cripples were walking through the aisles and walking up the steps to the platform. I cannot find words to describe these miracles. I had never spoken to or laid hands on them. The Lord was proving that the power came from Him and that He alone was doing the work of saving and healing. The congregation was moved; there was weeping and shouting all over the house.

A man arose in the congregation and wanted to give his testimony. Three years before when I was holding a meeting at San Jose, he came but did not know what was going on. He had to go inside. He had been a gambler and drunkard, was bad in every way, and was on the point of delirium tremens; the doctor told him he would die the next spell he had. He was miserable and was almost ready to commit suicide. He had met with a bad accident: his nose was broken, and his eye was puffed almost out on his cheek, his head and face were bandaged; it appeared like a hopeless case. He did not know why he went to the town. He was out walking but was not going to the meeting. Something drew him in. He arose and asked if there was any mercy or help for him, and he yielded to God. In a short time he was saved, all pain left him, his sight was perfectly restored, his nose was healed, and one little scar was left. He was delivered from all bad habits and was saved, kept by the power of God, and was very successful in the service of the Lord. His testimony was believed and had quite an effect on many; he was a great help. Praise the Lord!

The heavenly choir was great. Many had visions. Wonderful messages in tongues and interpretations were given. People came from nearly all the churches. Many got convicted for more of God, and that the coming of the Lord is very near. Many sought the baptism of the Holy Spirit. Dear Brother and Sister Montgomery were a great help to the work. Sister Piper, Dr. Smith, and his wife, who stood so nobly by us all through the revival twenty-seven years ago, joined us and rendered valuable assistance during the whole campaign. May the dear Lord keep them many years to hold up the banner of Jesus. Eternity alone will tell what the Lord did in the meeting at San Francisco, California.

Miracles Used to Convict, The Bridegroom Is Coming

(From *The Pentecostal Herald*)

Heaven is coming down to San Francisco, a notably wicked city. It is our honest conviction that God has chosen this Sodom of America to show forth some of the most startling miracles of the age to convince the people, if possible, that Jesus still lives and to give all a chance to get ready for the coming of the Bridegroom. At this date, January 20, the convention is in full swing, with two daily meetings in the Zion M. E. church. The pastor has given over the beautiful new and ideally appointed church building for an old-fashioned Pentecostal revival. The revival opened up strong from the beginning, and as if not a moment could be lost, God began at the very first meeting to pour out His Spirit, bringing salvation and healing.

Every meeting thus far has been a notable one for this city. The crowds are steadily increasing. It is now plainly evident that the commodious church will be far too small for the people desiring to hear the glorious gospel message and to witness the signs immediately following, as promised. Practically all who enter are stricken with awe at the conscious presence of God. People get healed in their seats. Others get healed and saved at the same time when the prayer of faith is offered. One lady, while in prayer for her daughter, who was being prayed for, was healed herself. The long altar is too small for those seeking God for salvation, healing, and the baptism. San Francisco is a cosmopolitan city. Almost every nation under the sun has a strong representation here. Many nationalities are pressing in for God's best. Many Spanish-speaking people are being healed, saved, and some filled with the Spirit. All glory to our God and His Christ.

No disease is hard for our Christ when the saints are dwelling in sweet unity, as is seen here at present. The Word goes forth with no uncertain sound. We are feeling the necessity in Glad Tidings Assembly of having the *"signs following"* (Mark 16:20) to show forth the real, full Gospel. Let every reader offer believing prayers that *"all may be one"* (John 17:21), even as Christ and the Father are one. For them His glory shall shine forth.

—*Robert J. Craig*, Pastor

Revival Continues

To Brother Brinkham and Readers of *The Pentecostal Herald*:

San Francisco has had a really great spiritual awakening. People who have long resided here claim that the greatest revival that this city has ever known has visited it during the past two months. Sister Woodworth-Etter continued here about seven weeks in active campaign work. For the last two weeks of this special effort, the meetings were held in the National Theater, with a seating capacity of fifteen hundred. On the last Sunday night, it was estimated that about that number were present during the meeting. The power of God fell in a marked degree at nearly every meeting. The mark of a genuine revival is this: that after the evangelists are gone, the revival continues. That feature is practically true in this case. Let the coming King receive all the homage and the glory, for it belongs unto Him. People in various parts, whom we never even met, were either healed or saved or both in this revival. The meetings go forward grandly. A splendid hall, seating about seven hundred and fifty people, is now being specially fitted up for the Pentecostal work in this city. It will be located at 1636 Ellis Street, near Filmore Street.

It is strongly believed that could Sister Etter have continued for two months longer, the Lord would have shaken the whole city, and since she has gone, we expect God to do it anyway.

The manifestations of the Spirit were inspirational, and many times God came forth in solemn warning of the Master's imminent return or in calling attention to sins and weights in the lives of the people who should be stripped for the race.

Heaven's recording angel has the record preserved of the large number who were saved and baptized in the Holy Spirit with the sign following.

Our hearts are filled with thanksgiving and gladness that after standing in our lot at this point for three and a half years, God is so pouring out His Spirit.

—*Robert J. Craig*, Pastor
Glad Tidings Assembly, 1636 Ellis Street, San Francisco

Healed through Anointed Handkerchief

During this meeting a handkerchief was sent to Ayton, Ontario, Canada, where a woman was almost dead with stomach trouble. Medicines and doctors could do nothing more for her, as she was rapidly failing in strength. Hearing of the work God was doing, she sent for a handkerchief and had it anointed. When she applied it to her body, she soon felt the healing virtue. Not long after came the report that she had the victory, was up and around, and could eat again.

Raised from Sickness by the Spirit

Another sister was sick in bed. While looking to God to strengthen her so that she could go to the meeting, the Spirit raised her up. She ran about nine blocks. On the way to the meeting, she found a sick man on the street and brought him along with her. This man was about to go to a hospital for an operation. He also was deaf and had bad, running sores on his leg. God saved and healed him.

Husband Learns through a Dream of the Conversion of His Wife, Later Saved and Baptized

I was saved in the Woodworth-Etter meeting, February 4. While this took place, my husband was at home in bed, asleep. While I received salvation, he had a dream in which an angel appeared to him, telling him the angels in heaven were rejoicing because his wife gave her heart to God. Later I called him over the phone, telling him the good news. He answered that he knew all about it, that an angel had revealed it unto him. The next night he got saved and baptized. I also received my baptism. The Lord healed me also of a chronic bowel trouble, which

I had suffered from all my life; at one time my bowels did not move for over two months. My appetite was good during that time. When I was prayed for, I got healed, and now I am well and happy. Our home is a little paradise on earth.

—*Mrs. C. H. E.*, San Francisco, California

A Professional Testimony

(Regarding meetings held in San Francisco, California,
by Mrs. Woodworth-Etter, February, 1916)

Speaking of spiritual gifts, Paul said, *"To another the gifts of healing by the same Spirit"* (1 Cor. 12:9). We have known Mrs. Woodworth-Etter for twenty-seven years, and I, as a regularly qualified physician, registered in this state, a graduate of Trinity College, Dublin, and licensed by the Rotunda Lying-In Hospital, Dublin, do vouch for the results I have seen with my own eyes as to definite and miraculous healing of multiform diseases through the laying on of her hands and prayer. The facts are indisputable. Critics may call it fakery, mesmerism, spiritualism, or whatever, but for my own part, as an unbiased Christian man, I believe these exploits are derived from one Source alone, and that is the all-powerful God and Father, the all-powerful Son, and the all-powerful Holy Spirit. The lame man walks. The deaf man hears. The dumb speak. The blind, even blind from birth, see. Such achievements are accomplished outside all the vaunted surgical and medical science of the age. Things are done, and done from a Bible standpoint, in the name we recognize to be above all names.

In Christ's day, critics sought to demonize His miracles by shouting, "Beelzebub," but He showed them Satan is not such a fool as to be divided against himself. (See Matthew 12:24–28.) I have witnessed immense goiters that pressed on the jugulars and carotids, threatening suffocation, disappearing. I have witnessed a woman, for seven years bedridden and never walking during that time, carried into the meeting and commanded by Mrs. Etter to rise in the name of Jesus from where she lay in her invalid chair amid the crowd; she stepped out boldly and ascended the steps to the platform, walking and praising God. I have seen another, who from fourteen years old was a sufferer of exaggerated heart trouble, kidney and bladder disease, brought in before my eyes so exhausted as to be almost dead from cardiac failure; yet after a few minutes the sufferer was completely healed, walking at a brisk rate up and down before us all, and has continued in this state ever since. But there is no need of multiplying cases. Scores and scores have been healed and many saved through becoming involuntary witnesses of the power of God in these meetings. If this is diabolical, then Satan must have become a new creation in Christ Jesus, because God is glorified, souls are saved, diseases fly, saints rejoice, and Jesus Christ goes about doing good and healing all who are no longer oppressed by the devil (Acts 10:38), perhaps because he (Satan) has relegated the job to others. But, my friends, Satan is still Satan. He oppresses, depresses, and suppresses the truth, as it is in Jesus. Happy are those who have escaped from the clutches of the destroyer, either for spirit, soul, or body. Praise God, *"who hath delivered us from the power of darkness, and hath translated us into the kingdom of his dear Son"* (Col. 1:13).

—G. *Sidney Smith*, B. A. T. C. D., M. D.
3145 East 27th Street, Fruitvale, East Oakland, California
February 26, 1916

God Working in San Francisco

As we write, we are in the midst of the Mid-Winter Convention in the charge of Pastor Craig, with Mrs. M. B. W. Etter holding meetings twice every day. These meetings are held in the Zion M. E. Church, and they will continue until February 13. It is difficult to find words to describe the blessedness of these meetings. Many of God's dear children, who have been baptized with the Holy Spirit in Pentecostal fullness, are gathered here from different places, and again and again as the spirit of worship comes upon the people, the Dove of God sings the beautiful strains of the heavenly chorus through them, giving a foretaste of the wondrous, ecstatic joy and praise when the Lord will descend from heaven and catch up His waiting ones to be with Himself forever.

We have had strong sermons from Mrs. Etter and from Brother Argue, many of them very solemn, showing the nearness of the Lord's coming and the impending judgments in the earth. There have been remarkable messages in tongues with interpretation, most of these pleading with people to yield to God before the greater storms of God's judgment break over the earth, and also prophecies of the Lord's near coming. Altogether these meetings have been of great power and sweetness, and we praise God for answered prayer. It is marvelous to see Mrs. Etter, at the age of seventy-one, so filled with the life of God and so sustained in her continuous and heavy ministries, which have gone on year after year for over forty years with scarcely a break.

—*Mrs. C. J. Montgomery*

Healed of Spinal Trouble

Mrs. Mary Murry, past seventy years, of the Crocker Home for Aged People, in San Francisco, was carried to the meeting one day. She seemed to have had everything the matter with her, besides a severe spinal trouble. She had been in this condition for the last seven years, had not been able to lay on either side, and had to be propped up in bed day and night, suffering severely. She has had the best specialists of the city and state. They all said nothing could be done for her. She felt that God would heal her. While Sister Etter talked to inspire faith in her, she got up and walked up a small flight of stairs onto the platform and demonstrated before the audience that she was healed, walking by herself. All her friends thought it was marvelous. The power of God was present to heal.

Healed of Goiter; Saved and Baptized

Mrs. M. F. Reuch, 1620 Gery Street, reported: "I had a goiter about the size of a fist on the inside of my neck for the last fifteen years. It grew in such a way that it would have pressed out my eyes in a short time. I also had a lump in my mouth about the size of an English walnut. After I was prayed for, both goiter and lump soon disappeared."

Healed of Heart Trouble and Dropsy

Mrs. H. W. Pope, 289 West San Carlos Street, San Jose, California, had heart trouble since she was fourteen years old and had also severe bladder and female trouble. Five of the best physicians had given her up to die. When they brought her to the meeting, she was in a dying condition, unable to walk. Her heart fluttered as if it would burst. After she was prayed for, she walked back and forth alone on the platform. Night after night she testified. She demonstrated that she was healed. Her heart got normal. Her other troubles also left her. Her limbs were swollen from dropsy. Water immediately began to ooze out of the pores and run down her limbs. The swelling disappeared in a very short time. She is a well and happy woman today.

Healed of Blindness

Mrs. F. Eagle, 280 Seventh Street, Oakland, gave this testimony: I was prayed for by Sister Etter at Hot Springs, Arkansas, nearly three years ago.

I had been totally blind for nearly a year. All the eye specialists said I would never see again. A. T. Vaughan, reputed by some to be the best eye specialist in the world, held out no hope for me. A peculiar disease had set in, which made me go blind. When Sister Etter prayed for me, my eyes opened at once so that I could tell her granddaughter what kind of dress she had on. Now, after three years, I have two large, blue, perfect eyes. A day after I was prayed for, I experienced salvation, and a week later I got my baptism. My mother had to be helped in the same meeting, suffering with sciatic rheumatism in the hip for twenty years. She also had heart trouble so bad that doctors said she was dying with it. Mentally and physically she was a wreck and was in a backslidden condition, thinking she had sinned against the Holy Spirit. When she was prayed for, the power came upon her, and all her troubles soon left her. She also got saved and baptized, and we have both been in the work ever since.

Cured of Epilepsy

H. W. Appearus, 1810 O'Farrell Street, had epileptic spells for ten years. He took as many as twenty in a day. He had treated with all kinds of doctors, but no one could help him. After he was prayed for, he never took another spell. His father bore witness to the truth of his testimony.

Healed of Eye Trouble

W. R. Kelley of Oakland, California, had eye trouble for three years. His eyes would bleed almost continuously from hemorrhages, so that he was nearly blind. Seven famous eye specialists of Oakland and San Francisco said he was a hopeless case. Sister Etter prayed for them, and they began to heal up. Now he sees as well as ever.

Heard the Angels Sing

H. B. Ostrander of Auburn, Nebraska, wrote these words: "One day while we were singing in the choir, suddenly I heard heavenly music, which was most wonderful. At first I thought that it must be coming from the piano, but soon noticed that it came from above, circling around over the choir. It sounded like the voice of many waters. Then came the message through Sister Etter on *"the voice of a great multitude, and as the voice of many waters"* (Rev. 19:6). God wonderfully poured out His Spirit during the meeting. This experience has been a great encouragement to me.

Much Interest in Meetings; The Angelic Host is Present

The meetings started on January 13 in a Methodist Church. They grew daily in interest and power until the church got too small. At the end of six weeks, the audience swelled in number to nearly fifteen hundred people in the National Theater, where the meetings had been transferred.

The Spirit sang through the saints during this campaign in a marvelous way. A number of times when this took place, a number of saints also heard the angelic host singing the most marvelous music.

In a vision a brother saw Jesus standing on the water, with people trying to press around Him. He said unto them, "You cannot reach Me until you forsake all your sins."

At another time a sister saw Jesus standing on the platform, clothed in priestly and then in kingly garments. She also heard these words: "Jesus is coming soon." And again she saw Him come in the clouds in great power and glory.

An elderly preacher, who had been in Bible work for forty years, but in a backslidden condition for some time, was reclaimed and filled with the Spirit. He testified continually of the wonderful way the Spirit was being poured out. He also understood and interpreted part of a message in tongues one day, it being in a Hindu dialect.

A Jew Is Saved, Healed, and Baptized; Gives Messages in Tongues

Every day, many hearts surrendered to God and experienced genuine salvation. Many of these dear souls soon received their baptism and came out speaking in other tongues as the Spirit gave utterance, sometimes being understood by some of those who stood by. A number of these were Jews. One young man (a Jew) staggered in one evening, dying with consumption. His mother said the doctors gave him only two months to live. When he got prayed for, he soon received salvation and his baptism of the Holy Spirit. Time after time he demonstrated on the platform that he was healed by pounding his lungs with his fist. The change in him was wonderful. He also spoke short messages in tongues, which were interpreted.

Evil Spirits Driven Away—Guardian Angel Protects

A lady was prayed for one afternoon for double rupture. In the evening meeting she testified that the ruptures had disappeared and that she threw away her trusses. Her face fairly shone with joy as she gave testimony.

A woman who keeps a rooming house brought a handkerchief to be prayed over to drive evil spirits out of a room, which made their appearance night after night, terrifying those who occupied the room. She herself got scared when she slept in the room and they made their appearance. After the handkerchief was prayed over, she took it and slept in the room, not waking up all night. In the morning, when she woke up, she saw a beautiful guardian angel standing by her bed, protecting her.

What God Did for Two Individuals

God snatched some individuals from the very strongholds of Satan. Miss P. Vogel, a leader of the IWWs (Industrial Workers of the World), called by them the "Queen of the Unemployed," got saved and baptized. She has lectured to thousands and speaks eight different languages. She had been in the Indian and Chinese revolutions. Her career has been wonderful in her short life. Many of the saints in the various missions in San Francisco have prayed for this woman. While she was honest in heart, she could not get rid of her anarchistic spirit. In these meetings she saw the power of God demonstrated and accompanied with signs, as she had never seen before. The Spirit began to work on her and brought her under deep conviction. While this was going on, the police began to connect her name with the present Chinese revolutionary spirits in the city.

The saints invited her out to the Home of Peace in Oakland to pray and tarry with her. She soon experienced salvation and then received the Holy Spirit and began to speak in other languages. She has since interceded for hours in the Spirit for others. Reports come continually that she is out and out for God, and that she longs to get out and preach that Jesus is the Living Christ.

One evening when the church was crowded, a boy about twelve years old was prayed for. He began to speak in other tongues and interpret. Suddenly a man burst forth from the gallery, saying, "God must be an awful wicked God for permitting such a spell to be put on a child." The man who made the disturbance was J. E. M., called the "Revolutionary Poet" of the labor movement of America. With him were a number of his friends. They actually thought a spell had been put on the child. Later some of them acknowledged that it was some other power. Prayer was offered for them. Someone got under deep conviction and made inquiries about salvation. He had such a restless spirit in him that he could not bear to be where the saints prayed. He struggled until the last day of the meeting, when Sister Etter and a few of the workers prayed for him. He at once testified that he felt much better. With his six-year-old girl, he went into the tarrying room to seek God. As he came in, the power fell on his little girl and she came out speaking in other tongues. This broke his heart. Soon the power fell on him, and in less than an hour after he was prayed for, he lay back in the tarrying room, praising God in another language.

God is now using both him and the girl in the work.

The last day a flaming sword was seen hanging over the pulpit. The sword of the Spirit is still doing its work. Since Mrs. Etter left, reports have arrived that people continue to get saved, healed, and baptized right along, as many as four receiving the baptism in one day. Let us all praise and magnify God for His wonderful works unto the children of men.

—*August D. Feick*
Ayton, Ontario, Canada

60

CONFIRMATION OF GOD'S WORD

We were very sorry to close the meeting at San Francisco, for the convincing and awakening power was spreading in all the churches over the city. Many said if the meetings could have continued a few weeks longer, they believed thousands would have been brought to Jesus. We felt that our work was not done in that city, nor in many places in the state, so we all felt that in the near future God would send us back.

We started on the long journey over the plains and mountains; the Lord wonderfully strengthened us. When we arrived in Houston, Texas, we were met for the first time by Brother Morwood, the pastor, who, with a few saints, had made a brave effort to prepare for the largest Pentecostal convention that had ever been held in the city. Praise the Lord, they were not disappointed, for when we closed, he and with many others told a large audience that the meetings were successful in every way, much more than he expected, that miracles of healing and signs of the presence of God were far beyond anything he had ever seen.

Brother Ritchey and his son, from Zion City, Illinois, were present to help in most of the meetings; also Brother Caruthers was a blessing to all and encouraged me. From the first service until the last, they brought their sick, lame, blind,

486

deaf, and dumb—some on beds, some on crutches, some carried in—but there was none too hard for the Lord. Everyone who came in God's divine way was made to shout and praise the Lord for healing.

A man and wife came from South Dakota, a thousand or more miles. He was given up by all the best doctors and could hardly live coming on the train. They told me there was a man who was brought a long distance, who was nearly dead in the camp. I told them to bring him on the platform. He soon got saved, healed, and filled with heavenly virtue and resurrection life. He arose, walked, and praised God. His wife also got saved and healed and baptized. They were Lutherans and had never seen any demonstrations of the Spirit. When his wife began to seek the baptism, he told her if she would fall on the floor under that power, he would go home and leave her. While at the altar, she was struck down. The sisters stood around her so that he could not see her. When they looked around, they saw him lying in another part of the house, under the mighty power of the Lord, having visions. When both he and his wife arose from the power, they testified that God is surely visiting His people, that they got saved, healed, and filled with the Holy Spirit. On the way home, they testified at every opportunity what they saw and heard and what God had done for them. When they got home, they stirred up the whole neighborhood, so that a request came back for a meeting, saying we must have one, for they are hungry for the deep things of God.

A railroad conductor and wife from Iowa came to the meeting. He had been hurt in a wreck, so that he was crippled in the spine and other places. He had been laid off from his work for many months. His wife was an invalid of long standing. When he saw the mighty works of God, he said that half had not been told. He knew there was a living merciful Christ; he wanted to get saved and healed and was not disappointed. His spine was soon made straight and strong. His crooked, partially paralyzed limbs were made straight. He left his wife at the meeting and went home. Soon one letter after another came back, telling how God had saved and healed him.

A woman, who had been very low for many weeks, was brought on a cot. She was starving to death; nothing would stay on her stomach. They carried her from a back room to the platform. We put her in the arms of Jesus and covered her with the blood. In a few minutes she arose, walked, and shouted, shaking hands and praising God. She stayed for the night meeting and came to almost every meeting, helping others, singing in the Spirit, telling how God had healed her.

As soon as she got healed, she said, "Wire to my children that I am healed and am hungry and can eat now."

A woman was brought from her bed in her nightgown, carried in like a helpless child, all bloated from head to foot with dropsy. She had been operated on several times; the doctors said she could not live to have another operation. She was healed in the presence of all, like they all are. She came day after day, sitting up and walking; the swelling going down and getting stronger. Cancers, tumors, Bright's disease, rupture, and almost every disease and plague of the worst kind were healed. The blind, the deaf, and the dumb were made to see, hear, and sing by the power of God. The heavenly choir, spiritual dancing, strong messages in other tongues, interpretations, and prophecies were given, accompanied with the presence of God; this made sinners and saints alike tremble.

We always have the best of order. People are afraid to laugh and mock in the presence of God. We never allow fanaticism or other spirits, contentions or doctrines to be aired in the meetings. Everything that God does through the Holy Spirit is edifying. The best of order is always maintained, so every honest person will have to admit that it is God working through His people.

The Spirit of love is felt and seen in all and through all, so that everyone will say, "Of a truth God is here." Brother Morwood is a lovely Christian man. He stood like a brave soldier and was very kind to me. His wife and all the band did everything they could to help me and make me comfortable.

Now, after some months, we just received a letter from him telling how the interest was deepening. They have had a meeting every night since we left. Many were saved and baptized, and some great healings were wrought in the name of the Lord.

May the good work ever go on.

Successful Preaching

(Abbreviated Report)

Sister Etter is, without doubt, one of the greatest evangelists of today. She has been preaching the Gospel successfully for the last thirty-five years, and while she is now past seventy years of age, she is as strong and vigorous as when she first started. The fruits of her ministry are to be found in almost every section of the country, and her converts are spoken of everywhere as the most stalwart

Christians and the best workers in the community where they live. Many of them have themselves become ministers of the Gospel and have carried the Good News all over the world.

A very attractive feature of these meetings, and one that appeals to the natural mind more than trances and visions, is the cases of divine healing. One of the signs that Jesus said would follow believers is that *"they shall lay hands on the sick, and they shall recover"* (Mark 16:18).

Place of meeting, 1122 Franklin Avenue, Corner of San Jacinto Street, Houston.

—*Pastor F. A. Hale*, Kingsville, Texas

God Is Present

(From *The Pentecostal Herald*)

Houston, Texas, March 18, 1916

I am glad to report great success in Houston. The papers have taken notice and have written it up. The people cannot understand what it is; they have left God out so long that they don't recognize Him when He makes His appearance. The conditions in Houston were favorable for a revival. There were no serious divisions, and the saints were working in harmony, so the Lord could manifest Himself from the very start. Outsiders are becoming interested, and many who have never heard of Pentecost before are becoming hungry for the experience. About the first thing that took place was a holiness preacher got the baptism and spoke in tongues as the Spirit gave utterance. He said he used to preach himself under conviction when he preached on the baptism of the Holy Spirit, but now that he has the genuine experience, he can preach it with greater power.

The writer has known Sister Etter for many years and can say that her faith is as strong today as it was when she was a young woman, and that her power of physical endurance is even greater than in former years. Brother E. N. Ritchie, pastor of the Bruner Tabernacle, this city, testified in this meeting to being healed of leakage of the heart in Sister Etter's meeting at Decatur, Illinois, thirty years ago.

Jesus is coming soon and is bringing His reward with Him. Therefore, we should press the battle to the gates, trusting Him to be with us, and with many other words encourage His people to work for the salvation of those who are lost.

We are greatly encouraged, for we know that God is with us. Praise the Lord.

Your brother in Christ,
—*F. A. Hale*

The revival that began in Houston, Texas, March 11, at the Full Gospel Mission, 1122 Franklin Avenue, at the corner of San Jacinto Street, still goes on with great interest, and many feel that God is visiting this city as never before. The sick are being healed of all kinds of diseases, tumors, cancers, fevers, lameness, deafness, blindness, and many other things produced by the enemy; all have yielded to the prayer of faith, according to James 5:15. Many soul-stirring messages have gone forth through the preaching of Sister Etter, inspiring our hearts to a closer walk with God; and in every meeting the Lord sends forth messages through tongues and interpretation, warning us of the soon coming of Jesus and exhorting all to flee from the wrath that is coming upon the earth and to hide away in Jesus Christ, the only place of refuge from the storms and tribulations that are soon to come. Let all take heed to the voice of God. He is surely visiting this city in a marvelous way, with signs and wonders done in the name of Jesus. One young man was saved and healed in the congregation before he came forward to be prayed for. Many wonderful things are taking place; someone in the congregation saw a vision of Jesus and an angel standing on the platform as the choir was singing a heavenly anthem.

There are many things we could say in regard to the Etter meeting. We are all sure, both saint and sinner, that Sister Etter is a real, true servant of God, and the signs are following. Many of the saints feel that this city is getting her last call, and this is indeed the day of her visitation, just as when Jesus wept over Jerusalem and cried, *"How often would I have gathered thy children together, as a hen doth gather her brood under her wings, and ye would not!"* (Luke 13:34) and did not know the day of her visitation. God grant that we may heed the day of our visitation.

After Sister Etter leaves, meetings will be continued at the same place, 1122 Franklin Avenue, corner of San Jacinto Street.

—*William Morwood*, Pastor
Houston, Texas, March 29, 1916

I want to praise the Lord for what He has done for me. Praise His holy name. On the fourth of this month, I sprained my ankle so badly that I could not walk on it without great pain; also I had rheumatism in my upper and lower limbs. But thank the Lord, I am healed, both spiritually and bodily, by the great healing power of the Lord, through Sister Etter, who is conducting a meeting here at present. Praise His name. Amen.

—C. T. Wallis
2602 Glass Street, Houston, Texas

I came to Houston, Texas, on March 25, sick and suffering from gallstones and stomach trouble. I had suffered intensely for six weeks, unable to eat nor sleep, sometimes not able to retain ice or ice water on my stomach. For ten days no one was allowed in my room, but, praise God, after Sister Etter laid hands on me and prayed for my healing, I was free from pain and could eat anything, sleep well, and talk to people. I must have talked to a thousand, and it did not make me nervous. *"I am the LORD that healeth thee"* (Exod. 15:26) is true today.

—Mrs. Martha Johnson
110 Lelia Street, Waco, Texas

I praise the Lord for His wonderful baptism of power. I have been a holiness preacher for more than a year. I thought I had the baptism of the Holy Spirit. I preached a clean life and sanctification as the baptism. I saw that I needed more power and was honest about it; and when I met the Lord's conditions, He gave me the baptism of the Holy Spirit with the Bible evidence of speaking in other tongues as the Spirit gave utterance. Praise His dear name for it all. I am looking for Jesus to come soon. Your brother in Jesus,

—E. Bohannon

Whole families are being healed in this meeting. Mrs. L. C. Williamson, eighty-two years old, her daughter, Mrs. Walkup, two granddaughters, and a great grandson were all prayed for and are testifying to being healed.

While visiting my aunt in Houston, Texas, I went to Sister Woodworth-Etter's meeting and saw the wonderful healing power of the Lord manifested there, and I cannot praise the Lord enough for what He has done for my baby. She was born without a frontal bone, and a large lump pressed out between her eyes; her eyes were all out of shape, and she had no bridge in her nose; but, praise God, through Sister Etter's prayers, the dear Lord has healed her. The lump is nearly gone, and her eyes and nose are coming to the right shape. But that isn't all. I received the baptism of the Holy Spirit in Sister Etter's meeting. Glory be to His dear name!

—*Mrs. Wm. Schafer*
97 E. High Street, Detroit, Michigan

I want to thank God for what He has done for me during this meeting. I have had sciatica for thirty-five years, and for the last fifteen years have been confined to the house, and a good deal of the time to bed; but I can now truthfully say that I am healed. When Sister Etter laid hands on me and prayed, the Lord took all the pains away. My age is seventy-six. Glory to God!

—*L. Lestarjette*, 1404 Main Street, Houston, Texas

A Little Girl's Dream

Dear Sister Etter:

I dreamed I saw the prettiest angels up in the sky. They looked so pretty in their white robes. It looked as if each one of them had a long trumpet in his mouth. Then I saw Christ up in the clouds in my dream. Some people seemed to be afraid and wanted to run from Him, but I said, "Stand still; He will do you no harm." I think this is a warning to the people to get right with God.

Gets Saved, Healed, and Baptized

Glory, praise, and honor to Jesus.

I am rejoicing, because I know I have a real Savior. It's so sweet to trust in Jesus.

He has saved me and baptized me with the Holy Spirit, with the Bible evidence of speaking in other tongues as the Spirit gives utterance. Glory to His name!

Sister Etter prayed for me, and, thanks be to God, He touched my body. I had been afflicted with paralysis for eleven years, with no feeling in my lower limbs, but am now getting the sense of feeling and can feel the lightest touch. Praise God! I am trusting God for complete healing. I am so glad I've found this wonderful way. Glory to God!

—*John Ward*
Houston, Texas

Lame Made to Walk

Houston, Texas, March 23, 1916

I am so glad I can join my testimony in with others' to praise God for His mighty healing power.

I was about two years old when I had the slow fever, and it settled in my left leg and made it shorter than the other, and after I got up and could walk around, I cut my foot very badly on a piece of glass, which severed the ligaments and caused my foot to grow crooked. I have found it very hard to walk around and to do my work.

I have been saved and baptized in the Holy Spirit for almost six years, and I have trusted God that someday I would get healed. However, I did not get a real touch for healing until I went to the meeting that Sister Etter was holding in the city. On the nineteenth day of March, God wonderfully touched me. Praise His dear name! I was standing on the platform singing, when I felt the Spirit of God moving upon me. Sister Etter was sitting in a chair just a little way from me. There was no healing service going on at the time, but the Spirit said to me, "Step over to her," and I obeyed. She said that God showed her He wanted to pour out His Spirit on me, and she put one hand on me and told me to look up; and as I did so I felt the power of God go through my leg from my hip to my toes. Not until then did Sister Etter notice that I was crippled. Then, laying both hands on my shoulders, she said, "Jesus heals you now." And then the power went through my limbs like an electric shock, and this set me to leaping and praising God.

From that time until this, my leg has begun to grow longer and stronger, and my foot has continued to straighten out. Bless His name forever.

—Mrs. L. C. Nelson
1218 Washington Street

Marvelous Case of Sense of Smell Restored

Houston, Texas, March 19, 1916

On the fourteenth of March, I was healed of an offensive sore in my nose. It would get worse in the winter, and I never had any sense of smell since I can remember. I could not even smell the worst odors or the fragrance of beautiful roses. I would see people smelling flowers and talking about them, and I would wish I could smell them, too. My parents thought I had catarrh and spent a great deal of money on patent medicines trying to get a cure for me, but nothing did me any good.

When I was three years old, I had the measles; when I got almost well, I took cold and had a setback. My parents thought the trouble started from that time. As I grew up, they found out that I could not smell at all; it would be so embarrassing at times, when someone would put something under my nose to smell, and I would have to tell them I could not smell.

To prove to one and all that I could not smell, I will tell you what happened when I was a little girl. I went out in the fields one day and ran across a beautiful little black animal with a white stripe down its back. I killed it and carried it home to give to my mother. When my mother smelled the odor and saw the polecat in my hands, she made me drop it pretty quick and took me out in the barnyard and gave me a bath and change of dress.

I had a big nose but no sense of smell. Some people would laugh at me, and many times I would make out like I could smell to keep people from laughing at me. However, when I got saved from sin on April 7, 1905, I could not deceive people that way any more.

So on last Tuesday night, I was healed. Sister Etter laid her hands on my nose, and when she prayed for me, I instantly felt the healing stream of Jesus go through my nose. I shouted the victory. Then the devil said to me, "How do you know you can smell?" I opened my eyes and right in front of me was a woman with a bouquet of roses pinned on her dress. You know God provided the sacrifice for Abraham just at the time he needed it, and so He provided the roses for me just when I needed them. I asked the sister for the roses, and she handed them to me, and for the first time in my life I smelled the sweet fragrance of God's beautiful rose. Oh, such a wave of glory went through and through my very being. Words cannot express the joy that I felt.

This is not the first time I have been healed by God's mighty power. My husband and I and five children trust God for both soul and body, for which I praise Him and give Him all the glory.

—Mrs. A. J. Fauss
1218 Washington Avenue
Houston, Texas

Healed of Asthma, Bronchitis, and Catarrh

Houston, Texas, March 26, 1916

About sixteen months ago I took sick with asthma, bronchitis, and catarrh in Watertown, South Dakota. I had the best doctors, but no cure. They advised me to go south. I came to Kingsville, Texas, last November. I was just improving slowly, when, praise God, I heard of Sister Etter coming to Houston.

Before attending her meetings, I was barely able to walk a few blocks. When Sister Etter laid hands on me and rebuked the disease, I was instantly healed. I got up and walked without my cane and walked many blocks without being tired. I can never cease to praise God for what He has done for me. Glory! Hallelujah to His holy name!

—*Mr. Ole S. B. Olson*

Healed of Nervous Prostration

Kingsville, Texas, March, 1916

I am sending in my testimony that the Lord may be glorified, and in hopes that some poor afflicted one may seek Jesus as Healer. For three years I had been a complete invalid, the greater part of the time being confined to the bed with "neurasthenia," or nervous prostration, which affected the motor nerves principally at intervals of three, four, and seven months. I was then bedfast, unable to walk at all. After trying masseurs, osteopaths, electric massages, and for three months the live nerve cells of animals injected in the hip, I still could not walk.

Doctor's Advice

My doctor at this time, being a devout man and fully persuaded that I'd never walk unless God undertook for me, advised me to obey James 5:14–15, which I did. This enabled to walk to and from a table three or four times a day, a distance of about one dozen steps, and to drive several times a week for the past nine months, but no more was possible. But I knew the Lord had undertaken for me and was dealing with me. Hearing that the Etter meeting was going to be held in Houston, I undertook the trip with great difficulty. I knew the Lord was going to bless me. I prayed earnestly that there would be some physical demonstration in my body when the disease was rebuked, but there was no such sign given me. I had to take God's words on simple faith and obey.

After the disease was rebuked, I was able to walk three and four blocks every day while in Houston, attending both afternoon and night services for a week.

While I'm not in a normal condition as yet, I know that the death stroke has been applied to the disease and that the effects will have to leave sooner or later. I am confident the Lord will give me to possess every bit of ground I set my foot on.

Money could not replace the joyful experiences of my Houston trip. I also received a glorious anointing. Please pray for me that I may see the Bible evidence of the baptism in the Holy Spirit by speaking in tongues soon.

God be with you and bless you, and continue to confirm the Word as you preach.

—*Mrs. Enoch Gordon*

Daily Letters Come Reporting Victory

Healed of Rupture

Dear Sister in Christ:

This leaves me well and happy in Jesus. Amen. You probably will remember me. I am still the little old man who brought the tomatoes and beans. Well, I do praise the dear Lord for His saving, keeping, and healing power. I will try to tell you about what God has done for me. Amen and Amen.

I had been afflicted for many months with a severe pain in my left side, especially after eating my supper. My wife would have to put a hot iron on my side. Many times it seemed it would blister before I would get relief. Finally, we examined and found that I had a rupture, in a wedge shape and about eight inches long and two and a half inches wide, starting near the lower part of my abdomen. The last day of your meeting at 1315 South Main Street, Los Angeles, California, the dear Lord heard your prayer for me and healed me. Oh, praise His dear name.

—*R. B. Frisbey*
1865 West 38th Place, Los Angeles, California

Healed of Gallstones

League City, Texas

I came to Sister Etter's meetings at Houston, where I was prayed for and healed of gallstones, deafness, and weakness of the lungs. I am perfectly healed. I can hear perfectly. Gallstones were removed, and I have felt no pain since. I was prayed for in Jesus' name. He healed me. Glory to His name!

I am seventy-seven years old and the happiest man on earth.

—J. H. Cravey

Spoke in Tongues in 1888

(From The Weekly Evangel, May, 1916)

While attending a meeting conducted by the evangelist M. B. Woodworth (now Mrs. Woodworth-Etter) in the fall of 1886, I received a wonderful anointing and enduement of power. I had been saved about nine months previous to this experience. From that time on, I labored for Jesus, and He honored us (my wife and I) with many souls. Sometimes I have seen a whole roomful of people slain like men in battle under the mighty power of God. One night in October of 1888, while many were slain, I became as a drunken man. I began to stutter, or stammer, and then suddenly began speaking in other tongues. Always after this, there seemed to be a greater anointing upon me, but I concluded that it was only a strange operation of the Spirit. In 1912 I attended a camp meeting conducted by Brother Haywood in Indianapolis, Indiana, with the purpose of receiving the baptism in the Holy Spirit. I received Him in great glory and spoke in tongues. Then I knew that it was the same as I had received in 1888.

Since then my wife has gone home to be with the Lord; an angel, or white form, was standing at the foot of the bed, saying, "I am sent for your wife." Before leaving, she asked many questions about the "bright ones" around her.

I now see many lonely days, but Jesus seems more precious than ever before. I had thought she would remain with me until Jesus came, but *the dead in Christ shall rise first: then we which are alive and remain shall be caught up together with them in the clouds, to meet the Lord in the air; and so shall we ever be with the Lord"* (1 Thess. 4:16–17).

—A. P. Dennis, of Scottsburg, Indiana

61

"TRY THE SPIRITS"

Sermon Preached to Ministers and Workers at Montwait, Massachusetts

Beloved, believe not every spirit, but try the spirits whether they are of God" (1 John 4:4). There are many spirits we do not want to have anything to do with. There are our own spirits, the flesh, and the devil. There are many spirits contending, and many times we let our own spirits rule and convince ourselves it is God; the same with the flesh and the devil.

Sometimes we know it is not God, but we want to have our own way. If we have the Holy Spirit, we can prove the spirits, because everything the Holy Spirit does is confirmed by the Word. We do not want to trust to tongues and interpretations; you must measure things by the Word; we must measure tongues and demonstrations by the Word, and if they do not agree with the Word, we must not accept them. Everything must be measured by the Word.

We do know God and the voice of God, but the devil can come as an angel of light. When you are in the Holy Spirit, that is the time the devil tries to get in and lead you astray. The Holy Spirit is revealing some secret things; at the same time the devil comes in, and if you are not careful, you will listen to what he has to say and follow him.

Once I was having a wonderful vision, and right in the midst of it, the devil said to me, "You are going to die." I was in poor health and had worked nearly to death. I listened to the devil for a moment; then I stopped to hear what God wanted to teach me.

I said, "What is this God is showing me? Does this agree with what God is showing?" I saw there was a big difference. God touched my forehead, the seat of intellect and reason, and my mouth, signifying courage and power to give forth the message, and I could not die if I was to do this. If I was to give the people His message, I was not going to die.

There was someone here in the meeting God was blessing. He wanted to use her, but the devil came in and made her think she could do any outrageous thing and it would be of God.

See how the devil can lead us astray. She was talking in tongues and praying, and she said, "Lord, if you want me to kill anyone, I will do it; if you want me to set the camp on fire, I will do it."

That is the way in spiritualism. The Holy Spirit never does anything like that; He does not come to kill and knock people's heads off; He deals with them in love and tenderness. People have even offered up children in sacrifice. If you listen to God, the devil will be put to one side.

These things hurt the Pentecostal movement; God is in it, but the devil is in it, too. Many people are honest, but they do not understand. God shows great things that are going to happen, and the devil comes in and makes them set a date.

Daniel did not understand the vision he had for some time; an angel appeared to him to make him understand the vision. Be careful the devil does not come in and give you another meaning that is altogether different from what God wants you to have.

So many prophesy this or that, and it never comes true; the prophecy was not according to the Word of God. Someone gives a person a message, and he believes God sent it, when it is not according to the Word.

When God calls you out for His work, He will take care of you, give you something to eat, and clothe you. There are so many who run before they are sent; it would be better not to go at all. Sometimes the devil uses tongues to upset things generally. The devil can speak in tongues, and so can your flesh.

When God speaks in tongues, it means something, and you want to look for the interpretation. God says to ask for the interpretation. Sometimes God gives it through someone else, but give the person who speaks in tongues a chance to interpret. Be careful you do not give an interpretation in your own spirit; this hurts the work everywhere. Let us try the spirits and not get in the flesh.

Some people, if they do not like a person, will give a message in tongues or a rebuke and nearly knock the person's head off. This is the work of the devil. Then someone will get up—some people are so silly—and say, "Don't lay hands on that; it is the Holy Spirit," and no one dares to touch it, and the devil has control of the whole thing.

It gets about that the leader sanctions what is going on, and people do not want to have anything to do with the ministry. The leader may have discernment, but someone will pull his coattail and say, "Don't lay hands on that; don't touch it." Instead of being so afraid, let us search the Scriptures. God never told anyone to rebuke in an ugly tone.

There was a great work being done in the West. One woman, especially, said the United States was going to be destroyed, and they should go to Japan. They went. People who could not spare the money helped them; they went to escape the wreck.

The whole thing was of the devil. The United States was not destroyed; they could not speak the Japanese language; they were stranded, and a number backslid; they tried to raise money for a great building but never accomplished it. They had been doing a good work here, but other spirits got in.

God gave me a special commission to take the precious from the vile, and I do not want you to get into the snare of the devil. So many young people, after their baptism, give up work and go to preaching. In a few days they tell all they know, then tell something they don't know; bread and butter does not come in, and many of them backslide.

If God doesn't send you out, don't give up your job; then you will have something to give. This mistake is made by many missionaries who go abroad. Some sell all they have, break up their homes, separate from their wives, and God has not called them.

The Holy Spirit makes us levelheaded. Those who stayed in the camp got as much as those who went to the battlefront. (See 1 Samuel 30:21–25.) Be God's stewards, and give the Lord His part. The cattle upon a thousand hills are His, but He works through our instrumentality. He gives you everything you have—physically, financially, and spiritually—and He expects you to use all your powers for Him; if you give out, He will supply.

He expects you to take Him into partnership and give Him what belongs to him, and He will bless you. The Gospel has to be supported.

Water is free, but it costs money to lay the pipes and keep the water running. Angels can fly, but men have to pay fares, and someone has to help. If you help to keep the pipes in order, the Gospel will be given out. You need to help with your prayers and hold up the hands of those who work. If you trust God and walk with Him, that is the work God wants of you.

Don't take up with every vision that comes along. In the Pentecostal movement in some places, they have discarded the Word of God. They don't want a leader, but God always has a leader. When there is none, the devil takes the chair. God has given some as pastors and teachers (Eph. 4:11).

How do people know when God calls them to the ministry? Someone has said that when God calls anyone to do His work, you can hardly get him into the pulpit; but when the devil calls him, you can't keep him out of it.

Some people want to talk so much, bringing in a bone of contention, and it is hurting the work everywhere. Leave outside issues. God will teach people what to eat, what to wear, and where to go. Many of God's children are nagging about these things. The Lord said that if you don't think it is right to eat meat, don't do it; but don't judge another who does (1 Cor. 8:8–9).

When we open our mouths, let us say something. If you have the baptism, you need not tell it; people will know it. Let God speak to you. Do not wait for someone to speak in tongues and tell you God wants you to go to India; let God speak to you.

People who go because someone else says so get homesick and discouraged and try to come back again. Let the Lord be our guide; if we do His will, we shall know His will.

Hold up Jesus, and try to get the people so full of the Holy Spirit that they will live in unity. We do not want to lay hands on anyone suddenly (1 Tim. 5:22).

If we do anything in a spirit of contention, the first thing we know, everything is in a jumble, and we have done more harm in one meeting than can be imagined.

Hold up Jesus and the Resurrection. Let us *"walk in the light, as he is in the light"* (1 John 1:7). Christ is the great Headlight, and I am on the stretch for more light than I ever saw in my life; you have fellowship when you walk in the light. We are the lower lights, and He will show us what to do next.

He will say to you, "Now you can do this." You may say, "I did not know before that You would trust me." Again His answer, "You can do it now."

Until God shows you a thing you're doing wrong, it is not a sin, but after He shows it to you, if you do it, it is a sin. Consecrate everything to God, day by day. He will not call you to do a thing unless He is going to give you strength and grace.

When you go into a meeting, listen to the teaching; if it does not suit you and you want something else, the best thing you can do is to go out quietly and drum up a crowd yourself. Some say you have no need for any man to teach you (1 John 2:27); the natural man cannot teach you, but the spiritual man can teach you.

We know what we are talking about; the spiritual man can teach you. We know nothing as we should, and there is so much for us to know.

Be careful not to lay hands suddenly on anyone. Regarding the recent disturbance here, we profess to be saints, and we want to show forth the Spirit of Christ. We must be firm but kind. Do not speak roughly. The crowds want to see. I would have nearly broken my neck when I was young to see what you are seeing.

When they became noisy, it would have been useless to attempt to use force; it would only have ended in a fight, and the plan of the enemy would have been accomplished. God led me in the only way by which the disturbance could be quelled and order restored; God fought for us. Do not speak roughly to the boys; each one is some mother's boy. God can smite with conviction; the battle is His, not ours.

"Try the spirits." In one of our meetings there was a colored woman who had wonderful experiences spiritually; that is the kind the devil gets after. One day she commenced to go about on her knees, twisting about like a serpent. God does not tell anyone to do that. She spoke in tongues; then she said, "I don't want to do it; I don't want to do it."

Everyone knew it was not of God, and I said to her, "That is not God; the enemy has got hold of you." At first, she didn't want to give up, but the next day God showed her, and she asked to be delivered. The devil had got in and made her do things that were not right to kill her influence.

A woman came to me and said, "I am afraid this spirit on me is not of God; I was baptized in the Holy Spirit; I went into a mission where they did everything by tongues, and they got me so mixed up, I did not know where I was; then, this spirit got hold of me; it shakes my head and makes my head ache."

That is spiritualism. Some people, when they pray for anyone and lay on hands, throw the slime off. That is spiritualism. Don't ever do anything like that.

When you lay hands on a person, God takes care of the evil spirit. If you are filled with the Holy Spirit, the devil is outside you; keep him out. Be careful who lays hands on you, for the devil is counterfeiting God's work.

For two years, that woman could not give a testimony. God rebuked the shaking spirit, the power of God came in her hands and in her voice, and she gave a testimony for God.

That is what ails the Pentecostal movement; so much of this has crept in. Some people accept every foolish thing as the Holy Spirit. There are two extremes operating: one keeps the Holy Spirit from working except in a certain narrowly defined way, and the other thinks everything is of the Holy Spirit: "Don't lay hands on it." One is as bad as the other. Let everything be done by the Word of God.

We are living in the last days, and there has got to be a higher standard for the Pentecostal movement. Christ is coming, and we cannot move along in the old rut. God is sifting us today, and we have got to rise above errors; we have to rise up and go forward. By the grace of God we will. Praise His name!

Where the Blood Can Heal

Do you seek relief for your sin-sick soul?
    You to Christ, then, must make appeal.
There's no other one who can make you whole,
    You must come where the blood can heal!

REFRAIN

You must come where the blood can heal,
You must come where the blood can heal;
There's no other one who can make you whole,
You must come where the blood can heal!

Vain are all your hopes of another cure,
    Be persuaded, you now, to feel,
Help alone, through Christ, that you can secure,
    You must come where the blood can heal!

Other proffered aids can but you deceive,
    At your will, unto life, they steal!
You must look to Christ if you'd hope receive,
    You must come where the blood can heal!

Hear you not? 'Tis there a decoying voice,
    Striving ever to quench thy zeal;
Would you from Him turn, refuge safe to find,
    You must come where the blood can heal!
If you would arise from your bed of pain,
    To the counsel of Christ then kneel,
'Tis prescribed by Him, and your only hope,
    You must come where the blood can heal!

62

WORK OF THE HOLY SPIRIT

Sermon by Mrs. M. B. Woodworth-Etter

In John 15:26, Jesus is speaking of the coming of the Holy Spirit: *"But when the Comforter is come, whom I will send unto you from the Father...he shall testify of Me."* He is the Holy Spirit. The Lord speaks of the Holy Spirit as a person as much as He would of one of the apostles.

On the Day of Pentecost, they were all in one accord, in one place (Acts 2:1), and something happened. It will every day if you have the Spirit. *"Suddenly there came a sound from heaven as of a mighty rushing wind"* (v. 2). This was the Holy Spirit when He came to stay. Cloven tongues of fire appeared sat upon each of them (v. 3). *"And they were all filled with the Holy Ghost, and began to speak with other tongues, as the Spirit gave them utterance"* (v. 4).

"When this was noised abroad, the multitude came together" (v. 6). What was noised abroad? That these people were all speaking in other languages. The news went through Jerusalem, and the multitude came together and were bewildered, because every man heard them speaking in his own language; and those who came were of every nation under heaven (v. 5).

They heard these hundred and twenty speak in their own native languages. This is what drew the crowds. "*They were all amazed and marvelled, saying one to another, Behold! are not all these which speak Galileans? And how hear we every man in our own tongue, wherein we were born?*" (Acts 2:7–8). "We hear them speak in our own tongues of the wonderful works of God" (v. 11).

The Holy Spirit is a wonderful person, not a myth or shadow. Pentecost is the greatest thing that ever happened in God's work, when the Holy Spirit came in to stay. He came and took possession of one hundred and twenty men and women; He sat upon their heads in cloven tongues of fire and went in and took possession of their bodies, then of their vocal organs; and they spoke, everyone, as He gave them utterance.

They spoke in languages they had never learned and did not know what they were saying. The Holy Spirit took possession of their tongues and spoke through them; He spoke through the clay as you would speak through a telephone. The Holy Spirit's words told about Jesus: "*He shall testify of me.*"

Jesus told the apostles that they should be witnesses. The Holy Spirit, when He came, knew all about it, and He told through them of the wonderful works of God. When this was noised abroad, multitudes gathered; it was the speaking in tongues that drew the people. When they heard them, they were perplexed and said, "What could this mean?" (Acts 2:12).

I want you to notice this point: It was speaking in tongues that confounded them. The Holy Spirit spoke through unlearned men who had never been to college to learn other languages. It was one of the most wonderful things God ever did; it is now, when God speaks through you.

The Lord said through the prophet, many hundred years ago, "*Whom shall he teach knowledge?…Them that are weaned from the milk*" (Isa. 28:9). The wisdom of the world was to be confounded through these unlearned people, and it proved to be so.

Jesus had been on earth, healed the sick, cast out devils, cleansed the temple; but the Jews rejected and crucified Him. Now, on the Day of Pentecost, when they heard the Holy Spirit speak through these one hundred and twenty unlearned men and women, they were confounded.

They heard them tell of Jesus, whom they had crucified, and were convinced that this was the work of divine power. Some said that these people are drunk, filled with new wine; but Peter said that they couldn't be drunk so early in the day. (Acts 2:13–15).

He went back to the Old Testament Scriptures and told what the prophet had said about the coming of the Holy Spirit: *"This is that which is spoken by the prophet Joel"* (v.16). The Holy Spirit had been with the apostles in a wonderful way, but they had not spoken with other tongues until Pentecost.

Isaiah prophesied, *"With stammering lips and another tongue will he speak to this people....Yet they would not hear"* (Isa. 28:11–12). God Almighty was speaking through other tongues; Pentecost was proving the prophecy was fulfilled.

They would not believe Jesus, so they had to be convinced by the Word of God that what they heard was the Holy Spirit, as spoken by the prophets. Peter preached to them, taking the Old Testament as proof (Acts 2:14–36). They were convicted of sin and converted, three thousand of them (v. 41).

They cried out for mercy, *"Men and brethren, what shall we do?"* (v. 37). Peter said to them, "What you see is from the Father; repent of what you did, turn to God, and you will receive the gift of the Holy Spirit" (v. 38). They got saved and baptized in the Holy Spirit.

"The promise is unto you, and to your children" (v. 39). You can all have the same power we have and do the same things, you and your children; you can get this baptism and teach it to your children. Everyone can have it: *"...and to all that are afar off, even as many as the Lord our God shall call"* (v. 39).

God sends the Holy Spirit to come into the human body; He takes charge of the vocal organs, and the person has nothing to do with it. However, for all that God does in such a wonderful thing, some of you will not believe it. Tongues are for a sign to unbelievers (1 Cor. 14:22), and these were the worst kind of unbelievers: they had crucified the Lord. Yet they were made to believe in Jesus Christ by this sign. They were convinced by this sign that Jesus was the Messiah when everything else had failed.

These were unlearned men, all Galileans, yet they spoke all these tongues, representing the different nations, in a wonderful way. It takes years and years to master other languages, and very few ever speak them fluently like natives. These were unlearned people, yet they spoke fluently, like the natives, because God Almighty spoke through them.

Everyone who is baptized in the Holy Spirit today, as he ought to be, speaks in another language, and the first words almost always are, "Jesus is coming soon!"

The pouring out of the Holy Spirit in this way is a sign that we are in the last days. When He comes in His fullness, He shall take possession and talk through you of the death, Resurrection, and Ascension of Jesus. When Jesus went away, He said, "Don't go out preaching yet, but wait in Jerusalem until you receive power, after the Holy Spirit comes upon you; then you will be My witnesses" (Luke 24:49; Acts 1:8).

After their training of three years, they had much to tell, but He told them not to talk about it, to stay together and watch until the power came, and then they could testify of Him. Now, when the Holy Spirit came and took possession of them, remember they kept still until the Holy Spirit testified through them; then they could be witnesses.

They had to keep still until the Holy Spirit testified through every one of them. In other languages, He told the wonderful works of God; Jesus died and rose again, went to God's right hand, and sent the Holy Spirit to testify of Him. This is so wonderful to me; the Holy Spirit spoke first, the rest waiting until He had finished.

Then Peter took the Scriptures, for the people always believed in the prophets. He took the witness stand and brought to them the proof that the promise of the Father had literally come to pass in the fullness of time. God had spoken in other tongues through men. Peter took up the Word and confirmed what the Holy Spirit had done. He confirmed it by the Old Testament.

Jesus said, "When the Holy Spirit comes in, He will testify of Me; then you will be witnesses." "*In the mouth of two or three witnesses, every word* [shall] *be established*" (Matt. 18:16). When the Holy Spirit comes in to abide, He comes into the body like rivers of living water. The power comes from the heart, not the head. We talk through the intellect; the Holy Spirit talks through the Spirit. The Holy Spirit testifies when it is God's work.

Peter said, "*This is that,*" this special thing. These people, acting like drunken men; these, talking in other languages—all this is "*that spoken by the prophet*" (Acts 2:15). God said when His Spirit was poured out, He would speak with stammering lips and another tongue; but some will not believe it.

The cloven tongues are seen today. In Dallas and Chicago, fire was seen upon the heads of some. It is the same Holy Spirit speaking in other tongues; why not see the cloven tongues of fire?

When the Holy Spirit comes in, He will take possession of the house, take the uppermost seat, and speak Himself. Paul showed that it is a wonderful thing for God to speak through you in unknown tongues by the Holy Spirit. He quoted the prophets of thousands of years ago.

Paul wrote: *"I would that ye all spake with tongues.....I thank my God I speak with tongues more than ye all: yet in the church I had rather speak five words with my understanding, that by my voice I might teach others also, than ten thousand words in an unknown tongue....Forbid not to speak with tongues"* (1 Cor. 14:5, 18–19, 39).

This is one of the last signs of the soon coming of Jesus. For almost everyone who is baptized with the Holy Spirit, the first words they speak in an unknown tongue, when interpreted, are, "Jesus is coming soon; get ready." Everyone who speaks in an unknown tongue should pray that he might interpret (1 Cor. 14:13).

Paul said, *"Desire spiritual gifts.....He that speaketh in an unknown tongue speaketh not unto men, but unto God: for no man understandeth him; howbeit in the spirit he speaketh mysteries,... [and he] edifieth himself,...except he [or someone else] interpret, that the church may receive edifying"* (1 Cor. 14:1–2, 4–5).

Tongues are for a sign to unbelievers that Jesus is coming soon and that the Holy Spirit is poured out. Those who have the gift of tongues can speak at will, or any time that the Spirit is moving. Some even lose their experience and still speak any time, anything they want to, casting aspersions on the cause; this is in the flesh or not of God.

John the Baptist was filled with the Holy Spirit from his birth, yet he was under the law. The mother of Jesus was filled with the Holy Spirit, but she had to receive the baptism with the rest. The apostles had received the Holy Spirit and had the love of God shed abroad in their hearts, yet were baptized on the Day of Pentecost.

Follow on, and get the real baptism, and you will *"be filled with all the fulness of God"* (Eph. 3:19). Jesus did not have the fullness of power until He finished His work, laid down His life, and God raised Him from the dead. When He arose, He was a mighty conqueror; then He had all authority and power. He breathed upon the apostles and said, *"Receive ye the Holy Ghost"* (John 20:22). Their understanding was opened, and they knew more than they ever did before. They were wonderfully blessed.

You must be full of joy before you get the baptism. They were full of joy, and all of one mind and one spirit. Glory to God! They went to the upper room, they were ready, they believed, and they waited at Jerusalem; they continued with one accord, not praying and begging all the time, but waiting.

Stop begging and get joy in your heart! Then you will get something. God had been moving in power, and they had cast out devils; but they waited until the power came upon them, and then they spoke in new tongues.

Just as far as you believe, you will receive. Everyone, after the baptism, is supposed to speak with tongues. They had the testimony of the prophets, and Christ said they should speak with tongues. They were prayed up-to-date, they believed, expected, praised, and the Holy Spirit came down upon them. They were full of joy; every doubt was gone; they did not care about the results, only that He came; and everyone was filled with the Holy Spirit. You must have something else, the other gifts—casting out demons, healing the sick, poison or the deadly serpent not harming you.

The apostles had had nearly all the gifts; they were looking for tongues. Many people have spoken with tongues only once; they are not looking for other gifts. To the extent you believe, you will get every blessing. We ask God to sanctify us and bless us, and just as far as our faith reaches, we get what we ask for.

In these days, we have too much light for God to wink at ignorance. We see miracles done, showing that the Holy Spirit is poured out, and God wants us to step out for all the gifts. There is the poison. Some running sores are putrid and full of poison; people come here like that. When we ask God to rebuke that and believe He will, it will be cleansed.

If you accidentally drink poison, believe, give Him the glory, and the poison won't hurt you. A viperous serpent fastened on Paul's hand; he shook it off and suffered no harm; and they thought he was a god (Acts 28:3–6). All these things are the work of the Holy Spirit.

Many people teach today that no one has the Holy Spirit until baptized with the Holy Spirit. The Holy Spirit comes in different degrees, the filling of the Spirit and the baptism in the Spirit. The baptism comes down on your head like a cloud.

When the prophets were anointed, the oil was poured over their heads; then the Holy Spirit came upon them. The Holy Spirit must come upon our heads; then all through us, taking possession of us. Many people do not think of anything but speaking in tongues; they lay everything else aside.

Thirty-five years ago, I was baptized with the Holy Spirit and fire, and I stood alone. When the Pentecostal movement broke out, and some said they would not have anything but tongues, I was kept back and could not do much with the movement at first. There was so much false teaching that the Holy Spirit was driven away from many people; they wanted the Holy Spirit to work this way and not that way. Let the Holy Spirit work in any way that agrees with the Word of God.

The apostles had faith; they knew they were going to have power as they had never had it before. God has given us light, and He expects us to have faith that we will receive the Holy Spirit in such a wonderful way that He will speak through us.

I believe the Holy Spirit will speak in tongues through everyone who receives the baptism, and you will receive the other gifts also, if you believe for them. In these last days, God is raising up a people who will blow the trumpet.

How can we sing in the heavenly choir unless we are filled with the Spirit? John heard the song of the redeemed like the rushing of mighty waters. It is the Holy Spirit; it rolls up and sounds like the rushing of many waters.

We have heard the heavenly music, and many times there are sounds like instruments playing; the Holy Spirit sings through people. God is working in mysterious ways these days, and I bless Him for it.

The early rain and the latter rain much more abundant, were promised in the same month, with the same power and gifts as in the early church.

"*Greater works than these shall [y]e do, because I go unto my Father*" (John 14:12). He has left His work in our hands. It means something wonderful to be baptized in the Holy Spirit. The Jews were unbelieving until they heard the Holy Spirit speaking in other tongues through those unlearned people; they knew it was God; they realized they had crucified the Lord, that He had risen and gone to glory, and they cried out, "*What shall we do?*" (Acts 2:37).

Jesus prayed on the cross, "*Father, forgive them; for they know not what they do*" (Luke 23:34). When the Holy Spirit came, they knew what they had done. The tongues were a sign to unbelievers; it is today one of the greatest things God ever did.

The Holy Spirit will sing through us; He is training us to sing at the marriage supper of the Lamb. "*We shall not all [die], but we shall all be changed*" (1 Cor. 15:51); we will have a glorious body, like Jesus, and will rise to meet Him in the air, full of joy.

People who are healed are full of joy and sometimes jump and dance when the healing power comes into them. The Holy Spirit takes all the deadness and stiffness out of them. Sometimes God slays them and lays them down so He can talk to them.

Men and women, rejoice, seek the baptism, and receive the gifts. You shall have them if you believe for them, and you shall be witnesses. May God seal this to some heart, in the name of Jesus.

63

JAMES' COMMISSION TO THE CHURCH TO PRAY FOR THE SICK

Sermon by Mrs. M. B. Woodworth-Etter

The last chapter of James is for the church. Remember, it is not for sinners. *"Is any sick among you? Let him call for the elders of the church; and let them pray over him, anointing him with oil in the name of the Lord: and the prayer of faith shall save the sick, and the Lord shall raise him up; and if he have committed sins, they shall be forgiven him."* (James 5:14–15).

"Confess your faults one to another" (v. 16). You have to be pretty straight when you come to God. *"Pray one for another, that ye may be healed. The effectual fervent prayer of a righteous man availeth much."*

Elijah was a man like other men, not an angel, and he prayed that it might not rain, and it rained not for three years and six months. He prayed again and God heard him and sent the rain (vv. 17–18). This chapter is for us; it applies to us. All through the chapter, it refers to the days we are living in.

When these things come to pass, know that the end draws near. This chapter brings us down to the last days.

About verse seven, in the east they had the early rain to start the grain. They could not tell anything about the harvest until they received the latter rain. If it came abundantly, there would be a good harvest.

Verses seven and eight say to us, "Wait for the latter rain; also be patient unto the coming of the Lord." When the latter rain is falling, we know the coming of the Lord is near. We are getting the early rain and will get the latter rain before long. He is getting the bride ready.

The apostle is speaking to the church. If anyone is sick among you, don't run for the doctor, or send him to the hospital, but let the sick ones send for the elders. The elders were supposed to be men endued with the Holy Spirit, who would come and pray over him, anointing him with oil, and he should be raised up; and if he had sinned in any way, he must confess it, and through prayer, be forgiven.

Some people say this is spiritual healing. They are blind because they want to be. Anointing with oil is a symbol of the anointing with the Holy Spirit. A barrel of oil would not heal, but if you are anointing with faith and obedience, you get the blessing.

It is the healing virtue of Jesus, the power of God. After the disease is cast out, the healing power of Jesus comes in. The prayer of faith saves the sick; the power of God cleanses the soul; and the sick one is raised up, both soul and body.

Any of God's children, filled with the Holy Spirit, can pray with the sick, anointing with oil, in the name of the Lord, and— you can rely upon it—the person will be raised up.

You can do that without any special gift. Pray for one another. People may die before help can reach them. Call in the neighbors, and unite in prayer. If there has been any backbiting, confess it.

The prayer of faith is effective and avails much. If you cannot get anyone with a special gift, pray for each other. I know many people who have not had a doctor in the family; parents pray for the children, and children pray for the parents. Little ones who can hardly talk will pray, and the sick are raised up.

Pray one for another. Wherever you are, Jesus is; He is the Healer and also the Baptizer. He gives the resurrection life. Today, many are wonderfully healed while alone with God. God is moving in a marvelous way. We must exercise faith and obedience.

Elijah had great power with God, and he was a man just like you. Elisha had twice as much power as Elijah. Moody said we ought to have much more and do greater things than he did. This was away back in the moonlight of the church. We, in the sunlight, today, ought to do four times as many miracles as they did.

Great miracles ought to be performed, and they are being performed in these days when the bride is getting herself ready to meet the Bridegroom and go up into the air with Him. God will do greater works in the last days.

All the people who are baptized in the Spirit believe that Jesus is coming soon. Half the world knows it. How? By the Word and signs. God wants to move His people; when the Gospel of the coming King is preached in all the world, then He will come (Matt. 24:14).

This Gospel of the coming King is to cover the earth and give every professing child of God a chance to come into the power of the Holy Spirit. If we do not blow the trumpet and give forth the right sound, the Tribulation will be upon us, and their blood will be required at our hands.

We are told to watch and pray as we see the day approaching. What is the signal of danger? The great Day of the Lord is at hand. How could we blow the trumpet, if we did not know the signal? I am glad we do know it.

This chapter shows the power of God in the church. Every child of God should have power enough to bring down a blessing. There must be faith and obedience. Expect something from the Lord just now, and He will answer quickly.

You see how quickly prayer is answered and different diseases healed; you see it here every day. God says the prayer of faith will save the sick. Everyone does not have to anoint with oil; some have gifts; there are different gifts.

Jesus said, "*These signs shall follow them that believe; in my name shall they cast out devils; they shall speak with new tongues; …they shall lay hands on the sick and they shall recover*" (Mark 16:17–18). One point I want to make clear.

It says anoint with oil, but it does not say pray for every sinner. This is for the saints; if they have backslidden, let them confess, and they will be forgiven.

Sinners cannot expect to be healed unless they give their hearts to God. Jesus said, "*Thy sins are forgiven*" (Luke 7:48), then He healed. God expects you to come the same way. I cannot pray for your body unless you give yourself to God. If you want God to heal you, you must stop sinning.

If you promise me you will, God will take your promise through our faith. God did not promise to heal sinners and let them go forth to serve the devil; He said, "*Sin no more, lest a worse thing come unto thee*" (John 5:14). You will sin unless you get saved.

They should know in every church what to do: send for the elders. Until recently very few people would lay hands on the sick without anointing with oil; I have been criticized for this, all the way.

I received my anointing thirty-five years ago when God raised me up from the sick bed. God showed me I must preach healing, and I told the people how God raised me up. After a while, I was holding a meeting in Indiana and worked nearly to death, sometimes nearly all night.

The Spirit of the Lord came upon me; God was trying to show me He wanted me to preach healing for the sick, but I was afraid it was the enemy. It seemed like presumption. Many souls would be saved through divine healing, and the devil knew it.

Healing is the great drawing card in the New Testament. Finally, I settled the question. I knew it was the Lord, and I said, "Whenever You want me to pray for someone, bring them to me, or take me to them, and I will do it."

The first place I went, we had a wonderful meeting. There was a man who had been a great skeptic; I met a man who asked me to go and visit the man's daughter, who was dying; five doctors had given her up.

She had been converted a few weeks before in our meeting. I did not see how I could go, but I felt the hand of the Lord was in it, and I said, "If I cannot go, I will pray for her, and I believe God will heal her."

The next morning, I was very weak, but felt I must go to her, when the Lord said to me, "You pray for her, and I will heal her." A few days later in another town, I received word that He had fulfilled His promise. You talk about hypnotic power or my power; I never saw this woman.

Concerning laying on of hands, I was holding a meeting in Indiana; there were few people to pray the power down. Dr. Daggett, a physician, came to the meetings whenever he could and would lead in prayer.

Sometimes he had to go out, he suffered so with pain in his knees. The Lord began to say to me, "That man ought to be healed." He impressed this upon me so much that I had to go to him and say, "I wish you did not have to go out; I need you here." He said, "I am very sorry, but I am suffering so much I have to leave."

I asked him if he did not believe God could heal him, and I told him that I believed God wanted to heal him. God was working with him in the same way. I called the congregation together and said, "Are there any Christians here who believe God can heal? If you really believe, come and help me. I am going to pray for healing."

Several came. I did not know what to do any more than a baby. I began to pray. The power of the Lord raised my right arm up until it was over the knee and then stopped, for I did not like to touch it. The power of God was in my hand, and He wanted me to lay my hand on that man's knee.

When I understood what God wanted, I laid my hand on the knee and asked God to take the disease out. He sprang to his feet, healed. He had been that way for twelve years; everyone knew him, and everyone was amazed.

Once when there were thousands of people present, I called out, "Is Dr. Daggett in the congregation?" He was making his way through the crowd, running to a place on the platform. He told how wonderfully he was healed, and I heard of him twelve years afterward.

That was the first person I ever laid hands on. "*They shall lay hands on the sick, and they shall recover*" (Mark 16:18). That was the way God led me out. I have been criticized all along the way by those who anoint with oil.

After Pentecost, you never read of the apostles anointing with oil. They did as Jesus directed: they laid their hands on the sick, and they recovered.

God does not lead everyone alike. Anyone He leads to anoint, it is all right. However, God did not lead me to minister that way; He led me to pray the prayer of faith and lay hands on, and cast out demons in the name of Jesus.

Anyone who has faith to comply with the commission James gives can pray the prayer of faith for the sick, and they will be healed.

64

"EYE HATH NOT SEEN NOR EAR HEARD"

Sermon by Mrs. M. B. Woodworth-Etter

Eye hath not seen, nor ear heard, neither have entered into the heart of man, the things which God hath prepared for them that love him. But God hath revealed them unto us by his Spirit: for the Spirit searcheth all things, yea, the deep things of God.   (1 Corinthians 2:9–10)

This Scripture text is not understood by anyone unless he has the Holy Spirit. Many today apply this to eternity, to the other world; they think we never know these things until we get into another world. I am glad the Scripture explains itself. *"Eye hath not seen,"* in the natural state. God has—in the present—revealed unto us by His Spirit. How? By His Spirit, in this world. *"The Spirit searcheth all things; yea, the deep things of God."*

I desire to call your attention, especially, to the fourteenth verse. *"The natural man receiveth not the things of the Spirit of God: for they are foolishness unto him: neither can he know them, because they are spiritually discerned"* (1 Cor. 2:14).

The natural man cannot understand this wonderful Scripture. There are two classes of men, the spiritual man and the natural man. The natural man is in the *"gall of bitterness"* (Acts 8:23), but the spiritual man is born of God and walks in the Spirit; he gets out into the deep. The natural man can never discern spiritual things, never hear and understand the work of the Lord; these things pass all human understanding. The wisdom of this world, intellect, and science can never understand the spiritual things of God.

There are two kinds of wisdom. *"The wisdom of this world is foolishness with God"* (1 Cor. 3:19). The wisdom from above, the natural man cannot comprehend; it never enters his imagination to think of the things God has prepared for those who love Him.

He has prepared already, and He has revealed them to us by His Spirit. His Spirit lets us down into the deep things, even the deep things of God. This is what we preach, what we practice, and what we stand on. The work of the Spirit is foolishness to the natural man; but he who has the Spirit can discern spiritual things.

There are many kinds of power, and many spirits going out in the world today; and we are told to try the spirits; they are many. Everything is revealed by God through His blessed Holy Spirit. There is only one Spirit we want anything to do with; not our own spirit, nor any other spirit, but the Spirit of the living God. *"As many as are led by the Spirit of God, they are the sons of God"* (Rom. 8:14); and He will lead us into all truth, all the way; will lead us where we can get the truth. The child of God will be led into the baptism of the Holy Spirit and fire, the Pentecostal baptism.

Then we can go from one deep thing to another. The Holy Spirit is sent to us by Jesus Christ, and all gifts come through the Holy Spirit. Jesus said that the Spirit, when He comes to you, will not speak of Himself, but will glorify Christ, and that He will speak to you and show you the things to come. (See John 16:13–14). We believe it. Glory to God!

This is the Holy Spirit who came at Pentecost and turned Jerusalem upside down. Jesus said that when the Holy Spirit came, He would abide with us forever, even unto the end. The work of the Spirit is foolishness to the natural man, who cannot comprehend it.

Unless you will hear the voice of God, the voice of the natural man will make you attribute what you see to excitement or to some other power. When the Holy

Spirit is poured out, there are always two classes: one is convinced and convicted, and accepts it; the other says, "If I accept this, I will have to lead a different life and be a laughingstock to the world." They are not willing to pay the price, so they begin to draw back. First they wonder at the strange acts, and then when they won't accept, they begin to despise them. All who continue to despise the works of the Spirit will perish.

There are many powers in the world that are not of God; they are counterfeit. But where there is a counterfeit, there is always a genuine. No one ever tries to counterfeit anything that is not genuine; that is a sure evidence that it is genuine.

The devil shows his power in a good many ways to deceive people; he tries to substitute some other power for the power of God. It was so in the time of Moses and the time of the prophets. God's power was especially in the world at certain times, and then magicians would come along with their power and show something that seemed similar. One was God; the other was the devil.

Moses went to Egypt to lead the people out. He threw down his rod before Pharaoh, and it became a live serpent. The magicians said they had the same power, so they threw some rods down, and they became serpents. One was of God, and the other was of the devil. Moses did not get scared and run away; he knew God and wouldn't have run if all the serpents in Egypt had come before him.

He stood his ground, and I admire him for it; I do not like a coward. What was the result? Moses' serpent-rod swallowed the others up (Exod. 7:12)! There was nothing left of them. Those who are trying to overthrow the power of God and substitute something else will have a Day of Judgment. The time is coming when the Almighty power of God will swallow them up in the day of His wrath.

The Lamb of God left the realm of glory and came down here to be footsore, dusty, weary, spit upon. He said, *"I come to do thy will, O God"* (Heb. 10:9). If He had not borne all these things, if He had not gone all the way to the cross, the Holy Spirit never could have come. If Christ had been left in the tomb, the Holy Spirit never could have come. As soon as He arose from the dead and ascended into heaven, the Holy Spirit could come.

God gave His Son the highest place before all the hosts of heaven; then He sent the Holy Spirit to dwell in these bodies, His temple.

The Holy Spirit is a great power; He is compared to wind, water, and fire. At Pentecost the Spirit came like a cyclone, a mighty rushing wind (Acts 2:2); He is to come like *"rivers of living water"* (John 7:38). He comes as fire; tongues of fire sat upon each of them at Pentecost (Acts 2:3). Wind, water, and fire—the most destructive elements we have, yet the most useful.

God uses them to denote the mighty power of the Holy Spirit, and He was to be given after Jesus was to be glorified (John 7:39). We see many demonstrations of His mighty power, and *"we cannot but speak the things which we have seen and heard"* (Acts 4:20) of His glory, His majesty. Then we know these things, we are witnesses to His power, His majesty, and His glory. Glory to God!

He is a mighty power, and He lives in these bodies. He lets down an *"eternal weight of glory"* (2 Cor. 4:17) upon us here, and when we are filled with glory, we have to vent it, or we would explode. What are we? Only worms of the dust; we cannot stand the glory of God; one breath from Him lays us prostrate.

In the Bible we read how men fell when they had a glimpse of God's glory. Paul warned us there are those who have a form of godliness, but deny the power thereof; we are to turn away from such (2 Tim. 3:5). *"In the last days perilous times shall come"* (v. 1), and those who have reprobate minds will withstand God's children to their faces, even as the magicians withstood Moses (v. 8).

In the last days, there will be some people living very near to God; but the devil will have his workers, too, who will attribute signs and wonders to any power except the power of Christ. The Lamb of God, the Lion of the tribe of Judah, has never lost His power, and never will lose His power, and I would hate to say by my actions that I thought the devil had more power than God.

There is a wonderful difference between the power of God and any of those other powers. The Holy Spirit comes only in Christ; He only comes into the bodies of those who love God. When He takes possession of us, He takes us away into the sweetest experience this side of heaven, alone with God. He talks to us and reveals to us *"things to come"* (John 16:13).

It is wonderful! God puts us under the power, and God takes us out. No man can bestow this power upon another; it comes only through Jesus Christ. There are two kinds of power, and people who do not know the difference will stand up today and say wisdom is foolishness.

Many people today have an intellectual faith, a historical faith; they believe. Well, the devils believe and tremble. Belief is one thing; faith is another. *"The letter killeth, but the Spirit giveth life"* (2 Cor. 3:6). If the truth is hid, it is hidden to those who are lost.

We may have intellectual imaginations, go through a course of study, learning the doctrines of men; no one but the Holy Spirit can even give us knowledge of "the things of God." They seem foolishness to the natural man. Sometimes the Holy Spirit gives a spirit of laughter, and sometimes of weeping, and everyone in the place will be affected by the Spirit.

I have stood before thousands of people and could not speak, just weeping. When I was able to see, people were weeping everywhere; that is one way the Holy Spirit works. I have stood an hour with my hand raised, held by the mighty power of God. When I came to myself and saw the people, their faces were shining.

The God I worship "moves in mysterious ways, His wonders to perform." Jesus said, *"Behold, I and the children whom the* LORD *hath given me are for signs and for wonders in Israel"* (Isa. 8:18.) We believe in *"signs and wonders,"* not from below but from above. We are a people to be wondered at; we are for a sign among the people.

The heaven of heavens cannot contain God, yet He tabernacles with men; He comes and dwells in us. His gifts are demonstrated through us, that people may know God dwells in Zion. We have a bodyguard of angels. The angels of the Lord encamp around those who love God. "Our citizenship is in heaven," and we are on the way.

The Holy Spirit works in many ways. People saw the fire on the disciples' heads at Pentecost; they staggered like drunken men; then the Holy Spirit took possession of their tongues. God Almighty spoke through one hundred and twenty of His children, and they were telling of His wonderful works. They did not know what they were saying, but every man heard them speak in his own tongue wherein he was born.

I am glad God does the same thing today. People who are not saved hate the power of God; the cold, dead formalists cannot understand the power of God; it is foolishness to them; they think people are excited, hypnotized, have lost their mind.

May God have mercy upon us if we do not know God's power from hypnotic power or devil power! If any man speak against the Holy Spirit, it shall never be forgiven him; to attribute the work of the Holy Spirit to the devil or to any unclean spirit cannot be forgiven; that is the unpardonable sin.

Some people are calling the Holy Spirit the devil, and they had better beware. There are different kinds of spirits and different kinds of power; and the natural man cannot understand the work of the Holy Spirit—shining faces, singing, shouting as one, *"to make one sound"* (2 Chr. 5:13); sometimes staggering and falling, drunken, but not with wine (Acts 2:15); sometimes speaking with *"other tongues"* (v. 4).

Praise God, some of the redeemed are getting so filled with the Holy Spirit that He is singing through them songs that none but the redeemed can sing. *"There are diversities of gifts, but the same Spirit"* (1 Cor. 12:4). Paul told us that the Spirit will work in someone in one way, and in another in another way; you know it is the same Spirit, and you do not get jealous because the other is blessed; no matter how the Spirit works, every member of the body profits.

People examine these things. They see us lift up holy hands to God, and they don't like it. They are so dead, they could not get their hands up. Paul said, *"I will therefore that men pray every where, lifting up holy hands"* (1 Tim. 2:8). The psalmist wrote, *"O clap your hands, all ye people; shout unto God with the voice of triumph."* (Ps. 47:1).

People go to the theater and clap their hands, but when we get our grave clothes off and begin to clap our hands, they think it is an awful thing. David danced with all his might before the ark (2 Sam. 6:14), and sometimes the Spirit of God gets into our feet and makes them *"like hinds' feet"* (Ps. 18:33).

David said, *"By my God have I leaped over a wall"* (2 Sam. 22:30). How much more so in these last days, when we are getting ready for a flight in the air! We must get a good supply of this power; the same power that took Jesus up will take us up one day.

We want more of it, don't we? More of this mighty power. No matter what people say—foolishness, hypnotism, and every other thing—that doesn't make it so. The Spirit will take us out into the deep things, even *"the deep things of God."*

Many things recorded in the Old Testament are types of the work of the Spirit in the New. Many of the movements of God through His children seemed foolishness, and the messages He gave His prophets to carry, humanly speaking, seemed very foolish.

He gave Noah a plan of the ark; only one window, only one door. He built it according to God's plan, not heeding the jeers of the people, who thought he was losing his mind. He was a laughingstock for everybody, but he went on with the building and proved the wisdom of God in the end.

He built the ark, and God provided the water, more water than they wanted, too much water for them. What happened? God took those who believed Him into the ark and shut the door. The water rose, and the ark went above the tree-tops—as we are going someday. God is building the ark now, and the works of the Holy Spirit are foolishness to the people who are fighting them.

The ark sailed away, and the world went down, all except Noah and his family. Not many are going into the ark God is building; people are crying, "Foolishness." One time there was a great battle; the enemy had gathered like grasshoppers. God knew there were a lot of cowards among His people, and He tested them until only three hundred were left to meet the enemy.

God can work by the few as well as the many. He told Gideon what to do: Gideon "*divided the three hundred men into three companies, and he put a trumpet in every man's hand, with empty pitchers, and lamps within the pitchers*" (Judg. 7:16). Then he said, "When I give the signal, blow the trumpets on every side of the camp, and say, '*The sword of the Lord and of Gideon*'" (Judg. 7:18).

As they obeyed their leader, something happened—God always has a leader. At the signal, they blew the trumpets, broke the pitchers, revealing the lamps; and they shouted, "*The sword of the Lord and of Gideon.*"

At the shout and the light, the enemy was frightened to death and started to run; but God sent confusion among them. That little band of three hundred "cranks" put the whole host of the enemy to flight. What they did seemed foolish, didn't it? But what was the outcome? The whole army of the enemy was conquered.

God used a vision—He does sometimes. He let Gideon go down to the enemy's camp, and He heard a man tell his fellows a vision or dream about how a "*cake of barley bread tumbled into the host of Midian, and came into a tent, and smote it that it fell, and overturned it, that the tent lay alone*" (v. 13).

The other interpreted it, "*This is nothing else save the sword of Gideon,…into his hand hath God delivered Midian, and all the host*" (v. 14). So Gideon believed and took courage.

Children of God, you who think you are something—you are nothing. When you realize you are nothing, God fights for you. How foolish did this method of fighting the Midianites seem! Israel might have said, "If we break the pitchers, the lamps will show the enemy where we are, and they will shoot us." When God tells you to go forward, obey Him. He takes care of His own.

Truly, God moves in a mysterious way. Remember the fall of Jericho. It had great walls around it, and all the people were shut in. God said to Joshua that he and his men of war should march around the city once a day for six days, seven priests bearing before the ark seven trumpets of rams' horns; on the seventh day they were to march around the city seven times, the priests blowing with the trumpets; and when they made a long blast, the people were to shout, and the walls should fall down. (See Joshua 6.)

It took faith to do all that marching without any sign of victory, to shout; anyone can shout after the walls fall. Humanly speaking, how foolish this all was, don't you see? No preparation for war, only marching and blowing rams' horns. But that was God's way, and they were silly enough to obey God! What was the result? The walls went down.

So we could go all through the Word of God; so many things that seem so silly, things people would laugh at, but it was God's way, and His servants were willing to obey Him. The result showed His wonderful wisdom and brought victory through a visible display of His power.

When these visible signs came, they put a fear of God upon the people. So it is with the works of the Holy Spirit. The ways of God are foolishness to the natural man, and the works of the Spirit are foolishness to the natural man, but what is the outcome?

Paul said, *"If any man among you seemeth to be wise in this world, let him become a fool that he may be wise"* (1 Cor. 3:18). Later he said, *"I will come to visions and revelations of the Lord"* (2 Cor. 12:1). He said he was carried away to the third heaven—whether in the body or out of the body, he could not tell (v. 2)—he could not tell whether his whole body went or not; he was so light he could not tell whether he had left his body here or not.

Paul declared, *"God knoweth"* (vv. 2, 3), and he heard unutterable things. Another time, Paul was praying in the temple and fell under the power of God; he fell into a trance; he appeared to be unconscious to the world, but he was never so wide awake to God in his life (Acts 22:17–18).

It is then the Spirit of God lets us down into the deep things, even the deep things of God. Peter fell into a trance upon the housetop and God spoke to him three times (Acts 10). Paul and Silas started out to visit converts. Paul had a vision; he saw a man of Macedonia holding out his hands and saying, *"Come over...and help us"* (Acts 16:9). He knew it was the call of God, so they changed their course and went to this place, altogether different from their plans.

When they began to preach and were arrested, they might have thought they had been mistaken, but Paul knew God, and he never doubted it was God who had called him. They might have said, "If we had not come here we would have had many people to preach to; now we have come to this strange place, have been put in prison, with our feet fast in the stocks." The devil put them in there, but God permitted it, and God delivered them. (See Acts 16.)

There are many wonderful things all about us in these last days, things the natural man cannot understand, demonstrations of God's power. There are other powers, too, and many do not know the difference. God's power is the greatest and is the only power that will bring peace to your soul.

God wants you to be pure and holy, filled with the Holy Spirit, but the devil is right here, too; if you do not know the difference, you will be listening to him. He comes sometimes as an angel of light (2 Cor. 11:14). One word in the Garden of Eden upset the world; the little word "not."

When God talks to you, the message agrees with the written Word; the Holy Spirit never says anything that doesn't correspond with the Word. A message that comes from heaven must correspond with the Word; if otherwise, do not accept it.

The things of the Spirit that seem foolishness to the world antagonize the devil, and he sometimes does things that look very similar; but to the person who understands, there is a wonderful difference. I have been carried away in the Spirit many, many times.

Once I was under the power of God for seven hours. I have been examined at such a time by medical doctors and found to be in a normal condition. Many I know of have been honest enough to say the power was not hypnotic, even when they could not understand it.

One of the greatest hypnotists in the world came to our meeting in St. Louis; he had been there two or three days before I knew anything about it. He was surprised to see a man lying there whom hundreds of hypnotists had tried to get under their power; he himself had tried it. He went to him and tried to bring him out, but could not. After a while, the hypnotist came to me to have an interview with me. He said he was going to call his friends together and tell them he had found something he could not understand.

He said, "If there is a God, I believe this is His power." He could not put anyone under that power or bring anyone out. When the doctors examined me when I was lying under the power, they said my pulse was regular, my blood flowing naturally, my heart in a natural condition.

I am told that when a person is hypnotized, the blood does not flow naturally; the person is unconscious and simply does what he is told; someone has to put him in that state and brings him out again.

God does lay His people down under His power, and then He talks to them. I have known people to be under the power of God for a whole week. May He seal these truths to our hearts!

I know nothing about hypnotic power; I never saw a person hypnotized. But I do know something of the power of God, of the power of the Holy Spirit. It is God himself who sends this power. We can press the button, but God sends the power.

Talk about excitement! This power is the best thing in the world to settle the nerves. These people go down praising God while they are there, and when they are up, they are still giving God praise.

"Let everything that hath breath praise the Lord" (Ps. 150:6). People ask why we tell them to praise the Lord. If you do not feel it at first, praise as a "sacrifice," and after a while the praise will come of itself from a soul filled with joy. Hallelujah!

If you will search your Bible, you will find the things I have told you are true. My words do not amount to anything unless they are backed up by God's Word. The Lord gave me this message tonight, and I have given it to you.

When the power of the Spirit has been so maligned, it is time for you to take a stand for the truth. When a ship is in danger, the sailors come to the front if they are not cowards. Let us come to the front, not run away.

I stand here in defense of the Gospel. If we are faithful, all things must work together for God's glory. Praise His name.

65

THE FIRE AND GLORY OF GOD
FILLING THE TEMPLE

A Symbol of the Outpouring of the Holy Spirit on the Day of Pentecost Sermon by Mrs. M. B. Woodworth-Etter (*Abbreviated*)

> *It came to pass when the priests were come out of the holy place....It came to pass, as the trumpeters and singers were as one, to make one sound to be heard in praising and thanking the LORD; and when they lifted up their voice with the trumpets and cymbals and instruments of music, and praised the LORD, saying, For He is good; for His mercy endureth for ever: then the house was filled with a cloud, even the house of the LORD; so that the priests could not stand to minister by reason of the cloud; for the glory of the LORD had filled the house of God.* (2 Chronicles 5:11, 12–14)

I want you to see how they came; one hundred and twenty of them with different instruments, yet all making the same sound; the Levites arrayed in white linen, emblematic of purity.

There were one hundred and twenty priests blowing trumpets; there were singers and instruments of music, but they were as one, to make one sound.

The one hundred and twenty priests who were supposed to minister stood like statues, and the Holy Spirit took over the meeting. The entire building was filled with the glory of God.

All this demonstration, the house filled with the glory of God, was brought about by the one hundred and twenty priests blowing the trumpets; the sounding of the different instruments was mingled with the voice of the great company of singers, the whole object being to glorify God, and all making one sound.

God wants perfect harmony—no one criticizing, no one finding fault, but all sounding forth His praise—and in the white robes of purity. If we go out to meet God clothed in white, washed in the blood of the Lamb; if we go out, all making the same sound; if we go out to glorify God, God will honor all the noise.

It is not excitement. God comes down to acknowledge the praise. They pressed the button, and the power of God came down. That same power will either save or destroy us some day. The house was filled with the power and glory of the Lord.

There was no preaching then, but singing, shouting, praising the Lord, and all that praise glorified God. The house was filled with His glory. The people were still standing, Solomon ready to dedicate the temple. The temple represents the church, but it also represents our bodies: *"Know ye not that your body is the temple of the Holy Ghost, which is in you?"* (1 Cor.. 6:19).

The first two or three verses of the seventh chapter are like Pentecost, represent Pentecost. *"When Solomon had made an end of praying"* (2 Chr. 7:1). So many people never look to God to answer; they would be frightened if He did. Solomon stretched out His hands and prayed to God (1 Kings 8:54), and God heard him.

"When Solomon had made an end of praying," something happened. God will come forth if you are not afraid of the power, if you are ready to stand for God with all there is of you. As Pentecostal people we should always be "prayed up," so we can get hold of God quickly and be sure it is for the glory of God.

"The fire came down from heaven and consumed the burnt offering and the sacrifices; and the glory of the LORD filled the house" (v. 1). Some people talk as if God never had any glory, as though the glory of God was never seen at any time.

Paul wrote, "*If the ministration of death, written and engraved in stones, was glorious,....shall not the ministration of the Spirit be rather* [more] *glorious?*" (2 Cor. 3:7–8).

The glory under the law did not last; but the Holy Spirit came at Pentecost to stay, and the manifestations under the ministry of the Holy Spirit are to be with much greater glory, to "*exceed in glory*" (v. 9). The power under the law was only a shadow of what we ought to have under grace. This is the ministry of life, not death.

The house was filled with the glory of the Lord; they saw and felt it; it was not a shadow. I am glad the glory of God has been seen here a number of times. Many times in our ministry the glory of God has been seen over us. God is here. What you see and hear, "*this is that*" (Acts 2:16). This is the promise of the Father; this is the Holy Spirit.

The priests could not enter into the house; they could not get in at all, because the glory of the Lord had filled the Lord's house. "*When the children of Israel saw how the fire came down, and the glory of the* LORD *upon the house, they bowed themselves with their faces to the ground upon the pavement, and worshipped and praised the* LORD, *saying, For he is good, for his mercy endureth forever*" (2 Chr. 7:3).

Everything connected with this represents this glorious age. Paul said that God can reveal His doctrine, which was hidden from all ages. Those who crucified the Lord did not know about the mystical body of Christ. This divine life in us they did not know, or they would not have crucified Him. (See 1 Corinthians 2:7–8.)

It could be revealed only when the Holy Spirit came down from God to make men understand the new covenant. The glory that belongs to the ministration of death did not come to stay. The glory came from the ark of the covenant, containing the tables of stone on which the law was written, the Ten Commandments.

There were the cherubim, two angels, facing each other, with wings outspread over the ark and mercy seat, where God dwells in His temple. In His tabernacle nothing is supposed to be in the heart but God's Word, the new and everlasting covenant, written on the fleshy tables of the heart, not on stone, but with the finger of God Almighty.

If, when the people obeyed, the glory of God came down and the people fell prostrate, how much glory ought there to be today? There was just one tabernacle and two tables of stone. Today your body is the temple of the living God. Our bodies are the temple of the Holy Spirit—and God with His own finger writes His Word in our hearts.

The ancient temple in all its glory represents each one of our bodies. If we are filled with the Holy Spirit as we ought to be, the body will be flooded with rivers of water flowing out to others, and it will be on fire for God.

The glory of the Lord was seen over the ark; inside the tabernacle the lamp was always burning, being kept supplied with oil; it never went out. In the temple of the body, God puts His love in our hearts, and He wants us to keep the light always burning, never to let it go out.

By keeping all obstructions out of the channel of faith, we get a supply of oil continually; and the light will shine through the tabernacle always. If the oracle written on stone was glorious, how much more glorious under grace! The Holy Spirit will abide with you always.

Jesus said if we keep His commandments, the Father and He would both take up their abode with us (John 14:23). They dwell with us, and we are flooded with the Holy Spirit, people to be wondered at. *"I and the children God hath given me"* (Heb. 2:13). There should be perfect fellowship and harmony; we should all make one sound. The glory came down at Solomon's prayer. At a glimpse of that glory, they lost their strength, and the whole multitude went down.

When we are praying for people to get saved or healed, some shout, some praise, some pray, but all are making the same sound. We put on the blood by faith and get a glimpse of His glory. Is it any wonder people lose their strength and fall prostrate under the new life that comes to them?

Is it strange we are people to be wondered at? You have seen all this here: singing, playing, making the same sound. Is it any wonder these people who come here, especially to get under the blood as never before, when they get a glimpse of Jesus, is it any wonder they fall prostrate?

You must prove God has changed, has taken His power away, before you condemn us. *"For the gifts and calling of God are without repentance"* (Rom. 11:29). He never changes; He is the same yesterday, today, and forever.

No one has any right to condemn us, to say the people are hypnotized, crazy, have lost their minds, or that I have put a spell on them. Great God! Awaken the people before the thunders of judgment shall arouse them! You must throw the

Bible away, or you must prove the gifts and callings have been taken from the church before you reject us.

We are going the Bible route, and you have no business to teach anything else; you must stick to the Word of God. We do not hold anything up but the Word of God. It is good enough for me. "*I am not ashamed of the gospel of Christ*" (Rom. 1:16), nor of His power.

What a wonderful people we are in our privileges! Today everyone may be God's priest. If we abide in Him and His words abide in us, we may ask what we will, and it shall be done (John 15:7). We indeed have wonderful privileges. The power of the Lord shines forth a hundred times greater than under the law; the power then was typical of Pentecost.

Get your Bibles, and search out these things; you are getting the light of God, and He expects you to walk in the light, even if you get it from a little weak woman. In His name we tell you these things are true. What do you care for man's opinion when you stand before God? Dried up opinions and traditions of men all go to destruction, but it is the living Word that we are preaching to you.

When John the Baptist was in prison, he began to doubt a little whether Jesus was the Christ, and he sent his disciples to ask, "*Art thou he that should come?*" (Matt. 11:3). Jesus did not say, "I belong to the church or I belong to a college." He said, "Go and tell John the things you have heard and seen here: the lame walk, the blind see, diseases are healed, the dead are raised, and the poor have the Gospel preached to them. Blessed is he, whoever shall not be offended in me" (vv. 4–6). Men get mad at the signs of the Holy Spirit, jealous, spitting out hatred, trying to tear down God's work.

If John did not believe in Christ through the signs, no eloquence would be of value. If he did not believe what the witnesses told him, he would not believe anything—neither will you! There is a devil's counterfeit, and there is a genuine, as sure as you live.

If you only look on, it will seem foolishness to you as we praise God, and as people get filled with the Holy Spirit and get gifts; but it is Jesus first, last, and all the time. We hold up Jesus and praise His name. We see bright, happy faces; we see pain go out of bodies, and we go home rejoicing, feeling we have heaven here below.

Resist the devil in the name of the Lord. Sometimes when I am standing up preaching, the devil would make me drop dead, if I would listen to him. I resist in the name of the Lord, and he has to go. We have such a wonderful Savior!

You shall lay hands on the sick, it does not say where. He commissioned me, and I obey God rather than man. Neither the deadly serpent nor any poison shall harm you. You will cast out devils; I believe every bit of it, and I have seen it all. Hallelujah!

I got my commission from the Lord, and I did not go until He called me, nor until I was baptized and qualified; I get my message from heaven. I do not know what I am going to talk about; but God knows everyone here and just what everyone needs, and He will give you something.

The power Jesus promised His disciples, when He told them to tarry at Jerusalem (Luke 24:49), was to change their lives and qualify them to transact the business of heaven. After they were baptized with the Holy Spirit, they would be true to their Master and be witnesses for Him.

They went down from that mountain praising the Lord. They were filled with a great joy as they went back to Jerusalem to await the fulfillment of the promise. They had confidence in God; He said so, and they began to praise.

Are you full of joy, having not a doubt about Jesus being your Lord and Savior? You want power to do the work of God; you want to be clothed with power. God says He will baptize with fire, bestowing wisdom, knowledge, and gifts. He will make you to understand the deep things of God; and as you teach them and live them, God will be with you.

You must believe you are going to get this blessing. "They were all with one accord" (Acts 2:1). God help us to get to that place. God wants us of one accord, hearts running together like drops of water.

A little company like that could shake a city in a day. We are not in one accord when one is pulling one way and one another; when we hear "maybe this," and "maybe that." Do you suppose God will bless you in that?

You cannot understand the first principles. Once you have the newborn joy in your heart, when you see it in someone else, you know it is of God. Be of one mind; no matter how much you have to praise God for, we always want more.

At Pentecost, suddenly they heard a sound like a mighty, rushing wind. This Holy Spirit we are holding up is a mighty power; He came from heaven like a windstorm, as floods of water filling the vessels, and as fire upon the heads of one hundred and twenty people. As it were, cloven tongues of fire sat upon their heads; then the Holy Spirit went in and took possession of the temple, took full possession of the machinery, wound it up, and set it running for God. They staggered like drunken people and fell. This mighty power took possession of their tongues and spoke through them in other languages.

It was said by the prophet: *"With stammering lips and another tongue will he speak to this people"* (Isa. 28:11). Think of that! God doing such a mighty thing! But some do not want to believe. That is the way the Holy Spirit came, and comes today; yet people say it is some other power.

They did not lose their minds; they had just found them! They got the spirit of love and a sound mind. We never have a sound mind until we get the mind of Christ. People who cannot understand it say these things are foolishness. We are told the wisdom of this world is foolishness with God. This is the power of God and the wisdom of God, not the work of the devil; people saying so doesn't make it so.

God had complete control. He came in and took possession. The Holy Spirit is in the world today. You must prove He has been taken away, and also the gifts and callings, before you have a right to lay hands on God's people.

The things called foolishness today are the power of God unto salvation. Step out in the deep with God. Paul tells us the Lord ascended into heaven and sent down gifts *"for the perfecting of the saints, for the work of the ministry, for the edifying of the body of Christ"* (Eph. 4:12).

The ministry does not lack the gifts today. Saints, that is, Christians, are baptized with the Holy Spirit so that the whole body may be edified, no matter how much you have got. When God is working, every one of His children is edified. If God works through someone else, I am edified and encouraged, and I rejoice.

The working of the Holy Spirit is the visible sign of the presence of Jesus. They went from Jerusalem to preach the Gospel everywhere, and *"the hand of the Lord was with them"* (Acts 11:20). I love that word. He is in heaven? Yes, but He is with us also.

The Lord was with them, confirming the Word. How? With signs and wonders following. Amen. Wherever they went, they saw faces shine, someone healed, someone speak in tongues. This you see and hear; it is the Holy Spirit, and it is for the work of the ministry.

If I did not know Jesus was by my side and His loving arms around me, I could not stand here today. I would not have the strength if I did not know that

He dwells in this body. If I did not know by experience that these things are true, I could not stand here.

I have tested the truth; I know it is of God. How can we help talking of the things we have seen? I have seen things by the Spirit and in visions. I have seen Jesus, the heavens open, the marriage supper, hosts of angels, the glory of God. I have seen them, glory to God! I know what I am telling you. I know Jesus lives and is standing by my side, more truly than I know you are here. These things are truths!

I am not ashamed of the Gospel of Christ. Glory to God! When a weak woman comes here to tell you what strong men ought to have told you, what are you going to think about it? I say these things are true; and when people say they are foolishness and fanaticism, do they dare attempt to prove it by the Word? I dare them to do it.

When they can prove the Holy Spirit has been taken out of the world, away from God's people, I am ready to go to prison, but not before.

Open the Pearly Gates

We are marching upon the King's highway,
We'll shout and sing, and we'll watch and pray;
No time to idle, no time to wait,
But hasten on to the golden gate.

CHORUS

Open, open the pearly gates,
Open, open the pearly gates;
Open, open the pearly gates,
And let the redeemed pass in.

With joy and gladness upon each head,
We're marching up where the feast is spread;
For a royal banquet will there be giv'n
To all who enter the gates of heav'n.

No unclean thing shall go up thereon,
No lion there, oh no, not one;
But those arrayed in pure garments white,
With souls prepared for the mansions bright.

With our battles fought and our victories won,
Our warfare weapons all laid down,
We'll strike our golden harps and sing,
And crown our Christ as a conq'ring King.

66

DANCING IN THE SPIRIT

Dancing in the Spirit Always Means Victory
Sermon by Mrs. M. B. W. Etter

David danced with all his might before the Lord. The Word is full of dancing. Where dancing is mentioned in the Bible, it always signifies victory for the Lord's hosts. It was always done to glorify God. The Lord placed the spirit of power and love of the dance in the church. Wherever the Scripture speaks of dancing, it implies that they danced by inspiration and were moved by the Spirit, and the Lord was always pleased and smiled His approval. However, the devil stole it away and took advantage of it. In these last days, when God is pouring out His Spirit in great cloudbursts and tidal waves from the floodgates of heaven, and the great river of life is flooding our spirits and bodies, baptizing us with fire and resurrection life and divine energy, the Lord is doing His acts, His strange acts, in dancing in the Spirit and speaking in other tongues, and many other operations and gifts. The Holy Spirit is confirming the last message of the coming King with great signs and wonders and miracles. If you read carefully what the Scripture says about dancing, you will be surprised, and will see that singing, music, and dancing have a humble and holy place in the Lord's church. Read these verses: *"Let them praise his name in the dance: let them sing praises unto him with the timbrel and harp"* (Ps. 149:3); *"Praise him with the timbrel and the dance: praise him with stringed instruments and organs"* (Ps. 150:4); *"Then shall the virgin rejoice in the dance, both young men and old together"* (Jer. 31:13).

David Danced before the Lord

"David danced before the LORD with all his might" (2 Sam. 6:14). His wife did not like it; she scolded him and made light of him, said he was dancing before the maidens like a lewd fellow, and made out as if he was base and low. But David answered, "I was not dancing before men, but before the Lord" (2 Sam. 6:21), showing that he had lost sight of the world and what they thought or said, but was moved and controlled entirely by the Holy Spirit for the glory of God. All the great company was blessed but Michal, and she was stricken with barrenness until the day of her death (v. 23), because she sinned in making light of the power of God in the holy dance (just as some do today), and attributed it to the flesh or the devil. They always lose out, and many are in darkness until death.

Women Sing and Dance

The news of King David's great victory, how he had killed the giant Goliath and destroyed the great army of the Philistines, spread quickly over the land, and as David returned from the slaughter, *"the women came out of all the cities of Israel, singing and dancing, to meet king Saul, with tabrets, with joy, and with instruments of music"* (1 Sam. 18:6). Now notice, in all their cities the women went out in the streets and danced with their music; men are not mentioned there, just women, who danced unto the Lord, in honor of God and king Saul, prompted by the Spirit of God to praise Him in the dance. It took courage to honor the king in this way, but the Lord smiled His approval by having it written by holy men of old and sent down to us in His precious Word.

The lame beggar took Peter's hand, and he stood up, and leaped and praised God (Acts 3:7–8). Paul said to the cripple, "'*Stand upright on thy feet.' And he leaped and walked"* (Acts 14:10).

Moses' Sister Leads Women in Dance while Playing Instruments

"And Miriam the prophetess…took a timbrel in her hand; and all the women went out after her with timbrels and with dances. And Miriam answered them, Sing

ye to the LORD, for he hath triumphed gloriously; the horse and his rider hath he thrown into the sea" (Exod. 15:20–21). God has never done a greater miracle nor demonstrated His presence in so great a cloud of glory as at that time. While under the inspiration and light of His presence, their whole bodies and spirits going out in love, the whole multitude of women, Miriam the prophetess and leader, leading them forth to praise the Lord with dancing, shouting, and music, singing a new song just given by the Spirit that had never been sung, do you call that foolishness? No, they were praising the Lord in the dance and song as they were moving in and by the mighty power of God.

Moses Leads the Host. They Sing and Dance in the Spirit.

Moses also led the hosts in the same way, with music and dancing and a new song given for the occasion by the Spirit. So the Holy Spirit is falling on the saints of God today, and they are used the same way. Those who never danced one step are experts in the holy dance; those who do not know one note from another are expert musicians in playing many different instruments of music; and often the sound of the invisible instruments as heard from the platform, the sounds can be plainly heard all over the house. And I say in the fear and presence of God, the singing and demonstration puts the fear of God on the people and causes a holy hush to come over the people. The strange acts are coming more and more, showing that they are something new, that Jesus is coming soon, and the Lord is getting His bride ready to be translated and dance and play at the great marriage of the Lamb, which will soon take place, for the bride is making herself ready.

Elder Son Hears Music and Dancing

"Now his elder son was in the field; and as he came and drew nigh the house, he heard music and dancing. And he called one of the servants, and asked what these things meant" (Luke 15:25–26). The servants told him that his brother had come home, and his father had killed the fatted calf, because he has received him safe and sound. He was angry and would not go in, but the feast and rejoicing went on just the same. His father said that it was right that they should be merry and rejoice, for his brother who was dead and who was lost, had returned home safe and sound. (See Luke 15:25–32.) All will agree with me that this was an old fashioned Holy Spirit revival. The lost son is a sinner whom the Spirit brought out of darkness to light; the saints are filled with the Spirit.

Dancing in the Spirit of the Lord

I was very slow to accept the dancing in the Spirit, for fear it was in the flesh, but I soon saw it was the cloud of glory over the people that brought forth the dancing and playing invisible instruments. The sounds of sweet, heavenly music could often be heard. Several times I asked that those of the congregation who heard this music from the platform—where they knew there were no instruments to be seen—to be honest and raise their hands. Many hands went up from saints and sinners. The stillness of death went over the people when they heard the sounds of music accompanied with the heavenly choir. Often a message in tongues was given in one or more languages, and then the interpretation. As I saw the effect on the people by the Holy Spirit in convincing them that they were in the presence of God, I concluded that this is surely part of the Lord's strange work and His strange acts (Isa. 28:21). I saw as many as nine of the most noted ministers dancing at one time on the platform; they danced singly, with their eyes closed. Often some fell, slain by the mighty power of God. These things convinced me. I also saw men and women who have been crippled join in the dance with wonderful grace. One lady who had been on crutches for five years, who got healed in her seat, afterwards danced over the platform, singing heavenly music. The virgins, the young men, and the old men, all join in the dance together. Praise the Lord. *"Let us be glad and rejoice...for the marriage of the Lamb is come, and his wife hath made herself ready"* (Rev. 19:7). The Lord is quickening our mortal bodies for the translation.

67

THE OUTPOURING OF THE HOLY SPIRIT IN THE LAST DAYS

Sermon by Mrs. M. B. Woodworth-Etter

The Lord is in our midst. Be still and know the voice of God. "*The LORD is in his holy temple: let all the earth keep silence before him*" (Hab. 2:20). Let us try to realize His wonderful presence. We must all meet Him sooner or later, as individuals; it is a good thing to get acquainted with Him now.

This Scripture applies to us today:

It shall come to pass in the last days, saith God, I will pour out of My Spirit upon all flesh, and your sons and your daughters shall prophesy, and your young men shall see visions, and your old men shall dream dreams: and on my servants and on my handmaidens I will pour out in those days of my Spirit, and they shall prophesy: and I will show wonders in heaven above, and signs in the earth beneath; blood, and fire, and vapor of smoke: the sun shall be turned into darkness, and the moon into blood, before that great and notable day of the Lord come. (Acts 2:17–20)

This is a wonderful Scripture, and many do not understand it. There is a certain time spoken of here, when certain great and wonderful things are to take place, and people will know that prophecy is being fulfilled. *"It shall come to pass in the last days,…I will pour out My Spirit,"* and there will be signs in the heavens and the earth—signs of Jesus' coming. The Holy Spirit will be poured out before the *"notable day of the Lord"* comes.

This prophecy was first spoken eight hundred years before Jesus came to earth. Peter, standing up on the Day of Pentecost, recited the prophecy and confirmed it. Under the inspiration of the Holy Spirit, on fire with the Holy Spirit from head to foot, speaking with a tongue of fire, he said these things would come to pass in the last days.

We believe and know by the Word of God and by the signs, that we are now living in the last days—the very times Peter spoke about—which we were to know by the mighty things taking place. We are the people, and this is the time, just before the *"notable day of the Lord"* bursts upon the world. We believe we are the people, yes, we know it; we have a right to our belief, for it is based upon the Word of God, and no man or woman has any right to denounce our teaching or to injure us in any way until it can be proved by the Word of God that the things we teach are not true.

You should give us a hearing; then take the same Word of God and prove by it that the things we teach are not true—if you can. You must first prove that the Holy Spirit, working in all His mighty miraculous power, has been done away with, before you have any right to denounce us as frauds and hypocrites on account of these things, which we say come from God.

Whenever anyone, minister or lawyer, can take the platform and prove by the Word of God that the Holy Spirit and His mighty, miraculous power have been taken away from the church, we are willing to go to prison—but not before. It cannot be done. God never recalls His gifts; God never changes. My Bible says, *"Jesus Christ the same yesterday, and to day, and for ever"* (Heb. 13:8). There are many ways besides the working of the Holy Spirit by which we know we are in the last days.

Joel, in speaking of the last days, told us many things we cannot go into today, but which show us that we are in this time. Nahum said that when this time comes, it will be the *"day of his preparation"* (Nah. 2:3), preparing men so that they may be taken out of the world first, before the Tribulation comes.

Before the flood, Noah was commanded to build an ark. He was just five years building the ark—though many believe it was much longer than that—and the time he was building it was the preparation time in those days. Noah, at God's command, was preparing a place for himself and family, where they should be in safety, above the storm that was coming, above the waves and billows. At the same time the old world was getting a warning, Noah was building the ark.

Jesus compared Noah's day of preparation to this time in these last days. It is a short period and has been going on for some time. It was prophesied that there will be great signs in the earth—blood, fire, and smoke; earthquakes, great destruction—all these things have been coming upon the earth in the last few years. God has a time for everything. Daniel said that in *"the time of the end, many shall run to and fro, and knowledge shall be increased"* (Dan. 12:4). Nahum wrote, *"The chariots shall rage in the streets,…they shall seem like torches, they shall run like the lightnings"* (Nah. 2:4). (See the sermon on "The Second Coming of Christ," Chapter 36.)

Jesus sent the Holy Spirit with mighty signs and wonders. He took possession of men, and they staggered like drunken men; they were drunk, but not with wine. They spoke with *"stammering lips and another tongue"* (Isa. 28:11). These things happened when Pentecost first came to set up the church in power; that was the early rain.

In the last days, the time of preparation, God will cause to come again the early rain as at Pentecost, and He will also give the latter rain abundantly in the same month (Joel 2:23). What do you think of that? The early disciples went by the death route. It will take a double portion of the Spirit to fill our bodies, to make us sound in spirit, soul, and body. When Jesus comes like a flash of lightning, He shall change these bodies of ours in a moment, and they shall be made like His glorious body (Phil. 3:20).

"I show you a mystery…we shall all be changed" (1 Cor. 15:51), and shall rise to meet the Lord in the air. When are these things to be? At the end of the day of preparation, just before the Tribulation bursts upon the world. We are to watch for the signs and not forsake the assembling of ourselves together, and so much the more as we see the Day approaching (Heb. 10:25)! Glory to God! The Jews understood something of this. They say one to another, "We have been wounded;

we have gone through many troubles; let us turn to the Lord: '*After two days will he revive us; in the third day he will raise us up*'" (Hos. 6:2). The Holy Spirit was first poured out at Pentecost.

We are now down at the end of the second thousand years since Christ set up His kingdom. What about the Jews? The Jews today have great liberty in Palestine, so much so that they are going back by thousands and building up the waste places (Isa. 58:12). Modern improvements are there today, and they are hoping for something, but they do not know what. After the Tribulation the Jews will return to the Lord.

"*In the last days,…I will pour out of my Spirit*" (Acts 2:17), not sprinkle a few drops, but pour out—a cloudburst—on all flesh! Just at the end; it will continue until the saints are taken away; then the Tribulation will burst upon the earth. The signs will be for some, not everybody: "*Your sons and your daughters shall prophesy*" (Acts 2:17). It is very plain that everyone may understand. There is to be a wonderful ministry in the last days. Paul said male and female are one in Christ (Gal. 3:28); both shall prophesy in the last days. That is the effect of the outpouring of the Holy Spirit. Other signs of the last days are: devils shall be cast out; hands shall be laid on the sick and they shall recover; many shall speak with new tongues; if anyone drinks poison accidentally, it shall not hurt him; serpents shall not be able to hurt (Mark 16:17–18).

See the power given man today; he has even chained the lightning. It is the day for preparation. Men run to and fro and fly over the land. Hurry up! The ark will soon be finished, and then God will say, "Come up." The ark went up above the waters; the world went down. God is preparing His spiritual ark today; the body of Christ will soon be complete; and when it is complete, it will sail above the treetops to meet our Lord and King in the air. We are in the day of preparation of the King of Glory, and His bride is making herself ready; rejoice and be glad, for the marriage of the Lamb is at hand (Rev. 19:7). The bride must be arrayed in white linen, the robe of righteousness, clothed in the power of the mighty God through His outpoured Spirit.

She is getting her garments ready to meet the Bridegroom. I praise the Lord I am living in this day. The bride will be caught up just before the Tribulation bursts upon this sin-cursed earth. The bride must be very beautiful. She is represented as a queen dressed in a robe of finest needlework. What is that fine wedding dress, the garments the bride will wear when she meets the Lord in the air? She will shine with the gifts and jewels of the Holy Spirit. We have this treasure in earthen vessels; but *"they that be wise shall shine as the brightness of the firmament"* (Dan. 12:3), and the wise shall know when these things are coming, when the ark is about ready to go up. The Lord will not keep any secrets from them. As there is perfect confidence between bride and Bridegroom, so Jesus will reveal secrets to His bride. He will show us the deep things of God, and we will know when the end is drawing near. You must make your own wedding garments; you cannot hire them made. The time is coming; people do not usually begin to make wedding garments until the wedding day is near. A bride is very happy, is willing to forsake her father's house, her friends, everything, and go with her bridegroom, even to a foreign country. She loves those she leaves, but he is dearer to her than anything else. We must be willing to leave anything and everything to go with Jesus. The bride will be taken out from among men, and men and women will be left. (See Matthew 24:39–42.) You may say, "I do not believe it." I believe it!

Do you suppose I would leave home, friends, my only child that I have, to spend my life for others, if I did not know these things were so? God has revealed these things by His Word and by signs, and I know they are true. God is almighty and is putting His seal upon this truth every day. He is putting the seal of the Holy Spirit upon people every day. The Holy Spirit is a witness to you, by mighty signs and wonders, that we are preaching the Word of God. I call God to witness that the Holy Spirit is putting His seal upon the work here. There are signs here every day. What are you going to do about it? If you believe the Bible, you must accept it. We have the eternal Word to stand on, and greater is He that is with us than all in the world that can be against us (1 John 4:4).

After Pentecost, they went out and preached the Holy Spirit sent by the ascended Jesus; and He confirmed the Word with signs following. I say before God, He is confirming the Word here every day; and these miracles are put down in heaven's record. Jesus Christ is the Healer and the Baptizer. John the Baptist said, *"He that cometh after me is mightier than I....He shall baptize you with the Holy Ghost, and with fire"* (Matt. 3:11), and I praise God that some of the fire has struck this place. You can make flowery speeches, and the devil laughs, but this work stirs the devil. It is *"by my Spirit,"* says the Lord (Zec. 4:6).

Paul said his *"preaching was not with enticing words of man's wisdom, but in demonstration of the Spirit and of power"* (1 Cor. 2:4). That shakes the world; and it is just the same today. You say, I do not like this power; well, the devil does not like it either. I have been out in the work thirty-five years, and people fell under the power by the thousands before I preached healing. There were mighty out-pourings of the Spirit that made the devil howl. It shows how little we know of the real fullness of the Gospel when we take the letter of the law (2 Cor. 3:6); it is like skimmed milk. No man can understand the deep things of God except by the Spirit (1 Cor. 2:10).

Paul had much knowledge, but he said that the wisdom of this world was foolishness in the sight of God (1 Cor. 3:19). True wisdom comes from heaven. The Word must be preached in simplicity (2 Cor. 1:12; 11:3). Jesus had the elo-quence of high heaven at His command, yet He used language that the most uneducated could understand.

Preach in a simple way, and demonstrate; the seal is put upon the Word by the Holy Spirit. Many say that when we lay hands upon the people, they get mesmerized. I am sorry they do not know more of the power of God. There was a great revival at Samaria (see Acts 8:14–24); the people were baptized, but none of them had been baptized with the Holy Spirit. Peter and John went to Samaria and laid their hands on them, and they received the Holy Spirit. He was imparted to them in some way through the laying on of the apostles' hands. Simon the sorcerer recognized the power was different from sorcery, and he wanted it; he offered them money to give him this power that whomsoever he laid hands on, they might receive the Holy Spirit.

The apostles were horrified. They said, "*Thy money perish with thee, because thou hast thought that the gift of God may be purchased with money*" (v. 20). The Holy Spirit and His power are gifts of God; you cannot buy them. Many people today do not understand any more than Simon did. The apostles told him to repent or he would be lost: "*Thou art in the gall of bitterness*" (v. 23). May God open the eyes of the people!

By the laying on of the apostles' hands, something happened; the Holy Spirit fell on those people, and they had great blessing. There were great demonstra-tions in those days when the Holy Spirit fell on the people. The thought is that when hands were laid on, something happened; they spoke in other languages, their mouths were filled with laughter, and sometimes they fell like dead men.

You must prove that God has taken this power away before you judge us harshly. Peter said the things they saw on the Day of Pentecost were the things the prophets said would come. You ask why the people go down? What is our little strength under the power of God? Whenever people get a glimpse of God's glory, they lose their strength and fall. Paul said that in his vision, he did not know whether he was in the body or out of the body (2 Cor. 12:3). John the Revelator, when he saw the glory of God, he fell as though dead (Rev. 1:17). In Daniel's vision, he fell upon his face and was stunned with his face to the ground (Dan. 8:17–18); then a hand touched him and set him upon his knees and hands—you have never seen anything like that—then he was taken up, strengthened, and saw a great vision. The men that were with Daniel fled, so they did not see the vision; but Daniel fled not, and he saw it, but he fell prostrate. Just a little manifestation of God's power, and we lose our strength and go down.

Some of you do not understand the working of the Spirit; you are not near enough to God to know it is the work of the Spirit. Peter was on the housetop praying; and he lost his strength and went down; a voice from heaven called him three times. Sometimes God teaches us more in ten minutes when we are lost to this world than we would otherwise learn in months. Paul, as he journeyed to Damascus while persecuting the Christians, was struck to the earth when a light shone from heaven and those who were with him also fell to the earth. Paul said the light was above the brightness of the sun; yet it was at midday when the sun was at its strength. All those men fell from their horses and rolled in the dust when the glory of God passed by. Paul was struck blind and was blind three days. (See Acts 22:4–9; 26:13–14.)

When Jesus went to the grave, He went down a corpse, but when He arose from the dead, the guards were stricken down at the manifestation of God's power and glory (Matt. 28:4). You must prove God no longer manifests His power and glory before you condemn us. Remember the first martyr, Stephen; he was a man full of faith, wisdom, and power, full of the Holy Spirit. The wise men tried to confound him but could not do it; then they were jealous and wanted to get rid of him. They hired men of the baser sort—that is the kind for that work—who lied about this mighty servant of God. (See Acts 6:9–7:60.)

They arrested him, and there he was before the great assembly. He did not try to defend himself, but he took the opportunity offered to preach to them about Jesus. He was filled with the Holy Spirit; his face was as the face of an angel, and those who swore his life away saw it. He did not look like a liar and a hypocrite. He was a servant of Almighty God.

You can see that light today sometimes in the faces of God's children. Stephen looked up into heaven, and saw the glory of God; he saw Jesus who had risen from the dead, standing at the right hand of God, and he told the people. Oh, Lord, open the eyes of these people, and let them see the angels of the Lord encamped around about us and Jesus standing in the midst! When Stephen told what he saw, they gnashed their teeth; they did not intend to repent; they dragged him out and stoned him to death; but the Lord received him and permitted it. God promises His people shall be protected, and it is no sign that He forsakes them because trouble comes. Stephen's enemies did not like it because God received him, nor did they like to see his face shine with the glory of God. His body was lying a bruised mass, but he rose to meet the Lord. He had a glorious vision. Do you believe he saw the throne and Jesus standing there? People talk about these things as though they were fables.

God says before Jesus comes, these same signs and wonders shall come to pass: the sick will be healed, devils cast out, people will speak with tongues—just before He comes. I am so glad for these days. When Jesus came before, He rebuked the Jewish leaders. He told them they could discern the face of the sky, but not the signs of the times (Matt. 16:3) that pointed to His coming. "Why weren't you looking for Me?" How much more will He upbraid people when He returns? "Why didn't you see the signs? Why didn't you listen to My messengers? Why didn't you look at the Word and see whether they were telling the truth or if they were impostors?" Excuses won't do when we stand before Jesus. The light has come. Let us arise and shine and give God the glory!

Nothing but the mighty Holy Spirit will ever take you up in the clouds; He will quicken these mortal bodies, and they will be changed. We won't have wings, but our hands and feet will be made light. Our feet will be like "hinds' feet," as we run, skip, and almost fly. We will know the power of resurrection life. We will be so filled with the Holy Spirit that our bodies will be made light.

Sometimes my body is made so light that I feel as if I can hardly stay. My feet are on the earth, but my hands seem on the throne. Christ arose from the dead, and He is the Resurrection and the Life. People want to get the blood of Jesus over them, over their diseased bodies, in His name.

Do you believe right now? If you believe, praise the Lord in faith, and it shall be done. If you do not feel the joy, offer praise as a sacrifice, and ask God to give you the joy. When the unclean spirit is driven out, the disease goes, and the resurrection life comes in; then you lose what little strength you have and go down like Daniel, John, and the rest of them, and lie down in green pastures.

Some dance, shout, and praise the Lord as the life of Jesus thrills through them. I declare to you on the authority of God and from my own experience, I know it is the power of God through Jesus Christ. It does not take Jesus long to do the work, but it takes some of us a long time to get there. Five minutes will do the work. Then the peace of God will flow through you like a river, and you will have joy in the Holy Spirit. As you go home, don't think about your sins. Don't commit any more, and don't worry about the past—it is under the blood.

God gave me a message, and He has given me the strength to stand here and deliver it. He asks you in a loving way to meet the Lord in the air, to attend the marriage supper. Will you meet me there? He is coming so soon; I often think I shall live until He comes. I praise Him today that I know these things. Sometimes people get into the flesh and make too much demonstration, but that is better than never to talk, pray, or sing. Let us not condemn, but let us all try to get nearer to God; that is what I am striving for today.

Oh, God, I have held up your Son today; I have honored His name with all the strength You have given me. Take the scales off the eyes of those who do not see, and make them to see the truths that have been brought out! May they think of them again and again, and may they go to You to find out whether these things are so.

You know how I have pleaded with people not to lay hands on the ark, or on the Lord's anointed. Open the eyes of those who have only known dead forms, and make them to know I am Your servant. Lord, I want the joy bells to ring in heaven because they are on the way, but You cannot take them against their will. I pray I may meet them at the marriage supper of the Lamb.

68

THE GREAT REVIVAL
IN JERUSALEM

Sermon by Mrs. M. B. Woodworth-Etter, at Montwait

*And great fear came upon all the church, and upon as many as heard these
things. And by the hands of the apostles were many signs and wonders wrought
among the people (and they were all with one accord in Solomon's porch).*

(Acts 5:11–12)

This was the greatest revival given in the New Testament, greater in
many ways than Pentecost. Then they were all with one accord in one
place, awaiting the outpouring of the Spirit. They all made the same sound. You
get there, and God will shake the country.

Signs and wonders were wrought, and *"of the rest durst no man join himself
unto them"* (v. 13). They were so full of fire no one dared to say falsely, "I am one of
you." They were afraid God would strike them dead. God wants to get a people so
full of power, His power, that others full of wildfire will not say, "God sent me."

What was the result? Believers were added. To the church? No, *"to the Lord; multitudes both of men and women"* (v. 14). Some say that this excitement, this fanaticism is good enough for women, but there was a multitude of strong-minded men here, too.

"They brought the sick into the street and laid them on beds and couches, that at the least the shadow of Peter passing by might overshadow some of them" (v. 15). What a cranky set they were! I wish we were just like that. Excitement rose higher and higher.

The whole country was stirred. There came a multitude out of the cities near Jerusalem, bringing the sick and those vexed with unclean spirits; and they were healed, every single one (v. 16); healed because they came right. A wonderful revival, was it not?

In the midst of it, it was broken up. The high priest and Sadducees arrested the apostles and put them in prison. Bless God, they didn't stay there long. God sent His angel and brought them out and told them to go into the temple and preach to the people.

It took some grace to do that, did it not? To go right back there and preach the Word, not leaving out divine healing, but showing all the signs and wonders. In the morning the council sent to bring them out. They found the prison locked but no one there; those they sought were out preaching.

It is better to obey God. We are determined to obey God and let the result be what it may. God's people must meet persecution. People say this work is not of God. That is the kind of talk the devil likes to hear. All the devil has to do is to blow his whistle, and his army comes running to do his work.

God has to blow and blow before He can get His people to do His work; yet we have the promise, *"One [shall] chase a thousand"* (Deut. 32:30). The devil hates holiness and power; he persecutes, and persecution is all that makes men fit for heaven.

This was a great revival. Every one of the apostles seemed to be there, and God gave them wonderful power. Many mighty signs and miracles were done by them, because they were of one accord, preaching and believing. Because of this, the fire of God fell upon the church, and sinners began to tremble.

I believe in preaching in such a way that the power of God will make people tremble, preaching holiness, coming up to the front to do His will. *"The fear of* the LORD *is the beginning of wisdom"* (Prov. 9:10). The first we know of God, a holy awe comes over us. When we want God to work, to cause His presence to be felt in our midst, we must feel He has the power to work among His people; and it is a terrible thing to resist.

We must put on the full armor and rush into the battle. *"Turn* [back] *the battle to the gate"* (Isa. 28:6). Vain is the help of man. There is no shelter except in the wounded side of Jesus. It is the only place on earth to which we can flee. We learn there the way of righteousness, and we know what awaits the sinner if he does not accept this shelter.

In the Old Testament, we read of God's workings among His people. When someone was sent with a message, it often seemed very foolish, humanly speaking. What was the outcome? God will always show Himself and put His seal upon His work. When the message was delivered, He came forth with the supernatural, with the sign of His invisible presence.

He manifested His presence in miraculous ways. That put the fear of Him on the heathen. They said there is no God like the Hebrews', because of His wonderful works. He was a God to be feared.

In the New Testament, signs and wonders were done before the people. Wherever Jesus went, the people followed Him. God was with Him, putting fear on the people through miracles, signs, and wonders that God wrought through Him.

He said, "I don't do these things of myself; *'but the Father that dwelleth in me, he doeth the works'"* (John 14:10). The apostles said the same: *"According to the working of his mighty power"* (Eph. 1:19). *"Not I, but Christ"* (Gal. 2:20). It is the same today.

With signs and wonders today, it is also *"not I, but Christ."* He dwells in these bodies, and the work is done by the mighty power of the Spirit. *"Know ye not that your body is the temple of the Holy Ghost?"* (1 Cor. 6:19). The Spirit of Christ dwells in us. We are God's powerhouse.

It was by the hands of the apostles, not of angels, that God did His mighty works; and people believed when the signs followed. Jesus commanded the unclean spirits to come out, and they had to come. The power of the Holy Spirit went through the apostles' hands and that is just the way God works today.

The apostles were not afraid of persecution, the sword, or anything else. They faced death in any form rather than disgrace the cause of Christ by being cowards. It is a mighty God we serve, and today, Jesus Christ who ascended into heaven is here by my side. He will lead His hosts on to victory. Let us press the battle to the gates.

This sect is always spoken against, misrepresented, and lied about; but Jesus Christ is leading on His hosts. God permitted Jesus to be nailed to the cross and laid in the grave, but He came forth like the sun.

God permitted the apostles to be arrested and put in prison. Then He had an opportunity to show His power. He sent His angel and delivered them. The angel of the Lord is with His own. Our citizenship is in heaven. We are children of the King.

Around us day and night are *"ministering spirits, sent forth to minister for them who shall be heirs of salvation"* (Heb. 1:14). We can afford to be misrepresented, or even put in prison, if only we are looking for the manifestation and the glory of translation, to go sweeping through the gates.

The apostles were persecuted, and the meeting broken up in Jerusalem, where the Lord was crucified. The meeting was held in Solomon's porch, one of the prominent places in the city. It seems the apostles were in this great porch, and they brought the sick into the street on beds and couches and every way, and laid them all around—the sick, blind, and those vexed with unclean spirits, a great multitude.

What would the preachers think if we brought the sick around the church in this way? When they were preaching one of those fine sermons, firstly, secondly, thirdly, if someone dropped a sick person down in the midst, they would send for a policeman quickly; you know they would.

The paralytic did not break up the meeting when he was brought to Jesus and dropped down through the roof, while He was preaching. Jesus is our example. He was glad to have something like that, because it gave Him a chance to show His power. He forgave him all his sins and then made him rise, take up his bed, and walk. (See Mark 2:1–12.)

The people began to shout, "Glory," the same way you do here; you cannot help yourselves. If you have not done it, you will. A consumptive woman was brought in here in her night robe. I did not care what she had on; she was healed. Hallelujah!

When the paralytic was healed, they gave glory to God. People say today, "You never heard such a crazy set." If they had only heard them then! We have something to make a fuss about. Dead people never make much noise, do they? There is not much noise in a graveyard.

Some people are frozen and have their feet in grave clothes. May God take off the grave clothes and set us free! David danced before the Lord with all his might. His wife did not like it; she thought he had disgraced her before the handmaidens, and she began to grumble.

David said he was not dancing before the handmaidens but before the Lord. It is dangerous to lay your hand on the work of the Lord. She had no child to the day of her death. It was a great disappointment to the Jewish woman, as each one hoped to be the mother of the Lord.

Do not lay your hand upon the work of the Lord. It meant sudden death to lay your hand upon the ark of the Lord. Beware of sin against the Holy Spirit. That is the unpardonable sin and cannot be forgiven. Sometimes the Holy Spirit comes like a mighty rushing wind from heaven and makes a great commotion among the people; sometimes silently. He comes to us here.

You want to take down your umbrellas and get your buckets right side up. God will fill the vessels and make you a powerhouse for Him. Then God will show Himself mighty to pull the strongholds of the devil and build up the kingdom of Christ.

You will have power to preach, and signs and wonders will be wrought as in the days of the apostles. The Lord was with them. He was invisible, but He was with them, *"confirming the Word with signs following"* (Mark 16:20); and He will never forsake us if we obey Him.

Signs and wonders following. Following what? The preaching of the Word. He is here, and you will see Him with what we call visible signs. Peter said, "What you see is the Holy Spirit." If you are willing, you will see it here, for God is coming in a wonderful way.

They saw the fire on the apostles' heads and heard them speak in other tongues as the Spirit gave them utterance; they saw them stagger like drunken men. Wherever the Holy Spirit is poured out, you will see signs.

That was a great meeting; the sick were brought on beds and cots, and God, by the hands of the apostles, wrought many signs and wonders (Acts 5:12). The fear of God fell on the people. Thousands and thousands were converted to God.

Their names were written in heaven; they were filled with the Holy Spirit, the glory of God; the power of God was so great they could not get close enough to have hands laid on all the sick. Peter seemed to be the leader in this divine healing movement, and they tried to get the sick near enough that Peter's shadow might overshadow some of them (v. 15).

The power was of the Holy Spirit. He who believes on Jesus Christ will have such power that *"out of his* [inward parts] *shall flow rivers of living water"* (John 7:38). The Holy Spirit is like a river. Pentecost filled the apostles, and people were healed even watching for Peter's shadow.

The power of the Holy Spirit struck the sick ones and healed them, and the people marveled. Jesus did many mighty works, and He told the apostles they should do greater things than these if they believed on Him (John 14:12).

Men and women, God wants you to get into that place. Don't you see God works through human instrumentality? God will use us if we are swallowed up in Him. In Chicago, people were healed sitting in their seats, and way up in the gallery, some fell like dead people.

The power of God is going out while I am talking. You know I am speaking the truth; believe it, accept it, and get more of Jesus. If we take in and take in and do not give out, we are like a sponge that needs to be squeezed. Let us get so full that it will run right out through us, not absorb and absorb and never give out.

Many of you are baptized with the Holy Spirit. You ought to send the power this way while I send it that way, and when the two come together, something would happen. I could not keep my feet if you would do this, glory! Glory to God!

Take a picture of that revival. Did they act like crazy folks? Some of the best people in Jerusalem took part in that revival. All classes were there. People were lying all around, getting healed, or running to bring someone else to be healed, and multitudes were saved.

It was the greatest revival. Divine healing was the drawing card. When people are healed, it does not mean simply healing, but it brings people to Christ. Take the man healed at the beautiful gate of the temple. Peter took the miracle as his text and preached. The authorities laid hands on him and commanded him not to speak or teach in the name of Jesus, but Peter and John said that they would preach in that name anyway. They prayed and the Holy Spirit came in great power. The outgrowth of that healing in the temple was a great revival. (See Acts 3:2–26.)

Notice the mighty power that went from Peter's body. His very shadow healed people (Acts 5:15). Paul did special miracles; from his body were sent out handkerchiefs, and the people were healed through them (Acts 19:11–12). This is different than any other miracle in the New Testament, but God is doing the same thing today.

The Holy Spirit works through our hands, through our bodies! We are sending out thousands of handkerchiefs all over the country, over land and sea. I could tell you wonderful stories of the work they do; five were healed from one handkerchief.

As we hold up Jesus, God sends His power through us as He did in apostolic days. Let us arise and shine and give God the glory.

When I first started out to preach, I did not know I was to pray for anyone to be healed, but God showed me I was to preach divine healing. The devil tried to keep me back, but thousands have been healed and saved through healing.

I lay on hands in the name of Jesus. 'Tis Jesus makes you whole. Sometimes the power is so great they are healed instantly, leaping and jumping and praising God. The Lord is here; we can have as great a revival as they had in Jerusalem, and the fear of God will be upon the people.

God wants you to march to the cross and give glory to God. We need to get to work here. Let Him do the work in your soul first. We are going to have a revival here like the one in Jerusalem, with many signs and wonders.

Receiving divine healing isn't like going to the doctor. Get baptized with the Holy Spirit before you leave. Then when you get home you will not backslide. Glory to God!

The Communings of Jesus

Not a sound invades the stillness,
   Not a form invades the scene,
Save the voice of my Beloved,
   And the person of my King.

REFRAIN

Precious, gentle, holy Jesus,
   Blessed Bridegroom of my heart,

In the secret inner chamber,
    Thou wilt whisper what Thou art.

And within these heavenly places,
    Calmly hushed in deep repose,
There I drink with joy absorbing,
    All the love Thou wouldst disclose.

Wrapt in deep adoring silence,
    Jesus, Lord, I dare not move,
Lest I lose the smallest whisper,
    Meant to catch the ear of Love.

Rest thou, O my soul, contented,
    Thou hast reached thy happy place,
In the bosom of thy Savior.
    Gazing up in His dear face.

69

BLASPHEMY AGAINST THE HOLY SPIRIT

God's Cyclone of Power, a Great Leveler
A Sermon by Mrs. M. B. Woodworth-Etter

In the Stone Church, Chicago, Illinois, July 6, 1913

(As recorded in *The Latter Rain Evangel*)

Dear friends, we have met in the presence of the most high God. We have come to do business for Jehovah. Let us do it well. We shall meet again in eternity. Let us be very solemn. God's reporter is taking note of every thought, every action here tonight, of those who are against Him and those who are for Him. So let us turn our minds from the fleeting things of life, the things that are passing away, and be close with God this hour.

The message the Lord has brought before us tonight will be found in Matthew:

Wherefore I say unto you, All manner of sin and blasphemy shall be forgiven unto men: but the blasphemy against the Holy Ghost shall not be forgiven unto men. And whosoever speaketh a word against the Son of man, it shall be forgiven him: but whosoever speaketh against the Holy Ghost, it shall not be forgiven him, neither in this world, neither in the world to come.

(Matt. 12:31–32)

This message comes to us from Jesus tonight as much as if He were standing here. Hear the eternal Word from the lips of the Son of God now reigning in glory. The words are just as powerful as directly from His lips, if they go out by the power of the Holy Spirit. This subject is considered one of the deepest in the Word of God. You have often heard the question asked, "What is the unpardonable sin?" And some people are very much concerned about having committed it. John said, *"There is a sin unto death: I do not say that [you] shall pray for it"* (1 John 5:16), but other sins are not unto death, and through prayer God will wash them all out.

Blasphemy against God and all kinds of sin against Him and against mankind will be blotted out, but whosoever speaks against the Holy Spirit has no forgiveness either in this world or in the world to come. Christ said this because they said He had an evil spirit and did His mighty works through that agency. So, you see, it is an unpardonable sin to attribute any of the mighty works of the Holy Spirit to the devil. There has never been a time since the early church, when there was so much danger of people committing the unpardonable sin as there is today, since the Pentecostal fire has encompassed the earth and tens of thousands have received the Holy Spirit, feeling His presence, backed up by signs and wonders and diverse operations of the Spirit.

When men and women come in contact with this work of the Holy Spirit, hearing His words and seeing His works, there is danger that they may attribute the power present to some other agency other than the Spirit of God. There is danger that they may condemn the power and condemn God's servants. How often have we heard ministers say, when they heard men and women and children speaking in other tongues, "Oh, it is the work of the devil." Now you hear what God says about it; they are speaking against the Holy Spirit. God has been working in this city and is going to work in much greater measure. We expect to see greater signs and wonders. If the saints stand together as one, pray together, and shout victory, God will show himself a mighty God and a Savior.

He will not only come in healing power, but will manifest Himself in many mighty ways. On the Day of Pentecost, Peter said, "[God] *hath shed forth this, which ye now see and hear*" (Acts 2:33). And from what they heard and saw, three thousand realized it was the power of God and turned to Christ. Others stifled conviction and turned away, saying, "This is the work of the devil." When the Holy Spirit is poured out, it is either life unto life or death unto death (1 Cor. 2:16). It is life unto life to those who go forward and death unto death to those who blaspheme against the Holy Spirit. So we want to be careful what we say against the diverse operations, supernatural signs, and workings of the Holy Spirit. Some people look on and say, "It looks like hypnotism," or "I believe it is mesmerism." To others it appears mere foolishness, even as Scripture says of the natural man: *"The things of the Spirit of God...are foolishness unto him; neither can he know them, because they are spiritually discerned"* (1 Cor. 2:14).

It was the same on the Day of Pentecost, when a multitude saw the disciples staggering about under the power of the Spirit, speaking in tongues. While some said, "They are drunk," others knew the mighty power of God was there. There is a power here that is not of earth, a power lifting people up, making men and women upright, making them good neighbors, good husbands and wives; it is the mighty presence of Almighty God. Watch the lives of these people; they do not seek worldly amusements, but the power of God is manifested in them. What did the power bring on the Day of Pentecost? The people who crowded together were amazed and said, "We never saw this before." Everybody began to get convicted; though some, not willing to accept it, not willing to be called fools for Christ's sake, rejected it and, to ease their guilty consciences, said, "They are drunk." They knew better. They knew the mighty power of God was there, and if there was a question, God settled it. Peter got up in the midst of the brothers and said: "These are not drunken, as you say. Men don't get drunk at nine o'clock in the morning; but this is that which was spoken by Joel the prophet: 'In the last days I will pour out my Spirit upon all flesh. Your young men shall see visions, your old men shall dream dreams.' This is the Holy Spirit that you now see and hear" (Acts 2:15–18). It is the same Holy Spirit tonight.

The Holy Spirit is the Spirit of God. He is a person and works under the direction of Jesus Christ, under His orders. He doesn't do anything but what Christ tells Him to do. When we are ready to receive Him, Jesus sends the Holy Spirit to impart to us His own gifts. The Holy Spirit cleanses these temples and comes in to dwell. He fills these bodies, and His power in us gives us utterance in tongues and works through us in other ways. Now, in order to guard against committing the unpardonable sin, we must know a little of what the Holy Spirit is. He could not come until Christ was glorified. Christ was on the earth in His human body for only a short time, but at Pentecost He came through the Holy Spirit to stay.

Jesus said that when the Holy Spirit should come, whom the Father would send in His name, "He will guide you into all truth. He will not speak of Himself, but what He hears, He will say" (John 16:13). I love the Holy Spirit because He is always witnessing for Jesus, and He comes to bring us power. He is the Comforter, the Spirit of truth, who will abide with us forever (John 14:16). He brings all things to our remembrance. We are so forgetful in our natural state; but we have a spiritual mind, and God writes His Word on our minds, and the Holy Spirit brings these messages to us at the right time—a message to this one in sin, that one in sorrow, encouraging the weak and helping the strong with some message from heaven, always pointing us to Jesus, the great Burden-Bearer—rivers of living water flowing from the individual, healing virtue going out.

Virtue went out from Peter so that the sick were healed upon whom his mere shadow fell. Power went out from Paul so that they sent handkerchiefs and aprons from his body, and through them, when they were laid on the afflicted, streams of healing went forth and devils were driven out. Water is a symbol for the Holy Spirit. *"I will pour water on him that is thirsty, and floods upon the dry ground: I will pour my spirit upon* [him]" (Isa. 44:3). A tidal wave of glory is coming this way. God help us to be as empty vessels so that the Holy Spirit's power may fill us to overflowing. The Holy Spirit is spoken of as "fire," "wind" and "water"—three of the most destructive elements in the world and three of the most useful.

We could not live without fire, wind, or water. When a cyclone comes, men and women turn pale. When God's cyclone through the Holy Spirit strikes the people, it is a great leveler. They lose sight of their money, and all hatred and ill will are swept away as a cyclone carries all before it. When a tidal wave strikes a city, it submerges everything; so, in a tidal wave of the Holy Spirit, everything goes under. Oh, we want a cyclone of God's power to sweep out of our lives everything that encumbers us, and a tidal wave to submerge us in God.

God uses these great elements—fire, wind, and water—in all their force to give us an idea of the mighty power of the Holy Spirit. Our bodies are His temples; and, as great pieces of mechanism are moved by electricity, so our bodies, the most wonderful piece of mechanism ever known, are moved by the power of the Holy Spirit sent down from heaven. He filled the one hundred and twenty on the Day of Pentecost with power to witness for Jesus. At the hands of the apostles,

God healed the sick, and He heals today by the same power that was on the apostles. God pours out rivers of living water. What manner of people are we to be?

If we don't have the power, let us confess it and ask God to give us the power He gave the first disciples. If those who come to the Lord will be filled as they were on the Day of Pentecost, we will have streams of living water rushing through us and flowing to the very ends of the earth. Jesus Christ was baptized in the Holy Spirit, but He did not have all power until He had finished His course. He could have turned away and not have gone to the cross, but He went all the way and cried, "It is finished." His last act was this going down into death.

But God Almighty raised Jesus up, and when He came up, all power was given Him—all power! He sent His disciples out in His name and said that those who believed on Him should cast out devils, should speak in new tongues, should lay hands on the sick, and if they drank any deadly things (accidentally, of course), it would not hurt them (Mark 16:17–18). He said to the disciples, "Do not marvel at what you see. These things you will do if ye believe in Me, and greater works than these will you do because I go to the Father" (John 14:12). Now when Pentecost came, they were all in the upper room waiting. They were all saved and all pure and of one accord—no divisions, no controversy. They did not know how the *"promise of the Father"* (Acts 1:4) was going to come, but they were waiting for it. Suddenly the Spirit, like a cyclone, came and filled the whole building; a great tidal wave of power was turned upon them, and they were all filled with living water.

The Spirit's tongues of fire were upon their heads, and they all *"began to speak with other tongues, as the Spirit gave them utterance"* (Acts 2:4). The people who came running up were amazed and said, "What does this mean? Are not all these who speak Galileans? Aren't they ignorant of these foreign languages? Yet everyone hears them speak in his own native language" (vv. 6–8). It was the Holy Spirit who gave them utterance in languages. The Lord had said, *"With men of other tongues and other lips will I speak unto this people; yet for all that will they not hear me"* (1 Cor. 14:21). He put the emphasis on other tongues, and the people heard and knew what was said, yet they mocked and cried out that the men had been drinking. The Holy Spirit came to testify of Jesus. The Spirit preached the first sermon on Jesus' resurrection through Peter, who got up and brought forward the Scripture to prove that this manifestation was of the Holy Spirit and that He witnessed of Christ.

People who had not believed that Jesus was the Christ—even though He did works that no one else did and spoke as no other man spoke—were now brought under conviction, and three thousand souls were converted on that day. Many in Jerusalem, when they saw the operations of the Holy Spirit, believed, and *"a great company of the priests were obedient to the faith"* (Acts 6:7).

The Holy Spirit is here tonight bringing Jesus into our midst. He is healing the sick by the power of God today, devils are being cast out, and miracles are being wrought in the mighty name of Jesus through the power of the Holy Spirit. God is giving visions. The Bible says, *"Where there is no vision, the people perish"* (Prov. 29:18). People are having visions today of the second coming of the Lord, visions of the marriage supper of the Lamb, and of the Rapture. The Holy Spirit comes with weeping. He makes you weep because of what is coming on the earth. Oh, there is a sign of trouble! The unbelieving world is going to be cast out into darkness; but while we sigh and weep at the sad condition of the world, we rejoice to know that Jesus is coming soon.

We were holding meetings in Moline. One night an evangelist came in whom we had never seen before. We were talking about the baptism of the Holy Spirit, which she had heard about and was hungry for. I said to her, "You are going to get the baptism tonight." There was not much sign of it as I got up to give the Word. She sat in front of me, and while I was speaking, she looked as if she was asleep, but the power of God was upon her. The Word was going out, and the lightning struck. When I got through speaking, the power was on her in a wonderful way, and she commenced speaking in tongues and interpreting.

Then she wailed the saddest wail I ever heard; it struck me it was like the voice of lamenting and great mourning that was heard, Rachel bitterly weeping for her dead children (Matt. 2:18); so painful, so doleful was it that everyone was made sad. I said, "This is the signal of some great sorrow, great distress, great anguish, and trouble that is coming on the people." God showed me it was a signal of distress, of awful calamity that was coming. At the same time, a sister said that she saw a great earthquake and described how the water swept over the corpses and down the street. The next day there came out in the papers an account of the dreadful destruction caused by an earthquake in Kingston, Jamaica.

Do you not see the hand of God in that vision? It was something that, coming true immediately, would convince the people. In Dallas last year, the Lord showed us many things that took place in Turkey when the armies came together. An old brother in Dallas had visions of the battles before they took place and saw multitudes being killed. One night there was the sound of a loud report like a terrible explosion. About sixty saints heard it, and the whole congregation felt the shock. As soon as the news could reach us, we heard about it through the papers.

The Holy Spirit brings gifts, miracles, discerning of spirits. We laugh and cry in the Spirit; we shout and dance and leap; our bodies get so light we scarcely touch the earth. The Spirit gives heavenly music.

At our last meeting at Long Hill, Connecticut, the heavenly choir surpassed anything I had ever heard. We had it two or three times a day, and there was no dissonance or discord heard. It was the Holy Spirit making harmony through these bodies, and the singing was no earthly singing, but heavenly. Sometimes I would be a little late in getting to the meeting, and as I came up the hill, the sound of the heavenly choir was wafted down. It sounded as if it came from heaven; it was the song of the redeemed.

God is getting His children ready to sing at the marriage supper of the Lamb. They sing a song no one can sing except the redeemed. No outsiders can join them. The Spirit has shown me the coming of the Lord is very near, and I know it now more than ever. God baptized me over twenty-five years ago with a wonderful baptism, but I am hungrier today than I ever was. I see greater possibilities today than ever before. Let us go on from one degree to another. Blessed is the servant who, when His master comes, is found at His post, giving to the household their portion of meat in due season. This is your opportunity, your day of God's visitation.

"*His* [bride] *hath made herself ready*" (Rev. 19:7). You cannot go to the tailor and order your suit to go to the banquet; you have to make it yourself. The bride has made herself ready, and it is going to be the most wonderful wedding garment you ever heard of. It takes skill to weave the pure linen garment and to embroider the "*fine linen, clean and white*" (v. 8), and when she is ready, He will greatly admire her. There will be a great company of guests in the banquet hall. But some of us are not ready; we don't have our garments. The time has come to get ready. Oh, it means something to dress for the marriage supper of the Lamb. When there is a banquet in honor of the King's son or daughter, it is a great occasion, and the musicians are trained for it long before. Now this banquet that is going to take place in the skies, this marriage supper of the Lamb, will be the greatest wedding that was ever known.

The King of Glory will be married to His bride. Don't you know that every good thing the world enjoys God is going to let us enjoy a thousandfold? That will be the greatest banquet, the most wonderful occasion ever heard of, when we eat bread and drink wine in the kingdom.

The bride is now in training. The Holy Spirit is the Dove; the singing is the cooing of the Dove before the storm. Did you ever hear the doves before the storm calling to their mates to seek shelter? So the Holy Spirit is cooing and chirping, calling us to seek shelter from the tribulation storms that are coming upon the earth. The Lord is having us in training, making our bodies light and supple so that we can go up. May the Lord help us to be filled with the Holy Spirit so that we can rise. The Spirit is the only moving power in the church of Christ, the mighty agent He has sent to carry on business through His body. Let us get the fire from heaven that will enable us to do business for God and be careful that we do not attribute the power of God to the devil, lest we commit the unpardonable sin.

70

THE BLOOD OF
THE LAMB AND THE WORD
OF THEIR TESTIMONY

Petoskey Meeting Is In Session while Book Goes to Press

Just an added chapter as the new book goes to press. In the midst of many calls from the North, South, East, and West, the Spirit has drawn me the second time to Petoskey, in northern Michigan. God is working mightily in our midst, and yet there is more to follow.

Remarkable visions are given with testimonies. Lights are seen in different parts of the tabernacle; also angels hovering over the mercy seat. Wonderful healings are taking place daily—crooked limbs are straightened, eyesight restored, the lame made to leap for joy, demons cast out—and God places His seal on the work.

Who shall say anything against God's elect (Rom. 8:33)? It is the Spirit who bears witness. Mockers are silenced. Unbelievers are confounded, the proud are humbled, and *"blessed are the meek"* (Matt. 5:5).

Yes, and glory be to God, that I, under this widespread canvas and waving forest, am permitted on this twenty-second day of July, to count another milestone to my three score and eleven years—with vigorous pulse beatings and feet swift to respond to the Spirit's call. Sometimes it seems this prison of clay must break and my ransomed spirit soar to everlasting bliss. But, no, what greater bliss than to lead souls into the kingdom and hear the chants of new-born souls! What greater honor than to be a messenger to tell the glad tidings and blow the gospel trumpet!

To Mary He said, *"Go and tell"* (Mark 16:7), and He still honors His handmaidens. Glory to His holy name!

Stephen Feith, of 1164 Grenfield Avenue, Milwaukee, Wisconsin, came to the meeting. He had been badly afflicted for two and a half years with inflammatory rheumatism. His foot had been badly swollen and drawn out of shape, suffering pain in it continually. In these few years he lost about seven hundred dollars by not being able to work. On his journey up here, they assisted him as a cripple. The Lord made it plain to him and his wife that he must come to these meetings to be healed. On the journey, God gave him Scripture texts, showing him that he would get his healing.

When they brought him to the altar, he was weeping from pain and because of his backslidden condition. He had been prayed for many times, but he was getting worse. We prayed the prayer of faith for both soul and body; immediately the burden of sin rolled away, and he felt the pain go out of his ankles and foot and the swelling go down. He at once began to praise God, springing to his feet, and demonstrating on the platform that he was healed by leaping and stamping his sore foot on the floor.

The power of God came upon him. With tears streaming down his cheeks, he told the audience what God had done for him. His exhortations in the Spirit were wonderful, convincing everybody that God had performed a great miracle. He has since received the baptism of the Holy Spirit, speaking in other tongues, as evidence, and has also interpreted messages in English.

Many people testify that they were prayed for two years ago, some for goiters, tumors, weak eyes, and many incurable diseases, and today they are perfectly well. They can and do demonstrate that they are well.

The Spirit is leading many this way. Interest deepens, and the people ask, "What meaneth this?" Surely His hand is not shortened that He cannot save, nor

568 ⁓ *Maria Woodworth-Etter: Collected Works*

His ear heavy that He cannot hear. He still declares that with "stammering lips and other tongues" will I speak to this people, and I will get Myself glory. Jesus is the same yesterday, today, and forever, strong to deliver and mighty to save. "Be patient, therefore, brethren, unto the coming of the Lord. Behold, the husband-man waiteth for the precious fruit of the earth, and hath long patience for it, until he receives the early and the latter rain" (James 5:7).

The Latter Rain is Falling

By Pastor

Thousands are seeing and feeling and hearing the wonderful works of God. Sister M. B. Woodworth-Etter is at her best, and God's power is with her as she rebukes diseases in the mighty name of Jesus; demons fear and flee for other quarters as in ancient days. People are gathering in from almost every state in the Union. It will take eternity to reveal the souls that have been saved, healed, and baptized as in Acts 2:4. The tide is still rising, and the end is not yet, praise the Lord. "*Eye hath not seen, nor ear heard,….the things which God hath prepared for them that love him*" (1 Cor. 2:9).

Your servant has been trying to preach the Gospel for over twenty-five years, but since the meetings commenced, I have seen and heard more *Gospel* demonstrated than in the twenty-five years.

Your brother in Jesus,
—F. W. Jewell

Pastor's Report at Close of Meeting

Come and see the wonderful works of God. We have just closed the second annual camp meeting conducted by Sister Woodworth-Etter and her helpers. The time of modern miracles has not passed. We have seen almost every disease cured by the power of God in these meetings. We are living in the day when God is demonstrating the Gospel with signs following. People have come from almost every state in the Union to see and to hear the wonderful things of God. The teaching has been, "*Thus saith the Lord*" (Exo. 4:22). Lives have been made better. The unity has been brought about and in almost every meeting God's mighty power has been demonstrated in healing, saving, and baptizing.

About twenty-five have followed Jesus through the baptismal service in water, and people have been led to say, "This is God!" when they saw God's handmaiden, over seventy-two years preaching the Gospel with such power and authority. We feel that tongue is too frail and pen will not be able to describe the great good that has been accomplished through this wonderful camp meeting, and to Him who is worthy, we ascribe all the glory.

Your servant for the cause of Christ,
—F. W. Jewell
Petoskey, Michigan

A Wonderful Vision

By a Missionary

Sunday night the Lord held me in prayer for Sister Etter, the workers, and the great multitude that thronged the tent, so filled with unbelief. The Lord gave assurance of victory. The heavens opened; then I saw a mighty angel fly from heaven and overshadow the tent. He was mighty and very powerful, and his attitude was of protection. I heard a voice say, "Gabriel."

Again, I saw God's people fleeing from the wrath to come. They were running up a steep mountainside. It seemed impossible to go farther, so I cried out, "How can I go farther on?" Immediately a ladder was let down from heaven and put within my reach, and a voice said, "Faith." So I climbed until I could see over the crest of the mountain, and there I beheld the beauty and glory of heaven. I began praying the Father to send down the glory of His Son upon His people; then I saw the tent filled with saints. I saw a flame of fire sitting upon each head, as they waited upon God. Then very suddenly I saw a cloud of glory descend and fill the place. We could not see each other for the exceeding brightness of the presence of God.

—N. Diamond Gill

Powerful Meetings

(Taken from Word and Work)

The Woodworth-Etter meetings in Petoskey, Michigan, have begun with wonderful interest and power. The interest and attendance are rapidly increasing.

People have come and are coming from near and far. A minister from the state of New York writes, "I am coming to get Pentecostal power in my life." We are looking for an unusual outpouring of God's Spirit in these meetings. "*The signs of the times*" (Matt. 16:3), as they are being manifested among the warring nations this summer, almost demand that God's people have corresponding signs and demonstrations of His power in their camps. Let us pray that this may be so.

Last night, the third night of the meeting, the power of God fell like large drops of rain all over the tent. Saints were praying, weeping, shouting all over the congregation as the power fell upon them. A woman in the back of the audience came hastily forward with her friend to the altar and began to weep and pray her way through to God. In just a few minutes, the power fell on her. She rose and almost ran up onto the platform to Sister Etter and asked her to forgive her for speaking evil against her and of the power of God, saying that she thought it was hypnotic power and that she prayed for God to smite her if it was not His power. God's smiting power came, but it fell on her so that, with heavy tears and prayer, she asked God to forgive her for speaking evil of His power.

Already quite a number have been saved, healed, and baptized with the Spirit, having the evidence of tongues. Wonderful testimonies on healing of two years ago are being given. These souls demonstrate that the work that the Spirit wrought in their bodies two years ago has been permanent. The shout of victory is all over the camp. Let all the saints pray that this whole northern peninsula may become enlightened with Pentecostal truth and power.

—*August D. Feick*, Secretary

Power from on High

Sister Woodworth-Etter, who has been holding meetings in Petoskey, Michigan, writes us, July 18, that the meetings are fine, and the power falls and people get saved, healed, and baptized. On Sunday two came up from Detroit and in the evening both received the baptism. On another occasion a young couple came from Detroit, and the husband received his baptism the same day and his wife a few days later, and they also got healed. Last night a number got their baptism. We are glad to hear that God is using our dear sister and we shall never forget the meeting she held here at Montwait. There were many healed and blessed during the month she was here. Praise the Lord!

—Editor

Editor, *Pentecostal Herald*, Chicago, Illinois

Dear Brother Brinkman:

Grace and peace unto you! It has been my privilege, pleasure, and profit to visit for four days the camp meeting being held at Petoskey, Michigan, by Sister M. B. Woodworth-Etter, at whose request I give you this little report of God's working in that place.

First, let me say that it was a delightful surprise to me to find in Sister Etter a humble, sweet-spirited handmaiden of the Lord, full of the Holy Spirit and wisdom, and one who, like Abraham of old, "believe[s], *even God*" and *"stagger[s] not at the promise of God through unbelief"* (Rom. 4:17, 20). I say it was a surprise, because I had heard very derogatory reports concerning her meetings. But now for the report of God's working: I am reminded of Jesus' reply to John the Baptist, when he sent men to ask if Jesus was truly the One they were looking for. Jesus replied, *"Go your way and tell John what things ye have seen and heard; how the blind see, the lame walk, the lepers are cleansed, the deaf hear, the dead are raised, to the poor the gospel is preached"* (Luke 7:22). While we did not see the dead raised or actual lepers cleansed, we saw some who had been *"as good as dead"* (Heb. 11:12), rejoicing in God's resurrection life in answer to prayer at this meeting and the one held here two years ago.

One sister testified that she was dying of hemorrhage, was prayed for by Sister Etter and workers, and was able to come to the meeting with wonderful deliverance. Lepers? No, there were no literal cases of this disease, but some very similar; cancers, blood-poisoning, and the like all have to yield to the irresistible power of the prayer of faith.

Sister Black, formerly of St. Louis, was there, a living testimony to God's healing power. Two years before she had been brought in an almost helpless condition, but now she dances before the Lord. Another sister who was healed of goiter in such a terrible condition that she could scarcely breathe and was a great sufferer, was there to tell of God's miracle of healing in her behalf—absolutely no sign of goiter was left. A deaf and dumb girl had never spoken plainly in her life before, until prayed for. I had the privilege of hearing her say, "Praise God," "I shall yet speak," "Believe God,"

"Hide away," and other things that I do not now recall. She has also received the baptism of the Holy Spirit. A young man from Milwaukee, who came to the meetings scarcely able to walk because of disease in his feet, was healed and also received the baptism of the Holy Spirit, speaking in tongues and with the gift of interpretation. A lady doctor was there who had a disease of the mouth and was scarcely able to speak. She was prayed for and now able to speak plainly.

These are only a few cases, but they were there from many different states and some from Canada with similar testimonies. Souls are also yielding to God and being beautifully saved. God's power manifested in a vision brought a man and his wife—who had been Roman Catholics and great opposers of the work—under conviction. They truly repented of their sins and were saved, and they also received the baptism as at Pentecost.

One of the impressive things about these meetings is the spirit of worship manifested in the heavenly music or, as Paul wrote, "*Making melody in* [their] *heart to the Lord,*" as well as "*psalms and hymns and spiritual songs*" (Eph. 5:19), also the dancing before the Lord. The saints are encouraged to be free and recognize the Holy Spirit's presence, or as Sister Etter puts it, "Let the Dove sing." "*The time of the singing of birds is come*" (Song 2:12). Some have argued that this was too mechanical in Sister Etter's meeting. Well, perhaps it may seem so at times, but she does not desire that but urges the people according to Ephesians 5 to be filled with the Spirit and worship God, and this is certainly scriptural, and at times the presence of God was manifested in a wonderful way. We say, God bless Sister Etter and her band of noble workers and give them many more such splendid campaigns in behalf of lost souls.

Yours for Jesus,
—*Pastor J. R. Kline*
Pentecostal Assembly, Detroit, Michigan

Inspired by the Spirit

Petoskey, Michigan, July 19

Sister Etter came to us for the second time, and God is still with her in mighty power. Two years ago all the country around was thrilled and stood amazed at the wonderful demonstrations of the power of God in our midst; the lame were made to walk and the blind to see, the deaf to hear, and the saints lifted to higher ground. Glory be to God in the highest! Many of those who, two years ago, were delivered from some awful power of sin and made whole in Christ are here today, rejoicing and pressing on. Praise God! Some are prosperous businessmen in our city. Others have gone to carry the good tidings to distant lands. To Him be all the glory, it is just the same today. The heavenly choir is with us at nearly every session, and God gives the messages full of faith and glory. Many fall under the power, and the people in the homes around feel and enjoy it and are drawn to the meetings. Often every seat in the great tent is taken; yes, and they are coming, coming from far away—Canada, Texas, Florida, Dakota, etc., many having come from the inspiration from reading her book, *Acts of the Holy Spirit*.

—Mrs. J. P. Howard
Eleventh District President of the Woman's
Christian Temperance Union, Petoskey, Michigan

Healed of Six Deadly Diseases

My testimony.

Sunday, July 30, 10:30 a.m., at the opening of the morning session, I was healed of six deadly diseases: paralysis, sciatic rheumatism, bladder trouble, Bright's disease, a cancerous rectal trouble, heart failure, and neurasthenia (nervous prostration). When Sister W. Etter and Brother Feick laid hands in Jesus' name upon the diseased organs, I felt the power of the risen Lord streaming through my body, and within a few minutes pains, lameness, and disease had to flee and had to leave my pain-ridden body before the quickening power of our Lord and God. Hallelujah! In the presence of many witnesses, I fairly leaped and jumped, praising God with a loud voice for His love, power, and goodness toward a poor suffering sinner.

Some weeks previous to my healing, the pains in my body were so intense, especially at night from midnight to two a.m., that I asked my heavenly Father to take me home. For four consecutive years I was not without pain, day or night, still believing, teaching, and preaching, also practicing divine healing as given us in the Atonement according to Isaiah 53:4–6. At last the time of my deliverance had finally come! Praise Jesus for evermore! Amen.

As we listened to the great number of testimonies, given by people from all parts of the United States and from years back, telling the same story of redemption and deliverance, we were convinced more and more of the restoration of the apostolic faith to the saints and the preparation of God's people for our Lord's speedy coming in these days of the latter rain. Returning to Detroit, we gave in our August sixth services a brief report of God's work at Petoskey. The altar calls given at the close of the evening service were answered by the majority present, who came to seek more of God, to get deeper in Him, to consecrate themselves anew and fully to God. So our dear Lord is doing a new work of blessing and spiritual preparation on Mt. Horeb, of which place He said in a sevenfold promise, "Mt. Horeb is Mine!" "*God is no respecter of persons*" (Acts 10:34), and He is a rewarder of all those who diligently seek Him (Heb. 11:6). May saint and sinner realize that now is the accepted time. Therefore watch and pray; soon He will come and the door will be shut to the foolish virgins (Matt. 25:1–13).

Your brother in His blessed service,
—*Benjamin Wittich*

A Few Visions

A Remarkable Thing about This Meeting Has Been the Many Wonderful Visions Seen by the Saints

I beheld Jesus nailed to the cross and saw the nails in His hands and in His feet, and the crown of thorns on His head. I began to weep and fell down at His feet and began to cry. He said He had died for this sinful world. I saw Him taken down from the cross and laid in a large tomb, rough on the inside, and then I saw some men with ugly countenances roll a big stone up by it. It took about twenty of them to roll the stone up. I saw Him suddenly get up from the tomb and saw Him walk out. The stone was rolled away. He went out by the riverside and met some men and talked to them. He said, "I am going up to my Father. I am coming back again. Tarry until I endue you with power from on high." Many people were gathered around, then He was lifted up and went into the clouds in glory.

One sister was caught away in the Spirit and found herself before the throne, pleading for greater power. She then saw the power falling all over the people in the tent like glittering jewels, and a mighty angel descending and hovering over with outstretched wings.

In another vision many angels were seen; their brightness was as the sun. They were hovering around the tent. Jesus was standing in the center of them.

His glory shone brighter than the sun. His hands were outstretched over the people. As we sang, He smiled. A look of tenderness and pleading came over His face, then a voice spoke and said, "As your voice goes out in thanksgiving and praises in the Spirit, the angels carry your songs before the throne as sweet incense to the Father." No words or pen can describe the beauty of this vision.

At another time a light or glory was seen rising a little above the horizon. It appeared as if it was the sun; the glory and splendor of it was so great that the natural eye could not gaze steadily upon it. Just above the light was a brilliant cross and over the cross, in a rainbow shape, were these words, written in letters of gold, "*Behold I come quickly,…unto you that fear my name shall the Sun of righteousness arise with healing in his wings*" (Rev. 22:12; Mal. 4:2).

A ring of light, having rainbow colors, was seen all around the tent, emanating from a pillar of fire. Jesus was also seen with outstretched hands in the tent.

While a sister was resting in her tent, she saw a ball of fire, about ten inches in diameter, fall through the tent and explode with a loud report; then the tent seemed to be filled with glittering diamonds. This same sister woke up one morning about two A.M. and heard the loveliest music, which resembled a band of alto cornets. Spirit-filled saints often hear music like this. Many times they hear the angels sing. God has wonderful things prepared for those who pay the price and go all the way with Him. Balls of fire coming down from heaven and falling around the tent were seen so much in our big revival at Dallas, Texas, a few years ago.

Jesus was seen marshaling His hosts together. He is on the white horse of His power, and He is soon to burst through the clouds of heaven. It is so real. I could see Him just as plain as I see you. Jesus is coming soon. The trials and tribulations of this world will soon be so great that God's children cannot stay here.

I saw a bright light, and in this light there was a throne, and on the throne sat God. I could not see Him face-to-face because there was so much glory. Jesus said, "I am coming soon. Go out and preach the Gospel. I am with you. I will be with you always." I told Him that He would have to provide everything because I did not know anything and did not have a Bible and did not know very much Scripture. He said He would fill me and open up the way. He asked me again if I would preach the Gospel, and I answered, "Yes."

I saw a great many golden instruments, and Jesus said, "I am letting people play these nowadays. I am pouring out My Spirit. I am coming soon to catch My bride away. I will soon let loose the four winds." Jesus left me for a few minutes, and an angel stood before me. Jesus broke forth in a cloud over me. He was in all His glory. A lot of angels followed. I saw the saints rise up to meet Him.

A Few Cases of Healings

Healed of Various Diseases

I want to praise God for the meetings at Petoskey, because they have meant so much for my husband and me. He healed me of adenoids, goiter, catarrh, and bronchial trouble. He also baptized me with the Holy Spirit and fire. Glory be to His name.

—Mrs. Abbie Thomas
35 Pomlow Street, Columbus, Ohio

Healed and Baptized with the Holy Spirit

About eight years ago, I was hit by a baseball that struck me just below the appendix. The injury gave me great pain, and I was badly swollen at times. I took a lot of medicine, but none of it helped me. I also had heart trouble and other diseases. Sister Etter laid hands on me and rebuked the diseases and, praise God, they all left. I also received my baptism of the Holy Spirit and spoke in other tongues.

My mother was prayed for by Sister Etter about twenty years ago for a bad cancer in her eye. It dried up almost at once after she was prayed for, and today you cannot even see a scar where it had been.

—Grace Boggs
R. R. 1, Litts, Iowa

I am a missionary from the mountains of Kentucky. I had the grippe, which left me with a very bad cough. I coughed until I tore my side, and that became a bleeding cancer. I sent a handkerchief to Sister Etter to be anointed, and in the letter they returned to me, they said there would be a meeting in Petoskey. I decided to go if I did not get any better, with the thought in my mind that I would be healed. The doctor said I should not go unless I went on a cot. I replied that I would trust God and go on my own feet. I came from Jackson, Kentucky, and thought I would surely die. I suffered such intense pain, but with the Lord's help

I arrived in Petoskey on Saturday morning. On Sunday morning in the meeting, I thought I would sit back and wait until I had received more teaching and my faith was increased, but Sister Etter saw me and asked me if I was sick, told me to step out and be prayed for. She prayed for me, and I was healed of a cancer from which I was bleeding to death, also kidney trouble and heart trouble. I give my testimony to the glory of God for this healing.

—Mrs. M. Banfill
Nooksack, Washington

Miscellaneous

On July 4 two young men came in to see what was going on. They soon got under conviction, came forward, and gave their hearts to God. The power soon fell on one so that he got up on the platform and began to prophesy in the Spirit and admonished the saints to keep lowly at the feet of Jesus. He was only a farmer's boy, about sixteen years old, I understand.

A man and his wife came all the way from North Dakota. The first evening while he was sitting in the meeting, the healing power came upon him and went all through his body. He demonstrated how he got healed.

A sister from Alanson, Michigan, got healed of acute appendicitis.

A woman from Tiffin, Ohio, brought her child, about six years old, to the meeting to be prayed for. He had inherited an awful disease and was a mass of scabs and corruption. The mother said there were places on his body where the corruption seemed to be half an inch deep. After he got prayed for, he soon showed indications of healing. In about a week's time a good part of his body had healed up—a marvel to everybody—even to doctors who examined him. Since then, the mother wrote that the child had been almost completely healed.

Sense of Smell and Taste Restored

Last January I took the grippe, which totally destroyed my senses of smell and taste. Food would burn on the stove while cooking because I could not smell the strongest odor. I could not even taste salt or pepper. A person has no idea how trying this has been to me. When I was prayed for at the Petoskey meeting, the power of God came on me and went all through my body. With my eyes closed, I sat calmly in the chair, when suddenly I smelled a rose. When the power came on me, a brother got a rose and held it a few inches from my nose to see if I could smell. I immediately got out of the chair and told everybody—I can smell. Also my sense of taste came back to me. After about a month's time, my senses of smell and taste are still perfect. Oh, how I do praise God that I came to the meeting. My son-in-law came with me and received his baptism of the Holy Spirit.

—*Mrs. George Simmins*
127 W. Division Street, Boyne City, Michigan

Healed of Spinal Curvature and Nervous Prostration

I praise the Lord for wonderfully healing me on July 20, at Petoskey, Michigan. Sister Etter prayed for me and instantly the healing balm was sent through my whole body, and all pain that I had left me. I had nervous prostration and curvature of the spine since childhood, having fallen on a stone flat on my back, and was nearly gored to death by a cow when eight years old. I have used a pillow on my back for years. Now I am healed. He has also baptized me and spoken through me in other tongues, to His glory.

—*Minnie Kapp*
454 Monroe Street, Tiffin, Ohio

A Wonderful Case of Healing

Dear People:

I'm telling my wonderful healing, which I received at Sister Etter's Petoskey, Michigan, camp meeting. I was sick for twelve years from blood poisoning that I received when my boy was born. I have had seven operations, having organs and tumors removed, and have been at death's door many times. When I came to the meetings, I had an abscess and adhesions, terrible constipation, headaches, and pain. I went to the doctor nearly every other day and could not do any work.

I came to these meetings, and seeing and hearing what was going on, I believed and came forward to the altar and asked God to forgive me of all my sins. When I felt that He had, I asked Sister Etter to pray for my healing. I got it, praise Jesus, I got it. I have not had any pain nor taken any medicine since. I have also worked hard since without ill effects. I can write chapters about my sufferings. For two days my bowels had not worked at all. When Sister Etter prayed for me, I felt my intestines draw up, and they soon began to move in a normal way again, far better than when I dosed them with medicine three times a day. This is the truth—no guess so maybe. I can run and lie flat on my back without pain, where I used to suffer so much. I sleep well, too. Now I am sorry that I ever said anything against this work and Sister Etter. I asked them all to forgive me.

My daughter got saved and baptized in these meetings, with speaking in tongues as evidence. My son was healed of adenoids.

—*Mrs. Minnie Bowman*
1215 Emmet Street, Petoskey, Michigan

Healed of Paralysis and Dropsy

A little over two years ago I came to Sister Woodworth-Etter's meetings at Petoskey, Michigan, and was healed of paralysis of the right side, which I had for five years. The doctors could do nothing for me. After I was prayed for, I ran up and down on the platform and aisle and have been well ever since. For some time I have been troubled with dropsy of the heart. A doctor examined me on the campground and said I was in a bad condition, that he hardly knew how I was able to get here myself. I got Sister Etter and the workers to pray for me. I had been so full of fluid that a few days later my waist measurement had gone down five inches. I am healed. My case was a marvel to the doctor.

—*Joseph Walker*
Box 116, Niles, Michigan

Many Miracles Seen

Darby, Pennsylvania, December 14, 1914

My Dear Sister Etter:

I hope that you will forgive me for not writing my testimony of the camp meeting that was held at Philadelphia, a little sooner. I have been in the camp meeting work held by the Holiness people for fifteen years, but I never saw or heard the full Gospel preached like it was at the camp meeting at Philadelphia. I went there with prejudice in my heart, but I heard you say about the Lord telling the people to roll the stone away from Lazarus' grave, and you only spoke a few words, and the stone was removed from my heart.

Praise the Lord! I saw the blind led on the ground and walk off the ground with their sight, also the deaf hear, the dumb speak, and the lame people throw away their crutches, and they would walk and jump and dance for joy. Many deadly cancer cases were healed, and I myself was healed from nervous headaches, which I had for many years. By the touch of your hand, the Lord healed me, and I have been healed ever since. Praise the dear Lord. I met a colored lady at a meeting in Philadelphia who had been to the camp meeting; she had been blind, and the Lord restored her sight to her again, and she is praising the Lord for healing her eyes.

I praise the Lord for His goodness to me, and my life has been changed since the camp meeting. I have been reading the Word of God ever since, and I am digging into the deep things of God. I was awfully disappointed because I did not get to the meetings that were held in Chicago, but it may have been all for the best, on account of your being taken sick. I expect to go to another meeting that you and your workers will hold when you get well and able to preach the Gospel once again.

Hoping that this little testimony will be of some help to you and a blessing to many souls who may read it. The Lord bless you and your workers is my earnest prayer. I remain yours in the Master's service,

—*Harry W. Tyler*
8 North Sixth Street,
Darby, Pennsylvania

A Few Interpretations of Messages in Other Tongues

I am He that lives; My Word shall not return unto Me void, but it shall accomplish that which I purpose.

This meeting will be a judgment of life unto life for those that accept, death unto death for those that reject. My words must be preached with mighty signs and wonders in this day and time.

Behold I have said that My people should never be ashamed. I work a work in your midst before which the gainsayers shall shut their mouths. Behold the time has come. I am about to fulfill the prophecies that I have spoken of in My holy Word. Those who work the works of God shall stand up in all the power of their Savior.

Listen to the warnings that are being given from time to time. There is a calamity coming; then you will wish for one of these days that you might get ready to meet God, but these days will be past then. The judgments will come, and you will be counted to sit on the left hand of the judgment seat, and the Judge will say, "Accursed ones, depart into the lake of fire prepared for the devil and his angels." Come while the door of mercy is open.

Behold, I will come. The time is near when you shall cry for the rocks and mountains to hide you from the face of Him who sits upon the throne. Heaven and earth will flee away from His presence. The earth shall reel as a drunken man to and fro. Where will you be in that day? Behold, I have warned you; I have told you these things.

My people, heed the warnings that have been hurled forth from this place. You stiff-necked and hard-hearted, come to Jesus while you may. You will see the day when you will call for the rocks and the mountains to cover you, and it will be too late. Oh, heed the warnings! Behold, I come quickly—every eye shall see Me. Be ready, for in such an hour as you think not, the Son of Man will come. I will have a people that will be looking for Me when I come again. Keep on the wedding garment, and be ready. Now is the sifting time. Who will be able to stand? Who will be true to the words that I have given them to speak? Who will do My will? Behold, I have sent my Son to the world to suffer, bleed, and die upon Calvary's cross so that you might have life and that you might be redeemed from your sins. And for all that, you will not believe. But turn, for why would you die? Come now while My arm is stretched out to save you. The darkness of the wrath of God will be poured out on this earth on account of sin and iniquity, because you have trampled the blood of My Son under your feet and called it unholy. Oh, forget everything but that Jesus died on the cross so that you might have life and have it more abundantly.

For some time you have been looking for signs in the church. Now we are in the midst of them. These signs shall follow them that believe. Now you are stripped of your excuse. This is what was spoken of by the prophet Joel as that which should come and is a testimony against you. Behold, if you will lift up your eyes, you can see. You look over this world, read My Word, and compare. See the darkness stealing upon the earth. See the great wars and pestilences coming right now! Realize that we are living in the last days. Oh, you should get ready to meet your God.

Now the wrath of God is being poured out into this earth; don't you know it? Do you not know that I am just withholding these awful plagues and awful things that I may seal My children in their foreheads? The day is at hand; you should be hidden away in Me. Come closer. Hide away in Me, and let Me protect you.

The days are at hand when the inhabitants of the earth shall mourn, when the sun shall burn as an oven, and when only you who are hidden away in Me can stand these things. Behold the days are at hand when I shall smite this earth with plagues and pestilences. These are just the beginning of sorrows that you feel now.

I have spoken through stammering lips and other tongues, and I have warned you of the judgments to come. Prepare to meet your God, because the wrath of God is to be poured out upon this earth. Have I not said unto you that you should cry for the rocks and mountains to hide you from Him who sits upon the throne? Behold, your house is left unto you desolate. How often would I have gathered you unto Me even as a hen gathers her brood, and ye would not? Many signs and wonders have been done in your midst, and for all that, ye have stiffened your neck and hardened your heart. Behold My servants' hands are clear of your blood. They have warned you, pleaded with you, and shown you of My wrath to come, and for all that, some of you would not believe.

Lift Jesus Up

A Message Given in Tongues by the Spirit

Come, My people, march to Zion. Jesus is calling you; rise up steadfast in faith, run with your feet prepared with the Gospel of peace and righteousness. Look forward, still forward to the Lamb of God, the Spotless One, and He will lead you out and on, still farther, for you are His chosen ones, and you are sealed to the day of redemption.

I have always loved My people. Have I not given My life for them? Although the path is narrow, walk in it, and be saved. Now, go, proclaim to the nations, shout it from the rooftops that the kingdom of heaven is at hand, and all who follow Me must proclaim the glad tidings of salvation. Come hither, My children, follow Me. I will be your Compass, your Guide, and your Physician. If you would inherit eternal life, believe and receive. Wake up and shout, people, that Jesus saves. Let it be proclaimed as at Pentecost, "a flame of fire across the sky." Shout the message into whatever land you go. Lift Jesus up, and point the people to the Lamb of God.

Multitudes shall be saved if Jesus is lifted up. I will be with you to strengthen and keep you, My people, in this life and in the life to come. Amen.

A Few Closing Remarks

Well, beloved readers, as the meetings are closed, I will write more of God's wonderful works and outstretched hands in Petoskey.

Surely the people of this city and surrounding country will have no cloak for their sins.

The Holy Spirit has also borne witness to the Word with signs, wonders, and gifts of the Spirit, spiritual significations, and diverse operations, which Paul says are profitable to all.

The convention has continued six weeks without intermission, with three meetings a day and an early morning prayer service almost every day.

The interest in the meeting has increased in power and number from the first to the last. Jesus said, "If I am lifted up, I will draw all men unto Me, and wherever the body is (or pure strong meat is held up), there will the eagles be gathered together" (John 12:32; Luke 17:37). We praise the Lord that God's saints, or eagles, came from many parts; the pastor says they have come from almost every state in the Union. The Master of Assemblies has honored the feast with His glorious presence and continually supplied the table with the bounties of heaven. Oh, praise the Lord, He prepares the table in the presence of our enemies, and they cannot taste of the feast! Oh, see the beautiful whiteness, the shining brightness of the great loaves of "living bread" dropped down from heaven, not like the manna in the wilderness, after which people died, but whoever eats of this Bread will live forever (John 6:51). Oh, see, the table is filled with "a feast of fat things, a *feast of wine on the lees, of fat things full of marrow, of wines on the lees well refined"* (Isa. 25:6). See the strong meat to make us mighty in the Lord, the oil to make us shine that the beauty of the Lord may be seen in us.

Praise God for the many hungry hearts who have continued to gather here. Many were very timid at first and felt their unworthiness, yet the Master of the feast was always present to welcome and drive away their fears. As He began to reveal Himself to them, they fell in love with the Nazarene. As they let Him have His way with them, His love and brightness began to shine forth through them until, like Stephen, they looked like angels.

As they left for their homes, their testimonies rang out with shouts and tears that they had received much more than they had expected, and they must get busy in every way possible to show by word and life that Jesus will soon come to catch us away.

The Lord revealed His presence in many ways to saints and sinners. A Catholic man and wife were brought to Christ and received healing. They also were baptized in the Holy Spirit by the glory of God's brightness lighting up their room so that they were frightened and tried to hide. Many were healed in their homes, also in their seats. Many saw bright lights in the tent and saw it a blaze of glory. Many displays of the fire and glory of the Lord were seen in and around the tent. Often the whole tent, or parts of it, were seen lit up with the glory of God. The Lord was seen on the platform and in different parts of the tent.

Through the Spirit-filled saints the soft, sweet, dove-like song of the redeemed, in almost every meeting, rolled out through the tent and was heard by people far away. John described this as being like rolling thunder or the roaring of a lion (Rev. 10:3–4). The people looked on in wonder. A stillness like death settled over the people; then as God began to speak from heaven in other languages, through little children, old men and women, young men and maidens, plainly, fluently, intelligently, with great power, one at a time; and each message was interpreted, in the same voice as was given, by the one who gave the messages in the unknown language. Little children often interpreted their own messages, all speaking and telling the wonderful works of God, quoting strong prophecies that many did not know anything about, singing new songs about Jesus and His coming in words that never were heard before, then singing them in English. The congregation was spellbound in wonder and amazement. The fear of God rested on them. Many wept and trembled at the presence of God.

The Lord revealed Himself and put His seal on the work.

As the saints came together from day to day, the power and glory increased until the last day of the feast. The glory of God rested over the tabernacle, and many ministers, evangelists, and those who were about to start out in the battle came forward and were prayed for by the laying on of hands for gifts and stirring up those that they already had for fresh anointing and endowments of power. They were not disappointed, for the power of God fell on each one. Several received their baptism, speaking in plain tongues, and stepped right out and stood and preached to the people in a way that put the fear of God on the people. Many were baptized in the Holy Spirit in these meetings and received different gifts, many the gift of interpretation.

Beloved readers, the evil days are on us. The awful storm and darkness of the Tribulation is now sweeping over us with such force, and unless we get deep, yes, deeper in God, we will not be able to stand against all the powers of hell that soon will be let loose. Let us go forward. Do not tarry in the plains. Be willing to forsake every earthly thing, leave our earthly father's house and worship Him only, and He will reveal Himself to us as never before. Oh, join the bridal procession, run from the storm, and receive a crown of life! Amen.

The Coming King

Blow ye the trumpet, all ye Zion's host,
  Sound the alarm o'er ev'ry hill and plain,
Till all nations the warning message shall have heard
  That Jesus is coming again!

REFRAIN

He's coming again,
    O Zion's glorious King!
He's coming again,
    And reward for our labor He'll bring.
Send out the message over land and sea,
  Let all the earth take up the glad refrain,
Soon His glory transcendent ev'ry eye shall see,
  When Jesus to earth comes again.

Oh, then prepare to meet the coming King!
    Washed in His blood with garments pure and white,
For a crown of rejoicing He will with Him bring
    For all who have fought the good fight.

71

PUT A MARK ON EVERY MAN AND WOMAN

That Sighs and Cries for the Abominations Done in the Land

(Scripture text: 9th chapter of Ezekiel)

A Sermon by Mrs. Woodworth-Etter Petoskey, Michigan, July, 1916

The same things are taking place today that took place at the time of the destruction of Jerusalem, as revealed in the vision that the Lord gave the prophet Ezekiel nearly twenty-seven hundred years ago. *"He cried also in my ears with a loud voice, saying, Cause them that have charge over the city to draw near, even every man with his destroying weapon in his hand"* (Ezek. 9:1). This refers to the great army that destroyed Jerusalem. *"Behold, six men came from the way of the higher gate [men of authority], which lieth toward the north, and every man a slaughter weapon in his hand; one man among them was clothed in linen, with a writer's inkhorn by his side"* (v. 2). This man represents the baptized saints before the destruction of Jerusalem, with the Holy Spirit in them, going around baptizing people with blood and fire. *"And he called to the man clothed with linen, which had the writer's inkhorn"* (v. 3). He also represents the church today.

The Lord's instructions were, "*Go through the midst of the city, through the midst of Jerusalem, and set a mark upon the foreheads of the men that sigh and that cry for all the abominations that be done in the midst thereof. And to the others he said in mine hearing, Go ye after him through the city, and smite: let not your eye spare, neither have ye pity: slay utterly old and young, both maids, and little children, and women: but come not near any man upon whom is the mark; and begin at my sanctuary....And he said unto them, Defile the house, and fill the courts with the slain: go ye forth"* (vv. 4–7).

"*Then they began at the ancient men which were before the house....And they went forth and slew in the city*" (Ezek. 9: 6–7). In the vision Ezekiel witnessed God's orders being carried out: "*And it came to pass, while they were slaying them, and I was left, that I fell upon my face, and cried, and said, Ah Lord GOD! wilt thou destroy all the residue of Israel in thy pouring out of thy fury upon Jerusalem?*" (v. 8).

"*Then said he unto me, The iniquity of the house of Israel and Judah is exceeding great, and the land is full of blood, and the city full of perverseness: for they say, The LORD has forsaken the earth and the LORD seeth not*" (vv. 8–9). That is what they are saying today, that the Lord does not see any more. But God says, "*Mine eye shall not spare, neither shall I have pity, but I will recompense their way upon their head*" (v. 10).

"*And the LORD said unto him, Go through the midst of the city, through the midst of Jerusalem, and set a mark upon the foreheads of the men that sigh and that cry for all the abominations that be done in the midst thereof*" (v. 4). When it was done he came back and reported that the task was done, he had finished, the last one was sealed, and the door closed: "*And, behold, the man clothed with linen, which had the inkhorn by his side, reported the matter, saying, I have done as thou hast commanded me*" (v. 11).

Ezekiel had this vision nearly seven hundred years before Jesus came, and now it is about twenty-seven hundred years since he saw that vision—the vision of Jerusalem, of the church, and of the conditions of the world, especially of the church. The time that we are living in today is parallel in the world and the church, and the same wonderful things are taking place today just before the Great Tribulation, just before the wrath of God is poured out without mercy on the people. The same things are going on today. The Lord showed the prophet the awful condition of the church, and these things came upon the Jewish nation. But this time it will come on the whole world. The Jewish nation had sinned against God. They were God's peculiar people, God's called-out people. He said that He did not call them out because they were the most populous nation, for they were the fewest of all people (Deut. 7:7). God's chosen people have always been the fewest.

The Lord had called them out, chosen them, and set His love upon them because of His covenant with their forefathers who loved Him and kept His commandments (vv. 8–9). And unto these people came the law, the prophets, and then came Christ. God gave the law amidst mighty signs and wonders. When the temple was dedicated, the presence of God was seen. God appeared, gave them priests and prophets, revelations from heaven, spiritual signs and visions. Angels appeared. God talked from heaven and did all these things while His people obeyed. But by and by they got proud, haughty, and lifted up; and they began to glory in multiplying numbers, taking in people from other nations, who were uncircumcised in heart and not right with God, and gave them high places in the church, gave them great advantage, gave them charge of God's holy vessels; and they ruled the holy people with a rod of iron. The spiritual temple, the church, had one door—only one way to enter, one right foundation, and that was the circumcision of the heart and flesh.

As with Jeremiah, God wanted Ezekiel to warn His people that they have left the Fountainhead of living waters and hewn out broken cisterns that would not hold water (Jer. 2:13); they had begun to follow the wisdom of men. The glory of God appeared to Ezekiel, picked him up by the hair of his head, carried him through space between heaven and earth, and set him down at Jerusalem (Ezek. 8:3). He told him to look and see the awful things; the holy places were filled with pictures of serpents, like devil worship today, things that were unclean. God showed him all the abominations, took him into the holiest place where twenty-five men sat with their backs to God and worshipped the sun (v. 16). God wanted him to go and take the pattern of the temple in all its glory, when the glory of God filled the house, and warn these people; to take the pattern of the glorious temple, go and compare it with the existing pattern, show them where they failed, and see if they would repent. (See Ezekiel 43:10–11.) They were warned.

Ezekiel was not sent to the heathen, but to the people of the house of Israel. However, they failed to know that the prophet of God was in their midst; and when he stood and warned them, it did not do any good; and pretty soon the last prophet came, and they rejected him. They who had felt the power of God and watched the wonderful signs were left adrift, and for nearly four hundred years, perhaps more, the children of Israel were left without holy priests, without prophets, and without visions or revelations except a few humble little ones. They began to ask, "How long? There is no one that can tell us any more. We have no prophets, no priests, no visions, no revelations." They were once God's chosen people, and He was with them. But when they backslid, they lost connection—the pipe got filled up, the living water failed, and they began to hew themselves out broken cisterns—man's wealth and knowledge—which are an abomination without God.

That is what the condition was when Jesus Christ came. After they had been looking for Him for four thousand years, they did not know Him. Christ asked them, "Why is it that you do not discern the signs of this time? Your prophecies are fulfilled, and you are living in the days when the Son of Man is to come." (See Matthew 16:1–4.) But they were saying, "God has forsaken the earth. God doesn't see. God has left the earth, and the signs and wonders are all gone." They were following men's wisdom. They didn't want the power of God. They had left the fountains of living water. They didn't want to hear a shout in the camp, didn't want to see God's power. And so it is now.

Still, when Jesus came, He gave them another call just like the *"latter rain"* (Joel 2:23), but they spurned Him and turned Him away, just as they are doing today. And finally one day, He spread His hands out over them and wept and cried, "O Jerusalem, how often would I have gathered you from the storm that is coming!" (Matt. 23:37). And that is what He is saying tonight, but you are so blind you won't see, so deaf you won't hear. This day your house will be left desolate and your city will be destroyed. The enemy is coming in; the armies are coming in to lay your place desolate; the blood will flow like rivers.

But Jesus had a people who had accepted Him, who had followed the Lamb. One day Christ told them when speaking of the temple, "The day is coming when that beautiful temple will be torn down, not one stone left upon another, and the city will be destroyed." And they asked Him what would be the sign of His Coming, and of the ending of the world (Matt. 24:3). So Jesus told them.

Jesus is soon coming and we are concerned about the signs. The Lord told His disciples how they would know. He gave them signs and said, "When you see certain things come to pass, prepare to flee to the mountains; make ready to

591 Signs and Wonders

escape. And then other signs, and finally a certain sign—when you see this sign, if you have not made all preparations for flight, if you are on the housetop and have left anything in the house, don't take it, but flee to the mountains, because the gates will be closed, and you will be shut in" (Matt. 24:4–22). They believed what God said. They took His word by faith; they believed the Word and felt the responsibility. They loved their people, and they knew that unless they accepted Jesus Christ, they would not escape. They were sighing and crying for their own people according to the flesh and for their neighbors, and crying on account of the evil things coming, yet they were shut in with God. They had the mark of God upon them. When you see the things that are making the world turn pale and tremble, lift up your head and rejoice when these things come to pass, because it will soon be over. So the saints of God see these things and sigh and cry, yet they rejoice because they know they are saved.

To the Holy Spirit people, in a short time, all these things are coming. Get busy; warn the people whether they will bear or forbear; warn the people. See the saints of God, filled with the Holy Spirit. We see them go through the stores and business places, and here are the people who are coming in this army of destruction, going back and forth to their businesses, all unconcerned; so today we are getting ready for the great war.

Judgment is coming; destruction is coming; the city will be taken. They were laughed at as fools, fanatics, and enemies. They would not listen. But the saints knew that when the destruction came, the city would be taken, and their business would be no good; the enemy would take everything; their houses and lands would amount to nothing. The only thing they could do was to use their money to warn the people that destruction was coming. So their money and their gold and silver and their land would not do any good; neither will it do you any good. God help you to see it.

Blow the trumpet in Zion; sound the alarm (Joel 2:1). Jerusalem will be taken; the Tribulation is coming. The Day of the Lord is near; it hurries greatly. It is even at the door. Warn the people that they must have the seal of God on their foreheads (Ezek. 9:4). So we are going around, getting the people saved, giving the Word in the Holy Spirit so that they may be sealed with the finger and mark of God in the forehead. They had to have the mark of God in their foreheads to understand those things. Go through the streets of the city; note those who sigh and cry, and put the mark on them—that is what God is doing today. Glory to God!

That is what the disciples did, and the Word went out. They felt the scorn, persecution, and everything else, and saw the signs coming faster. They hid away in the mountains, and every day they felt worse because of their friends and neighbors; they would hasten into the city and try to show the people that these things were true. Even though the people did not believe, that did not change the fact.

At that time of the great feast, rabbis and many people from all over the world were there. The people of the Jewish nation were gathered there in the city. The city was full for the great feast. The Lord had told them, "When you see a certain signal, get out quickly. Don't go back to take anything out of your house; make haste to get out of the city." They would not believe anything and were having a good time. But at last a certain signal came; the gates were closed, and they were shut in with nothing to eat. But those who had the seal of the living God upon them were caught up—taken out—just like we will be when the time comes. Josephus, the historian, tells us that not one of the followers of Jesus Christ ever went down in the slaughter. They believed God, prepared for night, and escaped. Hallelujah!

We are a nation that is hated, a nation not desired, a nation despised. This sect is spoken against everywhere, but Paul said, "I am glad I am one of them." When Jesus comes again, you will be willing to be called a fanatic, a Holy Roller, or anything else. The day is coming. God help you to see it.

They were all taken unawares, the enemy came, the gates were shut, and the greatest calamity that the world ever saw fell upon the Jews. The army went into the city, into the inner court where the holy men—twenty-five of them—sat with their backs to God. They commenced at these fat priests and heads of the church, and they were slaughtered like oxen. We are told that they had no provisions, were shut in there, and literally starved to death. Delicate women ate their own children. Delicate women who would not put their feet on the ground ate their own children during that siege. Never had such a thing happened before—you know all about those things—some were carried away in captivity, only a few despised little ones left as slaves. But to God's people who had the mark, God revealed this knowledge to them, and every last one was taken out. Oh, Hallelujah!

But the prophet is looking down on us today, in just the same way. When Jesus comes, there will be such tribulation on the earth and such a time of trouble as was never known. That was only a little storm. The great preparation is going on over our country now and all over the world; the darkness will be so great that it can be felt; there will be such a time as the world never heard of, when Jesus comes to catch His bride away. All who sigh and all who cry for the abominable things that are going on in the world, those who have the mark are children of the day. You will not be overtaken as a thief in the night, for you are the children of light. The wise shall know, glory to God. History tells us that many rich men and many great men went down in the siege, but those who were called, who had God's mark, who were wanderers and pilgrims, and had to leave their homes and leave their wealth, they escaped with their lives and a few little things that they could take away to provide for their comfort. When Jesus comes, you won't take anything: all will be left for the devil to work with, because the world will go on just as it is now. When Jesus comes, it is not the end of the world. The disciples asked, *"What shall be the sign of thy coming, and of the end of the world?"* (Matt. 24:3). The bride, the saints, will be taken up when Jesus comes.

Every day watching, every day ready, but some won't go until you see a certain signal; you better get out quick. If you don't hurry, they will get you. You will be shut out.

Dear friends, we are living in a time parallel to that. Jesus is coming again. God is visiting the earth again, pouring out His Spirit. The church has gone back. When I was a girl, the Methodist Church was the most spiritual. People fell under the power of God, danced, and did lots of other things. They had an "amen" corner in every church, and when the preacher would come, he would not stop for anything, but go into the pulpit, open the Bible, and begin. No secondly, or thirdly, he did not have time. The "amens" came from all over the house. They had God, and they were a happy people. But now they are just like the Jews. We don't know God. He left us. We don't see Him. He is away. We don't like the fuss they are making, and what is the need of all that; and if any sister shouts, three or four sisters get around her, and she never shouts again.

Dear friends, if they (your own fathers, mothers, and grandfathers) were right, you would not like to have anyone say they were crazy. If they were right before God, someone is wrong today. But today, whenever they see any people get together and shout and praise God, they set them down as cranks.

The stiff-necked Jews did not know, but they wished they were one of the despised ones when they found out that they had been spared. They found out when it was too late. Likewise, after the cranks are taken away, they will say, "These people were not so cranky, after all."

God is pouring out His Spirit again—on all the nations of the earth, all over the world. God has a baptized people; saints of every nation and every tribe are in this country, baptized in the Holy Spirit and fire. They are working, getting people saved and baptized with the Holy Spirit and fire.

Get under the blood, and get the mark of the living God in the forehead. God is visiting you again on the eve of the awful Tribulation. Men and women will eat their own flesh, eat their own children. Look at the families that have gone down, bodies thrown in the ocean for the sharks to eat, and now they want flesh and want to get after the living. God says that it will be that way, and that devilish appetite is going to get into animals of all kinds, into the wild beasts, and more so because famine is coming and animals will leave the wilderness and come into the cities to get something to eat. There will be war, famine, and pestilence, and all these things at one time. If you escape the war, the wild beasts will get you; if you escape the lion and the bear and enter your own house and lean up against the wall to die in peace, a serpent will bite you. Great God, don't you see these things are coming? God has not left you without warning.

Watch the signs, and read the Word—read the Word, and watch the signs. These are the things the prophet saw in vivid pictures way back there. These things were seen twenty-seven hundred years ago. One day with the Lord is only a little while; a thousand years, only a day (2 Pet. 3:8). We are among the people on the stage of action today who will be in this great army of slaughter and blood. All saints will be taken out; those who will become saints here on the earth today. This generation will never die until Jesus comes. Some of these living here tonight will never see death until they see the Son of God coming in glory.

So we see every day the signs being fulfilled everywhere that Jesus is coming. One great sign is that God's real saints are making such an effort to go through the world, running the risk of everything to enlighten the people, finding hearts that will receive the message, get saved, and let God mark them and seal them with the seal of the living God in their foreheads. Make the vision plain. God help me. Will the people see that we are actors in this vision? Make it plain so that those who receive the message and the seal will run to get ready. That is what we are trying to do.

Now, beloved, we must have this mark of God, not only saved but sealed. Get baptized with the Holy Spirit, get sealed with the seal of the living God. It may be that if you get deep enough, you will be hid away from all these awful things that are coming on the earth. Be shut in with God.

The angels represented as holding back the four winds of the earth are letting loose now, as sure as God lives. We wonder about these things. Angels see the condition of the earth—the cup of iniquity is full. O why can't we let loose? Hold back the destructive powers. May we let loose; may the sun be turned on to scorch men? Can the high winds tear down the cedars; can the tidal waves sweep the towns away; can the earthquakes shake the earth? But the great angel of Jesus Christ says, Hold on a little while, hold on a little while. Do not let loose. Hold back the power of the sun; hold back the greatest tidal waves, the greatest winds, the greatest earthquakes, the greatest calamities, until we seal the servants of God with the seal of the living God in their forehead.

You who are the servants of God tonight must be sealed with the seal of God, with the blood and fire mark, sealed with the seal of the living God. Hold back all the calamities; it would be a great inconvenience to the saints. They are the lights of the world. For the sake of the souls who want to be saved, He will give the people a little more time to work. Hold back! What for? Until we have sealed the saints of God with the seal of the living God in the forehead.

My God, help these people to see why the sun did not get two or three degrees hotter and kill millions. Don't you see the signs of what is coming? One hundred fell in Chicago in the heat. A few more degrees and millions would have gone down. All these things are coming. Watch and pray. Be in an attitude of prayer or praise all the time that you may be counted worthy to escape these awful calamities and stand before the Son of God. Don't you see we have no time for foolish talking for what this one or that one said? I am here to tell what Jesus said. I don't steal words from my neighbor.

God help us to get where we can believe and get hold of God.

Two will be in the fields; one will be taken, the other left (Matt. 24:40). One will be watching and praying, the other idly talking and jesting, and you answer him because you have to listen, but soon you will look around—he doesn't answer. Why, what is the matter, Tom? You are alone; he is gone. Where did he go? You find him if you can. He escaped. Two will be sleeping in the same bed; one will be caught away, and the other will snore away. He escaped before the gates were shut, glory to God. Caught away.

That is just going to be the way it is when Jesus comes. He will take them up alive *"in the twinkling of an eye"* (1 Cor. 15:52). Not another body but this body will be so light. We are not waiting for wings, but we are looking for the dynamo from heaven to lighten these bodies. We will rise like He did. Hands and feet will be like wings. We will go sailing through the air—up over the stars—up to meet the Lord with a shout. Glory to God!

But for those who are left, it will be so, so different. Those who rejected Christ will be left to go down. Oh, God, how we ought to be sighing and crying for the ones who will be left. We don't sigh enough; we don't cry enough. But at the same time we are so full of joy, we have to give vent or explode. Be glad because you are living in the time of the latter rain. Rejoice and be glad. At the same time, we are sighing and crying because of the calamities that are coming. Many times I cry out, the Holy Spirit in me crying out. It came to me like the prophet said when he was speaking of this time, *"My bowels, my bowels! I am pained at my very heart"* (Jer. 4:19). His body was a burning waste, and his head was a fountain of tears, for the destruction that is going on in the earth, the awful days that are coming. Jesus is weeping over Jerusalem. How the Holy Spirit weeps through me; it seems as though I would cry until I would die. But I go on.

God is putting a mark on us to guard us against the damnable things that are coming on the earth. Dear friends, don't you see? The angels are holding back the four winds. They are about to let loose. Oh, can we let loose for they are so wicked? Let the people go. No, not yet; not until we have sealed the servants of God with the seal of the living God in their forehead. Go through the streets, and put a mark upon everyone who sighs and cries. Put the mark of God on them. Let them be baptized in the Holy Spirit. Jesus Christ will baptize you with the Holy Spirit and fire. He will give us wisdom, seal us with knowledge. You will not be left in the dark, but you shall know. You who are saved and living pure holy lives before God, if you don't get down and seek more of God and be sealed, you are going to be left in the dark. If you don't get where you can feel the everlasting arms of Jesus around you, you will be carried away in the press, and you will not be ready to go up when Jesus comes. Oh, hold until the servants of God get the light and are sealed with the seal of the living God in their forehead.

No wonder I don't rest—I am trusting in God to carry me through. I know these things are true. God help us. We are getting pretty well shut in now. So many false doctrines of the devil are coming in. You must keep under the blood, or you will be carried away. I praise God for the knowledge that Jesus is coming soon. Praise His name forever. These awful tribulations are just now on the earth. You know the Lord said certain things would happen, and these are only the beginning of sorrows. The nations are mad. They are crazy, filled with jealous hatred, killing each other. One nation against another, several have gone down. Look at them. No one knows the real truth; the best ones in the country are going down. May God help you to see it.

This is the beginning of sorrows. The four angels are going to let loose, as sure as you live. Let me ask you, travelers to the bar of God, if this is the beginning of sorrows, what will the end be? You may escape the worst things and be hid away. The prophet looking down to the last days saw the saints going up. He says, "Come up, My people, and enter into the place prepared for you, and shut the doors after you, and hide for a little while, for the Lord is coming down to punish the inhabitants of the earth, and their blood shall flow like the dust and their flesh lie like dung, and they will not be buried. Tens of thousands are being burned in piles and rotting." You know, you have heard these things. Nobody knows where the end will be. Isn't that being fulfilled now? If this is only the beginning of sorrows, what will the end be? God is holding back the worst until they have been warned, and warned again.

God gave a wonderful vision to a man who was raised to be a Catholic priest. Two angels visited him in the night and revealed to him the things that are about to come to pass and told him he must go and warn that great congregation, about two thousand of them.

God is warning the people here, giving them another chance to be sealed with the seal of the living God, and the last one will soon be sealed. God is calling this country in mercy, but He will soon call at the mouth of the cannon. The best thing is to hide away. God help us to be up and doing, clothed in linen with the power of the Holy Spirit working through us. Blow the trumpet; get right with God. Ask God for knowledge and wisdom, get the resurrection power in your body, and when Jesus comes, be snatched out of this world.

We who are alive and remain will not prevent those who are asleep. The dead in Christ shall rise first and shake off the dust and worms like dew and will go up with a shout. Praise the Lord. They will meet us. Don't be afraid for the dead who died in Christ, for when Jesus comes, God will bring them with Him, so God is coming to His Son's wedding to meet the bride. We don't need to worry about the dead ones. They will come up. Oh, the time is near; it will not be very long until we will see our loved ones. Some will be laid away the very day He comes, at the very last minute. I laid my dear husband away a little over two years ago, and when he went he said, "I am not looking to the grave at all." But his body is there, and different ones have seen him come up in his glorified body, and he will be one of the first to meet me when I rise in the air. Many dear saints have died shouting, "Gone to glory!" They will be raised, and I will meet them. O dear friends, all who have died in Christ will be raised first. We will rise in our glorified, immortal bodies to meet the Lord in the air.

Now, beloved, don't let this run off; let it go down and burn; let it burn in your heart, because it is a message from the Lord. Hallelujah! Something you have never heard, but you hear it now.

You see the parallel with the time of the prophet Ezekiel; you see the danger; you are being warned. Take your Bibles; ask God about these people who are so foolish. Oh, glory to God, I am glad I am clearheaded enough to believe God. I am glad I am light enough to go up in the air when He comes. Hallelujah! Glory! I am looking to go up in the sky—up in the air, not to the grave. Glory to God! Hallelujah! Amen!

THE HOLY SPIRIT

CONTENTS

EARLY LIFE AND EXPERIENCE IN THE WORK

I was born in New Lisbon, Ohio, on July 22, 1844, the fourth daughter of Samuel Underwood. My parents were not Christians, but when I was ten years old, they joined the Disciples' Church. One year later, my father, who was a drunkard, got struck by lightning in a terrible storm and died. It was an awful blow to all our young hearts to see our father carried cold and stiff into the house and our mother fainting as fast as they could bring her to. There were eight of us children, and soon my older sisters and I had to go out and work to provide for the family. I longed for an education, but this seemed impossible.

At the age of thirteen, I attended a meeting that a Dr. Belding was holding. When I heard the story of the Cross, my heart was filled with the love of Jesus and my eyes were like a fountain of tears. When the invitation to seek God was given, I was the first one to respond. It seemed so far to the front, but I said,

> I can't but perish if I go,
> I am resolved to try,
> For if I stay away I know
> I shall forever die.

The minister took a great interest in me and said many things to encourage me. If he could have looked forward and seen my lifework for the Master, he would have rejoiced to know how kindly he had spoken to the poor little orphan girl. But I did not get fully converted then. The next day, as they took me down to the creek to baptize me, I heard someone say, "Maybe she will be drowned." It scared me a little. I thought, "Maybe I will." But I said, "Lord, I will go through if I do." So I asked the Lord to save me. While I was going down into the water, a light came over me, and I was converted. The people saw the change and said that I had fainted. Then began my new life of peace and joy in the Savior's love. I also felt that I had a calling to go out into the highways and byways and gather in the lost sheep.

The church in those days did not believe that women had a right to publicly preach Jesus. Had I told them my heart's desire, they would have mocked me.

Later, I married a Mr. Woodworth. I hoped that now the way would open for me to go out in the work for Jesus. But one trial and hardship after another was my lot. I felt happy with the few little children that God gave us, but soon the Angel of Death took away my bright, blue-eyed, darling boy. One year had hardly passed before another one was taken away.

About this time, my little daughter, Georgia, was converted. We loved so much to talk about the goodness of God and longed for the time when we could meet the little ones over on the other shore. In a short time, she took sick and died. For weeks before she died, her face was all lighted up with the glory of God. She would say, "Oh, Mamma, if you could go with me, I would be so happy." I said, "Georgia, I will try." But that would not do. She said, "Oh, Mamma, say you will. I cannot die unless you promise to meet me in heaven." I said, "Georgia, by the grace of God, I will meet you in heaven." She said, "Now I am ready. I know you will come."

The Sabbath before she died, she called me to her bedside and said, "Mamma, I am going to leave you this week," and she began to set her house in order. She gave her Testament to me. Just before she passed away, she said, "Oh, Mamma, I see Jesus and the angels coming for me." It seemed to me that I could see them as they went sweeping through the gates into the New Jerusalem. It was like death to part with my darling, but Jesus was precious to my soul. I could say with David, "They cannot come back to me, but I can go to them." (See 2 Samuel 12:1–23.) Praise the Lord for the Christians' hope.

From the time of the sad occurrences just mentioned, my health was very poor. I seemed to hover between life and death many times. Now I know that all this time God was preparing me for my life's work. I could never dismiss from my mind the call that I had, and Jesus began to give me such wonderful visions. Heaven is a place; its inhabitants are real and not imaginary. I saw Jerusalem in it and talked face to face with Jesus. But I was not willing to go.

When I was alone, I missed my darling so much that I wept as though my heart would break. Then I would always pray; as I prayed, I would forget everything earthly and soar away by faith to the Golden City. There I would see my darlings all together shining in glory and looking at me and saying, "Mamma, do not weep for us, but come this way." I would always end by praising and giving glory to God for taking them to such a happy place. Lizzie, our oldest child, aged sixteen, was all we had left of six sweet children.

In all these trials, God was preparing me and opening the way for the great battle against the Enemy of souls; now the great desire of my heart was to work for Jesus. I longed to win a star for the Savior's crown. But when I thought of my weakness, I shrank from the work.

Sometimes when the Spirit of God was striving and calling so plainly, I would yield and say, "Yes, Lord; I will go." The glory of God came upon me like a cloud, and I seemed to be carried away hundreds of miles and set down in a field of wheat where the sheaves were falling all around me. I was filled with zeal and power, and I felt as if I could stand before the whole world and plead with dying sinners. It seemed to me that I must leave all and go at once. Then Satan would *come in like a flood* (Isa. 59:19) and say, "You would look nice preaching, being a laughingstock for the people to make sport of. You know you could not do it." I would think of my weakness and say, "No, of course I cannot do it." Then I would be in darkness and despair. I wanted to run away from God, or I wished I could die. But when I began to look at the matter in this way, that God knew all about me and was willing and able to qualify me for the work, I asked Him to qualify me.

I want the reader to understand that at this time, I had a good spiritual experience, a pure heart that was full of the love of God, but I was not qualified for God's work. I knew that I was but a worm. God would have to take a worm to hammer out a mountain. Then I asked God to give me the power He gave the Galilean fishermen—to baptize me for service. I came like a child asking for bread. I looked for it. God did not disappoint me. The power of the Holy Spirit came down as a cloud. It was brighter than the sun. I was covered and wrapped up in it. My body was as light as the air. It seemed that heaven came down. I was baptized with the Holy Spirit and with fire and power, which have never left me. Oh, praise the Lord. There was liquid fire, and the angels were all around in the fire and glory. It is through the Lord Jesus Christ and by this power that I have stood before hundreds of thousands of men and women and proclaimed the unsearchable riches of Christ.

The time finally came when I felt I had to promise God or die. I promised God that if He would restore my health and show me the work, I would do it. I got better immediately. Soon we moved to another settlement, and they took me to church. God seemed to say to me, "I brought you here; go to work." I was very timid. When I rose to testify, I trembled like a leaf; I began to make excuses, saying, "O God, send someone else."

Then the Lord caused me to see the bottomless pit, open in all its horror and woe. There was weeping, wailing, and gnashing of teeth (Matt. 8:12; 13:42). It was surrounded by people who seemed unconscious of their danger and who, without a moment's warning, would tumble into that awful place. I was above them on a narrow plank walk that wound up toward heaven, exhorting and pleading with the people to escape that awful place. This vision left a great impression on my mind. In meetings, when I felt I should talk or pray, I would resist as long as I could; then this awful vision would rise before me, and I would see souls sink into eternal woe. Again I would hear the voice of Jesus whisper, "I am with you; do not be afraid." In a moment, I would be on my feet or knees. I would have been glad to preach if I had been a man and not had so much opposition from my husband and friends.

Several ministers whom I had never seen before told me that God was calling me to the ministry and that I would have to go. Then I thought of going through a course of studies, but I could not get my mind on any study. Everything seemed empty and vacant.

In a vision one night, Jesus asked me what I was doing on the earth. I said, "I am going to work in Your vineyard." He asked, "When?" I answered, "When I get prepared." Jesus said, "Souls are perishing. Go now and tell the people what I have done for you, and I will be with you." I told Him I did not understand the Bible well enough. Then a large open Bible appeared upon the wall, and the verses stood out in raised letters. The glory of God shone around the book. I looked, and I could understand it all. Then Jesus said again, "Go, and I will be with you." I cried, "Lord, where shall I go?" Jesus said, "Go here, go there, wherever souls are perishing."

The first meeting that I undertook to hold was in a little town among my husband's people, where we had lived before. I said, "In the name of the Lord, I will try and leave the results with God." As I rose to speak, this text came to me: "Set thine house in order: for thou shalt die, and not live" (Isa. 38:1). The timid spirit left me, and the words came faster than I could give them utterance. People got converted all through the neighborhood.

Soon after this, God led me to a place called the Devil's Den. It was distinguished for infidelity and skepticism. There was an old free church there, in which no one was ever known to be converted. Some of the best ministers had tried to hold meetings there but had left the place in disgust. When I arrived, a large crowd came to see me out of curiosity and expected me to back out. They said, "No one will come." I told them, "If they do not come, I will be alone and pray to God to pour out His Spirit on the people." I also scheduled day meetings.

God came to my rescue. The fire fell. The news spread like fire, and Christians, singers, and ministers came in from miles around. There were hundreds who could not get in the church. An old man and his wife and nine children got converted. Some of the hardest sinners in the whole country got converted. I organized a Sunday school of one hundred and fifty students and appointed a man as superintendent who had been a noted drunkard. From this time forth, "Macedonian calls" (see Acts 16:9) came in constantly, and people would fall like dead men when the power fell. They would lie there for days at a time and have visions and come out brightly converted.

Since the early part of my ministry, which has now been going on for over forty years, some came out of the experience speaking in other tongues. I never felt led to speak much about this experience, but I knew it was of God and that it was according to the Bible. God also gave me the ministry of healing. He showed me that I was to lay hands on the sick and pray for their recovery. The first person that I laid my hands on publicly and prayed for was instantly healed of an incurable disease and turned out to be a wonderful Christian worker in the meeting. This gave me hope and courage. In my ministry I have prayed for hundreds and thousands of people. Almost innumerable people from all walks of life have been healed of all manner of diseases that mankind is susceptible to. Healing for the body, like salvation for the soul, is in the Atonement and belongs to the Gospel. They should never be separated. I have traveled the continent many times and preached to thousands of people in all the large cities of this country. While always weak in the natural, I followed where the Spirit led and trusted Him for the anointing whenever needed. He has never left me. He bears me up under the anointing and makes me as bold as a lion in bearing witness for my Master. Amen.

For a more complete record of my life, please refer to my book *Signs and Wonders*.[1]

> Oh, the wonders of creation,
>   And the work of nature's God,
> Call forth songs of admiration
>   As we travel life's rough road.

---

1. See Maria Woodworth-Etter, *Signs and Wonders* (New Kensington, PA: Whitaker House, 1997).

1

THE SPIRIT REVEALS THE DEEP THINGS OF GOD

Eye hath not seen, nor ear heard, neither have entered into the heart of man,
the things which God hath prepared for them that love him. But God hath
revealed them unto us by his Spirit: for the Spirit searcheth all things, yea,
the deep things of God.
—1 Corinthians 2:9–10

This passage is not understood by anyone unless he has the Holy Spirit. Many people today apply this to eternity, to the other world; they think that we never know these things until we get into the other world. I am glad that the Scripture explains itself. *"Eye hath not seen"*—in the natural state. God has, in the present, revealed things to us by His Spirit, by His Spirit in this world. *"The Spirit searcheth all things, yea, the deep things of God."*

I desire to especially call your attention to 1 Corinthians 2:14: *"The natural man receiveth not the things of the Spirit of God: for they are foolishness unto him: neither can he know them, because they are spiritually discerned."*

The natural man cannot understand this wonderful Scripture. There are two classes of men: the spiritual man and the natural man. The natural man is *"poisoned by bitterness and bound by iniquity"* (Acts 8:23 NKJV); the spiritual man is *"born of God"* (1 John 3:9) and walks in the Spirit; he gets out into the deep. The natural man can never discern spiritual things; he can never hear and understand the work of the Lord. These things pass all human understanding. The wisdom of this world, intellect, and science can never understand the spiritual things of God.

There are two kinds of wisdom. *"The wisdom of this world is foolishness with God"* (1 Cor. 3:19). The natural man cannot comprehend the wisdom from above (James 3:17). It never enters his imagination to think of the things God has prepared for those who love Him. He has prepared them already, and He has revealed them to us by His Spirit. His Spirit lets us down into the deep things, even the *"deep things of God."* This is what we preach, what we practice, and what we stand on. The work of the Spirit is foolishness to the natural man; but he who has the Spirit can discern spiritual things.

Various Kinds of Spirits

There are many kinds of power and many spirits going out in the world today. We are told to *"try the spirits"* (1 John 4:1); they are many. Everything is revealed by God through the blessed Holy Spirit. There is only one Spirit that we want anything to do with: not our own spirits, nor any other spirit, but the Spirit of the living God. *"As many as are led by the Spirit of God, they are the sons of God"* (Rom. 8:14).

The Spirit will lead us into all truth, all the way. He will lead us where we can get the truth. The child of God will be led into the baptism of the Holy Spirit and of fire (Matt. 3:11), the Pentecostal baptism. Then we can go from one deep thing to another. The Holy Spirit is sent to us by Jesus Christ, and all gifts come through the Holy Spirit. Jesus said of the Spirit, "'He shall not speak of himself,' but of Me. He will speak to you and 'show you things to come' (John 16:13)." We believe it. Glory to God!

This is the Holy Spirit who came at Pentecost and turned Jerusalem upside down. Jesus said that when the Holy Spirit came, He would abide with us forever (John 14:16), even unto the end. The work of the Spirit is foolishness to the natural man; he cannot comprehend it.

Unless you will hear the voice of God, the voice of the natural man will make you attribute what you see to excitement or to some other power. When the Holy Spirit is poured out, two kinds of people are revealed: one is convinced and convicted, and accepts it; the other says, "If I accept this, I will have to lead a different life and be a laughingstock for the world." They are not willing to pay the price, so they begin to draw back. At first they are amazed at the strange works of God. Then, when they won't accept them, they begin to despise them. Everyone who continues to despise the works of the Holy Spirit will perish.

Counterfeit Power

There are many powers in the world that are not of God but are counterfeit. However, where there is a counterfeit, there is always the genuine. No one ever tries to counterfeit anything that is not genuine; that is a sure evidence that it is genuine.

The Devil shows his power in a good many ways in order to deceive people. He tries to substitute some other power for the power of God. It was so in the time of Moses and the time of the prophets. God's power was especially in the world at certain times, and then magicians would come up with their power and show something that seemed similar. One was of God; the other was of the Devil.

Moses went to Egypt to lead the people out. He threw down his rod before Pharaoh and it became a live serpent. The magicians said they had the same power, so they threw some rods down and they became serpents. One was of God, and the other was of the Devil.

Moses did not get scared and run away. He knew God, and he wouldn't have run if all the serpents in Egypt had come before him. He stood his ground, and I admire him for it; I do not like a coward. What was the result? Moses' serpent swallowed the others up, head and tail! There was nothing left of them. Those who are trying to overthrow the power of God and substitute something else will have a Day of Judgment. The time is coming when the almighty power of God will swallow them up in the *"day of his wrath"* (Rev. 6:17).

The Coming of the Spirit

The Lamb of God left the realm of glory and came down here to be footsore, dusty, weary, and spit upon. He said, *"I come to do thy will, O God"* (Heb. 10:9). If

He had not borne all these things, if He had not gone all the way to the cross, the Holy Spirit never could have come. If Jesus had been left in the tomb, the Holy Spirit never could have come. As soon as He arose from the dead and ascended into heaven, the Holy Spirit could come.

God gave His Son the highest place, before all the hosts of heaven. Then He sent the Holy Spirit to dwell in these bodies of ours, His temple (1 Cor. 3:16). The Spirit was to be given after Jesus was glorified. The Holy Spirit is a great power. In the Bible, He is compared to wind, water, and fire.

At Pentecost, He came like a cyclone, a *"rushing mighty wind"* (Acts 2:2). He comes like *"rivers of living water"* (John 7:38). He comes like fire; tongues of fire sat upon each of the disciples at Pentecost (Acts 2:1–4). Wind, water, and fire—the most destructive elements we have, yet the most useful.

God uses these images to denote the mighty power of the Holy Spirit. We see many demonstrations of His mighty power, and *"we cannot but speak the things which we have seen and heard"* (Acts 4:20) of His glory and His majesty. When we know these things, we are witnesses to His power, His majesty, and His glory. Glory to God!

He is a mighty power, and He lives in these bodies of ours. He lets down upon us here an *"eternal weight of glory"* (2 Cor. 4:17), and when we are filled with glory, we have to release it in some way, or we would explode. What are we? We are only worms of the dust. We cannot bear the glory of God; one breath from Him lays us prostrate. In the Bible, we read how men fell when they had a glimpse of God's glory.

Paul tells us that there are those who have a form of godliness but who deny the power thereof; from such we are to turn away (2 Tim. 3:5). *"In the last days perilous times shall come"* (v. 1), and those who have reprobate minds will oppose God's children to their faces, even as the magicians opposed Moses.

In the last days, some people will be living very near to God, but the Devil will have his workers, too, who will attribute signs and wonders to any power except the power of Christ. The Lamb of God, the Lion of the Tribe of Judah, has never lost His power and never will lose His power. I would hate to say by my actions that I thought the Devil had more power than God.

God's Power Is Unlike Any Other

There is a wonderful difference between the power of God and any of those other powers. The Holy Spirit only comes in Christ. He only comes into the bodies of those who love God. When He takes possession of us, He takes us away into the sweetest experience this side of heaven; we are alone with God. He talks to us and reveals to us *"things to come"* (John 16:13).

It is wonderful! God puts us under the power, and God takes us out. No man can bestow this power upon another; it comes only through Jesus Christ. There are two kinds of power, and people who do not know the difference will stand up today and say that wisdom is foolishness.

Many people today have an intellectual faith, a historical faith; they believe. Well, *"the devils also believe, and tremble"* (James 2:19). Belief is one thing; faith is another. *"The letter killeth, but the spirit giveth life"* (2 Cor. 3:6). If the truth is hidden, it is hidden to those who are lost.

Spiritual Manifestations

We may have intellectual imaginations and go through courses of study, learning the doctrines of men. Yet no one but the Holy Spirit can give us a real, abiding, tangible, definite knowledge of the *"things of God."* They seem foolish to the natural man. Sometimes the Holy Spirit gives a spirit of laughter, and sometimes of weeping, and everyone in the place will be affected by the Spirit.

I have stood before thousands of people and been unable to speak; I could only weep. When I was able to see, people were weeping everywhere; that is one way the Holy Spirit works. I have stood for an hour with my hand raised, held by the mighty power of God. When I came to myself and saw the people, their faces were shining.

"God moves in mysterious ways, His wonders to perform." He is the God I worship. Jesus says, "Here am I, and the children You have given me." (See John 17:9–11, 24.) We believe in signs and wonders, not from beneath but from above. We are a people to be wondered at; we are to be a sign among the people.

The heaven of heavens cannot contain God, yet He tabernacles with men. He comes and dwells in us. His gifts are demonstrated through us, so that people may know that God dwells in Zion (Ps. 9:11). We have a bodyguard of angels.

The angels of the Lord encamp around those who love God (Ps. 34:7). *"Our citizenship is in heaven"* (Phil. 3:20 NKJV), and we are on the way there.

The Holy Spirit works in many ways. People saw the fire on the disciples' heads at Pentecost. They staggered like drunken men; then the Holy Spirit took possession of their tongues. God Almighty spoke through one hundred and twenty of His children, and they told of His wonderful works. They did not know what they were saying, but every man in that multitude in Jerusalem heard them speak in his own native tongue. (See Acts 2:1–13.)

I am glad God does the same thing today. People who are not saved hate the power of God. The cold, dead formalists cannot understand the power of God; it is foolishness to them. They think people are excited, hypnotized, or have lost their minds.

May God have mercy upon us if we do not know God's power from hypnotic power or the Devil's power! If any man speaks against the Holy Spirit, it will never be forgiven him; to attribute the work of the Holy Spirit to the Devil or to any unclean spirit cannot be forgiven; that is the unpardonable sin. (See Matthew 12:31–32.)

Some people are calling the work of the Holy Spirit the work of the Devil, and they had better beware. There are different kinds of spirits and different kinds of power, and the *"natural man"* (1 Cor. 2:14) cannot understand the work of the Holy Spirit: shining faces, singing, shouting *"as one, to make one sound"* (2 Chron. 5:13), sometimes staggering and falling, *"drunken, but not with wine"* (Isa. 29:9), sometimes speaking *"with other tongues"* (Acts 2:4).

Spiritual Manifestation in Angelic Singing

Praise God, some of the redeemed are getting so filled with the Holy Spirit that He is singing songs through them that none but the redeemed can sing. (See Revelation 14:3.) *"There are diversities of gifts, but the same Spirit"* (1 Cor. 12:4). Paul tells us that the Spirit will work in you in one way and in someone else in another way. You know it is the same Spirit who is working, and you do not get jealous when the other person is blessed. No matter how the Spirit works, every member of the body benefits. (See 1 Corinthians 12:1–7.)

People look on these things—they see us lift up holy hands to God, for example—and they don't like it. They are so dead that they cannot get their hands up. Paul said, *"I will therefore that men pray every where, lifting up holy hands"* (1 Tim. 2:8). The psalmist said, *"O clap your hands, all ye people; shout unto God with the voice of triumph"* (Ps. 47:1).

People go to the theater and clap their hands, but when we get our grave clothes off and begin to clap our hands, they think it is an awful thing. David danced with all his might before the ark of the Lord (2 Sam. 6:14), and sometimes the Spirit of God gets into our feet and makes them like *"hinds' feet"* (2 Sam. 22:34).

David said, *"By my God have I leaped over a wall"* (2 Sam. 22:30). How much more will He enable us in these last days, when we are getting ready for a flight in the air! We must get a good supply of this power. The same power that took Jesus up to heaven will take us up one day.

We want more of it, don't we? More of this mighty power. No matter what people say—that it is foolishness, hypnotism, and every other thing—that doesn't make it so. The Spirit will take us out into the deep things, even the *"deep things of God."*

Old Testament Types Revealed in the New

Many things recorded in the Old Testament are types of the work of the Spirit in the New Testament. Many of the movements of God through His children seemed to be foolishness; the messages He gave His prophets to carry seemed very foolish, humanly speaking.

He gave Noah the plans for the ark. There was to be only one window and only one door. Noah built it according to God's plan. He did not heed the jeers of the people, who thought he was losing his mind. He was a laughingstock to everybody; but he went on building, and he proved the wisdom of God in the end.

He built the ark, and God provided the water, more water than they wanted, too much water for them. What happened? God took those who believed Him into the ark and shut the door. The water rose, and the ark went above the tree-tops—as we are going someday. God is building the ark now, and the works of the Holy Spirit are foolishness to the people who are fighting them.

The ark sailed away, and the world went down, all except Noah and his family. Not many are going into the ark God is building. People are crying, "Foolishness!"

Obedience to God

One time there was a great battle in the land of Israel. The enemy had gathered like consuming grasshoppers. God knew there were a lot of cowards among His people, and He tested them until only three hundred were left to meet the enemy. God can work by the few as well as the many. He told Gideon what to do; Gideon divided the men into three companies and *"put a trumpet in every man's hand, with empty pitchers, and lamps within the pitchers"* (Judg. 7:16). He said, "When I give the signal, blow the trumpet and say, 'The sword of the LORD, and of Gideon' (v. 18)."

God always has a leader. As they obeyed their leader, something happened. At the signal, they blew the trumpets and broke the pitchers, revealing the lamps. They shouted, *"The sword of the LORD, and of Gideon."*

At the shout and the light, the enemy was frightened to death and started to run, but God sent confusion among them. That little band of three hundred "fanatics" put the whole host of the enemy to flight. What they did seemed foolish, did it not? But what was the outcome? The whole army of the enemy was conquered.

God used a vision—He does sometimes. He told Gideon to go down to the enemy's camp, where Gideon heard a man tell his friend a vision or dream he had had: *"A loaf of barley bread tumbled into the camp of Midian; it came to a tent and struck it so that it fell and overturned, and the tent collapsed"* (Judg. 7:13 NKJV).

His friend interpreted it: *"This is nothing else but the sword of Gideon!...Into his hand God has delivered Midian and the whole camp"* (v. 14 NKJV). So Gideon believed and took courage. (See Judges 6:1–7:23.)

Children of God, those of you who think you are something are really nothing. When you realize you are nothing, God fights for you. How foolish the method of fighting the Midianites seemed! Israel might have said, "If we break the pitchers, the lamps will show the enemy where we are, and they will shoot us." When God says, "Go forward," obey Him; He takes care of His own.

Truly, God moves in mysterious ways. Remember the fall of Jericho? The city had great walls around it, and all the people of Jericho were shut inside to protect themselves from the Israelites. God told Joshua that he and his men of war should march around the city once a day for six days, with seven priests bearing before the ark of the covenant seven trumpets of rams' horns. On the seventh day, they were to march around the city seven times, with the priests blowing the trumpets. When they made a long blast on the trumpets, the people were to shout, and the walls would fall down. (See Joshua 6:1–20.)

It took faith to do all that marching without any sign of victory and to shout. Why, anyone can shout after the walls fall. Humanly speaking, don't you see how foolish this all was? They had made no preparations for war, only marching and blowing rams' horns. But that was God's way, and they were silly enough to obey God! What was the result? The walls went down.

We could go all through the Word of God in this way. There are so many things that seem so silly, things people would laugh at, but it was God's way, and His servants were willing to obey Him. The result showed God's wonderful wisdom and brought victory through a visible display of His power.

Spiritual Revelation

When these visible signs came, they put a fear of God upon the people; it is the same way with the works of the Holy Spirit. The ways of God and the works of the Spirit are foolishness to the *"natural man"* (1 Cor. 2:14), but what is the outcome?

Paul said, *"If any man among you seemeth to be wise in this world, let him become a fool, that he may be wise"* (1 Cor. 3:18). Later, he said, *"I will* [now] *come to visions and revelations of the Lord"* (2 Cor. 12:1). He said that he had been carried away to the *"third heaven"*—whether in the body or out of the body, he could not tell (v. 2). He could not tell whether his whole body went or not; he was so light that he could not tell whether he had left his body here or not, but he said, *"God knoweth"* (v. 2). There he heard unutterable things (v. 4).

At another time, Paul was praying in the temple and fell under the power of God; he fell into a trance (Acts 22:17–18). He appeared to be unconscious to the world, but he was never so wide awake to God in his life.

It is during these times that the Spirit of God lets us down into the deep things, even the *"deep things of God."* Peter fell into a trance on the housetop, and God spoke to him three times (Acts 10:9–16). Paul and Silas started out to visit converts. Then Paul had a vision; he saw a man of Macedonia holding out his hands and saying, "Come over and help us." He knew it was the call of God, so they changed their course and went there; this was altogether different from their original plans.

When they began to preach and were arrested, they might have thought they had been mistaken; but Paul knew God, and he never doubted it was God's voice that had called him. They might have said, "If we had not come here, we would have had many people to preach to. Now we have come to this strange place and been put in prison, with our feet fastened in the stocks." The Devil put them in there; but God permitted it, and God delivered them. (See Acts 16:9–10, 16–34.)

There are many wonderful things all around us in these last days, things the natural man cannot understand, demonstrations of God's power. There are other powers, too, and many do not know the difference. God's power is the greatest, and it is the only power that will bring peace to your soul.

God wants you to be pure and holy, filled with the Holy Spirit, but the Devil is right here, too. If you do not know the difference, you will be listening to Satan. He comes sometimes as an *"angel of light"* (2 Cor. 11:14). One word by the Devil in the Garden of Eden upset the world—the little word *"not"* (Gen. 3:4).

When God talks to you, the message agrees with the written Word. The Holy Spirit never says anything that doesn't correspond with the Word. A message that comes from heaven must correspond with the Word; if it is otherwise, do not accept it.

The things of the Spirit that seem foolishness to the world antagonize the Devil, and he sometimes does things that look very similar; but to the one who understands, there is a wonderful difference.

I have been carried away in the Spirit many, many times. Once I was under the power of God for seven hours. I was examined by medical doctors and found to be in a normal condition. Many doctors I know of have been honest enough to say that the power was not hypnotic, even though they could not understand it.

Celebrated Hypnotist Baffled

One of the greatest hypnotists in the world came to our meeting in St. Louis. He had been there two or three days before I knew anything about it. He was surprised to see a man lying there whom hundreds of hypnotists had tried to get under their power; he himself had tried it.

He went to him and tried to bring him out of it, but he could not. After a while, the hypnotist came to me to have an interview. He said he was going to call his friends together and tell them he had found something he could not understand. He could not put anyone under that power or bring anyone out. He said, "If there is a God, I believe this is His power."

When the doctors examined me as I was lying under the power, they said that my pulse was regular, my blood was flowing naturally, and my heart was in a natural condition. I am told that when a person is hypnotized, the blood does not flow naturally. The person is unconscious and simply does what he is told. Someone has to put him in that state and bring him out again.

God does lay His people down under His power, and then He talks to them. I have known people to be a whole week under the power of God. May He seal these truths to our hearts!

I know nothing about hypnotic power, and I have never seen a person hypnotized. But I do know something of the power of God, the power of the Holy Spirit. It is God Himself who sends this power; we can press the button, but God sends the power.

Talk about excitement! This power is the best thing in the world to settle the nerves. These people go down praising God; they continue while they are there, and when they are up, they are still giving God praise.

"*Let every thing that hath breath praise the Lord*" (Ps. 150:6). People ask why we tell them to praise the Lord. If you do not feel it at first, praise as a "*sacrifice*" (Heb. 13:15), and after a while the praise will come by itself from a soul filled with joy. Hallelujah!

If you will search your Bible, you will find that the things I have told you are true. My words do not amount to anything unless they are backed up by God's Word. The Lord gave me this message, and I have given it to you.

When the power of the Spirit has been so maligned, it is time for you to take a stand for the truth. When a ship is in danger, the sailors come to the front, if they are not cowards. Let us not run away but come to the front.

I stand here in defense of the Gospel. If we are faithful, all things must work together for God's glory (Rom. 8:28). Praise His name.

2

"TRY THE SPIRITS"

Beloved, believe not every spirit, but try the spirits whether they are of God:
because many false prophets are gone out into the world.
—1 John 4:1

There are many spirits that we do not want to have anything to do with. There are our own spirits, the flesh, and the Devil. There are many spirits contending; many times we let our own spirits rule, and we make ourselves think it is God. The same thing happens with the flesh and the Devil.

The Holy Spirit and the Word

Sometimes we know it is not God, but we want to have our own ways. If we have the Holy Spirit, we can prove the spirits, because everything the Holy Spirit does is confirmed by the Word. We do not want to rely on tongues and interpretations alone; we must measure things by the Word. We must measure tongues and demonstrations by the Word, and if they do not agree with the Word, we must not accept them. Everything must be measured by the Word.

We do know God and the voice of God, but the Devil can come as an *"angel of light"* (2 Cor. 11:14). When you are in the Holy Spirit, that is the time the Devil tries to get in and lead you astray. The Holy Spirit is revealing some secret things, and at the same time, the Devil comes in. If you are not careful, you will listen to what he has to say and follow him.

Once I was having a wonderful vision, and right in the midst of it, the Devil said to me, "You are going to die." At the time, I was very sick and had worked myself nearly to death, and I listened to the Devil for a minute. Then I stopped to hear what God wanted to teach me.

I said, "What is this that God is showing me? Does this agree with what God is showing?" I saw there was a big difference. God touched my forehead, the seat of the intellect and reason, and my mouth, signifying courage and power to give forth the message. If I was to give the people His message, I was not going to die; I could not die if I was to do this.

There was someone who attended these meetings whom God was blessing. He wanted to use her, but the Devil came in and made her think that she could do any outrageous thing, and it would be of God.

Do you see how the Devil can lead us astray? She was speaking in tongues and praying, and she said, "Lord, if you want me to kill anyone, I will do it. If you want me to set the camp on fire, I will do it."

That is the way it is with Spiritualism. The Holy Spirit never does anything like that. He does not come to kill and knock people's heads off. He deals with them in love and tenderness. People have even offered up children in sacrifice. If you listen to God, the Devil will be put to one side.

These things hurt the Pentecostal movement. God is in it, but the Devil is in it, too. Many people are honest, but they do not understand. God shows them great things that are going to happen, and the Devil comes in and makes them set a specific date for when it will occur.

For some time, Daniel did not understand the vision that he had received. An angel appeared to him to make him understand the vision. (See Daniel 8:1–26.) Be careful that the Devil does not come in and give you another meaning that is altogether different from what God wants you to have.

So many people prophesy this or that, and it never comes true; the prophecy was not according to the Word of God. Someone gives a person a message, and he believes God sent it, but it is not according to the Word.

When God calls you out for His work, He will take care of you. He will give you something to eat and clothe you. There are so many who run before they are sent; it would be better for them not to go at all. Sometimes the Devil uses tongues to upset things generally. Remember that the Devil can speak in tongues, and so can your flesh.

When God speaks in tongues, it means something, and you need to look for the interpretation. God says to ask for the interpretation. Sometimes God gives it through someone else, but we should give the person who speaks in tongues a chance to interpret (1 Cor. 14:13). Be careful that you do not give an interpretation in your own spirit; this hurts the work of God everywhere. Let us *"try the spirits"* and not get in the flesh.

Some people, if they do not like someone, will give a rebuke or a message in tongues and nearly knock the person's head off. This is the work of the Devil. Then someone will get up—some people are so silly—and say, "Don't touch that; it is from the Holy Spirit." They act as if discerning the spirit and motivation of a message were the same thing as "touching God's anointed" or doing harm to a prophet. (See 1 Chronicles 16:22.) Therefore, no one dares to touch it, and the Devil has the whole thing. Then word gets out that the leader of the group sanctions all that, and people do not want to have anything to do with it. The leader may have discernment, but someone will exert pressure on him and say, "Don't touch that." Instead of being so afraid, let us search the Scriptures. God never told anyone to rebuke in an ugly tone.

There was a great work being done in the West. One woman who was in the group said that the United States was going to be destroyed, and that they should go to Japan. They went. People who could not spare the money helped them; they went to escape the destruction.

The whole thing was of the Devil. The United States was not destroyed, they could not speak the Japanese language, they were stranded, and a number of them backslid. They tried to raise money for a great building but never accomplished it. They had been doing a good work here, but deceiving spirits got in.

God gave me a special commission to take the *"precious from the vile"* (Jer. 15:19), and I do not want you to get into the snare of the Devil. So many young people, after their baptism, quit their jobs and start preaching. In a few days, they tell everything they know about the Gospel; then they tell something they don't know. Money to live on does not come in, and many of them backslide.

If God doesn't send you out, don't give up your job; then you will have money to give to God's work. This mistake is made by many missionaries who go abroad. Some sell all they have, break up their homes, and separate from their wives, yet God has not called them.

Gifts and Requirements

The Holy Spirit makes us levelheaded. Remember, those who stayed in the camp got as much as those who went to the battle. (See 1 Samuel 30:1–24.) Be God's stewards, and give the Lord His due. The *"cattle upon a thousand hills"* (Ps. 50:10) are His, but He works through our instrumentality. He gives you everything you have—physically, financially, and spiritually—and He expects you to use all your abilities for Him. If your resources give out, He will supply.

He expects you to take Him into partnership and give Him what belongs to Him, and He will bless you. The Gospel has to be supported. Water is free, but it costs money to lay the pipes and keep the water running. Angels can fly, but men have to pay for transportation; someone has to help with this.

If you keep the pipes in order, the Gospel will be given out. You need to help by praying, by holding up the hands of those who work. (See Exodus 17:12.) If you trust God and walk with Him, that is the work God wants of you.

Don't take up with every vision that comes along. In some places in the Pentecostal movement, people have discarded the Word of God. They don't want a leader, and God always has a leader. When there is none, the Devil takes the chair. God has given some to be pastors and teachers (Eph. 4:11).

Then how does anyone know if God has called him to the ministry? Someone has said that when God calls anyone to do His work, you can hardly get him into the pulpit, but when the Devil calls him, you can't keep him out of it! Those are people who just like to hear themselves talk. Some people want to talk a great deal, bringing in a bone of contention, and it is hurting the work of God everywhere. Leave outside issues alone. God Himself will teach people what to eat, what to wear, and where to go. Many of God's children are fussing about these things. The Lord said that if you do not think it is right to eat meat offered to idols, don't do it, but don't judge another. (See 1 Corinthians 8:1–13.) Therefore, when we open our mouths, let us say something of real spiritual value.

If you have the baptism of the Spirit, you do not need to talk about it; people will know it. Also, let God speak to you. Do not wait for someone to speak in tongues and tell you that God wants you to go to India. Let God speak to you. When people go to a place because someone else has told them that they should go, they get homesick and discouraged and try to get back again. Let the Lord be our Guide. If we do His will, we will know His will.

Lift up Jesus, and try to get people so full of the Holy Spirit that they will live in unity. For example, we do not want to lay hands on anyone suddenly. If we do anything in a spirit of contention, the first thing we know is that everything is in a jumble, and we have done more harm in one meeting than can be imagined.

Lift up Jesus and the Resurrection. Let us *"walk in the light, as he is in the light"* (1 John 1:7). Christ is the great Headlight, and I am earnestly seeking more light than I have ever seen in my life. You have fellowship when you walk in the light (v. 7). We are the lower lights, and He will show us what to do next.

He will say to you, "Now you can do this." You may say, "I did not know before that You would trust me to do this." His answer will be, "You can do it now."

Until God shows you something you're doing wrong, it is not a sin. But after He shows it to you, if you do it, it is a sin. Consecrate everything to God, day by day. He will not call you to do something unless He is going to give you strength and grace.

Having a Teachable Spirit

When you go into a meeting, listen to the teaching. If it does not suit you, and you want something else, the best thing you can do is to go out quietly and drum up a crowd yourself. Some say that you do not need anyone to teach you. (See 1 John 2:27.) It is true that the natural man cannot teach you; however, the spiritual man can teach you.

We know what we are talking about: the spiritual man can teach you. We know nothing as we should, and there is so much for us to know.

As I said earlier, be careful not to lay hands on anyone suddenly. Regarding the recent disturbance here, we profess to be saints, and therefore we want to show forth the Spirit of Christ. We must be firm but kind. Do not speak roughly.

The crowds want to be able to see what is going on. Do not speak roughly to the boys. Each one is some mother's boy. When I was young, I would have nearly broken my neck to see what you are seeing.

When they became noisy, it would have been useless to attempt to use force; it would only have ended in a fight, and the plan of the Enemy would have been accomplished. God led me in the only way by which the disturbance could be quelled, and order was restored. God fought for us. God can smite with conviction. The battle is His, not ours.

"Try the spirits." In one of our meetings, there was a black woman who had wonderful spiritual experiences; that is the kind the Devil goes after. One day she commenced to go about on her knees, twisting about like a serpent. God does not tell anyone to do that. She spoke in tongues; then she said, "I don't want to do it; I don't want to do it."

Everyone knew it was not of God, and I said to her, "That is not God. The Enemy has gotten hold of you." At first, she didn't want to give it up; but the next day God showed her, and she asked to be delivered. The Devil had gotten in and caused her to do things that were not right, in order to kill her influence.

Spiritual versus Spiritualism

A woman came to me and said, "I am afraid that this spirit that is upon me is not of God. I was baptized in the Holy Spirit. I went into a mission where they did everything by tongues, and they got me so mixed up, I did not know where I was. Then, this spirit got hold of me; it shakes my head and makes my head ache."

That is Spiritualism. For two years, this woman could not give a testimony. But God rebuked the shaking spirit, the power of God came into her hands and voice, and she gave a testimony for God.

Some people, when they pray for and lay hands on a person, throw the slime off. Again, that is Spiritualism. Don't ever do anything like that. When you lay hands on a person, God takes care of the evil spirit. If you are filled with the Holy Spirit, the Devil is outside you; keep him out. Be careful who lays hands on you, for the Devil is counterfeiting God's work.

That is what ails the Pentecostal movement; so much of this has crept in. Some people take every foolish thing as if it is from the Holy Spirit. There are two extremes: some Christians prevent the Holy Spirit from working except in a certain way. Others think everything is of the Holy Spirit. They say, "Don't touch it; it is of God." One is as bad as the other. Let everything be done by the Word of God.

We are living in the last days, and there has got to be a higher standard for the Pentecostal movement. Christ is coming, and we cannot continue in the old rut. God is sifting us today, and we have to rise above errors; we have to rise up and go forward. By the grace of God, we will. Praise His name!

3

THE UNPARDONABLE SIN

Dear friends, we have met in the presence of the Most High God; we have come to do business for Jehovah. Let us do it well. We will meet again in eternity. Let us be very solemn. God's reporter is taking note of every thought, every action here tonight, of those who are against Him and those who are for Him. So let us turn our minds from the fleeting things of life, the things that are passing away, and be shut in with God this hour.

The message the Lord has brought before us is found in Matthew 12:31–32:

Wherefore I say unto you, All manner of sin and blasphemy shall be forgiven unto men: but the blasphemy against the Holy Ghost shall not be forgiven unto men. And whosoever speaketh a word against the Son of man, it shall be forgiven him: but whosoever speaketh against the Holy Ghost, it shall not be forgiven him, neither in this world, neither in the world to come.

This message comes to us from Jesus, as much as if He were standing here. Hear the eternal Word from the lips of the Son of God now reigning in glory. The words are just as powerful today as when they came from His lips, if they go forth by the power of the Holy Spirit.

This subject is considered one of the deepest in the Word of God. You have often heard the question asked, "What is the unpardonable sin?" And some people are very much concerned about having committed it. John says, "*There is a sin unto death: I do not say that* [you] *shall pray for it*" (1 John 5:16); but other sins are not unto death (v. 16), and through prayer God will wash them all out.

The Danger of Blasphemy

Blasphemy against God and all kinds of sin against Him and against mankind will be blotted out, but whoever speaks against the Holy Spirit has no forgiveness, either in this world or in the world to come. Christ made this statement because the Pharisees said He had an evil spirit and did His mighty works through that agency. So, you see, it is an unpardonable sin to attribute any of the mighty works of the Holy Spirit to the Devil. Since the early church, there has never been a time when there was so much danger of people committing the unpardonable sin as there is today. This is because the Pentecostal fire has encircled the earth, and tens of thousands have received the Holy Spirit, feeling His presence. This has been backed up by signs and wonders and diverse operations of the Spirit.

When men and women come in contact with this work of the Holy Spirit, hearing His words and seeing His works, there is danger lest they attribute the power present to an agency other than the Spirit of God, lest they condemn the power and condemn God's servants. How often have we heard ministers say, when they heard men and women and children speaking in other tongues, "Oh, it is the work of the Devil." Now you hear what God says about it; they are speaking against the Holy Spirit. God has been working in this city and is going to work in much greater measure. We expect to see greater signs and wonders. If the saints stand together as one, pray together, and shout victory, God will show Himself as a mighty God and a Savior.

The Spirit Comes in Many Ways

God will not only come in healing power, but will manifest Himself in many mighty ways. On the Day of Pentecost, Peter said, "[Jesus] *hath shed forth this, which ye now see and hear*" (Acts 2:33). And from what they saw and heard, three thousand acknowledged that it was the power of God and turned to Christ. Others stifled conviction and turned away, saying, "This is the work of the Devil." When the Holy Spirit is poured out, it is either *"life unto life"* or *"death unto death"* (2 Cor. 2:16). It is *"life unto life"* to those who go forward and *"death unto death"* to those who blaspheme against the Holy Spirit. So we want to be careful what we say against the diverse operations, supernatural signs, and workings of the Holy Spirit. Some people look on and say, "It looks like hypnotism" or "I believe they are mesmerized." To others, it appears to be mere foolishness, even as the Scripture says of the *"natural man"*: *"the things of the Spirit of God...are foolishness unto him...because they are spiritually discerned"* (1 Cor. 2:14).

It was the same on the Day of Pentecost, when a multitude saw the disciples staggering about under the power of the Spirit, speaking in tongues. While some said, "They are drunk" (see Acts 2:13), others knew that the mighty power of God was there.

There is a power here that is not of earth, a power lifting people up, making men and women upright, making them good neighbors, good husbands and wives. It is the mighty presence of Almighty God. Observe the lives of these people. They do not seek worldly amusements, but the power of God is manifested in them.

What did the power bring on the Day of Pentecost? The people who came together were all amazed and said, "We never saw anything like this before." Everybody began to get convicted, though some, who were not willing to accept it, not willing to be called fools for Christ's sake, rejected it. To ease their guilty consciences, they said, "They are drunk."

They knew better. They knew that the mighty power of God was there; if there was a question about it, God settled it. Peter got up in the midst of them and said, "These men are not drunk, as you say. Men don't get drunk at nine o'clock in the morning. Rather, this is what was spoken by Joel the prophet: *'In the last days, saith God, I will pour out of my Spirit upon all flesh: and your sons and your daughters shall prophesy, and your young men shall see visions, and your old men shall dream dreams'* (Acts 2:17). This is the Holy Spirit that you now see and hear." (See Acts 2:15–17, 33.)

It is the same Holy Spirit today. The Holy Spirit is the Spirit of God. He is a person, and He works under the direction of Jesus Christ, under His orders. He doesn't do anything except what Christ tells Him to do. When we are ready to receive Him, Jesus sends the Holy Spirit to impart to us His own gifts. The Holy Spirit cleanses these temples of ours and comes in to dwell. He fills our bodies, and His power in us gives us utterances in tongues (see Acts 2:4) and works through us in other ways.

The Mission of the Holy Spirit

Now, in order to guard against committing the unpardonable sin, we must know a little of what the Holy Spirit is. He could not come until Christ was glorified. Christ was on the earth in His human body for only a short time, but at Pentecost, He came to stay through the Holy Spirit.

Jesus said that when the Holy Spirit comes, "*whom the Father will send in my name*" (John 14:26), He will abide with us forever (v. 16). And He will not speak on His own; rather, He will say what He hears (16:13).

I love the Holy Spirit because He is always witnessing for Jesus, and He comes to bring us power (Acts 1:8). He is "*the Comforter…the Spirit of truth*" (John 15:26) who will abide forever (14:16). He brings all things to our remembrances (14:26). We are so forgetful in our natural state. But we have spiritual minds, and God writes His Word on our minds and on the tablets of our hearts (Heb. 10:16). The Holy Spirit brings these messages to us at the right time—a message to this one who is in sin, that one who is in sorrow—messages from heaven that encourage the weak and help the strong and always point us to Jesus, the great Burden-Bearer.

"*Rivers of living water*" (John 7:38) flow from us through the Holy Spirit, and healing power goes out. Power went out from Peter, so that the sick whom his mere shadow fell upon were healed (Acts 5:14–16). Power went out from Paul, so that handkerchiefs and aprons that he had touched were taken to the sick, and when they were laid on the afflicted, streams of healing went forth and devils were driven out (Acts 19:11–12).

The Holy Spirit is called "*water*": "*I will pour water upon him that is thirsty, and floods upon the dry ground: I will pour my spirit upon thy seed, and my blessing upon thine offspring*" (Isa. 44:3). A tidal wave of glory is coming this way. May God help us to be as empty vessels, so that the Holy Spirit's power may fill us to overflowing. In addition to "*water*," the Holy Spirit is spoken of in the Bible as "*fire*" (Matt. 3:11) and "*wind*" (Acts 2:2)—three of the most destructive elements in the world, and three of the most useful. We could not live without fire, wind, or water.

Mighty Winds and Heavenly Zephyrs

When a cyclone comes, men and women turn pale. When God's cyclone through the Holy Spirit strikes the people, it is a great leveler. They lose sight of their money bags, and all hatred and ill will are swept away, just as a cyclone carries away everything before it. When a tidal wave strikes a city, it submerges everything. In the same way, in a tidal wave of the Holy Spirit, everything goes under. Oh, we need a cyclone of God's power to sweep out of our lives everything that hinders us and a tidal wave to submerge us in God.

God uses these great elements, fire, wind, and water, in all their force to give us an idea of the mighty power of the Holy Spirit. Our bodies are His temples. As great pieces of machinery are moved by electricity, so our bodies, the most wonderful pieces of machinery ever known, are moved by the power of the Holy Spirit *"sent down from heaven"* (1 Pet. 1:12). On the Day of Pentecost, the Spirit filled the one hundred and twenty disciples with power to witness for Jesus. At the hands of the apostles, God healed the sick, and He heals today by the same power. God pours out *"rivers of living water"* (John 7:38). Therefore, what manner of people ought we to be?

If we don't have the power, let us confess it and ask God to give us the power He gave the first disciples. If those who come to the Lord will be filled as the disciples were on the Day of Pentecost, we will have streams of living water rushing through us and flowing to the very ends of the earth. Jesus Christ was baptized in the Holy Spirit, but He did not have *"all power"* (Matt. 28:18) until He had finished His course. He could have turned away and not gone to the cross, but He went all the way and cried, *"It is finished"* (John 19:30). His last act was this going down into death.

But God Almighty raised Him up, and when He was resurrected, *"all power"* was given to Him (Matt. 28:18)—all power! He sent His disciples out in His name and said that those who believed in Him would cast out devils, speak in new tongues, and heal the sick by the laying on of hands; if they drank anything deadly (accidentally, of course), it would not hurt them (Mark 16:17–18). He said to the disciples, "Do not marvel at what you see. You will do these things if you believe, and *'greater works than these shall* [you] *do; because I go unto my Father'* (John 14:12)."

The Pentecost Shower Falls

Now, when Pentecost came, the disciples were in the Upper Room, waiting. They were all saved and pure and of one accord—there were no divisions and there was no controversy (Acts 1:13–14). They did not know how the *"promise of the Father"* (v. 4) was going to come, but they were waiting for it. Suddenly, the Spirit came like a cyclone and filled the whole building; a great tidal wave of power was turned upon them, and they were all filled with *"living water"* (John 7:38). The Spirit's tongues of fire were upon their heads (Acts 2:2–3), and they all began to speak in other tongues as the *"Spirit gave them utterance"* (v. 4).

The people who came running up were amazed and said, "What does this mean? Are not all these Galileans who are speaking? Are they not ignorant of these foreign tongues? Yet everyone hears them speak in his own native language!" (See Acts 2:7–8.) It was the Holy Spirit who gave them these utterances in other languages. The Lord had said, *"'With stammering lips and another tongue will* [I] *speak to this people,'* but for all that, they will not believe" (Isa. 28:11–12). He emphasized that, and the people heard and knew it; yet in spite of all that, they mocked and cried out that the men had been drinking.

Peter Preaches in the Power of the Spirit

The Holy Spirit came to testify of Jesus. The Spirit preached the first sermon on Jesus' resurrection through Peter, who got up and brought forth the Scriptures to prove that this manifestation was of the Holy Spirit and that the Spirit witnessed of Christ.

People who had not believed that Jesus was the Christ—though He did works that no one else did (John 15:24) and spoke as no man had ever spoken (7:46)—were now brought under conviction, and three thousand souls were converted on that day. When they saw the operations of the Holy Spirit, many in Jerusalem believed, *"and a great company of the priests were obedient to the faith"* (Acts 6:7).

The Holy Spirit is here today bringing Jesus into our midst. He is healing the sick by the power of God; devils are being cast out, and miracles are being worked in the mighty name of Jesus through the power of the Holy Spirit. God is giving visions. Proverbs 29:18 says, *"Where there is no vision, the people perish."* People are having visions today of the Second Coming of the Lord, of the Marriage Supper of the Lamb, and of the Rapture.

The Holy Spirit comes with weeping. He makes you weep because of what is coming on the earth. Oh, there are signs of trouble! The unbelieving world is going to be cast out into darkness; but while we sigh and weep at the sad condition of the world (see Ezekiel 9:4), we rejoice to know that Jesus is coming soon.

Prophecy Comes True

We were holding meetings in Moline, Illinois. One night an evangelist came in whom we had never seen before. We were talking about the baptism of the Holy Spirit, which she had heard about and was hungry for. I said to her, "You are going to get the baptism tonight." Well, there was not much sign of it happening as I got up to give the Word. She sat in front of me, and while I was talking, she looked as if she were asleep; however, the power of God was upon her. The Word was going out, and the lightning struck. When I finished talking, the power was on her in a wonderful way, and she commenced speaking in tongues and interpreting.

Then she wailed the saddest wail I ever heard. It struck me that it was like the daughters of Jerusalem weeping over the destruction of the temple. (See Luke 23:28–31.) It was so painful, so doleful, that everyone was made sad. I said, "This is the signal of some great sorrow, distress, anguish, and trouble that is coming on the people." God showed me that it was a signal of distress, of awful calamity that was coming. At the same time, a sister said that she saw a great earthquake and described how the water swept over the corpses and down the street. The next day in the newspapers, there was an account of the dreadful destruction by earthquake that had occurred in Kingston, Jamaica.

Do you not see the hand of God in that vision? It was something that, coming true immediately, would convince the people. In Dallas last year, the Lord showed us many things that took place in Turkey when the armies came together. An old brother in Dallas had visions of the battles before they took place, and he saw multitudes being killed.

The Spirit Gives Heavenly Music

The Holy Spirit brings gifts, miracles, and the discerning of spirits. We laugh and cry in the Spirit; we shout and dance and leap; our bodies get so light we scarcely touch the earth.

At our last meeting in Long Hill, Connecticut, the heavenly choir surpassed anything I have ever heard before. We had it two or three times a day, and there wasn't any discord. It was the Holy Spirit making harmony through these believers, and the singing was not earthly singing, but heavenly. Sometimes I would be a little late in getting to the meeting, and as I came up the hill, the sound of the heavenly choir wafted down. It sounded as if it came from heaven; it was the song of the redeemed.

A Song Only the Redeemed Can Sing

God is getting His children ready to sing at the Marriage Supper of the Lamb. They sing a song no one can sing except the redeemed. (See Revelation 14:3.) No outsiders can join them. The Spirit has shown me that the coming of the Lord is very near, and I know it now more than ever.

God baptized me over twenty-five years ago with a wonderful baptism, but I am more spiritually hungry today than I ever was. I see greater possibilities today than ever before.

Let us advance from one degree of glory to another. (See 2 Corinthians 3:18.) Blessed is the servant who, when his master comes, is found at his post, giving to the household their portion of *"meat in due season."* (See Matthew 24:45–46.) This is your opportunity, your day of God's visitation. The bride has *"made herself ready"* (Rev. 19:7). You cannot go to the tailor and order your suit for the banquet; you have to make it yourself. The bride has made herself ready, and it is going to be the most wonderful wedding garment you ever heard of.

It takes skill to weave the garment of pure linen and to embroider the finely made linen work. (See Psalm 45:14.) When the bride is ready, the Bridegroom will greatly admire her. There will be a great company of guests in the banquet hall. But some of us are not ready; we do not have our garments. The time has come to get ready. Oh, it means something to dress for the Marriage Supper of the Lamb. When there is a banquet in honor of a king's son or daughter, it is a great occasion, and the musicians are trained for it long beforehand. Now, this Banquet that is going to take place in the skies, this Marriage Supper of the Lamb, will be the greatest wedding ever known.

The King's Bride

The King of Glory will be married to His bride. Don't you know that every good thing the world enjoys, God is going to let us enjoy ten-thousandfold? When we eat bread and drink wine in the kingdom (see Matthew 26:29; Luke 22:30), it will be the greatest Banquet, the most wonderful occasion ever heard of.

The bride is now in training. The Holy Spirit is the Dove; the singing is the cooing of the Dove before the storm. Have you ever heard doves, before a storm, calling to their mates to seek shelter? In a similar way, the Holy Spirit is calling to us to seek shelter from the Tribulation storms that are coming upon the earth.

The Lord has us in training. He is making our bodies light and supple so that we can go up to meet Him in the air. May the Lord help us to be filled with the Holy Spirit so that we can rise. The Spirit is the only moving power in the church of Christ, the mighty Agent. He was sent to continue the ministry of Jesus through the body of Christ.

Let us get the fire from heaven that will enable us to do business for God, and let us be careful that we do not attribute the power of God to the Devil, lest this leads to the unpardonable sin.

4

CHRIST'S GREAT REVIVAL ON THE PLAINS

And it came to pass in those days, that he went out into a mountain to pray, and continued all night in prayer to God. And when it was day, he called unto him his disciples: and of them he chose twelve, whom also he named apostles....And he came down with them, and stood in the plain, and the company of his disciples, and a great multitude of people out of all Judaea and Jerusalem, and from the sea coast of Tyre and Sidon, which came to hear him, and to be healed of their diseases; and they that were vexed with unclean spirits: and they were healed. And the whole multitude sought to touch him: for there went virtue out of him, and healed them all.
—Luke 6:12–13, 17–19

This was one of the greatest revivals that Jesus Christ ever held. There were great and wonderful results. We find much preceding these verses: the Son of God had healed a lame man who had a withered arm (Luke 6:6–10), the Devil had stirred up the Pharisees, and they began to plot how they might kill the Son of God (v. 11). However, He slipped away from the crowd and went into the mountains and prayed all night alone with God. If the Son of God found it necessary to pray all night alone with God, don't you think we ought to spend some time alone with God?

He was probably fasting. When Jesus Christ fasted, something happened afterward. If God puts a fast upon you, and you do as He directs, something will happen afterward—and it will not be that your body is afflicted and that you are all out of sorts and making everybody miserable around you when you are finished. That is not God's fast. When Jesus went out and fasted and prayed, some great miracle always took place afterward.

When Jesus received His baptism at the Jordan, the Holy Spirit came upon Him to stay, and He was led into the wilderness. He was alone with God for forty days, fasting all that time, and was among the wild beasts (Mark 1:12–13). After the forty days, the fasting and praying were over, and He was hungry. He was not hungry all the time He was fasting; however, we are told that afterward, He was hungry.

The Devil is always at hand, so the Devil tempted Him in an amazing way by asking Him to make bread out of stones. Of course, He could have done it, but you see, while He was fasting with God and communing with the Spirit, He got power to counter the Devil. The Devil came with all his force. But Jesus had won the victory in prayer while He was alone with God, and He was enabled to drive the Devil back. (See Matthew 4:1–11.)

Another time, after He had been alone in the mountains praying, a great storm came. The disciples thought the ship was about to go down, but He calmed the tempest and the sea became as glass. (See Matthew 14:23–32.)

In our Scripture text, He was alone with God all night in prayer on the mountain. He was not talking to the wind; He was talking with His Father, the God of heaven. He was about to undertake something requiring great wisdom and mighty power from God. He was about to select the pillars that were going to establish the church of Christ—the church of the living God.

Jesus Christ could not be hidden, and if you are filled with God as you ought to be, you cannot be hidden, either. He could not be hidden, and when He came out of His hiding place, he saw the disciples and a great multitude who were watching and waiting for Him. He called the disciples together to do a mighty work. He had many thousands following Him who had been healed and wonderfully blessed and who knew a great deal about the Son of God, so He had a mighty responsibility to choose the right apostles.

He selected twelve and ordained them. He clothed them with power. He gave them license from heaven—God-given authority. He filled them with the Holy Spirit. He loaned them the same power that He had over all devils and unclean spirits. He told them to go out two by two and preach the same Gospel He was preaching, in the same way. He told them to exercise the same faith He had exercised with God—to cast out devils and heal the sick. He qualified them and ordained them with power from on high to go forth to accomplish the same results that He had accomplished. This was wonderful.

We read that Jesus and all the disciples went down from the mountain into the plains. We are told that great multitudes followed Him from Judea—a multitude is not less than five hundred people—and multitudes came out of all Judea and Jerusalem, from the seacoast of Tyre and Sidon, and out of towns all along the seacoast and from every direction.

There must have been many thousands out there in the hot sun. What did they come for? They came to hear Jesus, not just to get healed, like some of you. They came to hear about Jesus, to get acquainted with Him, to see Him whom to know is *"life eternal"* (John 17:3). They came to hear the Word that He brought from heaven, to find out the way that they might be saved and healed. They had a wonderful meeting there.

Remember, they came to hear the Word and to see. "Faith cometh by hearing"—hearing the Word of God (Rom. 10:17). How can they hear the Word of God without a preacher, and how can he preach the Word of God unless God has sent him (vv. 14–15)? How are people to get faith for healing today when you preach against it? How will they get faith about the coming of the Son of God when you don't talk about it? Faith comes by hearing the Word of God. No man can get down into the mysteries of God without the enlightening power of the Holy Spirit. If the Bible is sealed, it is sealed to those who are lost, who are blinded by the *"god of this world"* (2 Cor. 4:4). But this glorious Gospel brings you into communication with Jesus, God Almighty's dear Son, and with the Father who sent Him.

A Divine Healing Meeting

So these people were gathered there to hear and get acquainted with Jesus and to find the way to be healed. The first thing Jesus did after ordaining the disciples for the ministry was to take them into the greatest revival He ever held and give them a start for the great work they had to do. It was a divine healing meeting from start to finish. Jesus Christ preached the Glad Tidings—salvation for the soul and healing and redemption for the body. He preached the double cure; otherwise, His fame never would have gone out over that country. They heard about the Great Physician, about His mighty love and power. No case was too hard for Him. No one was too poor or too rich, if they came in God's way. He healed everyone, and He not only healed but He also saved them, for He gave them the double cure. He Himself took our infirmities and bore our sicknesses, and by His stripes we are healed today (Isa. 53:5).

"Which is easier, to say, 'Your sins are forgiven you,' or to say, 'Rise up and walk'?" (Luke 5:23 NKJV). One is as easy as the other. Both are miracles, God's power being demonstrated. The same power saves the soul and heals the body, and it will take us up to glory. It will make us so light that we will rise without wings. Hallelujah!

So the Lord preached the Word to these people, and they were healed, every one. *"Man, thy sins are forgiven thee"* (Luke 5:20). *'Behold, thou art made whole: sin no more, lest a worse thing come unto thee'* (John 5:14). Go and tell your friends, every one, what great things the Lord has done. Don't forget it. Don't be so forgetful of His benefits. Serve God, give glory to God, and that disease will never come back. Go—you are whole. Go, and sin no more, lest it come back and you die or something worse comes." Glory to God. You must see how much glory God is to get out of this. Hallelujah! When He healed the body, He saved the soul.

All kinds of people gathered in the plains came out to see Jesus. Did you come here to see Jesus, or did you come here out of curiosity? I hope that if you came through curiosity, you are satisfied by this time. They came to see Jesus, to get acquainted with Him and to hear the blessed doctrine He was preaching. They came to learn the way to God and to get this great salvation. It cost such a terrible price, but God is offering it to you *"without money and without price"* (Isa. 55:1). Glory to God. Accept it.

Shocks from the Heavenly Battery

These disciples were initiated in a great revival. Jesus preached as no man had ever preached. (See John 7:46.) He preached the Glad Tidings: salvation from sin and healing from their diseases. He preached the Word and made it plain. He gave them to understand that *"whosoever will"* may come (Rev. 22:17). Oh, you nervous people, you who are going to have an operation, God can keep you from all these things. *"I am…the God of all flesh"* (Jer. 32:27). Is there anything too hard for Jesus? (See verse 27.) No. He can move the mountain of tumor in a minute. He can remove the cancer and soothe your nerves. You who are afraid that the excitement will make you nervous: get a shock from the battery of heaven, and you will sleep like a baby. He is the very same Jesus, the wonder-working Jesus, *"the same yesterday, today, and forever"* (Heb. 13:8 NKJV). Glory! I am a witness.

Jesus went out to preach, and He did not have a lot of music to accompany Him. There were no pianos, but the power of God was there. It is not so much music, singing, long prayers, or preaching that is effective, but the Spirit of the living God. When Jesus opened His mouth, He spoke as no man had ever spoken (John 7:46), because there was something behind it. His Word was like the hammer that breaks the hard rock, like coals of fire on the mind. It lodged in the heart; it was like arrows dipped in the blood of Jesus, shot out by the lightning of God's power to strike men in the forehead, causing them to fall like dead men.

Go to the Cross

Move out of the city of destruction; move to the cross. Get out of the plains, and start for glory. They had a wonderful meeting there. Jesus preached the Word. He showed them it was for them. He showed them how to come. He showed them what they had to do, and they met the conditions. Every last one of them had to believe in Jesus and get close enough to touch Him.

Someone touched me. Glory! How do I know? I felt the power going out. (See Mark 5:25–34.) If you touch Jesus Christ with faith, God will come, even if He has to bring heaven down. It isn't the long prayer or the flowery prayer that is effective, but the prayer of faith—faith that touches God and brings heaven down. Hallelujah!

The preaching was over; the altar call was given; they began to make their way to Jesus, and they stood on the watch. Faith comes by watching. Faith came to them as they heard and saw the wonderful testimonies that were occurring right in front of them. We see them trying to come, trying to get there first. Everyone who came received. If they had faith, it did not take two or three hours for the flash of light to come from heaven.

These people accepted it. They did not carry their sick back over those plains in the hot sun. Rather, they touched Him, and the result was that the diseases left and the demons went out like dogs. The healing power of Jesus went in, and their bodies were healed. Then they went out to bring in others. Is that what you are doing? Or are you sitting down and waiting for the power to come back? Bless the Lord.

So their faith grew into knowledge. When they first came, they saw and heard, but now they knew it was so. They saw it before their eyes. They saw people running, leaping, and skipping in every direction. The "excitement," as many call it today, ran high, and everyone got in the battle. When you begin to get your eyes on Jesus Christ, you can tell it. So their faith grew, and pretty soon the multitudes decided they would all just rush forward. Then the whole congregation—thousands of people—made a rush to try to touch the Son of God, and everyone who touched Him was made whole.

He cast out devils, saying, "You deaf spirit, you dumb spirit, come out." Jesus Christ came to destroy the works of the Devil. So the multitude tried to touch Him, and everyone got the double cure: salvation for the soul and body. They got joy in their hearts. Do you believe it? Praise the Lord!

So this was a great revival. Jesus cast out the demons. Those possessed with demons will do all kinds of foolish, devilish things to torment everyone. But when Jesus came, the demons knew they had to leave. It is the same way today. The demons will have to leave if you come into the truth. Christ has given you authority and power to cast out devils in His name. The devils will run like dogs. *Resist the devil, and he will flee from you* (James 4:7). But you have to keep the devils out, or they will try to get in again. (See Luke 11:24–26.) You keep them out.

The demoniac in Luke 8:26–33 represents tribulation. The man had had these devils all his life. But Jesus said, "You come out of him, and don't you ever go in anymore." He will cast the devils out of you, but you have to keep them out yourself. If you get your house full of the glory of God and give the Lord the key, you will not be bothered anymore.

The Double Cure

This was a glorious revival, and Jesus initiated His disciples into ministry there to give them courage. They went out with gladness, filled with the Spirit of mighty power. They went into the villages and cities and preached the Gospel—the double cure (Luke 9:1–6, 10). They had never heard it before, but they preached the Gospel and healed the sick everywhere. Wherever they preached the double cure, somebody believed and was healed. If they had not preached it, no one would have known anything about it. Glory to God! You find this all through the Word of God. Some of the greatest work that Jesus ever did was healing the sick and casting out devils.

We are told that Jesus Christ was anointed by God and began to preach and heal the sick of all kinds of diseases, *"for God was with him"* (Acts 10:38). He was anointed by God to do this. Preach the Gospel, and demonstrate and prove it to be from God by healing the sick. Wherever Jesus went, He did that. The greatest revivals in the New Testament after Pentecost were the direct result of people witnessing one or more divine healings of the body.

The incidences of healing in the Word of God show us that healing is the most effective way in which people are drawn to Christ. Nearly all of the great revivals were brought about by divine healing, and sometimes only one was healed. The man at the Beautiful Gate was healed and got the double cure. Peter and John were just going in to the temple to preach. The result was that five thousand men were converted that day, and Peter and John were thrown into prison. (See Acts 3:1–4:4.) If you are all right, you are going to be persecuted. But Peter and John began to shout and rejoice; they had results and were willing to sit in prison when they thought of the souls that had been saved. Hallelujah!

Hundreds have been healed here. Look how hard your hearts are! You would not believe God if He walked across the platform. May God sweep away this damning sin of unbelief. We find that Jesus gave to His disciples the same power that He had. He ordained seventy and sent them out. He first chose twelve, and a few days later, He chose seventy and gave them power over all kinds of devils. They went out and had great success. As soon as they believed Jesus Christ, they had power. (See Luke 10:1–20.)

The Word was demonstrated by signs and wonders following (Mark 16:17–18), and so God's Word must be demonstrated today. All through the Word, from Genesis to Revelation, whenever God gave a message to one or two—the message looked very foolish from a human standpoint; it took wonderful faith to go out and carry the message, but they knew God—whenever they went out and carried a message in God's way, something happened. The Lord God came in a visible way with signs from heaven that all the people could see. God demonstrated that message. So these visible signs of the Spirit are the Word demonstrated.

Demons of Witchcraft and Sorcery

The working of God's Spirit is foolishness to man (1 Cor. 2:14). You go to some hypnotist or Spiritualist and let him call up the dead, and he can pull the wool over your eyes; yet you would rather believe that than believe Jesus Christ. Satan's workers always try to counterfeit the real, don't they? God works today, and the Devil works. In Bible times, there were witches and sorcerers, but God's people knew Him, and all through the Old Testament, God demonstrated His Word. The Israelites acted like crazy people, but God was with them. He always came to the rescue, and those who laugh last, laugh best. The result of Jesus' disciples going out preaching the Gospel and healing the sick was that the fire of God fell on the people. They thought these men must be connected with heaven.

So the working of the Holy Spirit is foolishness to the natural mind. The Holy Spirit is not discerned by the natural man. But if you go to God and get the oil of heaven, you will have light on the blessed Word of God. God will talk to your heart, and Christ will be real, salvation will be real, and heaven will be real because the Spirit of God will let you down into the *"deep things of God"* (1 Cor. 2:10). Glory to God!

It was so on the Day of Pentecost when the Holy Spirit came. Some said that the disciples were drunk. (See Acts 2:1–13.) They lied about the Holy Spirit, and people have been lying about Him ever since, but the work went on just the same. Glory to God! People have always persecuted the work of God, grieved the Holy Spirit, and treated the blood of Christ as something unholy.

If you don't know, if you don't believe, if you don't understand, ask God about these things. Don't go to some old infidel. Go to God. You say, as they did then, "What do you think of it? Have any of the scribes believed?" This is what they said before: "Have any of our smart men believed yet?"

You better believe in Christ and seek the wisdom that comes from above. (See James 3:17.) He will make you wise in spiritual things. They are foolishness in the sight of man; however, the wisdom of God, the things of God, are eternal, and they are what will take us to heaven. I praise God for this wonderful salvation.

Now I want to say a few more words concerning the work I know about. I have been standing before the public for forty years, and God has given me grace and courage to stand. I have preached the Gospel in nearly every denomination. Thousands have gone out as ministers and workers. Many saints have gone home to glory.

We have been praying for the sick. If you have read my book *Signs and Wonders*, you will remember that when I started out, I did not know I would have to pray for the sick; but I was sick myself, and God healed me and raised me from my deathbed. My friends said, "Somehow, I believe God is going to raise you up." I did not look like it, but I knew inside that God wanted me to do something. I promised God that if He would raise me up and show me His way, I would do it.

I started out after God baptized me in the Holy Spirit. I knew God was calling me for public service. I knew I would die unless God came to me like He did to the fishermen. I told the Lord that if He would baptize me with power and knowledge, I would undertake the work. I would go to the ends of the earth and live a thousand years, if I might take one soul to heaven. So the Lord wonderfully baptized me and sent me out. I did not try to heal then—I don't now; God does the healing. But after a while, God showed me I must pray for the sick. I had a big battle; I nearly lost my soul before I would consent. He had to give me power. Bless God, He did.

After that, I began to pray for the sick. When God comes, the Devil comes. I was holding meetings in a big skating rink. The Devil kept telling me, "Oh, if you start praying for the sick, they will bring wagonloads of people. Nobody will be saved, and your original purpose will not be accomplished." And I felt that this was so. I fought through this for about three nights; for about three nights I lay awake. But I believed God knew His own business, so I said, "Lord, if you want me to pray, you send them to me, and by the grace of God, I will do it." Since that time, thousands and thousands have been saved as a result of the healings, who might never have been saved otherwise—they might have died in their sins.

Dear friends, the people came and got convicted, saved, and healed. I have been in Chicago three times, and some of you know that the people came by the hundreds, rushing down the balconies, sides, and aisles. The altar was full from one side to another. Everyone was trying to get there first. The whole place was crowded, and people tried to get in the back way.

The Power of God

In the first meeting in the big stone church, many hundreds came to be healed and saved, and they came so thick and fast that I could not stand it. I told the preachers that they had to help me. I called a brother over and said, "You take this chair and pray for the sick." He said, "Oh, I can't pray for the sick." I said, "Yes, you can. I will pray for you." He said, "Give me an easy one." I gave him the most seriously crippled person I could find, and I said, "Never mind, God can heal that one as easy as any."

They thought they were in for it. We had five chairs on that large platform, and two or three ministers to pray for the sick, but you would have been surprised to see how many were healed. It is Jesus who does it. When a few were healed, they had faith for the next one. It is wonderful how those people jumped and ran, shouting and praising God. Soon we had five rows of chairs, and I would go back and forth and encourage them. God did mighty works. The next place we go, we expect to see people coming by the hundreds.

Sometimes the power is very great when the saints are in one accord. People who are afflicted come to us from St. Louis, California, Alabama, and all over. Some come bringing their grave clothes along, but not one has died yet that we know of. Jesus is a mighty Savior. Sometimes the power has been so great that I have walked along large, long altars, telling the people, "I have no time to talk much. You know what to expect. The power of God is here. You give everything to God." In a few minutes, they would be leaping and running in all directions.

The power of God will go out like rivers of water. If you are looking to God in faith, you can get your baptism in the Spirit without waiting two or three weeks. It is not men or women, but God who does the work. Jesus Christ is the divine Healer and Baptizer. God gave Him power to give life to everyone who will come to God in His way.

In one meeting, they came by the hundreds, and we never could get around to each person individually. We only had two or three minutes, and there were fifty or one hundred people trying to come up. But the power of God was very great. By faith, we sprinkled the blood of Christ on them and looked to God. It was so late that I said, "The power of God will come, if you believe." I said, "By faith Moses took the blood of lambs and sprinkled the people, and I take the blood of the real Lamb, Calvary's Lamb, by faith, and sprinkle it over the people." I asked God to rebuke the diseases and take away people's sins. Right there, the power of God fell in every direction. God did the work. Oh, glory to God, who has given such wonderful powers to His church, through Jesus Christ, our Lord!

5

THE POWER OF THE WORD

The words of God have been sent down from heaven to us by Jesus Christ and the holy apostles, spoken by the Holy Spirit. They are from God, and they go forth a living power. Jesus said,

> *Believest thou not that I am in the Father, and the Father in me? the words that I speak unto you I speak not of myself: but the Father that dwelleth in me, he doeth the works. Believe me that I am in the Father, and the Father in me: or else believe me for the very works' sake.* (John 14:10–11)

Jesus also said that His works testified that the Father was in Him and with Him (John 10:38).

> *In the beginning was the Word, and the Word was with God, and the Word was God. The same was in the beginning with God. All things were made by him; and without him was not any thing made that was made....And the Word was made flesh, and dwelt among us.* (John 1:1–3, 14)

God spoke the worlds into existence. "God said, 'Let there be light'; and there was light" (Gen. 1:3 NKJV). As He spoke the Word, the earth, land, light, darkness, mighty seas, lakes, mountains, and valleys with all the fruits and flowers sprang into life, into existence and beauty. He spoke the Word, and every living creature stood before Him. From the mighty monsters of the sea, the lions of the forest, and the wild beasts of every kind, down to the little singing bird, they all stood looking in wonder and awe at the Mighty God who had, by the word of His mouth and the power of His voice, called them into this beautiful world. They said, by their very presence, "We know You are the great Jehovah, the God who inhabits eternity!"

The Words of God

That which was from the beginning, which we have heard, which we have seen with our eyes, which we have looked upon, and our hands have handled, of the Word of life; (for the life was manifested, and we have seen it, and bear witness, and show unto you that eternal life, which was with the Father, and was manifested unto us;) that which we have seen and heard declare we unto you, that ye also may have fellowship with us: and truly our fellowship is with the Father, and with his Son Jesus Christ. (1 John 1:1–3)

When the high priest sent the officers to apprehend Jesus, the question was asked them, "Why did you not bring Him?" They said, *"Never man spake like this man"* (John 7:46). With His voice, the dead are raised and the lepers are cleansed. The blind see; they have their sight restored.

The raging storm on the Sea of Galilee was hushed at His word, and the roaring sea became as a sea of glass. The words of God spoken by the Holy Spirit have the same effect today. There is as much power in the name of Jesus today as in New Testament times. Through the Holy Spirit, His words come like coals of fire, burning through the minds and hearts of men. They are shot out like arrows dipped in the blood of Jesus; they are shot out like lightning, piercing the King's enemies in their heads and lodging in their hearts, so that they fall like dead men. They are like the little stones that David used to slay Goliath; we throw them at a venture, and God directs them so that they never return void (Isa. 55:11) but instead bring life or death, heaven or hell. They stand forever, for by the Word we will be justified or condemned.

When the disciples were arrested and put into prison, as recorded in Acts 5:19–20, *"the angel of the Lord by night opened the prison doors, and brought them forth, and said, Go, stand and speak in the temple to the people all the words of this life.*" You see that God sent the angel to set them free and to tell them to go back, amid all the threats and danger, and preach "*all the words of this life.*" His words are life; do not hold back any part of the message.

False Teachings

Jesus said, "*Whosoever therefore shall be ashamed of me and of my words...of him also shall the Son of man be ashamed, when he cometh in the glory of his Father*" (Mark 8:38). Oh, may God help all who pretend to preach the Word to see what is at stake! Will you please men or God? Will you deceive the people and come forward at the Judgment with your hands dripping with the blood of souls?

"*Behold, the LORD's hand is not shortened, that it cannot save; neither his ear heavy, that it cannot hear*" (Isa. 59:1).

> *For your hands are defiled with blood, and your fingers with iniquity; your lips have spoken lies, your tongue hath muttered perverseness....The way of peace they know not; and there is no judgment in their goings: they have made them crooked paths: whosoever goeth therein shall not know peace.* (vv. 3, 8)

Jesus is saying, "You have given them smooth sayings, trusting in good works and a moral life. You worship Me in vain, teaching the doctrines and traditions of men, which will perish with the using." (See Matthew 15:9.)

Jesus said what He will do when He comes in all His glory. Yes, He is coming soon. This is the time of the end; we see the signs everywhere. In this "*wicked and adulterous generation*" (Matt. 16:4), in these last days, the churches have gone after the wisdom and power of men, instead of the wisdom and power of God. "*Having a form of godliness, but denying the power thereof: from such turn away*" (2 Tim. 3:5). Read the third chapter of the second epistle of Timothy to gain an understanding of this.

God is calling as never before, in thunder tones, to those who pretend to preach His Word: "Blow the trumpet in Zion" and "Sound an alarm in the Holy Mountain":

> *Blow ye the trumpet in Zion, and sound an alarm in my holy mountain: let all the inhabitants of the land tremble: for the day of the LORD cometh, for it is nigh at hand.* (Joel 2:1)

Let all the people tremble. What is the signal to make the people tremble? The Day of the Lord is at hand. It is even at your doors.

> *The great day of the LORD is near, it is near, and hasteth greatly, even the voice of the day of the LORD: the mighty man shall cry there bitterly. That day is a day of wrath, a day of trouble and distress, a day of wasteness and desolation, a day of darkness and gloominess, a day of clouds and thick darkness, a day of the trumpet and alarm against the fenced cities, and against the high towers. And I will bring distress upon men, that they shall walk like blind men, because they have sinned against the LORD: and their blood shall be poured out as dust, and their flesh as the dung. Neither their silver nor their gold shall be able to deliver them in the day of the LORD's wrath; but the whole land shall be devoured by the fire of his jealousy: for he shall make even a speedy riddance of all them that dwell in the land.* (Zeph. 1:14–18)

It Pays to Endure to the End

Hear the angel shout, "The hour of His judgment has come. Repent and worship God, who made heaven and earth and the sea and all that are therein." (See Revelation 14:7.)

The time has come when men *"will not endure sound doctrine"* (2 Tim. 4:3), but are turning the people to *"cunningly devised fables"* (2 Pet. 1:16), turning away from the truth. They are *"men of corrupt minds, reprobate concerning the faith"* (2 Tim. 3:8), *"having a form of godliness, but denying the power thereof: from such turn away"* (v. 5). "Of him I will be ashamed when I come in all My glory." (See Mark 8:38.)

The last invitation is going forth, "Come to the Marriage of the Lamb and to the Supper of the Lamb." (See Revelation 19:9.) The Gospel of His coming kingdom is being preached as a witness to all nations (Matt. 24:14). This work will soon be done. What are you doing? Preach *"all the words of this life"* (Acts 5:20). Oh, what a calling! Oh, what a privilege! The angels who stand before the throne cannot do this work.

Jesus said, *"Tarry...until ye be endued with power from on high"* (Luke 24:49) and *"Ye shall receive power, after that the Holy Ghost is come upon you"* (Acts 1:8). Then you will

*cast out devils; [you] shall speak with new tongues; [you] shall take up ser-
pents; and if [you] drink any deadly thing, it shall not hurt [you]; [you] shall
lay hands on the sick, and they shall recover.*   (Mark 16:17–18)

People will have visions. Tell them that Jesus is coming soon. Show them
the signs. The wise will know the times. (See Daniel 2:21–22; 12:10.) The wise
will shine as the firmament (12:3). They will reign; they will be kings, with
kingly authority, and will bless the people as priests for one thousand years. (See
Revelation 20:6.)

The Bridal City

Do you not think that it will pay to be a true messenger, or herald, of His
soon coming, when we will be like Him and will have glorious bodies like
His? "Of such will I be well pleased when I come in all my Father's glory." (See
Matthew 16:27.) Oh! Can you not understand? He is coming as the Prince of
Glory to meet His bride in the air, to escort His bride back to the Great City, to
be present at the Wedding, at the Marriage of the Lamb, when Jesus will present
His bride to the Father. He will welcome His Son's wife. He is coming in all the
glory of all His holy angels.

Oh, what a picture! Oh, what brightness! See, oh, see, the shining hosts! See
Gabriel, who stands before God (Luke 1:19). They are getting ready. They are
warming up the heavenly choir. They are coming. They are coming to meet us in
the air! *"For the Lord himself shall descend from heaven with a shout, with the voice
of the archangel, and with the trump of God: and the dead in Christ shall rise first"*
(1 Thess. 4:16). They will come in the clouds of glory. We will all be caught up
in the air, changed in a moment, have glorious bodies like our Lord and Savior,
Jesus Christ, and be forever with the Lord (1 Thess. 4:17). Oh, this is wonderful,
but it is true.

Don't Miss the Glory

*Whosoever therefore shall be ashamed of me and of my words in this adulter-
ous and sinful generation; of him also shall the Son of man be ashamed, when
he cometh in the glory of his Father with the holy angels.*   (Mark 8:38)

652 ⌐ Maria Woodworth-Etter: Collected Works

Dear brothers and sisters in the ministry, can we miss this *"eternal weight of glory"* (2 Cor. 4:17)? When Jesus comes, will He be ashamed of us? The wicked will be completely ignored and banished from the Lord and from His glorious presence forever, because they were ashamed of Christ or of His words or of His supernatural and divine power or of the works of the Spirit, which are foolishness to the world and to the natural man. Will you miss all this for a high position or a high salary or a social position or to please the people? Oh, what will you do in that Day?

May God help us to preach *"all the words of this life"* (Acts 5:20) and *"earnestly contend for the faith…once delivered unto the saints"* (Jude 3).

As God sent Jesus into the world to deliver His messages, so Jesus sends us into the world as His ministers to preach the Gospel faithfully. Woe to us if we do not preach the whole truth or are ashamed or offended at any of His mighty works.

> But though we, or an angel from heaven, preach any other gospel unto you than that which we have preached unto you, let him be accursed. As we said before, so say I now again, If any man preach any other gospel unto you than that ye have received, let him be accursed. For do I now persuade men, or God? or do I seek to please men? for if I yet pleased men, I should not be the servant of Christ. But I certify you, brethren, that the gospel which was preached of me is not after man. For I neither received it of man, neither was I taught it, but by the revelation of Jesus Christ. (Gal. 1:8–12)

Notice that Paul said he had been taught by the revelation of Jesus Christ, by inspiration; no man had taught him. You see that the Bible is a sealed book to those who are lost. No one can preach the Gospel except by inspiration and revelation of the Holy Spirit through Jesus Christ, for He takes of the things of God and brings them to us; the Lord reveals them to us by His Spirit (John 16:13–15): *"But God hath revealed them unto us by his Spirit: for the Spirit searcheth all things, yea, the deep things of God"* (1 Cor. 2:10).

With man's wisdom, you can only learn historical knowledge and the dead letter that kills (2 Cor. 3:6) and condemns. However, the Spirit gives life (v. 6) and power. He takes into our hearts and minds thoughts from our loving Father, who says He will reveal His secrets to His sons. Jesus and the Father will come in and abide with us; they will manifest themselves to us. Oh, beloved, do not handle the Word of God deceitfully! Rather, as in the sight of God, preach the Word in the light and power of the Holy Spirit. Paul is our example. We should follow Paul as he followed Christ (1 Cor. 11:1):

> *I was with you in weakness, and in fear, and in much trembling. And my speech and my preaching was not with enticing words of man's wisdom, but in demonstration of the Spirit and of power.* (1 Cor. 2:3–4)

> *For the gifts and calling of God are without repentance.* (Rom. 11:29)

This song was composed by a minister sitting in the congregation, from a sermon preached on "The Great Day of His Wrath":

> In the awful day that's coming,
>   When Gabriel's trump shall sound
> And call the world to judgment,
>   Oh! where shall we be found?
> Shall we cry for the rocks and the mountains
>   To hide us in that day,
> From Him who comes in glory
>   With all His bright array?

> The Lord is coming shortly,
>   According to His word,
> Taking vengeance on the wicked
>   And them that know not God.
> Oh! who will then be able
>   In that awful day to stand?
> "Thou shalt be no longer steward!"
> Will be the stern command.

> Shall we begin to tremble
>   While looking on that sight
> And take our march in anguish
>   Down to eternal night?

Oh! what an awful picture!
  To some it will come true;
And, oh! my brother, sister,
  Shall it be I or you?

6

THE PRAYER OF FAITH WILL
SAVE THE SICK

Is any sick among you? let him call for the elders of the church; and let them
pray over him, anointing him with oil in the name of the Lord: and the
prayer of faith shall save the sick, and the Lord shall raise him up; and if
he have committed sins, they shall be forgiven him. Confess your faults one
to another, and pray one for another, that ye may be healed. The effectual
fervent prayer of a righteous man availeth much. Elias was a man subject to
like passions as we are, and he prayed earnestly that it might not rain: and it
rained not on the earth by the space of three years and six months.
—James 5:14–17

The apostle James sent this letter out across the world to all churches, ministers, and members of the body of Christ. All these teachings and blessings are for every child of God who will accept them. He wanted the church to know that the power to heal the sick and teach divine healing was not confined to the apostles, but that elders of each and every church had the gift of healing or the power to heal, and that by meeting the conditions given, every one of the followers of Christ would positively be healed.

He delivered this doctrine of divine healing of the body to be taught and practiced in every church, so that each member would know his privilege and duty to God. If he were sick, instead of sending only for a doctor, perhaps a non-Christian doctor, he should send at once for the elders and let God glorify Himself by manifesting the healing power in raising him up.

Some teachers refuse to walk in the God-given light, and they say that this text means spiritual healing. I am glad the Word of God is so plain that anyone who wants the light can have it. *"The prayer of faith shall save the sick, and the Lord shall raise him up; and if he have committed sins, they shall be forgiven him."* You see the line between the raising up of the sick one and the forgiving of sin. If the sick person has backslidden or sinned in any way that brought on the sickness, he should have faith in the promises of God in sending for the elders, as God has commanded.

The elders come and anoint with oil. This is a symbol of the Holy Spirit or healing power, which must come from Jesus, on and through the sick one—soul and body. They pray together the prayer of faith, and when they have met the conditions in this way, the Lord honors their faith. He comes with His mighty power and raises up the sick one to health and restores peace and joy in his soul. *"Pray one for another, that ye may be healed."*

You see that the power of the Lord is ever present with His children to heal. The command is given to every child of God. If the elders cannot come, then get a few of God's children together in the true Spirit of Christ and pray for one another so that you may be healed.

Some have gifts of casting out devils and healing by the laying on of hands. Oh, let us not forget these blood-bought benefits. *"[He] forgiveth all [our] iniquities; [He] healeth all [our] diseases"* (Ps. 103:3). He promises to heal soul and body; the verb is in the present tense: *"The effectual fervent prayer of a righteous man availeth much."*

Unwavering Faith

The Lord shows us that we must have the righteousness of Christ, meet every other condition, and ask the Lord for what we want, in faith, without wavering. If we waver or doubt, we should not expect anything, for God will not hear us.

God will answer the prayer of faith, even if He has to bring all heaven down, in order to prompt us to greater faith to ask the Lord for greater things.

James referred us to the dark days of famine and condemnation in which Elijah lived, and he said, "[He] *was a man subject to like passions as we are.*" He was not an angel, but a man, with the same human nature and passions that we have. "*He prayed earnestly that it might not rain: and it rained not on the earth by the space of three years and six months.*" Elijah prayed again, and the rain came (James 5:18). He also prayed for God to send fire from heaven so that the people might know there was a true God, that he was God's servant, and that the Lord was leading him. (See 1 Kings 18.)

The Lord wants us to ask for great signs and wonders. The fire that came from heaven and brought the people down before God was a symbol of the Holy Spirit. The Lord wants to send signs and wonders into our midst, in answer to our prayers.

Elijah represents Christ—the church. When Elijah was taken up to heaven, a double portion of his spirit came upon Elisha, and Elisha did many more signs and wonders than Elijah did. Jesus said:

> *Verily, verily, I say unto you, He that believeth on me, the works that I do shall he do also; and greater works than these shall he do; because I go unto my Father. And whatsoever ye shall ask in my name, that will I do, that the Father may be glorified in the Son. If ye shall ask any thing in my name, I will do it.* (John 14:12–14)

> *If ye abide in me, and my words abide in you, ye shall ask what ye will, and it shall be done unto you.* (John 15:7)

You see, Christ's will and our wills come together with the same desire to glorify the Father. The Spirit of Christ prompts us to ask for great things so that the Lord will have a chance to let down His "*right hand of power*" (Matt. 26:64) and let the people see the visible signs of the "LORD *of hosts, which dwelleth in mount Zion*" (Isa. 8:18).

Every one of us ought to be anointed with the same power and gifts that God has given to the church, so that the world may believe that the Father has sent Christ into the world and that the Father has loved us as He has loved Christ (John 17:23).

"In my name shall they cast out devils....They shall lay hands on the sick, and they shall recover" (Mark 16:17–18). These are the special gifts. I praise the Lord that He has given these gifts to me! In His name, through His name, thousands of unclean spirits have been cast out. Demons causing deafness, muteness, lameness, blindness, paralysis, and cancer have been driven out. Thousands of diseases have fled when I have laid my hands on the sick in His name; those who were sick have been made whole.

Healing in the Atonement

Divine healing is taught in the Atonement, as much as the salvation of the soul is. Consider these Scriptures:

He was wounded for our transgressions, he was bruised for our iniquities: the chastisement of our peace was upon him; and with his stripes we are healed.
(Isa. 53:5)

That it might be fulfilled which was spoken by Esaias the prophet, saying, Himself took our infirmities, and bare our sicknesses. (Matt. 8:17)

Gifts and Workings of the Spirit

For to one is given by the Spirit the word of wisdom; to another the word of knowledge by the same Spirit; to another faith by the same Spirit; to another the gifts of healing by the same Spirit; to another the working of miracles; to another prophecy; to another discerning of spirits; to another divers kinds of tongues; to another the interpretation of tongues....For by one Spirit are we all baptized into one body....Ye are the body of Christ....God hath set some in the church [body of Christ], first apostles, secondarily prophets, thirdly teachers. (1 Cor. 12:8–10, 13, 27–28)

Together we have the promise of apostles, prophets, teachers, and evangelists in the church of Christ. What a glorious church is the real body and bride of our Lord!

Signs were to follow those who believe in Christ (Mark 16:17): *"For the perfecting of the saints, for the work of the ministry, for the edifying of the body of Christ"* (Eph. 4:12). You see that God placed all the gifts and workings of the Spirit in the church, and they were to remain with the people of God *"till we all come in the unity of the faith"* (v. 13) *"by the same Spirit"* (1 Cor. 12:8). *"The manifestation of the Spirit is given to every man to profit withal....But all these worketh that one and the selfsame Spirit"* (vv. 7, 11). There is one Lord and one Spirit (Eph. 4:4–5).

The Holy Spirit is the agent of Christ, sent by God to work through the church, the body of Christ. Each member is to possess one or more of these gifts as the church walks in the light and believes and accepts these blessings or gifts.

Ignorance Inexcusable

Paul said, *"Concerning spiritual gifts, brethren, I would not have you ignorant"* (1 Cor. 12:1). *"Till we all come in the unity of the faith, and of the knowledge of the Son of God, unto a perfect man, unto the measure of the stature of the fulness of Christ"* (Eph. 4:13).

Dearly beloved, when will we all come up to this measure? Not until the last one of the little flock is ready to be translated. We must be filled with the fullness of God, with wisdom and power. These signs and gifts must follow until the church goes out to meet the Lord, the Bridegroom. She will go out to meet Him with the same power that the apostles had after they were filled with the Holy Spirit on the Day of Pentecost. Oh, praise the Lord, all these signs are with us and are manifested in our meetings!

7

SIGNS AND WONDERS TO LEAD PEOPLE TO CHRIST

All of us who have read the Acts of the Apostles know that the apostles' ministry was marvelously successful. Here are a few brief reports of some of their revivals from the book of Acts:

Then they that gladly received his word were baptized: and the same day there were added unto them about three thousand souls. (2:41)

And the Lord added to the church daily such as should be saved. (2:47)

Howbeit many of them which heard the word believed; and the number of the men was about five thousand. (4:4)

And believers were the more added to the Lord, multitudes both of men and women. (5:14)

And the word of God increased; and the number of the disciples multiplied in Jerusalem greatly; and a great company of the priests were obedient to the faith. (6:7)

Then had the churches rest throughout all Judaea and Galilee and Samaria, and were edified; and walking in the fear of the Lord, and in the comfort of the Holy Ghost, were multiplied. (9:31)

While Peter yet spake these words, the Holy Ghost fell on all them which heard the word. (10:44)

And the hand of the Lord was with them: and a great number believed, and turned unto the Lord. (11:21)

But the word of God grew and multiplied. (12:24)

And the next sabbath day came almost the whole city together to hear the word of God. (13:44)

And so were the churches established in the faith, and increased in number daily. (16:5)

And some of them believed, and consorted with Paul and Silas; and of the devout Greeks a great multitude, and of the chief women not a few. (17:4)

Therefore many of them believed; also of honourable women which were Greeks, and of men, not a few. (17:12)

And fear fell on them all, and the name of the Lord Jesus was magnified. And many that believed came, and confessed, and showed their deeds. Many of them also which used curious arts brought their books together, and burned them before all men: and they counted the price of them, and found it fifty

thousand pieces of silver. So mightily grew the word of God and prevailed.
(19:17–20)

Three Reasons for the Disciples' Success

There were three reasons or causes that gave the disciples this phenomenal success.

First, they preached the Gospel of the kingdom, which is, as I have already stated, a full Gospel for spirit, soul, and body. They preached exactly as the Lord told Jeremiah to preach:

> *Thus saith the LORD: Stand in the court of the LORD's house, and speak unto all the cities of Judah, which come to worship in the LORD's house, all the words that I command thee to speak unto them; diminish not a word.*
> (Jer. 26:2)

They also preached as the Lord told Jonah to preach: "*And the word of the LORD came unto Jonah the second time, saying, Arise, go unto Nineveh, that great city, and preach unto it the preaching that I bid thee*" (Jonah 3:1–2).

The apostles did not diminish a word of the Gospel of the kingdom. They preached precisely the Gospel that Christ commanded them to preach. God will always honor and bless such preaching.

In the second place, they preached this Gospel under the power of the Holy Spirit, whom they had received on the Day of Pentecost. This is such an essential and all-important factor in preaching that Jesus would not permit them to enter into their great lifework until they had received the divine anointing. Had they not tarried in Jerusalem until this anointing came, the Acts of the Apostles would never have been written, for there would not have been any acts on their part that needed to be recorded, and the revivals mentioned above would never have been reported.

In the third place, God bore witness to their preaching with signs and wonders and with various miracles and gifts of the Holy Spirit (Heb. 2:4). This was as important a factor in their success as either of the others. I am convinced that without these miracles, the Gospel would have made but little progress in pushing its way through the heathen world.

Notice the apostles' prayer, which shows the estimation they placed upon miracles, especially the miracle of healing, as an auxiliary to their work:

And now, Lord, behold their threatenings: and grant unto thy servants, that with all boldness they may speak thy word, by stretching forth thine hand to heal; and that signs and wonders may be done by the name of thy holy child Jesus. (Acts 4:29–30)

Notice now a significant fact. Read the following:

And by the hands of the apostles were many signs and wonders wrought among the people....Insomuch that they brought forth the sick into the streets, and laid them on beds and couches, that at the least the shadow of Peter passing by might overshadow some of them. There came also a multitude out of the cities round about unto Jerusalem, bringing sick folks, and them which were vexed with unclean spirits: and they were healed every one. (Acts 5:12, 15–16)

The significant fact is that, in this passage, there is a parenthesis, which reads as follows:

(and they were all with one accord in Solomon's porch. And of the rest durst no man join himself to them: but the people magnified them. And believers were the more added to the Lord, multitudes both of men and women.) (vv. 12–14)

Why did Luke insert that parenthesis? Did those miracles have anything to do with that multitude of believers, both men and women, being added to the Lord? They constituted a powerful factor in that revival. That was the result in nearly every instance: where miracles were performed, great revivals followed. Read these words:

And the word of God increased; and the number of the disciples multiplied in Jerusalem greatly; and a great company of the priests were obedient to the faith. And Stephen, full of faith and power, did great wonders and miracles among the people. (Acts 6:7–8)

Is there any relationship between the miracles that Stephen worked and the multiplication of disciples in Jerusalem? There is a most intimate and vital relationship. Take another example:

> *Then Philip went down to the city of Samaria, and preached Christ unto them. And the people with one accord gave heed unto those things which Philip spake, hearing and seeing the miracles which he did. For unclean spirits, crying with loud voice, came out of many that were possessed with them: and many taken with palsies, and that were lame, were healed. And there was great joy in that city.* (Acts 8:5–8)

Did the miracles of casting out unclean spirits and healing the lame have anything to do with the people giving heed with one accord to the things that Philip spoke and filling that city with joy? Very much. Take still another example:

> *And it came to pass, as Peter passed throughout all quarters, he came down also to the saints which dwelt at Lydda. And there he found a certain man named Aeneas, which had kept his bed eight years, and was sick of the palsy. And Peter said unto him, Aeneas, Jesus Christ maketh thee whole: arise, and make thy bed. And he arose immediately. And all that dwelt at Lydda and Saron saw him, and turned to the Lord.* (Acts 9:32–35)

Raising Dorcas to life was another case that had the same effect (see verses 36–41): "*And it was known throughout all Joppa; and many believed in the Lord*" (v. 42).

If ministers could cast out devils today in the name of Jesus and lay hands on the sick and have them restored to health, they would not preach to empty benches or mourn over the dearth of revivals. On the contrary, every minister who could do that would have crowded houses and a perpetual revival. That is what God wants His ministers to do, and it is not His fault if they are not able to do it.

There is nothing the Devil hates with more infernal malevolence than divine healing. That is something that is visible, tangible, real, and valuable.

When a lame man is enabled to walk, or a poor epileptic is made well, that is something the unsaved world can see and appreciate. It convinces them of the goodness and loving-kindness of God.

A book is lying here in front of me. It is entitled, *Back to the Bible*. I've seen another book advertised, entitled, *Back to Pentecost*. Does it occur to these authors that to get back to the Bible and to Pentecost is to get back to miracle-working power?

Such a return would not only secure the baptism of the Spirit, but it would secure the gifts of the Spirit in the working of miracles. Is there anyone taking the track back in that direction?

8

THE CLOSING OF THE GENTILE AGE

The LORD shall rise up as in mount Perazim, he shall be wroth as in the valley of Gibeon, that he may do his work, his strange work; and bring to pass his act, his strange act. Now therefore be ye not mockers, lest your bands be made strong: for I have heard from the Lord GOD of hosts a consumption, even determined upon the whole earth.
—Isaiah 28:21–22

In all the history of the Bible, and in all God's dealings with the world, He sent and offered mercy and deliverance first and did everything to persuade people to trust and obey Him and escape the coming judgments. But they still kept on sinning until the pent-up wrath of God was poured out, and they were all destroyed. Yet with a strong hand and a supernatural power, He was with His people in the *"spirit of justice"* and *"strength"*—with *"those who turn[ed] back the battle at the gate"* (Isa. 28:6 NKJV).

When mercy ceased to be a virtue, judgments came like a desolation, and destruction like a whirlwind. Hear what God said: "You will seek me very early, but your cries will come too late; I will not answer. I will laugh at your calamities and mock when your fear comes." (See Proverbs 1:26–30.)

In all the threatened dangers, and in the midst of awful judgments, the Lord caused His supernatural presence to be seen in signs through His children. While showing wrath, He worked His *"strange work"* through, and by, the Holy Spirit.

With all these past warnings and examples of mercy and awful calamities that came with or followed the loving voice of God—who so tenderly called people to Himself from their evil ways, called them to fly to His outstretched arms—with all these past warnings and examples, the poor, blinded, debauched world does not, and will not, take warning. Instead, after six thousand years, she keeps on sinning. She still seems to take the management from God, saying, "God does not know. He does not care. We will run the machinery ourselves."

People are running wild after wealth and status, worshipping the wisdom of men and their mighty inventive powers. Even in their professed worship, they have left the Fountainhead of living waters and have hewn out *"cisterns, broken cisterns, that can hold no water"* (Jer. 2:13). They have turned their backs to God and are facing the sun of human wisdom and power that has risen and blinded them so that they are satisfied with the gods of this world. (See 2 Corinthians 4:4.)

Hear one of the last warning notes from the eternal throne, from the loving Father: "In vain you worship Me, going after the doctrines and traditions of men, which will perish with the using." (See Mark 7:7–9.)

The time for trifling is about over. God is calling modern-day Elijahs, who are clothed with the power of God, and King Ahabs to come face to face and test their gods. We must come to a halt and put our gods to a test. We will serve the one who answers by fire. That is God's test. (See 1 Kings 18:17–40.)

"It will come to pass in the last days," says the Lord, "that I will plead with all flesh, with the sword and fire, *'and the slain of the Lord shall be many.'"* (See Isaiah 66:16.)

The sword is the Word of God. The fire is the Holy Spirit. The slain of the Lord are those who fall under conviction or who fall like dead men under the power of God.

The Lightning of His Power

He will send out His arrows. His Word dipped in the blood of Jesus will be shot out with the lightning of His power, and the arrows will wound the King's enemies in the head. They will fall at His feet. Oh, praise His name. When God has His way, the ground of the meeting tent looks like a battlefield: men, women, and children lying everywhere, like dead men.

According to God's Word, the time of trouble, such as men have never seen or known, or ever will see again (Matt. 24:21), has already commenced and will end with the battle of the Great God.

We are in the last days of His preparation; Jesus is coming soon for His bride (1 Thess. 4:16–17), and she is getting ready. He is sending His angels, His servants, with the sound of a trumpet, calling the elect together, so that we may all be baptized with one faith, one Spirit, and one mind; so that we may be among the wise, who will *"shine as the brightness of the firmament"* (Dan. 12:3).

Isaiah 28, the chapter from which our text is taken, refers to the last church mentioned in the book of Revelation, the Laodicean church. This church is the *"vine of the earth"* (Rev. 14:18), the vine of man's planting. Jesus Christ shows us that in the awful destruction in which this *"vine"* will be utterly destroyed, the saints who are going through to victory will be clothed with power. (See Revelation 3:14–21.)

"The LORD shall rise up as in mount Perazim, he shall be wroth as in the valley of Gibeon, that he may do his work, his strange work," that He may work and bring to pass His strange acts in the last call of mercy. He will stir up the elements: *"Behold, the Lord hath a mighty and strong one, which as a tempest of hail and a destroying storm, as a flood of mighty waters overflowing, shall cast down to the earth with the hand"* (Isa. 28:2). He will bring distress upon men, because they have sinned against God, *"and their blood shall be poured out as dust, and their flesh as the dung. Neither their silver nor their gold shall be able to deliver them in the day of the LORD's wrath"* (Zeph. 1:17–18). He will rise in His wrath and work His *"strange work."*

God's Strange Acts in Old Testament Times

He will help His saints today, as he helped David at Mount Perazim and Gibeon. He will bring the powers of heaven, the destructive elements together, to accomplish His work through His saints.

The hosts of the enemies had gathered against David. He asked the Lord to help him. The Lord told him not to go near them but to take his forces back and to go under the mulberry trees and pay no attention to them. They were to rest and wait until he heard the sound of the *"going"* (2 Sam. 5:24) in the tops of the mulberry trees. Then he was to take his army and go forth to battle; he was to go after the enemy, for the Lord had gone before them, and He would smite the hosts of the Philistines.

The enemies heard the noise of the great hosts, the *"going"* in the treetops, the sound of war, of approaching armies. God confused them, and they were frightened, for they thought that David had engaged all the armies in the land against them.

It took great faith for David to obey the voice of God and to rest so peacefully under the trees when the hosts of enemies were ready to destroy them. But he knew that the battle was the Lord's (1 Sam. 17:47), and that, unless He fought for them, they were lost.

David was waiting for help from heaven; the armies of heaven were coming down to fight the battle. The Israelites had to wait until they heard the bugle blast, the rolling of chariots, the cannonading, and the noise of marching hosts. Oh, yes, our God of Battles gave them the victory, and their enemies fled before the Lord. (See 2 Samuel 5:17–25; 1 Chronicles 14:8–17.)

The Lord will also help his saints today as He helped Joshua. The enemy had gathered five kings with all their armies at Gibeon, and they were sure of victory. They were trusting in the *"arm of flesh"* (2 Chron. 32:8), but the Mighty God of heaven was coming with His armies. *"And the Lord said unto Joshua, Fear them not: for I have delivered them into thine hand; there shall not a man of them stand before thee"* (Josh. 10:8).

As the armies fled from Israel, the Lord followed them and cast down great stones from heaven, so that more men died from the hailstones than by the sword (v. 11).

The Lord God will work His *"strange work"* for us, as in Gibeon. The battle was on; the enemy was strong, and defeat was sure, unless the God of Battles came to the rescue. The only hope was for God to work a miracle, to do a *"strange act."*

Then the Lord told Joshua to command the sun to stand still, and the sun stood still in the midst of the heavens; it did not go down for a whole day. The Lord told Joshua to command the moon to stand still and not to go down until they had gained a victory. There had never been a day like it, in which the Lord listened to the voice of a man. The Lord fought for them. (See Joshua 10:1–15.)

The Lord says He will *"rise up"* in wrath and work His *"strange work,"* His strange acts, as He did in Gibeon; the whole land will be destroyed. He will make a speedy riddance of the whole land. Two-thirds of the tribes of the earth will perish (Zech. 13:8) by storms, earthquakes, hail, cyclones, floods, pestilence, and famine in this time of trouble. (See Matthew 24:7; Revelation 16:18, 21.)

And there fell upon men a great hail out of heaven, every stone about the weight of a talent [one hundred pounds or more]: and men blasphemed God because of the plague of the hail; for the plague thereof was exceeding great. (Rev. 16:21)

God's Strange Acts in the Early Church

God is pouring out His Spirit in these last days (Acts 2:17) of the *"latter rain"* (Joel 2:23), and His people are seeking and receiving the baptism of the Holy Spirit with all the Pentecostal gifts and blessings. God has risen up and is working His *"strange work,"* His strange acts, the acts of the apostles, through His baptized saints.

When the paralytic was healed by Jesus and took up his bed and walked, all the people shouted with a loud voice, giving glory to God. The fear of God fell on all. They walked softly, saying, "We have seen strange things today." (See Mark 2:1–12.) Oh, praise God. Praise His holy name forever and ever.

When the Holy Spirit came on the Day of Pentecost like a rushing wind, this was His *"strange act,"* similar to bringing His hosts of armies through the treetops. When the tongues of fire rested on the heads of the hundred and twenty disciples, and they were all filled with the Holy Spirit and began to speak in other tongues as the Spirit gave utterance (Acts 2:4), this was God's *"strange act,"* His *"strange work."* (See Acts 2:1–4.)

While Peter was preaching at the home of Cornelius, the Holy Spirit was poured out on everyone, and they spoke with new tongues and magnified God. This was His *"strange work,"* His *"strange act."* (See Acts 10.)

This is the day; this is the time spoken of. He has risen up in majesty, like a mighty *"man of war"* (Isa. 42:13) and of power.

Hear the Spirit of the Conqueror, "Come up, my people, come up to the help of the Lord, against the mighty." The Devil is mighty in these last days, but *"the battle is the Lord's"* (1 Sam. 17:47).

The hosts of evil have not only gathered against us, but against the Lord of Hosts. The *"captain of the LORD's host"* (Josh. 5:15) has come down to fight our battles. He is in our midst. He goes before us with a *"two-edged sword"* (Rev. 1:16 NKJV); He has bowed the heavens and come down (Ps. 144:5). He is making the people tremble. He is moving the mountains of difficulty and of sin, of tumors and of cancers. He is tearing down the Devil's works and breaking the hearts of stone. (See Ezekiel 11:19.) Yes, the Lord is bringing the powers of heaven and the destroying elements together. They are rising up in His wrath.

When His judgments are in the earth, some will repent. Yes, we see the great calamity, the sinking of the mighty SS *Titanic*, causing travail and gloom and sorrow and awakening people all over the world. We see great loss of life in floods, fires, and earthquakes. We see the terrifying storms and cyclones. Men and women turn pale from fear and from watching and wondering what will happen next. Yes, the Lord is working through the elements and through the *"strange work"* of the Holy Spirit through His children: the great work of giving the last warning, the last call, for people to escape these things that are coming upon the earth and to stand before the Lord at His coming (Luke 21:36).

The Lord is sending His angels, His saints, with the sound of a great trumpet. The Gospel is the trumpet, and it is blown in Zion. *"Blow ye the trumpet in Zion, and sound an alarm in my holy mountain"* (Joel 2:1). Let all the people tremble. The great Day of the Lord is near; it is near, even at your doors. (See Matthew 24:33.) It is the last call to be saved before the *"great and notable day of the Lord come[s]"* (Acts 2:20).

> *Therefore be ye not mockers, lest your bands be made strong: for I have heard from the Lord GOD of hosts a consumption, even determined upon the whole earth.* (Isa. 28:22)

We can all see the *"strange work"* in the workings of the Holy Spirit through, and with, the baptized saints. As it was in the early church, this "sect" is spoken against everywhere (Acts 28:22). The workings of the Holy Spirit are foolishness to men. People cry out and say, "They are drunk." However, they do not mean that they are drunk with wine or strong drink. They say, "They are hypnotized and mesmerized." Many are mockers. They see the strange and supernatural with the natural eye, and they hear with their ears the wonderful works of God. They confess that there was and is great power demonstrated. They cannot deny the great miracles. It makes them fear and tremble. But many turn away, drive away their conviction, and become mockers.

They commit the unpardonable sin, and their chains are made strong; they are lost forever. The Lord says He will consume them in His wrath. They will not mock then, when the tornado is raging, when the earth is rocking and reeling under the earthquake. But now they greatly mock, and they say of the strange and supernatural, "It is true that a work has been done, but it is the work of the Devil."

In his vision, Daniel heard one saint ask another, "When will all these wonders cease?" The answer was, "When the shattering of the power of the holy people has been accomplished, all these wonders will cease." (See Daniel 12:5–7.) The Gospel of His coming kingdom must first be preached, as a witness to all nations (Matt. 24:14). God will have many witnesses out of every nation, tongue, and people on the earth.

Signs, Wonders, and Works

These signs, wonders, works, and demonstrations, and the power of the Holy Spirit, must be dispersed through baptized saints. This is our work today: calling the elect together, so that they may see, feel, and receive the baptism of the Spirit and be sealed with the knowledge of God; so that they may be among the wise who will know when Jesus is coming. (See Daniel 2:21–22; 12:10.) Then they will shine like the sun in our Father's kingdom (Matt. 13:43).

The Lord of Hosts is with us today *"for a crown of glory, and for a diadem of beauty, unto the residue of his people"* (Isa. 28:5) and with great power *"to those who turn back the battle at the gate"* (v. 6 NKJV).

He is giving His wisdom to the weak. To those who do not naturally have the wisdom of this world, He is teaching knowledge and bringing understanding. To those who are weaned from the milk—little children and those who are not learned—He is revealing and manifesting Himself. Yes, He reveals the *"deep things of God"* (1 Cor. 2:10), causing us to speak in new tongues as the Spirit gives utterance (Acts 2:4), showing the *"wonderful works of God"* (v. 11).

He is speaking in other languages—fluently, plainly, distinctly, and with power—what no one can learn at school, except after a long time. "With stammering lips and other tongues I will speak unto this people, yet for all that, you will not believe." (See Isaiah 28:11–12.) Oh, readers, do not be mockers, lest your chains be made strong, lest you be consumed. Hear Him say so. Hear, friend.

The apostle Paul referred to the above warning hundreds of years after it was solemnly spoken by the prophet. (See 1 Corinthians 14:21–22.) The outpouring of the Spirit in the gift of tongues is one of the last signs God is giving to the lost world that He is moving in our midst and that Jesus is coming. Yes, it is a special sign that Jesus is coming soon. Yet with all this, you will not believe. Be careful how you hear and how you act. It is the last call. God is working His *"strange work"* and His *"strange act."* The Holy Spirit is seen in many ways. He is seen in bright lights, in balls of fire, in hundreds of stars, and in companies of angels, over and in the tent in our meetings.

The Lord of Hosts says He will work as He did when the sun and moon stood still at the command of Joshua. We will not be surprised at anything our God does. His people are a people of power. *"All thy works shall praise thee, O LORD; and thy saints shall bless thee. They shall speak of the glory of thy kingdom, and talk of thy power"* (Ps. 145:10–11).

9

"WILL YOU ALSO GO AWAY?"

Jesus said, "As the living Father hath sent me, and I live by the Father: so he that eateth me, even he shall live by me" (John 6:57). If a person keeps on eating and believing, he will never die spiritually: "This is that bread which came down from heaven: not as your fathers did eat manna, and are dead: he that eateth of this bread shall live for ever" (v. 58).

Many of His followers said, "This is an hard saying; who can hear it?" (v. 60). Jesus knew their murmuring, and He gave them a little insight into the great Resurrection: "What and if ye shall see the Son of man ascend up where he was before?" (v. 62). He added, "Therefore said I unto you, that no man can come unto me, except it were given unto him of my Father" (v. 65). That is a wonderful truth. No man ever made his way to Jesus without God. No man ever made his way to Jesus unless the Father sent His Spirit and drew him.

"From that time many of his disciples went back, and walked no more with him. Then said Jesus unto the twelve, Will ye also go away?" (vv. 66–67). I don't think Jesus was ever more sad than at that moment. He saw the multitude turn away; they would not walk in the light. Peter answered Him, "Lord, to whom shall we go? thou hast the words of eternal life. And we believe and are sure that thou art that Christ, the Son of the living God" (vv. 68–69).

Many do not believe that today. Many do not know it, but that is the key to the whole Word of God: *"And we believe and are sure that thou art that Christ, the Son of the living God."*

"As the living Father hath sent me, and I live by the Father" (John 6:57)—we must live in the same way, by the power of Almighty God. Glory to God.

We can see by what we have read that the Lord had many thousands of followers by this time. His fame had gone out all over the land. He had five thousand converts when He supplied them with bread in the wilderness. Another time, there were seven thousand who saw the mighty power of Almighty God through Jesus Christ when they ate and were filled, and many basketfuls were taken up from what remained of the few loaves and fishes with which they had started. Thousands came to Him for salvation and healing; when they were healed, they always received salvation. He gave them the double cure.

Christ said, "Which is easier: to take away sins or heal the body?" (See Mark 2:9.) One is as easy as the other. After He healed the invalid at the pool of Bethesda, He said, *"Behold, thou art made whole: sin no more, lest a worse thing come unto thee"* (John 5:14). The people Christ healed got the double cure: they were saved and healed. They were pretty well acquainted with Christ and His love and mercy and mighty power. They had heard of His fame, and every day His power was greater and more wonderfully demonstrated.

One day, when Jesus and His disciples were in a boat, a great storm arose. The waves were going over the ship; it was going down, and everyone was about to be drowned. Yet when the disciples had faith to come and call Him, He stepped out and said, *"Peace, be still"* (Mark 4:39). The mighty wind ceased, and the rolling waves suddenly became as a sea of glass through the mighty power of Christ. The mighty power of God fell upon the disciples, and they came forward and said, "Behold, what manner of man is He anyway? Is there no limit to His mighty power? This Man, this Messiah, says He is the Son of God. We are following Him from day to day, and every day we see more of His mighty power. There is no limit to it; even the winds and the waves obey Him." (See verse 41.) Everyone on the ship fell at His feet and acknowledged Him as the Son of God.

So His fame went everywhere, not so much because of what He said, but because of the mighty manifestations.

Jesus said, "If you don't believe what I say, believe Me for the works' sake. (See John 14:11.) They testify that I came from God and am the Son of the living

God. (See John 5:36; 10:25, 38.) Even though I spoke as no man has ever spoken (see John 7:46), you seem to have a cloak around you; however, before the mighty signs and wonders, you stand before God naked."

The people had seen the mighty miracles; they had heard Him speak; they had seen His majesty and power in so many ways. But now He began to tell them about being filled with God, giving themselves up to the fullness of God, being baptized with the Holy Spirit, being kept by the authority of God.

Jesus said, *"I live by the* [living] *Father"* (John 6:57). He was sustained and kept continually by the power and presence of the living God, for the Father never left Him for a moment. He said, "The works that I do, I do not do, but my Father does the works. The words I say, I do not say, but my Father gives me the words. (See John 14:10.) Whatever the Father tells me to do, I do." He gave the Father credit for everything.

He was sustained by the mighty power of the living God, and we also must come to the point where we can be sustained and kept in the same way, by the power of God through Jesus Christ. This is a hard saying; who therefore can be saved? (See Matthew 19:25.) We are not to live by natural bread alone (Matt. 4:4); to get to heaven, the spiritual man must be sustained and fed by the Bread of Heaven, by the Holy Spirit. We need to drink from the Fountain that never runs dry.

The sixth chapter of John shows us that many of Jesus' followers did not understand this and did not want to. In the same way, many people today don't want to walk in the light, and they turn away and are lost forever. The question is, *"Who then can be saved?"* (Matt. 19:25).

The people in Jesus' day began to murmur and grumble as they do today. God knows when people grumble. Many thousands of those people who were saved and had had all those blessings, turned away and never followed the Son of God anymore. Jesus looked at the few who were left, and His heart must have been broken for those who were so blind. He asked His disciples, "Will you also go away?"

He is saying the same thing to us. So many Christians have backslidden and are going off into delusions. It is the sifting time as never before. God is looking at us, especially those who are baptized in the Spirit. He asks, "Will you also forsake Me? Will you also turn back, or will you go forward all the way?" Peter's answer was, *"'To whom shall we go?'"* (John 6:68). We cannot find a better way.

This has been a glorious way, and we are willing to go all the way. *'Thou hast the words of eternal life'* (v. 68). We don't guess—*'we believe and are sure that thou art that Christ, the Son of the living God'* (v. 69)."

Earlier, Jesus had said to those who were offended by His words, "What if you should see Me ascend to heaven?" (See verse 62.) He wanted to show them the mighty power of the Holy Spirit. He wanted to show the resurrection life and that the saints would go up by the same power. "I am the Living Bread that comes down from heaven; he who eats of Me will live by Me, and if he continues to eat, he will never die spiritually." (See verse 51.)

They Laughed at the Signs

Jesus said to the few who remained, *"Will ye also go away?"* (v. 67). And they answered, "We know truly that You are the Christ, the Son of the living God, whom you have been telling us about." (See verse 69.)

Oh, glory to God! Dear friends, God's people were always the fewest of all the people on earth. God said to the children of Israel, "I did not choose you because you were the wisest or the wealthiest people; you were the fewest of all the people on the earth. Yet I have called you, chosen you, put my love upon you." (See Deuteronomy 7:6–8.) We find that the previous followers of the Lord God always diminished instead of increased. We find that, way back at the beginning, at the time of the Flood, when the ark finally sailed away, only eight souls had faith enough to sail away with it, and all the rest went down to an awful doom. They saw the mighty signs and wonders, but they would not believe God. They laughed at the sign. They thought that Noah was a fool and that the ark was the craziest building they had ever seen. They turned away after having had the light.

Even before the great inferno on the plain of the Jordan, when the judgments and fire of God came down and destroyed the proud cities of Sodom and Gomorrah, God sent an angel from heaven to warn the people, but only three souls escaped to the mountains. The people had their chance; they had their opportunity. But they turned back; they took the wrong way. God gave mercy first, until finally His mercy ceased. They lost their opportunity; judgments came. Judgments have always followed and always will follow the backslider who refuses to obey God. It is judgment unto death. Where Christ is, the disobedient can never go. We find that all through the Word of God, there were just a few who obeyed God. At the destruction of Jerusalem, the people had the call, they all had a chance, but not many escaped.

Only Twelve Left

Now I want to come back to my main point. I said earlier that after the multitudes abandoned Christ, and there were only twelve disciples left, Jesus asked these few, *"Will ye also go away?* (John 6:67). Peter answered, *"Lord, to whom shall we go? thou hast the words of eternal life"* (v. 68). The rest never followed Him anymore; we never hear of them. These people had been saved, but they did not follow the Son of God anymore.

After Jesus rose from the dead, He appeared to His disciples. He asked for fish and ate it in their presence. He called Thomas to come and put his finger into His side, and He proved to them that He had the same body that had been laid in the grave. Many different times, He appeared to them to take away every doubt and prove that He was the risen Christ, the Son of the living God, and would soon ascend back to God where He came from. Different times, He met with them. At one time after He rose from the dead, He was seen by five hundred disciples.

Many believe that this instance was the time He ascended to heaven. He went out on the mountain, talked to His disciples for the last time, and gave the Great Commission. (See Matthew 28:16–20.) The disciples watched Him ascending into heaven until the angels appeared and said, *"Why stand ye gazing up into heaven? this same Jesus, which is taken up from you into heaven, shall so come in like manner as ye have seen him go into heaven"* (Acts 1:11). And they remembered that He had charged them, "Don't preach sermons or teach the people or do anything, but wait at Jerusalem until you have been endued with power from on high." (See Luke 24:49.) They had a great deal to preach about concerning Christ's sufferings, death, and resurrection, but He told them, "You will not have entered into this wonderful life until you have been endued with power from on high."

Glory to God! I want you to see that Christ wanted to select men and women to set up His spiritual kingdom. He wanted to qualify them to establish the Holy Spirit religion in the world. But after all they had seen and heard, and after these five hundred had seen Jesus and were thoroughly convinced that He was the Son of God, there were only one hundred and twenty out of the five hundred, to say nothing about any of the rest, who really believed and were willing to face the music—to face death or anything else—until God qualified and sent them out.

It seems as if His work may have diminished after He was taken to heaven. May God help you to see whose fault it was that some did not come to the Upper Room and wait to be initiated into the Holy Spirit baptism and the secrets of heaven. Perhaps only the one hundred and twenty who were present in the Upper Room believed that God would fulfill the promise made hundreds of years earlier to the prophets, a promise that Jesus had confirmed. When the Day of Pentecost came, there was only a small company of disciples there with God to be qualified to establish the Holy Spirit church. They were saved and full of joy; they believed they would receive the Holy Spirit, and they went back to Jerusalem and waited, continually blessing and praising God. They were filled with joy. If you are seeking the baptism, get saved first, get filled with joy, get off the judgment seat, and be of one accord, of one mind, praising the Lord, just as the early believers were. (See Acts 1:14; 2:1.)

A Blaze of Pentecostal Power

Christ's church was set up in a blaze of Pentecostal power. Common, unlearned men and women went to the Upper Room trusting God, and the power of heaven came down. (See Acts 2:1–4.) They knew God was coming, and they were not being critical about how He would come, but were willing to leave all that in God's hands. Suddenly, while they were praising and blessing God, they heard a sound from heaven like a *"rushing mighty wind"* (Acts 2:2). The whole building was shaken, and the tidal wave filled the place. The power of God struck them, and the Holy Spirit came to rest on each of them like tongues of fire.

God was initiating them into the *"deep things of God"* (1 Cor. 2:10) and making them pillars in the church of the living God (Rev. 3:12). This was where the church was established, where the church was organized, the *"church of the firstborn"* (Heb. 12:23). Glory to God! These few disciples were all that the Lord had to depend on to establish the church and spread the glad news of what had happened. "You will receive power after the Holy Spirit has come upon you, and then you will know how to testify of Me. (See Acts 1:8.) Tell them in a way that people will believe. I will be with you always (Matt. 28:20), and when you preach the Word, you will see the signs of the living Christ right in your midst."

Glory to God! Filled with the Holy Spirit, they began to preach the wonderful things, and the Lord Jesus Christ was with them. He was there invisibly. He was the Coworker with them, and He is working with His saints today. The Lord Jesus Christ confirms the Word with signs and wonders following. (See Mark 16:20.)

However, when the news went out, and the crowds came to see what was taking place on the Day of Pentecost, they said that these people were all drunk. They began to lie about the Holy Spirit, and they have been lying ever since. Peter quoted the ancient prophets and said, "You believe the prophets; then hear what they say. This is exactly what they said was coming, what God said would take place in the last days. What you are seeing with the natural eye and what you are hearing (and we know they felt it)—this is the power of God. It is the Holy Spirit sent down from heaven." (See Acts 2:5–18.)

But the great company that had followed Jesus previously and seen the mighty miracles refused to walk in the light. When we are born of the Spirit, we have some of the light of heaven in our souls. Jesus is giving us more light, and He is giving us degrees of glory. As long as we walk in that light, we have fellowship with one another, and the blood of Jesus Christ, His Son, cleanses us from sin (1 John 1:7).

You are either going forward or backward. As long as you walk in the light, you have fellowship with and love for your brothers and sisters in Christ, and you have a present salvation. However, when you refuse to walk in the light, you go backward, and you lose that sweet fellowship with God and with the saints.

God is testing us, just like He did the Jews, down to the end of the age. Christ will not return until there is a falling away from the faith (2 Thess. 2:3). God knows there is a falling away today. The church of Jesus Christ was inaugurated in a blaze of glory and celestial fireworks, but she must be taken up in a greater blaze of glory. *"Fear not, little flock; for it is your Father's good pleasure to give you the kingdom"* (Luke 12:32). The Holy Spirit will continue to take us down into the *"deep things of God"* (1 Cor. 2:10), and we will be filled with all the fullness of God, with our garments white (Rev. 3:5) and our lamps brightly burning. (See Matthew 25:1–13.)

The church will soon leave this world in a cloud of glory. God is calling out a people for a prepared place (John 14:2–3), and He is preparing a people to finish up His work in the church of the living God. She must be a glorious church, pure and white and clothed with the power of Almighty God—a prepared people, a special nation, a called-out nation from all the nations of the earth, a separate nation, a holy priesthood (1 Pet. 2:9), children of the living God, God's sons and daughters.

So now, the Lord is calling us to eat the *"strong meat"* (Heb. 5:14). He is calling the saints of God to get deeper in Him. We must be filled with the Holy Spirit; we must eat of the Living Bread. By continuing to eat, we will never die spiritually. The time has come in which we must have strong meat. We must receive it or be left behind in the Great Tribulation that is coming. One calamity after another is sweeping over the earth. Unless we get deep in God, the waves and tribulations will sweep us away. Blessed is that servant whom Jesus will find giving the saints of God their *"meat in due season"* (Matt. 24:45) when He comes to catch His bride away. This Gospel of His kingdom must be preached to all nations, and then the end will come (v. 14). This Gospel must be backed up by mighty signs and wonders, by people filled with the Holy Spirit, baptized in the fire.

Refusing to Walk in the Light

People don't want to walk in the light; they don't like the way. They say, "We will be despised, and they will call us all kinds of names." If they can call us any worse than they did the Son of God, I'd like to know about it. But if we suffer with Him, we will reign with Him (2 Tim. 2:12). He has promised us everything in this life, *"with persecutions"* (Mark 10:30). We all want the good things but not the persecution. Yet those who desire to live in a godly way will suffer persecution (2 Tim. 3:12). Bless God, He is around us like a wall of fire. He who is in us and around us is greater than he who is against us (1 John 4:4).

Will you belong to the royal line? Will you accept the invitation and eat of the *"strong meat"* (Heb. 5:14)? Will you be baptized in the Holy Spirit? May God help us to say yes. Will you go on the mountaintop and help make up the little flock that will fill the earth with a blaze of glory? The wise, those who know the *"deep things of God"* (1 Cor. 2:10), will shine as the sun (Matt. 13:43) when Jesus comes. Those who are wise will even outshine the sun. Don't you see how you can glorify God? He is coming *"in the glory of his Father"* (Matt. 16:27), in the glory of all the angels. He is coming for His bride. The saints who are alive in that day will be taken up alive. *"We shall not all sleep, but we shall all be changed"* (1 Cor. 15:51).

Bless God! He makes our feet like hinds' feet (2 Sam. 22:34). He makes us jump and dance with joy. It is the resurrection power.

You say, "Oh, I don't want to be a fool." But you are one already. I would rather be a fool for God than for the Devil. To everyone who is not saved, He says, "*Thou fool*" (Luke 12:20). I would rather be one of God's wise little ones, even if all the people in the world called me a fool. For the wisdom of this world is foolishness in the sight of God (1 Cor. 3:19). The wisdom of this world will perish. Men are trusting in their money and education and the like instead of trusting in the arm of Almighty God. All these things will perish. But look at the Great White Throne (Rev. 20:11); see the River of Life (Rev. 22:1); see the wonderful things God is preparing. The things we see here will perish, but the things we see in the Spirit up in heaven will last forever.

God will gather us up and take us where the people never get old! There will be no death! No children will be crying for bread! There will be no prairie fires! No wars! Bless God, we are going! Don't you want to join the procession? Don't you want to sell everything and go? Leave the city of destruction and run from the storm; don't linger in the plain. Prepare to meet God. Prepare for the coming of the Lord, because He is coming.

Let us not be foolish, like the great company of those disciples who had the light. Some had been healed; many had been saved. They had come to know that God is good. But people are saying today, as they said then, "Have any of the priests believed? No, not many? Well, I guess I won't then, either." There will be some priests who will go to hell; ministers will, too, if they don't get right with God. Priests and ministers all have to go the same way, through the narrow gate; they have to wash in the fountain and be made white in order to receive eternal life. If you expect to go up, you must wait at your Jerusalem and be filled. In heaven, we won't be mortal or in the grave; the Holy Spirit will quicken our mortal bodies. Like David, we will say, "*For by thee I have run through a troop; and by my God have I leaped over a wall*" (Ps. 18:29).

God gives you power to dance, power to get out of the mud and run up the mountains. Bless God! Let us get out of the mud. Let us get cleaned up and dressed up for heaven. Join this race. God is filling the people. There are great degrees of glory, but everyone can advance another degree, and another, and another—and they won't have to pay any money, either—until they come into the perfect image of Jesus Christ. (See 2 Corinthians 3:18.) But you say, "I don't want to give up this, and I don't want to give up that." If you had any of the love of God in your heart, you would not want to do these things, because you would be a new creature. Old things would pass away, and everything would be new (2 Cor. 5:17). But the trouble is that you don't want to walk in the light.

Stubborn or Fearful

Many people see the light, but they are too stubborn to walk in it. They don't want to follow that path and be laughed at and all that. Dear friends, what do you care? How many of you draw back through fear—fear of being laughed at, fear that you will lose your position or be "thrown out of the synagogue"? (See John 9:22.) Bless God, they cannot throw you out of heaven.

God is pouring out His Spirit; many have had the real Pentecostal power, but they are not willing to acknowledge it. They are not willing to go forward, and they begin to draw back, sinning against the light. Refusing to walk in the light, they get leanness of soul. The first thing you know, if you fail to walk in the light, you cease to have fellowship with Jesus, the blood ceases to cleanse, and you begin to invent excuses to ease your own guilty conscience. (See 1 John 1:7–8.) You were not willing to acknowledge that you did not know it all. "Behold, I show you a new thing." (See Isaiah 43:19.) You did not know it yesterday. "Behold, I will show you new things from this day. Things you never knew before." So many of us do not want to acknowledge that we don't know it all. We don't know anything as we ought to, and there is so much more for us. Let us leave the shoreline and get where the Spirit lets us down into the deep things of God.

People are not willing to walk in the light. Thousands of people who have come up against the Pentecostal movement have declared that it is of the Devil or something similar, and when we refuse to walk in the light, it is death to our souls, especially if we "lay hands on the ark." It is spiritual death to that man's soul if he does not make it right. (See 2 Samuel 6:2–7.)

So there is great confusion. At the same time, there are a great many who have just been saved and who are being filled with God and baptized in the Holy Spirit. God is revealing wonderful things to them, and they are going on and on in the Lord, thanking God for what they have and advancing in glory. Some are in a place of affliction, where everything is against them—all the Devil's old rubbish. It is the sifting time. They are going upstream, but they will land on the mountaintop when Jesus comes to catch His bride away. We find that after Jesus takes the saints away, He will come back with them, and they will return on white horses. Imagine this little flock coming back on white horses!

Jesus is coming back! We are told that He is coming on a great white horse with a great army from heaven behind Him, all on white horses (Rev. 19:11–14). The bride of Christ will be shouting glory to Him who bought us with His own blood. This little flock will be taken up very soon. Jesus will take them away from earth and bring them home to heaven. He will make them kings and priests to God, and they will reign for one thousand years (Rev. 20:6).

At Pentecost, when the few out of many thousands were willing to be called fanatics, then God, true to His promise, owned and accepted them with a cloudburst of glory and filled their bodies with the Holy Spirit. God spoke through them in other languages. They were ignorant, unlearned people, but God took possession of them and got hold of their tongues and spoke through them, as He had said He would: *"With stammering lips and another tongue will [I] speak to this people"* (Isa. 28:11); yet for all that, some don't want to hear (v. 12). The believers at Pentecost could afford to be laughed at and eventually brought to death, in order to have such a visitation from heaven and to have God smile on them.

A Royal Line

Jesus must become to us the fairest *"among ten thousand"* (Song 5:10) and the *"altogether lovely"* (v. 16) One, and we must be willing to leave everything and everyone on earth to follow Him. The great holy Bridegroom is getting ready to come and take away His bride. *"Fear not, little flock; for it is your Father's good pleasure to give you the kingdom"* (Luke 12:32).

Are we going to backslide instead of walking in the light? Are we going to eat the *"strong meat"* (Heb. 5:14), or are we going to say the way is too hard and go off and grumble and growl and be lost forever? We are a royal line, the King's sons and daughters, a company of nobles, children of the living God who will go up to meet Christ—a great company. Every last one of us will be a king and a priest. Bless God, we are going to ride on the white horses and come back to the great Battle of Armageddon. But we must have the white robes on down here and follow the Lord wherever He goes.

If you are persecuted for Christ's sake, *"great is your reward in heaven"* (Matt. 5:12). However, if you are persecuted because you are walking in a crooked way, you ought to be persecuted enough to humble yourself and get right with God. If you are wrong, it will take persecution to get you right, but if you are a child of God and these persecutions come, then you can look up and rejoice because *"great is your reward in heaven."*

Jesus is coming soon. He is giving you an invitation to the Wedding. Will you accept it? Will you be one of the little flock? The angels are holding back the four winds (see Revelation 7:1) and they are crying, "Shall we let loose?" No, not until we have sealed the servants of God in the forehead with the seal of the living God. (See Ezekiel 9:4; Revelation 7:3.) Perhaps you are a servant of God; you need to be sealed, baptized, filled with new life. One of these days, we will burst these chains and go up to meet the Lord in the air. You who love Jesus will be tested. God is asking us the question: "Will you go away also?"

Is the way too hard? Is the price too great? Make up your mind that you will stand on the rock and that even if the whole world leaves, you won't, because Christ will be sufficient. We are going to be tested as never before. It is going to be harder every day, even among the people of God, because so many false teachers are coming in. It is a day of delusions; all kinds of delusions are coming. Keep under the blood, keep white, keep holy, keep pure, and God will give us wisdom. Glory to God!

10

THE GREAT REVIVAL
IN JERUSALEM

*And great fear came upon all the church, and upon as many as heard these
things. And by the hands of the apostles were many signs and wonders
wrought among the people;
(and they were all with one accord in Solomon's porch.)*
—Acts 5:11–12

This was the greatest revival of the New Testament, greater in many
ways than Pentecost. The disciples were all of one accord in one
place, awaiting the outpouring of the Spirit. They all made the same sound. (See
2 Chronicles 5:13.) If you get to that place, God will shake the country.

Now, in this great revival, signs and wonders were effected, and *"none of the
rest dared join them"* (Acts 5:13 NKJV). They were so full of fire that no one dared
to say falsely, "I am one of you." They were afraid that God would strike them
dead. God wants to get a people so full of power, His power, that others who are
merely full of wildfire will not say, "God sent me."

What was the result? Believers were added. To the church? No, *"to the Lord, multitudes of both men and women"* (v. 14). Some say that this excitement, this fanaticism, is well and good for women; however, there was a multitude of strong-minded men there.

"They brought forth the sick into the streets, and laid them on beds and couches, that at the least the shadow of Peter passing by might overshadow some of them" (v. 15). See what a "fanatical" lot they were! I wish we were just like that.

The excitement rose higher and higher. The whole country was stirred. A multitude came out of the cities around Jerusalem, bringing the sick, and they were all healed—every one (v. 16). They were healed because they came in the right way. This was a wonderful revival, was it not?

Yet the revival was broken up right in the middle of it. The high priest and Sadducees arrested the apostles and put them in prison. Bless God, they did not stay there long. God sent His angel down, brought them out of prison, and told them to go into the temple and preach to the people (vv. 17–20).

It took some grace to do that, did it not, to go right back there and preach all the Word, not leaving out divine healing, but showing all the signs and wonders? In the morning, the high priest and the others sent to have them brought out. They found the prison locked but no one there; those whom they sought were out preaching (vv. 21–25).

One Will Chase a Thousand

It is better to obey God than men (Acts 5:29). We are determined to obey God, whatever the result is. God's people must meet persecution. People say that this work we are doing is not of God. That is the kind of talk the Devil likes to hear. All the Devil has to do is blow his whistle, and his army runs to do his work. God has to blow and blow on His whistle before He can get His people to do His work, yet we have the promise, *"One man of you shall chase a thousand"* (Josh. 23:10). The Devil hates holiness and power; he persecutes, and persecution is all that makes men fit for heaven.

This revival recorded in Acts 5 was a great revival. Every one of the apostles seemed to be there, and God gave them wonderful power. Many mighty signs and miracles were done by them because they were of one accord, preaching and believing. As a result of this, the fire of God fell upon the church, and sinners began to tremble.

I believe in preaching in such a way that the power of God will make people tremble—preaching holiness, coming up to the front to do His will. *"The fear of the* LORD *is the beginning of wisdom"* (Ps. 111:10). When we first know about God, a holy awe comes over us. When we want God to work, to cause His presence to be felt in our midst, we must believe He has the power to work among His people; it is a terrible thing to resist Him.

We must put on the full armor (Eph. 6:11) and rush into the battle. We must press the battle to the gates (Isa. 28:6). The help of man is vain. There is no shelter except in the wounded side of Jesus. It is the only place on earth to which we can flee. There we learn the way of righteousness; we know what awaits the sinner if he does not accept this shelter.

God Confirms His Word

In the Old Testament, we read of God's workings among His people. When someone was sent with a message from God, it often seemed very foolish, humanly speaking. Yet what was the outcome? God will always show Himself and put His seal upon His work. When the message was delivered, He came forth with the supernatural, with the sign of His invisible presence.

He manifested His presence in miraculous ways. That put the fear of God upon the heathen. They said that there was no god like the God of the Hebrews, because of His wonderful works. He was a God to be feared.

In the New Testament, signs and wonders were done before the people. Wherever Jesus went, the people followed Him. God was with Him, putting the fear of God upon the people through the miracles, signs, and wonders that God worked through Him. Jesus said, "I do not do these things on my own. It is the Father who does the works." (See John 5:19; 14:10.) The apostles said the same: "By the mighty power of the Holy Spirit, Jesus does the works." (See Acts 2:32–33.) As the apostle Paul said: *"Not I, but Christ"* (Gal. 2:20).

It is the same today. In the signs and wonders that are occurring today, it is *"not I, but Christ."* He dwells within us, and the work is done by the mighty power of the Holy Spirit. *"Know ye not that your body is the temple of the Holy Ghost?"* (1 Cor. 6:19). Jesus Christ dwells in us. We are God's power plant.

It was by the hands of the apostles, not of angels, that God did His mighty works, and people believed when the signs followed (Mark 16:20). Jesus commanded the unclean spirits to come out, and they had to come. The power of the Holy Spirit went through the apostles' hands, and that is just the way God works today.

The apostles were not afraid of persecution, the sword, or anything else. They faced death in any form rather than disgrace the cause of Christ by being cowards. We serve a mighty God, and Jesus Christ who ascended into heaven is here by my side today. He will lead His hosts on to victory. Let us press the battle to the gates (Isa. 28:6).

This "sect" is always spoken against, misrepresented, and lied about (see Acts 28:22), but Jesus Christ is leading on His hosts. God permitted Jesus to be nailed to the cross and laid in the grave, but He came forth like the sun in the Resurrection. God permitted the apostles to be arrested and put in prison. Then He had an opportunity to show His power. He sent His angel and delivered them. The angel of the Lord is with His own. *"Our citizenship is in heaven"* (Phil. 3:20 NKJV). We are children of the King.

Around us, day and night, are ministering spirits, sent to minister to those who are heirs of salvation (Heb. 1:14). We can afford to be misrepresented or even put in prison, if we are only looking for the manifestation and the glory of translation, if we are only looking to go sweeping through the gates of heaven.

Persecution Comes When God Works

The apostles were persecuted, and the meeting was broken up in Jerusalem, where the Lord was crucified. The meeting was held in Solomon's porch, one of the prominent places in the city. It seems that the apostles were in this great porch; the sick were brought into the street on beds and couches, in every way, and placed all around—those who were sick, blind, and troubled by unclean spirits, a great multitude.

What would the preachers think if we brought the sick and placed them around the church in this way? In the first place (and in the second and third places, also), if they were preaching one of those fine sermons and someone dropped a sick person down in the middle of the congregation, they would send for a policeman quickly; you know they would.

In another New Testament incident, the paralytic did not break up the meeting when he was brought to Jesus and dropped down through the roof while the Lord was preaching. He is our example. Jesus was glad to have something like that happen, because it gave Him a chance to show His power. He forgave all of the man's sins and then made him rise, take up his bed, and walk. (See Mark 2:1–12.) The people began to shout "Glory" the same way you do here; you cannot help yourselves. If you have not done it, you will. A woman with tuberculosis was brought in here in her nightgown. I did not care what she had on; she was healed. Hallelujah!

When Jesus healed the paralytic, the people gave glory to God. People say today, "You never heard such a fanatical group!" If they had only heard the people giving glory to God then! We have something to make a fuss about. Dead people never make much noise, do they? There is not much noise in a graveyard. Some people are frozen; they're wearing grave clothes. May God take off our grave clothes and set us free!

David danced before the Lord with all his might. His wife Michal did not like it; she thought he had disgraced her before the handmaidens, and she began to grumble. He said he was not dancing before the handmaidens, but before the Lord. It is dangerous to meddle with a genuine work of the Lord. Michal had no child to the day of her death. (See 2 Samuel 6:14–23.) Barrenness was a great disappointment to a Jewish woman, as each one hoped to be the mother of the Lord.

Do not touch the work of the Lord. It meant sudden death to lay your hand upon the ark of the Lord. (See 2 Samuel 6:1–7.) Sometimes the Holy Spirit comes like a *"rushing mighty wind"* (Acts 2:2) from heaven and makes a great commotion among the people; other times, He comes silently. He comes to us here.

You need to take down your umbrellas and get your buckets right-side up. God will fill the vessels and make you a power plant for Him. Then God will show Himself mighty to pull down the strongholds of the Devil and build up the kingdom of Christ. (See 2 Corinthians 10:4–5.) You will have power to preach, and signs and wonders will be worked, as in the days of the apostles. The Lord was with them. He was invisible, but He was with them, confirming the Word with signs and wonders (Mark 16:20). He will never forsake us if we obey Him.

The Scripture says there were *"signs following"* (v. 20). Following what? The preaching of the Word. The Spirit of the Lord is here, and you will see Him with what we call "visible signs." Peter said, "What you see is the Holy Spirit."

(See Acts 2:33.) If you are willing, you will see Him here, for God is coming in a wonderful way.

At Pentecost, the people saw the fire on the apostles' heads and heard them speak in other tongues *"as the Spirit gave them utterance"* (Acts 2:4); they saw them stagger like drunken men. Wherever the Holy Spirit is poured out, you will see signs.

The Power of the Holy Spirit

Returning to our text, that revival in Jerusalem was a great meeting. The sick were brought on beds and cots, and God, through the apostles, worked many signs and wonders. The fear of God fell on the people. Thousands and thousands were converted to God. Their names were written in heaven. They were filled with the Holy Spirit, the glory of God; the power of God was great. Not all the sick could get close enough to have hands laid on them for healing. Peter seemed to be the leader in this divine healing movement, and they tried to get the sick near enough so that Peter's shadow might fall on some of them. Pentecost filled the apostles, and people were healed even watching for Peter's shadow.

The power was of the Holy Spirit. He who believes in Jesus Christ will have such power that out of his inward parts will flow *"rivers of living water"* (John 7:38). The Holy Spirit is like a river. The power of the Holy Spirit struck the sick ones and healed them, and the people marveled. Jesus Himself did many mighty works, and He told the apostles that they would do even greater things if they believed in Him (John 14:12).

Men and women, God wants you to get into that place. Don't you see that God works through human instrumentality? God will use us if we are swallowed up in Him. In our meetings in Chicago, people were healed sitting in their seats, and away up in the gallery, some fell completely under the power of God.

The power of God is going out while I am talking. You know I am speaking the truth; believe it, accept it, and get more of Jesus. If we take in and take in and do not give out, we are like a sponge that needs to be squeezed. Let us get so full that it will run right out through us, and not absorb and absorb, and never give out.

Many of you are baptized with the Holy Spirit. You ought to send the power toward me while I send it toward you, and when the two come together, something will happen. I could not stay on my feet if you would do this. Glory! Glory to God!

Get a clear picture of that revival in Jerusalem. Did they act like crazy folks? Some of the best people in Jerusalem took part in that revival. All classes of people were there. They were under the power of the Spirit, getting healed, or running to bring someone else to be healed. Multitudes were saved.

Healing the Sick Is Part of the Gospel

It was the greatest revival, and divine healing was the drawing card. When people are healed, the end result is not just healing; people are also brought to faith in Christ. The account of the man healed at the Beautiful Gate of the temple is an example of this. Peter took the miracle of healing as his text, and he preached to the people. Then the authorities apprehended Peter and John and commanded them not to speak or teach in the name of Jesus. But Peter and John said that they would preach in His name anyway. They prayed, and the Holy Spirit came in great power. The outgrowth of that healing in the temple was a wonderful revival. (See Acts 3:10–4:4.)

Returning to the great revival in Jerusalem, notice the mighty power that went from Peter's body. His very shadow healed people. Paul also did special miracles; handkerchiefs and aprons that he had touched were sent out, and the people were healed through them. This is different from any other miracle in the New Testament, but God is doing the same thing today.

The Holy Spirit works through our hands, through our bodies! We are sending out thousands of handkerchiefs all over the country, over land and sea. I could tell you wonderful stories of the work they do; five were healed from one handkerchief.

As we lift up Jesus, God sends His power through us, as He did in apostolic days. Let us rise and shine and give God the glory.

When I first started out to preach, I did not know I was to pray for anyone to be healed, but God showed me I was to preach divine healing. The Devil tried to hold me back, but thousands have been healed and saved since.

I lay hands on the sick in the name of Jesus. It is Jesus who makes us whole. Sometimes the power is so great that people are healed instantly, leaping and jumping and praising God. The Lord is here; we can have as great a revival as they had in Jerusalem, and the fear of God will be upon the people.

God wants you to march to the Cross and give glory to God. We need to get to work here. Let Him do the work in your soul first. We are going to have a revival here like the one in Jerusalem, with many signs and wonders.

Getting divine healing isn't like going to the doctor. Get baptized with the Holy Spirit before you leave; then, when you get home, you will not backslide. Glory to God!

11

THE FIRE AND GLORY
FILLING THE TEMPLE

*The house was filled with a cloud, even the house of the LORD; so that the
priests could not stand to minister by reason of the cloud: for the glory of the
LORD had filled the house of God.*
—2 Chronicles 5:13–14

I t came to pass, when the priests were come out of the holy place" (2 Chron. 5:11).
I want you to see how they came: one hundred and twenty of them with
different instruments, yet all making the same sound. The Levites were arrayed
in white linen, emblematic of purity.

It came even to pass, as the trumpeters and singers were as one, to make one
sound to be heard in praising and thanking the LORD; and...they lifted up
their voice with the trumpets and cymbals and instruments of music, and
praised the LORD.   (v. 13)

There were one hundred and twenty priests blowing trumpets; there were singers and instruments of music; but they *"were as one, to make one sound."* They praised God, saying, *"For he is good; for his mercy endureth for ever"* (v. 13).

The house was filled with a cloud, even the house of the LORD; *so that the priests could not stand to minister by reason of the cloud: for the glory of the* LORD *had filled the house of God.*

The one hundred and twenty priests who were supposed to minister stood like statues, and the Holy Spirit took over the meeting. The entire building was filled with the glory of God.

All this demonstration, the house being filled with the glory of God, was brought about by the one hundred and twenty priests blowing the trumpets. The playing of the different instruments was mingled with the voices of the great company of singers. The whole object was to glorify God, with everyone making one sound.

God wants perfect harmony. He doesn't want anyone criticizing or finding fault; He wants everyone sounding forth His praise, in purity. If we go out to meet God clothed in white, washed in the blood of the Lamb; if we go out, all making the same sound; if we go out to glorify God, God will honor all the noise.

It is not just excitement. God Himself comes down to acknowledge the praise. They praised and honored God, and the power of God came down. That same power will either save or destroy us someday. The house of God was filled with the power and glory of the Lord.

Living Temples Praise God

There was no preaching then, but singing, shouting, and praising the Lord, and all who praised glorified God. The house was filled with His glory. The people were standing, and Solomon was ready to dedicate the temple. The temple represents the church of Jesus; it also represents our bodies. *"Know ye not that your body is the temple of the [living God]?"* (1 Cor. 6:19).

What happens in 2 Chronicles 7:1–3 is like Pentecost; it represents Pentecost. The first verse reads, *"When Solomon had made an end of praying."* So many people never look to God to answer their prayers; they would be frightened if He did. Solomon stretched out His hands and prayed to God, and God heard him.

When he had finished praying, something happened. God will come forth if you are not afraid of the power, if you are ready to stand for God with everything that is within you. As Pentecostal people, we should always be "prayed up," so that we can get hold of God quickly and be sure it is for the glory of God.

"*The fire came down from heaven, and consumed the burnt offering and the sacrifices; and the glory of the* LORD *filled the house*" (2 Chron. 7:1). Some people talk as if God never had any glory, as though the glory of God was never seen at any time.

The apostle Paul wrote,

> If the ministration [ministry] of death, written and engraven in stones, was glorious, so that the children of Israel could not stedfastly behold the face of Moses for the glory of his countenance; which glory was to be done away: how shall not the ministration [ministry] of the spirit be rather glorious?
> (2 Cor. 3:7–8)

The glory under the law did not last; but the Holy Spirit came at Pentecost to stay. The manifestations under the ministry of the Holy Spirit are to be with much greater glory; they are to exceed in glory. The power under the law was only a shadow of what we ought to have under grace. This was the ministry of life, not death.

I am glad that the glory of God has been seen here a number of times. Many times in our ministry, the glory of God has been seen over us. God is here. This is what you see and hear (Acts 2:33). "*This is that which was spoken by the prophet Joel*" (v. 16). This is the promise of the Father; this is the Holy Spirit.

As I said earlier, when Solomon had finished praying, the house of the Lord was filled with God's glory. The people saw and felt it; it was not a shadow. The priests could not enter into the house; they could not get in at all, because the glory of the Lord had filled the Lord's house.

> When all the children of Israel saw how the fire came down, and the glory of the LORD upon the house, they bowed themselves with their faces to the ground upon the pavement, and worshipped, and praised the LORD, saying, For he is good; for his mercy endureth for ever. (2 Chron. 7:3)

Everything connected with this represents our present glorious age. The apostle Paul said that God can reveal His doctrine, which has been hidden for all ages (Col. 1:26). Those who crucified the Lord did not know about the mystical body of Christ. They did not know the divine life we have received, or they would not have crucified Him. It could be revealed only when the Holy Spirit came down from God to make men understand the new covenant.

The glory that belonged to the *"ministration of death"* (2 Cor. 3:7) did not come to stay. The glory came from the ark of the covenant, which contained the tablets of stone on which the law was written, the Ten Commandments. On the mercy seat of the ark of the covenant, there were the cherubim, two golden angels, facing each other, with wings outspread over the mercy seat, where God dwells in His temple. In His tabernacle—that is, in us, who are the temples of the Holy Spirit (1 Cor. 6:19)—nothing is supposed to be in the heart but God's Word, the new and everlasting covenant. It is written on the tablets of the heart, not on stone, by the finger of God Almighty (2 Cor. 3:3).

We May Always Be Filled with God's Glory

If, when the Old Testament people obeyed, the glory of God came down and the people fell prostrate, how much glory ought there to be today? Then there was just one tabernacle and two tablets of stone. Today your body is the temple of the living God. Our bodies are the temples of the Holy Spirit, and God writes His Word in our hearts with His own finger.

The ancient temple in all its glory represents each one of our bodies. If we are filled with the Holy Spirit as we ought to be, our bodies will be flooded with *"rivers of living water"* (John 7:38) that flow out to others.

We will also be on fire for God. The glory of the Lord was seen over the ark. Inside the tabernacle, the lamp was always burning. Since it was kept supplied with oil, it never went out. In the temple that is each of our bodies, God puts His love in our hearts. He wants us to keep the light always burning and never let it go out. By keeping all obstructions out of the channel of faith, we get a supply of oil continually; the light will always shine through the tabernacle. If the oracle written on stone was glorious, how much more glorious is the ministry of the Spirit under grace! The Holy Spirit will abide with us always.

Jesus said that if we keep His commandments, He and the Father will both take up their abode with us (John 14:23). They will dwell with us, and we will be flooded with the Holy Spirit. We are a people to be wondered at. Jesus said, "Here am I, and the children You have given me." (See John 17:9–11, 24.)

There should be perfect fellowship and harmony among believers; we should all make *"one sound"* (2 Chron. 5:13). The glory came down at Solomon's prayer. At a glimpse of that glory, they lost their strength, and the whole multitude bowed down to the ground and worshipped God.

When we are praying for people to get saved or healed, some shout, some praise, some pray, but all are making the same sound. We put on the blood of Jesus by faith and get a glimpse of His glory. Is it any wonder that people lose their strength and fall prostrate under the new life that comes to them? Is it strange that we are people to be wondered at? You have seen all this here: singing, playing, making the same sound. Is it any wonder that these people who come here especially to get under the blood as never before fall prostrate when they get a glimpse of Jesus?

You must prove that God has changed, that He has taken His power away, before you condemn us. *"The gifts and the calling of God are irrevocable"* (Rom. 11:29 nkjv). He never changes. He is the same yesterday, today, and forever (Heb. 13:8).

No one has any right to condemn us, to say that the people are hypnotized or crazy or have lost their minds or that I have put a spell on them. Great God, awaken the people before the thunders of Judgment arouse them! You must throw the Bible away, or you must prove that the gifts and callings have been taken from the church, before you reject us.

We are going the Bible route, and you have no business teaching anything else; you must stick to the Word of God. We do not hold anything up but the Word of God. It is good enough for me. *"I am not ashamed of the gospel of Christ"* (Rom. 1:16) or of His power.

What a wonderful people we are in our privileges! Today, every believer may be God's priest (Rev. 1:6). If we abide in Him, and His words abide in us, we may ask what we will, and it will be done (John 15:7). We indeed have wonderful privileges. The power of the Lord shines forth a hundred times greater than under the law; the power then was typical of Pentecost.

Get your Bibles and search out these things; you are getting the light of God, and He expects you to *"walk in the light"* (1 John 1:7), even if you get it from a little weak woman like me. In His name, I tell you these things are true. What do you care about man's opinion when you are standing before God? Dried opinions and the traditions of men all go to destruction, but it is the living Word that I am preaching to you.

The Signs of the Holy Spirit

When John the Baptist was in prison, he began to doubt a little whether Jesus was the Christ, and he sent his disciples to ask Him, *"Art thou he that should come, or do we look for another?"* (Matt. 11:3). Jesus did not say, "I belong to the church" or "I belong to a college." He said, "Go and tell John the things you have seen here: the lame walk, the blind see, different diseases are healed, and the poor have the Gospel preached to them. Blessed is he who will not be offended because of Me." (See verses 4–6.) Men get mad at the signs of the Holy Spirit. They get jealous; they spit out hatred; they are trying to tear down God's work.

If John did not believe in Christ through the signs, no eloquence would be of value. If he did not believe what the witnesses told him, he would not believe anything, and neither will you! There is the genuine, and there is the Devil's counterfeit, as surely as you live.

If all you do is stand back and watch, it will seem like foolishness to you as we praise God and as people get filled with the Holy Spirit and receive gifts. But it is Jesus first, last, and all the time. We lift up Jesus and praise His name. We see bright, happy faces; we see pain go out of bodies. We go home rejoicing, feeling as if we have heaven here below.

Resist the Devil in the name of the Lord. Sometimes, when I am standing up preaching, the Devil tries to interfere. He would make me drop dead, if I would listen to him. I resist in the name of the Lord, and he has to go. (See James 4:7.) We have such a wonderful Savior!

The Scripture says, "[You] *shall lay hands on the sick"* (Mark 16:18). God commissioned me, and I obey God rather than man (Acts 5:29). Neither the deadly serpent nor any poison will harm you. You will cast out devils. (See Mark 16:17–18.) I believe every bit of it, and I have seen it all. Hallelujah!

I got my commission from the Lord, and I did not go until He called me and until I was baptized and qualified. I get my message from heaven. I do not know what I am going to talk about, but God knows everyone here and just what everyone needs, and He will give you something.

Power for Service

The power that Jesus promised His disciples when He told them to wait at Jerusalem was to change their lives and qualify them to transact the business of heaven. When they were baptized with the Holy Spirit, they would be true to their Master and be witnesses for Him. Therefore, after the disciples watched Jesus ascend into heaven, they went down from the mountain praising the Lord. They were filled with a great joy as they went back to Jerusalem to await the fulfillment of the promise. They had confidence in God. He had said it would happen, and they began to praise Him in anticipation.

Are you full of joy, with no doubts that Jesus is your Lord and Savior? You need power to do the work of God; you need to be clothed with power. God says He will baptize you with fire, bestowing on you wisdom, knowledge, and gifts. He will cause you to understand the *"deep things of God"* (1 Cor. 2:10). As you teach them and live them, God will be with you.

Be of One Accord

You must believe that you are going to receive this blessing. The disciples were *"with one accord"* (Acts 1:14). May God help us to get to that place. God wants us of one accord, our hearts running together like drops of water.

A little company of believers like that could shake a city in a day. We are not of one accord when one is pulling this way and another is pulling that way—when we hear "maybe this" and "maybe that." Do you suppose God will bless you in that?

You cannot understand the first principles. Yet once you have the newborn joy in your heart, when you see it in someone else, you will know it is of God. Be of one mind; no matter how much there is to praise God for, we always want more.

At Pentecost, the disciples suddenly heard a sound like a mighty, rushing wind (Acts 2:2). This Holy Spirit we are holding up is a mighty power. He came from heaven like a windstorm, like floods of water filling up vessels, like fire upon the heads of one hundred and twenty people.

"Cloven tongues…of fire" (v. 3), as it were, sat upon the disciples' heads. Then the Holy Spirit went in and took possession of the temple, took full possession

of the machinery, wound it up, and set it running for God. They staggered and fell like drunken people. This mighty power took possession of their tongues and spoke through them in other languages.

Way back in the time of the prophets, it was said, "*With stammering lips and another tongue will he speak to this people*" (Isa. 28:11). Think of that! God doing such a mighty thing! But some do not want to believe. That is the way the Holy Spirit came, and that is the way He comes today. Yet people say it is some other power.

The disciples had not lost their minds; they had just found them! They had received the spirit of love and a sound mind (2 Tim. 1:7). We never have sound minds until we receive the mind of Christ. People who cannot understand this say that these things are foolishness. We are told that the "*wisdom of this world is foolishness with God*" (1 Cor. 3:19). This is the power of God and the wisdom of God, not the work of the Devil—people saying so doesn't make it so.

God had complete control. He came in and took possession of the disciples at Pentecost. Now, the Holy Spirit is in the world today. If you disagree, you must first prove that He has been taken away, as well as the gifts and callings, before you have a right to lay hands on God's people.

The things called foolishness today are the "*power of God unto salvation*" (Rom. 1:16). Step out into the deep with God. Paul told us that the Lord ascended into heaven and sent down gifts "*for the perfecting of the saints, for the work of the ministry, for the edifying of the body of Christ*" (Eph. 4:12; see also verses 7–8, 11).

God's Children Built Up in Christ

The ministry does not lack the gifts today. Saints, that is, Christians, are baptized with the Holy Spirit so that the whole body may be edified, no matter how much a believer has already received. When God is working, every one of His children is edified. If God works through someone else, I am edified and encouraged, and I rejoice.

The working of the Holy Spirit is the visible sign of the presence of Jesus. The disciples went from Jerusalem to preach the Gospel everywhere, and the Lord "*was with them*" (Acts 11:21; see Mark 16:20). I love that truth. Is He in heaven? Yes, but He is with us also.

The Lord was with them, "*confirming the word*" (Mark 16:20). How? "*With signs* [and wonders] *following*" (v. 20). Wherever they went, they saw faces shine, someone healed, someone speaking in tongues. What you *"now see and hear"* is of the Holy Spirit (Acts 2:33), and it is for the work of the ministry.

If I did not know that Jesus is by my side with His loving arms around me, I could not stand here today. I would not have the strength if I did not know that He dwells in this body. If I did not know by experience that these things are true, I could not stand here.

I have tested the truth; I know it is of God. How can we help talking of the things we have seen? (See Acts 4:20.) I have seen things by the Spirit and in visions. I have seen Jesus, the heavens open, the Marriage Supper, hosts of angels, the glory of God. I have seen them, glory to God! I know what I am telling you. I know that Jesus lives and is standing by my side, more truly than I know you are here. These things are verities.

"I am not ashamed of the gospel of Christ" (Rom. 1:16). Glory to God! When a weak woman comes here to tell you what strong men ought to have told you, what are you going to think about it? I say that these things are true. When people say they are foolishness and fanaticism, do they dare to attempt to prove it by the Word? I dare them to do it.

When they can prove that the Holy Spirit has been taken out of the world, away from God's people, I am ready to go to prison, but not before.

12

THE FORMER AND THE
LATTER RAIN

The Lord is in our midst. Be still and know the voice of God: "*The Lord is in his holy temple: let all the earth keep silence before him*" (Hab. 2:20). Let us try to realize His wonderful presence. We must all meet Him sooner or later as individuals; it is a good thing to get acquainted with Him now.

This Scripture applies to us today:

> *It shall come to pass in the last days, saith God, I will pour out of my Spirit upon all flesh: and your sons and your daughters shall prophesy, and your young men shall see visions, and your old men shall dream dreams: and on my servants and on my handmaidens I will pour out in those days of my Spirit; and they shall prophesy: and I will show wonders in heaven above, and signs in the earth beneath; blood, and fire, and vapour of smoke: the sun shall be turned into darkness, and the moon into blood, before that great and notable day of the Lord come.* (Acts 2:17–20, quoting Joel 2:28–31)

This is a wonderful Scripture, and many do not understand it. There is a certain time spoken of here, when certain great and wonderful things will take place and people will know that prophecy is being fulfilled. *"It shall come to pass in the last days, saith God, I will pour out of my Spirit upon all flesh"* (Acts 2:17). There will be signs in the heavens and the earth—signs of His coming. The Holy Spirit will be poured out before the *"notable day of the Lord come[s]"* (v. 20).

This prophecy was first spoken eight hundred years before Jesus came to earth. Peter, standing up on the Day of Pentecost, recited the prophecy and confirmed it. Under the inspiration of the Holy Spirit, on fire with the Holy Spirit from head to foot, speaking with a tongue of fire, he said that these things would come to pass in the last days.

We Are in the Last Days

We believe and know by the Word of God and by the signs that we are now living in the last days, the very times Peter spoke about, which we were to know by the mighty things taking place. We are the people, and this is the time, just before the *"notable day of the Lord"* bursts upon the world. We believe we are the people; yes, we know it. We have a right to our belief, for it is based upon the Word of God, and no man or woman has any right to denounce our teaching or to injure us in any way until it can be proved by the Word of God that the things we teach are not true.

You should give us a hearing. Then take the same Word of God and prove by it that the things we teach are not true—if you can. You must first prove that the Holy Spirit, working in all His mighty miraculous power, has been done away with before you have any right to denounce us as frauds and hypocrites on account of these things that we say come from God.

As I wrote earlier, whenever anyone, minister or lawyer, can take the platform and prove by the Word of God that the Holy Spirit and His mighty, miraculous power have been taken away from the church, I am willing to go to prison, but not before. It cannot be done. God never recalls His gifts (Rom. 11:29). God never changes. My Bible says, *"Jesus Christ the same yesterday, and to day, and for ever"* (Heb. 13:8).

There are many ways besides the working of the Holy Spirit by which we know we are in the last days. Joel, in speaking of the last days, tells us many things I don't have time to mention today, which show us that we are in this time. Nahum tells us that when this time comes, it will be the *"day of his preparation*" (Nah. 2:3). God is preparing men so that they may be taken out of the world before the Tribulation comes.

Before the flood, Noah was commanded by God to build an ark. It took him just five years to build the ark—though many believe it was much longer than that—and the time he was building it was the preparation time in those days. Noah, at God's command, was preparing a place for himself and his family where they would be in safety, above the storm that was coming, above the waves and billows. At the same time that the old world was getting a warning, Noah was building the ark.

Signs of the Last Days

Jesus compared that day of preparation to our time in these last days. (See Matthew 24:37–44.) It is a short period and has been going on for some time already. It is prophesied that there will be great signs in the earth: blood, fire, smoke, earthquakes, great destruction. All these things have been coming upon the earth in the last few years. God has a time for everything. The book of Daniel says that in the *"time of the end: many shall run to and fro, and knowledge shall be increased"* (Dan. 12:4). Nahum said, *"The chariots shall rage in the streets, they shall justle one against another in the broad ways: they shall seem like torches, they shall run like the lightnings"* (Nah. 2:4).

Jesus sent the Holy Spirit with mighty signs and wonders. He took possession of men, and they staggered like drunken men; they were drunk but not with wine. They spoke with *"stammering lips and another tongue"* (Isa. 28:11). These things happened when Pentecost first came, in order to establish the church in power. That was the early rain (James 5:7).

In the last days, the time of preparation, God will cause the early rain to come again as at Pentecost, and He will also give the *"latter rain"* (v. 7) abundantly in the same month. What do you think of that? The early disciples went to heaven by the death route. It will take a double portion of the Spirit to fill our bodies, to make us sound in spirit, soul, and body. When Jesus comes like a flash of lightning (Matt. 24:27), He will change these bodies of ours in a moment, and they will be made like His glorious body (Phil. 3:21).

"Behold, I show you a mystery; we shall not all sleep, but we shall all be changed" (1 Cor. 15:51) and will rise *"to meet the Lord in the air"* (1 Thess. 4:17). When

are these things to be? At the end of the day of preparation, just before the Tribulation bursts upon the world. We are to watch for the signs and not forsake the *"assembling of ourselves together"* (Heb. 10:25)—and so much the more as we see the Day of the Lord approaching! Glory to God!

The Jews understood something about heeding the warnings of God. They said one to another, "We have been wounded; we have gone through many troubles; let us turn to the Lord. (See Lamentations 3:1–40.) *'After two days will he revive us: in the third day he will raise us up'* (Hos. 6:2)."

We are now down to the end of the second thousand years since Christ set up His kingdom. Now, what will happen to the Jews? The Jews today have great liberty in Palestine, so much so that they are going back by the thousands and building up the waste places. Modern improvements are there today, and they are hoping for something, but they do not know what. After the Tribulation, the Jews will return to the Lord.

The Holy Spirit was first poured out at Pentecost. *"In the last days...I will pour out of my Spirit upon all flesh"* (Acts 2:17). The prophecy does not say that He will sprinkle a few drops, but *"pour out...upon all flesh"*—a cloudburst! This will happen just at the end; it will continue until the saints are taken away. Then the Tribulation will burst upon the earth. Some of the signs will be, *"Your sons and your daughters shall prophesy"* (v. 17). It is very plain so that everyone may understand. There is to be a wonderful ministry in the last days. Paul said that male and female are one in Christ (Gal. 3:28). Both will prophesy in the last days. That is the effect of the outpouring of the Holy Spirit. Other signs will be the following: devils will be cast out; hands will be laid on the sick, and they will recover; many will speak with new tongues; if anyone drinks poison accidentally, it will not hurt him; and serpents will not be able to harm believers. (See Mark 16:17–18.)

The Bride Is Almost Ready

See the power that has been given to man today: he has even chained the lightning. It is the day for preparation. Men *"run to and fro"* (Dan. 12:4) and fly over the land. Hurry up! The ark will soon be finished, and then God will say, "Come up." The ark went up above the waters; the world went down. God is preparing His spiritual ark today. The body of Christ will soon be complete, and when it is complete, it will go above the treetops to meet our Lord and King in the air (1 Thess. 4:17). We are in the day of preparation of the King of Glory, and His bride is making herself ready (Rev. 19:7). Rejoice and be glad, for the Marriage of the Lamb is at hand. The bride must be arrayed in white linen, the robe of right-eousness, clothed in the power of the mighty God through His outpoured Spirit.

She is getting her garments ready to meet the Bridegroom. I praise the Lord that I am living in this day. The bride will be caught up just before the Tribulation bursts upon this sin-cursed earth. The bride must be very beautiful. She is rep-resented as a queen dressed in a robe of finest needlework (Ps. 45:13–14). What is that fine wedding dress, the garments the bride will wear when she meets the Lord in the air? She will shine with the gifts and jewels of the Holy Spirit. *"We have this treasure in earthen vessels"* (2 Cor. 4:7), but they who are wise will shine as the brightness of the sun (Dan. 12:3). The wise will know when these things are coming, when the ark is about ready to go up. (See Daniel 2:21–22; 12:10.)

The Lord will not keep any secrets from them. As there is perfect confidence between bride and Bridegroom, so Jesus will reveal secrets to His bride. He will show us the *"deep things of God"* (1 Cor. 2:10), and we will know when the end is drawing near. You must make your own wedding garments; you cannot hire someone to make them. The time is coming. People do not usually begin to make wedding garments until the wedding day is near.

A bride is very happy, is willing to forsake her father's house, her friends, everything, and go with her bridegroom, even to a foreign country. She loves those she leaves, but he is dearer to her than anything else. We must be willing to leave anything and everything to go with Jesus. The bride of Christ will be taken out from among men, and many men and women will be left behind. You may say, "I do not believe it." I believe it!

Do you suppose that I would leave my home, my friends, and the only child that I have, to spend my life for others, if I did not know these things were so? God has revealed these things by His Word and by signs, and I know they are true. God is almighty. He is putting His seal upon this truth every day; He is putting the seal of the Holy Spirit upon people every day. The Holy Spirit is a witness to you, by mighty signs and wonders, that we are preaching the Word of God. I call God to witness that the Holy Spirit is putting His seal upon the work here. There are signs here every day. What are you going to do about it? If you believe the Bible, you must accept it. We have the eternal Word to stand on, and stronger is He who is with us than all that can be against us. (See 1 John 4:4.)

Signs Follow the Word

After Pentecost, the disciples went out and preached the Holy Spirit sent by the ascended Jesus, and He confirmed the Word *"with signs following"* (Mark 16:20). I say before God that He is confirming the Word here every day, and these miracles are written down in heaven's record. Jesus Christ is the Healer and the Baptizer. John the Baptist said, *"He that cometh after me is mightier than I...he shall baptize you with the Holy Ghost, and with fire"* (Matt. 3:11). I praise God that some of the fire has struck this place. You can make flowery speeches, and the Devil will just laugh, but this work stirs the Devil. It is *"by my spirit, saith the LORD"* (Zech. 4:6).

Paul said that his teaching was *"not with enticing words of man's wisdom, but in demonstration of the Spirit and of power"* (1 Cor. 2:4). That shook the world, and it is just the same today. You say, "I do not like this power." Well, the Devil does not like it, either. I have been ministering for thirty-five years, and people fell under the power of God by the thousands before I preached healing. There were mighty outpourings of the Spirit that made the Devil howl. It shows how little we know of the real Gospel when we take the letter of the law (see Romans 7:6); it is like skimmed milk.

No man can understand the *"deep things of God"* (1 Cor. 2:10) except by the Spirit. Paul had much knowledge, but He said that the wisdom of this world is foolishness in the sight of God (3:19). True wisdom comes from heaven. The Word must be preached in simplicity. Jesus had the eloquence of high heaven at His command, yet He used language that the most uneducated could understand.

Preach in a simple way and demonstrate. The seal is put upon the Word by the Holy Spirit. Many people say that when we lay hands upon people, they get mesmerized. I am sorry that they do not know more of the power of God.

The Bible tells us that there was a great revival in Samaria through Philip's ministry. Simon the sorcerer and many others had been baptized in water in the name of the Lord Jesus, but none of the believers there had been baptized with the Holy Spirit. Then Peter and John went to Samaria and laid their hands on the new Christians, and they received the Holy Spirit. The Spirit was imparted to them in some way through the laying on of the apostles' hands. Simon recognized that the power was different from sorcery, and he wanted it. He offered the apostles money in exchange for this power, so that whoever he laid hands on might receive the Holy Spirit. (See Acts 8:5–19.)

The apostles were horrified. Peter said, *"Thy money perish with thee, because thou hast thought that the gift of God may be purchased with money"* (v. 20). The Holy Spirit and His power are gifts of God; you cannot buy them. Many people today do not understand that any more than Simon did. The apostles told him to repent, or he would be lost: *"Repent therefore of this your wickedness, and pray God if perhaps the thought of your heart may be forgiven you. For I see that you are poisoned by bitterness and bound by iniquity"* (vv. 22–23 NKJV). May God open the eyes of the people!

The Workings of the Spirit

Something happened by the laying on of the apostles' hands. The Holy Spirit fell on those people, and they had great blessing. There were great demonstrations in those days when the Holy Spirit fell on the people. The thought is that when hands were laid on people, something happened: they spoke in other languages, their mouths were filled with laughter, and sometimes they fell prostrate like dead men.

You must prove that God has taken this power away before you judge us harshly. Peter told the multitude that the things they saw on the Day of Pentecost were the things the prophets had said would come. (See Acts 2:14–36.) You may ask why people fall down in our meetings. What is our little strength under the power of God? Whenever people get a glimpse of God's glory, they lose their strength and fall.

The Impact of God's Glory

When Paul described the vision he had received from God, he said he did not know whether he had been in the body or out of the body at that time, but that God knew. (See 2 Corinthians 12:1–4.) When John the Revelator saw the glory of God in a vision, he fell *"as [one] dead"* (Rev. 1:17). When Daniel had a vision, he fell on his face; then a hand touched him and placed him on his hands and knees—you have never seen anything like that—and he was taken up, strengthened, and saw a great vision. The men who were with Daniel fled, so they did not see the vision. Daniel did not flee; he saw it, but he fell prostrate. (See Daniel 10:1–12:13.) When we experience just a little manifestation of God's power, we lose our strength and fall down.

Some of you do not understand the working of the Spirit. You are not near enough to God to know that it is the work of the Spirit.

Peter was on the housetop, praying, and he lost his strength and went down. A voice from heaven called him three times. (See Acts 10:9–16.) Sometimes, God teaches us more in ten minutes when we are lost to this world than we would otherwise learn in months. Paul, as he journeyed to Damascus persecuting the Christians, was struck down to the earth when the light shone from heaven, and those who were with him also fell to the earth. Paul said that the light was brighter than the sun, yet this happened at midday when the sun was at its strength. All those men fell from their horses and rolled in the dust when the glory of God passed by. Paul was struck blind and was blind for three days. (See Acts 9:1–9.)

When Jesus went to the grave, He went down as a corpse. But when He rose from the dead, the soldiers fell down at the manifestation of God's power and glory. (See Matthew 28:1–4.)

You must prove that God no longer manifests His power and glory before you condemn us. Remember the first martyr, Stephen. He was a man full of faith, wisdom, and power; he was full of the Holy Spirit (Acts 6:5, 8). Learned men tried to confound him, but they could not do it; then they were jealous and wanted to get rid of him. They hired men of the baser sort—that is the kind for that work—who lied about this mighty servant of God.

They arrested Stephen, and there he was before the great assembly. He did not try to defend himself, but he took the opportunity offered to preach to them about Jesus. He was filled with the Holy Spirit. His face was as the face of an angel, and those who bore false testimony against him, so that he lost his life, saw it. He did not look like a liar and a hypocrite. He was a servant of Almighty God.

You can sometimes see that light today in the faces of God's children. Stephen looked up into heaven and saw the glory of God. He saw Jesus who had risen from the dead, standing at the right hand of God, and he told the people about it. (Oh, Lord, open the eyes of these people, and let them see the angels of the Lord encamped around us and Jesus standing in the midst!)

When Stephen told what he saw, they gnashed their teeth; they did not intend to repent. They dragged him out and stoned him to death, but the Lord permitted it and received him. God promises that His people will be protected, and when trouble comes, it is not a sign that He has forsaken them. Stephen's enemies did not like the fact that God received him, nor did they like to see his face shine with the glory of God. His body was lying as a bruised mass, but his spirit rose to meet the Lord. He had a glorious vision. (See Acts 6:8–7:60.) Do you believe he saw the throne of God and Jesus standing there? People talk about these things as though they were fables.

The Signs of the Times

God says that before Jesus comes, these signs and wonders will come to pass: the sick will be healed, devils will be cast out, and people will speak with tongues. (See Mark 16:17–18.) I am so glad for these days. When Jesus came the first time, He rebuked the Jewish leaders. He told them they could discern the face of the sky but not the signs of the times (Matt. 16:3). *"How is it that ye do not discern this time?"* (Luke 12:56). How much more will Jesus upbraid people when He returns? "Why didn't you see the signs? Why didn't you listen to My messengers? Why didn't you look at the Word and see whether they were telling the truth or were impostors?" Excuses won't do when we stand before Jesus. The light has come. Let us rise and shine and give God the glory!

Nothing but the mighty Holy Spirit will ever take you up in the clouds. He will quicken these mortal bodies (Rom. 8:11), and they will be changed. Christ rose from the dead, and He is the *"resurrection, and the life"* (John 11:25). We will know the power of the resurrection life. We will be so filled with the Holy Spirit that our bodies will be made light. We will not have wings, but our hands and feet will be made light. Our feet will be like *"hinds' feet"* (2 Sam. 22:34) as we run, skip, and almost fly. Sometimes my body is made so light, I can hardly stay. My feet are on the earth, but my hands seem to be near the throne.

People need to have the blood of Jesus covering them, covering their diseased bodies in His name. Do you believe right now? If you believe so that you praise the Lord in faith, it will be done. If you do not feel the joy, offer praise as a sacrifice, and ask God to give you the joy. When the unclean spirit is driven out, the disease goes, and the resurrection life comes in. Then you lose the small amount of human strength that you have, and you go down like Daniel, John, and the rest of them, and you lie down in green pastures.

Some people dance, shout, and praise the Lord as the life of Jesus thrills through them. I declare to you on the authority of God and from my own experience, I know that this is the power of God through Jesus Christ. It does not take

Jesus long to do the work, but it takes some of us a long time to get there. Five minutes will do the work. Then the peace of God will flow through you like a river, and you will have joy in the Holy Spirit. As you go home, don't think about your sins; don't commit any more, and don't worry about the past—it is under the blood.

God gave me a message, and He has given me the strength to stand here and deliver it. He asks you in a loving way to meet the Lord in the air, to attend the Marriage Supper. Will you meet me there? He is coming so soon. I often think that I will live until He comes.

I praise Him today that I know these things about the Holy Spirit. Sometimes people get into the flesh and make too much of a demonstration, but that is better than never to talk, pray, or sing. Let us not condemn, but let us all try to get nearer to God. That is what I am striving for today.

Oh, God, I have held up your Son today. I have honored His name with all the strength you have given me. Take the scales off the eyes of those who do not see, and cause them to see the truths that have been brought out! May they think of them again and again, and may they go to You to find out whether these things are so. You know how I have pleaded with people not to lay hands on the ark of the covenant or on the Lord's anointed. Open the eyes of those who have known only dead formality, and cause them to know that I am Your servant. Lord, I want the joy bells to ring in heaven because they are on the way, but you cannot take them against their will. I pray that I may meet them at the Marriage Supper of the Lamb.

13

THE BLOOD AND FIRE MARK

Today, the same things are taking place that took place at the time of the destruction of Jerusalem. Nearly twenty-six hundred years ago, the Lord gave the prophet Ezekiel this vision:

> He cried also in mine ears with a loud voice, saying, Cause them that have charge over the city to draw near, even every man with his destroying weapon in his hand. And, behold, six men came from the way of the higher gate [men of authority], which lieth toward the north, and every man a slaughter weapon in his hand; and one man among them was clothed with linen, with a writer's inkhorn by his side [he represents the baptized saints before the destruction of Jerusalem, with the Holy Spirit in them, going around baptizing people with blood and fire]....And he called to the man clothed with linen, which had the writer's inkhorn by his side; and the LORD said unto him, Go through the midst of the city, through the midst of Jerusalem, and set a mark upon the foreheads of the men that sigh and that cry for all the abominations that be done in the midst thereof. And to the others [the destroying army] he said in mine hearing, Go ye after him through the city, and smite: let not your eye spare, neither have ye pity: slay utterly old and young, both maids, and little children, and women: but come not near any man upon

whom is the mark; and begin at my sanctuary. Then they began at the ancient men which were before the house. And he said unto them, Defile the house, and fill the courts with the slain: go ye forth. And they went forth, and slew in the city. And it came to pass, while they were slaying them, and I was left, that I fell upon my face, and cried, and said, Ah Lord GOD! wilt thou destroy all the residue of Israel in thy pouring out of thy fury upon Jerusalem? Then said he unto me, The iniquity of the house of Israel and Judah is exceeding great, and the land is full of blood, and the city full of perverseness: for they say, The LORD hath forsaken the earth. (Ezek. 9:1–9)

That is what they say today, that the Lord does not see anymore. "*As for me also* [He caused me to know that He lives], *mine eye shall not spare, neither will I have pity, but I will recompense their way upon their head*" (v. 10).

"*And, behold, the man clothed with linen, which had the inkhorn by his side, reported the matter, saying, I have done as thou hast commanded me*" (v. 11). It is done; I have finished. The last one is sealed, and the door is closed.

Ezekiel had this vision nearly six hundred years before Jesus came, prior to the destruction of Jerusalem, and now it has been about twenty-six hundred years since he saw that vision—the vision of Jerusalem, of the church, and of the conditions of the world, especially of the church. Today, we are living in a time in the world and the church that is parallel to the time of the destruction of Jerusalem. The same remarkable things are taking place today—just before the Great Tribulation, just before the wrath of God is poured out without mercy on the people. The Lord showed the prophet the awful condition of His people, and these things came upon the Jewish nation. But this time they will come upon the whole world.

The Jewish nation had sinned against God. They were God's special people—God's called-out people. He said, "I did not call you out because you were the greatest people, the strongest people, the wealthiest people, the best people, for you were the fewest of all. Yet I have called you, chosen you, set My love upon you." (See Deuteronomy 7:6–8.) God's chosen people have always been few.

To the Jewish people came the Law and the Prophets, and then Christ. God gave the Law from Mount Sinai amid mighty signs and wonders. When the temple was dedicated, the presence of God was seen. Over the years, God appeared to His people. He gave them priests and prophets, revelations from heaven, spiritual signs, and visions. Angels appeared. God talked from heaven and did all these things while His people obeyed. But soon they got proud, haughty, and lifted up. They began to glory in their multiplying numbers; they began to take in people from other nations whose hearts were not right with God and to give them power and high places of authority and great advantage. These people were given charge over God's holy people, and they ruled them with a rod of iron.

God's people began to follow the wisdom of men. He warned them and warned them and finally began to show them that they had left the Fountainhead of living waters and had hewed out broken cisterns that could not hold water (Jer. 2:13).

The glory of God appeared to Ezekiel, picked him up by the hair on his head, carried him through space between heaven and earth, and set him down in Jerusalem. God told him to look and see the dreadful things. The holy places were filled with pictures of serpents, like Devil worship today, things that were unclean. God showed him all the abominations. He took him into the holiest place where twenty-five men sat with their backs to God and worshipped the sun. (See Ezekiel 8:1–16.)

Then God told Ezekiel, "Now you go and take the example of the temple in all its glory, when the glory of God filled the house (Ezek. 10:4), and you warn these people. Take the example of the glorious temple, and go and compare it with the example today. Show them where they have failed, and see if they will repent." God said they would never do it (Ezek. 3:7). But God does not say we are to run things to suit ourselves. They were warned.

"Son of man, I am not sending you to the heathen, but to the people of the house of Israel." (See Ezekiel 3:4–6.) But they would not hear. They failed to know that the prophet of God was in their midst. He stood and warned them, but it did not do any good.

Pretty soon, the last prophet came to Israel, and they rejected him. Then the love and mercy and glory of God left them. For nearly four hundred years, perhaps longer, the children of Israel were left without holy priests, without prophets, and without visions or revelations—except for a few humble believers, brokenhearted little ones, who were true to God.

The people began to say, "Oh, God, how long? There is no one who can speak to us anymore. We have no prophets, priests, visions, or revelations. Where are the signs?" All through the Word of God, when people were right with Him, they saw signs of the invisible God. But when they backslid, they lost the connection. The pipe got filled up, and the flow of living water stopped. They trusted in broken cisterns (Jer. 2:13)—man's wealth and knowledge, which is an abomination without God.

The Signs of the Times

That is the condition the Jews were in when Christ came. Yet after they had been looking for Him for nearly four hundred years, they did not know Him. He said to them, "Why is it that you do not discern the signs of the time? Your prophecies are fulfilled, and you are living in the days when the Son of Man has come." (See Luke 12:56.) But they were saying, "God has forsaken the earth. God doesn't see. God has left the earth, and the signs and wonders are all gone." (See Ezekiel 8:12; 9:9.) They began to follow men's wisdom. They did not want the power of God. They left the *"fountain of living waters"* (Jer. 2:13). They did not want to hear a shout in the camp (see 1 Samuel 4:5); they did not want to see God's power. And so it is now.

But God is love. God does hear, and He helps you to see that. God will visit the earth again.

When Jesus came, He gave the people another call just like the *"latter rain"* (Joel 2:23). Yet the apostle Paul said that the Day of the Lord would not come without a *"falling away"* (2 Thess. 2:3). God knows how they fell away. Before Jesus came, His coming was prophesied, and when He came, the Jewish nation had another chance—He offered them the kingdom. But they spurned Him and turned Him away, and finally one day He wept over them bitterly, saying, "O Jerusalem, how often would I have gathered you from the destruction that is coming. Now I leave you." (See Matthew 23:37–39; Luke 19:41–44.) And that is just what He is saying today. "This time your house is left unto you desolate (Matt. 23:38). Your city will be destroyed. The enemy is coming; armies are coming in to lay your place desolate (Luke 19:43), and the blood will flow like rivers."

But remember that God warned His faithful people about the destruction of Jerusalem that occurred in A.D. 70. He had a people who had accepted Christ, and they had followed the Lamb. They waited in Jerusalem until they were baptized with the Holy Spirit, and God revealed Himself and His Word to them. Christ had told his disciples one day, when speaking of the temple, "The day is coming when that beautiful temple will be destroyed. Not one stone will be left upon another, and the city will be destroyed." (See Matthew 24:1–2; Luke 19:43–44.) The disciples said, "Lord, tell us when that evil thing will happen. We want to know what will be the sign of Your second coming and of the end of the world" (Matt. 24:3). Jesus told them and gave them signs so that we can know them today.

Jesus is coming soon; the signs show He will come back soon. We are concerned about the signs. The disciples asked questions; they were serious about asking, and the Lord told them how they would know. He gave them signs and said, "When you see certain signs come to pass, prepare to flee to the mountains; make ready to escape. Then there will be other signs and finally a certain sign. When you see this sign, if you have not made all your preparations for flight, if you are on the housetop, do not go back into the house. If you are in the field, do not turn back to take your coat, but flee to the mountains. Get out of the city, because the gates will be closed, and you will be shut in." (See Matthew 24:3–18.)

The disciples believed what God said. They took His Word by faith; they believed the Word and felt the responsibility. They loved their people, and they knew that unless their people accepted Jesus Christ, they would not escape. They were in the right; they were baptized saints sighing and crying (see Ezekiel 9:4) for their families and for their neighbors, sighing and crying on account of the dreadful things going on. However, they were shut in with God. They had the mark of God upon them.

When you see the things that are making the world turn pale and tremble—when these things come to pass—lift up your heads and rejoice. Rejoice at every calamity, because it will soon be over. Although the disciples sighed and cried, they still rejoiced because they knew they were saved.

The man with the inkhorn represents the people of the Holy Spirit. In a short time, all these things are coming. Get busy and warn the people. "*Whether they hear or whether they refuse*" (Ezek. 2:5 NKJV), warn the people.

Imagine the early believers who were filled with the Holy Spirit. Imagine them going through offices and stores and business places in Jerusalem, doing their best to warn the people. The soldiers who were coming in that great army of destruction were going back and forth about their business. The man with the inkhorn was to do the work, to get ready for the great work, but no one in

Jerusalem knew what was going on. The saints of God were going everywhere, warning the people the best they could.

The believers told them, "Judgment is coming; destruction is coming; the city will be taken." The disciples were laughed at as fools, fanatics, and enemies. The people would not listen to them. But the saints knew that when the destruction came, the city would be taken, and the people's businesses would be no good. The enemy would take everything; their houses and lands would amount to nothing. The only thing they could do was to use their money to warn the people that destruction was coming. So their money, their gold, their silver, and their land would not do any good. Neither will yours do you any good. May God help you to see this truth and to use your time and resources to spread the Gospel.

God's Mark on the Forehead

"*Blow the trumpet in Zion*" (Joel 2:15)! Jerusalem will be taken; tribulation is coming. The Day of the Lord is near; it hurries greatly. It is even at the door (Matt. 24:33). Warn the people that they must have the seal of God on their foreheads (Ezek. 9:4; see also Revelation 7:3). That is why we are going around getting the people saved, baptized with the Holy Spirit, and sealed with the finger of the living God. They have to have the mark of God on their foreheads to understand these things. Go through the streets of the city; note those who sigh and cry, and seal them with the finger of God (Ezek. 9:4). That is what God is doing today. Glory to God.

That is what they did at the time of the destruction of Jerusalem. The Word went out. The believers were laughed at and scorned and persecuted, but they saw the signs coming faster. The more they did, the more the people laughed at them and persecuted them. They hid away in the mountains, and every day they felt worse about their friends and neighbors; they would hasten into the city and try to show the people that these things were true. The people did not believe, but that did not change the fact.

It was at the time of the great Feast of Passover that Jesus told His disciples what would be the signs of the destruction. Rabbis and many people from all over the world were there. While they were gathered there, the Lord told them, "When you see a certain signal, get out quickly. Don't go back to take anything out of your house, but get out of the city." (See Matthew 24:15–17.)

However, when the time came, they would not believe anything; they were having a good time. But at last a certain signal came, and the gates were closed; they were shut in, and they never got out. But those who had the seal of the living God upon them were "caught up"—taken out—just like we will be when the time comes. Josephus, the historian, tells us that not one of the followers of Jesus Christ went down in the slaughter. They believed God and prepared for the escape, and God took every baptized saint. Not one was permitted to be locked up in that city because they believed God and made preparations for flight. Hallelujah.

Today, the people of God are a nation that is hated, a *"nation not desired"* (Zeph. 2:1), a nation despised. This "sect" is spoken against everywhere (Acts 28:22), and I am glad I am one of them. When Jesus comes, you will be willing to be called a fanatic, a Holy Roller, or anything else. May God help you to see it.

The people of Jerusalem were all taken unawares. The enemy came, the gates were shut, and the greatest calamity that the world ever saw fell upon the Jews. When the army went into the city, they went into the inner court where the holy men—twenty-five of them—sat with their backs to God. (See Ezekiel 8:16.) They commenced with these fat priests and heads of the church, and they were slaughtered like oxen. We are told that the people in the city had no provisions; they were shut in there and literally starved to death. Delicate women ate their own children. Delicate women who would not put their feet on the ground ate their own children during that siege. Such a thing had never happened before. You know all about these things. Some were carried away in captivity, and only a few despised little ones were left as slaves. But God had revealed the knowledge of this destruction to His people who had the mark, and every last one escaped. Oh, hallelujah!

The prophet Ezekiel is looking down in history to us today, warning us in just the same way. When Jesus comes, there will be tribulation and a time of trouble on the earth such as was never known before. The darkness will be so great that people will be able to feel it. When Jesus comes to catch His bride away, there will be a time such as the world never heard of before. All who sigh and cry for the abominable things that are going on in the world, those who have the mark, are children of the day (Ezek. 9:4). You will not be overtaken as by a *"thief in the night"* (1 Thess. 5:2), for you are the children of light. The wise will know. Glory to God.

History tells us that many rich men and many great men went down in the siege; but those who were called, who had God's mark, who were wanderers and pilgrims and had to leave their homes and wealth, escaped with their lives and a few little things that they could take away to provide for their comfort. When Jesus returns for His bride, you won't take anything. All will be left for the Devil to work with, for the world will go on just like it is now. When Jesus comes, it will not yet be the end of the world. But the bride, the saints, will be taken up.

Dear friends, we are living in a day parallel to the time of the destruction of Jerusalem. Jesus is coming again. In preparation, God is visiting the earth again, pouring out His Spirit.

The church has gone back to a state of weakness. When I was a girl, the Methodist church was the most powerful and the most spiritual. People fell under the power of God, danced, and did lots of other things. They had an "amen corner" in every church. When the preacher came in, he would not stop for anything, but would go into the pulpit, open the Bible, and begin. He would not say, "My second point is..." and "My third point is..." for he did not have time. The amens came from all over the house. The people obeyed God; they were happy people, and they had great power.

But today people are saying, "We don't know God. He has left us. We don't see Him. We don't like these fanatical meetings." So today there is not an amen or a shout from anybody. If one sister gets blessed, and the power of God comes on her, and she shouts, three or four good sisters get around her, and she never shouts again.

Lots of people are wrong today if those good old people were right. Dear friends, if they were right, then your own fathers, mothers, and grandparents—and you yourself—would not like to have anyone say they were crazy. If they were right before God, someone is wrong today.

Now, listen, God is pouring out His Spirit again on all nations of the earth. Today God has a baptized people. Saints of every nation, tribe, and church are mixed up in this company who are baptized in the Holy Spirit and fire and who are risking everything to warn the people. They are working to get people saved and baptized with the Holy Spirit. Get under the blood, and get the mark of the living God on your forehead. God is visiting you again, and we are just on the eve of the awful tribulations.

War, Famine, and Pestilence

Men and women will eat their own children. There will be war, famine, and pestilence, and all these things in one day. God says that it will be that way. Devilish appetite is going to get into animals of all kinds, into the wild beasts. This problem will be compounded because famine is coming and the animals will leave the wilderness and come into the cities to get something to eat. (See Ezekiel 5:17.) If you escape the war, the wild beasts will get you. If you escape the lions and bears and stagger around in your own house for a quiet place to die, a serpent will bite you. (See Amos 5:19.)

Don't you see that these things are coming? God has not left you without warning. Read the Word of God and watch the signs; watch the signs and read the Word. These things were seen twenty-six hundred years ago. A day with the Lord is only a little while, and a thousand years is like only a day to Him (2 Pet. 3:8).

We are the people on the stage of action today, and the people living today will be in this great army of slaughter. But the saints will be taken out. They will never see death but will see the Son of God coming in glory.

So, every day, everywhere, we see the signs being fulfilled that Jesus is coming. One great sign is that God's real saints are making such an effort to go throughout the world with the Gospel. They are risking everything to enlighten the people, to find hearts who will receive the message, get saved, and let God seal them with the seal of the living God on their foreheads. Let us make the vision plain. May God help me to do so. Will the people see that we are actors in this vision? Let us make it plain so that those who hear may understand and, when they receive the seal of God, will run to get ready. That is what we are doing today.

Now, beloved, we must have this mark of God. We must not only be saved but sealed with the seal of the living God. It may be that if you go deep enough, you will be hidden away from all these things that are coming on the earth. Be shut in with God today—now.

The angels represented as holding back the four winds of the earth (Rev. 7:1) are letting loose now, as surely as God lives. Another great angel is crying, "Hold on a little longer." We wonder about these things. Angels see the awful condition of the earth: the cup of iniquity is full. They ask, "O Lord, can we let loose? Can the sun be turned on to scorch men? Can the cyclones tear down the cedars?

Can the tidal waves sweep the towns away? Can the earthquakes come?" But the great angel who carries the Gospel of Jesus Christ says, "Hold on a little longer; hold on a little longer. Don't let loose. Hold back the power of the sun; hold back the greatest tidal waves, the greatest cyclones, the greatest earthquakes, and the greatest calamities, until we have sealed the servants of God with the seal of the living God on their foreheads."

You may be a servant of God, but you must be sealed with the seal of God; you must have the mark of blood and fire; you must be sealed with the seal of the living God. Jesus is saying, "Hold back the great calamities; they would be a great inconvenience to My servants. They are the lights of the world (Matt. 5:14). For the sake of the souls who want to be saved, I will give my people a little more chance to work. Don't let loose."

Hold back! What for? Hold back until we have sealed the saints of God with the seal of the living God on the forehead. My God, help these people to see why the sun does not get two or three degrees hotter and kill millions. Don't you see the signs of what is coming? One hundred died in the heat in Chicago. If the sun had been a few more degrees hotter, millions would have died.

Watch and pray. Be in an attitude of prayer or praise all the time so that you may be counted worthy to escape these awful calamities and stand before the Son of God (Luke 21:36). Don't you see that we have no time for foolish talking about what this one or that one said? I am here to tell what Jesus Christ said. I don't steal words from my neighbor. It is what Jesus said that is important. We are to pay attention to *"Thus saith the Lord."* (See, for example, Ezekiel 2:4.)

In that day, two will be sleeping in the same bed; one will be taken and the other left. Two will be working in the field; one will talk and talk all kinds of foolishness, and the other will be obliged to answer; then suddenly there will be no answer. The first one will look up and say, "Why, what is the matter, my friend? Where did you go?" He is alone; his friend is gone. Find him if you can. He escaped before the gates were shut. Glory to God, he was caught away. (See Matthew 24:37–42.)

That is going to be just the way it is when Jesus comes. He will take His saints up alive; they will be changed quicker than a wink. We will not have other bodies, but our bodies will be very light. We are not waiting for wings; rather, we are looking for the power from heaven to lighten these bodies. We will rise like He did. Our hands and feet will be like wings. We will go sailing through the air—up over the stars—to meet the Lord with a shout. (See 1 Thessalonians 4:16–17.) Glory to God!

A Fountain of Tears

But for those who are left, it will be so different. Those who reject Christ will be left to go down. Oh, God, how we ought to be sighing and crying for the people who will be left. We don't sigh enough; we don't cry enough. But at the same time, we are so full of joy that we have to release it or explode. Be glad that you are living in the time of the *"latter rain"* (Joel 2:23). Rejoice and be glad.

Along with our joy, we are sighing and crying because of the corruption. Several times I have cried out—the Holy Spirit within me has cried out. It came to me like the prophet said when he was speaking of this day: *"My bowels, my bowels!"* (Jer. 4:19). His body seemed to be bursting, and his head was a fountain of tears, because of the destruction that is coming on the earth. Jesus is weeping over Jerusalem, and how the Holy Spirit weeps through me! It seems as though I will cry until I die. But I try to go on.

God is putting a mark on those who sigh and cry for all the abominable things that are coming on the earth. Dear friends, don't you see that the angels want to let loose the four winds? They are saying, "Oh, can we let loose? The people are so wicked; let the people go." No, not until we have sealed the servants of God with the seal of the living God on their foreheads. Go through the streets, and put a mark upon everyone who sighs and cries. Put the mark of God on them. Tell them to be baptized in the Holy Spirit. Jesus Christ will baptize you with the Holy Spirit and fire (Matt. 3:11). He will give us wisdom—the mind of Christ. He will seal us with knowledge, and we will not be left in the dark but will be children of light.

You say that you are saved and living pure, holy lives before God; however, if you don't get this baptism and get the everlasting arms of Jesus around you, you will be carried away in the throng, and you will not be ready to go up when Jesus comes. Oh, hold back until the servants of God get the light and are sealed with the seal of the living God on their foreheads.

There is not much time. The Lord is holding back these things. Are we about our Master's business? No wonder I don't rest—I am trusting God to carry me through. I know these things are true. God help us, the world is getting pretty well shut in now. There are so many false doctrines of the Devil coming in. People are believing in delusions. You must keep under the blood, or you will be carried away. I praise God for the knowledge that Jesus is coming soon. Praise His name forever.

These awful things are already on the earth. You know the Lord said that when certain things happen, it is the *"beginning of sorrows"* (Matt. 24:8). The nations are mad. Aren't they mad now? They are crazy. What are they fighting for? Jealous hatred. One nation is against another; several have gone down. Look at them. No one knows the real truth. May God help you to hear. This is the beginning of sorrows. The four winds are going to be let loose, as surely as you live. If this is the beginning of sorrows, what will the end be?

You may escape the worst things and be hidden away. The prophet, looking down to the last days, saw the saints going up. He says, "Come up, my people, and enter into the place prepared for you. Shut the doors after you, and hide for a little while, for the Lord is coming down to punish the inhabitants of the earth. Their blood will flow like the dust, and their flesh will lie like the dung (Zeph. 1:17); they will not be buried." In the World War, tens of thousands have been burned, and nobody knows where they are. Isn't that being fulfilled now? If this is only the beginning of sorrows, what will the end be? God is holding back the worst things. Europe has had the call. They have been warned and warned.

God gave a wonderful vision to a man who was raised to be a Catholic priest. Two angels visited him in the night and caused him to stand before a great congregation and warn the people of these awful calamities. He told two thousand people that Europe had been warned but that the people of Europe had turned their backs and rejected God, and now He is warning them at the mouth of the cannon.

The United States is the same way. God is giving the people here the last call—the last chance to be sealed with the seal of the living God, but they turn Him away. The last one will soon be sealed. God will call at the mouth of the cannon. This country will be bathed in blood after a while. The best thing is to hide away. May God help us to be up and doing, to be clothed in white linen, which is the righteousness of the saints, with the writer's inkhorn, which is the Holy Spirit working through us, calling the people to get right with God. Ask God for knowledge and wisdom; get the resurrection power in your body; and, when Jesus comes, be snatched out of this world.

"*We who are alive and remain until the coming of the Lord will by no means precede those who are asleep*" (1 Thess. 4:15 NKJV). The dead in Christ will rise first and shake off the dust and worms like dew and will go up with a shout. Praise the Lord! They will be ahead of us. Don't worry about the dead who died in Christ; when Jesus comes, God will bring them with Him. In honor of His Son's wedding, God is getting to meet the bride. The dead saints will be caught up first, and they will come with God the Father when Christ comes to catch His bride away. We do not need to worry about the dead who are in Christ. They will come up. But the time is near.

It will not be very long until we who are alive will meet them in the air. I will meet my husband who has died. He said, "I am not looking to the grave at all." But his body is there, and different saints in visions have seen him go up in his glorified body; he will be one of the first to meet me when I rise in the air. Many dear saints have died shouting and have gone to glory. They will be raised, and I will meet them. All our dear friends who have died in Christ will be raised first. We will rise in our glorified, immortal bodies to meet the Lord in the air.

Now, beloved, don't let this message run off you. Let it burn in your hearts, because it is a message from the Lord. Hallelujah. It may be something you have never heard before, but you are hearing it now. You see the parallel with the time of the prophet Ezekiel; you see the danger. Don't you see it? Oh, believe it: you are being warned. Take your Bibles; ask God about us whom you think are so foolish. Oh, glory to God; I am glad I am foolish enough to believe God. I am glad I am getting light enough to go up in the air when He comes. Hallelujah! Glory! Some of the resurrection power! Praise the Lord! I am looking forward to going up in the sky—up in the air—not to the grave. Glory to God. Hallelujah!

14

THE SEAL OF GOD ON HIS PEOPLE

Gather yourselves together, yea, gather together, O nation not desired; before the decree bring forth, before the day pass as the chaff, before the fierce anger of the Lord come upon you, before the day of the Lord's anger come upon you. Seek ye the Lord, all ye meek of the earth, which have wrought his judgment; seek righteousness, seek meekness: it may be ye shall be hid in the day of the Lord's anger.
—Zephaniah 2:1–3

This call is not to sinners, but to God's servants, to His children, to eat the *"strong meat"* (Heb. 5:14): *"Ye meek of the earth, which have wrought His judgment."*

You understand that you are saved, and you are working somewhat for the Lord, but He calls you to seek Him in a different way and for a different meekness. In this passage, He cries to you three times: to seek the Lord, to seek righteousness, and to seek meekness.

He is giving you the call to the Marriage Supper, calling you to get oil in your vessels (see Matthew 25:1–13), to get baptized with the Holy Spirit, to be sealed on the forehead with the seal of the living God, which is the seal of promise.

The Holy Spirit will also bear witness through you in other tongues, for you may have any of the gifts. You will have power as a witness after the Holy Spirit has come upon you (Acts 1:8).

The prophet Zephaniah warns you to escape the awful judgments that are now coming on the earth. It may be that you will be hidden in the Day of the Lord's anger. This is the only hope for you to escape the awful destruction that is about to sweep over the world, for there is no other hiding place, no other safety in the world. Oh, that you may be hidden in the Day of His wrath!

Yes, you may be, but whether or not you will be hidden in that Day depends on how far and how deep you get hidden away in God's love and power and will. You may be hidden. He shows that His judgments will burst on the earth like a whirlwind and that the wicked will be like chaff.

Dear reader, there is no doubt, according to God's Word and the signs all around us and the revelations and warnings the Lord is now giving us through His Spirit, that this is the time and we are the people. We have no time to lose, for "*behold, he cometh*" (Rev. 1:7) and is even now at the door (Matt. 24:33).

The text implies haste: Awake. Arise. Rouse yourselves. Flee to Christ. Get oil in your vessels. Shout the cry, "*Behold, the bridegroom cometh!*" (Matt. 25:6). Trim your lamps. Get sealed with wisdom so that you may be among the wise who will sit with Christ on His throne to judge the nations. Gather yourselves together. Yes, gather together.

"*O nation not desired.*" No one wants this people who have come out of darkness into this marvelous light (1 Pet. 2:9), this "*peculiar people*" (v. 9), who appear foolish on account of the supernatural power and visible works of the Spirit.

We are hated and despised and forsaken. Our name is cast out as evil; we are misrepresented and counted as the outcasts of the earth, but we are very much beloved in heaven.

When the prophet Daniel was asking God to explain these signs that we now see, Jesus appeared to him and sent the angel to him to make the vision clear. The angel said, "*O Daniel, a man greatly beloved, understand the* [vision and the] words" (Dan. 10:11). Then again, *"O man greatly beloved, fear not: peace be unto thee"* (v. 19).

The Sound of the Bugle Call

We are the people that the Lord was showing Daniel. Now the same loving words of cheer come to us through His Spirit, to the *"little flock"* (Luke 12:32), the bride that is making herself ready (Rev. 19:7): *"'To him that overcometh will I grant to sit with me in my throne'* (Rev. 3:21). Fear not, for I am with you; you are much beloved."

The Lord is sounding the bugle call through some believers in a most remarkable way by the Holy Spirit. It almost sounds as if the Judgment Day is here. It makes the people tremble. He is calling His saints together so that we will see eye to eye when He brings us to the heavenly Zion. *"Blow ye the trumpet in Zion, and sound an alarm in my holy mountain'* (Joel 2:1), among the saints. Let all the people tremble. Go gather My saints together, who have made a covenant with Me by sacrifice."

May God help us to make the right kind of sacrifice. Oh, praise the Lord, that is my calling today, to get the saints together in one spirit, one faith, and one mind (Phil. 1:27), filled with love and oneness in Christ, lost and swallowed up in Him and in His love and power.

In the chapter preceding our Scripture text, the Lord shows us the awful trials and the time of the Great Tribulation:

The great day of the LORD is near, it is near, and hasteth greatly, even the voice of the day of the LORD: the mighty man shall cry there bitterly. That day is a day of wrath, a day of trouble and distress, a day of wasteness and desolation, a day of darkness and gloominess, a day of clouds and thick darkness, a day of the trumpet and alarm against the fenced cities, and against the high towers. And I will bring distress upon men, that they shall walk like blind men, because they have sinned against the LORD: and their blood shall be poured out as dust, and their flesh as the dung. Neither their silver nor their gold shall be able to deliver them in the day of the LORD's wrath; but the whole land shall be devoured by the fire of his jealousy: for he shall make even a speedy riddance of all them that dwell in the land. (Zeph. 1:14–18)

He has given us this fearful warning; therefore, gather yourselves together. Oh, gather together, so that you may be hidden in the day of His wrath.

We are a nation among the nations:

But ye are a chosen generation, a royal priesthood, an holy nation, a peculiar people; that ye should show forth the praises of him who hath called you out of darkness into his marvellous light. (1 Pet. 2:9)

We are called out in this generation. We are a holy nation, a nation of kings and priests, called out from among men. We are royal because we are children of the King, a holy priesthood, heirs to a throne.

Unto him that loved us, and washed us from our sins in his own blood, and hath made us kings and priests unto God and his Father; to him be glory and dominion for ever and ever. Amen. (Rev. 1:5–6)

Thou wast slain, and hast redeemed us to God by thy blood out of every kindred, and tongue, and people, and nation; and hast made us unto our God kings and priests: and we shall reign on the earth. (Rev. 5:9–10)

This is the kind of praise that will go on in heaven after Jesus has taken His bride there. Shouting these praises will be the believers who were counted worthy to be hidden away in the City of Gold, the place prepared for them, which Jesus had promised (John 14:2–3). The great Marriage will have taken place. The long-waiting bride will have been made the Lamb's wife. They will all be enjoying the great Marriage Supper of the Lamb. They will be receiving their crowns and positions in glory. They will be taking their thrones and exalted stations, which their diplomas call for and which they had gained down here in the Holy Spirit school.

Hear the shouting; they make the heavens ring, amid all the brightness and glory of heaven. Oh, how wonderful is the meeting of the loved ones who will never part! They are safe, home safe at last.

Jesus is the attraction. He is the One. All eyes are on Him; all are trying to get nearest Him and to give Him all honor and glory, for through His blood and power they have entered into His glory.

Yes, the saints were safe in heaven while the dreadful work of destruction was going on in the earth. They knew they were coming back to earth to rule with kingly authority, to bless the people with priestly power. God has made them kings and priests unto Him, and they will reign on the earth a thousand years (Rev. 5:10; 20:6). *"The saints shall judge the world"* (1 Cor. 6:2). They are rejoicing because they are coming back to earth.

15

SOME WILL NOT TASTE DEATH

Verily I say unto you, There be some standing here, which shall not taste of death, till they see the Son of man coming in his kingdom. And after six days Jesus taketh Peter, James, and John his brother, and bringeth them up into an high mountain apart, and was transfigured before them: and his face did shine as the sun, and his raiment was white as the light.
—Matthew 16:28–17:2

H e was the Son of Man, and He was the Son of God. He *"shall come in the glory of his Father with his angels; and then he shall reward every man according to his works"* (Matt. 16:27), according to the deeds done while in the body.

Jesus said, *"Verily I say unto you, there be some standing here, which shall not taste of death, till they see the Son of man coming in his kingdom."* Six days later—literal days—Jesus took Peter, James, and James's brother John, and brought them up into a high mountain by themselves, and He was transfigured before them. His face shone as the sun, and His clothing was as white as the light.

And, behold, there appeared unto them Moses and Elias talking with him. Then answered Peter, and said unto Jesus, Lord, it is good for us to be here: if thou wilt, let us make here three tabernacles; one for thee, and one for Moses, and one for Elias. (Matt. 17:3–4)

731

Peter did not know what he was talking about. But God settled the question:

While he yet spake, behold, a bright cloud overshadowed them: and behold a voice out of the cloud, which said, This is my beloved Son, in whom I am well pleased; hear ye him. (v. 5)

Glory to God! Hallelujah! Glory to Jesus!

There is a great deal in this lesson. It shows the kingdom of Christ that is very close at hand now, and the translation of the saints. It shows the Tribulation that is coming on the earth. It shows the close of the Tribulation when Christ will come back with His saints, bind the Devil, destroy the Antichrist and his army, and set up the glorious Millennium.

Jesus had earlier said to His disciples, "*There be some standing here, which shall not taste of death, till they see the Son of man coming in his kingdom.*" These were six natural, literal days, for just six days afterward, the disciples saw on the Mount of Transfiguration what Jesus said they would see. However, these six days also apply to us. In prophetic terms, a day equals a year, and a day with the Lord is as a thousand years. (See 2 Peter 3:8.) There were four "days" before Christ came—four thousand years. The last two "days" bring us down to today, and make six thousand years. So we are on the stage of action today; we are right at the close of the last day. On the sixth day, close to the seventh day, we will be ushered into the great Millennium, the thousand years of rest, the Sabbath Day.

Jesus speaks to us with as much force today, and He applies this to us, as He did to them.

A Display of Heavenly Glory

"Some of you who are standing here will never experience death until you see My coming kingdom, for I will come in all the glory of My Father's kingdom, with all the holy angels, and I will come in My own kingly glory. I will give you a display of this glory; you will never experience death until you see this thing."

The disciples did not understand; but six days afterward, it came to pass. Jesus took Peter, James, and John—those who always seemed to be nearest the Master, more anxious to stand by Him than the rest—and they were initiated into a good many things the rest did not know. He took these three, slipped away from the rest, and brought them up into the mountain. That was six natural days from when He said, "There be some standing here, which shall not taste of death, till they see the Son of man coming in his kingdom."

Hallelujah to Jesus! Let us think about how this applies to us. The prophecies are fulfilled, and Christ's return will be just a very short time now, according to God's Word. I say to you today, this applies to us. "I am coming in My kingdom in all the glory of the eternal world to catch my bride away. Some of you will never experience death until you see this and take part in it." Glory to God! Hallelujah!

God Turns to His People Again

The prophecies point to this time. This is the end of the Gentile age (see Luke 21:24)—the Gentile age is to wind up at the close of the sixth day. The Jews are saying, "Come, let us return to the Lord, for we have been wounded and bruised, and He will heal us. The second day He will revive us, and early in the morning of the third day, He will raise us up. (See Hosea 6:1–2.)

This is the second day. The Jews are being wonderfully revived all over the land; they never had such renown. They are reviving; their chains are being broken. But early in the morning—it will only be a few days, bless God—He will raise us up. He will also raise them up from the grave, and wonderful things are going to take place. Before the Great Tribulation, the saints will be taken up. Jesus Christ will stand up for His people, and there will be a time of trouble on the earth such as the world has never known, and never will know again, when the dead in Christ will rise and the saints will be taken up.

So we are coming into the time when these prophecies are coming on the earth. These are the "beginning of sorrows" (Matt. 24:8), and if this is only the beginning, what will the end be? This is the preparation time when He will disseminate the power of the holy people all over the world as a witness. God will rise up in His power and majesty, and God will work His "strange work" (Isa. 28:21) by the Holy Spirit through His saints. Natural men do not understand this.

Jesus is coming in His kingdom. Get out of the city of destruction. Run up on the mountain. Bless God. Be ready for the "manifestation of the sons of God" (Rom. 8:19). This is the preparation time. This is the last message. Jesus said, "This Gospel of My kingdom will be preached in the last days of My preparation as a witness to all the world—to every nation. Then the end will come." (See Matthew 24:14.)

Christ will come and take a prepared people out for Himself—a people to be His bride—and then the awful darkness will cover the earth. The Tribulation time will set in; the time of trouble will continue until the Battle of Armageddon, when the Antichrist will be destroyed and two-thirds of all the earth will go down in war, famine, and pestilences (Matt. 24:7) and be devoured by wild beasts. But one-third will withstand the Antichrist and escape all the troubles and calamities that will come on this earth. (See Zechariah 13:8.) They will go through the fire, persecution, and famine, and when Jesus comes back to bind the Devil and cast him into the pit, one-third of the earth will run out to meet Him and acknowledge Him as their Lord of Lords. He will forgive their sins and call them His people; they will call Him their God (v. 9), and they will be restored at Jerusalem.

God has said it. He said that He will take His bride away; then, at the end of the Tribulation, He will return with His bride, riding on the white horse of power (Rev. 19:11–16). He will come back to build up the *"waste places of Jerusalem"* (Isa. 52:9) so that the remnant of men might seek the Lord. All the Gentiles who have called on His name will be in that company of the one-third who won't go down in the tribulations. He is coming back with the saints at the end of the Tribulation to destroy the Antichrist, and the blood will come up to the horses' bridles (Rev. 14:20).

The prophet John saw a great angel standing in the sun and calling with a loud voice to the fowls of the air, "Come gather yourselves together for the great supper of the great God, so that you may eat the flesh of the kings and of the mighty men of the earth, and those who sat upon horses, and the flesh of the horses, and so that you may drink their blood." (See Revelation 19:17–18.)

The Antichrist and his army will be destroyed when God calls the wild beasts and the fowls of the air to eat their carcasses, at the time when Jesus comes back and binds the Devil and casts him into the pit for one thousand years (Rev. 20:2–3). But the one-third who have gone through everything and escaped by the hand of God will come out to meet the Lord with gladness. He will accept them and forgive them, and He will call them His people. They will be established, and the glorious Millennium will be ushered in. But before this, the saints of God will be caught up to Christ (1 Thess. 4:17). He is coming to take His people out of the world, and everyone who is not ready to go up will be left behind and will go down when the Antichrist comes forth.

The time of the awful Tribulation is near. May the Lord help us to understand this, dear friends. The enemies of the Lord today are getting worse and worse. The cup of iniquity is full; the harvest of the earth is ripe and ready to be cut down and cast into the winepress of the wrath of God Almighty. So God is pouring out His Spirit. Glory hallelujah! He is bringing about signs and wonders through His holy vessels, which will scatter the power of God through the land. And the great angels are saying, "May we not loose the four winds?" (See Revelation 7:1.)

When will all these wonders—these unusual works of God coming up in the preparation time—cease? Not that they are wonders in themselves; they are wonders because they are part of God's time of preparation. There is no end to these unusual works of God.

God's Day of Preparation

The Lord says, "I will rise up and work my strange works in the day of preparation." Therefore, do not be mockers. Behold, I have the message from the Lord; the decree has gone forth, and He will make a speedy riddance of all the mockers on the face of the earth. They don't laugh at a cyclone; they don't laugh at a great fire; but they will laugh and mock at God's *"strange work"* (Isa. 28:21). Do not be mockers, for I have received the message from the Lord. It came from heaven, and the decree has already gone forth. God will make a speedy riddance of all the mockers on the face of the earth. (See verses 21–22.)

This is God's work. He is giving the people a warning. He is pouring out His Spirit upon the earth for the last time, in order to warn the people just before the *"notable day of the Lord come[s]"* (Acts 2:20). Repent and turn to the Lord, and you will be saved. Every nation will be warned through the mighty display of God's power. God's mighty works are the visible signs that He is here, the visible manifestations that this is God's message—the last message—and that God, through His people, is pouring out the Holy Spirit.

We do not have a dead God or a dead Christ. He lives forever, and He is here right now. God is dispersing power over the land and warning the people against the things that are coming. Everyone who has the mark of fire and blood will be caught up to heaven. Every last one. And then the Antichrist will come forth—the awful Antichrist, the Man of Sin. He will come forth in his awful power after the Hinderer, the One who restrains the lawlessness, is taken away. (See 2 Thessalonians 2:7 NKJV.)

Who is the Hinderer? The Holy Spirit, working through the body of Christ. *"Ye are the light of the world"* (Matt. 5:14). Jesus shines in the hearts of the saints just as He shines through their faces. Glory to God!

So God is warning you through His saints and getting people ready. He is sending out the warning in every direction, telling people to escape from the city of destruction and not to linger in the plains. Put on your wedding garments, accept the invitation, and get ready to take the flight through the air. When the saints are taken out of the world, there will be no restraining power, and the Devil will be let loose. People will sigh for the days in which we now live, after the Holy Spirit goes up with the body of Christ, the bride. They will sigh and cry, "There is no prophet anymore, no priests. We don't hear from heaven. There is no light; everything is darkness."

There will be awful darkness. The door will be shut, and no one will have an opportunity to join the bride. (See Matthew 25:10.) The bride is being prepared and adorned now. (See Revelation 21:2.) May God help us to see this. So the message is for you. Some of you here tonight will never experience death until you see the Son of Man coming in the clouds of heaven (Matt. 16:28). Hallelujah! Keep looking up. Are you ready to go? If you are not, come tonight.

The disciples did not understand what Jesus meant when He said, *"There be some standing here, which shall not taste of death, till they see the Son of man coming in his kingdom."* However, He took those who were nearest to Him—those who were watching and praying and looking for those things to come true—He took three of them and slipped away from everybody, and He brought them up into a high mountain. Nobody knew where He was.

That is a good place to be—way up above the world with the Devil under your feet. How beautiful on the mountain are the feet of those who are running up the mountain and hurling down the glad tidings that Jesus is coming! (See Isaiah 52:7.) That is a good place to go in order to pray, if you pray correctly. Bless the Lord, it is not the long prayer or the loud prayer that is effective but, hallelujah, the prayer of faith. Jesus took the disciples up the mountain to pray, and something happened. He had told them, "I am coming in all my Father's glory, and in all the glory of the holy angels, and some of you here are going to see this."

Just before Peter went to be with the Lord, he said, "There will be lying wolves (see 2 Peter 2:1–3), but don't forget what you have heard. I have been telling you that He is coming again, and I have not been telling you *"cunningly devised fables"* (2 Peter 1:16); I am telling you the truth. I saw the King transfigured, and I heard the voice of the great God of heaven. He came down to welcome the bride; He came down to be at the Wedding. The cloud of glory settled over us, and out of that cloud there was a great voice, the voice of God Almighty, and He introduced the bride to His Son: 'This is my Son. He is my Son, the King of Glory. I am pleased at the selection of His bride.'" (See verses 16–18.) Hallelujah!

In the Twinkling of an Eye

The disciples saw the manifestations. They saw Him just exactly as it is going to be when the saints go up. They had the picture, the vision. *"Fear not, little flock"* (Luke 12:32). In that vision, He brought before their eyes the saints who are going up one of these days. There are some living now who will not experience death until they see Jesus come. He brought the picture before them in a vision. Every tribe, tongue, and nation on earth will be in that company, witnesses out of every nation. These three disciples were permitted to see them all changed just like they will be when He comes. We will be all changed: *"We shall not all sleep, but we shall all be changed, in a moment, in the twinkling of an eye"* (1 Cor. 15:51–52). We will have glorious bodies like the Son of God (Phil. 3:21), and *"we shall be like him; for we shall see him as he is"* (1 John 3:2).

Now, then, John saw this picture twice. God has not left us in the dark. John was a man like we are, but God reveals the *"deep things of God"* (1 Cor. 2:10) to His saints. Near the end of his life, John had been banished to the Isle of Patmos. One time, when he was talking to the Lord, the Spirit of God was all over and around him; he saw an open door, and in a minute he was translated to heaven.

He saw the saints go up, and he went up with them. He saw thrones and those who sat upon them, and he saw Christ on the throne of His Father. (See Revelation 4:1–4.) *"To him that overcometh will I grant to sit with me in my throne, even as I also overcame, and am set down with my Father in his throne"* (Rev. 3:21). He overcame the Devil at the very end, and we must not only commence but also go on to the end. When He overcame at the end, He went up, and God gave Him a seat at His right hand—the highest place in the courts of glory—and He is there today. Stephen saw the glory of God, and He saw Jesus standing at the right hand of God in majesty on high. (See Acts 7:55–56.)

"To him that overcometh will I grant to sit with me in my throne, even as I also overcame, and am set down with my Father in his throne." He has not taken His own throne yet.

John saw the saints go up the second time. Then he saw Jesus take His throne, and he went up to the Marriage Supper. *"Blessed are they which are called unto the marriage supper of the Lamb"* (Rev. 19:9). Blessed are they that will eat bread at that Supper and drink wine in my Father's kingdom. (See Matthew 26:29.) We are going to be substantial people, aren't we? Glory to God! Sit down to the Marriage Supper of the Lamb. That is the place He is preparing for you. Oh, glory to God! Don't you want to be there?

We are a nation despised and hated, a *"nation not desired"* (Zeph. 2:1). The Devil hates us, and all his imps hate us. But Jesus says, "Come, hide away. Come together: bind yourselves together and get ready for the *'manifestation of the sons of God'* (Rom. 8:19). *'Fear not, it is your Father's good pleasure to give you the kingdom'* (Luke 12:32)." He will make us kings and priests in the sight of our God (Rev. 1:6). Kings and priests—glory to God!

So Jesus will come out and take the throne, and the bridal company will be the highest in heaven. There are great degrees of glory, but the overcomers—the bridal party—will sit with Jesus Christ the Lamb of God on His Great White Throne through all the ages. They will follow the Lamb wherever He goes. They are the ones whom Daniel saw: *"They that turn many to righteousness"* will shine as the sun (Dan. 12:3). There are degrees of glory. I would rather be one of the wise ones. (See verse 3.)

The glory of God knocked Paul blind, and it put the noonday sun in the shade. When the saints of God burst forth and their bodies are changed, they will eclipse the sun. Don't you think it will be great? Don't you think you had better advance a degree of glory today?

Jesus said to Peter, James, and John: "Don't tell any man about the vision until after I have gone to glory." (See Matthew 17:9.) So they saw something the rest did not know. This was because they were nearer to God. They wanted God to let them down into the *"deep things of God"* (1 Cor. 2:10). That teaches us a lesson, dear friends. There are degrees of glory. *"They that be wise shall shine as the brightness of the firmament"* (Dan. 12:3); those who are wise will know when Jesus comes.

Do you think that God would not reveal these things to His waiting bride? I tell you, no. We know a few things now. We know it is very soon. "You are not left in the dark; *'ye are all the children of light, and the children of the day'* (1 Thess. 5:5). You have been illuminated from heaven. You will not be overtaken by surprise."

Are we ready? Are we watching? Be ready to stand when the Son of Man comes. Always *"watch and pray"* (Mark 13:33). Watch the signs, and watch the prophecies, so that you may be counted worthy to escape the awful tribulations and stand before the Son of Man when He comes. *"Watch and pray."* You know the signs. You will not be overtaken as by a thief (see 1 Thessalonians 5:2), because I am warning you. You are the *"children of the day,"* and you will know. Glory to God!

So the Lord now shows us all these awful calamities that are coming on the earth. He says, "Do not be fearful when you see these awful things coming. Look up and rejoice. Lift your heads and see the break of day. The sun is rising. Lift up your heads. Rejoice, for *'your redemption draweth nigh'* (Luke 21:28)." Glory!

The secret of the Lord is with those who love Him, those whom He can trust. So God is revealing these things to us from day to day. We will not be surprised. When you see certain signs, know that it is even at your door. We know that now. We don't know the day or hour, but God gives us to understand that we will know a little while before we are taken up. And when you get to the point at which you cannot do anything else, just stand. Wait for the Son of Man to come and catch His waiting bride away.

The Bride Adorned for the Bridegroom

Make sure you understand this: there are great degrees of glory. Don't you want to be the beautiful bride and stand before the King of Glory? Her clothes are so beautiful with fine needlework. (See Psalm 45:14.) And, oh, how she loves her Bridegroom. She doesn't worship anybody but Him. She is not trifling with many lovers, but He has become the *"[fairest] among ten thousand"* (Song 5:10) to her. She is willing to leave all and go with her lover.

Sometimes, when a woman marries a stranger, there is a lot of opposition. Her father says, "If you go, I will disinherit you." But she leaves her parents, her home, and her money. She says, "I love my lover best. He is mine, and I am his. I will have to leave you." So she leaves everything, and she gets into the ship and sails with her strange lover to a strange land where she has never been, among strange people whom she has not known. He is so proud of her, and she is so proud of him. She says, "He is strange to the world, but he is mine, and I am his. I will be glad to go."

There are degrees of glory. God said, "The wise will know." (See Daniel 2:21–22; 12:10.) Don't think it is strange that none of the wicked will know about the coming of the Lord. Daniel saw the saints robed in white on land and sea and God dispersing the Holy Spirit through them. Daniel, one of the wise, will know. God reveals His secrets to the wise. Are you one of the wise? Is God letting you down into the "*deep things*" (1 Cor. 2:10)? Bless God, He will!

We are in the Holy Spirit school, going from one room to another, from one school to another, graduating, getting our diplomas. God wants us to get down into the "*deep things.*" He reveals His secrets to us just as He did to Peter, James, and John. He told them, "Don't tell anyone until after I am raised from the dead." It was hidden from the rest. That shows us, dear friends, that there are degrees in glory. Some will shine as stars, and some will eclipse the sun. A great many people will not know when Jesus comes. The wise will know when Jesus comes.

Many people think they will know, but they will be left. God is showing us these things and giving us this lesson. As Jesus told us, there will be two sleeping in one bed; one will be taken, and the other left. There will be two grinding at the mill; one will be taken, and the other left (Luke 17:34–35).

After Jesus was crucified and before His resurrection, the disciples were all in the dark. They lost their faith. In a parallel way, all power will be taken away when Christ is gone and the saints are gone from the earth. The Devil will be let loose, and the Antichrist will begin to show his power.

We find a type of this period in the story of the man who had the demons in him. The disciples could not cast the demons out. The father brought his son to Jesus and said, "The demons try to drown him, burn him, and knock his brains out." Jesus cast the demons out and commanded that they never enter into him any more. (See Matthew 17:14–21.) In the same way, the

Antichrist will burn some and drown some and knock the heads off others, as in the dark days. Then Jesus will come back, bind the Devil, and destroy the army of the Antichrist, including two-thirds of all the earth. Only one-third, who went through all the fires trusting God the best they could, are going to escape.

16

THE RESURRECTION
OF THE SAINTS

Thou hast ascended on high, thou hast led captivity captive: thou hast received gifts for men; yea, for the rebellious also, that the LORD God might dwell among them.
—Psalm 68:18

After all the life of Jesus—after all His mighty signs and wonders and miracles, after people exclaimed, *"Behold the man!"* (John 19:5), *"Never man spake like this man"* (John 7:46), and *"What manner of man is this, that even the winds and the sea obey him!"* (Matt. 8:27)—after all this, if He had stopped short at Calvary or at going down into the cold grave, His work would have been a failure. Many people only see a dead Savior. They only have a dead religion of form and works. They have no life or power.

At the end of the Old Testament, Israel had forsaken the Lord, and He had taken His Spirit from her. For about four hundred years, she was in darkness. There were no prophets or priests. There was no communication from heaven, until the birth of John the Baptist and the birth of Christ were announced.

Remember that Jesus brought *"life and immortality to light"* (2 Tim. 1:10)—to us—through the Resurrection. No, the grave could not hold Him, though all hell was up in arms to try to hold Him cold in death. A hundred or more armed soldiers stood around His grave, for fear that His disciples would steal His lifeless body away. They also sealed the sepulcher with the governor's seal, and it was death to break that seal. (See Matthew 27:64–66.)

A mighty battle was fought. All the armies of heaven were engaged with the hosts of hell in fierce array around the rock casket or tomb where the mangled body of Jesus, our crucified Lord, lay cold in death. Hear the demons: "We have got Him, and we will hold Him captive. Where is your Prince? Where is your King?" But listen! The battle is turning; victory is near; help is coming. The Lord God Almighty Himself is coming with His great angel who rolls back the stone from the sepulcher and sits upon it. The Bible tells us that *"his countenance was like lightning, and his raiment white as snow: and for fear of him the keepers did shake"* (Matt. 28:3–4). They fell and lay as dead men.

God, with His mighty presence, sent a great earthquake. With a great shout over death and hell and the grave, we see the Conqueror come forth, holding the keys to unlock the prison house of the dead.

We see the women who were the last at the cross and the first at the grave. The angel said,

Fear not ye: for I know that ye seek Jesus, which was crucified. He is not here: for he is risen, as he said. Come, see the place where the Lord lay. And go quickly, and tell his disciples that he is risen from the dead. (Matt. 28:5–7)

As they went with great joy, Jesus met them, saying, "Fear not, but go and tell my brothers that I will meet them in Galilee." (See verse 10.)

The women were commanded by the angels, and later by the Lord Himself, to preach the first news of the Resurrection.

No, He is not dead. *"The Lord is risen indeed"* (Luke 24:34). Oh, praise God for a living Christ, a living church, and our soon-coming King and Lord!

After His resurrection, the graves were opened, and many of the bodies of the saints that slept in their graves arose, came out, went into the city, and appeared to many. (See Matthew 27:52–53.) The Scripture says, *"And many bodies of the saints which slept arose"* (v. 52). The word *many* here implies thousands or more, and I believe that most of those saints were the prophets and priests: Abraham, Isaac, Jacob, and Joseph, in addition to those holy men of old who spoke as they were moved by the Holy Spirit (2 Pet. 1:21), including John the Baptist, who had recently been murdered for Jesus' sake.

Oh, praise God for the resurrection of these mighty men of old! Their bodies came up, and their spirits were united to them. They were living men; they were breathing and walking, and their bodies were free from corruption. See them going through the streets of Jerusalem, going from one place to another and making themselves known.

Oh, praise God for the resurrection of our bodies! Praise God that we will know each other!

Yes, the Devil held their bodies captive for hundreds of years in the grave. But see the mighty Conqueror break the chains, take them captive from the Devil and from the power of the grave, and—leading *"captivity captive"* (Eph. 4:8)—lead them away to some other world, where no doubt God is using them in some great way for His glory.

"Gifts to Men"

Jesus ascended on high and gave gifts to men (Eph. 4:8). Yes, He gave them even to the rebels, also. Jesus did not have *"all power"* (Matt. 28:18) until after God raised Him from the dead. No one could have the gift of God, eternal life, until after he was *"born of the Spirit"* (John 3:6).

Jesus has all power. He was raised up with all power. (See Romans 1:4.) The Holy Spirit was with the disciples, but Jesus said, *"The Spirit of truth…shall be in you"* (John 14:17). When the disciples were all together, Jesus met with them, and He opened their spiritual minds. He breathed on them and said, *"Receive ye the Holy Ghost"* (John 20:22). They received Him and became *"partakers of the divine nature"* (2 Pet. 1:4). They received the gift of God, were enlightened, and cried out, with Thomas, *"My Lord and my God"* (John 20:28). No one had ever had that experience before that time. They were sons of God by the new birth. It was the gift of God, eternal life. Yes, *"for the rebellious also."* This is the most important of all gifts, for without this gift you can never get inside the pearly gates.

When the sinner stops his rebellion, and repents, God gives him faith to accept Christ. God gives him power to become a son of God who is born not of man or of the will of men, not of flesh and blood, but by the power of God. (See John 1:12–13.) He is then no longer a rebel but a son, for he has received the gift of God and has been born of the spiritual family of God. His name has been written in the family record by the finger of God, and it has been said, "This man was born in Zion." (See Psalm 87:5.) The finished work on Calvary atones for his sin and uncleanness, and he is now a child of God, ready for any or all of the gifts of the Pentecostal baptism and power. He is God's man.

Jesus received gifts for men (Eph. 4:8). When He was giving His last blessing to His disciples on the mountain before going up to heaven, He said the following to them:

> *Tarry ye in the city of Jerusalem, until ye be endued with power from on high.* (Luke 24:49)

> *But ye shall receive power, after that the Holy Ghost is come upon you: and ye shall be witnesses unto me.* (Acts 1:8)

> *All power is given unto me in heaven and in earth.* (Matt. 28:18)

> *Go ye into all the world, and preach the gospel to every creature….These signs shall follow them that believe* [in Me]; *in my name shall they cast out devils; they shall speak with new tongues; they shall take up serpents; and if they drink any deadly thing, it shall not hurt them; they shall lay hands on the sick, and they shall recover.* (Mark 16:15, 17–18)

In this last Scripture, Jesus was saying to His disciples, in effect, "These are some of the gifts that I will give to men."

These were the last words our Savior spoke on earth before He was taken up out of the disciples' sight in a visible manner. After that, they got the promised baptism and greatest gift; they went forth preaching the Word everywhere, *"the Lord working with them, and confirming the word with signs following"* (Mark 16:20).

The disciples could not see the Lord in person as in days past, but they saw the visible signs of His invisible presence. These signs and gifts could be seen and heard with the natural eye and ear. Jesus was with them, with all gifts, signs, miracles, and diverse operations of the Spirit. With these, He confirmed and put His seal on the truth and on their preaching.

At Pentecost, He sent the *"promise of the Father"* (Acts 1:4). The Holy Spirit came as a *"rushing mighty wind"* and sat on all their heads like *"cloven tongues…of fire"* (Acts 2:2–3). These cloven tongues were a sign of the new tongues; they were tongues of fire and of the Spirit, for all the disciples were filled with the Spirit and began to speak *"as the Spirit gave them utterance"* (v. 4).

It was at the time of the great Jewish Feast of Pentecost, and Jewish people from *"every nation under heaven"* (v. 5) were gathered there. They saw and heard the wonderful demonstration of the Holy Spirit, the gifts, and the glory of God. They were amazed, saying, "What does this mean? *'How hear we every man in our own tongue, wherein we were born?'* (v. 8)." Jesus had sent down gifts for men and women. The Holy Spirit had come to stay. He was given now without measure. (See John 3:34.)

In the book of Acts, we read that God sent Peter down to Caesarea to hold a revival among the Gentiles. While he was preaching, the Holy Spirit fell on those who heard the Word, for they spoke with tongues and magnified God. (See Acts 10.)

The Holy Spirit, with all the accompanying gifts, was poured out on the Gentile nations, just as He had been poured out on the Jews at Pentecost. *"For the promise is unto you, and to your children, and to all that are afar off, even as many as the Lord our God shall call"* (Acts 2:39). Praise God, beloved, for that includes you and me!

Jesus sent these gifts with all the Pentecostal power and glory. Our bodies are God's power plants; they are channels for the Holy Spirit to flow out of like *"rivers of living water"* (John 7:38). In reference to this *"living water,"* the Scriptures tell us, *"This spake he of the Spirit, which they that believe on him should receive"* (v. 39).

Signs of His Presence

Thou hast ascended on high, thou hast led captivity captive: thou hast received gifts for men; yea, for the rebellious also, that the Lord God might dwell among them.

This is the evidence to the lost world that God is with us: the signs of His invisible presence. We are a people to be wondered at. "Father, here am I, and the children whom You have given." (See John 17:9–11, 24.) God's purpose is that we would work signs and wonders in Israel from the Lord of Hosts, who dwells in Zion (Isa. 8:18)—down here, not in heaven. *"He led captivity captive, and gave gifts unto men....He gave some, apostles; and some, prophets; and some, evangelists; and some, pastors and teachers"* (Eph. 4:8, 11). These imply and include all the gifts and workings of the Holy Spirit.

Why did He send this power and these gifts to men—to His disciples and to the church? *"For the perfecting of the saints, for the work of the ministry, for the edifying of the body of Christ"* (v. 12). Christ gave gifts in order to make the saints, God's men, perfect and to lead them in the same Pentecostal power and gifts.

Ministers need the power of God, and they must have the seal of the Holy Spirit, with all these signs and gifts, to encourage them. Not only are these signs and gifts God's seal to them, but they are also the visible signs to the world that God is with His people, working together with them, confirming the Word with visible signs (Mark 16:20).

When the disciples were put into prison and their lives were threatened on account of the great power that was with them in healing and miracles, they were forbidden to preach in the name of Jesus, for the authorities saw that the power came through His name. (See Acts 4:1–21.)

The disciples met together, and they knew that the demonstration of the power of God had caused all their persecution. They knew that if they had a form of religion but denied the power (see 2 Timothy 3:5), they would have no more trouble with the authorities. But, beloved, they said, "We will be true to God. We will preach the Word if we die." Then they prayed to the Lord, saying,

Lord, behold their threatenings: and grant unto thy servants, that with all boldness they may speak thy word, by stretching forth thine hand to heal; and that signs and wonders may be done by the name of thy holy child Jesus.
(Acts 4:29–30)

You see that these ministers needed power to give them boldness to stand up for Jesus, to preach *"all the words of this life"* (Acts 5:20).

When they preached, they knew they must see in their meetings the signs of the presence of the invisible Christ, who would be present to confirm the Word and their message. Jesus had said, "*I am with you alway, even unto the end of the world*" (Matt. 28:20). With the signs of Christ's presence, they could say to the people, like Peter had at Pentecost, "What you see and hear and feel is the promise of the Father; it is the Holy Spirit." (See Acts 2:33.)

The Son was pleased with the disciples' prayer (see Acts 4:29–30) and with their faith and courage, and the building where they were assembled was shaken. They were all filled with the Holy Spirit and spoke the Word with boldness (v. 31).

See, beloved, this was a greater baptism. They needed it to prepare them for the work they had to do. After this, they had greater success. God did mighty signs and wonders through the apostles; great fear fell on all the church and on all who heard and saw these things. "*Multitudes both of men and women*" (Acts 5:14) came flocking to Christ and were added to the Lord. (See verses 11–14.)

"*Multitudes*" means thousands. They came from Jerusalem and all the surrounding cities, bringing their sick folk on beds and cots and placing them along the streets so that the shadow of Peter passing by might fall on them (vv. 15–16). You see that the power went forth from the disciples' bodies. The same thing happened when handkerchiefs that had touched Paul's body were sent to the sick; the devils or diseases went out, and people were healed (Acts 19:11–12).

Oh, praise God, I am a witness to these things! We see the same thing today: some of the greatest miracles of healing and salvation I have ever seen have been done in the same way, hundreds of miles away. He "*gave gifts unto men*" (Eph. 4:8).

Read carefully the twelfth chapter of the first epistle to the Corinthians. Paul showed that the church is in possession of all the gifts, power, calling, and work of the Holy Spirit; they are in the body of Christ, His church.

Oh, beloved, we ought to live in this way, in all places, in these last days when the bride is making herself ready (Rev. 19:7). Paul said he did not want us to be ignorant concerning spiritual gifts (1 Cor. 12:1). "*Covet earnestly the best gifts*" (v. 31). "*Follow after charity* [love], *and desire spiritual gifts*" (14:1), for God has set them in the church.

Gifts are "*for the rebellious also.*" Thank God, the sinner no longer needs to be rebellious. He can fall at God's feet and settle the old account. God says He has a gift for you. Oh, *"the gift of God is eternal life"* (Rom. 6:23). When you receive this gift, then you are God's man. You are no longer a stranger or foreigner, but have been brought near by the blood of Christ. Through Him, you will have access to the Father by one Spirit. You are a citizen with the saints and of the household of God; you are a living stone (1 Peter 2:5 NKJV) in the building that is being fitly framed together, a holy temple in the Lord. (See Ephesians 2:12–22.)

Beloved, you are a son and an heir to all the Pentecostal blessings, gifts, and power. Press your claims at the court of heaven. Seek the baptism of the Holy Spirit and power. You can be a *"pillar in the temple of…God"* (Rev. 3:12). You will go in, and will go out no more (v. 12).

Let all who read this take warning: "He who knows My will and does not do it, will be beaten with many lashes." (See Luke 12:47.) Be among the wise who will know of the Lord's coming, the wise who will *"shine as the brightness of the firmament"* (Dan. 12:3).

17

THE MARRIAGE SUPPER
OF THE LAMB

Blessed are they which are called unto the marriage supper of the Lamb.
—Revelation 19:9

Oh, beloved, have you been called? Let us be glad and rejoice and give honor to Him, for the Marriage of the Lamb has come. The bride must be arrayed in linen, pure and white.

Yes, His wife has made herself ready; see the King coming out of His ivory palace, which He has made ready to receive His bride. His garments are overflowing with sweet scents. They smell of *"myrrh, and aloes, and cassia"* (Ps. 45:8).

The bride is rejoicing in His love. Listen, O daughters! Beloved, are we the blessed who are called to the banquet, to this heavenly Marriage Supper in the skies? Oh, consider, and incline your ears to hear the whispers of His love. We must forget our own people and our Father's house (v. 10). Our beloved Bridegroom is very jealous. We must love Him with our whole heart and our whole being. We must long for Him, so that He will greatly desire our beauty. He is our Lord, and we must worship Him (Ps. 45:11).

We must be ready to leave all at any moment when the herald shouts, "Behold the Bridegroom. Behold, He comes; go forth to meet Him." (See Matthew 25:6.) Oh, are you ready to leave all to sail away with our Beloved to that heavenly kingdom, to those mansions in the City of Gold that He has been preparing and adorning for so many years with all the wealth and jewels of heaven? Oh, that City of Gold!

Do our hearts leap for joy? Do we cry, "Come, oh, come quickly, my Redeemer, my Beloved, and my King"? Oh, Most Mighty, with Your glory and Your majesty, You are fairer than all the sons of men! *"Thy throne, O God, is for ever and ever: the sceptre of thy kingdom is a right sceptre"* (Ps. 45:6).

Oh, look at the lovely bride. They are all honorable women—kings' daughters. Behold, on His right hand stands the queen robed in the shining glory of Ophir. (See verse 9.)

The king's daughter is all glorious within: her clothing is of wrought gold. She shall be brought unto the king in raiment of needlework: the virgins her companions that follow her shall be brought unto thee. (vv. 13–14)

Oh, glory to God! Look at the virgins, the guests at the wedding. They will go in with gladness; they will be brought into the King's palace, rejoicing with great joy (v. 15).

Streets like Transparent Glass

Oh, the very gates of solid pearl! The walls are jasper and the city is pure gold, like clear glass. The streets are pure gold, like transparent glass. The very foundations are built and *"garnished with all manner of precious stones"* (Rev. 21:19; see also verses 18–21).

Oh, behold! Let us rise on the wings of faith and in the Spirit take a view of our eternal home. *"The city is laid out as a square"* (Rev. 21:16 NKJV). It is fifteen hundred miles long, fifteen hundred miles wide, and fifteen hundred miles high. Oh, those pearly gates and jasper walls! How they shine in the glorious brightness and light of God and of the Lamb. Oh, beloved, if the outside is so glorious, what will it be like to live in the city, to roam through the courts of glory?

Our Lord says that we will go in with joy and rejoicing. (See Psalm 45:15.) Oh, our Lord will have many surprises for us as He takes us through our beautiful mansions. We will sit with Him on His throne (Rev. 3:21) and be surrounded with all the brightness and glory of heaven.

We will see the River of Life running out from beneath the throne of God, like a sea of clear glass (Rev. 22:1). There will be the nation of kings, with their gold-crowned heads. (See Revelation 4:4.)

We will eat of the Tree of Life that bears twelve kinds of fruits every month (Rev. 22:2). Oh, this beautiful tree on each side of the River! We will eat of its fruit.

Jesus said, "*I say unto you, I will not drink henceforth of this fruit of the vine, until that day when I drink it new with you in my Father's kingdom*" (Matt. 26:29). Yes, we will eat and drink with our Bridegroom in His kingdom. Jesus said, "*I appoint unto you a kingdom, as my Father hath appointed unto me; that ye may eat and drink at my table in my kingdom*" (Luke 22:29–30). Oh, praise the Lord, this is strong proof that the kingdom is literal and natural. And it will be free from the curse of sin. "*Blessed are they which are called unto the marriage supper of the Lamb.*"

See the Feast: the Lord will "*make…a feast of fat things, a feast of wines on the lees, of fat things full of marrow, of wines on the lees well refined*" (Isa. 25:6). He will swallow up death in victory (1 Cor. 15:54). And the Lord God Himself will wipe all tears from all faces (Rev. 7:17). The rebuke will be forever taken off His people.

Oh, hasten the day when the kingdoms of this world will become the kingdoms of our Lord and of His Christ. He will reign, and we will reign with Him for the ages of ages. (See Revelation 11:15; 22:5.) Oh, blessed King, come and take up Your great power, and reign!

We now bear the image of Adam, the first man, but our fleshly bodies will be changed and made "*like unto his glorious body*" (Phil. 3:21). Our mortal bodies will be changed into immortal bodies (1 Cor. 15:53–54). In the same body He had before His crucifixion, Jesus ate fish with His disciples after He rose from the dead; it will be the same with us, for "*we shall be like him*" (1 John 3:2). Our bodies will be resurrected or translated and glorified.

Beloved, "*we shall not all sleep, but we shall all be changed, in a moment, in the twinkling of an eye*" (1 Cor. 15:51–52). "*Then we which are alive and remain shall be caught up together with them* [the risen and glorified dead] *in the clouds, to meet the Lord in the air: and so shall we ever be with the Lord"* (1 Thess. 4:17).

The time is about up: Jesus will come to take out a people to be His bride and will give her His name. Yes, we will be called the bride, the Lamb's wife; she will be His pride and glory. He will be glorified in her through the ages of the ages.

As they travel through the many beautiful worlds, He will present her, in all her beauty; and she, in her pride and glory, will point to her royal Bridegroom and tell of His wonderful redeeming love.

The Time Is at Hand

Yes, the time is at hand. Jesus has given us many signs so that we would know when to look for His return, so that we would know that His coming is near, *"even at the doors"* (Matt. 24:33). He said that the wise would know (Dan. 12:10). *"And they that be wise shall shine as the brightness of the firmament"* (v. 3).

Oh, beloved, are we watching? Are we waiting? Will we be ready to escape all the awful things that are coming on the earth? To many who are looking, it will be a day of darkness, and there will be no light in it for them. He will come as suddenly as a flash of lightning, and we will be taken as quickly.

He will come with all the brightness of heaven. The saints will see all His glory and will hear all the bells of heaven ringing. Amid the singing of the great angelic choir, they will be caught away, swallowed up in all this brightness and glory. But the poor lost world will sleep on, not knowing what has happened. Remember, two will be sleeping in one bed; one will be taken, and the other will be left to sleep on. Two will be at the mill, grinding; one will be taken, the other left. Two will be in the field; one will be taken, the other left. (See Luke 17:34–36.)

So suddenly will this appear that they will not know it until it is too late. Then they will realize what has happened, when they see that all these foolish "fanatics," these people, have disappeared.

No, the world is too blinded in darkness and sin. She cannot behold the glory of the Rapture as the saints go shouting through the air.

Hark! We can almost hear them marshaling the hosts of heaven, the angels tuning their harps of gold. We can almost see the Banquet, the table spread for the Marriage Supper in the air. Many have seen the table, reaching across the skies. The great preparation is soon coming. Oh, dear reader, will you accept the invitation to the Marriage Supper in the skies? Oh, glory to God, I will meet you there!

18

CHRIST AND HIS BRIDE

The apostle Paul wrote that Christ *"loved the church, and gave himself for it"* (Eph. 5:25) so that she might be *"a glorious church, not having spot, or wrinkle, or any such thing; but that it should be holy and without blemish"* (v. 27).

She must be a glorious church, not having *"spot, or wrinkle"* or any such thing. She must be *"holy and without blemish."* Oh, beloved, it means much to be a member of this church. Let us now see how the church is to be the bride of Christ.

In the third chapter of Revelation, Jesus Himself gave John a description of the Philadelphian church, whose name signifies love:

And to the angel of the church in Philadelphia write: These things saith he that is holy, he that is true, he that hath the key of David, he that openeth, and no man shutteth; and shutteth, and no man openeth; I know thy works: behold, I have set before thee an open door, and no man can shut it: for thou hast a little strength, and hast kept my word, and hast not denied my name. Behold, I will make them of the synagogue of Satan, which say they are Jews, and are not, but do lie; behold, I will make them to come and worship before thy feet, and to know that I have loved thee. Because thou hast kept the word of my patience, I also will keep thee from the hour of temptation, which shall come upon all the world, to try them that dwell upon the earth. Behold, I come quickly: hold that fast which thou hast, that no man take thy crown. Him that overcometh will I make a pillar in the temple of my God, and he shall go no more out: and I will write upon him the name of my God, and the name of the city of my God, which is new Jerusalem, which cometh down out of heaven from my God: and I will write upon him my new name.

(Rev. 3:7–12)

The book of Revelation, attributed to the apostle John, is the most wonderful book of the New Testament. Peter once asked Jesus about John's future: "*And what shall this man do?*" (John 21:21). Jesus had answered Peter, "*If I will that he tarry till I come, what is that to thee? follow thou me*" (v. 22). After that, the report went out that John would never die.

Tradition says that when John was quite old, the enemies of Christ tried to kill him. They threw him into a kettle of boiling oil, but the Lord did not let it hurt him. Then his enemies were frightened; they banished him to the lonely island called Patmos, and he was left there to die. He had been such a true witness for Jesus and His Word that it was the darkest hour of his life, but he was alone with God, filled with the Spirit.

As I said, the book of Revelation is a wonderful book. About sixty-four years after John and the other disciples saw Jesus go up to heaven, Christ came back to earth and appeared to John. He gave John great, moving pictures of the church, starting from the Day of Pentecost.

Oh, what power! What a force! What a light He brought to John in those dark days in which the church then lived! "*All things are possible to him that believeth*" (Mark 9:23).

Jesus came back to John in all His kingly power and glory. He had been gone a long time. The change was so great, and John felt so little in His presence, that when he saw Him, he "*fell at his feet as dead*" (Rev. 1:17). John said that Jesus laid His right hand on him, saying, "'*Fear not...I am alive for evermore*' (vv. 17–18). John, do you know me? We fished together, walked together, and slept together. Many times you have rested your weary head on my chest."

Can you imagine the joy John experienced when he heard the familiar voice of the Galilean, which had quieted the disciples' fears so often, when the sweet voice said, "It is I; do not be afraid. I have come back to bring you important messages. I want you to write all you hear, and send it to the churches"?

The first three chapters of Revelation give the history of Christ's body, or church, from the time she was established at Pentecost down to the last believer who overcomes, and on to the close, where the church is taken up to glory and seated on the throne with Jesus, executing judgment on the lost world. These chapters also show all that will take place through the end of Christ's thousand-year reign. (See Revelation 20:4.)

The first thing John heard was a loud voice that sounded like a trumpet. He looked to where the voice came from, and he saw seven golden candlesticks, representing the seven churches, or types of Christians, down to the last. He saw Jesus in the midst of the candlesticks, in all His power and glory. His eyes were like a blaze of fire, His feet like a blazing furnace. His voice was like the sound of many waters. In His right hand were seven stars. Out of His mouth came a two-edged sword. His countenance was like the sun, shining in all its strength. (See Revelation 1:10–16.) Oh, glory to God! What a Prince! What a King! What a living, wonder-working power is our Christ in His church. He is in us, beneath us, around us, like a wall of fire!

He shows us that our greatest trials and battles will be with the Devil in the enemies of Christ who are also the enemies of His true church. But hear Him say, "Behold, I will make them come and fall at our feet and acknowledge that God loves us and that we are His true witnesses." (See Revelation 3:9.)

Today, Christ is on trial for His honor and glory as never before. When so-called "great preachers" are denying the atoning blood of Christ and everything except the dead letter of the law (see Romans 7:6), hear Him say, "I hold the key. I will open for you." No man or power can close the door against us. We will keep His Word and not deny His name or be ashamed of His works. (See Revelation 3:7–8.)

He warns us that we will have trouble. We will be persecuted. We will be misrepresented by false prophets who call themselves *"Jews"*—or, in today's terms, "great Christians" and "leaders"—but who are of the *"synagogue of Satan"* (Rev. 2:9), who lie, and who do not practice the truth (v. 9; see also 1 John 1:6).

Come out of the "Laodicean" church, which represents spiritual lukewarmness, and become a "Philadelphian." (See Revelation 3:7–12; 14–21.)

The Rapture of the Saints

The fourth chapter of Revelation shows the Rapture of the saints and that their seat is on Christ's throne. All through the book of Revelation, Jesus describes the condition of the church, and His message still applies to us who are living on earth today.

The Laodicean church is the last, or great, church of today; it includes all organizations or groups in the world having a nice *"form of godliness, but denying the power thereof: from such turn away"* (2 Tim. 3:5). There has been a falling away from the doctrine of Christ and from the Holy Spirit, apostolic power, and wisdom, to a cold formality and to a teaching of the *"tradition[s]"* and *"doctrines of men"* (Col. 2:8, 22).

> *And unto the angel of the church of the Laodiceans write; These things saith the Amen, the faithful and true witness, the beginning of the creation of God; I know thy works, that thou art neither cold nor hot: I would thou wert cold or hot. So then because thou art lukewarm, and neither cold nor hot, I will spue thee out of my mouth. Because thou sayest, I am rich, and increased with goods, and have need of nothing; and knowest not that thou art wretched, and miserable, and poor, and blind, and naked: I counsel thee to buy of me gold tried in the fire, that thou mayest be rich; and white raiment, that thou mayest be clothed, and that the shame of thy nakedness do not appear; and anoint thine eyes with eyesalve, that thou mayest see. As many as I love, I rebuke and chasten: be zealous therefore, and repent. Behold, I stand at the door, and knock: if any man hear my voice, and open the door, I will come in to him, and will sup with him, and he with me. To him that overcometh will I grant to sit with me in my throne, even as I also overcame, and am set down with my Father in his throne. He that hath an ear, let him hear what the Spirit saith unto the churches.* (Rev. 3:14–22)

This is what concerns us. God is calling His people out of the Laodicean church. Thousands have heard the call: *"Come out of her, my people, that ye be not partakers of her sins, and that ye receive not of her plagues"* (Rev. 18:4). The last call is going forth. The Lord is shouting in a voice of thunder through His bride, "Come out quickly." You may have time to be an overcomer *"in the temple of my God"* (Rev. 3:12). Of such He says, *"He shall go no more out"* (v. 12).

The High Rank of the Family of God

The bride must graduate in the highest honors of the Holy Spirit. Those who sit on His throne will be the highest rank of the whole family of God. They will be *"heirs of God, and joint-heirs with Christ"* (Rom. 8:17); they will have kingly power with Christ to rule the nations for one thousand years. They are called the *"wise"* and are those whom Daniel saw: *"And they that be wise shall shine as the brightness of the firmament; and they that turn many to righteousness as the stars for ever and ever"* (Dan. 12:3).

The *"wise shall shine as the brightness of the firmament"* or *"as the stars for ever."* There are degrees of glory: one for the sun, another for the moon (1 Cor. 15:41). We thought years ago that the winning of souls was the greatest work. *"They that turn many to righteousness [will shine] as the stars for ever and ever."* However, *"the wise shall shine as the brightness of the firmament."* They will *"shine forth as the sun in the kingdom of their Father"* (Matt. 13:43).

None of the wicked will know anything about when Jesus comes, but the wise will know. Hear Jesus shout, *"To him that overcometh will I grant to sit with me in my throne, even as I also overcame, and am set down with my Father in his throne"* (Rev. 3:21). Oh, praise the Lord! The wise will sit with Christ on His throne.

The wise will know just when Jesus will come for His bride. They will be pillars in His temple (v. 12), in His body, or church. They will be initiated into the *"deep things of God"* (1 Cor. 2:10), and they will know His secrets. They will go in, never to go out. Oh, let us be sure that we are faithful and true. Then He will save us in that hour of trial, or tribulation, that is coming on all the world.

He Himself will come to take His bride, to take us, if we are part of His bride, to the Marriage Supper of the Lamb in the skies. He says, "I am coming quickly," meaning "soon" (Rev. 22:7). Hold fast to all you have received until He comes. See that no man takes your crown. *"Him that overcometh will I make a pillar in [My church]"* (Rev. 3:12).

"Watch and pray" (Mark 13:33) so that you may be counted worthy to escape all these things that are coming on the earth and to stand before the Lord.

A Royal Nation in Royal Robes

We are strangers in a strange land (see Exodus 2:22), but we are princes in disguise; our royal robes shine, but the world cannot see them. They cannot see the table our Father has prepared for us, spread out in shining brightness and snowy whiteness. It is covered with royal delicacies: rich wine to make us glad, meat to make us strong, heavenly bread to keep us alive forevermore, and oil to make us shine as bright lights in this dark world.

Our enemies cannot taste of the feast. Oh, praise the Lord, He is calling out a people for a special purpose in these last days. He calls them the wise ones, a chosen generation, a nation called out from among the nations, a royal kingly nation or nation of kings, a holy priesthood, a special people, who confess that they are not of this world, for our citizenship and kingdom are not of this world. (See Daniel 12:3, 10; 1 Peter 2:9; John 18:36.) We confess that we are pilgrims and strangers in this world (Heb. 11:13).

As living stones, we are being built up into a spiritual house (1 Pet. 2:5). Oh, glory to God! We are God's temple, in which He lives and moves. He molds us as clay in order to show His glorious presence, and so the world can see that the treasure is in our earthen vessels and that it is all of God (2 Cor. 4:7).

We are a holy priesthood so that we may offer up spiritual sacrifices to God through Jesus Christ. We are a living church, a spiritual body of Jesus, the living Head. Christ is the Head, and we are the living members of His body.

Christ is the Firstborn. It has pleased God, through Jesus, the Captain of our salvation (Heb. 2:10), to bring many sons and daughters into the kingdom, for He does not call us servants but sons (Gal. 4:7). Because we are the sons of God, He *"hath sent forth the Spirit of his Son into* [our] *hearts, crying, Abba, Father"* (v. 6).

The church of God and of our Lord Jesus Christ was set up in a blaze of glory on the Day of Pentecost. It was built on the foundation laid by the apostles and prophets, Jesus Christ being the Cornerstone (Eph. 2:20). The disciples were the one hundred and twenty "pillars" (Rev. 3:12) who were present at Pentecost and received the Pentecostal baptism. The three thousand who were saved, who received the gift of the Holy Spirit that day, became *"living stones"* (1 Pet. 2:5 NKJV) and were placed in God's building.

The Marriage of the Lamb

"And his wife hath made herself ready....Blessed are they which are called unto the marriage supper of the Lamb" (Rev. 19:7, 9). Psalm 45 tells us,

Kings' daughters [will be] among [His] honourable women: upon [His] right hand [will] stand the queen in gold of Ophir....The king's daughter is all glorious within: her clothing is of wrought gold. (vv. 9, 13)

Oh, hear the shouts around the throne, from one end to the other, as *"the voice of a great multitude, and as the voice of many waters, and as the voice of mighty thunderings, [shouting] Alleluia: for the Lord God omnipotent reigneth"* (Rev. 19:6). Beloved, what is all this about? Do we comprehend that we are causing all this rejoicing?

All heaven is waiting to hear the shout, "Go forth to meet her." Something wonderful is going to take place soon. The Mighty God, who inhabits eternity, and all the heavenly hosts have been waiting thousands of years for this great event: for the mystical body to come together—Christ our living Head, and the bride, the living body—for the Marriage of the Son of God, the Great Jehovah. *"For the marriage of the Lamb is come"* (Rev. 19:7).

Oh, dearly beloved, let us *"abstain from fleshly lusts, which war against the soul"* (1 Pet. 2:11). Let our words be few and well chosen; let our conversation be in heaven (Phil. 3:20), from which we are expecting a message from the King, telling us that He is coming. We can almost hear the bugle call of the angels, getting the armies of heaven ready for marching; we can almost hear the angelic choir, tuning their harps of gold. All heaven is getting excited.

"To him that overcometh will I grant to sit with me in my throne, even as I also overcame, and am set down with my Father in his throne" (Rev. 3:21). Jesus has not yet taken His throne, and He will not do so until He takes up His bride.

This promise is only to the wise of the bridal party. Those who will sit with Christ on His throne will have the highest rank of all the hosts of heaven. This is only promised to the overcomers in the last days, to those who will be taken up from among men. This is the close of the bride's tenure on earth.

In the first verse of Revelation chapter 4, we see a picture of the church's translation to heaven. John was carried to heaven; he represents the Rapture:

Immediately I was in the spirit [or changed, as we will be in the twinkling of an eye]; and, behold, a throne was set in heaven, and one sat on the throne. And he that sat was to look upon like a jasper...and there was a rainbow round about the throne. (vv. 2–3)

The brightest jewels are mentioned to help us to comprehend a little of the brightness and splendor of the glory of Christ and His bride.

John saw Jesus taking His throne and seating the bride with Him in the midst of the throne:

> *And out of the throne proceeded lightnings and thunderings and voices: and there were seven lamps of fire burning before the throne, which are the seven Spirits of God. And before the throne there was a sea of glass like unto crystal: and in the midst of the throne, and round about the throne, were four beasts full of eyes before and behind.* (Rev. 4:5–6)

The Glory of the Bride

The description of these beasts is symbolic of power, the wings and the eyes signifying that they are full of light, power, and knowledge. They are so swallowed up in the sunlight of glory that their crowns cannot be seen.

Now these are not beasts, but the overcomers, shining as the brightness of the sun, seated with Christ on His throne, just like He promised. We see the twenty-four crowned heads seated around the throne, as if in council; yet they are not on the throne (v. 4). We hear these overcomers shouting the loudest praises to the Lamb and to the Lord God Almighty, who was and is and who has come to take His great power and to reign. (See verse 8.)

When the overcomers give glory to Him who sits on the throne, "*who liveth for ever and ever*" (v. 9), they do not fall down, but the twenty-four elders fall before the throne and worship Him, casting their crowns at His feet, saying, "*Thou art worthy, O Lord, to receive glory and honour and power*" (v. 11). You see that the beasts or overcomers on the throne do not fall down; the others fall down in honor of what the living creatures are saying.

However, in Revelation 5:8–10, we read:

> *And when he had taken the book, the four beasts and four and twenty elders fell down before the Lamb, having every one of them harps, and golden vials full of odours, which are the prayers of saints. And they sung a new song, saying, Thou art worthy to take the book, and to open the seals thereof: for thou wast slain, and hast redeemed us to God by thy blood out of every*

kindred, and tongue, and people, and nation; and hast made us unto our God kings and priests: and we shall reign on the earth.

You see here that the living creatures, that is, the overcomers, and elders all fall down before the Lamb, *"having every one of them harps, and golden vials full of odours, which are the prayers of saints."* Oh, hear again the shouts of the overcomers with the elders:

Thou art worthy…for thou wast slain, and hast redeemed us to God by thy blood out of every kindred, and tongue, and people, and nation; and hast made us unto our God kings and priests: and we shall reign on the earth.

In Revelation 5:13, we hear all the hosts of heaven and earth raise a shout, giving glory to Him who sits on the throne. The four living creatures say, *"Amen"* (v. 14). Then *"the four and twenty elders [fall] down and [worship] him that liveth for ever and ever"* (v. 14).

When the overcomers say *"Amen,"* the elders fall down and worship, but the living creatures do not fall down, showing that they were redeemed by His blood from all nations and are clothed with the highest honor and power. They are *"joint-heirs with Christ"* (Rom. 8:17) in power and glory.

In Revelation 6, you see the living creatures, the overcomers, on the throne with Christ, executing judgments on the earth during the Great Tribulation. As one after another shouts, *"Come and see"* (Rev. 6:1), one judgment after another comes on the earth.

"'Do ye not know that the saints shall judge the world' (1 Cor. 6:2) and that the saints will judge fallen angels?" (See verse 3.) They will come back with Christ to fight the last great battle when the Antichrist and all his army will be destroyed. After this, they will reign as kings and priests for one thousand years (Rev. 20:6), when all the remnant of men will seek after the Lord and all the Gentiles will call on His name. Oh, hasten the day when the knowledge of God will cover the earth, as the waters cover the great and mighty deep (Isa. 11:9).

19

DANCING IN THE SPIRIT
AS VICTORY

D avid danced with all his might before the Lord (2 Sam. 6:14). The
Word is full of people dancing. Where dancing is mentioned in the
Bible, it always signifies victory for the Lord's hosts. It was always done to glorify
God. The Lord placed the spirit of power and love of the dance in the church.
Wherever the Scripture speaks of dancing, it implies that people danced by inspiration and were moved by the Spirit, and the Lord was always pleased and smiled
His approval. However, the Devil stole dancing away and made capital of it.

In these last days when God is pouring out His Spirit in great cloudbursts
and tidal waves from the floodgates of heaven, and the great river of life is flooding our spirits and bodies, baptizing us with fire and resurrection life and divine
energy, the Lord is doing *"his act[s], his strange act[s]"* (Isa. 28:21). There is dancing in the Spirit, speaking in other tongues, and many other operations and gifts.
The Holy Spirit is confirming the last message of the coming King with great
signs and wonders and miracles.

If you read carefully what the Scriptures say about dancing, you will be surprised; you will see that singing, music, and dancing have a humble and holy place
in the Lord's church:

Let them praise his name in the dance: let them sing praises unto him with the
timbrel and harp. (Ps. 149:3)

Praise him with the timbrel and dance: praise him with stringed instruments
and organs. (Ps. 150:4)

Then shall the virgin rejoice in the dance, both young men and old together.
(Jer. 31:13)

David Danced before the Lord

As I mentioned earlier, *"David danced before the Lord with all his might"*
(2 Sam. 6:14). His wife Michal did not like it; she scolded him and made light
of him. She said he was dancing before the maidens like a lewd fellow and made
it seem as if he was base and low. But he answered, "I was not dancing before
men, but before the Lord," showing that he had lost sight of the world and what
they thought or said and was moved and controlled entirely by the Holy Spirit
for the glory of God. All of the great company of people were blessed except
Michal, and she was stricken with barrenness until the day of her death. (See
2 Samuel 6:12–23.) So you see, she sinned in making light of the power of God
in the holy dance. Some do the same thing today, attributing it to the flesh or the
Devil. They always lose out, and many are in darkness until death.

Women Sang and Danced in Victory

Earlier in David's life, the news of his great victory—how he had killed the
giant Goliath and destroyed the great army of the Philistines—spread quickly
over the land. As the Israelite army was returning from the slaughter, the women
came out of all the cities of Israel to meet King Saul. They were singing and dancing with great joy and instruments of music. Now, notice, in all their cities, the
women went out in the streets and danced with their music. Men are not mentioned there, just maidens, and women danced unto the Lord in honor of God
and the king, prompted by the Spirit of God to praise the Lord in the dance. It
took courage to honor the king in this way, but the Lord smiled His approval by

having it recorded by holy men of old and sent down to us in His precious Word. (See 1 Samuel 17:21–18:6.)

Moses' Sister Led Dancing

Another example of dancing in the Bible is when Miriam and the other Hebrew women danced after God saved the Israelites by parting the Red Sea and destroying the Egyptian armies.

> *And Miriam the prophetess, the sister of Aaron, took a timbrel in her hand; and all the women went out after her with timbrels and with dances. And Miriam answered them, Sing ye to the Lord, for he hath triumphed gloriously; the horse and his rider hath he thrown into the sea.*   (Exod. 15:20–21)

God has never done a greater miracle nor demonstrated His presence in so great a cloud of glory as at this time. While they were under the inspiration and light of His presence, their whole bodies and spirits going out in love, the whole multitude of women praised the Lord with dancing, shouting, and music. Miriam, the prophetess and leader, led them forth, and they sang a new song that had just been given by the Spirit and had never been sung before. Do you call that foolishness? No, they were praising the Lord in the dance and song as they were moving in and by the mighty power of God.

Moses also led the children of Israel in the same way, with music and dancing, singing this new song given by the Spirit for the occasion. (See Exodus 15:1–19.)

Dancing in the New Testament

In the New Testament, we find that joyful leaping sometimes accompanied healing. When the lame man was healed through the ministry of Peter and John, *"he leaping up stood, and walked, and entered with them into the temple, walking, and leaping, and praising God"* (Acts 3:8). In another instance, the apostle Paul said to a man who had been crippled since birth, *"Stand upright on thy feet"* (Acts 14:10). What was the result? *"He leaped and walked"* (v. 10).

We discover a reference to dancing in the Parable of the Prodigal Son. The elder son was in the field. When he came near the house, he heard music and dancing, and he asked, "What does all this mean?" They said, "*Thy brother is come; and thy father hath killed the fatted calf, because he hath received him safe and sound*" (Luke 15:27). "[The elder son] *was angry, and would not go in*" (v. 28), but the feast and rejoicing went on just the same. The Father said, "*It was meet that we should make merry, and be glad: for this thy brother was dead, and is alive again; and was lost, and is found*" (v. 32).

All will agree with me that this was an old-fashioned Holy Spirit revival. The lost son represents the sinner whom the Spirit has brought out of darkness into light; the saints are filled with the Spirit.

Dancing in the Spirit Today

So the Holy Spirit is falling on the saints of God today, and they are being used in the same way. Those who never danced one step are experts in the holy dance; those who do not know one note from another are expert musicians in playing many different instruments of music. Often, the sound of invisible instruments is heard from the platform; the sounds can be plainly heard all over the building. I say in the fear and presence of God: the singing and demonstration puts the fear of God on the people and causes a holy hush to come over them. The strange acts (Isa. 28:21) are occurring more and more. They show that they are something new and that Jesus is coming soon. The Lord is getting His bride ready to be translated and to dance and play at the great Marriage of the Lamb. This will soon take place, for the bride is making herself ready (Rev. 19:7).

I was very slow to accept dancing in the Spirit, because I feared that it was of the flesh. However, I soon saw that it was the cloud of glory (see Exodus 16:10) over the people that brought forth the dancing and the playing of invisible instruments.

The sounds of sweet, heavenly music would often be heard in our meetings. Several times, I asked those in the congregation who heard this music coming from the platform (where they knew there were no instruments to be seen) to be honest and raise their hands. Many hands went up from saints and sinners. The stillness of death went over the people when they heard the sounds of music accompanied by the heavenly choir. Often, a message in tongues was given in one or more languages, along with the interpretation. As I saw the effect of the Holy Spirit on the people in convincing them that they were in the presence of God, I concluded that this was surely the Lord's strange work and His strange acts. (See Isaiah 28:21.)

I saw as many as nine of the most noted ministers dancing at one time on the platform. They danced singly, with their eyes closed. Often, some fell, slain by the mighty power of God. These things convinced me. I also saw men and women who have been crippled join in the dance with wonderful grace. One lady, who was on crutches for five years, got healed in her seat; afterward, she danced across the platform, singing heavenly music. I am reminded of the Scripture, "The virgins, the young men, and the old men all join in the dance together." (See Jeremiah 31:13.) Praise the Lord. *"Let us be glad and rejoice, and give honour to him: for the marriage of the Lamb is come, and his wife hath made herself ready"* (Rev. 19:7). The Lord is quickening our mortal bodies for the translation.

20

PREPARE FOR WAR

(Preached before World War I Began)

The following two quotations from Joel and Micah sound a little contradictory. I have heard people say so. But the statements refer to two
different parties and times:

For, behold, in those days, and in that time, when I shall bring again the captiv-
ity of Judah and Jerusalem, I will also gather all nations, and will bring them
down into the valley of Jehoshaphat….Proclaim ye this among the Gentiles;
Prepare war, wake up the mighty men, let all the men of war draw near; let
them come up: beat your plowshares into swords, and your pruninghooks into
spears: let the weak say, I am strong.   (Joel 3:1–2, 9–10)

But in the last days it shall come to pass, that the mountain of the house of the
LORD shall be established in the top of the mountains, and it shall be exalted
above the hills; and people shall flow unto it. And many nations shall come,
and say, Come, and let us go up to the mountain of the LORD, and to the
house of the God of Jacob; and he will teach us of his ways, and we will walk
in his paths: for the law shall go forth of Zion, and the word of the LORD from

Jerusalem. And he shall judge among many people, and rebuke strong nations afar off; and they shall beat their swords into plowshares, and their spears into pruninghooks: nation shall not lift up a sword against nation, neither shall they learn war any more. But they shall sit every man under his vine and under his fig tree; and none shall make them afraid: for the mouth of the LORD *of hosts hath spoken it.* (Mic. 4:1–4)

The first Scripture quotation under consideration, "*Beat your plowshares into swords, and your pruninghooks into spears*" (Joel 3:10), means "Get ready for battle," and it refers to this present time, a time of war. The second Scripture, "*Beat [your] swords into plowshares, and [your] spears into pruninghooks*" (Mic. 4:3), means "Get ready for a time of great farming."

The first one calls us to prepare for the greatest battle the world has ever heard of; the other refers to the time when war will be no more.

"Prepare for war; wake up the mighty men of war; let the nations gather together for battle" (see Joel 3:2, 9) refers to this time of the end that we are now living in, when the time of the Gentiles (Rom. 11:25) has been completed or is coming to a close.

A Mighty Man of War

You see the awful slaughter, massacre, and deadly hatred that is causing the nations to kill and destroy each other. God has risen up like a "*mighty…man of war*" (Isa. 42:13). He will roar and shout out from Jerusalem (Joel 3:16) until all nations are gathered in deadly combat, until the blood flows like a river.

In the text in Joel, the call is primarily to the Holy Land, where the great Battle of God Almighty will be fought. This is the Battle of the great Day of God, when the angel is standing in the sun calling all the fowls of the air to come to the supper of the great God, to eat the flesh of all the mighty men, the great men of the world, and the rich men. They are invited to eat and drink the blood and get fat on the flesh, on the carcasses of kings and princes of the world, who will soon fall in the "*notable day of the Lord*" (Acts 2:20). (See Revelation 19:17–18.)

The Lord will awaken and shout out as a "*man of war*" (Isa. 42:13). He will "*roar out of Zion, and utter his voice from Jerusalem; and the heavens and the earth shall shake*" (Joel 3:16) when the nations are gathering for this great Battle with the Lamb and His army from heaven.

The apostle John wrote,

> *And I saw heaven opened, and behold a white horse; and he that sat upon him....His eyes were as a flame of fire, and on his head were many crowns.... And he was clothed with a vesture dipped in blood....And the armies which were in heaven followed him upon white horses, clothed in fine linen, white and clean.* (Rev. 19:11–14)

Oh, praise the Lord! Let me give you the background of this verse. The saints have been translated to heaven. The Marriage of the Lamb and His bride has taken place, with shouting and hallelujahs that have shaken all heaven and earth. The great Marriage Supper, with all its grandeur and glory and greatness, is over. The saints have been with the Lord, executing judgments on the earth during the awful Tribulation.

Now the cup of wickedness is full. The God of heaven has been defied long enough. He has stood up in His wrath. All nations of the earth are gathering to the "*valley of Jehoshaphat*" (Joel 3:2). The Antichrist has gathered his army and is about to destroy God's children. The "KING OF KINGS AND LORD OF LORDS" (Rev. 19:16), with all His armies of heaven, comes riding in triumph, down through the skies. Enoch saw the Lord coming with "*ten thousands of his saints*" (Jude 14). All the armies will gather together against Jerusalem to fight, but then the Lord will come from heaven and fight this great Battle. The saints do not have to fight: the Lord Himself does the fighting.

Millennial Kingdom

Following this, the millennial kingdom will be set up, and Satan will be chained during the thousand years. During this time, the curse and its effects, including all weeds, thistles, and anything that would produce disease and the like, will have been taken away. "*They shall not hurt nor destroy in all my holy mountain*" (Isa. 11:9). The time is coming when they will cease to make war, and the Devil will be taken out of the hearts of the people.

Today, people are just like wild beasts that are thirsting for each other's blood. They are burying the living and the dead together. Pestilence also has already begun its deadly havoc.

Have you ever heard of a great war breaking out so quickly, the way it has in Europe? For years past, the most talented men have been inventing weapons in order to see who could make the most deadly ones.

God has been holding back the tidal waves and other destructive forces. His angel has shouted, "Wait until the servants of God are sealed with the seal of God." (See Revelation 7:3.)

The chapters in the book of Joel have been divided poorly. The first verses of the third chapter are a continuation of the last verses of the second chapter and should not be separated from them.

"*And it shall come to pass in the last days, saith God, I will pour out of my Spirit*" (Acts 2:17, quoting Joel 2:28). God will baptize with the Holy Spirit and disseminate the power of the holy people.

God says, "I will rise up in My wrath in that Day." (See Joel 2:1–11.) When the judgments of God are in the earth, some will repent. (See verse 32.) "*In the last days, saith God, I will pour out of my Spirit.*" God says to wake up the heathen (Joel 3:9, 12).

God is sealing His saints, but that sealing time is pretty nearly over. That fact that the saints speak in "*new tongues*" (Mark 16:17) is a sign that the Lord is coming.

The power of the holy people will be disseminated. These are they who are clay in the Potter's hands. They are just clay, having no control over themselves at all. God Almighty speaks through them: "*With stammering lips and another tongue will* [I] *speak to this people....Yet they* [will] *not hear*" (Isa. 28:11–12).

Proclaim and tell it to the people. "*Blow ye the trumpet in Zion, and sound an alarm in my holy mountain*" (Joel 2:1). What is the danger? The Day of the Lord is coming; it is near at hand.

God's people are blowing the trumpet. They are sounding the alarm in Zion. What is the signal of danger? The great Day of the Lord is near.

It is time for the saints to get this knowledge, if they do not already know it. How can we give the signal if we do not know? How can we warn the people of danger?

If they escape when the sword is coming, good. But warn them anyhow. If we do not warn them, their blood will be on our hands. Wake up the heathen. Call up your mighty men. Call the soldiers into line. Get them ready. Get the weapons of war ready for the world's great conflict. There never has been anything like it, nor will there ever be again.

The nations are continually building new warships and manufacturing so many deadly weapons. Each nation is trying to build the largest ships and invent the most deadly weapons. Yet they are still crying, "Peace, peace." Right in the midst of this false peace and security, death and war and destruction have come like a whirlwind.

Men will be hunting around in the farmyards, old barns, stables, sheds, and everywhere for old plowshares and pruning hooks—for everything that they can beat into swords and spears to kill their neighbors with. Your neighbor will be hunting around for a piece of old steel to kill his neighbor with.

The time is coming in this glorious America when parties and factions will rise up—labor against capital, and other parties and factions. At that time, no one will be able to buy or sell unless they have the mark of the beast (Rev. 13:16–17). It will mean death, but to have the mark of the beast will mean the *"second death"* (Rev. 2:11).

There will be no safety or hiding place for him who goes out or in: *"As if a man did flee from a lion, and a bear met him; or went into the house, and leaned his hand on the wall, and a serpent bit him"* (Amos 5:19).

It is implied that the land will be infested with poisonous serpents, reptiles, and insects and that they will be turned loose among the people, with their deadly power to bite, sting, and destroy. So if a person runs away from the sword and pestilence and tries to hide in the house, he will rest his hand on the wall and be bitten by a deadly serpent. There will be no safety for him who goes in or out.

There will be awful, deadly hatred among the people, and they will be banded together hand in hand. They will make weapons of steel with which to kill and destroy one another. It is time to wake up from the sleep of death and call on God to give you life.

According to the Word of God and the signs of the times, we are now living in the commencement of these awful times, when many who read these lines will see a great deal more than I have written. You and your children will go down in death or go through this dreadful time of trouble, such as never has been or ever will be again.

Many of the best Bible students say that the eleventh chapter of Daniel refers to the Sultan, or ruling powers of Turkey. *"And he shall plant the tabernacles of his palace between the seas in the glorious holy mountain; yet he shall come to his end, and none shall help him"* (Dan. 11:45). They think that the book of Obadiah also refers to him.

The passage in Daniel does not refer to the Antichrist, for he will not be revealed or take his power until after the Hinderer is taken away (see 2 Thessalonians 2:7)—until Christ takes out a people for His name from among the Gentiles, until He comes and takes His bride.

He will come to his end in the *"time of the end"* (Dan. 11:40). At that time, Michael, the great prince, will stand up for God's people, and all whose names are written in the Book of Life will be delivered. (See Daniel 12:1.) The wise, who will know these things, will *"shine as the brightness of the firmament"* (v. 3).

It is reported that the Turks are building a large palace, or building; they are keeping it quiet and will not tell anyone what it is for. *"He shall plant the tabernacles of his palace between the seas in the glorious holy mountain; yet he shall come to his end, and none shall help him"* (Dan. 11:45). But he will not stay there very long; little by little, he will go down until he is entirely destroyed.

The Holy Land was to be trodden down by the Gentiles until the *"time of the end"* (8:17). Then, and at that time, Christ will come. The Jews will flock to Jerusalem and again possess the Holy Land.

Most of those who will go through the Tribulation will have had enough, and they will be ready to listen to the voice of the *"false prophet"* (Rev. 16:13).

If the angels are loosed (see Revelation 19:14–15), it will not be long before we take our flight. When these things begin to come fast, we will soon be taken out of the world. The worst trouble will come after the saints are taken out. The Antichrist will deny the blessed Christ and cause people to take his mark or be put to death. Those who do not go with Christ will have to go through this or go down in it.

Jesus will come to take a people out for His name, for His bride. He will come and take her away to the heavens. The great Marriage Supper will take place, after which the saints will be sitting with Christ on His throne and helping to execute judgment during this awful Tribulation.

Look at the terrible death and carnage and destruction you will experience if you do not go up with the bridal company. Those who go up when Christ comes are the Lamb's wife. Then He will return to build up the *"waste places of Jerusalem"* (Isa. 52:9). The soil will all be fertile then, and the people will not need to do much work. During the Millennium, it will be like a holy camp meeting all the time.

The first time Jesus returns, no one will see Him but the bride. The world hates her and cares nothing for her, and Jesus is going to take her away. Christ will come as quickly as the lightning flashes from the east to the west. (See Matthew 24:27.) Just that quickly, He will snatch His bridal company away, while the world sleeps in a drunken stupor.

But the next time He comes, all will know it. Every knee will bow and every tongue will confess that Jesus Christ is Lord (Phil. 2:10–11). Every eye will see Him (Rev. 1:7), and every slanderous tongue will have to confess before the world that the saints were God's chosen vessels. (See Revelation 3:9.)

This honor belongs to the saints. The world will have to confess that we were right and they were wrong. God is very proud of His bride. Children of God now deny themselves many of the things of the world. Yet we are heirs of the kingdom, even though many of us are poor in this world and are experiencing hard times. There is going to be a change in this old world. God is calling you to see this. Don't go a step further. Don't step over the mangled body of Christ any more, or it may be the last time.

As I said, the first time Christ returns, the bride will be caught away; the second time, the saints will come riding on white horses. (See Revelation 19:14.) Jesus will stand on Mount Olivet, and those who pierced Him will see Him (Rev. 1:7). You now know, down in your hearts, that Jesus is the Christ, that every believer present in this meeting is in earnest, that we hear something more than natural men hear. The wisdom we receive comes from God, who gives liberally. This has been my prayer more than anything else: "Give me wisdom." Why, even a blind man can see by looking at the signs of the times. Daniel said that the wise will know when the Lord comes.

You may say, "I don't believe." You just don't want to believe, and that Day will overtake you as a thief in the night. None of the wicked will understand the signs of Jesus' coming. You who are children of the light will know, and that Day will not overtake you unexpectedly. (See 1 Thessalonians 5:4–5.) God gave Daniel a picture of those who belong to the lost world, none of whom will know when He comes.

Who are the wise? Those who know the time of the Lord's coming. *"They that turn many to righteousness* [will shine] *as the stars"* (Dan. 12:3). But *"they that be wise shall shine as the brightness of the firmament"* (v. 3). They who are wise will know.

This is a wonderful message. Now you can have your choice. The greatest vengeance and pent-up wrath of God will be poured out on those who take the mark of the Antichrist. If we trust in God, we can have faith so that none of these things will hurt us.

Look up, dear children of the living God. Look up; our redemption is near (Luke 21:28), even at the door (Matt. 24:33). Oh, God, help us to awaken the sleeping virgins (see Matthew 25:5) and tell them to flee to Christ, to get the baptism of the Holy Spirit, to get sealed with the *"Spirit of promise"* (Eph. 1:13), to get ready to take the flight in the air.

Oh, accept the invitation to the Marriage Supper of the Lamb. He will come like a flash of lightning from the east. We will go in a moment. We will arise to meet Him in the sky.

Don't be looking to the grave. Look up. *"Behold, He cometh"* (Rev. 1:7). *"Glory to God in the highest"* (Luke 2:14). Come, O Redeemer; come quickly.

21

FEAR GOD,
AND GIVE HIM GLORY

And I saw another angel fly in the midst of heaven, having the everlasting gospel to preach unto them that dwell on the earth, and to every nation, and kindred, and tongue, and people, saying with a loud voice, Fear God, and give glory to him; for the hour of his judgment is come: and worship him that made heaven, and earth, and the sea, and the fountains of waters.
—Revelation 14:6–7

Our text describes certain things John saw in his Revelation. He was carried away in a trance, and he was not hypnotized, either. He saw an angel. He did not simply think so, but he saw it, flying *"in the midst of heaven, having the everlasting gospel to preach"* and saying, *"Fear God, and give glory to him."*

The image of an angel flying through the earth, preaching the everlasting Gospel, applies to us today in a wonderful way. We are living in the last days, right at the end of this glorious dispensation. God is calling out a people from among men, preparing the bride whom Jesus is coming to receive as His own. God is calling His servants for the ministry of the Gospel of His kingdom. They go over the land with swiftness. They are called eagles. The eagle has great power, and it soars over every difficulty. It is so with God's children in these days. God gives us strength and courage that has never existed before.

We are sent as angels to sound the trumpet. When God calls, we have to go, skipping across the ocean, running, flying, soaring over the world. Nothing can pull us down. God is calling us to give this old world the last call. He is taking men and women whom He can trust with His power to show forth His goods to the world. A traveling salesman shows his goods and secures orders. If he did not show his goods, he would not get the orders. People want to see the goods before they purchase them.

So God calls us to show the samples. We are not only to tell what God can do, but to put Him to the test and show what He can do. We must be clothed with the power of the King, showing such signs and wonders as the world has never seen. That will put the fear of the Lord on all those who see and hear.

Never before have we had a greater responsibility. The message is, "'Fear God, and give glory to him; for the hour of his judgment is come.' Worship God, 'which made heaven, and earth, the sea, and all that therein is' (Ps 146:6). Worship Him as never before."

There are as many gods being worshipped in America today as there are among the heathen. The God of heaven is left in the shade, and the Lord Jesus Christ is thrown down by many professing Christians. Give glory to Him, Him, Him, the God of heaven. Worship Him, "*and give glory to him; for the hour of his judgment is come.*" That time is here. "*Fear God, and give glory to him.*"

What is the message we are to give? Jesus is coming soon. God has given out the invitation to the Marriage Supper of His Son. We are invited to the Feast, and we are having our wedding garments made. There is everything to coax the bride away from her father's house, from everything that binds her, and to draw her to the Bridegroom.

"*Gather yourselves together*" (Zeph. 2:1). Those of you who follow Him, gather yourselves together—you who are despised and rejected. (See verse 1.) All men speak evil of this "sect." (See Acts 28:22.) Seek righteousness, meekness, and power from God. Hide away.

Watchman, what do you see of the morning? Glory to God! The sun is rising in the East. He is coming! What about the night? The night is coming soon.

Death and destruction are coming; the judgments of God are coming. *"Blow ye the trumpet in Zion"* (Joel 2:1) and sound the alarm in the Holy Mountain (v. 1). Let all the people tremble.

Why are the people going to get alarmed and tremble? What is the danger? The armies of the Devil are gathering. Hide, hide away in the rock from the wrath of God that is coming upon the earth. My God, warn the people! Let them tremble on account of their sins. We have to blow the trumpet, the signal of danger. We have to give the warning and let the people know. The angelic choir is getting ready. His people are being trained down here to sing the song of the redeemed. (See Revelation 14:3.) May the people tremble; may the fear of God come upon them. There is a great Day coming, a Day of black darkness, black as midnight. God's judgment is going to burst upon this earth. Give the signal of danger. The great Day of the Lord is coming; it is near at hand. He is at the door. (See Matthew 24:33.) If we know it, help us to tell it!

The ancient cities had great walls around them, and watchmen were placed day and night upon the walls. If they saw an army approaching, an enemy coming, or any danger threatening, they blew the trumpet, giving the warning to the men of war in the city who understood the signal, so that the people could escape. If the watchmen did not give the signal, the blood of the people was on their heads.

Watchmen, if you do not warn the people and the Enemy comes in and takes them, their blood will be upon your heads. God puts us upon the walls of Zion. Jesus is coming in this generation. The young people will not be old when He comes. According to His Word, the time is near. We are all either for Him or against Him. How can you give the signal of danger if you do not know it? Worship God, and give glory to Him, the God of heaven. If you blow the trumpet right, it will arouse the people. Then if they continue sleeping, your hands will be free from blood.

There never was such a responsibility on the people of God as there is today. There never was such a time for Jesus Christ to be lifted up as He is today. Gods of science and nature and other gods are on the earth today. At a gathering of twenty-three ministers in Boston, only three accepted the divinity of Christ. We have to drop all side issues and hobbies, everything else but Jesus; we must lift up Jesus.

In these days, our Lord is being crucified a thousand times worse than on the cross. In these days, His honor and His glory are at stake. Stand by Him, and defend His holy name. Hold up the fountain of Calvary that is opened wide; it cleanses from the effects of sin. It has power today, flowing from the wounded side of Jesus. Let us stand by Him in the battle against the world, the flesh, and the Devil. Men may call us every name that can be invented—hypnotists, fanatics, and crackpots—trying to strike those who are stepping out on God's promises. How the heart of Jesus must bleed! If we stand firm with Him, He will let the people know the work is of God. Stand firm; set your face like flint (Isa. 50:7). Prove the Word; He says He will stand by us to deliver us in the hour of temptation and in the hour of tribulation that is coming on the earth. Be true to Him; hold up the Atonement and the power of the blood. He will save us from the black darkness that is settling over the world.

We have to stand by Him and lift up Jesus, though men and devils howl and speak against Him and the wonderful works of the blessed Holy Spirit. Can He find messengers, men and women, who will interpret the Word correctly and show what the mighty power of God is? He says that if we will stand by Him now and blow the trumpet, the Word of God will encircle the earth. God will be here to judge His people, and the glory of heaven will be brought down to fight our battles. Let us lift up Jesus.

Don't talk about side issues; don't get a bone of contention and talk about it. When people know Him, they will know what to do, what to wear, how to get married, and how to live when they are married. Preach Jesus. Glory to God! People will not change their ideas to please you. God Almighty has to show them. These things break up meetings, and the people lose their power. Lift up Jesus. It is not by might or by power; it is Almighty God doing the work (Zech. 4:6). We must show forth what He is doing. Let us stand by Him during this short time when the command goes forth to blow the trumpet.

The great Day of the Lord is near at hand; it is at the door (Matt. 24:33). Give the signal of danger, and He will back it up by signs and wonders. If we are preaching the Word, we must have the signs and wonders to get people to believe in Him.

People are worshipping a mystical god; they are following *"doctrines of devils"* (1 Tim. 4:1). The wrath of God must come upon those who follow these things, and the blood will come up to the horses' bridles (Rev. 14:20). God is holding back the four winds (Rev. 7:1) to give us a chance to blow this trumpet, and He will back it up with power. The time is near at hand. There are temples of idols set up in this land, and a man sets himself up as if he is God. (See 2 Thessalonians 2:3–4.) They are getting ready; everywhere, federations are forming.

Don't go into these federations; keep out of them. Don't be afraid of their threats. Fear God, for the hour of His judgment is at hand. Can you not see these things? People are preaching the fatherhood of God and the brotherhood of man, but they are leaving out the blood of Christ entirely. Don't be afraid of their threats. Fear God; He will deliver. We see these things; we see them everywhere. Christ is at hand. Worship the God of heaven.

Who will stand for Jesus, the lowly Nazarene? Who will stand for Him when everyone is pointing the finger of derision? There are millions of professing Christians today who are denying the Lord who bought them. They deny the divinity of Christ, and they deny the power of the Holy Spirit. You can have the knowledge of these things if the blood of Jesus cleanses you. You may feed the poor and all that, but if you do not have the Spirit of God, all that you do outside of Jesus Christ will never build a ladder to take you to heaven. You cannot go there except through Christ. If you are in the flesh, and the Spirit of God does not dwell in you (compare Romans 8:9), then you are a reprobate. Yet, little children, you do know God (1 John 2:13). Praise His name. Give God the glory.

God has revealed by the Spirit that the Laodicean church will be spewed out (Rev. 3:14–16). The Sardian church has a reputation for being alive, but they are spiritually dead (v. 1). They have a beautiful outside form, but they deny the power of the Holy Spirit; "*from such turn away*" (2 Tim 3:5). They do not know the Holy Spirit or the blood that bought them. They stand off to one side and say that rather than being under the power of the Spirit, people are hypnotized, mesmerized, or drunk—as some said about the disciples on the Day of Pentecost. They do not want to investigate; they are afraid of being called fools by the world. I would rather be a fool in God's hands than a fool in front of the Devil. Wouldn't you?

David danced before the ark of the Lord with all his might (2 Sam. 6:14), yet they call us fanatics because we dance. May God give us more fanatics. Don't you see the darkness in the land? None of these people, judging by their actions, know anything about the Holy Spirit. When they come near us, there is a fear on them; they don't want to believe it. May God help us to know the difference between being mesmerized and being under the power of God. It is the power of God, yet they call it hypnotism when they see people laid out under His mighty power.

Don't you see how little they know of Jesus? He set us the example. He cast out demons and healed the sick. He sent the Holy Spirit down upon His disciples, and they staggered like drunken men and spoke in tongues (Acts 2:1–4). They were *"drunken, but not with wine; they stagger, but not with strong drink"* (Isa. 29:9). This is the way today. John the Baptist prophesied that Jesus would baptize with the Holy Spirit and fire (Matt. 3:11). What do you know about that? When people see the Holy Spirit working, they say we are crazy.

God's people are alive. Give glory to God, and worship Him, for the hour of the Judgment is at hand. You see some people worshipping a dead Christ, giving heed to *"doctrines of men"* (Col. 2:22) and *"doctrines of devils"* (1 Tim. 4:1). There is a power in education, wealth, and fine sermons. Yet may God help us to preach in the power of the Holy Spirit. They set Christ aside. If they had the blood of Christ applied to their hearts, how they would love God! Then they would know the power of the blood and the power of the Holy Spirit.

Christ said: "'I [will] *send the promise of my Father'* (Luke 24:49) and *'ye shall receive power, after that the Holy Ghost is come upon you'* (Acts 1:8). Then you will work miracles. Preach My Word, and I will be with you." (See Matthew 28:20.) He is with us. If you will believe correctly, you will cast out demons—legions are all around us. You will *"lay hands on the sick, and they shall recover"* (Mark 16:18). They will not be mesmerized, as some claim. Praise God!

Quit your grumbling, and get the experience of the baptism in the Holy Spirit so that you can praise God. Many make fun of the work of the Holy Spirit. You can see it in the city papers. God's work isn't being presented in its true light; it is being presented in a foolish, sensational way, to make people think it is of the Devil.

"When the Son of man cometh, shall he find faith on the earth?" (Luke 18:8). He will find only a little flock watching for Him. On the Day of Pentecost, Peter did not say, "There is no power here." He said it was the Holy Spirit, spoken of by the prophet Joel. (See Acts 2:14–18.) The people there saw the tongues of fire; they heard the sound as of a *"rushing mighty wind"* (vv. 2–3). It was the Holy Spirit, and He is here tonight. Be careful how you speak against Him. He is in these acts of healing and in the tongues. There is great power among the people who are giving the last warning before Jesus comes.

May God help us as never before to see Jesus in the power of His blood. Let us give Jesus the preeminence. Let us preach Jesus and the Resurrection.

Show He is coming by the signs, by the power to deliver the people. You know He is coming. Show the signs, and you won't have to do much preaching. The people will see the miracles, and many will be saved. Let us lift up Jesus as never before. Let the people see nothing but Jesus; they will soon drop everything that is unclean and go higher and higher and deeper still.

May God put His seal upon these truths in our hearts. The crisis is nearer than anyone thinks. Lift up Jesus, and God will show people the truth. God must show them by working through you. Glory to His name!

22

SET YOUR HOUSE IN ORDER

Thus saith the LORD*, Set thine house in order:*
for thou shalt die, and not live.
—Isaiah 38:1

My prayer is that the Lord will stop every sinner in his tracks who reads these words. I pray that you will understand the warning in the text to mean you, that you will take the nearest way to the Cross and throw yourself at the bleeding feet of the dying Lamb of God, and that you will let Him cleanse and wash out all the sin and filth from your heart and mind. I pray that you will let the Lord Jesus come in and take possession of your house, your self—that He will fill you with His love and presence, be the keeper of the house, and speak to You, so that you may obey like a dear child. His sheep hear His voice. When He leads, they follow (John 10:27).

Jesus has spoken to you many times by His Spirit and told you that this world is not your home and that it is not all of life to live or all of death to die, but that after death comes the Judgment. He has shown you that you are a sinner, lost and undone, that the wrath of God hangs over you. If you die in your sins, it will be an awful thing to "*fall into the hands of the living God*" (Heb. 10:31). If you go on in your sins, you will be arrested by the Sheriff of Heaven and be bound hand and foot; you will be cast into "*outer darkness,*" where the inhabitants weep and wail and gnash their teeth (Matt. 8:12). The Lord has told you that the time will come when you will cry for mercy. Yet the mercy door will be closed, and God will not hear you. He will laugh and mock at your fears and calamity. He will say, "*Depart from me, ye cursed, into everlasting fire,*" a place "*prepared for the devil and his angels*" (Matt. 25:41).

Heaven was prepared for you, but if you are not pure in heart, the pearly gates will be closed against you. This world will be wrapped in flames; it will burn as pitch and tar, and the wicked will be swept off into destruction.

In view of the terrible doom the text implies, make the preparation at once. You will have to die someday, and there is no repentance in the grave. As you go down in death, you will rise in the Judgment. Death is coming; that terrible eternity is before you! Before the sun rises or sets again, you may be cold in death, and your soul may be lost.

The Pale Horse

You will soon hear the clatter of the feet of the pale horse and his rider, the monster Death (Rev. 6:8), bearing down upon you. You will have a race with the pale horse, and he will run you down into the cold, icy river of death. You will die soon and meet your God, whether you are ready or not. The Lord says, "Prepare for death, '*for thou shalt die.*'"

"*As I live, saith the Lord God, I have no pleasure in the death of the wicked; but that the wicked turn from his way and live*" (Ezek. 33:11).

Hear Him call. Seek the Lord while He may be found. Call upon Him while He is near (Isa. 55:6). "*He will not always chide: neither will he keep his anger forever*" (Ps. 103:9). God has warned you through the rolling thunder, the flashing lightning, and the cyclone. The voice of God has spoken to you, saying, "Take warning; fly to Christ, and seek shelter from the storms of the great Judgment Day."

The Day of His wrath is coming, and who will be able to stand (Mal. 3:2)? Every funeral procession you see tells you that you, too, must soon die. Are you ready? When you stood by the bedside of one struggling in death or looked on the face in the coffin, the Lord said to you, "Prepare for death, and follow Me."

Every autumn you look upon the withered flowers and falling leaves. They tell you of death. Death is written on the breezes. Everything points to death and shows you that you will soon be laid away in the silent city of the dead and will soon be forgotten by the living.

Withering Leaves, Fading Flowers

You hear the solemn moaning of the winds through the leafy trees. They say to you, "This world is not your home; you did not come here to stay forever." Seek a home in heaven—a house not built with hands (2 Cor. 5:1), *"whose builder and maker is God"* (Heb. 11:10)—where you will soon meet all your loved ones, to be forever with the Lord.

When you walk over the withered flowers and faded leaves, and as they rustle beneath your feet, the voice of God speaks to you, saying, "You are passing away. You will soon be lying underneath the ground, and you will soon be forgotten." The thoughtless throng will walk over your moldering form and think no more of you than you do of the dead leaves you are crushing beneath your feet.

Dear reader, if you have not given your heart to Jesus, drop to your knees, confess your sins to Him, and accept Him as your personal Savior. Do not rise until the light of heaven shines down in your soul and you know you are saved. If you do not, you will soon find yourself swept out on the shores of eternity, lost, lost forever!

The Great Judgment Morning

I dreamed that the Great Judgment morning
    Had dawned, and the trumpet had blown;
I dreamed that the nations had gathered
    To Judgment before the White Throne.
From the throne came a bright-shining angel
    And stood on the land and the sea,
And swore with his hand raised to heaven,
    That time was no longer to be.

And, oh, what a weeping and wailing
    When the lost ones were told of their fate;
They cried for the rocks and the mountains,
    They prayed but their prayers were too late.

The rich man was there, but his money
    Had melted and vanished away;
A pauper he stood in the Judgment,
    His debts were too heavy to pay.
The great man was there, but his greatness
    When death came was left far behind,
The angel that opened the records
    Not a trace of his greatness could find.

The widow was there and the orphans,
    God heard and remembered their cries;
No sorrow in heaven forever,
    God wiped all the tears from their eyes.
The gambler was there and the drunkard,
    And the man who had sold them the drink, With the people
who gave him the license—
    Together in hell they did sink.

The moral man came to the Judgment,
    But his self-righteous rags would not do;
The men who had crucified Jesus
    Had passed off as moral men, too.
The soul that had put off salvation—
    "Not tonight; I'll get saved bye and bye;
No time now to think of religion!"
    At last they had found time to die.

EPILOGUE

Since my last book, *Signs and Wonders*,[2] was written, I have held meetings in a number of places, including some of the largest cities out West. In regard to our meeting in Sidney, Iowa, one of the local papers had this to report about the work:

> The crowd of spectators Sunday night was said to have been the largest ever seen at the city park on any occasion. They come back here sick and maimed, on crutches and in wheelchairs, and go away apparently sound and well and shouting hosannas to the Most High. Call it hypnotism or what you will, there is no dodging the fact that Mrs. Etter is exerting a power over these people that passeth common understanding. We give it up; we have no solution.

In addition, here are a few words taken from the *Fremont* (County) *Herald*:

> The big camp meeting is still in progress at the park and is more than ever the main topic of conversation on the streets and in the majority of the homes in Sidney. Each day brings a number of people from a distance,

---

2. See Maria Woodworth-Etter, *Signs and Wonders* (New Kensington, PA: Whitaker House, 1997).

on the train and in autos. The local reporter asked for the names of some of the people who were registered from a distance, but the joke was on her, for there were so many that the paper couldn't print them all. For the first time we can remember, a religious gathering has driven out a good show, and before they went, the members of the company, which was booked for the whole week before last at the opera house, went over to the camp meeting to see what had taken their crowds.

These meetings stirred this little town and its surrounding territory as nothing had ever done before. I remember that, on a Sunday, just as we had dismissed the meeting, the power of God fell on a little boy with a speech impediment. He was about twelve years old. He got up and walked back and forth on the platform, giving messages in tongues and exhorting the people to get down and pray, pray, pray! He would take his handkerchief and wipe off the perspiration and tears from his face, stamp his little feet, and plead with the people to get down and pray, hide away in God, and get ready for His coming. In a very short time, he had every saint and nearly all the sinners down on their knees, weeping and calling upon God.

From this little place, we headed for San Francisco, California. The saints in Salt Lake City, Utah, just a few in number, begged us to stop off at their city and hold a meeting. We did so, and we held a three-week campaign. God broke through the Mormon ranks. People got saved, healed, and baptized. I believe that if I could have stayed longer, the whole city would have been shaken. We held the meetings in the building in which prizefights were held. On the same blood-stained mat where the prizefights were being staged, sinners were weeping their way through to God, staining it with their tears. Surely this piece of canvas will be a witness for and against some people in the Day of Judgment. At this place, the glory of God was seen with the natural eye by about a dozen of the saints. The pastor, an evangelist, myself, and other Christian workers were among those who saw the wonderful sight—the glory of God like a cloud resting over the meeting.

New Tabernacle Built

I am very eager for the saints and the dear people everywhere to know why we have built the tabernacle in Indianapolis, Indiana. The Lord appeared before me in the night and brought the building before me. He told me to arise and build a house for the Lord. The message and plan came so forcibly before me that I knew it was the voice of God. I rose the next morning, laid the message and plan before my secretary, and told him that we must proceed at once to make arrangements for the building.

In about two months' time, the building was finished. We have a large, neat, comfortable tabernacle. Indianapolis is a large, beautiful, centralized city, a city that is easily accessible to the saints in the North, South, East, and West. All those traveling across the continent can conveniently stop off here. The Lord has made it plain that this place is prepared to call the saints together from all parts of the world and to get a special enduement with power from on high. It is qualified to do the last work and to get the last call, to gather in the hungry souls, to get them sealed with the seal of the living God and ready for the Rapture.

A brother in Canada wrote me that God showed him this is to be a lighthouse, that He is going to send the light out all over the world from this place.

God has put His seal on the building and the work in many ways. He has revealed to the saints in different places about establishing a work here. Some have had visions of the building before it was built.

The power and presence of the Lord have been present in a marvelous way from the first meeting, confirming the work with signs and miracles, and in a special manner displaying the supernatural. The heavenly choir has come forth many times accompanied by heavenly instruments. Angels have been seen and heard singing by many saints. The glory of God and Jesus has been seen over the pulpit and all over the tabernacle at times. Last Sunday, a brother saw Jesus appear on a throne over the platform. Streams of light and glory were going out from Him all over the building. This brother's face fairly shone as he testified to it. The next night, two sisters saw Him at about the same time. One was newly baptized. She saw Him close to her; the other one saw Him as He walked across the platform.

The saints are convinced that this is the time for God to do a mighty work. He wants to raise up workers who will go out under the anointing and in the unity of the Spirit to carry the work everywhere. We feel and know that this is the last call. What we do, we must do quickly.

Many People Healed, Saved, and Baptized

A Mrs. E. A. Moore was instantly healed of a stroke of paralysis that she had suffered. Her right side and bowels were paralyzed. For some days after the stroke, she was speechless, too. They brought her to the meeting and had to assist her onto the platform. When the prayer of faith was offered for her, she got up, walked, and gave praises to God. She demonstrated publicly that she had the use of the right side of her body again. Her neighbors consider it a great miracle. This sister has been well ever since. At another time, a black sister was brought in much the same condition. She was prayed for, and she came in about two weeks later without a sign of lameness.

Saints have come in from all the surrounding states, received what they came for, and gone back rejoicing. Some of them have come back the second time, bringing others with them.

A brother from Marcellus, Michigan, came down and got spiritually revived. He went back home and brought his mother, wife, two children, and some friends to the meeting. They all received the baptism of the Holy Spirit.

A number of hungry souls came in from Louisville, Kentucky. They also received the baptism.

One man came in from Virginia to get healed of tuberculosis. He got healed and baptized. When he got back home, he sent his wife here to be prayed for. She got healed and also received the baptism.

One brother came in from Oklahoma; he had been seeking the baptism of the Holy Spirit for a year. After he was here only a few days, he received a marvelous baptism. When he got back home, he sent his son, daughter, and a friend to Indianapolis. They also received the baptism; only the daughter was a little doubtful about whether she had received the baptism in its fullness.

As nearly as I can tell, about fifty have already followed Jesus in the ordinance of water baptism at this writing. When the first candidates were baptized in water in the baptistry, God put His seal on the ceremony in a wonderful way. Messages in tongues with interpretations came forth, and a number of the saints standing close by were slain in the Spirit and lay as though they were dead, under the mighty power of God. A group of angels was seen over the baptistry and was heard singing while the ceremony went on.

So many people are sending in handkerchiefs to have us pray over and anoint them that I believe I will say a few words about this part of my ministry. As in the days of Paul (see Acts 19:11–12), God is healing people through pieces of cloth. We have prayed for thousands of these cloths and handkerchiefs and have sent them out in the name of Jesus. The reports come in daily, and it is wonderful how God heals people through them. Others get saved and baptized in the Spirit.

I was just given a testimony from a man from Missouri. In this testimony, a man who had had tuberculosis for fifteen years, and whose relatives had all died from it, was instantly healed when an anointed handkerchief was placed on his body. He has had no more hemorrhages or coughing, and damp atmospheres have no effect whatsoever upon him anymore. He had been told by the doctors that he would not live three months if he stopped taking his medicine. This is only one out of the many such testimonies that we receive.

Now my prayer is that God will greatly bless this book. It will be prayed over as it goes out in the vineyard. What we do for Jesus and His cause must be done very quickly, because the coming of Jesus is right upon us. "*The Spirit and the bride say, Come....And let him that is athirst come. And whosoever will, let him take the water of life freely* (Rev. 22:17). Yes, "*come, Lord Jesus*" (v. 20). Amen.

ABOUT THE AUTHOR

The ministry of Maria Woodworth-Etter (1844–1924) is often called the most powerful of the modern era. She was born in Ohio, the fourth daughter of Samuel and Matilda Underwood, who eventually had eight children. Her father struggled with alcoholism, and the family lived in poverty. Her parents joined the Disciple Church one year before her father's death in 1855. After her father died, Maria and her sisters had to work to help support the family, but Maria longed for an education. At the age of thirteen, she went forward in a church service when the pastor gave an invitation to seek the Lord. However, Maria says she was not saved until she was taken to be baptized the next day. She wrote, "I asked the Lord to save me fully, trusting myself in His hands; and while going into the water, a light came over me, and I was converted. The people saw the change and said I had fainted."

Maria was filled with peace and joy, and she attended many church services each week. Her conversion had intensified her desire for an education because she wanted to better serve the Lord. She felt called to reach others for Christ, but her church denomination did not believe that women should be in the ministry except as missionaries. So, she kept her desire to minister to herself.

A few years later, she married Mr. Woodworth. Soon Maria's health failed. She wrote about this time, "Everything we undertook seemed to be a failure. I was away from all Christian influence and could not often attend the house of God...I had one trial after another, and temptations and discouragements beset me on every side." Maria suffered greatly when five of her six children also died.

Even though Maria still felt called to serve God, she did not feel qualified. Then, she was baptized in the Holy Spirit. She told God that if He would restore her health and show her what to do, she would obey Him and go into the ministry. She got better immediately. She began to hold meetings and many were converted, healed, and filled with the Holy Spirit. Eventually, her husband left his job, and together they went into the ministry full time.

After Maria's first husband died, she married Mr. S. P. Etter in 1902. Maria traveled North America many times and preached to thousands of people in all the large cities in the United States. Many dramatic healings of the most incurably sick occurred. Broken bones were instantly mended, the lame walked, demons were cast out, and even the dead were raised to life. Both she and her audiences reported many visions they had of heaven, angels, the New Jerusalem, and forthcoming events, including earthquakes and wars that subsequently occurred. Moreover, hundreds of thousands of people were saved through this remarkable ministry.